MAP SYMBOLS 4
SCALE 5
LATITUDE AND LONGITUDE 6
MAP PROJECTIONS 7–8
GEOGRAPHICAL INFORMATION SYSTEMS....................8

REMOTE SENSING   **9–17**

INTRODUCTION 10–11
ENVIRONMENTAL MONITORING 11
COLOUR COMPOSITES 12
VEGETATION AND LANDFORMS 13
URBAN REGENERATION 14–15
GEOLOGICAL INTERPRETATION 16

UNITED KINGDOM AND IRELAND   **17–48**

IRELAND: NORTH 18–19
         SOUTH 20–21
NORTHERN SCOTLAND 22–23
SOUTHERN SCOTLAND 24–25
NORTHERN ENGLAND 26–27
WALES AND SOUTH-WEST ENGLAND 28–29
SOUTH AND SOUTH-EAST ENGLAND 30–31
UK AND IRELAND: GEOLOGY 32
         RELIEF OF LAND 33
         CLIMATE 34–35
         ENVIRONMENT 36–37
         AGRICULTURE, INDUSTRY AND TRADE 38–39
         ENERGY 40–41
         TRANSPORT AND TOURISM 42–43
         COUNTIES AND REGIONS 44–45
         POPULATION TRENDS 46–47
         STANDARDS OF LIVING 48

THE WORLD   **49–122**

THE WORLD: RELIEF OF LAND 50–51
         COUNTRIES 52–53
ARCTIC OCEAN AND ANTARCTICA 54–55
EUROPE: RELIEF OF LAND 56
         COUNTRIES 57
         CLIMATE AND BIOMES 58
         POPULATION 59
EUROPEAN UNION/EUROPE 60–61
UK AND IRELAND 62
SCANDINAVIA AND THE BALTIC LANDS 63
CENTRAL EUROPE 64–65
FRANCE 66
SPAIN AND PORTUGAL 67
ITALY AND THE BALKAN STATES 68–69
EASTERN EUROPE AND TURKEY 70–71
ASIA: RELIEF OF LAND 72
         COUNTRIES 73
         CLIMATE AND BIOMES 74
         POPULATION AND WEALTH 75
RUSSIA AND NORTHERN ASIA 76–77
CHINA AND THE FAR EAST 78–79
CHINA: INDUSTRY AND HYDROELECTRICITY 80
JAPAN 81
SOUTH-EAST ASIA 82–83
SOUTH ASIA 84–85
THE MIDDLE EAST 86–87
         OIL AND WATER 88
ARABIA AND THE HORN OF AFRICA 89
AFRICA: RELIEF OF LAND 90
         COUNTRIES 91
         CLIMATE AND BIOMES 92
         POPULATION AND WEALTH 93
NORTHERN AFRICA 94–95
CENTRAL AND SOUTHERN AFRICA 96–97

OCEANIA 98–99
         CLIMATE AND POPULATION 100–101
PACIFIC OCEAN 102–103
NORTH AMERICA: RELIEF OF LAND 104
         COUNTRIES 105
         CLIMATE AND BIOMES 106
         POPULATION AND WEALTH 107
CANADA 108–109
UNITED STATES 110–111
NORTH-EAST UNITED STATES AND THE ST LAWRENCE ... 112–113
MEXICO, CENTRAL AMERICA AND THE CARIBBEAN 114–115
CARIBBEAN: HURRICANES 116
SOUTH AMERICA: RELIEF OF LAND 117
         CLIMATE AND BIOMES 118
         POPULATION AND WEALTH 119
SOUTH AMERICA 120–121
SOUTH-EAST BRAZIL 122

WORLD THEMES   **123–160**

THE WORLD: VOLCANOES AND EARTHQUAKES 124–125
         TEMPERATURE AND OCEAN CURRENTS 126
         PRESSURE, WINDS AND PRECIPITATION 127
         CLIMATE 128–129
         CLIMATE CHANGE 130–131
         CLIMATE STATISTICS 132–133
         BIOMES 134–135
         AGRICULTURE AND FOOD 136–137
         ENERGY AND MINERALS 138–139
         INDUSTRY AND TRADE 140–141
         TRAVEL AND TOURISM 142–143
         STANDARDS OF LIVING 144–145
         POPULATION DISTRIBUTION 146–147
         POPULATION TRENDS 148–149
         LANGUAGES AND RELIGION 150
         INTERNATIONAL ORGANIZATIONS 151
         HUMAN CONCERNS 152–153
         SOCIAL AND ECONOMIC STATISTICS 154–159
         PHYSICAL DIMENSIONS 160

INDEX   **161–184**

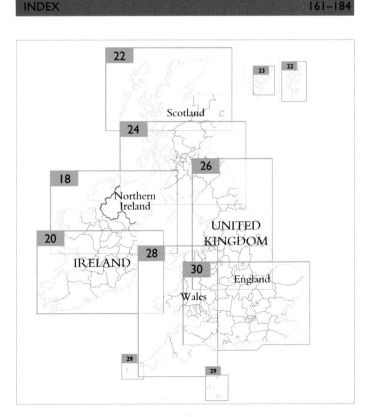

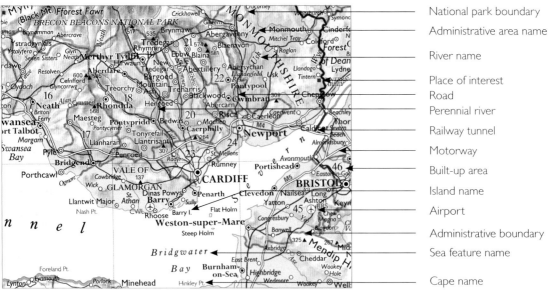

National park boundary

Administrative area name

River name

Place of interest

Road

Perennial river

Railway tunnel

Motorway

Built-up area

Island name

Airport

Administrative boundary

Sea feature name

Cape name

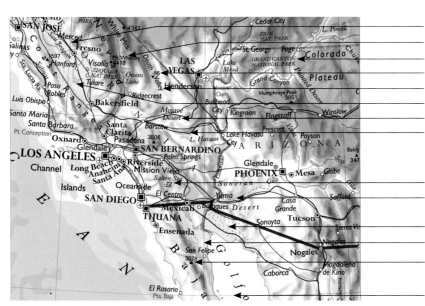

Permanent ice and glacier

Mountain range name

Mountain pass (m)

Regional name

Dam name

Lake name

Perennial lake

Capital city

Railway under construction

Disputed international boundary

International boundary

Dam

Canal

Aqueduct

Mountain peak name

National park name

Depth (m)

Valley name

Intermittent lake

Desert name

Railway

Height of lake surface (m)

Intermittent river

Sand desert

Line of longitude

Elevation (m)

Line of latitude

Settlement symbols and type styles vary according to the scale of each map and indicate the relative importance of towns rather than specific population figures

The scale of a map is the relationship of the distance between any two points shown on the map and the distance between the same two points on the Earth's surface. For instance, I inch on the map represents I mile on the ground, or 10 kilometres on the ground is represented by I centimetre on the map.

Instead of saying I centimetre represents 10 kilometres, we could say that I centimetre represents 1 000 000 centimetres on the map. If the scale is stated so that the same unit of measurement is used on both the map and the ground, then the proportion will hold for any unit of measurement. Therefore, the scale is usually written 1:1 000 000. This is called a 'representative fraction' and usually appears at the top of the map page, above the scale bar.

Calculations can easily be made in centimetres and kilometres by dividing the second figure in the representative fraction by 100 000 (i.e. by deleting the last five zeros). Thus at a scale of 1:5 000 000, I cm on the map represents 50 km on the ground. This is called a 'scale statement'. The calculation for inches and miles is more laborious, but 1 000 000 divided by 63 360 (the number of inches in a mile) shows that 1:1 000 000 can be stated as I inch on the map represents approximately 16 miles on the ground.

Many of the maps in this atlas feature a scale bar. This is a bar divided into the units of the map – miles and kilometres – so that a map distance can be measured with a ruler, dividers or a piece of paper, then placed along the scale bar, and the distance read off. To the left of the zero on the scale bar there are usually more divisions. By placing the ruler or dividers on the nearest rounded figure to the right of the zero, the smaller units can be counted off to the left.

The map extracts below show Los Angeles and its surrounding area at six different scales. The representative fraction, scale statement and scale bar are positioned above each map. Map I is at 1:27 000 and is the largest scale extract shown. Many of the individual buildings are identified and most of the streets are named, but at this scale only part of central Los Angeles can be shown within the given area. Map 2 is much smaller in scale at 1:250 000. Only a few important buildings and streets can be named, but the whole of central Los Angeles is shown. Maps 3, 4 and 5 show how greater areas can be depicted as the map scale decreases, down to Map 6 at 1:35 000 000. At this small scale, the entire Los Angeles conurbation is depicted by a single town symbol and a large part of the south-western USA and part of Mexico is shown.

The scales of maps must be used with care since large distances on small-scale maps can be represented by one or two centimetres. On certain projections scale is only correct along certain lines, parallels or meridians. As a general rule, the larger the map scale, the more accurate and reliable will be the distance measured.

1 1 : 27 000
I cm on the map represents 0.27 km on the ground

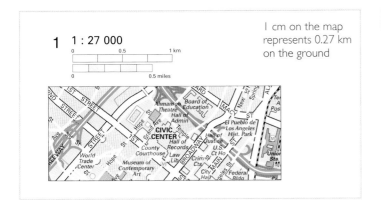

2 1 : 250 000
I cm on the map represents 2.5 km on the ground

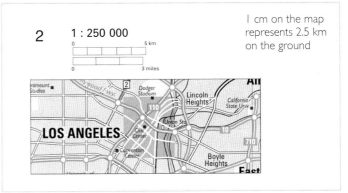

3 1 : 2 500 000
I cm on the map represents 25 km on the ground

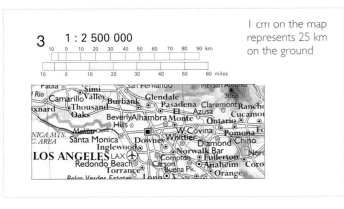

4 1 : 6 000 000
I cm on the map represents 60 km on the ground

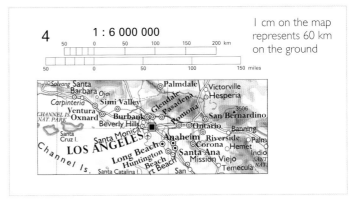

5 1 : 12 000 000
I cm on the map represents 120 km on the ground

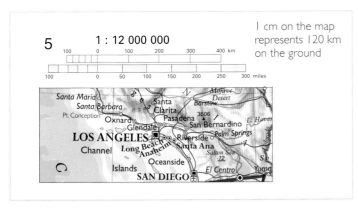

6 1 : 35 000 000
I cm on the map represents 350 km on the ground

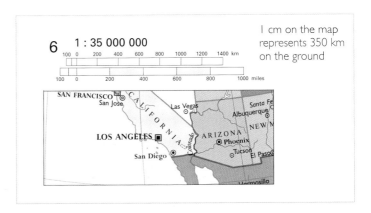

Accurate positioning of individual points on the Earth's surface is made possible by reference to the geometric system of latitude and longitude.

Latitude is the distance of a point north or south of the Equator measured at an angle with the centre of the Earth, whereby the Equator is latitude 0 degrees, the North Pole is 90 degrees north and the South Pole 90 degrees south. Latitude parallels are drawn west–east around the Earth, parallel to the Equator, decreasing in diameter from the Equator until they become a point at the poles. On the maps in this atlas the lines of latitude are represented by blue lines running across the map in smooth curves, with the degree figures in blue at the sides of the maps. The degree interval depends on the scale of the map.

Lines of longitude are meridians drawn north–south, cutting the lines of latitude at right angles on the Earth's surface and intersecting with one another at the poles. Longitude is measured by an angle at the centre of the Earth from the prime meridian (0 degrees), which passes through Greenwich in London. It is given as a measurement east or west of the Greenwich Meridian from 0 to 180 degrees. The meridians are normally drawn north–south vertically down the map, with the degree figures in blue in the top and bottom margins of the map.

In the index each place name is followed by its map page number, its letter-figure grid reference, and then its latitude and longitude. The unit of measurement is the degree, which is subdivided into 60 minutes. An index entry states the position of a place in degrees and minutes. The latitude is followed by N(orth) or S(outh) and the longitude E(ast) or W(est).

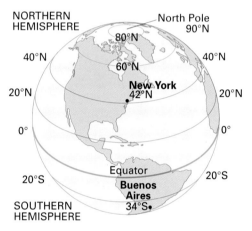

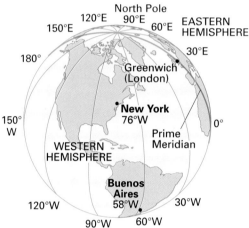

Latitude

Lines of latitude cross the atlas maps from east to west. The Equator is at 0°. All other lines of latitude are either north or south of the Equator. Line 40°N is almost halfway towards the North Pole. The North Pole is at 90°N.

Longitude

Lines of longitude run from north to south. These lines meet at the North Pole and the South Pole. Longitude 0° passes through Greenwich. This line is also called the Prime Meridian. Lines of longitude are either east of 0° or west of 0°. There are 180 degrees of longitude both east and west of 0°.

Using latitude and longitude

Latitude and longitude lines make a grid that can be printed on a map. You can find a place if you know its latitude and longitude. The degree of latitude is either north or south of the Equator. The longitude number is either east or west of the Greenwich Meridian.

HOW TO LOCATE A PLACE OR FEATURE

The two diagrams (right) show how to estimate the required distance from the nearest line of latitude or longitude on the map page, in order to locate a place or feature listed in the index (such as Helston in the UK and Mount McKinley in the USA, as detailed in the above example).

In the left-hand diagram there are 30 minutes between the lines and so to find the position of Helston an estimate has to be made: 7 parts of the 30 minutes north of the 50°0N latitude line, and 17 parts of the 30 minutes west of the 5°0W longitude line.

In the right-hand diagram it is more difficult to estimate because there is an interval of 10 degrees between the lines. In the example of Mount McKinley, the reader has to estimate 3 degrees 4 minutes north of 60°0N and 1 degree west of 150°0W.

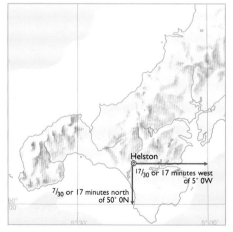

Helston, U.K. 29 G3 50°7N 5°17W
Helston is on map page 29, in grid square G3, and is 50 degrees 7 minutes north of the Equator and 5 degrees 17 minutes west of Greenwich.

Mt. McKinley, U.S.A. 108 C4 63°4N 151°0W
Mount McKinley is on map page 108, in grid square C4, and is 63 degrees 4 minutes north of the Equator and 151 degrees west of Greenwich.

A map projection is the systematic depiction of the imaginary grid of lines of latitude and longitude from a globe on to a flat surface. The grid of lines is called the 'graticule' and it can be constructed either by graphical means or by mathematical formulae to form the basis of a map. As a globe is three dimensional, it is not possible to depict its surface on a flat map without some form of distortion. Preservation of one of the basic properties listed below can only be secured at the expense of the others and thus the choice of projection is often a compromise solution.

Correct area
In these projections the areas from the globe are to scale on the map. This is particularly useful in the mapping of densities and distributions. Projections with this property are termed 'equal area', 'equivalent' or 'homolographic'.

Correct distance
In these projections the scale is correct along the meridians, or, in the case of the 'azimuthal equidistant', scale is true along any line drawn from the centre of the projection. They are called 'equidistant'.

Correct shape
This property can only be true within small areas as it is achieved only by having a uniform scale distortion along both the 'x' and 'y' axes of the projection. The projections are called 'conformal' or 'orthomorphic'.

Map projections can be divided into three broad categories – **'azimuthal'**, **'conic'** and **'cylindrical'**. Cartographers use different projections from these categories depending on the map scale, the size of the area to be mapped, and what they want the map to show.

AZIMUTHAL OR ZENITHAL PROJECTIONS
These are constructed by the projection of part of the graticule from the globe on to a plane tangential to any single point on it. This plane may be tangential to the equator (equatorial case), the poles (polar case) or any other point (oblique case). Any straight line drawn from the point at which the plane touches the globe is the shortest distance from that point and is known as a 'great circle'. In its 'gnomonic' construction any straight line on the map is a great circle, but there is great exaggeration towards the edges and this reduces its general uses. There are five different ways of transferring the graticule on to the plane and these are shown below. The diagrams below also show how the graticules vary, using the polar case as the example.

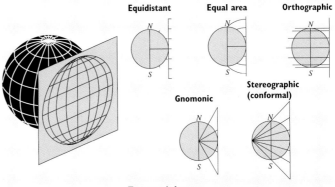

Polar case
The polar case is the simplest to construct and the diagram on the right shows the differing effects of all five methods of construction, comparing their coverage, distortion, etc, using North America as the example.

Oblique case
The plane touches the globe at any point between the Equator and poles. The oblique orthographic uses the distortion in azimuthal projections away from the centre to give a graphic depiction of the Earth as seen from any desired point in space.

Equatorial case
The example shown here is Lambert's Equivalent Azimuthal. It is the only projection which is both equal area and where bearing is true from the centre.

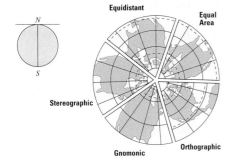

CONICAL PROJECTIONS
These use the projection of the graticule from the globe on to a cone which is tangential to a line of latitude (termed the 'standard parallel'). This line is always an arc and scale is always true along it. Because of its method of construction, it is used mainly for depicting the temperate latitudes around the standard parallel, i.e. where there is least distortion. To reduce the distortion and include a larger range of latitudes, the projection may be constructed with the cone bisecting the surface of the globe so that there are two standard parallels, each of which is true to scale. The distortion is thus spread more evenly between the two chosen parallels.

Simple conical with one standard parallel

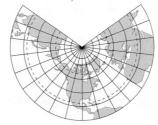

Bonne
This is a modification of the simple conic, whereby the true scale along the meridians is sacrificed to enable the accurate representation of areas. However, scale is true along each parallel but shapes are distorted at the edges.

Albers Conical Equal Area
This projection uses two standard parallels. The selection of these relative to the land area to be mapped is very important. It is equal area and is especially useful for large land masses oriented east–west, such as the USA.

MAP PROJECTIONS

CYLINDRICAL AND OTHER WORLD PROJECTIONS

This group of projections are those which permit the whole of the Earth's surface to be depicted on one map. They are a very large group of projections and the following are only a few of them. Cylindrical projections are constructed by the projection of the graticule from the globe on to a cylinder tangential to the globe. Although cylindrical projections can depict all the main land masses, there is considerable distortion of shape and area towards the poles. One cylindrical projection, Mercator, overcomes this shortcoming by possessing the unique navigational property that any straight line drawn on it is a line of constant bearing ('loxodrome'). It is used for maps and charts between 15° either side of the Equator. Beyond this, enlargement of area is a serious drawback, although it is used for navigational charts at all latitudes.

Mercator

Eckert IV
(pseudocylindrical equal area)

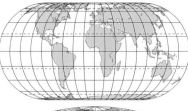

Hammer
(polyconic equal area)

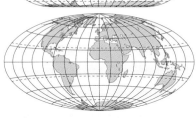

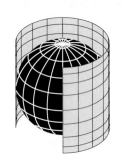

Simple cylindrical

Cylindrical with two standard parallels

GEOGRAPHIC INFORMATION SYSTEMS

A Geographic Information System (GIS) enables any available geospatial data to be compiled, presented and analysed using specialized computer software.

Many aspects of our lives now benefit from the use of GIS – from the management and maintenance of the networks of pipelines and cables that supply our homes, to the exploitation or protection of the natural resources that we use. Much of this is at a regional or national scale and the data collected from satellites form an important part of our interpretation and understanding of the world around us.

GIS systems are used for many aspects of central planning and modern life, such as defence, land use, reclamation, telecommunications and the deployment of emergency services. Commercial companies can use demographic and infrastructure data within a GIS to plan marketing strategies, identifying where their services would be most needed, and thus decide where best to locate their businesses. Insurance companies use GIS to determine premiums based on population distribution, crime figures and the likelihood of natural disasters, such as flooding or subsidence.

Whatever the application, all the relevant data can be prepared in a GIS so that a user can extract and display the information of particular interest on a map, or compare it with other material in order to help analyse and resolve a specific problem. From analysis of the data that has been acquired, it is often possible to use a GIS to create a computer 'model' of possible future situations and see what impact various actions may have. A GIS can also monitor change over time, aiding the interpretation of long-term trends.

A GIS may also use satellite data to extract useful information and map large areas, which would otherwise take many man-years using other methods. For applications such as hydrocarbon and mineral exploration, forestry, agriculture, environmental monitoring and urban development, these developments have made it possible to undertake projects on a global scale unheard of before.

To find out more about how GIS works and how it affects our lives, why not go the Ordnance Survey's Mapzone website at: https://www.ordnancesurvey.co.uk/mapzone/gis-zone

Examples of the type of information that can be added to a GIS

relief

drainage

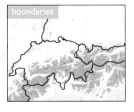
boundaries

GIS

locations

transport

names

REMOTE SENSING

The first satellite to monitor our environment systematically was launched as long ago as April 1961. It was called TIROS-1 and was designed specifically to record atmospheric change. The first of the generation of Earth resources satellites was Landsat-1, launched in July 1972. The succeeding decades have seen a revolution in our ability to survey and map our environment. Digital sensors mounted on satellites now scan vast areas of the Earth's surface day and night and at a range of resolutions from 0.3 m to several kms depending on the type of satellite. At any one time, up to 50 satellites may be in orbit. They collect and relay back to Earth huge volumes of geographical data, which is processed and stored by computers.

Satellite imagery and remote sensing

An ability to collect data of large areas at high resolution and the freedom from national access restrictions, have meant that sensors on these satellite platforms are increasingly replacing surface and airborne data-gathering techniques. Twenty-four hours a day, satellites are scanning the Earth's surface and atmosphere, adding to an ever-expanding range of geographic and geophysical data available to help us understand and manage our human and physical environments. Remote sensing is the science of extracting information from such images.

Satellite orbits

Most high resolution Earth-observation satellites are in a nearpolar, Sun-synchronous orbit. At altitudes of between 400–900 km, the satellites revolve around the Earth approximately every 100 minutes and on each orbit cross the equator at a similar local (solar) time, usually late in the morning. This helps to ensure that the sun is at a high elevation yet atmospheric moisture, which commonly increases throughout the day in warm climates, is relatively low. High resolution sensors can be pointed sideways from the orbital path, resulting in a 1–3 day interval, or 'revisit' time, between each opportunity.

Exceptions to these Sun-synchronous orbits include the geostationary meteorological satellites, such as the European Meteosat, American GOES and Russian Elektro satellites. These have an approximate 36,000 km high orbit and rotate around the Earth every 24 hours, thus remaining above the same point on the Equator. These satellites acquire frequent images showing cloud and atmospheric moisture movements for almost a full hemisphere.

In addition, there are constellations of global navigation satellite systems, each comprising 20–30 satellites, such as the American Global Positioning System (GPS), Russian GLONASS and, under

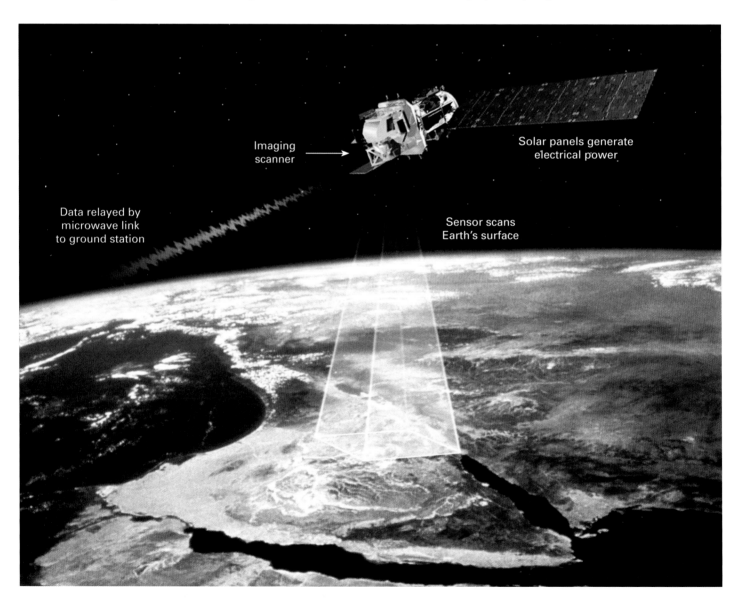

Data relayed by microwave link to ground station

Imaging scanner

Solar panels generate electrical power

Sensor scans Earth's surface

Landsat-8

This is the latest addition to the Landsat Earth-observation satellite programme, orbiting at 710 km above the Earth. With onboard recorders, the satellite can store data until it passes within range of a ground station. Basic geometric and radiometric corrections are then applied before distribution of the imagery to users.

development, the European Galileo system. These satellites circle the Earth at a height of 20,200 km in different orbital planes, enabling us to fix our position on the Earth's surface to an accuracy of a few centimetres. Although initially developed for military use, these systems now assist everyday life used by smart phones and in-car navigation systems. More precise corrections to location accuracy improves both terrestrial and aerial surveys, aircraft and marine navigation as well as guidance for precision agriculture.

Digital sensors

Early satellite designs involved images being exposed to photographic film and returned to Earth by capsule for processing. However, even the first commercial satellite imagery, from Landsat-1, used digital imaging sensors and transmitted the data back to ground stations (see diagram opposite).

Optical, or passive, sensors record the radiation reflected from the Earth for specific wavebands. Radar, or active, sensors transmit their own microwave radiation, which is reflected from the Earth's surface back to the satellite and recorded. This allows this type of sensor to operate twenty-four hours a day and in all weather. Synthetic Aperture Radar (SAR) images are examples of the latter.

Whichever scanning method is used, each satellite records image data of constant width but potentially several thousand kilometres in length. Once the data has been received on Earth, it may be split into approximately square sections or 'scenes' for distribution or, increasingly, customers provide a polygon of their 'Area of Interest' which is extracted from the full image strip.

Spectral resolution, wavebands and false-colour composites

Satellites can record data from many sections of the electromagnetic spectrum (wavebands) simultaneously. Since we can only see images made from the three primary colours (red, green and blue), a selection of any three wavebands needs to be made in order to form a picture that will enable visual interpretation of the scene to be made. When any combination other than the visible bands are used, such as near or middle infrared, the resulting image is termed a 'false-colour composite'.

The selection of these wavebands depends on the purpose of the final image – geology, hydrology, agronomy and environmental needs each have their own optimum waveband combinations.

ENVIRONMENTAL MONITORING

Fukushima Nuclear Power Station, Japan
This image was captured by the GeoEye-1 satellite, travelling at 6 km/sec and 680 km above the Earth. In front of the pylons, in the centre of the image, the damaged reactors in the heart of the irradiated area can be seen, following the March 2011 Japanese earthquake and tsunami. It allowed initial assessment of a very dangerous area to take place with minimum risk to human life. (©DigitalGlobe, Inc. All Rights Reserved)

Natural-colour and false-colour composites

These images show the salt ponds at the southern end of San Francisco Bay, which now form the San Francisco Bay National Wildlife Refuge. They demonstrate the difference between 'natural colour' (top) and 'false colour' (bottom) composites.

The top image is made from visible red, green and blue wavelengths. The colours correspond closely to those one would observe from an aircraft. The salt ponds appear green or orange-red due to the colour of the sediments they contain. The urban areas appear grey and vegetation is either dark green (trees) or light brown (dry grass).

The bottom image is made up of near-infrared, visible red and visible green wavelengths. These wavebands are represented here in red, green and blue, respectively. Since chlorophyll in healthy vegetation strongly reflects near-infrared light, this is clearly visible as red in the image.

False-colour composite imagery is therefore very sensitive to the presence of healthy vegetation. The bottom image thus shows better discrimination between the 'leafy' residential urban areas, such as Palo Alto (south-west of the Bay), and other urban areas by the 'redness' of the trees. The high chlorophyll content of watered urban grass areas shows as bright red, contrasting with the dark red of trees and the brown of natural, dry grass. (USGS)

Nishino-shima, Japan

This small volcanic island, in the Ogasawara chain, erupted into the world at the end of 2013 in the western Pacific Ocean some 1,000 km south of Tokyo. This natural-colour image was captured by Landsat 8 in August 2014 and shows the long white plume of volcanic gases. The continuing flowing out of lava on the eastern side of the island makes this a dangerous island to approach until conditions settle. *(NASA)*

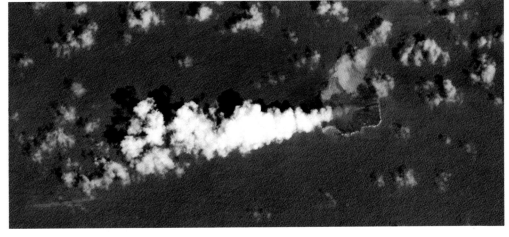

Piqiang Fault, China

By recording and processing the amount of energy reflected or emitted from the Earth in different ways, satellite images can help scientists see patterns in landforms that otherwise might be hard to make out with the naked eye. The colours assigned here clearly show the movement of the bands of sedimentary rocks along the fault line. The land has moved by about 3km along the fault. *(NASA)*

Kazakhstan/China

The startling contrast in land-use across the international border between Kazakstan, to the west, and China, to the east, is made clear in this Landsat 8 image. There is huge pressure on China to extract the maximum agricultural output from any suitable land, even when it requires irrigation. In the corresponding area of Kazakhstan, there is less need for intensive agriculture and therefore no irrigation. *(NASA)*

Niger Delta, West Africa

The River Niger is the third longest river in Africa after the Nile and Congo, and this false-colour image shows the different vegetation types. Deltas are by nature constantly evolving sedimentary features and often contain many ecosystems within them. In the case of the Niger Delta, there are also vast hydrocarbon reserves beneath it with associated wells and pipelines. Satellite imagery helps to plan activity and monitor this fragile and changing environment. *(USGS)*

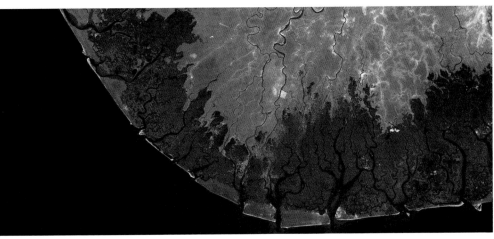

West India Docks, 1983

This vertical image shows the derelict site of the West India Docks, which were built between 1802 and 1870, as part of the London Docks which eventually stretched from Tower Bridge downstream to Beckton in the east.

The most successful year for the London Docks, in terms of tonnage handled, was 1961. However, by the 1970s they could no longer compete with coastal ports due to the containerisation of cargo and increased size of ships. This resulted in their rapid closure, consequent high unemployment and the economic decline in the area.

By 1981 the docks had closed. These images were taken as part of an aerial survey for the London Docklands Development Corporation, a new government Enterprise Zone covering all of the London Docks. Planning regulations were relaxed, transport infrastructure (the Docklands Light Railway) was constructed and financial incentives offered to attract businesses and property developers.

In this mosaic, made up of eight separate images and taken in 1983, the three docks making up the West India group can be seen. In the south dock empty Thames lighters, once used to move cargo from larger ships, are still visible. The warehouse at the western end of the middle spur was called 'Canary Wharf', where ships from the Canary Islands unloaded cargo, principally bananas and tomatoes. The name was subsequently adopted for the whole area. The building in the northeast corner, with the visible external roof supports, is Billingsgate Fish Market which moved from the City of London into this new building in 1982.

Aerial surveys from aircraft are still used by organisations such as the Ordnance Survey since they are efficient for large areas, provide higher resolution imagery than satellites and can be more flexible in areas such as the UK, where cloud cover often limits imaging opportunities. (©Tower Hamlets Local History Library and Archives)

Canary Wharf, 2014

Regeneration of the West India Docks site started in 1988. The whole 39 hectare area was renamed 'Canary Wharf' by the developers. The rapid construction of buildings such as One Canada Square (Canary Wharf Tower, the highest building in the area), and the extension of the Jubilee tube line from Green Park to Stratford attracted many companies to relocate from the City of London and elsewhere.

The satellite image, dating from 2014, shows how much the area has been developed. Over 100,000 people now work there, primarily in the financial and insurance sectors. To support these businesses, many others work in IT, retail and the legal profession.

Very little of what can be seen in the top image, in 1983, is visible here, with the newer buildings being constructed over parts of the North Dock. Billingsgate still occupies its place and is still London's fish market, most of its produce arriving by road from all over the country. In the northwest, the roofs of a group of the original former warehouses can be seen in both images. These are the earliest buildings on the site, dating from the early nineteenth century, and now partially house the Museum of London Docklands. The long shadows cast by the new buildings show how high they are.

Future developments include the planned opening of Crossrail in 2018 and the construction of more residential property, to the east of the main business centre, as well as the further commercial development of high-rise offices.

Satellite imagery is most useful for mapping areas in remote or inaccessible areas of the world, particularly where cloud cover is not too persistent. The ability to revisit and monitor small sites without the high cost of aircraft mobilisation is another benefit. (NPA Satellite Mapping, CGG)

Sichuan Basin, China

The north-east/south-west trending ridges in this image are anticlinal folds developed in the Earth's crust as a result of plate collision and compression. Geologists map these folds and the lowlands between them formed by synclinal folds, as they are often the areas where oil or gas are found in commercial quantities. The river shown in this image is the Yangtse, near Chongqing. *(China RSGS)*

Pingualuit Crater, Canada

The circular feature is a meteorite crater in the Ungava Peninsula, Québec, formed by an impact over 1.4 million years ago. It is 3.4 km wide and 264 m deep. The lake within has no link to any water sources and has been formed only by rain and snow. Thus the water is among the world's clearest and least saline. Sediments in the lake have been unaffected by ice sheets and are important for scientific research. *(NPA Satellite Mapping, CGG)*

Wadi Hadramaut, Yemen

Yemen is extremely arid – however, in the past it was more humid and wet, enabling large river systems to carve out the deep and spectacular gorges and dried-out river beds *(wadis)* seen in this image. The erosion has revealed many contrasting rock types. The image has been processed to exaggerate this effect, producing many shades of red, pink and purple, which make geological mapping easier and more cost-effective. *(USGS)*

Zagros Mountains, Iran

These mountains were formed as Arabia collided with Southern Eurasia. The upper half of this colour-enhanced image shows an anticline that runs east–west. The dark grey features are called diapirs, which are bodies of viscous rock salt that are very buoyant and sometimes rise to the surface, spilling and spreading out like a glacier. The presence of salt in the region is important as it stops oil escaping to the surface. *(USGS)*

UNITED KINGDOM AND IRELAND

1:1 000 000

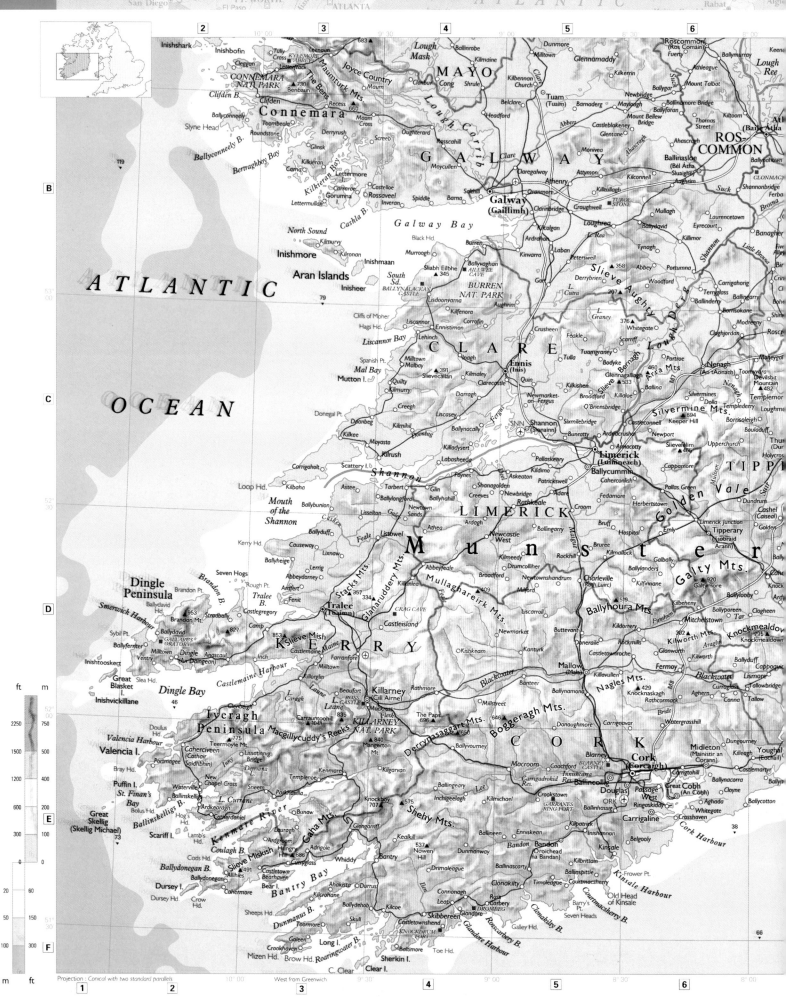

1:1 000 000

NORTH SEA

Pentland Firth

Caithness

Moray Firth

Easter Ross

MORAY

Buchan

Formartine

Garioch

ABERDEENSHIRE

Aberdeen

Mar

Cairngorm Mts.

CAIRNGORMS NAT.PARK

Braemar

Kincardine

Grampian Mountains

Badenoch

Monadhliath Mts.

Glen More (Great Glen)

PERTH AND KINROSS

Braes of Angus

ANGUS

Strathmore

Forest of Atholl

Rannoch Moor RANNOCH

COPYRIGHT PHILIP'S

5 0   10   20   30   40   50 km

5 0   5   10   15   20   25   30   35 miles

1: 1 000 000

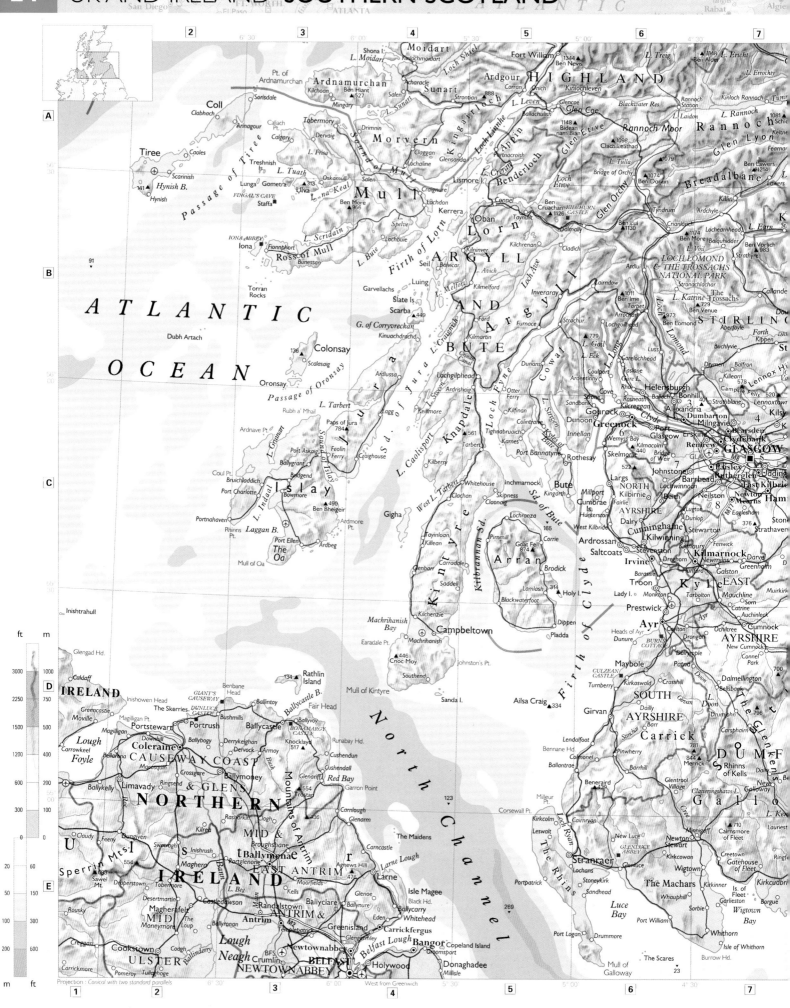

Projection : Conical with two standard parallels

West from Greenwich

NORTH

SEA

1:1 000 000

COPYRIGHT PHILIP'S

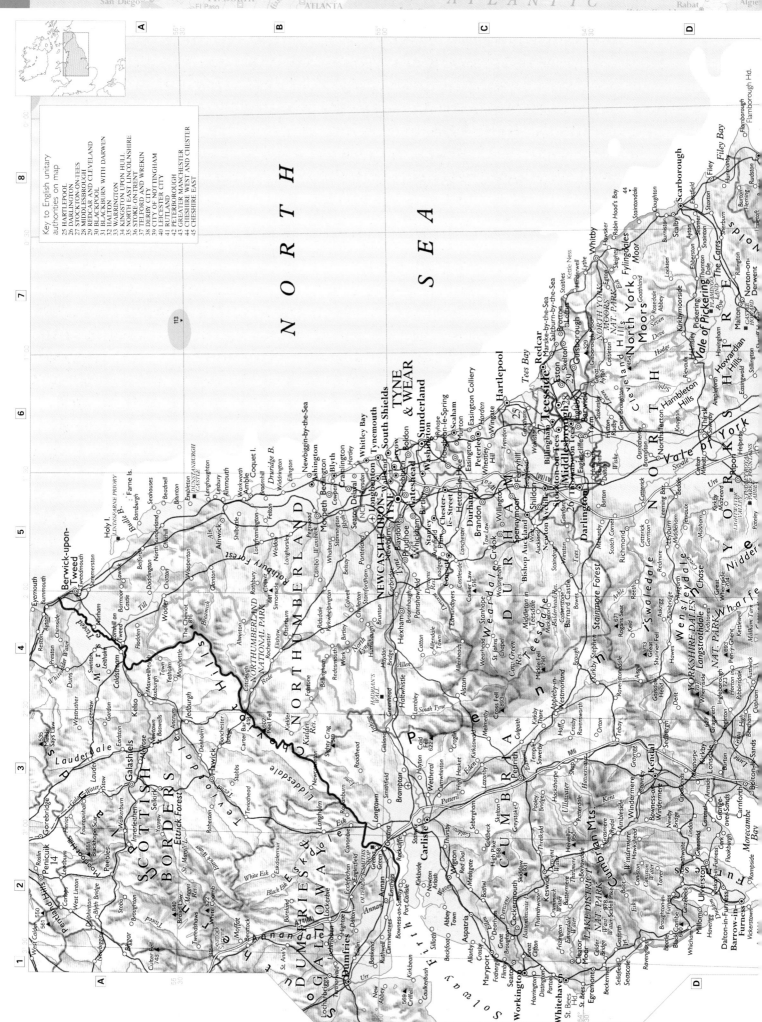

Key to English unitary authorities on map
25 HARTLEPOOL
26 DARLINGTON
27 STOCKTON-ON-TEES
28 MIDDLESBROUGH
29 REDCAR AND CLEVELAND
30 BLACKPOOL
31 BLACKBURN WITH DARWEN
32 HALTON
33 WARRINGTON
34 KINGSTON UPON HULL
35 NORTH EAST LINCOLNSHIRE
36 STOKE-ON-TRENT
37 TELFORD AND WREKIN
38 DERBY CITY
39 CITY OF NOTTINGHAM
40 LEICESTER CITY
41 RUTLAND
42 PETERBOROUGH
43 GREATER MANCHESTER
44 CHESHIRE WEST AND CHESTER
45 CHESHIRE EAST

NORTH SEA

IRISH SEA

Liverpool Bay

Cardigan Bay

Caernarfon Bay

Tremadog Bay

St. George's Channel

ANGLESEY

Isle of Anglesey

SNOWDONIA NATIONAL PARK

GWYNEDD

CONWY

DENBIGHSHIRE

FLINTSHIRE

WREXHAM

POWYS

CEREDIGION

CARMARTHENSHIRE

PEMBROKESHIRE

PEMBROKESHIRE COAST NATIONAL PARK

SHROPSHIRE

HEREFORDSHIRE

MONMOUTHSHIRE

GLOUCESTERSHIRE

BRECON BEACONS NATIONAL PARK

Black Mountains

Mynydd Eppynt

Clun Forest

Radnor Forest

LIVERPOOL

Chester

Shrewsbury

Hereford

Gloucester

Aberystwyth

Carmarthen

Haverfordwest

Milford Haven

Scale 1:1 000 000

5 0 10 20 30 40 50 km

5 0 5 10 15 20 25 30 35 miles

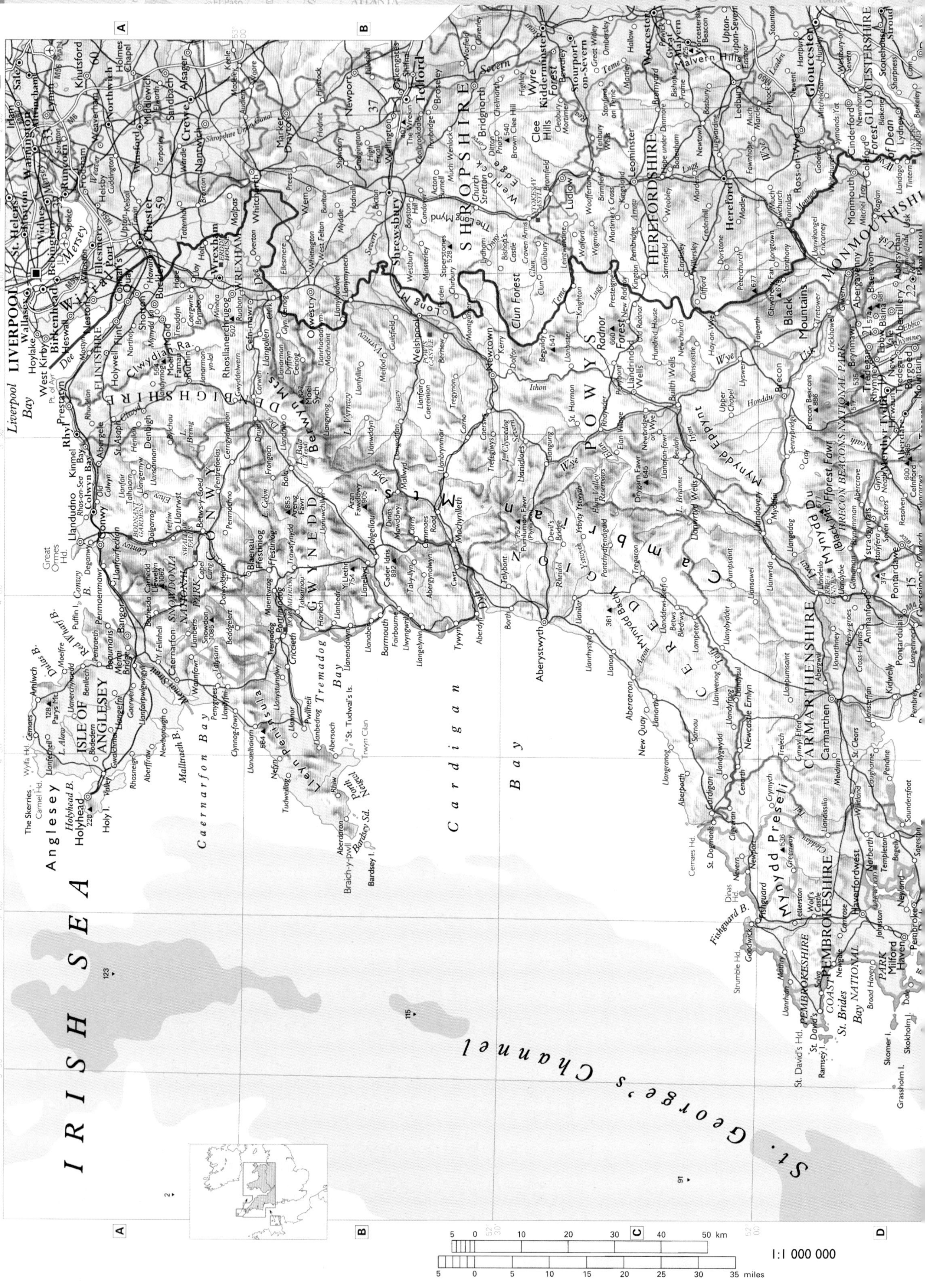

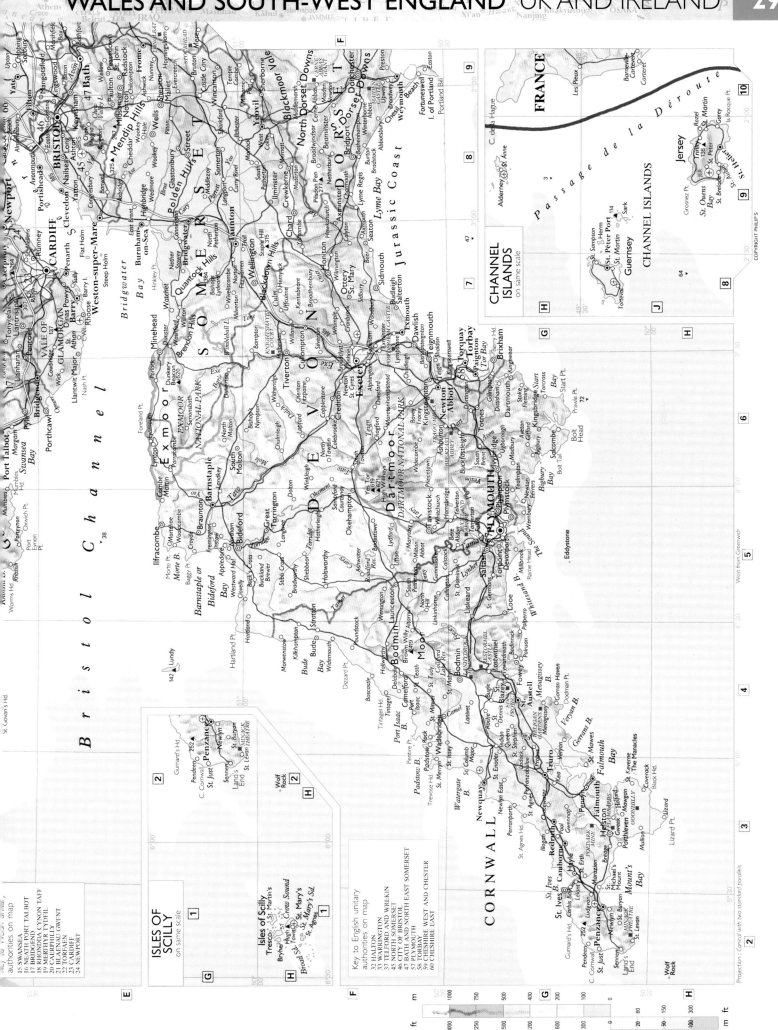

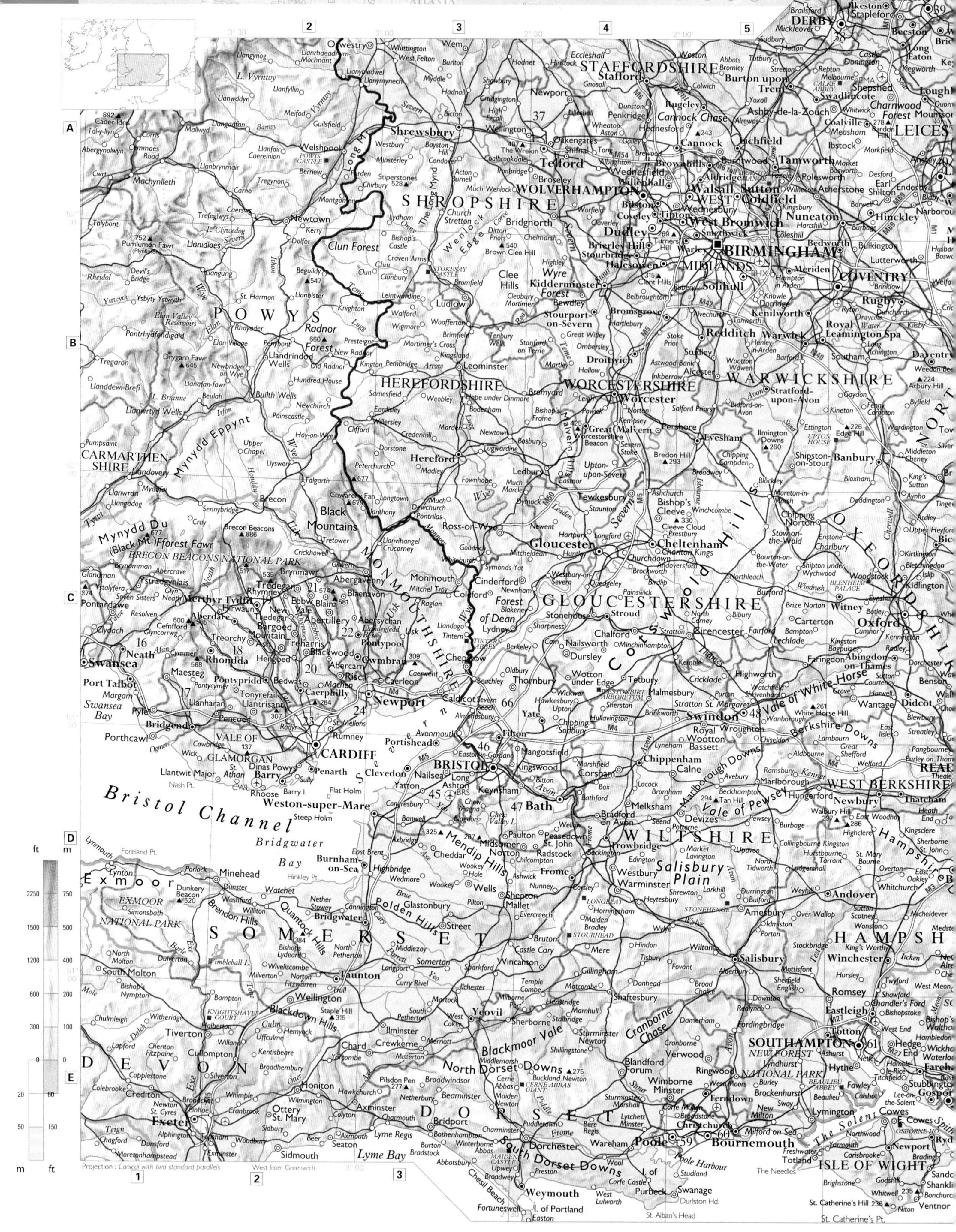

POWYS
SHROPSHIRE
STAFFORDSHIRE
HEREFORDSHIRE
WORCESTERSHIRE
WARWICKSHIRE
GLOUCESTERSHIRE
MONMOUTHSHIRE
OXFORDSHIRE
WILTSHIRE
SOMERSET
DEVON
DORSET
HAMPSHIRE
WEST BERKSHIRE
MIDLANDS
CARMARTHENSHIRE
VALE OF GLAMORGAN
ISLE OF WIGHT
BIRMINGHAM
WOLVERHAMPTON
COVENTRY
CARDIFF
BRISTOL
SOUTHAMPTON
NOTTINGHAM
DERBY
LEICESTER
Shrewsbury
Telford
Worcester
Hereford
Gloucester
Cheltenham
Swindon
Oxford
Bath
Salisbury
Winchester
Bournemouth
Poole
Exeter
Taunton
Newport
Swansea
Bristol Channel
Lyme Bay
The Solent
Exmoor
Black Mountains
Brecon Beacons
Cotswold Hills
Mendip Hills
Salisbury Plain
Vale of White Horse
Vale of Pewsey
Marlborough Downs
Berkshire Downs
Blackmoor Vale
Cranborne Chase
North Dorset Downs
South Dorset Downs
Quantock Hills
Blackdown Hills
Brendon Hills
Polden Hills
Clun Forest
Forest of Dean
NEW FOREST NATIONAL PARK
EXMOOR NATIONAL PARK
BRECON BEACONS NATIONAL PARK
Projection : Conical with two standard parallels
West from Greenwich

Key to English unitary authorities on map
37 TELFORD AND WREKIN
38 DERBY CITY
39 CITY OF NOTTINGHAM
40 LEICESTER CITY
41 RUTLAND
42 PETERBOROUGH
43 MILTON KEYNES
44 LUTON
45 NORTH SOMERSET
46 CITY OF BRISTOL
47 BATH AND NORTH EAST SOMERSET
48 SWINDON
49 READING
50 WOKINGHAM
51 WINDSOR AND MAIDENHEAD
52 SLOUGH
53 BRACKNELL FOREST
54 THURROCK
55 SOUTHEND-ON-SEA
56 MEDWAY
59 POOLE
60 BOURNEMOUTH
61 SOUTHAMPTON
62 PORTSMOUTH
63 BRIGHTON AND HOVE
64 BEDFORD
65 CENTRAL BEDFORDSHIRE
66 SOUTH GLOUCESTERSHIRE

Key to Welsh unitary authorities on map
16 NEATH PORT TALBOT
17 BRIDGEND
18 RHONDDA CYNON TAFF
19 MERTHYR TYDFIL
20 CAERPHILLY
21 BLAENAU GWENT
22 TORFAEN
23 CARDIFF
24 NEWPORT

1:1 000 000

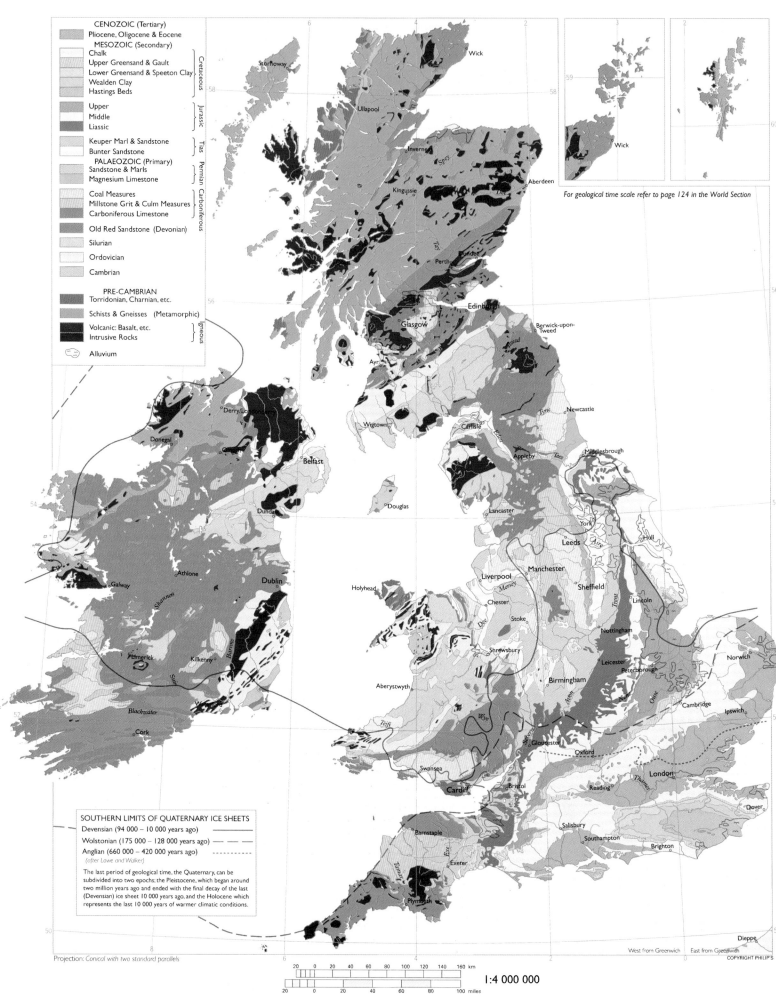

CENOZOIC (Tertiary)
Pliocene, Oligocene & Eocene

MESOZOIC (Secondary)
Chalk
Upper Greensand & Gault
Lower Greensand & Speeton Clay
Wealden Clay
Hastings Beds
— Cretaceous

Upper
Middle
Liassic
— Jurassic

Keuper Marl & Sandstone
Bunter Sandstone
— Trias

PALAEOZOIC (Primary)
Sandstone & Marls
Magnesium Limestone
— Permian

Coal Measures
Millstone Grit & Culm Measures
Carboniferous Limestone
— Carboniferous

Old Red Sandstone (Devonian)

Silurian

Ordovician

Cambrian

PRE-CAMBRIAN
Torridonian, Charnian, etc.

Schists & Gneisses (Metamorphic)

Volcanic: Basalt, etc.
Intrusive Rocks
— Igneous

Alluvium

For geological time scale refer to page 124 in the World Section

SOUTHERN LIMITS OF QUATERNARY ICE SHEETS
Devensian (94 000 – 10 000 years ago) ————
Wolstonian (175 000 – 128 000 years ago) – – – –
Anglian (660 000 – 420 000 years ago) · · · · · · ·
(after Lowe and Walker)

The last period of geological time, the Quaternary, can be
subdivided into two epochs; the Pleistocene, which began around
two million years ago and ended with the final decay of the last
(Devensian) ice sheet 10 000 years ago, and the Holocene which
represents the last 10 000 years of warmer climatic conditions.

Projection: Conical with two standard parallels

West from Greenwich   East from Greenwich
COPYRIGHT PHILIP'S

20 0 20 40 60 80 100 120 140 160 km
20 0 20 40 60 80 100 miles
1:4 000 000

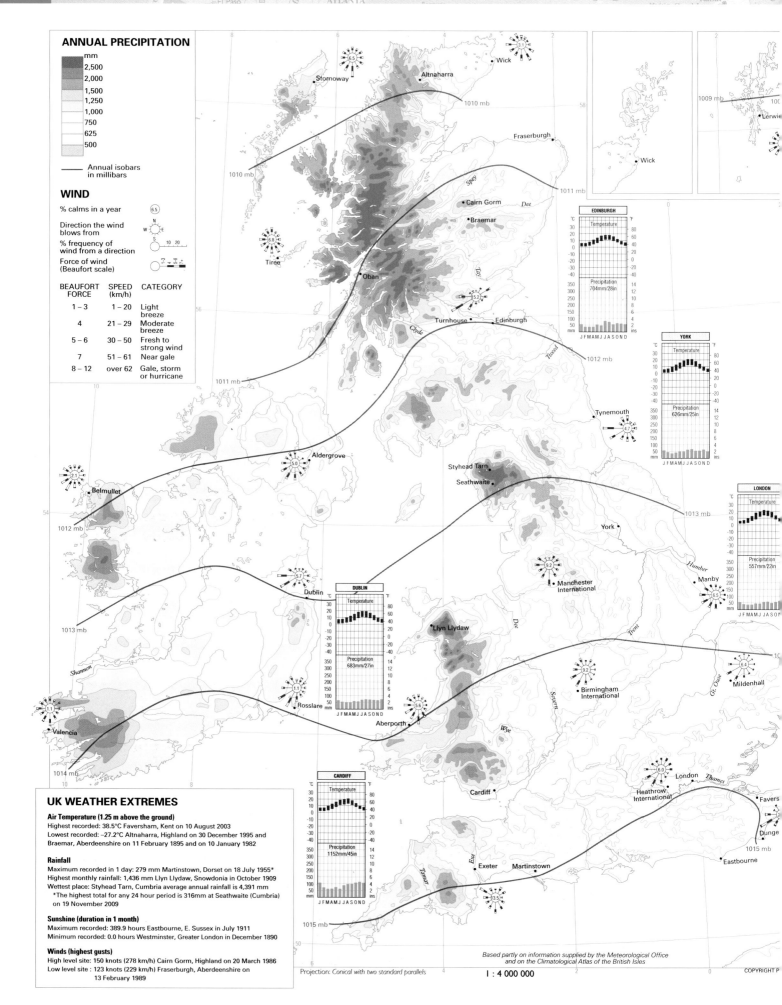

ANNUAL PRECIPITATION

mm
2,500
2,000
1,500
1,250
1,000
750
625
500

— Annual isobars in millibars

WIND

% calms in a year

Direction the wind blows from

% frequency of wind from a direction

Force of wind (Beaufort scale)

BEAUFORT FORCE	SPEED (km/h)	CATEGORY
1 – 3	1 – 20	Light breeze
4	21 – 29	Moderate breeze
5 – 6	30 – 50	Fresh to strong wind
7	51 – 61	Near gale
8 – 12	over 62	Gale, storm or hurricane

UK WEATHER EXTREMES

Air Temperature (1.25 m above the ground)
Highest recorded: 38.5°C Faversham, Kent on 10 August 2003
Lowest recorded: –27.2°C Altnaharra, Highland on 30 December 1995 and Braemar, Aberdeenshire on 11 February 1895 and on 10 January 1982

Rainfall
Maximum recorded in 1 day: 279 mm Martinstown, Dorset on 18 July 1955*
Highest monthly rainfall: 1,436 mm Llyn Llydaw, Snowdonia in October 1909
Wettest place: Styhead Tarn, Cumbria average annual rainfall is 4,391 mm
*The highest total for any 24 hour period is 316mm at Seathwaite (Cumbria) on 19 November 2009

Sunshine (duration in 1 month)
Maximum recorded: 389.9 hours Eastbourne, E. Sussex in July 1911
Minimum recorded: 0.0 hours Westminster, Greater London in December 1890

Winds (highest gusts)
High level site: 150 knots (278 km/h) Cairn Gorm, Highland on 20 March 1986
Low level site : 123 knots (229 km/h) Fraserburgh, Aberdeenshire on 13 February 1989

Based partly on information supplied by the Meteorological Office and on the Climatological Atlas of the British Isles

Projection: Conical with two standard parallels

1 : 4 000 000

COPYRIGHT P

JANUARY TEMPERATURE

Actual surface temperature

°C
- 7
- 6
- 5
- 4
- 3
- 2
- 1
- 0

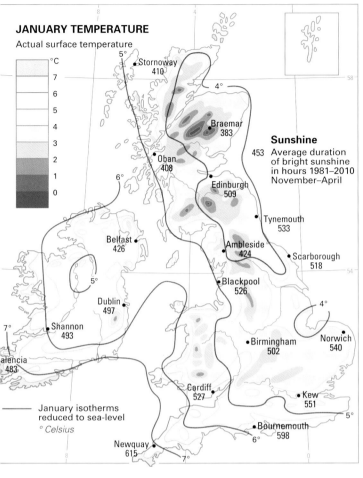

Sunshine

453 Average duration of bright sunshine in hours 1981–2010 November–April

— January isotherms reduced to sea-level
° Celsius

Stornoway 410
Braemar 383
Oban 408
Edinburgh 509
Tynemouth 533
Belfast 426
Ambleside 424
Scarborough 518
Blackpool 526
Dublin 497
Shannon 493
Valencia 483
Birmingham 502
Norwich 540
Cardiff 527
Kew 551
Bournemouth 598
Newquay 615

JULY TEMPERATURE

Actual surface temperature

°C
- 17
- 16
- 15
- 14
- 13
- 12
- 11
- 10

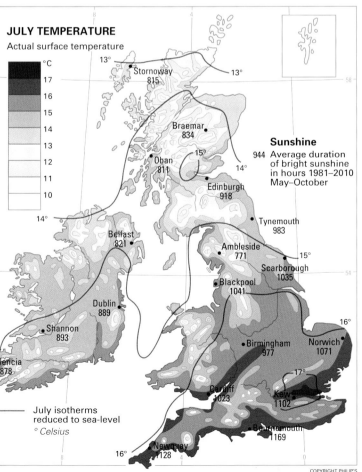

Sunshine

944 Average duration of bright sunshine in hours 1981–2010 May–October

— July isotherms reduced to sea-level
° Celsius

Stornoway 815
Braemar 834
Oban 811
Edinburgh 918
Tynemouth 983
Belfast 821
Ambleside 771
Scarborough 1035
Blackpool 1041
Dublin 889
Shannon 893
Valencia 878
Birmingham 977
Norwich 1071
Cardiff 1023
Kew 1102
Bournemouth 1169
Newquay 1128

COPYRIGHT PHILIP'S

CHANGES IN UK RAINFALL PATTERNS

Annual percentage change in precipitation, 1914-2007

- Over 10% increase
- 0 – 10% increase
- 0 – 2.5% decrease
- 2.5 – 5% decrease
- Over 5% decrease

Seasonal percentage change in precipitation, 1914-2007

region
increase
decrease

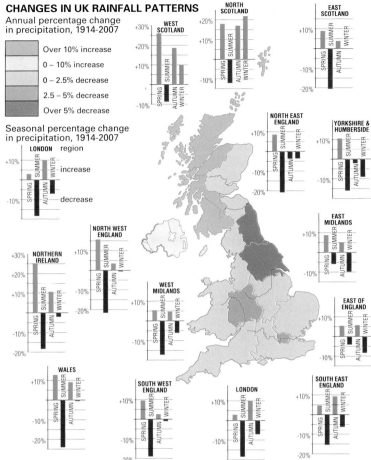

CHANGES IN SUMMER AND WINTER RAINFALL 1870–2010

Percentage change from 1961–1990 average
— High summer (July–August) in England and Wales
— Winter (December–March) in England and Wales

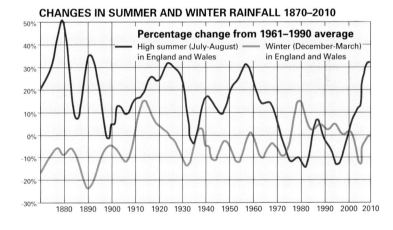

CHANGES IN AVERAGE SURFACE TEMPERATURE 1850–2010

Departures from 1961–1990 average
- Central England
- Global

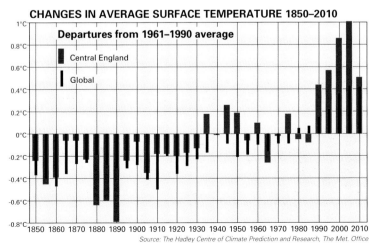

Source: The Hadley Centre of Climate Prediction and Research, The Met. Office

WATER SUPPLY

Regions of reliably high rainfall (more than 1,250 mm in at least 70% of the years)

(3) Major reservoirs (capacity over 20 million cubic metres, see list opposite for details)

→ Existing inter-regional transfers of water (by pipeline and river)

→ Proposed inter-regional transfers of water (by pipeline and river)

□ Proposed estuary storage site

▽ Proposed groundwater storage site

Principal sources of groundwater (porous and jointed aquifers)

THAMES WATER Water supply and sewerage companies in the UK

SCOTTISH WATER

NORTHERN IRELAND WATER

IRISH WATER

NORTHUMBRIAN WATER

YORKSHIRE WATER

UNITED UTILITIES

DWR CYMRU (WELSH WATER)

SEVERN TRENT WATER

ANGLIAN WATER

THAMES WATER

SOUTH WEST WATER

WESSEX WATER

SOUTHERN WATER

MAJOR RESERVOIRS
(with capacity in million m³)

England

1	Kielder Reservoir	198
2	Rutland Water	123
3	Haweswater	85
4	Grafham Water	59
5	Cow Green Reservoir	41
6	Thirlmere	41
7	Carsington Reservoir	36
8	Roadford Reservoir	35
9	Bewl Water Reservoir	31
10	Colliford Lake	29
11	Ladybower Reservoir	28
12	Hanningfield Reservoir	27
13	Abberton Reservoir	25
14	Draycote Water	23
15	Derwent Reservoir	22
16	Grimwith Reservoir	22
17	Wimbleball Lake	21
18	Chew Valley Lake	20
19	Balderhead Reservoir	20
20	Thames Valley (linked reservoirs)	
21	Lea Valley (linked reservoirs)	
22	Longendale (linked reservoirs)	

Wales

23	Elan Valley
24	Llyn Celyn
25	Llyn Brianne
26	Llyn Brenig
27	Llyn Vyrnwy
28	Llyn Clywedog
29	Llandegfedd Reservoir

Scotland

30	Loch Lomond
31	Loch Katrine
32	Megget Reservoir
33	Loch Ness
34	Blackwater Reservoir
35	Daer Reservoir
36	Carron Valley Reservoir

Ireland

37	Poulaphouca Reservoir
38	Inishcarra Reservoir
39	Carrigadrohid Reservoir

Kielder Water in Northumberland is the largest reservoir in the British Isles.

WASTE RECYCLING

The percentage of total household waste recycled in 2016/7

Over 50%
45 – 50%
40 – 45%
35 – 40%
Under 35%

SCOTLAND
NORTHERN IRELAND
IRELAND
NORTH EAST
NORTH WEST
YORKSHIRE & THE HUMBER
EAST MIDLANDS
WALES
WEST MIDLANDS
EAST
LONDON
SOUTH WEST
SOUTH EAST

JOURNEY TO SCHOOL IN THE UK

Mode of travel to school by children aged 5–16 in 2016/7

Other mode
Walking
Bus
Car

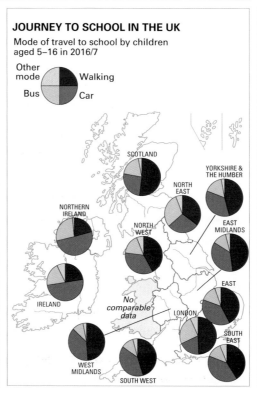

SCOTLAND
NORTHERN IRELAND
NORTH EAST
NORTH WEST
YORKSHIRE & THE HUMBER
EAST MIDLANDS
IRELAND
No comparable data
EAST
LONDON
SOUTH EAST
WEST MIDLANDS
SOUTH WEST

FLOOD RISK IN ENGLAND AND WALES

Areas at greatest risk from flooding (as designated by the Environment Agency)

SOILS

- Calcareous brown earth
- Brown earth
- Acid brown earth
- Podsol
- Peaty podsol
- Grey-brown podsol
- Gley
- Basin peat and alluvial gleys
- Peaty gley and blanket peat

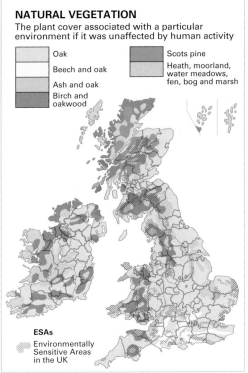

NATURAL VEGETATION

The plant cover associated with a particular environment if it was unaffected by human activity

- Oak
- Beech and oak
- Ash and oak
- Birch and oakwood
- Scots pine
- Heath, moorland, water meadows, fen, bog and marsh

ESAs
Environmentally Sensitive Areas in the UK

GREENHOUSE GAS EMISSIONS

Per capita Local CO2 emission estimates; industry, domestic and transport sectors 2016

- Over 20
- 12 –20
- 10 – 12
- 8 – 10
- 6 – 8
- Under 6

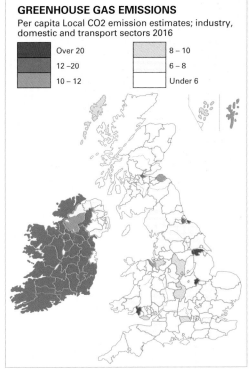

WORLD HERITAGE SITES

The settlement of Skara Brae is part of Neolithic Orkney.

Columns of basalt form the Giant's Causeway on the north coast of Northern Ireland.

Founded in the 6th century, Canterbury Cathedral has been enlarged and rebuilt, mainly in the Gothic style.

CONSERVATION

- National Parks
- Areas of Outstanding Natural Beauty (AONBs)
- National Scenic Areas (NSAs)
- Forest Parks, Regional Parks in Scotland and Special Protection Areas (SPAs)
- Green Belts (and the urban areas they surround)
- Heritage Coast (England and Wales)

✳ World Heritage Sites in the UK and Ireland

Other designated UK sites not shown:
St. Kilda, Atlantic Ocean
Henderson I., Pacific Ocean
Gough I. and Inaccessible I., Atlantic Ocean
St. George, Bermuda
Gorham's Cave Complex, Gibraltar

COPYRIGHT PHILIP'S

TYPES OF FARM

- Dairy cattle
- Beef cattle
- Sheep
- ● Pigs and/or poultry
- Mixed farming
- Market gardening (fruit and vegetables)
- Cereals
- Other crops (mainly potatoes, sugar beet)
- Northern limit of 9 month growing season
- Forests
- Built-up areas
- Areas with over 1,000 mm rainfall per year

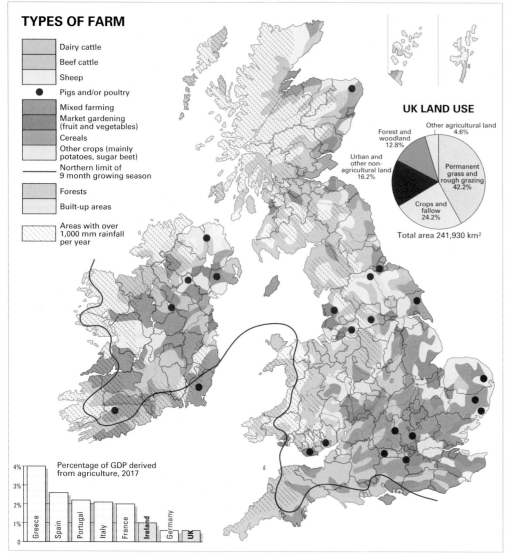

UK LAND USE

Forest and woodland 12.8%
Other agricultural land 4.6%
Urban and other non-agricultural land 16.2%
Permanent grass and rough grazing 42.2%
Crops and fallow 24.2%

Total area 241,930 km²

Percentage of GDP derived from agriculture, 2017

Greece, Spain, Portugal, Italy, France, Ireland, Germany, UK
(scale 0 to 4%)

CEREAL FARMING

The percentage of the total farmland used for growing cereals in 2016

- Over 40
- 25 – 40
- 10 – 25
- 5 – 10
- 0 – 5

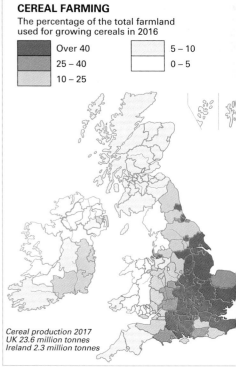

Cereal production 2017
UK 23.6 million tonnes
Ireland 2.3 million tonnes

DAIRY FARMING

The number of dairy cows per 100 hectares of farmland in 2016

- Over 40
- 30 – 40
- 20 – 30
- 10 – 20
- 0 – 10

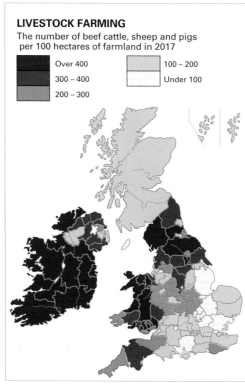

No comparable data

Milk Production (2016/17):
UK 14,251 million litres
Ireland 7,268 million litres

LIVESTOCK FARMING

The number of beef cattle, sheep and pigs per 100 hectares of farmland in 2017

- Over 400
- 300 – 400
- 200 – 300
- 100 – 200
- Under 100

FISHING

Major fishing ports by size of catch landed

- ▼ Demersal e.g. cod (Deep sea fish)
- ▼ Pelagic e.g. mackerel (Shallow sea fish)
- ▽ Shellfish e.g. lobster

▨ The most important inshore fishing ground

North Sea
263,100 tonnes

Total amount caught in each fishing region by UK vessels

Lerwick
Scrabster
Kinlochbervie
West Coast of Scotland 148,500 tonnes
Ullapool
Fraserburgh
Peterhead
Mallaig
North Sea 263,100 tonnes
Killybegs
Kirkcudbright
North Shields
Portavogie
Douglas
Bridlington
Kilkeel
Ardglass
Rossaveel
Howth
Holyhead
Dunmore East
Castletown Bearhaven
Milford Haven
Bristol Channel and Celtic Sea 13,900 tonnes
Shoreham
Newlyn
Plymouth
Brixham
West Ireland and Sole Bank 37,600 tonnes
English Channel 67,900 tonnes

1000 500 200 100 50 m Depth of sea in metres

EMPLOYMENT IN SERVICES

The percentage of the workforce employed in the service industry in 2017

- Over 90%
- 85 – 90%
- 80 – 85%
- 75 – 80%
- Under 75%

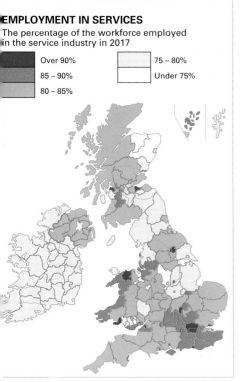

EMPLOYMENT IN MANUFACTURING

The percentage of the workforce employed in the manufacturing industry in 2017

- Over 15%
- 12.5 – 15%
- 10 – 12.5%
- 7.5 – 10%
- 5 – 7.5%
- Under 5%

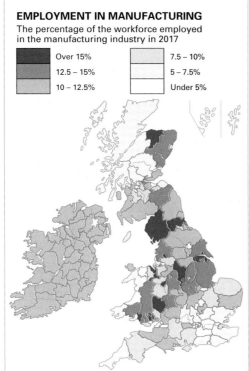

MOTOR MANUFACTURING IN ENGLAND AND WALES

Key manufacturing sites in 2018

- Car manufacturing sites
- Commercial vehicle manufacturing sites
- Selected engine manufacturing sites

Source: SMMT

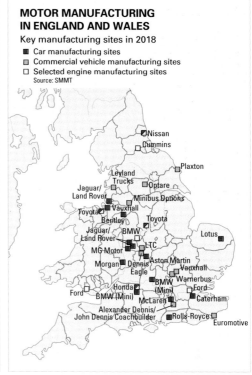

CHANGES IN EMPLOYMENT IN THE UK

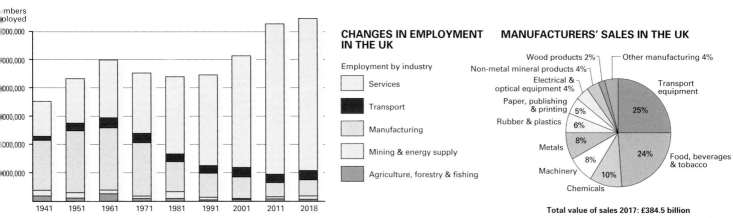

Employment by industry

- Services
- Transport
- Manufacturing
- Mining & energy supply
- Agriculture, forestry & fishing

MANUFACTURERS' SALES IN THE UK

- Wood products 2%
- Non-metal mineral products 4%
- Electrical & optical equipment 4%
- Paper, publishing & printing 5%
- Rubber & plastics 6%
- Metals 8%
- Machinery 8%
- Chemicals 10%
- Other manufacturing 4%
- Transport equipment 25%
- Food, beverages & tobacco 24%

Total value of sales 2017: £384.5 billion

UK FOREIGN TRADE

TOP TEN TRADING PARTNERS One container represents 1% of the total value of imports or 1% of the total value of exports in 2017

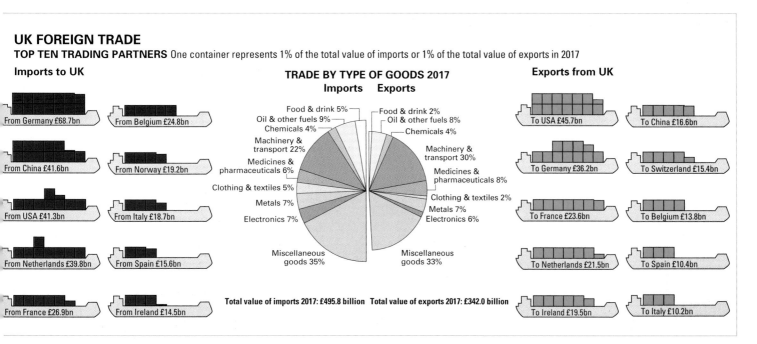

Imports to UK

- From Germany £68.7bn
- From Belgium £24.8bn
- From China £41.6bn
- From Norway £19.2bn
- From USA £41.3bn
- From Italy £18.7bn
- From Netherlands £39.8bn
- From Spain £15.6bn
- From France £26.9bn
- From Ireland £14.5bn

TRADE BY TYPE OF GOODS 2017

Imports   Exports

Imports:
- Food & drink 5%
- Oil & other fuels 9%
- Chemicals 4%
- Machinery & transport 22%
- Medicines & pharmaceuticals 6%
- Clothing & textiles 5%
- Metals 7%
- Electronics 7%
- Miscellaneous goods 35%

Exports:
- Food & drink 2%
- Oil & other fuels 8%
- Chemicals 4%
- Machinery & transport 30%
- Medicines & pharmaceuticals 8%
- Clothing & textiles 2%
- Metals 7%
- Electronics 6%
- Miscellaneous goods 33%

Exports from UK

- To USA £45.7bn
- To China £16.6bn
- To Germany £36.2bn
- To Switzerland £15.4bn
- To France £23.6bn
- To Belgium £13.8bn
- To Netherlands £21.5bn
- To Spain £10.4bn
- To Ireland £19.5bn
- To Italy £10.2bn

Total value of imports 2017: £495.8 billion   Total value of exports 2017: £342.0 billion

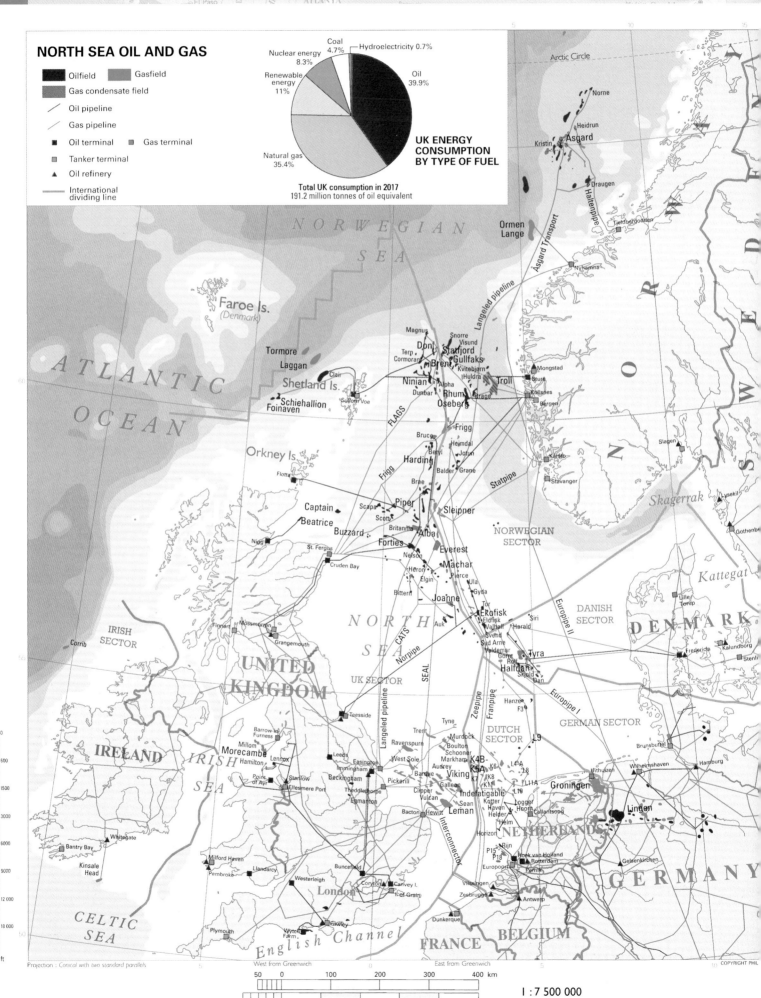

PRODUCTION OF PRIMARY FUELS IN THE UK 1975–2017

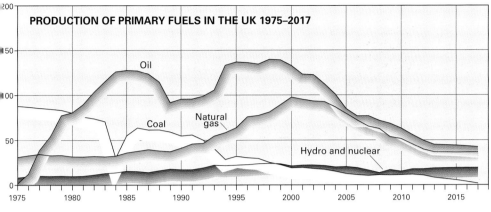

Oil
Coal
Natural gas
Hydro and nuclear

1975 1980 1985 1990 1995 2000 2005 2010 2015

UK ENERGY IMPORTS

Percentage of each type of fuel imported by the UK, 2015

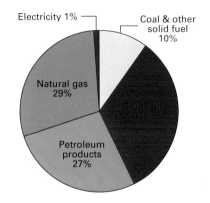

Electricity 1%
Coal & other solid fuel 10%
Crude oil 33%
Natural gas 29%
Petroleum products 27%

Total UK energy imports 2017 147.9 million tonnes of oil equivalent

PROSPECTING FOR SHALE GAS IN GREAT BRITAIN

□ Areas where licenses have been granted to prospect for shale gas

Rock outcrops where shale gas may occur
- Kimmeridge Clay
- Oxford Clay
- Liassic outcrops
- Millstone Grit
- Cambrian outcrops

COAL IN ENGLAND AND WALES

▽ Open-cast mines
□ Major coal-fired power stations
☐ Coalfields
← Coal imports

Drax
Fiddler's Ferry
West Burton
Cottam
Ratcliffe-on-Soar
Aberthaw

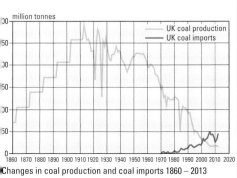

million tonnes
— UK coal production
— UK coal imports

1860 1870 1880 1890 1900 1910 1920 1930 1940 1950 1960 1970 1980 1990 2000 2010 2020

Changes in coal production and coal imports 1860 – 2013

RENEWABLE ENERGY IN THE UK

The amount of energy generated from renewable sources in GWh

- Over 25,000
- 20,000 – 25,000
- 10,000 – 20,000
- 5,000 – 10,000
- Under 5,000
- Possible sites for tidal power farm
- ✈ Major wind farm

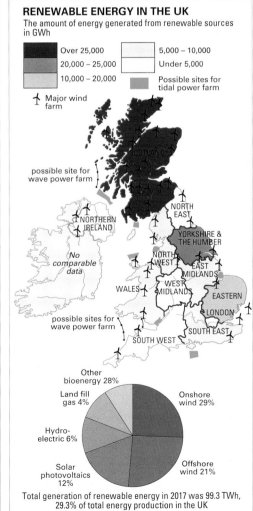

SCOTLAND
possible site for wave power farm
NORTHERN IRELAND
(No comparable data)
NORTH EAST
YORKSHIRE & THE HUMBER
NORTH WEST
EAST MIDLANDS
WALES
WEST MIDLANDS
EASTERN
LONDON
SOUTH EAST
SOUTH WEST
possible sites for wave power farm

Other bioenergy 28%
Land fill gas 4%
Hydro-electric 6%
Solar photovoltaics 12%
Onshore wind 29%
Offshore wind 21%

Total generation of renewable energy in 2017 was 99.3 TWh, 29.3% of total energy production in the UK

ELECTRICITY GENERATION

Power Stations (with capacity)
- □ Coal-fired (over 1,000 MW)
- ■ Peat-fired (over 100 MW)
- ■ Oil-fired (over 500 MW)
- ■ Combined cycle gas turbine (over 1,000 MW)
- □ Nuclear (over 1,000 MW)
- □ Proposed nuclear sites
- ▲ Pumped storage scheme
- ■ Hydro-electric (over 40 MW)
- □ Coal & gas-fired (over 1,000 MW)

Fasnakyle
Foyers
Peterhead
Rannoch
Errochty
Cruachan
Clunie
Lochay
Clachan
Sloy
Longannet
Torness
Hunterston
Ballylumford
Hartlepool
Heysham
Lough Ree
Saltend
West Offaly
Poolbeg
Fiddler's Ferry
Drax
South Humber Bank
Moneypoint
Edenderry
Dinorwig
Connahs Quay
West Burton
Cottam
Turlough Hill
Ffestiniog
Staythorpe
Tarbert
Ardnacrusha
Rheidol
Ratcliffe-on-Soar
King's Lynn
Aghada
Pembroke
Sizewell
Didcot
Aberthaw
Seabank
Grain
Hinkley Point
Dungeness

Fuel used in the generation of electricity in the UK 1980–2017

	0%	20%	40%	60%	80%	100%
1980						
1990						
2000						
2010						
2017						

- Coal
- Oil
- Natural gas
- Nuclear
- Renewable energy
- Other
- Net imports

ROADS AND FERRIES

- ▬M6▬ Motorways
- ─── Other main roads
- ········ Principal car ferry routes
- ─ ─ ─ Channel Tunnel

Scrabster, Stornoway, Wick, Kirkwall, Lerwick, Invergordon, Ullapool, Invergordon, Inverness, Aberdeen, Oban, Perth, Dundee, Glasgow, Edinburgh, Troon, Derry/Londonderry, Newcastle, Larne, Stranraer, Carlisle, Sligo, Belfast, Dundalk, Douglas, Morecambe, Galway, Dublin, Leeds, Hull, Dún Laoghaire, Holyhead, Liverpool, Manchester, Sheffield, Limerick, Shrewsbury, Leicester, Norwich, Waterford, Rosslare Europort, Birmingham, Cambridge, Killarney, Cork, Fishguard, Harwich, Felixstowe, Pembroke, Swansea, Oxford, London, Cardiff, Bristol, Dover, Dunkirk, Southampton, Portsmouth, Calais, Exeter, Poole, Weymouth, Newhaven, Boulogne, Plymouth, Penzance

RAILWAYS

- ─── Electrified lines
- ─── Other main lines
- ━━━ High-speed rail link London to Lille, Brussels and Paris
- ─ ─ ─ High Speed 2 (HS2) rail link (under con.) London to Birmingham, Leeds and Manchester

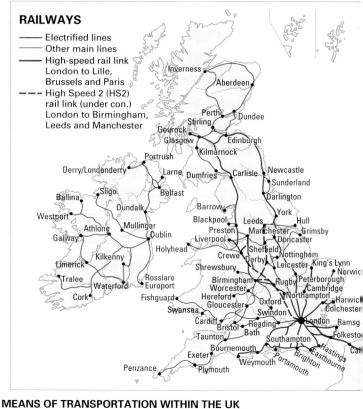

Inverness, Aberdeen, Perth, Dundee, Gourock, Stirling, Glasgow, Edinburgh, Kilmarnock, Portrush, Derry/Londonderry, Larne, Dumfries, Carlisle, Newcastle, Ballina, Sligo, Belfast, Sunderland, Darlington, Westport, Dundalk, Barrow, Blackpool, York, Athlone, Mullingar, Preston, Leeds, Hull, Galway, Dublin, Liverpool, Manchester, Grimsby, Doncaster, Kilkenny, Holyhead, Crewe, Sheffield, Nottingham, Limerick, Derby, Tralee, Waterford, Rosslare Europort, Shrewsbury, Leicester, King's Lynn, Cork, Fishguard, Birmingham, Rugby, Peterborough, Worcester, Hereford, Northampton, Cambridge, Gloucester, Oxford, Swindon, Colchester, Swansea, Cardiff, Reading, Bath, London, Harwich, Ramsg, Taunton, Southampton, Folkesto, Bournemouth, Brighton, Hastings, Exeter, Portsmouth, Eastbourne, Penzance, Weymouth, Plymouth

CHANNEL TUNNEL AND HIGH-SPEED RAIL LINKS IN EUROPE

Estimated journey times between London and other selected European cities

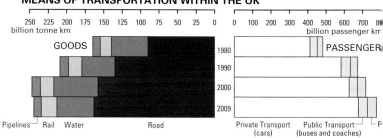

- London–Berlin
- London–Amsterdam
- London–Paris
- London–Brussels

Legend:
- 1990 — Best time achievable before opening of Channel Tunnel
- 2002 — Opening of Channel Tunnel in 1994 and completion of high-speed links in Europe
- 2018 — Journey time on high speed link from London St. Pancras to Folkestone

Scale: 5, 10, 15, 20 hours

MEANS OF TRANSPORTATION WITHIN THE UK

GOODS
250 225 200 175 150 125 100 75 50 25 0 billion tonne km

PASSENGER
0 100 200 300 400 500 600 700 8 billion passenger km

Years: 1980, 1990, 2000, 2009

Pipelines, Rail, Water, Road

Private Transport (cars), Public Transport (buses and coaches)

SEAPORTS

Goods traffic by port in million tonnes
- 60,000
- 30,000
- 10,000
- 5,000

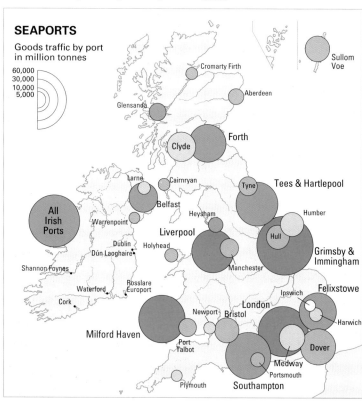

Sullom Voe, Cromarty Firth, Aberdeen, Glensanda, Forth, Clyde, Larne, Cairnryan, Tyne, Tees & Hartlepool, Belfast, Heysham, Humber, All Irish Ports, Warrenpoint, Liverpool, Hull, Dublin, Holyhead, Grimsby & Immingham, Dún Laoghaire, Manchester, Shannon Foynes, Felixstowe, Waterford, Rosslare Europort, Ipswich, Cork, London, Harwich, Newport, Bristol, Milford Haven, Port Talbot, Dover, Medway, Portsmouth, Plymouth, Southampton

AIRPORTS

Passenger traffic in millions
- 70,000
- 35,000
- 10,000
- 5,000
- 1,000

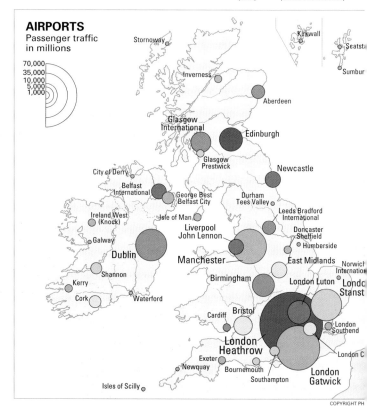

Stornoway, Kirkwall, Scatsta, Sumbur, Inverness, Aberdeen, Glasgow International, Edinburgh, Glasgow Prestwick, Newcastle, City of Derry, Belfast International, George Best Belfast City, Durham Tees Valley, Ireland West (Knock), Isle of Man, Leeds Bradford International, Galway, Liverpool John Lennon, Doncaster Sheffield, Humberside, Dublin, Manchester, East Midlands, Norwich International, Shannon, Birmingham, Kerry, London Luton, London Stanst, Cork, Waterford, Cardiff, Bristol, London Southend, Exeter, London Heathrow, Newquay, Bournemouth, London G, Southampton, London Gatwick, Isles of Scilly

LEISURE

- National Parks
- Areas of Outstanding Natural Beauty
- National Scenic Areas
- Built-up areas
- - - - Long distance footpaths
- ● Main tourist resorts
- ◆ Other tourist attractions

TRAVEL

- Motorways
- Other important roads
- Main Intercity railways
- Main ferry routes
- - - - Channel Tunnel
- ⊕ Main airports
- ○ Ports and other towns

TOP UK TOURIST ATTRACTIONS

- ◍ Museum or gallery
- ● Historic Property
- ○ Other attraction

		Total visits in millions (2017)
1.	British Museum, London	◍ 5.9
2.	Tate Modern, London	◍ 5.7
3.	National Gallery, London	◍ 5.2
4.	Natural History Museum, London	◍ 4.4
5.	Victoria & Albert Museum, London	◍ 3.8
6.	Science Museum, London	◍ 3.3
7.	Southbank Centre, London	○ 3.2
8.	Somerset House, London	○ 3.2
9.	Tower of London	● 2.8
10.	Royal Museums Greenwich	◍ 2.6
11.	National Museum of Scotland, Edinburgh	◍ 2.2
12.	Edinburgh Castle	● 2.1
13.	Chester Zoo	○ 1.9
14.	Royal Botanic Gardens, Kew	○ 1.8
15.	Tate Britain, London	◍ 1.8
16.	Scottish National Gallery, Edinburgh	◍ 1.6
17.	Stonehenge, Wiltshire	● 1.6
18.	St Paul's Cathedral, London	● 1.6
19.	Westminster Abbey, London	● 1.6
20.	Royal Albert Hall, London	○ 1.5

The British Museum in London is the UK's most visited attraction.

TOP IRELAND TOURIST ATTRACTIONS

- ◍ Gallery
- ● Historic Property
- ○ Other attraction

		Total visits in millions (2017)
1.	Guinness Storehouse, Dublin	○ 1.7
2.	Cliffs of Moher Visitor Experience, Clare	○ 1.5
3.	Dublin Zoo	○ 1.3
4.	National Aquatic Centre, Dublin	○ 1.1
5.	National Gallery of Ireland, Dublin	◍ 1.1
6.	Book of Kells, Dublin	○ 1.0
7.	Tayto Park, Meath	○ 0.7
8.	Castletown House Parklands, Kildare	○ 0.7
9.	Glendalough Site, Wicklow	○ 0.6
10.	St Patrick's Cathedral, Dublin	● 0.6

COPYRIGHT PHILIP'S

CENTRAL LONDON

VISITS ABROAD BY UK RESIDENTS

Total number of UK tourists 2017: 72.8 million

Millions of visitors from UK (2017)

0 1 2 3 4 5 6 7 8 9 10 11 12 13 14 15 16

- Spain
- France
- Italy
- Rep. of Ireland
- USA
- Germany
- Portugal
- Poland
- Netherlands
- Greece

ORIGIN OF TOURISTS TO THE UK

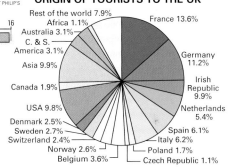

- Rest of the world 7.9%
- Africa 1.1%
- Australia 3.1%
- C. & S. America 3.1%
- Asia 9.9%
- Canada 1.9%
- USA 9.8%
- Denmark 2.5%
- Sweden 2.7%
- Switzerland 2.4%
- Norway 2.6%
- Belgium 3.6%
- France 13.6%
- Germany 11.2%
- Irish Republic 9.9%
- Netherlands 5.4%
- Spain 6.1%
- Italy 6.2%
- Poland 1.7%
- Czech Republic 1.1%

Total number of foreign tourists 2015: 13.9 million

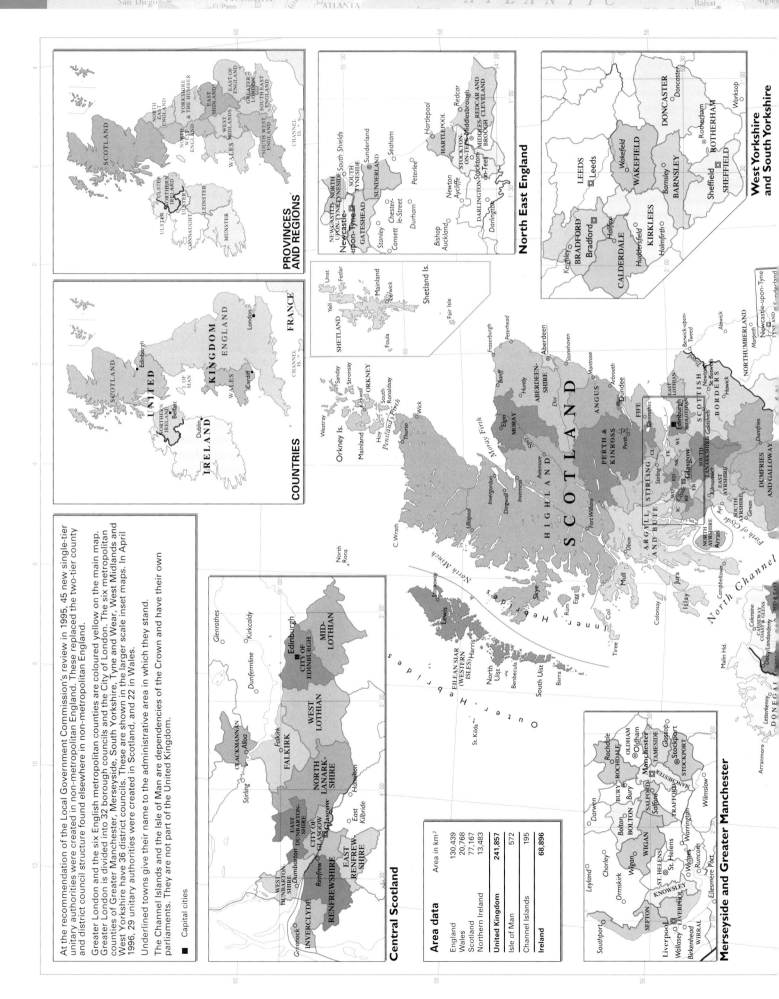

PROVINCES AND REGIONS

COUNTRIES

North East England

West Yorkshire and South Yorkshire

Central Scotland

Merseyside and Greater Manchester

At the recommendation of the Local Government Commission's review in 1995, 45 new single-tier unitary authorities were created in non-metropolitan England. These replaced the two-tier county and district council structure found elsewhere in non-metropolitan England.

Greater London and the six English metropolitan counties are coloured yellow on the main map. Greater London is divided into 32 borough councils and the City of London. The six metropolitan counties of Greater Manchester, Merseyside, South Yorkshire, Tyne and Wear, West Midlands and West Yorkshire have 36 district councils. These are shown in the larger scale inset maps. In April 1996, 29 unitary authorities were created in Scotland, and 22 in Wales.

Underlined towns give their name to the administrative area in which they stand.

The Channel Islands and the Isle of Man are dependencies of the Crown and have their own parliaments. They are not part of the United Kingdom.

■ Capital cities

Area data

	Area in km²
England	130,439
Wales	20,768
Scotland	77,167
Northern Ireland	13,483
United Kingdom	**241,857**
Isle of Man	572
Channel Islands	195
Ireland	**68,896**

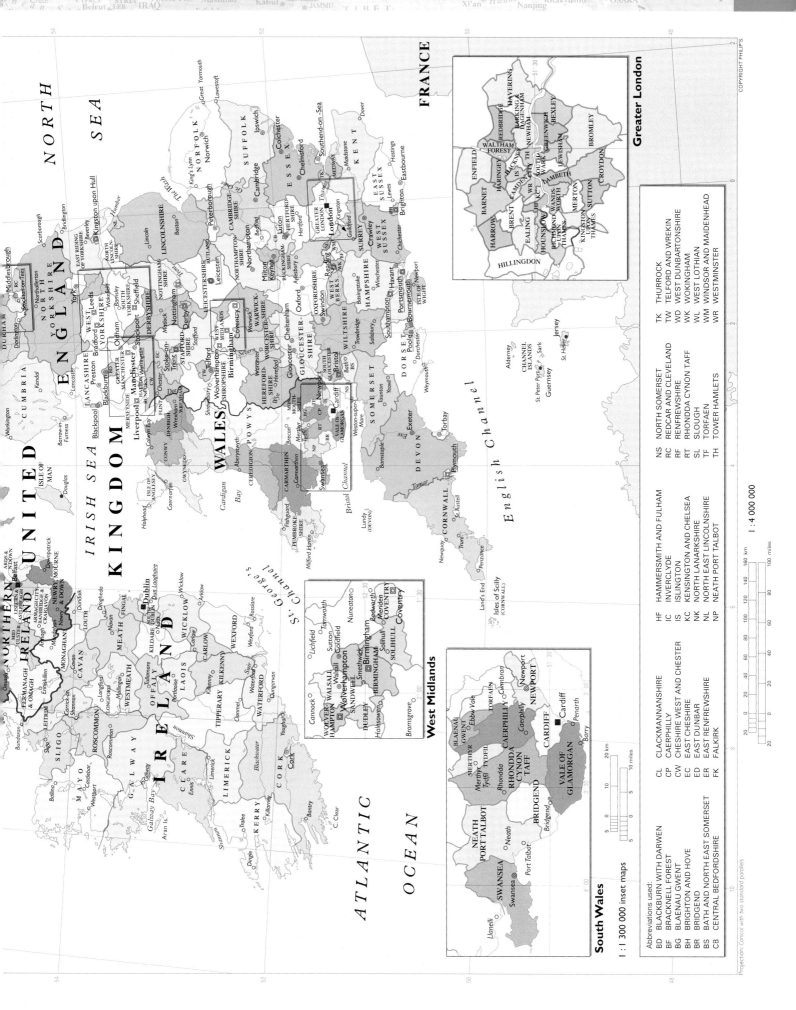

Greater London

West Midlands

South Wales

1 : 1 300 000 inset maps

Abbreviations used:
BD	BLACKBURN WITH DARWEN	CL	CLACKMANNANSHIRE
BF	BRACKNELL FOREST	CP	CAERPHILLY
BG	BLAENAU GWENT	CW	CHESHIRE WEST AND CHESTER
BH	BRIGHTON AND HOVE	EC	EAST CHESHIRE
BR	BRIDGEND	ED	EAST DUNBAR
BS	BATH AND NORTH EAST SOMERSET	ER	EAST RENFREWSHIRE
CB	CENTRAL BEDFORDSHIRE	FK	FALKIRK

HF	HAMMERSMITH AND FULHAM	NS	NORTH SOMERSET
IC	INVERCLYDE	RC	REDCAR AND CLEVELAND
IS	ISLINGTON	RF	RENFREWSHIRE
KC	KENSINGTON AND CHELSEA	RT	RHONDDA CYNON TAFF
NK	NORTH LANARKSHIRE	SL	SLOUGH
NL	NORTH EAST LINCOLNSHIRE	TF	TORFAEN
NP	NEATH PORT TALBOT	TH	TOWER HAMLETS

TK	THURROCK		
TW	TELFORD AND WREKIN		
WD	WEST DUNBARTONSHIRE		
WK	WOKINGHAM		
WL	WEST LOTHIAN		
WM	WINDSOR AND MAIDENHEAD		
WR	WESTMINSTER		

1 : 4 000 000

Projection: Conical with two standard parallels

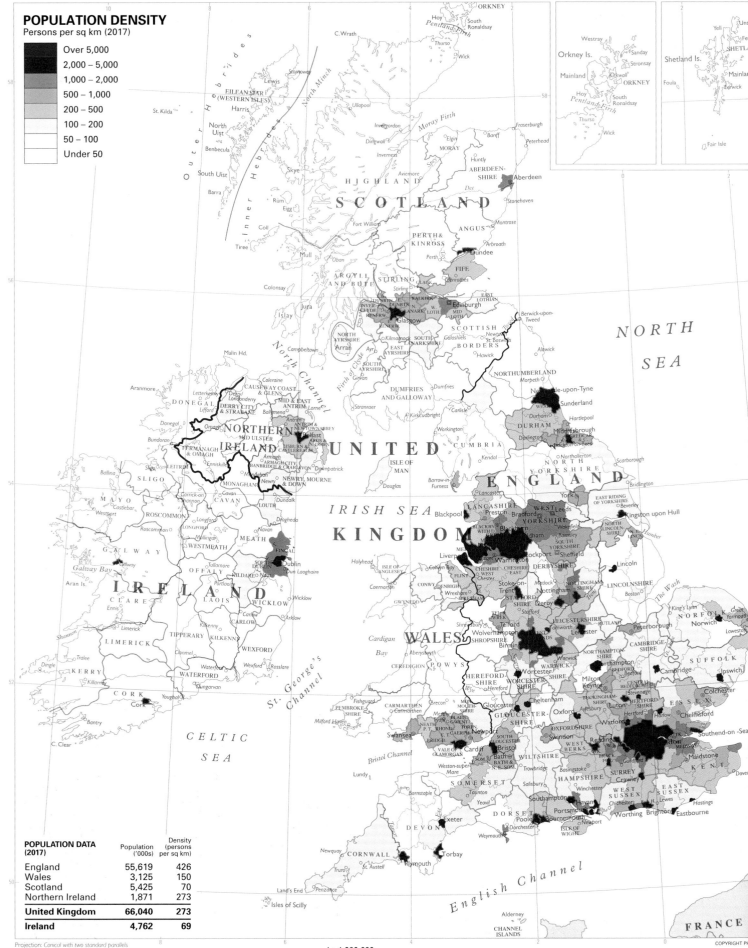

POPULATION DENSITY
Persons per sq km (2017)

- Over 5,000
- 2,000 – 5,000
- 1,000 – 2,000
- 500 – 1,000
- 200 – 500
- 100 – 200
- 50 – 100
- Under 50

POPULATION DATA (2017)	Population ('000s)	Density (persons per sq km)
England	55,619	426
Wales	3,125	150
Scotland	5,425	70
Northern Ireland	1,871	273
United Kingdom	**66,040**	**273**
Ireland	**4,762**	**69**

Projection: Conical with two standard parallels

1 : 4 000 000

COPYRIGHT P

POPULATION DENSITY IN 1891

Persons per sq km

- Over 1,000
- 500 – 1,000
- 200 – 500
- 100 – 200
- 50 – 100
- 25 – 50
- Under 25

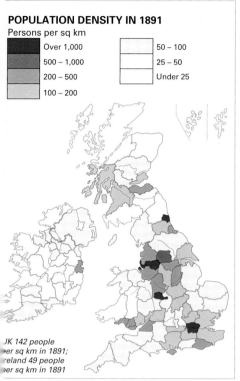

UK 142 people per sq km in 1891;
Ireland 49 people per sq km in 1891

NATIONALITY

Non-British as a percentage of total population in 2017

- Over 20%
- 10 – 20%
- 5 – 10%
- 0 – 5%

378 000   Total number of non-British people in each region

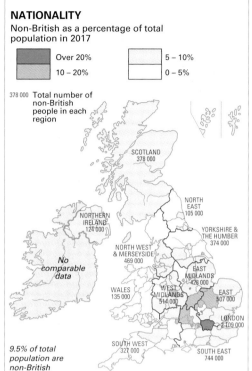

SCOTLAND 378 000

NORTHERN IRELAND 124 000

NORTH EAST 105 000

YORKSHIRE & THE HUMBER 374 000

NORTH WEST & MERSEYSIDE 469 000

EAST MIDLANDS 426 000

WALES 135 000

WEST MIDLANDS 514 000

EAST 507 000

LONDON 2 109 000

SOUTH WEST 327 000

SOUTH EAST 744 000

No comparable data

9.5% of total population are non-British

INTERNAL MIGRATION

The difference between the number moving in and the number moving away per 1,000 inhabitants 2017*

- Over 5 moved in
- 1 – 5 moved in
- 0 – 1 moved in
- 0 – 1 moved away
- 1 – 5 moved away
- Over 5 moved away

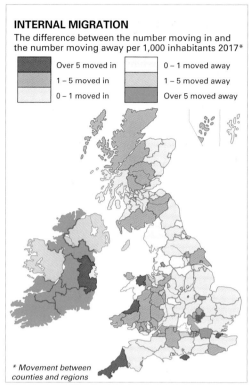

* Movement between counties and regions

NATURAL POPULATION CHANGE

The difference between the number of births and the number of deaths per thousand inhabitants in 2017

- Over 10 more births
- 5 – 10 more births
- 2.5 – 5 more births
- 1 – 2.5 more births
- 0 – 1 more births
- 0 – 2 more deaths

UK 2.7 more births than deaths;
Ireland 7.5 more births than deaths

YOUNG PEOPLE

The percentage of the population under 16 years old in 2017

- Over 21%
- 19 – 21%
- 17 – 19%
- Under 17%

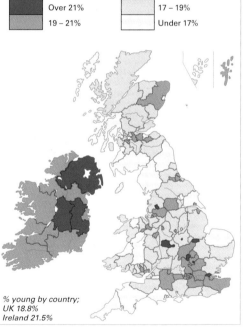

% young by country;
UK 18.8%
Ireland 21.5%

OLDER PEOPLE

The percentage of the population aged 65 and over in 2017

- Over 22%
- 20 – 22%
- 18 – 20%
- 16 – 18%
- 14 – 16%
- Under 14%

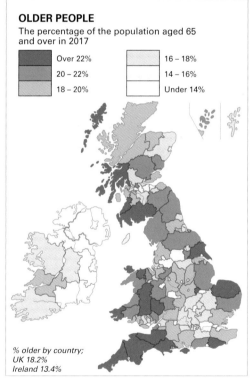

% older by country;
UK 18.2%
Ireland 13.4%

VITAL STATISTICS (1920–2017)

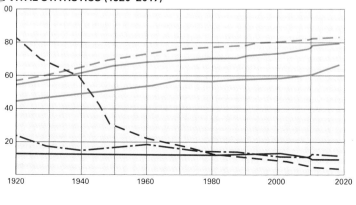

- Total population (in millions)
- Infant mortality (deaths per 1,000 live births)
- Birth rate (births per 1,000 of the population)
- Death rate (deaths per 1,000 of the population)
- Male life expectancy (in years)
- Female life expectancy (in years)

COPYRIGHT PHILIP'S

AGE STRUCTURE OF THE UK

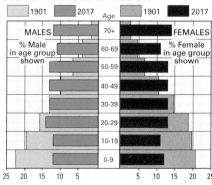

1901   2017   Age   1901   2017

MALES   FEMALES

% Male in age group shown   % Female in age group shown

70+
60-69
50-59
40-49
30-39
20-29
10-19
0-9

25 20 15 10 5   5 10 15 20 25

HOUSE PRICES

Annual change in house prices 2017-2018

- Over 5%
- 3 – 5%
- 2 – 3%
- 0 – 2%
- Under 0%

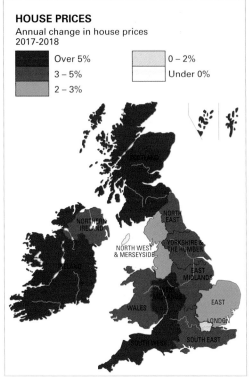

UNEMPLOYMENT

The percentage of the workforce unemployed in 2018

- Over 5%
- 4 – 5%
- 3 – 4%
- Under 3%

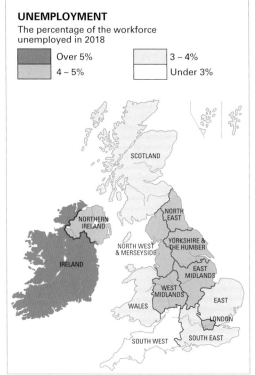

INCOME

The average gross weekly earnings of males and females in full employment in 2017

- Over £600
- £550 – £600
- £525 – £550
- £510 – £525
- £500 – £510

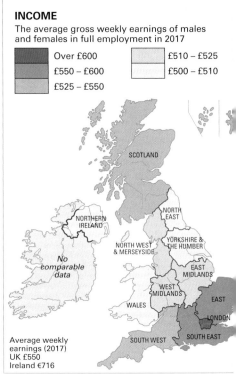

Average weekly earnings (2017)
UK £550
Ireland €716

EDUCATION

The percentage of pupils achieving 5 grade A*-C at GCSE (or equivalent) in 2015/6

- Over 60%
- 55 – 60%
- 50 – 55%
- 45 – 50%
- Under 45%

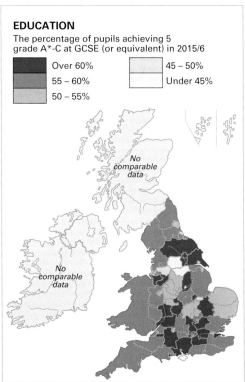

CRIME RATE

Total recorded crimes per 1,000 people in 2017

- Over 100
- 85 – 100
- 70 – 85
- 55 – 70
- 40 – 55
- Under 40

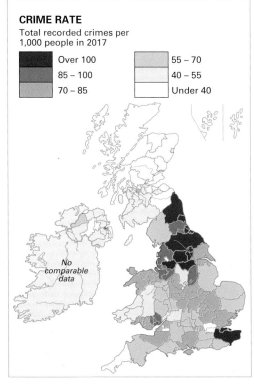

INTERNET USE

Frequency of internet use (%)

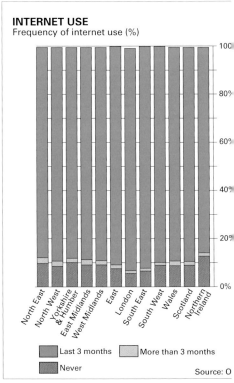

- Last 3 months
- More than 3 months
- Never

Source: O

COMPARISON OF HOUSEHOLD EXPENDITURE, 2017

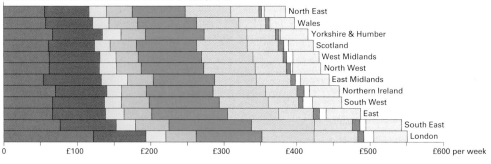

North East
Wales
Yorkshire & Humber
Scotland
West Midlands
North West
East Midlands
Northern Ireland
South West
East
South East
London

0   £100   £200   £300   £400   £500   £600 per week

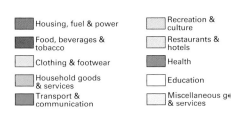

- Housing, fuel & power
- Food, beverages & tobacco
- Clothing & footwear
- Household goods & services
- Transport & communication
- Recreation & culture
- Restaurants & hotels
- Health
- Education
- Miscellaneous g & services

Average household expenditure per week in UK in 2017:

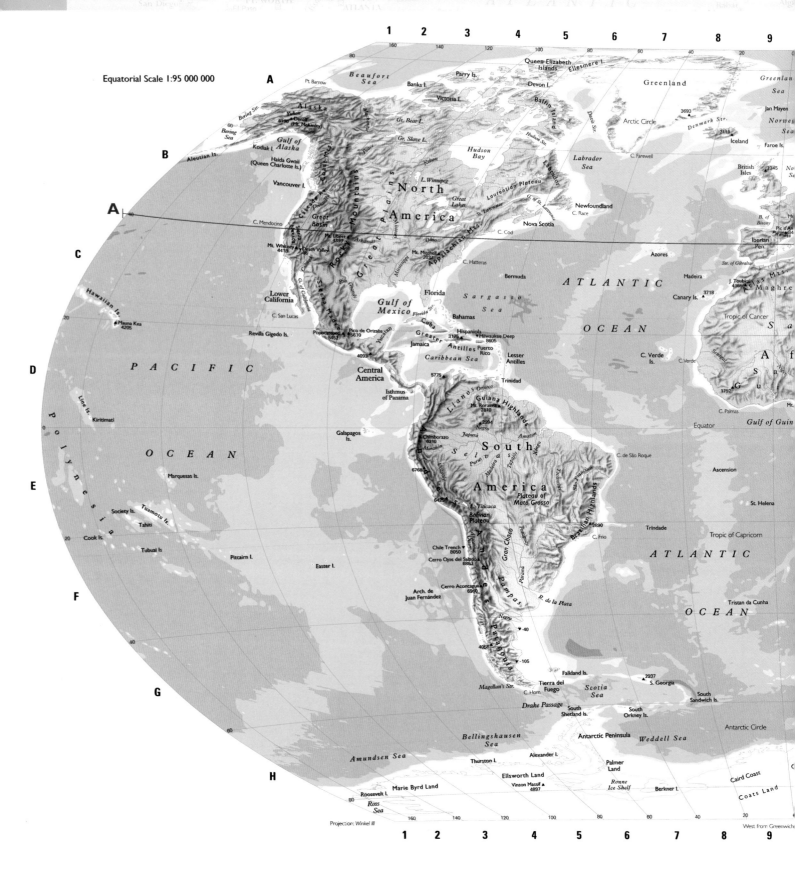

Equatorial Scale 1:95 000 000

Projection: Winkel III

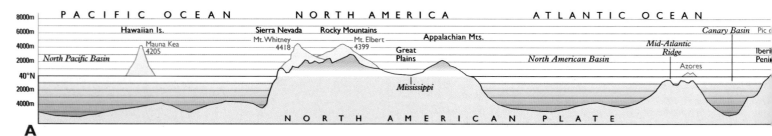

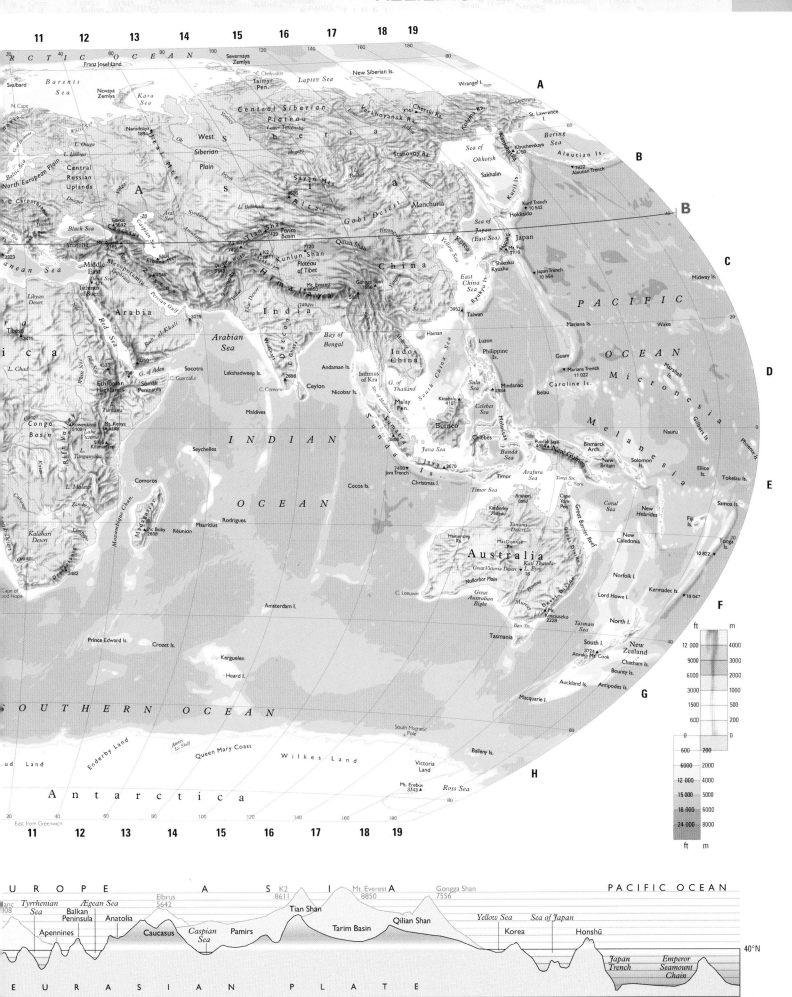

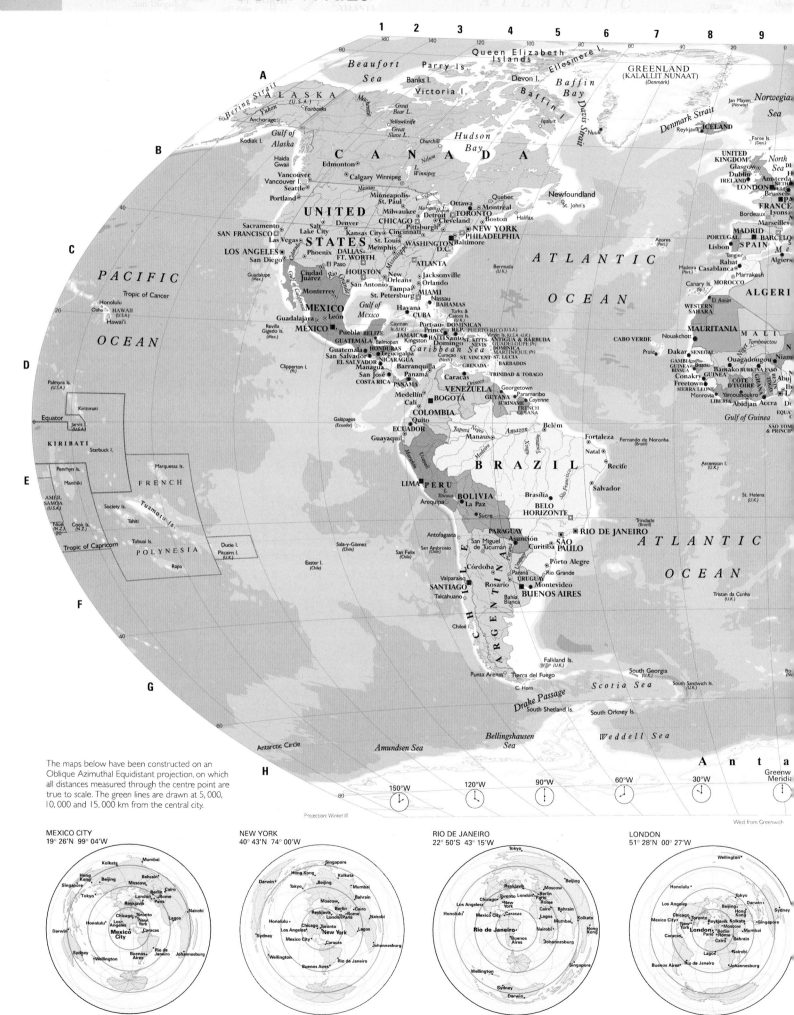

The maps below have been constructed on an Oblique Azimuthal Equidistant projection, on which all distances measured through the centre point are true to scale. The green lines are drawn at 5,000, 10,000 and 15,000 km from the central city.

Projection: Winkel III

West from Greenwich

MEXICO CITY
19° 26'N 99° 04'W

NEW YORK
40° 43'N 74° 00'W

RIO DE JANEIRO
22° 50'S 43° 15'W

LONDON
51° 28'N 00° 27'W

Equatorial Scale 1:95 000 000

ft	m
0	0
600	200
6 000	2000
12 000	4000
15 000	5000
18 000	6000
24 000	8000

30°E 60°E 90°E 120°E 150°E International Date Line 30°W

The time at this longitude when it is 12.00 (noon) at Greenwich

East from Greenwich

CAPE TOWN
33° 55'S 18° 35'E

DELHI
28° 39'N 77° 13'E

TOKYO
35° 33'N 139° 46'E

SYDNEY
33° 56'S 151° 10'E

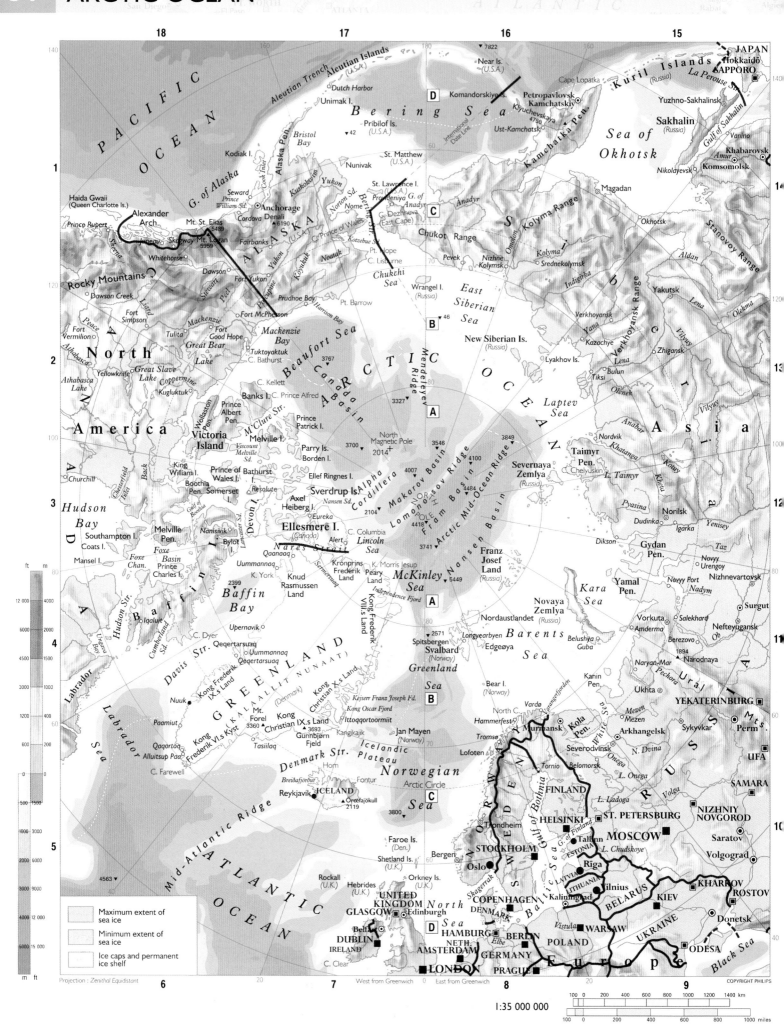

Projection : Zenithal Equidistant

West from Greenwich | East from Greenwich

COPYRIGHT PHILIPS

1:35 000 000

Maximum extent of sea ice

Minimum extent of sea ice

Ice caps and permanent ice shelf

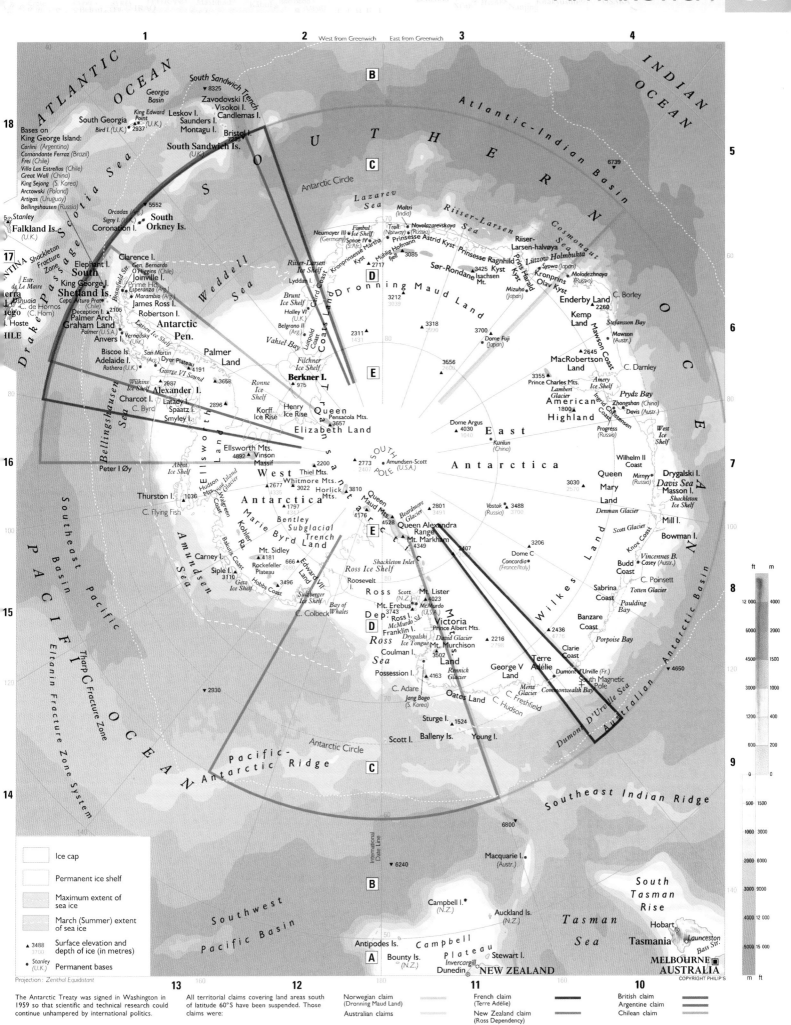

The Antarctic Treaty was signed in Washington in 1959 so that scientific and technical research could continue unhampered by international politics.

All territorial claims covering land areas south of latitude 60°S have been suspended. Those claims were:

Norwegian claim (Dronning Maud Land)

Australian claims

French claim (Terre Adélie)

New Zealand claim (Ross Dependency)

British claim

Argentine claim

Chilean claim

Projection: Zenithal Equidistant

Legend:

- Ice cap
- Permanent ice shelf
- Maximum extent of sea ice
- March (Summer) extent of sea ice
- ▲ 3488 / 3700 Surface elevation and depth of ice (in metres)
- ● Stanley Permanent bases

Bases on King George Island:
Carlini (Argentina)
Comandante Ferraz (Brazil)
Frei (Chile)
Villa Las Estrellas (Chile)
Great Wall (China)
King Sejong (S. Korea)
Arctowski (Poland)
Artigas (Uruguay)
Bellingshausen (Russia)

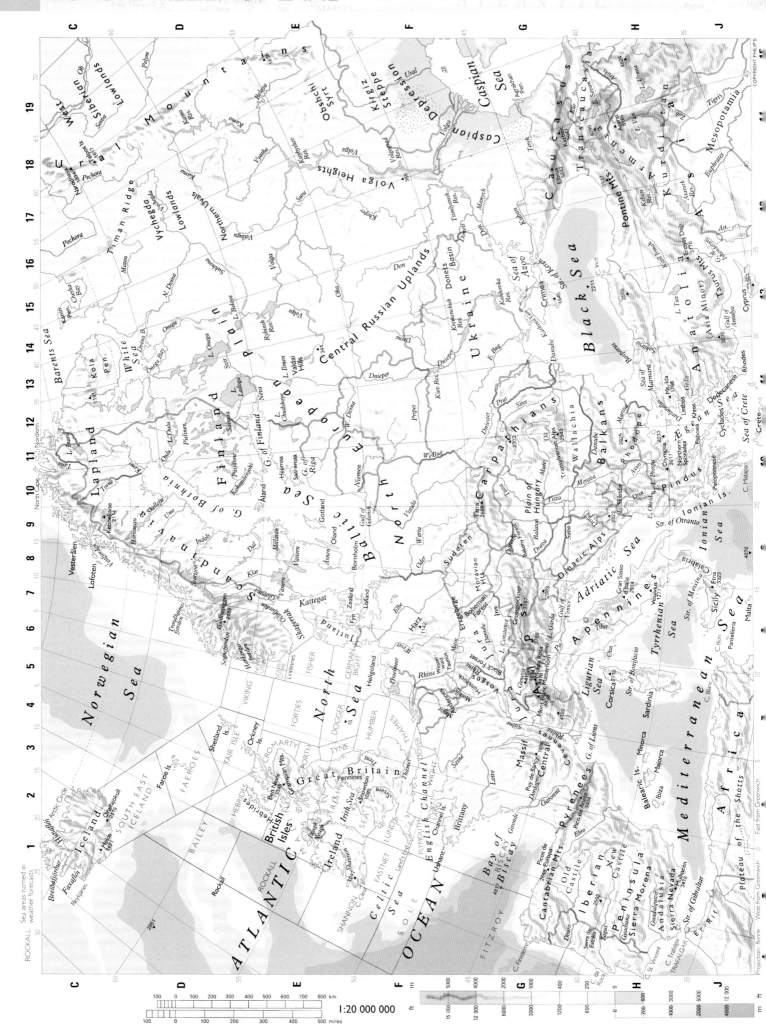

ATLANTIC

Ural Mountains

West Siberian Lowlands

Kirgiz Steppe

Caspian Depression

Caspian Sea

Caucasus

Transcaucasia

Armenia

Kurdistan

Mesopotamia

Pontine Mts

Anatolia (Asia Minor)

Taurus Mts

Black Sea

Volga Heights

Sea of Azov

Central Russian Uplands

Ukraine

Carpathians

Wallachia

Balkans

Rhodope

Pindus

Aegean Sea

Cyclades

Dodecanese

Sea of Crete

European Plain

Finland

Lapland

Barents Sea

White Sea

Kola Pen.

Onega Bay

Gulf of Finland

Gulf of Bothnia

Baltic Sea

North Sea

Scandinavia

Norwegian Sea

Vesterålen

Lofoten

Hebrides

Iceland

SOUTH EAST ICELAND

FAEROES

FAIR ISLE

Shetland Is.

Orkney Is.

Great Britain

British Isles

Ireland

English Channel

ATLANTIC OCEAN

Bay of Biscay

Pyrenees

Iberian Peninsula

Old Castile

New Castile

Sierra Morena

Sierra Nevada

Andalusia

Cantabrian Mts

Massif Central

Alps

Apennines

Dinaric Alps

Adriatic Sea

Ligurian Sea

Tyrrhenian Sea

Sardinia

Corsica

Balearic Is.

Ionian Sea

Mediterranean Sea

Africa

Plateau of the Shotts

Bohemian Forest

Black Forest

Sudeten

Plain of Hungary

Transylvanian Alps

1:20 000 000

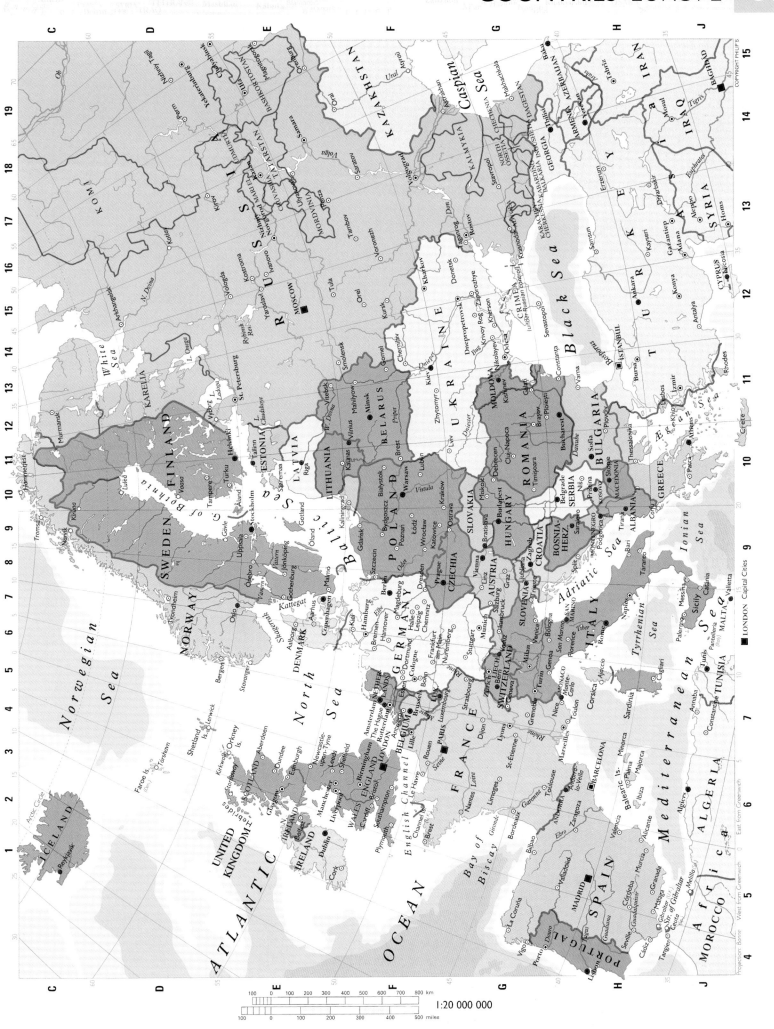

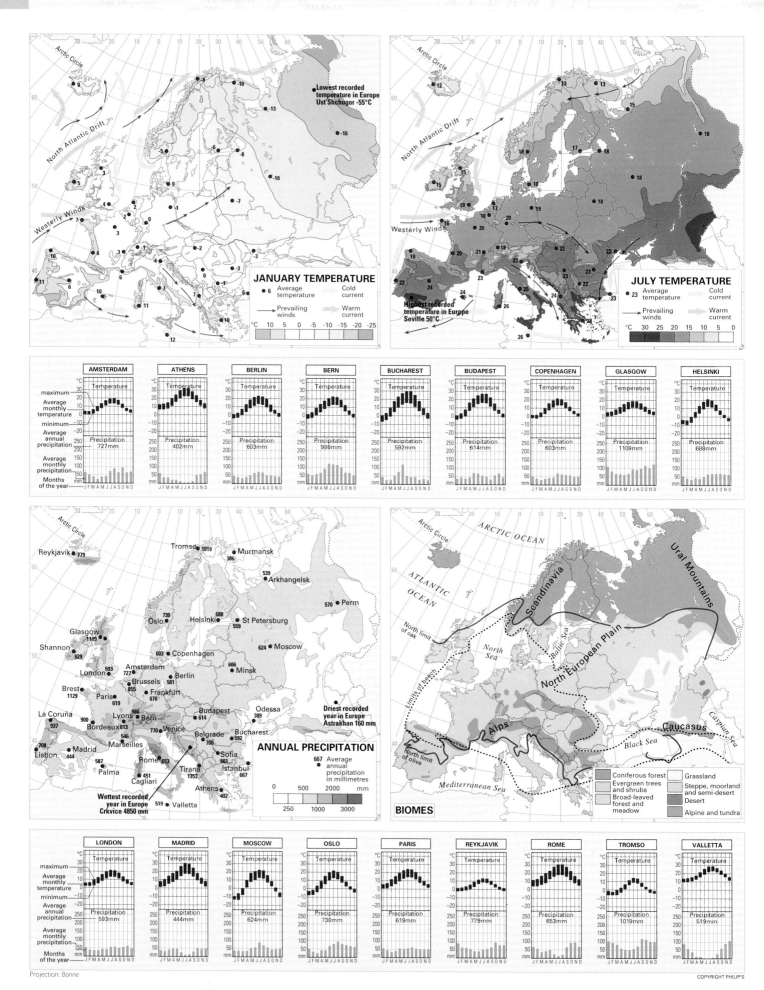

JANUARY TEMPERATURE

- • 6 Average temperature
- → Prevailing winds
- Cold current
- Warm current

°C 10 5 0 -5 -10 -15 -20 -25

Lowest recorded temperature in Europe
Ust'Shchugor -55°C

JULY TEMPERATURE

- • 23 Average temperature
- → Prevailing winds
- Cold current
- Warm current

°C 30 25 20 15 10 5 0

Highest recorded temperature in Europe
Seville 50°C

AMSTERDAM
Temperature
Precipitation 727mm

ATHENS
Temperature
Precipitation 402mm

BERLIN
Temperature
Precipitation 603mm

BERN
Temperature
Precipitation 986mm

BUCHAREST
Temperature
Precipitation 592mm

BUDAPEST
Temperature
Precipitation 614mm

COPENHAGEN
Temperature
Precipitation 603mm

GLASGOW
Temperature
Precipitation 1109mm

HELSINKI
Temperature
Precipitation 688mm

maximum — Temperature
Average monthly temperature
minimum —
Average annual precipitation — Precipitation
Average monthly precipitation
Months of the year — JFMAMJJASOND

ANNUAL PRECIPITATION

- • 667 Average annual precipitation in millimetres

0   500   2000   mm
250   1000   3000

Reykjavik 779
Tromsø 1019
Murmansk 386
Arkhangelsk 539
Perm 570
Oslo 730
Helsinki 688
St Petersburg 559
Glasgow 1109
Shannon 929
Moscow 624
Copenhagen 603
London 593
Amsterdam 727
Berlin 581
Minsk 606
Brussels 855
Brest 1129
Frankfurt 676
Paris 619
La Coruña 937
Lyons 986
Bern 614
Budapest 614
Odessa 389
Bordeaux 813
Venice 770
Belgrade 700
Bucharest 592
Marseilles 546
Rome 653
Sofia 661
Madrid 444
Lisbon 708
Palma 587
Cagliari 451
Tirana 1353
Istanbul 667
Athens 402
Valletta 519

Driest recorded year in Europe
Astrakhan 160 mm

Wettest recorded year in Europe
Crkvice 4850 mm

BIOMES

ARCTIC OCEAN
ATLANTIC OCEAN
Scandinavia
Ural Mountains
North European Plain
North Sea
Baltic Sea
Caspian Sea
Caucasus
Black Sea
Alps
Mediterranean Sea
North limit of oak
limits of beech
North limit of olive

- Coniferous forest
- Evergreen trees and shrubs
- Broad-leaved forest and meadow
- Grassland
- Steppe, moorland and semi-desert
- Desert
- Alpine and tundra

LONDON
Temperature
Precipitation 593mm

MADRID
Temperature
Precipitation 444mm

MOSCOW
Temperature
Precipitation 624mm

OSLO
Temperature
Precipitation 730mm

PARIS
Temperature
Precipitation 619mm

REYKJAVIK
Temperature
Precipitation 779mm

ROME
Temperature
Precipitation 653mm

TROMSO
Temperature
Precipitation 1019mm

VALLETTA
Temperature
Precipitation 519mm

maximum —
Average monthly temperature
minimum —
Average annual precipitation —
Average monthly precipitation
Months of the year — JFMAMJJASOND

Projection: Bonne

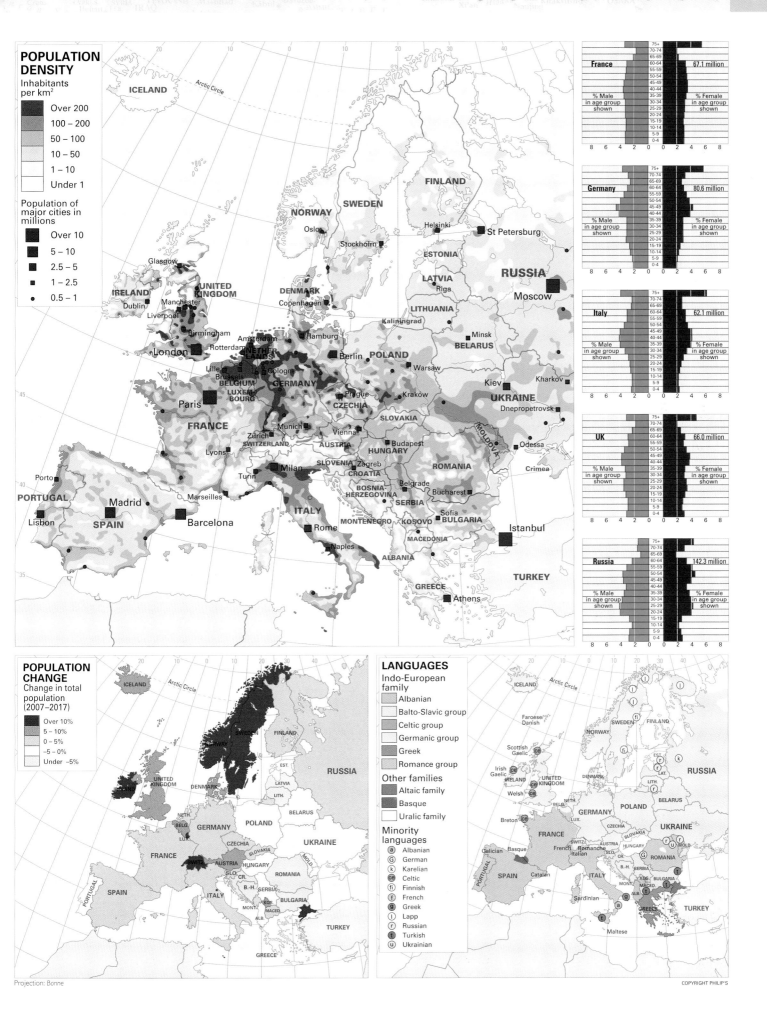

POPULATION DENSITY

Inhabitants per km²

- Over 200
- 100 – 200
- 50 – 100
- 10 – 50
- 1 – 10
- Under 1

Population of major cities in millions

- Over 10
- 5 – 10
- 2.5 – 5
- 1 – 2.5
- 0.5 – 1

France — 67.1 million
% Male in age group shown | % Female in age group shown

Germany — 80.6 million
% Male in age group shown | % Female in age group shown

Italy — 62.1 million
% Male in age group shown | % Female in age group shown

UK — 66.0 million
% Male in age group shown | % Female in age group shown

Russia — 142.3 million
% Male in age group shown | % Female in age group shown

POPULATION CHANGE

Change in total population (2007–2017)

- Over 10%
- 5 – 10%
- 0 – 5%
- –5 – 0%
- Under –5%

LANGUAGES

Indo-European family

- Albanian
- Balto-Slavic group
- Celtic group
- Germanic group
- Greek
- Romance group

Other families

- Altaic family
- Basque
- Uralic family

Minority languages

- a Albanian
- G German
- k Karelian
- ce Celtic
- fi Finnish
- f French
- g Greek
- l Lapp
- r Russian
- t Turkish
- u Ukrainian

Projection: Bonne

COPYRIGHT PHILIP'S

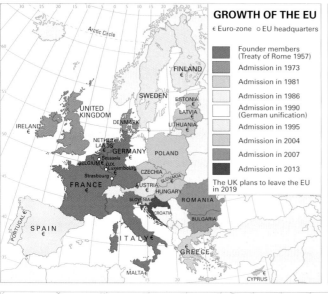

GROWTH OF THE EU

€ Euro-zone ○ EU headquarters

	Founder members (Treaty of Rome 1957)
	Admission in 1973
	Admission in 1981
	Admission in 1986
	Admission in 1990 (German unification)
	Admission in 1995
	Admission in 2004
	Admission in 2007
	Admission in 2013

The UK plans to leave the EU in 2019

EU COUNTRY COMPARISONS	Population (thousands)	Annual Income (US$ per capita)
Germany	80,594	50,200
France	67,106	43,600
United Kingdom	66,040	43,600
Italy	62,138	38,000
Spain	49,958	38,200
Poland	38,476	29,300
Romania	21,530	24,000
Netherlands	17,085	53,600
Portugal	10,840	30,300
Greece	10,768	27,800
Belgium	11,491	46,200
Czechia	10,675	35,200
Sweden	9,960	51,300
Hungary	9,851	28,900
Austria	8,754	49,200
Bulgaria	7,102	21,600
Denmark	5,606	49,600
Finland	5,518	44,000
Slovakia	5,446	32,900
Ireland	5,011	72,600
Croatia	4,292	24,100
Lithuania	2,824	31,900
Slovenia	1,972	34,100
Latvia	1,945	27,300
Estonia	1,252	31,500
Cyprus	1,222	36,600
Luxembourg	594	109,100
Malta	416	42,500
Total EU 2017 (28 countries)	**518,466**	**39,837**

REGIONS OF THE EU

Austria *(States)*

1 Niederösterreich	4 Kärnten	7 Tirol
2 Oberösterreich	5 Salzburg	8 Wien
3 Burgenland	6 Steiermark	9 Vorarlberg

Belgium *(Regions)*

1 Bruxelles	2 Vlaanderen	3 Wallonie

Bulgaria *(Regions)*

1 Severen tsentralen	3 Severozapaden	5 Yugozapaden
2 Severoiztochen	4 Yugoiztochen	6 Yuzhen tsentralen

Croatie

Cyprus *(member state with no corresponding division)*

Czech Republic *(Kraj)*

1 Jihovychod	4 Praha	7 Stredni Cechy
2 Jihozapad	5 Severovychod	8 Stredni Morava
3 Moravskoslezsko	6 Severozapad	

Denmark *(member state with no corresponding division)*

Estonia *(member state with no corresponding division)*

Finland *(Provinces)*

1 Åland	3 Väli-Suomi	5 Etelä-Suomi
2 Itä-Suomi	4 Pohjois-Suomi	

France *(Regions)*

1 Alsace	9 Franche-Comté	17 Normandie (Basse-)
2 Aquitaine	10 Ile-de-France	18 Normandie (Haute-)
3 Auvergne	11 Languedoc-Roussillon	19 Picardie
4 Bourgogne	12 Limousin	20 Poitou-Charentes
5 Bretagne	13 Loire (Pays de la)	21 Provence-Alpes-
6 Centre	14 Lorraine	Côte d'Azur
7 Champagne-Ardenne	15 Midi-Pyrénées	22 Rhône-Alpes
8 Corse	16 Nord-Pas-de-Calais	

Germany *(Länder)*

1 Baden-Württemberg	7 Hamburg	11 Rheinland-Pfalz
2 Niedersachsen	8 Hessen	12 Saarland
3 Bayern	9 Mecklenburg-	13 Sachsen
4 Berlin	Vorpommern	14 Sachsen-Anhalt
5 Brandenburg	10 Nordrhein-	15 Schleswig-Holstein
6 Bremen	Westfalen	16 Thüringen

Greece *(Regions)*

1 Anatoliki Makedonia kai Thraki	5 Epiros	10 Dytiki Makedonia
	6 Attiki	11 Kentriki Makedonia
2 Kriti	7 Sterea Ellas	12 Peloponnese
3 Voreio Aigaio	8 Dytiki Ellas	13 Thessaly
4 Notio Aigaio	9 Ionioi Nisoi	

Hungary *(Megyék)*

1 Del-Alfold	4 Eszak-Magyarorszag	7 Nyugat-Dunantul
2 Del-Dunantul	5 Kozep-Dunantul	
3 Eszak-Alfold	6 Kozep-Magyarorszag	

Ireland *(Regions)*

1 Border, Midland & Western	
2 Southern & Eastern	

Italy *(Regions)*

1 Abruzzo	8 Liguria	15 Sardegna
2 Basilicata	9 Lombardia	16 Sicilia
3 Calàbria	10 Marche	17 Toscana
4 Campánia	11 Molise	18 Trentino-Alto Adige/
5 Emilia-Romagna	12 Umbria	Südtirol
6 Friuli-Venézia Giulia	13 Piemonte	19 Valle d'Aosta
7 Lazio	14 Puglia	20 Véneto

Latvia *(member state with no corresponding division)*

Lithuania *(member state with no corresponding division)*

Luxembourg *(member state with no corresponding division)*

Malta *(member state with no corresponding division)*

Netherlands *(Regions)*

1 Noord-Nederland	3 West-Nederland
2 Oost-Nederland	4 Zuid-Nederland

Poland *(Voivodships)*

1 Dolnoslaskie	7 Mazowieckie	13 Swietokrzyskie
2 Kujawsko-Pomorskie	8 Opolskie	14 Warmińsko-Mazurski
3 Łódzkie	9 Podkarpackie	15 Wielkopolskie
4 Lubelskie	10 Podlaskie	16 Zachodniopomorski
5 Lubuskie	11 Pomorskie	
6 Mafopolskie	12 Śląskie	

Portugal *(Autonomous regions)*

1 Alentejo	3 Centro	5 Norte
2 Algarve	4 Lisboa	

Romania *(Regions)*

1 Bucureşti-Ilfov	4 Nord-Vest	7 Sud-Vest
2 Centru	5 Sud	8 Vest
3 Nord-Est	6 Sud-Est	

Slovak Republic *(Kraj)*

1 Bratislavsky Kraj	3 Vychodne Slovensko
2 Stredne Slovensko	4 Zapadne Slovensko

Slovenia *(member state with no corresponding division)*

Spain *(Autonomous communities)*

1 Andalucía	7 Cantabria	13 Madrid
2 Aragon	8 Castilla y Léon	14 Murcia
3 Asturias	9 Castilla-La Mancha	15 Navarra
4 Islas Baleares	10 Cataluña	16 Rioja (La)
5 País Vasco	11 Extremadura	17 Valencia
6 Islas Canarias	12 Galicia	

Sweden *(Regions)*

1 Stockholm	4 Västsverige	7 Övre Norrland
2 Östra Mellansverige	5 Norra Mellansverige	8 Småland med öarna
3 Sydsverige	6 Mellersta Norrland	

United Kingdom *(Regions)*

1 North East England	5 West Midlands	9 South West England
2 North West England	6 East of England	10 Wales
3 Yorkshire & The Humber	7 Greater London	11 Scotland
4 East Midlands	8 South East England	12 Northern Ireland

Projection: Bonne

COPYRIGHT PHILIP'S

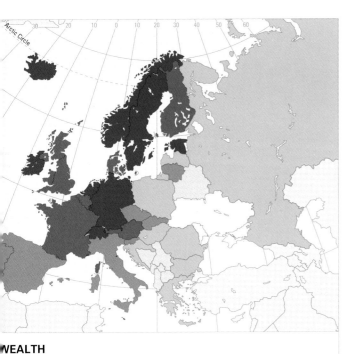

WEALTH
he value of total production divided
y population (US$ per person 2017)

	Over $50,000
	$40,000 – $50,000
	$30,000 – $40,000
	$20,000 – $30,000
	$10,000 – $20,000
	Under $10,000

Richest countries
Liechtenstein US$139,100
Monaco US$115,700
Luxembourg US$109,100

Poorest countries
Moldova US$5,700
Ukraine US$8,700
Kosovo US$10,400

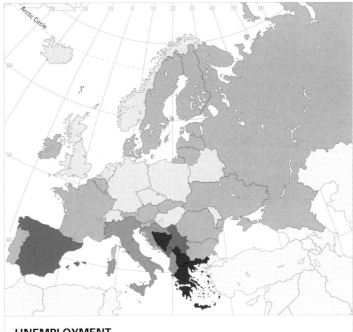

UNEMPLOYMENT
The percentage of the labour force without jobs (2017)

	Over 20%
	15 – 20%
	10 – 15%
	5 – 10%
	Under 5%

Highest unemployment
Kosovo 30.5%
Macedonia 23.4%
Greece 22.3%

Lowest unemployment
Monaco 2.0%
Liechtenstein 2.4%
Iceland 2.8%

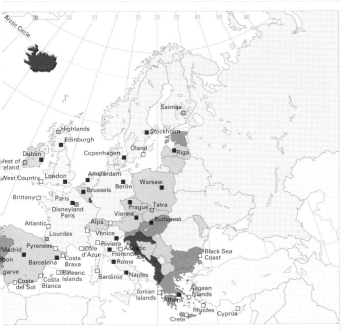

TOURISM
ourism receipts as a percentage
f Gross National Income (GNI)
2016)

	Over 10%
	5% – 10%
	2.5% – 5%
	Under 2.5%

Tourist destinations
■ Cultural & historical centres
□ Coastal resorts
□ Ski resorts
■ Centres of entertainment
■ Places of pilgrimage
■ Places of great natural beauty

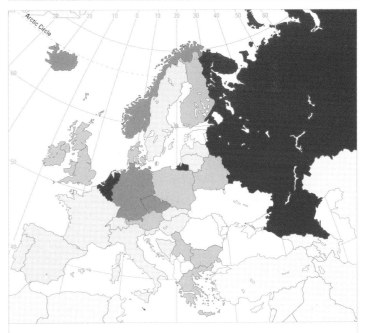
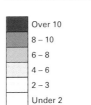

GLOBAL WARMING
Carbon dioxide emissions in tonnes per capita (2015)

	Over 10
	8 – 10
	6 – 8
	4 – 6
	2 – 3
	Under 2

Highest emissions (tonnes per capita)
Luxembourg 17.8
Malta 16.7
Netherlands 13.7

Lowest emissions (tonnes per capita)
Liechtenstein 1.2
Albania 1.4
Moldova 2.1

ATLANTIC

NORW

A T L A N T I C   O C E A N

Shetland Is.
(U.K.)
Yell
Unst
Fetlar
458
Mainland
Lerwick
Foula
Fair Isle

Bergen
Osøyro

NORW
Haugesund
Kopervik
Åkrahamn
Bø
Stavanger
Sandn
Bryr
Nærb

Stord
Bømlo

316

1224

North
Rona
Westray
Sanday
Stronsay
Orkney Is.
Mainland
Kirkwall
Hoy
481
South
Ronaldsay
C. Wrath
Pentland Firth

Flannan Is.
Stornoway
Thurso
Wick
Helmsdale

Lewis
Lairg
Golspie

St. Kilda
(U.K.)
789

Harris
Ullapool
1081
Tain
Dingwall
Invergordon
Nairn
Elgin
Buckie
Banff
Fraserburgh
Peterhead
Huntly
Inverurie

North
Uist
Portree
Inverness
L. Ness
Spey
Don
Aberdeen

Benbecula

South Uist
Skye
992
1182
Glen Mor
Aviemore
Dee
311
Ballater
Stonehaven

Barra
Rum
Eigg
Ben Nevis
1345
Fort William
1214
Forfar
Montrose

Coll
Tobermory
966
Oban
L. Awe
L. Lomond
973
Perth
St. Andrews

Tiree
Iona
Mull
Colonsay
Stirling
Glenrothes
Kirkcaldy
Dunbar

Jura
L. Fyne
Dumbarton
Dunfermline
Edinburgh
Berwick-upon-Tweed

Islay
Greenock
Paisley
GLASGOW
Cumbernauld
East Kilbride
Hamilton

N O R T H
238

S E A

16

Den He

Alk

NETHERLAN
The Hague
Hoek van Holland
ROTTERDA
Dordr
Zeeland
Vlissingen

Haarl

BELGIU
Gent Mech
BRUSSE
LILLE
Tournai

S C O T L A N D
Grampian Mts.
Tay

Tory I.
Malin Hd.
Buncrana
Coleraine
Ballymena
Larne
North Channel

Arranmore
Letterkenny
Lifford
Derry/Londonderry
Firth of Clyde
Arran
Campbeltown
Ayr
Southern Uplands
840
Hawick
816
Cheviot Hills
Alnwick

Donegal
Ulster
Omagh
Strabane
Antrim
Bangor
Kilmarnock
Irvine
Girvan
Stranraer
Kirkcudbright
Dumfries
Annan
Carlisle
Newcastle-upon-Tyne
South Shields
Sunderland

Bundoran
Lough Erne
Enniskillen
NORTHERN IRELAND
Lough Neagh
Lisburn
Belfast
Mull of Galloway
Whitehaven
Workington
Hexham
893
Gateshead
Durham
Hartlepool
Redcar

Sligo
Leitrim
Armagh
Newry
Craigavon
Whitehaven
Cumbrian Mts.
978
Darlington
Middlesbrough
Stockton-on-Tees
Scarborough

Ballina
L. Conn
Castlebar
Roscommon
Longford
Cavan
Clones
Carrickmacross
852
Douglas
620
I. of Man
Barrow-in-Furness
Lancaster
Pennines
Harrogate
Bridlington

Achill I.
Westport
Lough Mask
Connaught
Athlone
Mullingar
Boyne
Dundalk
Drogheda
KINGDOM
York
Beverley
Kingston upon Hull

Lough Corrib
Ballinasloe
Tullamore
Blackpool
Preston
Blackburn
Burnley
Leeds
Bradford
Huddersfield
Barnsley
Doncaster
Scunthorpe
Grimsby

Connemara
Galway
L. Derg
Portlaoise
Athy
Carlow
Wicklow Mts.
926
Arklow
Anglesey
Holyhead
MANCHESTER
Oldham
Stockport
Rotherham
Sheffield
Lincoln
Louth

Galway B.
953
Ennis
Nenagh
Thurles
Kilkenny
Bangor
Colwyn Bay
Chester
Crewe
Chesterfield
Mansfield
Boston
The Wash
Cromer

Aran Is.
920
Tipperary
Clonmel
Carrick-on-Suir
Wexford
Rosslare
1085
Snowdon
Wrexham
Pwllheli
Stoke-on-Trent
Derby
Nottingham
Granthan
Trent
King's Lynn
Norwich
Great Yarmouth
Lowestoft

Kilrush
Listowel
Tralee
Mallow
Suir
Waterford
Dungarvan
Cambrian Mts.
Shrewsbury
Telford
Stafford
Leicester
Nuneaton
Corby
Peterborough
Ely
Thetford
Bury St. Edmunds
Ipswich
Felixstowe

Dingle
Carrauntoohil
1041
Macgillycuddy's Reeks
Killarney
Blackwater
Youghal
Cardigan
Aberystwyth
Cardigan Bay
Welshpool
Wolverhampton
BIRMINGHAM
Redditch
Coventry
Rugby
Leamington Spa
Northampton
Bedford
Cambridge

Valencia
99
Cork
WALES
Hereford
Worcester
Cheltenham
Gloucester
Hemel
Milton Keynes
Stevenage
Hempstead
Harlow
Colchester
Chelmsford

C. Clear
Bandon
Kinsale
Fishguard
Haverfordwest
Milford Haven
Pembroke
Carmarthen
Merthyr Tydfil
886
Cotswold Hills
Oxford
High Wycombe
Luton
Watford
Slough
Basildon
Southend-on-Sea

Llanelli
Neath
Cwmbran
Rhondda
Cardiff
Bristol
Bath
Newbury
Reading
LONDON
Chatham
Margate

Swansea
Port Talbot
Newport
Swindon
Basingstoke
Guildford
Crawley
Maidstone
Canterbury
Dover
Folkestone

Bristol Channel
Weston-super-Mare
Salisbury
Winchester
Fareham
Hastings
Eastbourne

Barnstaple
Exmoor
Taunton
Yeovil
Southampton
Brighton
Worthing

Bude
618
Dartmoor
Exmouth
Bournemouth
Poole
Weymouth
Newport
Isle of Wight
Portsmouth
Havant

Newquay
Truro
Torbay
English Channel

St. Austell
Plymouth
Falmouth
Penzance

Land's End
Isles of Scilly

C E L T I C
S E A

UNITED

IRISH

SEA

DUBLIN
Dun Laoghaire
Bray

I R E L A N D
Limerick
Kells
Naas

Shannon

St. George's Channel

ENGLAND

FRANCE
C. de la Hague
Pte. de
Barfleur
Cherbourg-Octeville
Le Havre
Fécamp
Dieppe
Abbeville
Le Tréport
St. Quentin
Laon

Alderney
St. Peter
Port
Guernsey
St. Malo
Sark
St. Helier
Jersey
Channel Is.
(U.K.)
Valognes
Bayeux
Caen
Lisieux
Elbeuf
Rouen
Seine
Pays de Caux
Amiens
Picardie
Cambrai

Str. of Dover
Calais
Gris Nez
Boulogne-sur-Mer
Le Touquet-Paris-Plage
33
Dunkerque
St-Omer
Béthune
Bruay-la-Buissière
Lille
Douai
Valenciennes
Lens
Arras

NORW

Projection: Conical with two standard parallels
2 3 4
50   25   0   25   50   75   100   125   150   175 km
50   25   0   25   50   75   100 125 miles
1:5 000 000
West from Greenwich
East from Greenwich
COPYRIGHT PHILIP'S

ft m
3000 1000
1500 500
600 200
0 0
50 150
100 300
200 600
500 1500
1000 3000
2000 6000
m ft

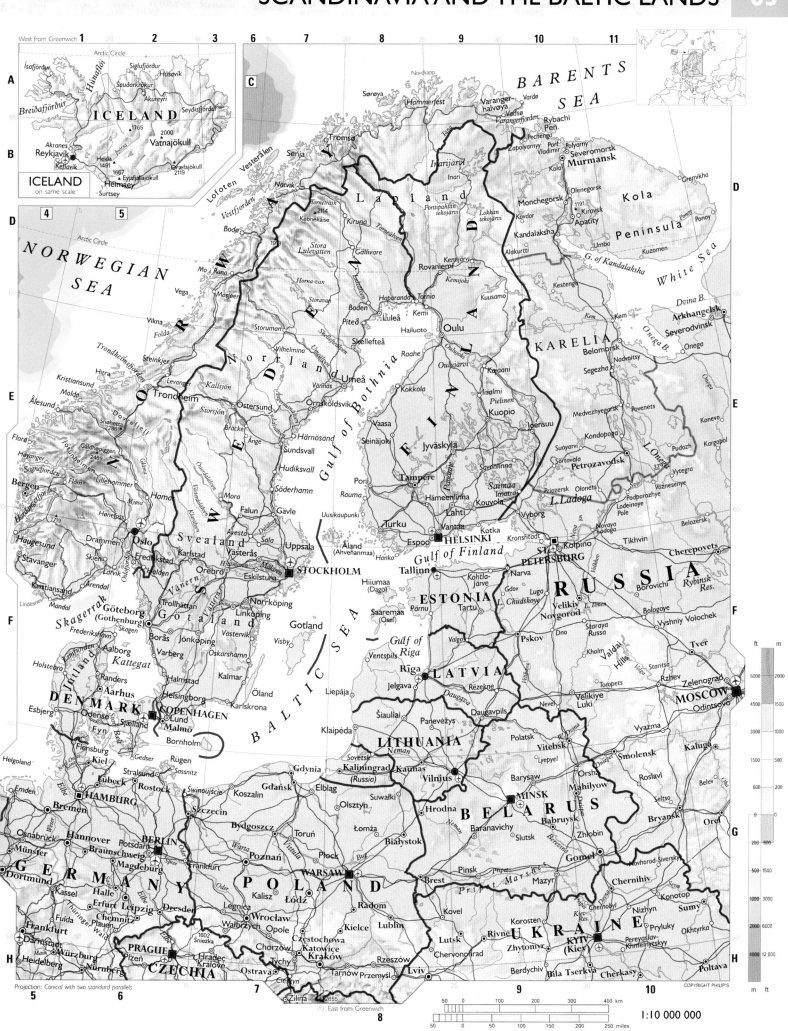

ICELAND

ICELAND on same scale

BARENTS SEA

NORWEGIAN SEA

Arctic Circle

Lapland

FINLAND

Kola Peninsula

White Sea

KARELIA

Gulf of Bothnia

RUSSIA

L. Onega

L. Ladoga

Gulf of Finland

ESTONIA

BALTIC SEA

Gulf of Riga

LATVIA

LITHUANIA

Kaliningrad (Russia)

MOSCOW

BELARUS

DENMARK

COPENHAGEN

GERMANY

POLAND

WARSAW

UKRAINE

KYIV (Kiev)

CZECHIA

PRAGUE

STOCKHOLM

OSLO

HELSINKI

ST. PETERSBURG

MINSK

VILNIUS

RĪGA

TALLINN

HAMBURG

BERLIN

Pripet Marshes

Projection: Conical with two standard parallels

COPYRIGHT PHILIP'S

1:10 000 000

West from Greenwich

East from Greenwich

NORTH SEA

BALTIC SEA

DENMARK

UNITED KINGDOM

NETHERLANDS

BELGIUM

LUXEMBOURG

GERMANY

FRANCE

SWITZERLAND

ITALY

AUSTRIA

CZECH

SLOVENIA

ADRIATIC SEA

Golfo di Génova

Golfo di Venézia

AMSTERDAM • The Hague • ROTTERDAM

BRUSSELS

PARIS

LONDON

HAMBURG • BERLIN • Potsdam

COLOGNE • Bonn • Düsseldorf • Essen • Dortmund

Frankfurt • Mainz • Wiesbaden • Mannheim • Stuttgart

MUNICH • Nuremberg • Augsburg

PRAGUE • Dresden • Leipzig • Chemnitz

ZÜRICH • Bern • Geneva • Basel

MILAN • TURIN • Venice • Bologna

LYON • MARSEILLES • MONACO • Nice

LJUBLJANA • SLOVENIA

Danube • Rhine • Elbe • Po

Projection: Conical with two standard parallels

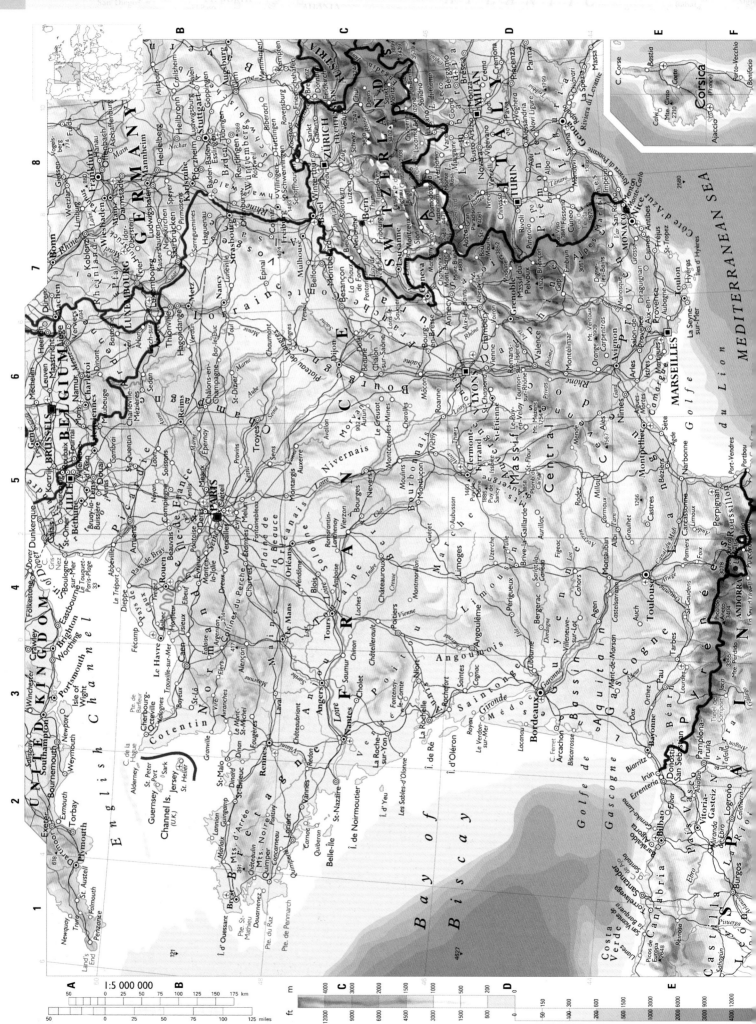

1:5 000 000

A   50   0   25   50   75   100   125   150   175 km   B

50   0   25   50   75   100   125 miles

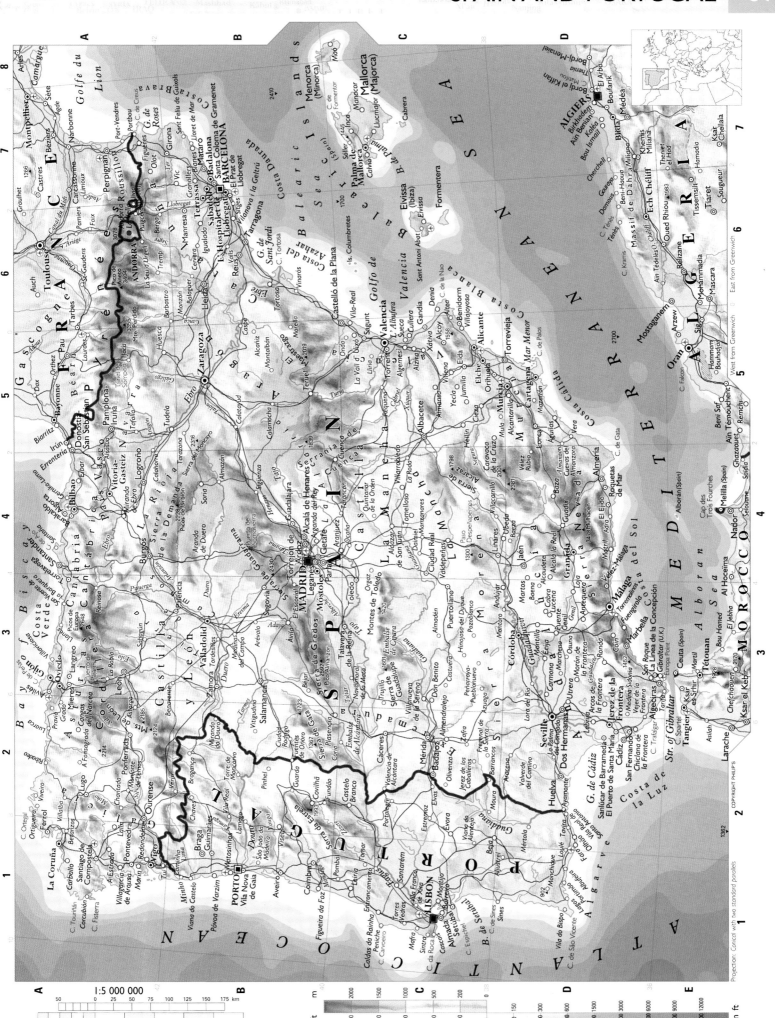

1:5 000 000

Projection: Conic with two standard parallels

MALTA
1:1 000 000

MEDITERRANEAN
SEA

Projection: Conical with two standard parallels

1:10 000 000

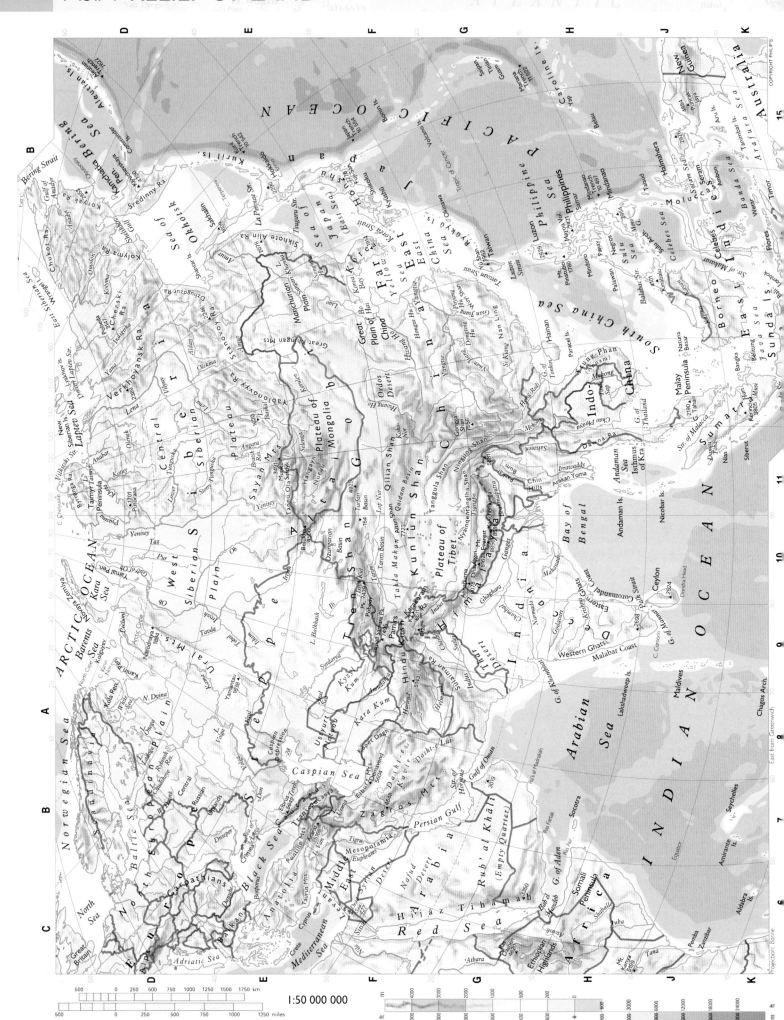

1:50 000 000

A · B · C · D · E · F

8 · 9 · 10 · 15 · 16 · 17 · 18 · 19

ARCTIC OCEAN

Severnaya Zemlya

Ostrov Komsomolets
Ostrov Oktyabrskoy Revolyutsii
965
Ostrov Bolshevik

Vilkitski Strait
C. Chelyuskin

Laptev Sea

East Siberian Sea

New Siberian Islands

Wrangel I. 1096

Ostrova Delonga
Ostrov Faddeyevskiy
Ostrov Novaya Sibir
374

Lyakhov Islands
Ostrov Kotelnyy
Dmitri Laptev Str.

Byrranga Ra.
Taimyr Peninsula
1146
621
Nordvik

Pyasina

Volochanka
Talnakh
Norilsk
1591
Gory Putorana 1678
1341

Kheta
Khatanga
Novorybnoye
Khatanga

Ust Olenek
Saskylakh
Tit-Ary
Tiksi
Ust Kuyga
Kazachye
Chokurdakh
Chersky
Ust Chaun
Pevek

Chukot Range

Anabar
Zhilinda
Olenek
Bulun
Kyusyur
Yana
Deputatskiy
Khonuu
Zyryanka
Nizhne Kolymsk

Ambarchik
Bilibino

Chukchi Sea

C. Dezhneva (East C.)
St. Lawrence I. (U.S.A.)
Ugolnyye Kopi
Egvekinot
1194
Vankarem
Anadyr
Gulf of Anadyr
Beringovskiy

Severnaya
naya
khansk
Noginsk
Lower Tunguska
1071

Yenisey
Tura

Udachnyy
962
Yessey

Olenek
Zhigansk
Verkhoyansk
2389

Batagai
Borogontsy
Ytyk-Kyuyel
2298

Srednekolymsk
Kolyma
Gora Chen 1827
Ust-Nera 3147

Poseda
Nayakhan 1603
Taskan
Omsukchan
Gizhiga
Evensk
Paren
Gizhiga 1684

Koryak Range
2453

Markovo
Yerepol
Penzhino
Kamenskoye

Sredinnyy Range

Talaya
Ossora
Ostrov Karaginskiy

Arctic Circle

R U S S I A

Stony Tunguska
Severo-Yeniseyskiy
1104

Kuyumba
Mutoray
Vanavara

Yerbogachen
599
Lensk

Vitim
Yenyuka
Olekma

Yuka
Chernyshevskiy
Mirnyy
Vilyuy Res.
Suntar
Nyurba
Vilyuysk
Verkhnevilyuysk
Namtsy
Nizhni
Yakutsk
Pokrovsk
Sinsk

Olekminsk
Tommot
Aldan
2264

Neryungri
Nogornyy

Ust-Mil
Ust Maya
Amga
Chagda
Ayan

Aldan
Uchur

Okhotskiy Perevoz
Khandyga
2959

Arkagala

Ulya
Nelkan
Maya
Ain

Ust-Omchug
Susuman
Yagodnoye
Ola
1691
Magadan

Omolon
Gizhiginskaya

Palatka
Oratukan
Orotukan

Shelikhov Gulf
Tigil
Palana

Klyuchi 4750
Kozyrevsk 2815
Ust-Kamchatsk
Ukelayat
2387

Kamchatka Peninsula

Bystrinskiye
Milkovo
3621

Sea of Okhotsk

Kirovskiy
Oktyabrskiy
Petropavlovsk-Kamchatskiy
Vilyuchinsk
2359

Bering Sea

Komandorskiye Islands

Lesosibirsk
Yeniseysk
Angara
chinsk
rovo
Krasnoyarsk
Krasnoyarsk Res.
Artemovsk
Chernogorsk
Minusinsk 2922
bakan
ayanogorsk

Kansk
Ilanskiy
Kondratyevo
Zheleznogorsk-Ilimskiy
Ust-Ilimsk
Makarovo

Boguchany
Ilanskiy
Tayshet
Alzamay
Nizhneudinsk
Tulun
Zima
Zalari

Bratsk
Bratsk Res.
1509

Ust-Kut
Magistralnyy
Severobaykalsk
Taksimo
Bodaybo
2999
Chara
Ust-Nyukzha
Kalakan

Mama
Mamakan

Karalon
2840
Bagdarin

Tynda
Skovorodino
Magdagachi
Ushumun

Stanovoy Range

Dzhugdzur Range
1906
2246
2371
Chumikan
Uda
Tugur

Shantar Is.
1806
Okha

Nikolayevsk-na-Amure
Lazarev

Neftegorsk
Noglik
Aleksandrovsk-Sakhalinskiy
Gora Lopatina 1609

Sakhalin

Ostrov Iturup 1819
Kurilsk
Ostrov Urup 1426
Ostrov Simushir 1538

Kuril Islands

Tatar Str.

Nizhneangarsk
Barguzin
1642
Bukachacha
Sretensk
Nerchinsk
Chita
Shilka
Baley

Mogocha
1903
Gulian

Shimanovsk
Svobodnyy
Zeya
Zeya Res.
1064

Belogorsk
Zavitinsk
Blagoveshchensk
Heihe

Bureya
Chegdomyn
Bureya Res.
Progress

Komsomolsk-na-Amure
Amursk
2078

Sovetskaya Gavan
Vanino
Shakhtersk
Uglegorsk
Poronaysk

Yuzhno-Sakhalinsk
Kholmsk
Korsakov

Dolinsk

La Perouse Str.
Wakkanai

Cheremkhovo
Usolye Sibirskoye
Angarsk
Irkutsk
Slyudyanka

Ulan Ude
Khilok
Petrovsk-Zabaykalskiy
Kyakhta
2519

Turan
Toora-Khem
Kyzyl
Samagaltay
3276
Erzin

Kuragino
Munku-Sardyk 3491
Hatgal
Zakamensk
Darkhan
Khövsgöl Nuur
Mörön

Hyargas Nuur
Dörö Nuur
Uliastay
3905
Tsetserleg

MONGOLIA

Aginskoye
Olovyannaya
Borzya
Klyuchevskoye
Krasnokamensk
Zabaykalsk

Manzhouli
Hulun Nur
Hailar

Aershan
Bukhedu

Zalantun
Baicheng
Taonan

Choybalsan
Tamsagbulag
Öndörhaan
Baruun-Urt

Great Khingan Mts.

Nenjiang
Fuyu
Yichun
Hegang
JIAMUSI
Suihua
QIQIHAR
DAQING
HARBIN
Daqing
JIXI
Mudan
MUDANJIANG
Dongning

Be'an

Yakeshi

Dalnerechensk
Spassk Dalniy
Arsenyev
Lesozavodsk
Kavalerovo
Dalnegorsk

Ussuriysk
Partizansk
Artem
Vladivostok
Nakhodka
Terney
Amgu

Sikhote-Alin Ra.

Hokkaido
Asahikawa 2290
Otaru
SAPPORO
Obihiro
Hakodate
Aomori
Hachinohe

Ulaanbaatar — **ULAN BATOR**

Choyr
Bayanhongor
Arvayheer
Mandalgovi
Buyant-Uhaa
Sainshand

Altai
3905

(Aerhtai Shan)
4266
4885
Hami

Dalandzadgad
Gaxun Nur

G o b i
Erenhot

C H I N A

Linxi
1949
Xilinhot

CHIFENG
CHENGDE
SHENYANG
JINXI
ANSHAN
Yingkou
FUSHUN
Tonghua
Fuxin

CHANGCHUN
Siping
JILIN
Yanji
Tumen

Songhua
2744

Ch'ŏngjin
Kimch'aek

NORTH KOREA
Hamhŭng
Wŏnsan
Dandong

Ganseong
Sokcho

Sea of Japan (East Sea)

Honshū

Akita
Niigata
Toyama

PYONGYANG
Nampo

SEOUL
INCHEON
SOUTH KOREA
DAEJEON
DAEGU
BUSAN
GWANGJU

Kanazawa

JAPAN
KYOTO
KOBE
OSAKA

BAOTOU · HOHHOT · ZHANGJIAKOU · **BEIJING** · TANGSHAN · **DALIAN**

Chengde
Ningkou

10 · 11 · 12 · 13 · 14

100 0 100 200 300 400 500 600 700 800 km
100 0 100 200 300 400 500 miles

1:20 000 000

COPYRIGHT PHILIP'S

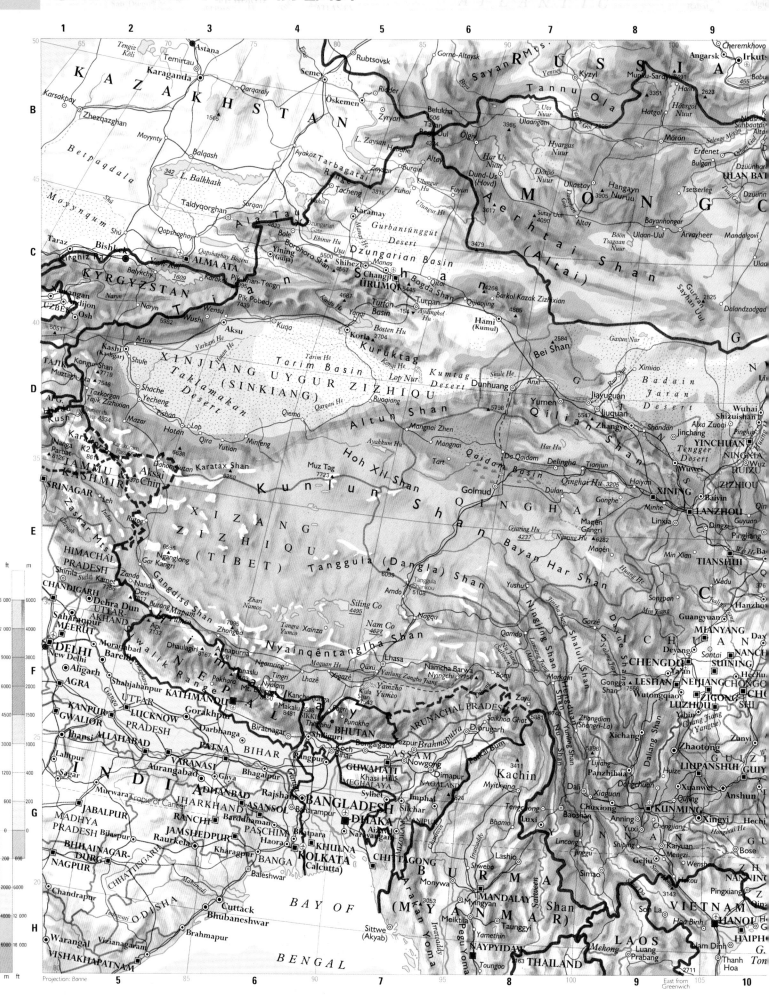

Ilan Ude
Baikal
Bukachacha
Yablonovyy Range
Chita
Olovyannaya
Borzya
Krasnokamensk
Priargunsk
Nerchinsk
Sretensk
Shilka
Gulian
Shimanovsk
Svobodnyy
Zeya
Chegdomyn
Amur
Aleksandrovsk-Sakhalinskiy
Poronaysk
Sakhalin
Dolinsk
Yuzhno-Sakhalinsk

RUSSIA
Khabarovsk
Birobidzhan
Komsomolsk-na-Amur
Vanino
Tatar Strait
Kholmsk

Ergun Youqi
Genhe
Yilehuli Shan
Blagoveshchensk
Heihe
Bureya
Obluchye
Ozero Bolon

Manzhouli
Yakeshi
Hailar (Hulunbuir)
Bei'an
Qianjin
Fujin
Ussuri

Hakkaido
SAPPORO
Muroran
Hakodate

RUSSIA
JAMUSI
Shuangyashan
Qitaihe
Hulin

QIQIHAR
DAQING
Anda
Suihua
HARBIN
Yichun
1047

JIXI
Mishan
Khanka
Spassk-Dalniy

CHANGCHUN
JILIN
MUDANJIANG
Vladivostok
Ussuriysk

SHENYANG
NORTH KOREA
P'YONGYANG

SEA OF JAPAN (EAST SEA)

YELLOW SEA

SOUTH KOREA
SEOUL
INCHEON

EAST CHINA SEA

PACIFIC OCEAN

SOUTH CHINA SEA

PHILIPPINES

HONG KONG, MACAU AND SHENZHEN
1:1 000 000

GUANGDONG
SHENZHEN
ZHONGSHAN
Lingding Yang
ZHUHAI
Macau (Aomen)
HONG KONG (Xianggang)
Hong Kong Island

1:15 000 000

EMPLOYMENT IN INDUSTRY

Industrial population by province in millions
20 10 4 2 1 0.5

HEILONGJIANG

JILIN

SINKIANG

INNER MONGOLIA

GANSU

BEIJING
LIAONING

NINGXIA HUI
TIANJIN
SHANXI
HEBEI
SHANDONG

QINGHAI

SHAANXI
HENAN
JIANGSU
SHANGHAI

TIBET

SICHUAN
CHONGQING
HUBEI
ANHUI
ZHEJIANG
HUNAN
JIANGXI

YUNNAN
GUIZHOU
FUJIAN
GUANGXI ZHUANGZU
GUANGDONG

MACAU HONG KONG

HAINAN

GDP per capita (US$)

Over $10,000
$7,500 – $10,000
$5,000 – $7,500
Under $5,000

INDUSTRIAL DEVELOPMENT

Core regions

▨ Industrial regions

● Major centres for industry and services

●• Other industrial centres

◉ Centres for iron and steel and chemicals

▨ Rapidly developing coastal regions

▪ Special Economic Zones (SEZ)

▼ Special Administrative Regions (SAR) 'One country, two systems'

Peripheral regions

▢ Densely populated and industrialized peripheral region

▨ Peripheral region with traditional heavy industry

▢ Remote undeveloped region

← Direction of future growth

— Important rail links

CHINA'S SHARE OF WORLD MANUFACTURING
(for selected goods)

China 20.0% Brazil 12.2% Canada 10.7% USA 9.2% Russia 4.7%
| **Hydroelectricity** |
World total: 3,471 billion kWh

China 25.7% USA 18.7% Japan 6.6% S. Korea 2.8%
| **Paper** |
World total: 399,100,000 tonnes

China 58.1% India 6.8% USA 2.0%
| **Cement** |
World total: 3,700,000,000 tonnes

China 47.4% USA 12.9% Australia 6.9% Indonesia 6.7% India 5.9% Russia 4.3% South Africa 3.7%
| **Coal** |
World total: 3,881,400,000 tOe

China 45.7% Russia 8.4% Canada 6.1% USA 5.1% UAE 3.8%
| **Aluminium** |
World total: 47,300,000 tonnes

China 49.2% Japan 7.0% USA 5.5% India 5.1% Russia 4.4%
| **Steel** |
World total: 1,582,500,000 tonnes

China 22.9% USA 12.3% Japan 11.8% Germany 6.7% S. Korea 5.4%
| **Motor vehicles** |
World total: 84,200,000 vehicles

China 43.8% USA 14.4% Morocco 12.5% Russia 5.5% Jordan 3.1% Brazil 3.0%
| **Phosphate fertilizer** |
World total: 224,000,000 tonnes

tOe = tonnes of oil equivalent

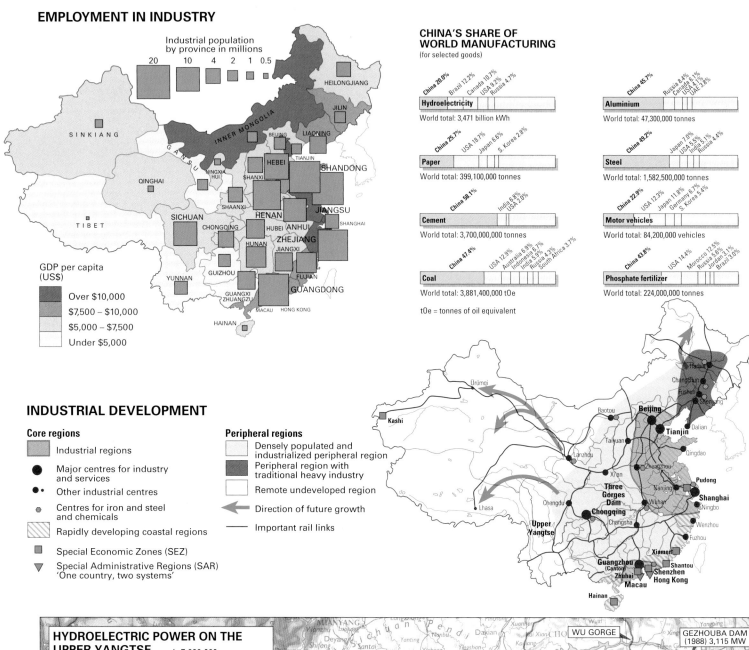

Ürümqi
Kashi
Baotou
Beijing
Harbin
Changchun
Fushun
Shenyang
Tianjin
Dalian
Taiyuan
Lanzhou
Qingdao
Xi'an
Zhengzhou
Pudong
Three Gorges Dam
Nanjing
Shanghai
Chengdu
Wuhan
Ningbo
Chongqing
Changsha
Wenzhou
Upper Yangtse
Lhasa
Fuzhou
Xiamen
Guangzhou (Canton)
Shantou
Zhuhai
Shenzhen
Macau
Hong Kong
Hainan

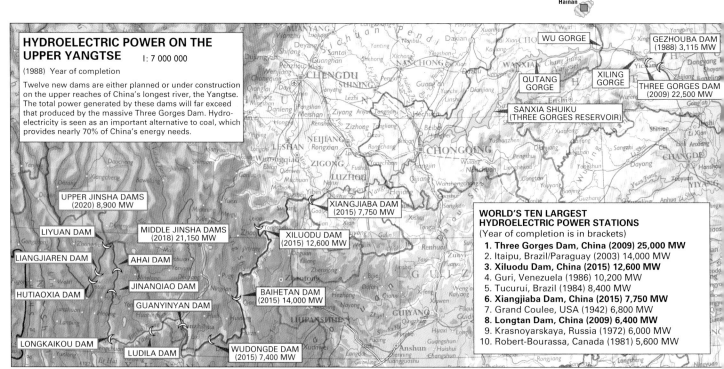

HYDROELECTRIC POWER ON THE UPPER YANGTSE
1: 7 000 000

(1988) Year of completion

Twelve new dams are either planned or under construction on the upper reaches of China's longest river, the Yangtse. The total power generated by these dams will far exceed that produced by the massive Three Gorges Dam. Hydroelectricity is seen as an important alternative to coal, which provides nearly 70% of China's energy needs.

WU GORGE
GEZHOUBA DAM (1988) 3,115 MW

QUTANG GORGE
XILING GORGE
THREE GORGES DAM (2009) 22,500 MW

SANXIA SHUIKU (THREE GORGES RESERVOIR)

UPPER JINSHA DAMS (2020) 8,900 MW

XIANGJIABA DAM (2015) 7,750 MW

LIYUAN DAM

MIDDLE JINSHA DAMS (2018) 21,150 MW

XILUODU DAM (2015) 12,600 MW

LIANGJIAREN DAM

AHAI DAM

HUTIAOXIA DAM

JINANQIAO DAM

BAIHETAN DAM (2015) 14,000 MW

GUANYINYAN DAM

LONGKAIKOU DAM

LUDILA DAM

WUDONGDE DAM (2015) 7,400 MW

WORLD'S TEN LARGEST HYDROELECTRIC POWER STATIONS
(Year of completion is in brackets)

1. **Three Gorges Dam, China (2009) 25,000 MW**
2. Itaipu, Brazil/Paraguay (2003) 14,000 MW
3. **Xiluodu Dam, China (2015) 12,600 MW**
4. Guri, Venezuela (1986) 10,200 MW
5. Tucuruí, Brazil (1984) 8,400 MW
6. **Xiangjiaba Dam, China (2015) 7,750 MW**
7. Grand Coulee, USA (1942) 6,800 MW
8. **Longtan Dam, China (2009) 6,400 MW**
9. Krasnoyarskaya, Russia (1972) 6,000 MW
10. Robert-Bourassa, Canada (1981) 5,600 MW

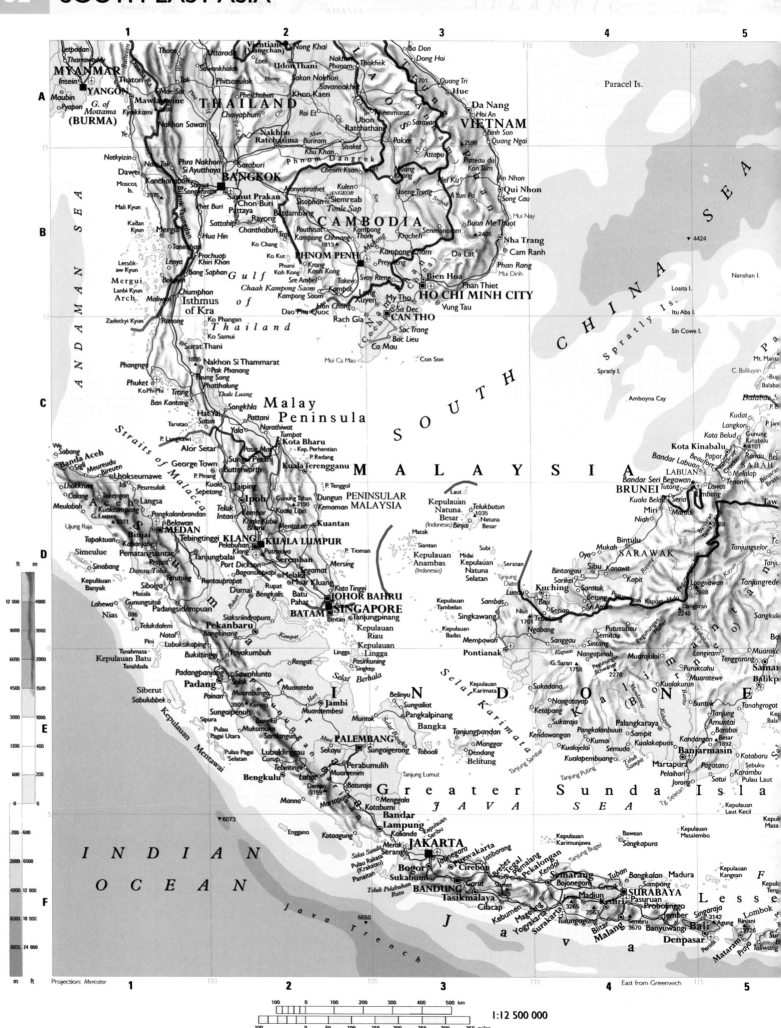

Projection: Mercator

1:12 500 000

East from Greenwich

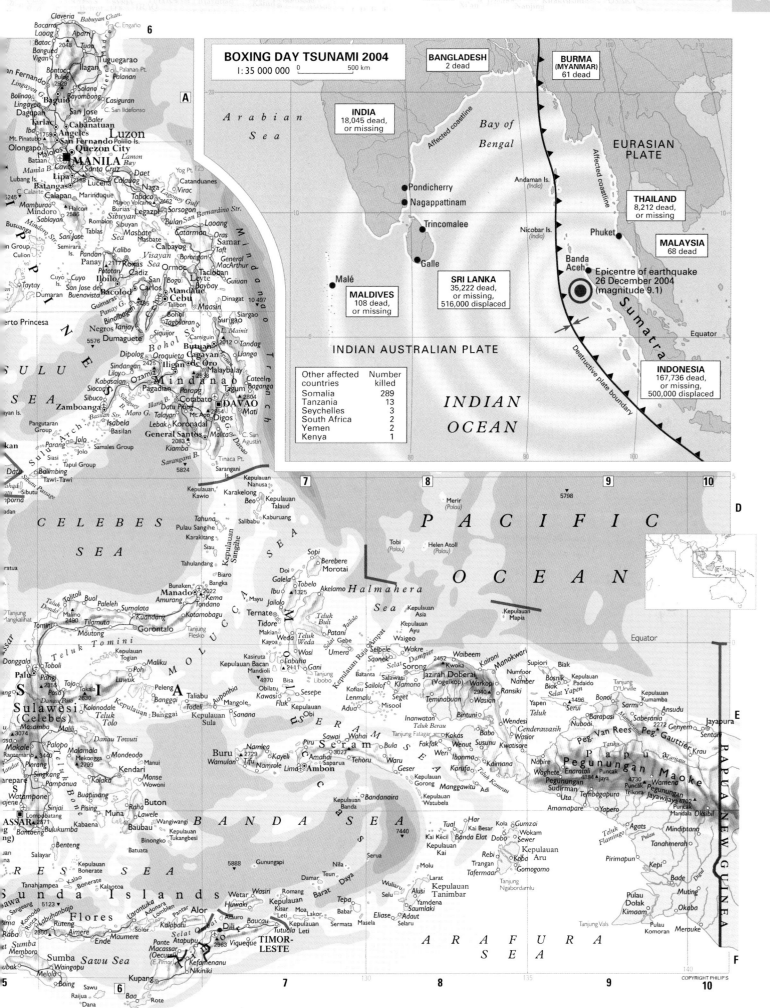

THE MONSOON 1:100 000 000

Monthly rainfall

mm		mm
400		50
200		25
100		0

→ Wind direction

━━ ITCZ (intertropical convergence zone)

In early March, which normally marks the end of the subcontinent's cool season and the start of the hot season, winds blow outwards from the mainland. But as the overhead sun and the ITCZ move northwards, the land is intensely heated, and a low-pressure system develops. The south-east trade winds, which are drawn across the Equator, change direction and are sucked into the interior to become south-westerly winds, bringing heavy rain. By November, the overhead sun and the ITCZ have again moved southwards and the wind directions are again reversed. Cool winds blow from the Asian interior to the sea, losing any moisture on the Himalayas before descending to the coast.

March – Start of the hot, dry season, the ITCZ is over the southern Indian Ocean.

July – The rainy season, the ITCZ has migrated northwards; winds blow onshore.

November – The ITCZ has returned south, the offshore winds are cool and dry.

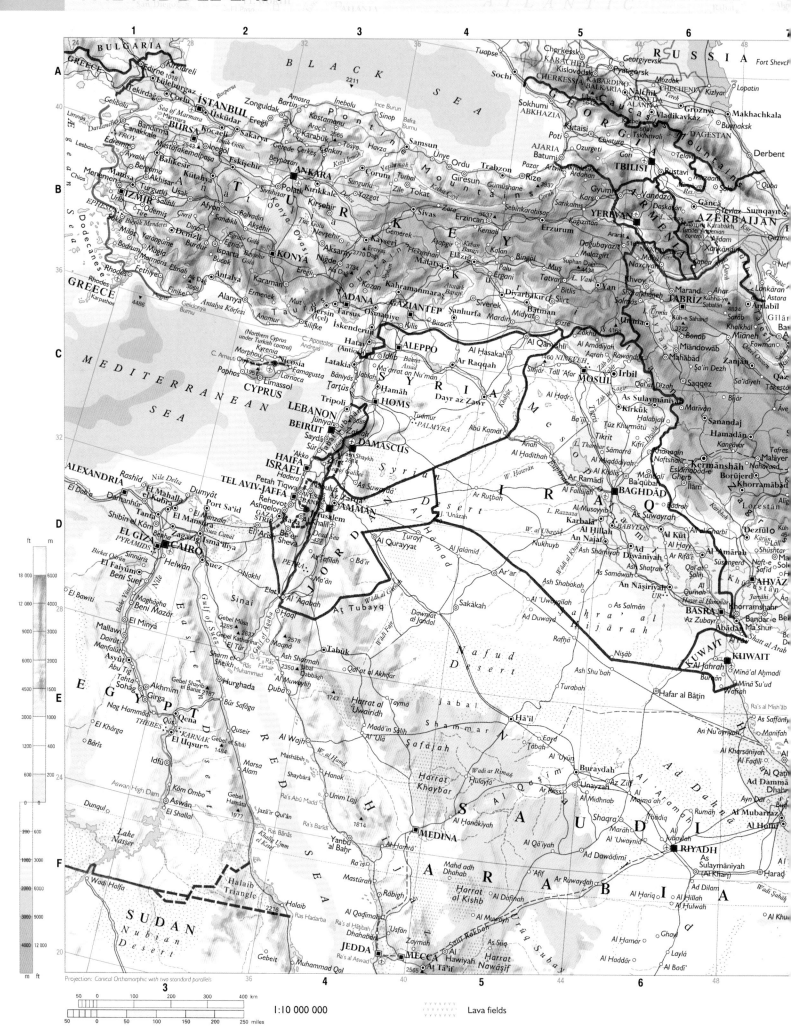

1:10 000 000

Lava fields

Projection: Conical Orthomorphic with two standard parallels

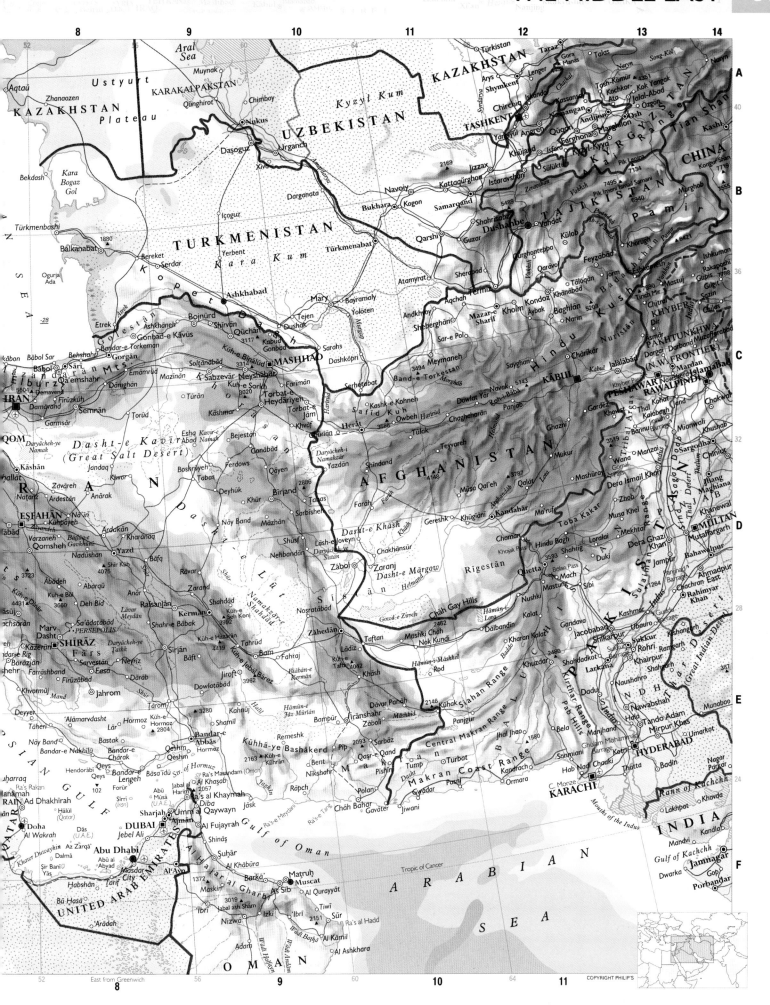

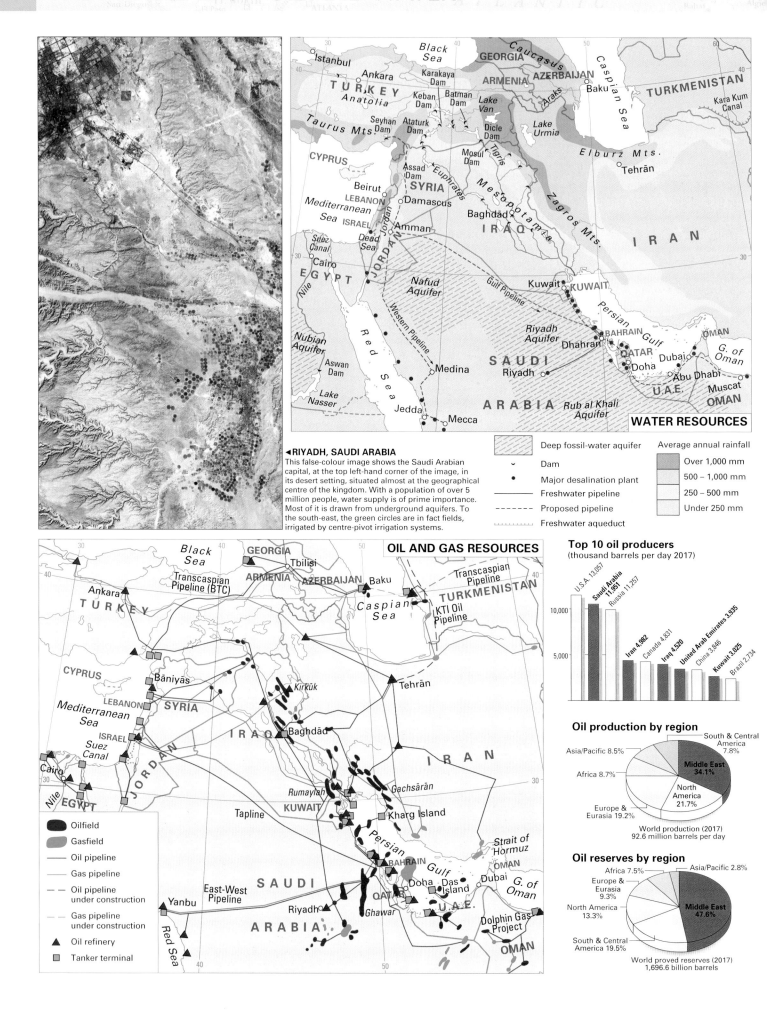

◄ RIYADH, SAUDI ARABIA
This false-colour image shows the Saudi Arabian capital, at the top left-hand corner of the image, in its desert setting, situated almost at the geographical centre of the kingdom. With a population of over 5 million people, water supply is of prime importance. Most of it is drawn from underground aquifers. To the south-east, the green circles are in fact fields, irrigated by centre-pivot irrigation systems.

WATER RESOURCES

Deep fossil-water aquifer
Dam
Major desalination plant
Freshwater pipeline
Proposed pipeline
Freshwater aqueduct

Average annual rainfall
Over 1,000 mm
500 – 1,000 mm
250 – 500 mm
Under 250 mm

OIL AND GAS RESOURCES

Oilfield
Gasfield
Oil pipeline
Gas pipeline
Oil pipeline under construction
Gas pipeline under construction
Oil refinery
Tanker terminal

Top 10 oil producers
(thousand barrels per day 2017)

U.S.A. 13,057
Saudi Arabia 11,951
Russia 11,257
Iran 4,982
Canada 4,831
Iraq 4,520
United Arab Emirates 3,935
China 3,846
Kuwait 3,025
Brazil 2,734

Oil production by region

South & Central America 7.8%
Middle East 34.1%
North America 21.7%
Europe & Eurasia 19.2%
Africa 8.7%
Asia/Pacific 8.5%

World production (2017)
92.6 million barrels per day

Oil reserves by region

Asia/Pacific 2.8%
Middle East 47.6%
South & Central America 19.5%
North America 13.3%
Europe & Eurasia 9.3%
Africa 7.5%

World proved reserves (2017)
1,696.6 billion barrels

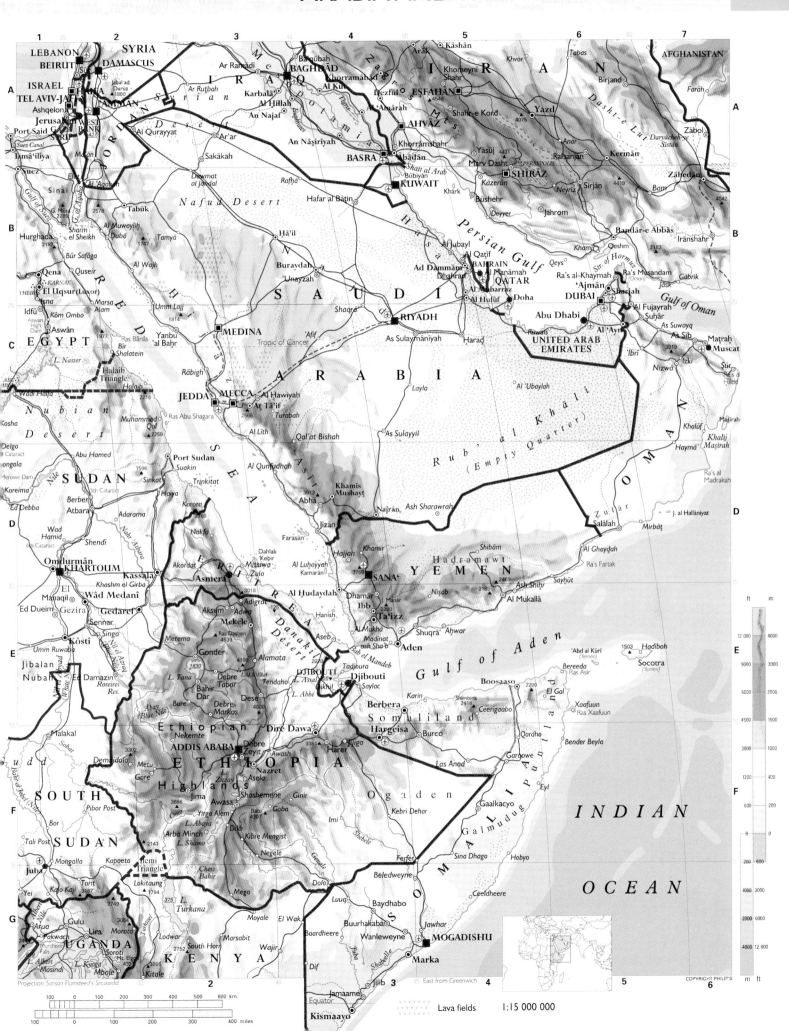

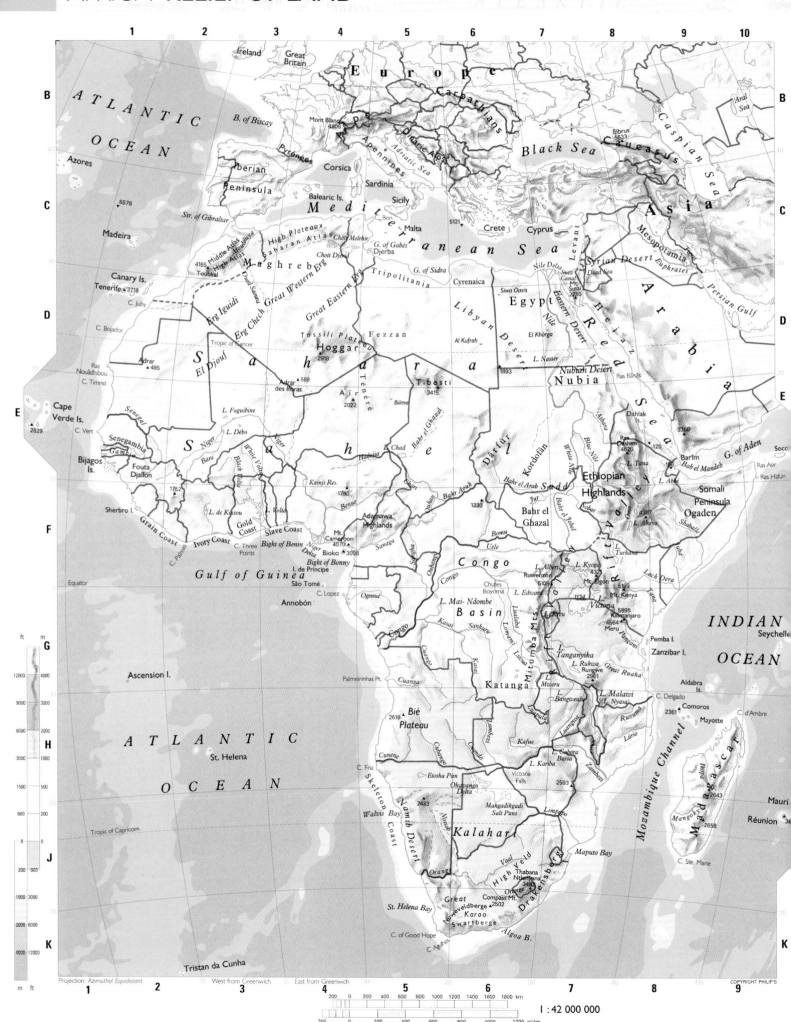

Projection: Azimuthal Equidistant

1 : 42 000 000

COPYRIGHT PHILIP'S

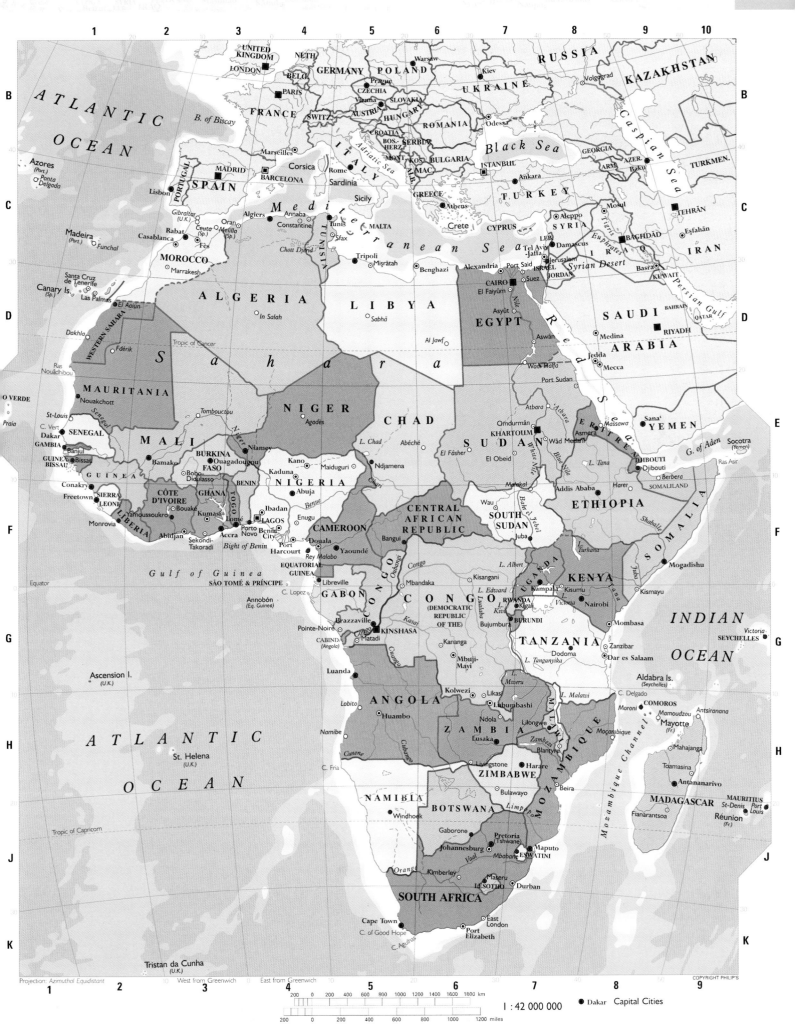

1 2 3 4 5 6 7 8 9 10

ATLANTIC OCEAN

UNITED KINGDOM
LONDON
NETH.
BELG.
GERMANY POLAND
Warsaw
PARIS
FRANCE
SWITZ.
CZECHIA
Prague
Vienna
AUSTRIA
SLOVAKIA
HUNGARY
ROMANIA
CROATIA
BOS.-HERZ.
SERBIA
MONT.
KOS.
MAC.
BULGARIA
ITALY
Rome
Corsica
Sardinia
Sicily
MALTA
GREECE
Athens
Crete
RUSSIA
Kiev
UKRAINE
Odessa
Black Sea
ISTANBUL
Ankara
TURKEY
CYPRUS
Volgograd
KAZAKHSTAN
GEORGIA
ARM. AZER.
Baku
Caspian Sea
TURKMEN.
TEHRÂN
IRAN

B. of Biscay
Marseilles
MADRID
BARCELONA
SPAIN
Lisbon
PORTUGAL
Gibraltar (U.K.)
Algiers
Oran
Annaba
Constantine
Tunis
Sfax
TUNISIA
Tripoli
Misrâtah
Benghazi
Alexandria
Port Said
CAIRO
El Faiyûm
Suez
Aswân
EGYPT
Aleppo
SYRIA
Damascus
Tel Aviv-Jaffa
ISRAEL
JORDAN
LEB.
Jerusalem
Mosul
BAGHDÂD
IRAQ
Basra
KUWAIT
Esfahân
Persian Gulf
BAHRAIN
QATAR
Medina
Mecca
Jedda
SAUDI ARABIA
RIYADH

Azores (Port.)
Ponta Delgada
Madeira (Port.)
Funchal
Santa Cruz de Tenerife
Canary Is. (Sp.)
Las Palmas
Rabat
Casablanca
Fês
MOROCCO
Marrakesh
Ceuta (Sp.)
Melilla (Sp.)
Chott Djerid
Dakhla
El Aaiún
WESTERN SAHARA
Fdérik
In Salah
Tropic of Cancer
ALGERIA
LIBYA
Sabhâ
Al Jawf
Asyût
Nile
Wâdi Halfa
Port Sudan
Red Sea
Atbara
KHARTOUM
Omdurmân
Wâd Medani
Massawa
Asmara
ERITREA
DJIBOUTI
Djibouti
SOMALILAND
Berbera
Ras Asir
G. of Aden
Sana'
YEMEN
Socotra (Yemen)

Ras Nouâdhibou
Nouakchott
MAURITANIA
St-Louis
C. Vert
Dakar
SENEGAL
Banjul
GAMBIA
Bissau
GUINEA-BISSAU
Conakry
Freetown
SIERRA LEONE
Monrovia
LIBERIA
Yamoussoukro
CÔTE D'IVOIRE
Bamako
MALI
Tombouctou
Senegal
Niger
Niamey
Agadès
NIGER
BURKINA FASO
Ouagadougou
Bobo-Dioulasso
Kano
Kaduna
Maiduguri
L. Chad
Ndjamena
Abéché
CHAD
El Fâsher
El Obeid
SUDAN
Malakal
Wau
White Nile
Blue Nile
L. Tana
Addis Ababa
Harer
ETHIOPIA
SOMALIA
Mogadishu
Kismayu
L. Turkana

O VERDE
St-Louis
Praia
BENIN
Lomé
TOGO
GHANA
Accra
Kumasi
Bouaké
Sekondi-Takoradi
Abidjan
Porto Novo
Benin City
Ibadan
LAGOS
NIGERIA
Abuja
Enugu
Benue
Port Harcourt
CAMEROON
Douala
Yaoundé
Malabo
EQUATORIAL GUINEA
Bight of Benin
SÃO TOMÉ & PRÍNCIPE
Libreville
GABON
C. Lopez
Annobón (Eq. Guinea)
CENTRAL AFRICAN REPUBLIC
Bangui
Oubangui
Congo
Mbandaka
Kisangani
SOUTH SUDAN
Juba
UGANDA
Kampala
L. Albert
L. Edward
L. Kivu
RWANDA
Kigali
BURUNDI
Bujumbura
KENYA
Nairobi
Kisumu
L. Victoria
Mombasa
INDIAN OCEAN
SEYCHELLES
Victoria

Equator
Ascension I. (U.K.)
CONGO
Brazzaville
Pointe-Noire
CABINDA (Angola)
KINSHASA
Matadi
CONGO (DEMOCRATIC REPUBLIC OF THE)
Kasai
Kananga
Mbuji-Mayi
Kolwezi
Likasi
Lubumbashi
Ndola
TANZANIA
Dodoma
Zanzibar
Dar es Salaam
L. Tanganyika
L. Mweru
L. Malawi
Aldabra Is. (Seychelles)
C. Delgado
COMOROS
Moroni
Mamoudzou
Mayotte (Fr.)
Antsiranana
Mahajanga

ATLANTIC OCEAN
St. Helena (U.K.)
Luanda
Lobito
Benguela
Namibe
ANGOLA
Huambo
Cunene
Cuando
ZAMBIA
Lusaka
Lilongwe
MALAWI
Blantyre
Zambezi
Livingstone
Harare
ZIMBABWE
Bulawayo
Beira
MOZAMBIQUE
Moçambique
Mozambique Channel
MADAGASCAR
Toamasina
Antananarivo
Fianarantsoa
MAURITIUS
St-Denis
Port Louis
Réunion (Fr.)

Tropic of Capricorn
NAMIBIA
Windhoek
BOTSWANA
Gaborone
Orange
Limpopo
Pretoria (Tshwane)
Johannesburg
Kimberley
Vaal
Maputo
Mbabane
ESWATINI
LESOTHO
Maseru
Durban
SOUTH AFRICA
Cape Town
C. of Good Hope
East London
Port Elizabeth
C. Agulhas

Tristan da Cunha (U.K.)

Projection: Azimuthal Equidistant
West from Greenwich
East from Greenwich
COPYRIGHT PHILIP'S

1 : 42 000 000   ● Dakar Capital Cities

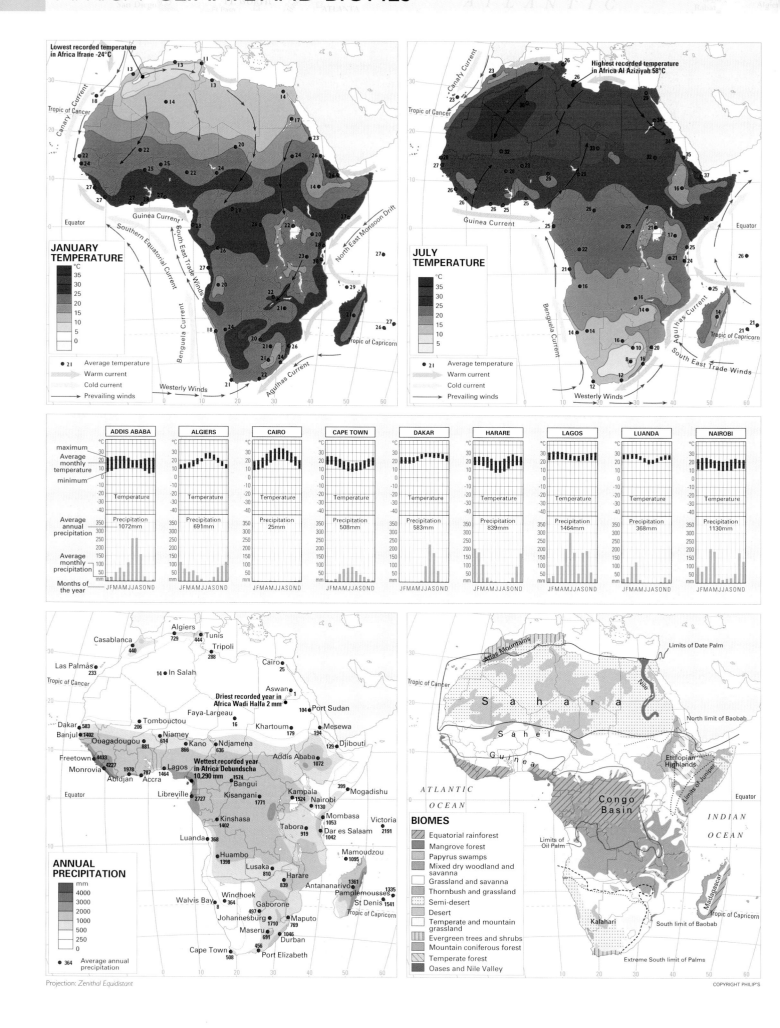

Lowest recorded temperature
in Africa Ifrane -24°C

JANUARY TEMPERATURE

°C
35
30
25
20
15
10
5
0

● 21 Average temperature
→ Warm current
→ Cold current
→ Prevailing winds

Canary Current
Tropic of Cancer
Guinea Current
Southern Equatorial Current
South East Trade Winds
Benguela Current
North East Monsoon Drift
Westerly Winds
Agulhas Current
Equator
Tropic of Capricorn

Highest recorded temperature
in Africa Al Aziziyah 58°C

JULY TEMPERATURE

°C
35
30
25
20
15
10
5

● 21 Average temperature
→ Warm current
→ Cold current
→ Prevailing winds

Canary Current
Tropic of Cancer
Guinea Current
Benguela Current
Agulhas Current
South East Trade Winds
Westerly Winds
Equator
Tropic of Capricorn

Climate graphs

maximum
Average monthly temperature
minimum

Average annual precipitation

Average monthly precipitation

Months of the year

Station	Precipitation
ADDIS ABABA	1072mm
ALGIERS	691mm
CAIRO	25mm
CAPE TOWN	508mm
DAKAR	583mm
HARARE	839mm
LAGOS	1464mm
LUANDA	368mm
NAIROBI	1130mm

ANNUAL PRECIPITATION

mm
4000
3000
2000
1000
500
250
0

● 364 Average annual precipitation

Algiers 729
Tunis 444
Tripoli 288
Casablanca 440
Cairo 25
Las Palmas 233
Aswan 1
Tropic of Cancer
In Salah 14
Driest recorded year in Africa Wadi Halfa 2 mm
Faya-Largeau 16
Port Sudan 104
Dakar 583
Tombouctou 206
Khartoum 179
Mesewa 194
Banjul 1402
Niamey 614
Ndjamena 636
Djibouti 129
Ouagadougou 881
Kano 866
Freetown 4433
Addis Ababa 1072
Monrovia 4227
Abidjan 1978
Accra 787
Lagos 1464
Wettest recorded year in Africa Debundscha 10,290 mm
Bangui 1574
Kampala 1524
Mogadishu 399
Libreville 2727
Kisangani 1771
Nairobi 1130
Equator
Kinshasa 1402
Mombasa 1053
Victoria 2191
Luanda 368
Tabora 919
Dar es Salaam 1042
Huambo 1398
Mamoudzou 1095
Lusaka 810
Harare 839
Antananarivo 1361
Pamplemousses 1335
Windhoek 364
St Denis 1541
Walvis Bay 8
Gaborone 497
Johannesburg 710
Maputo 769
Maseru 691
Durban 1046
Cape Town 508
Port Elizabeth 456

BIOMES

▨ Equatorial rainforest
Mangrove forest
Papyrus swamps
Mixed dry woodland and savanna
Grassland and savanna
Thornbush and grassland
Semi-desert
Desert
Temperate and mountain grassland
Evergreen trees and shrubs
Mountain coniferous forest
Temperate forest
Oases and Nile Valley

Atlas Mountains
Limits of Date Palm
Sahara
Sahel
North limit of Baobab
Guinea
Ethiopian Highlands
Limits of Juniper
Nile
ATLANTIC OCEAN
Congo Basin
INDIAN OCEAN
Equator
Limits of Oil Palm
Madagascar
Tropic of Capricorn
South limit of Baobab
Kalahari
Extreme South limit of Palms

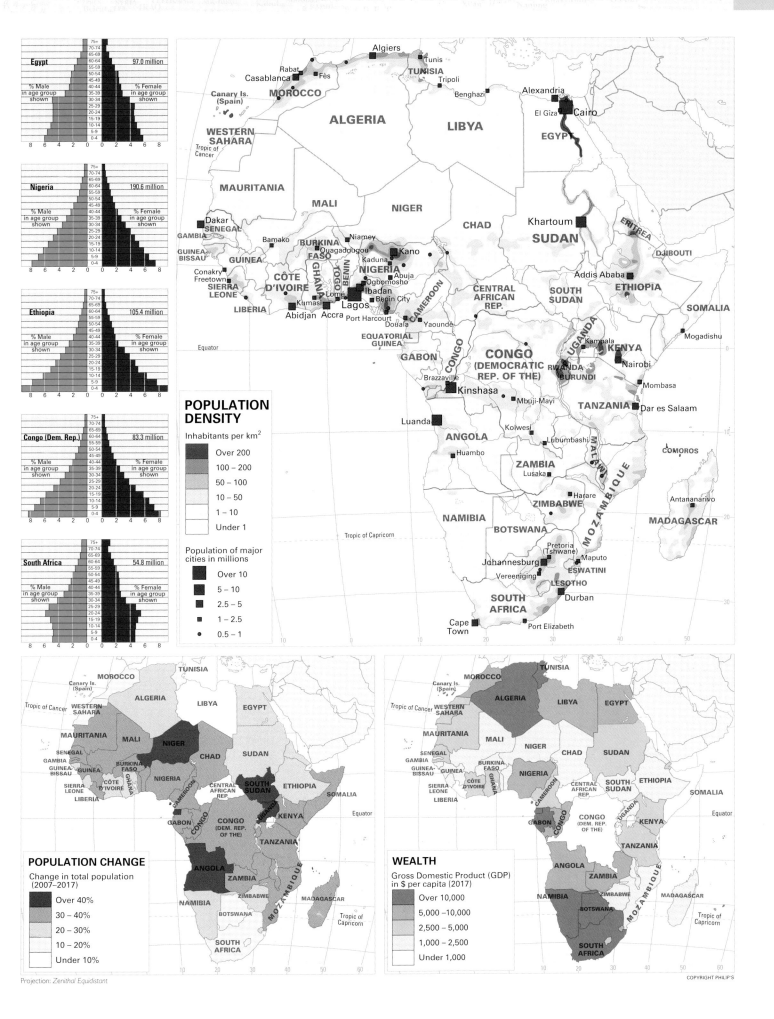

Egypt — 97.0 million

% Male in age group shown | % Female in age group shown
(age groups: 0-4, 5-9, 10-14, 15-19, 20-24, 25-29, 30-34, 35-39, 40-44, 45-49, 50-54, 55-59, 60-64, 65-69, 70-74, 75+)
8 6 4 2 0 2 4 6 8

Nigeria — 190.6 million

Ethiopia — 105.4 million

Congo (Dem. Rep.) — 83.3 million

South Africa — 54.8 million

POPULATION DENSITY

Inhabitants per km²

- Over 200
- 100 – 200
- 50 – 100
- 10 – 50
- 1 – 10
- Under 1

Population of major cities in millions

- Over 10
- 5 – 10
- 2.5 – 5
- 1 – 2.5
- 0.5 – 1

POPULATION CHANGE

Change in total population (2007–2017)

- Over 40%
- 30 – 40%
- 20 – 30%
- 10 – 20%
- Under 10%

WEALTH

Gross Domestic Product (GDP) in $ per capita (2017)

- Over 10,000
- 5,000 –10,000
- 2,500 – 5,000
- 1,000 – 2,500
- Under 1,000

Projection: *Zenithal Equidistant*

COPYRIGHT PHILIP'S

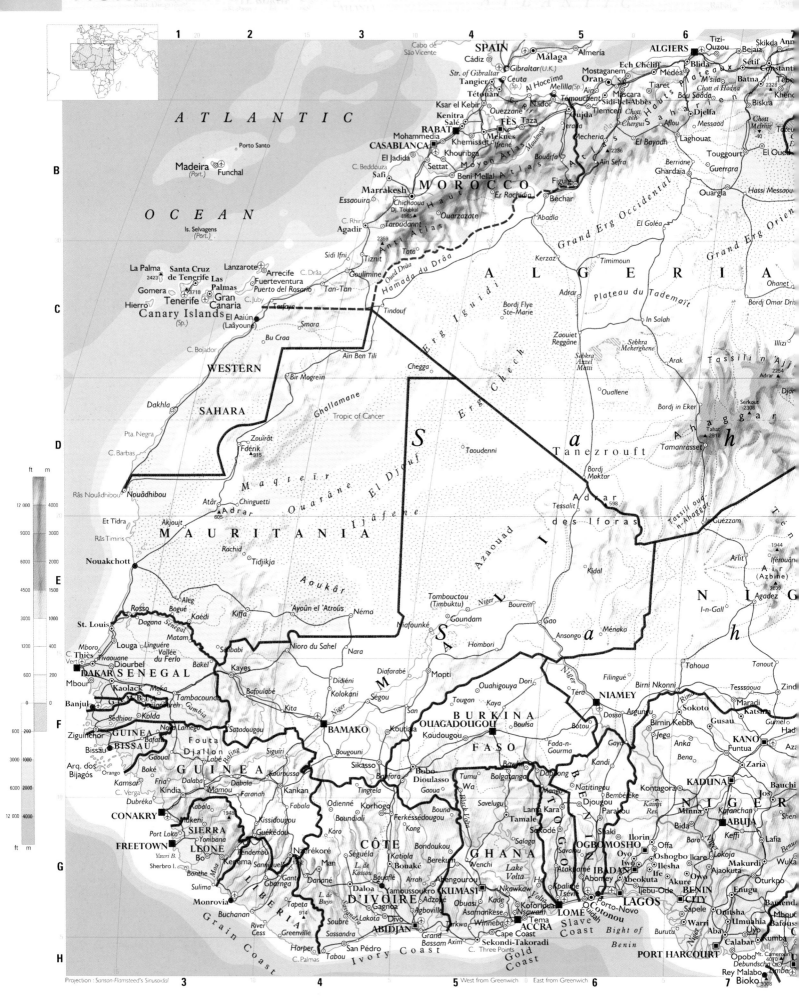

Lava fields

1:15 000 000

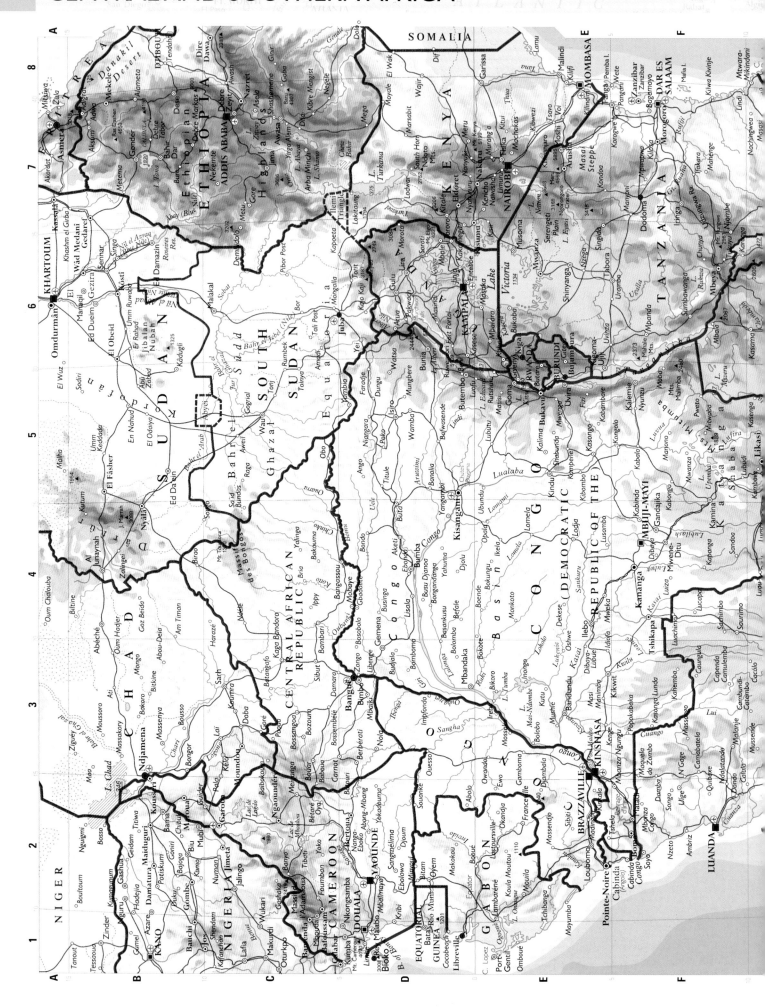

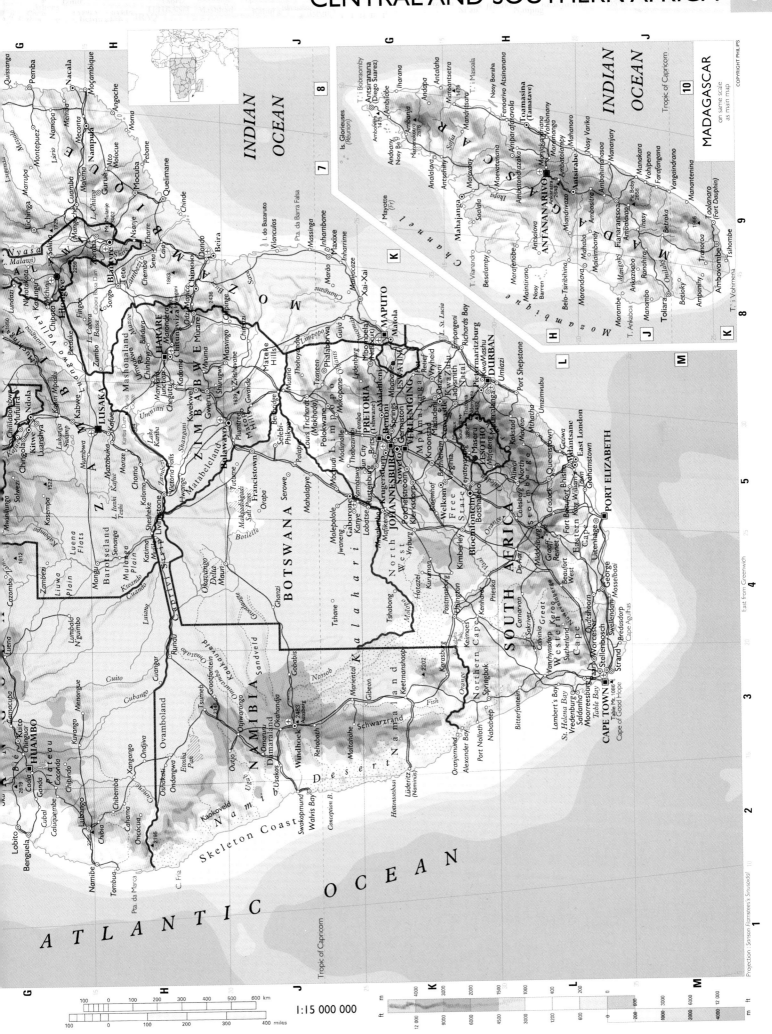

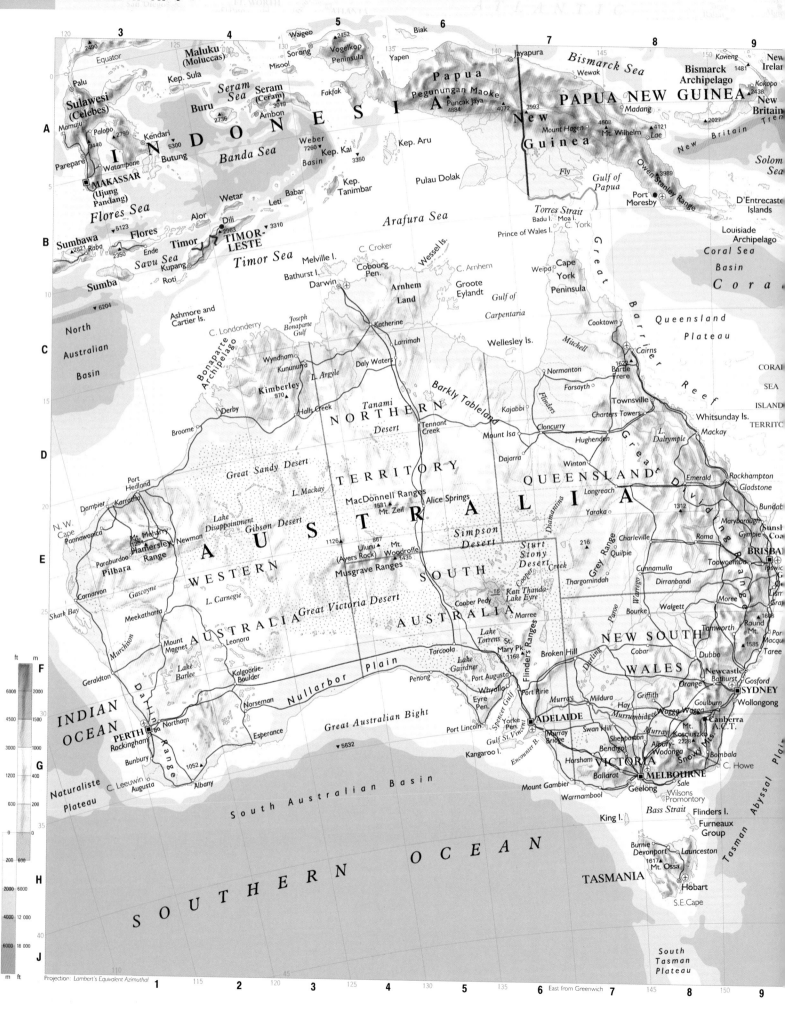

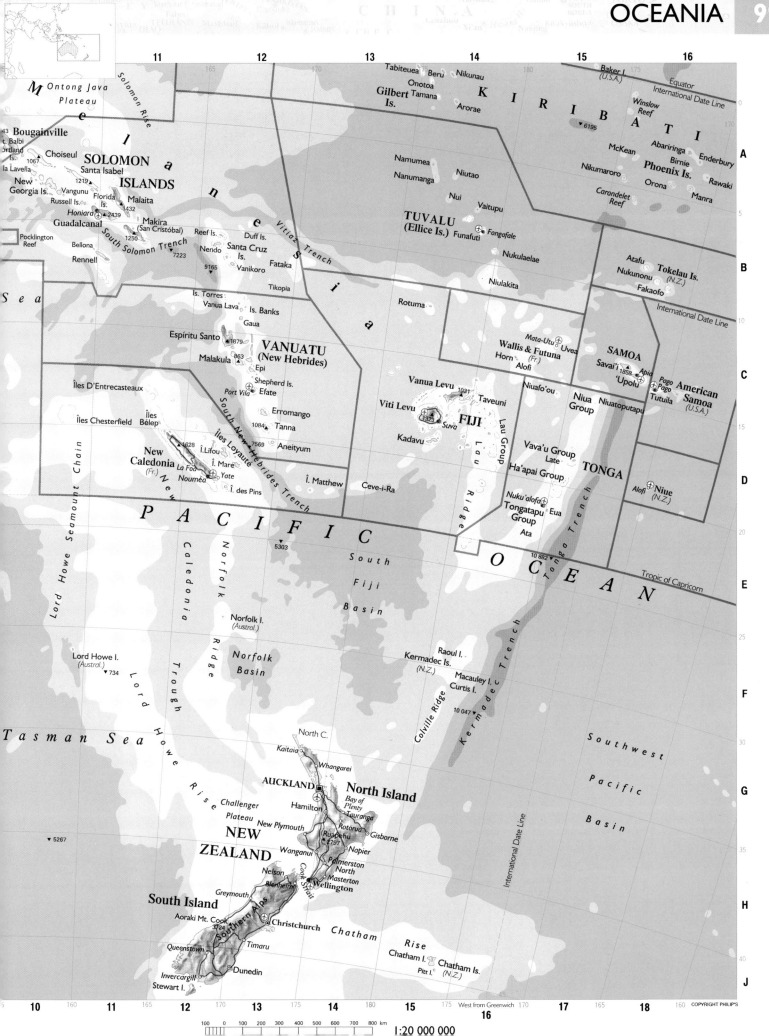

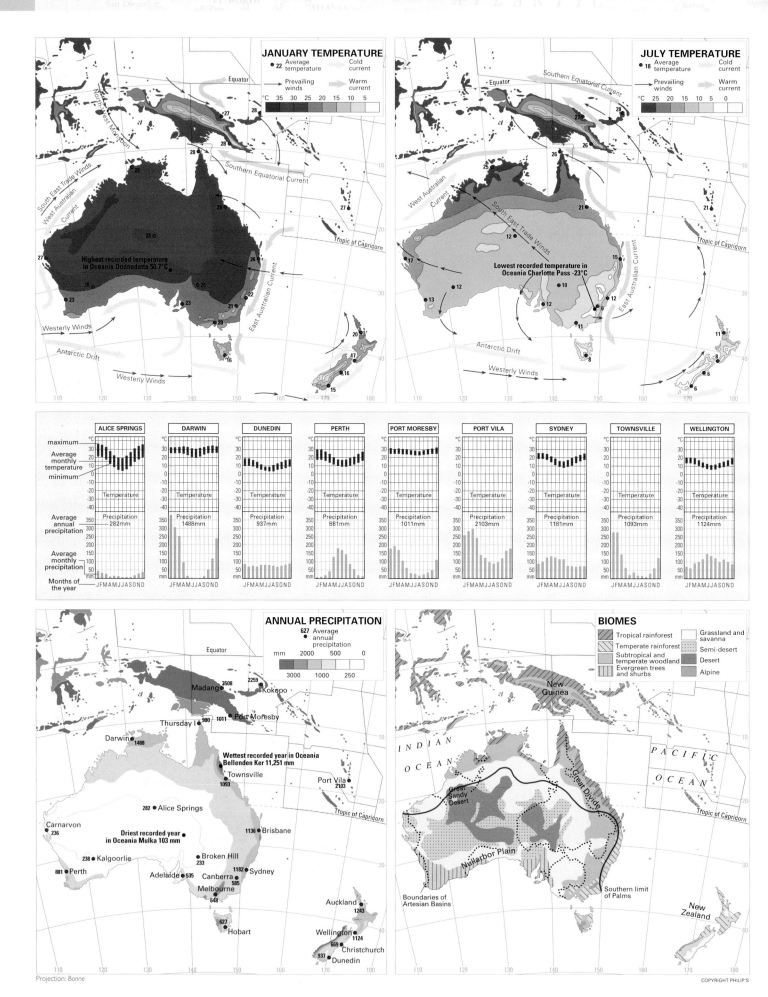

JANUARY TEMPERATURE
- 22 Average temperature
- Cold current
- Prevailing winds
- Warm current

°C 35 30 25 20 15 10 5

North West Monsoon
South East Trade Winds
West Australian Current
Southern Equatorial Current
East Australian Current
Westerly Winds
Antarctic Drift
Westerly Winds
Equator
Tropic of Capricorn

Highest recorded temperature in Oceania Oodnadatta 50.7°C

JULY TEMPERATURE
- 18 Average temperature
- Cold current
- Prevailing winds
- Warm current

°C 25 20 15 10 5 0

Southern Equatorial Current
West Australian Current
South East Trade Winds
East Australian Current
Antarctic Drift
Westerly Winds
Equator
Tropic of Capricorn

Lowest recorded temperature in Oceania Charlotte Pass -23°C

ALICE SPRINGS — Temperature — Precipitation 282mm
DARWIN — Temperature — Precipitation 1488mm
DUNEDIN — Temperature — Precipitation 937mm
PERTH — Temperature — Precipitation 881mm
PORT MORESBY — Temperature — Precipitation 1011mm
PORT VILA — Temperature — Precipitation 2103mm
SYDNEY — Temperature — Precipitation 1181mm
TOWNSVILLE — Temperature — Precipitation 1093mm
WELLINGTON — Temperature — Precipitation 1124mm

maximum — Average monthly temperature — minimum
Average annual precipitation
Average monthly precipitation
Months of the year — JFMAMJJASOND

ANNUAL PRECIPITATION
- 627 Average annual precipitation

mm 2000 500 0
3000 1000 250

Equator
Tropic of Capricorn

Madang 3508
Kokopo 2259
Thursday I. 900
Port Moresby 1011
Darwin 1488
Wettest recorded year in Oceania Bellenden Ker 11,251 mm
Townsville 1093
Port Vila 2103
Alice Springs 282
Carnarvon 236
Driest recorded year in Oceania Mulka 103 mm
Kalgoorlie 238
Perth 881
Brisbane 1136
Broken Hill 233
Adelaide 535
Canberra 585
Sydney 1182
Melbourne 648
Hobart 627
Auckland 1243
Wellington 1124
Christchurch 669
Dunedin 937

BIOMES
- Tropical rainforest
- Temperate rainforest
- Subtropical and temperate woodland
- Evergreen trees and shrubs
- Grassland and savanna
- Semi-desert
- Desert
- Alpine

New Guinea
INDIAN OCEAN
PACIFIC OCEAN
Great Sandy Desert
Great Divide
Nullarbor Plain
Boundaries of Artesian Basins
Southern limit of Palms
New Zealand
Tropic of Capricorn

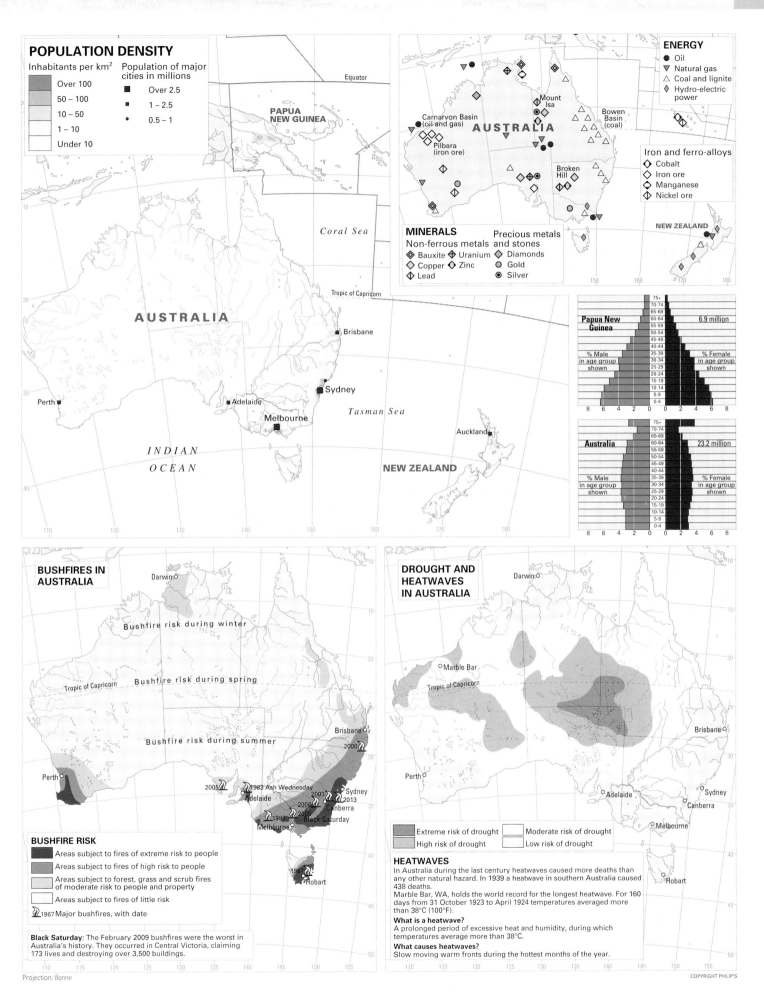

POPULATION DENSITY

Inhabitants per km²

- Over 100
- 50 – 100
- 10 – 50
- 1 – 10
- Under 10

Population of major cities in millions
- Over 2.5
- 1 – 2.5
- 0.5 – 1

Equator

PAPUA NEW GUINEA

Coral Sea

Tropic of Capricorn

AUSTRALIA

Brisbane

Sydney

Adelaide

Perth

Melbourne

Tasman Sea

INDIAN OCEAN

Auckland

NEW ZEALAND

ENERGY

- Oil
- Natural gas
- Coal and lignite
- Hydro-electric power

Mount Isa

Bowen Basin (coal)

Carnarvon Basin (oil and gas)

AUSTRALIA

Pilbara (iron ore)

Broken Hill

Iron and ferro-alloys

- Cobalt
- Iron ore
- Manganese
- Nickel ore

NEW ZEALAND

MINERALS

Non-ferrous metals
- Bauxite
- Copper
- Lead
- Uranium
- Zinc

Precious metals and stones
- Diamonds
- Gold
- Silver

Papua New Guinea — 6.9 million

% Male in age group shown / % Female in age group shown

75+, 70-74, 65-69, 60-64, 55-59, 50-54, 45-49, 40-44, 35-39, 30-34, 25-29, 20-24, 15-19, 10-14, 5-9, 0-4

Australia — 23.2 million

% Male in age group shown / % Female in age group shown

BUSHFIRES IN AUSTRALIA

Darwin

Bushfire risk during winter

Tropic of Capricorn

Bushfire risk during spring

Bushfire risk during summer

Brisbane

2000

Perth

2005

1983 Ash Wednesday

Adelaide

2003

2006

2006

2013

Sydney

Canberra

1983

2009

Black Saturday

Melbourne

1967

Hobart

BUSHFIRE RISK

- Areas subject to fires of extreme risk to people
- Areas subject to fires of high risk to people
- Areas subject to forest, grass and scrub fires of moderate risk to people and property
- Areas subject to fires of little risk
- 1967 Major bushfires, with date

Black Saturday: The February 2009 bushfires were the worst in Australia's history. They occurred in Central Victoria, claiming 173 lives and destroying over 3,500 buildings.

DROUGHT AND HEATWAVES IN AUSTRALIA

Darwin

Marble Bar

Tropic of Capricorn

Brisbane

Perth

Adelaide

Sydney

Canberra

Melbourne

Hobart

- Extreme risk of drought
- High risk of drought
- Moderate risk of drought
- Low risk of drought

HEATWAVES

In Australia during the last century heatwaves caused more deaths than any other natural hazard. In 1939 a heatwave in southern Australia caused 438 deaths.

Marble Bar, WA, holds the world record for the longest heatwave. For 160 days from 31 October 1923 to April 1924 temperatures averaged more than 38°C (100°F).

What is a heatwave?
A prolonged period of excessive heat and humidity, during which temperatures average more than 38°C.

What causes heatwaves?
Slow moving warm fronts during the hottest months of the year.

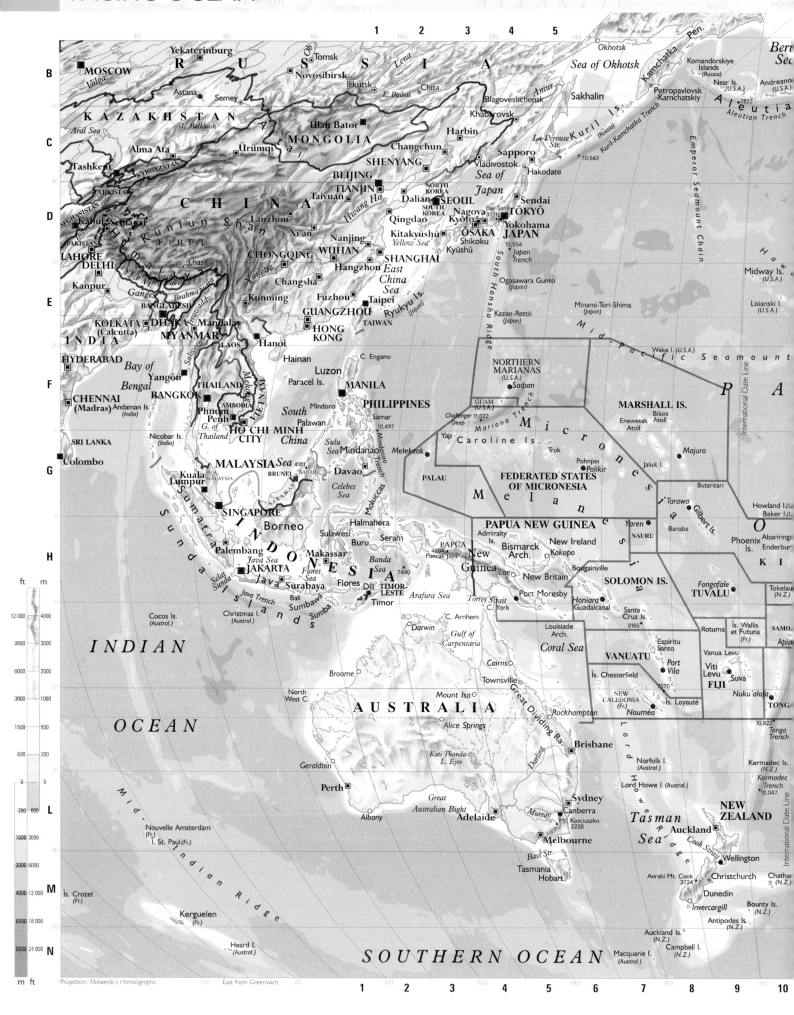

Projection: Mollweide's Homolographic   East from Greenwich

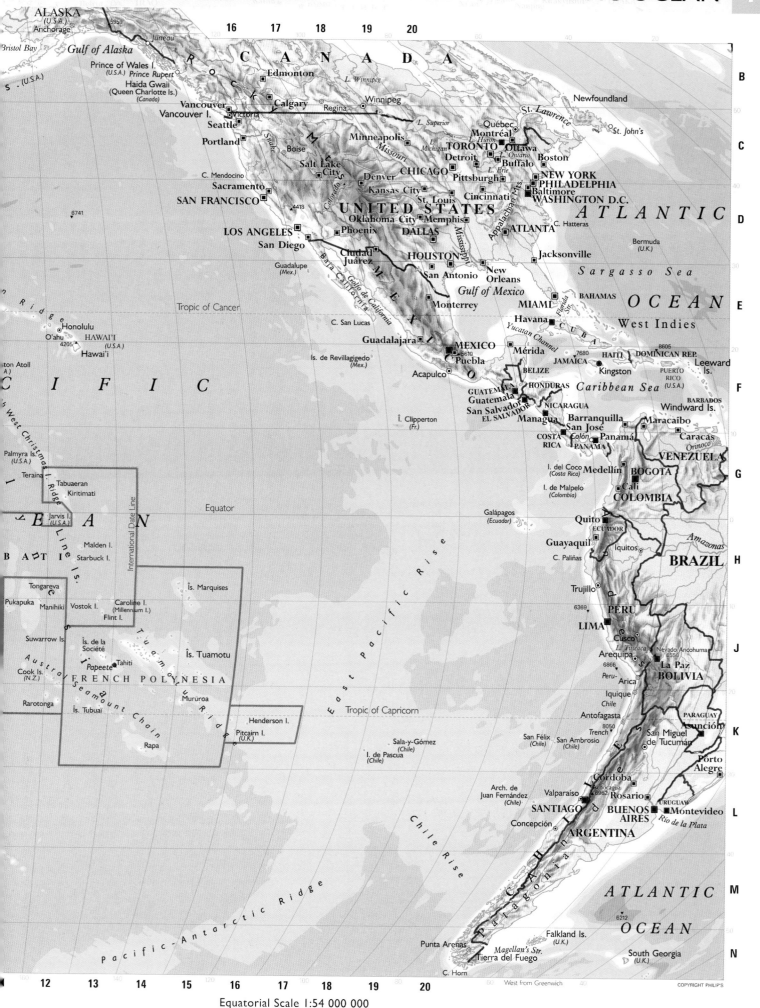

ALASKA
(U.S.A.)
Anchorage
Bristol Bay
Gulf of Alaska
Juneau
Prince of Wales I.
(U.S.A.) Prince Rupert
Haida Gwaii
(Queen Charlotte Is.)
(Canada)
Vancouver
Vancouver I.
Victoria
Seattle
Portland

CANADA
Edmonton
Calgary
Regina
Winnipeg
L. Winnipeg
Newfoundland

6959

CHINA

16 17 18 19 20

L. Superior
Minneapolis
L. Michigan
L. Huron
Québec
Montréal
St. Lawrence
Ottawa
Toronto
Detroit
Buffalo
St. John's
Boston
Pittsburgh
L. Erie
L. Ontario

Salt Lake City
Boise
C. Mendocino
Sacramento
SAN FRANCISCO
Denver
Kansas City
CHICAGO
St. Louis
Cincinnati
NEW YORK
PHILADELPHIA
Baltimore
WASHINGTON D.C.

6741
4418

UNITED STATES
Oklahoma City
Memphis
ATLANTA
ATLANTIC

LOS ANGELES
San Diego
Phoenix
DALLAS
Appalachian Mts.
C. Hatteras

Guadalupe
(Mex.)
Ciudad
Juárez
HOUSTON
San Antonio
New
Orleans
Jacksonville
Bermuda
(U.K.)

Baja California
Golfo de California
Mississippi
Gulf of Mexico
Monterrey
MIAMI
BAHAMAS
Sargasso Sea

Tropic of Cancer
OCEAN

C. San Lucas
Havana
CUBA
West Indies

Honolulu
O'ahu
HAWAI'I
(U.S.A.)
Hawai'i
4205

Is. de Revillagigedo
(Mex.)
Guadalajara
MEXICO
Puebla
Mérida
Yucatan Channel
HAITI
DOMINICAN REP.
8605
Leeward
Is.

6610
7680
JAMAICA
Kingston
PUERTO
RICO
(U.S.A.)

Acapulco
BELIZE
Caribbean Sea
BARBADOS

GUATEMALA
Guatemala
HONDURAS
Windward Is.

Î. Clipperton
(Fr.)
San Salvador
EL SALVADOR
NICARAGUA
Managua
Barranquilla
Maracaibo

COSTA
RICA
San José
Colón
PANAMA
Panamá
Caracas
Orinoco
VENEZUELA

I. del Coco
(Costa Rica)
Medellín
BOGOTA

I. de Malpelo
(Colombia)
Cali
COLOMBIA

Equator
Galápagos
(Ecuador)
Quito
ECUADOR

Guayaquil
C. Pariñas
Iquitos
Amazonas
BRAZIL

PACIFIC

Palmyra Is.
(U.S.A.)
Teraina
Tabuaeran
Kiritimati

Jarvis I.
(U.S.A.)
Malden I.
Starbuck I.

Tongareva
Îs. Marquises
Trujillo

Pukapuka
Manihiki
Vostok I.
Caroline I.
(Millennium I.)
Flint I.
6369
PERU

Suwarrow Is.
Îs. de la
Société
Îs. Tuamotu
LIMA
Cusco
L. Titicaca
Nevado Ancohuma
6550

Cook Is.
(N.Z.)
Papeete
Tahiti
FRENCH POLYNESIA
Arequipa
La Paz
BOLIVIA

Rarotonga
Îs. Tubuaï
Mururoa
6866
Peru-
Arica

Tropic of Capricorn
Iquique
Chile

Henderson I.
Antofagasta

Pitcairn I.
(U.K.)
Rapa
Sala-y-Gómez
(Chile)
San Félix
(Chile)
San Ambrosio
(Chile)
8050
Trench
PARAGUAY
Asunción

I. de Pascua
(Chile)
San Miguel
de Tucumán

Córdoba
6212
Porto
Alegre

Arch. de
Juan Fernández
(Chile)
Valparaíso
Aconcagua
6962
Rosario
URUGUAY
Montevideo

SANTIAGO
BUENOS
AIRES
Río de la Plata

Concepción
ARGENTINA

ATLANTIC

International Date Line
Line Is.
East Pacific Rise
Chile Rise

Pacific-Antarctic Ridge

OCEAN
Punta Arenas
Magellan's Str.
Tierra del Fuego
Falkland Is.
(U.K.)
South Georgia
(U.K.)
C. Horn

12 13 14 15 16 17 18 19 20
West from Greenwich
COPYRIGHT PHILIP'S

B C D E F G H J K L M N

Equatorial Scale 1:54 000 000

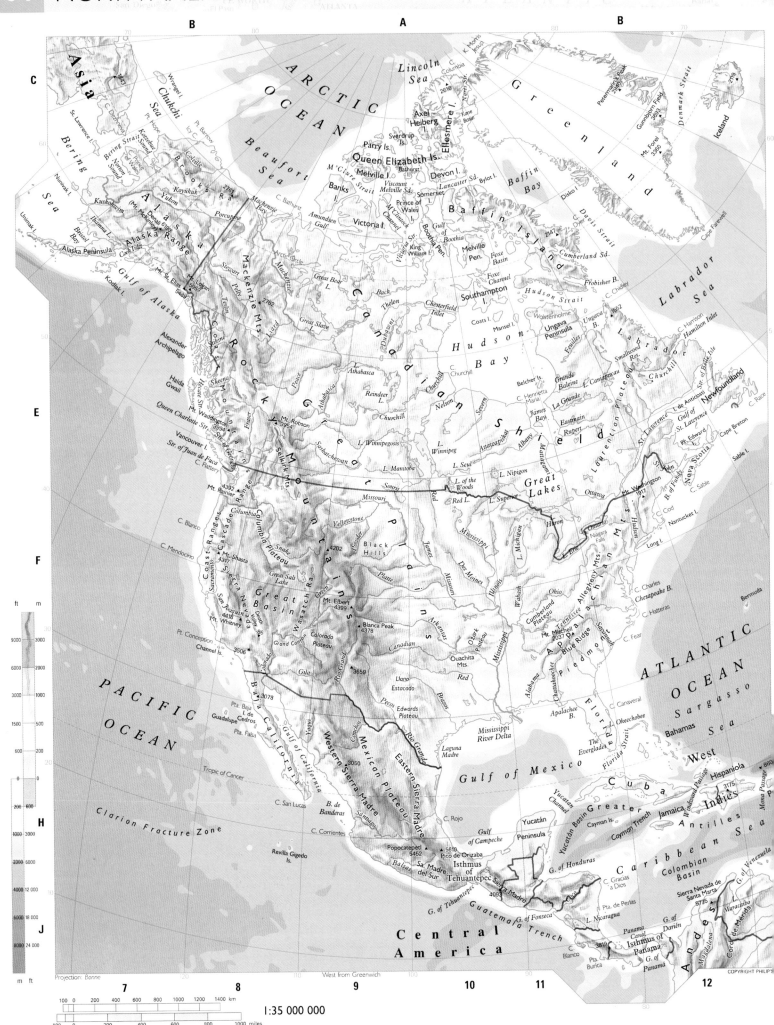

Projection: Bonne

West from Greenwich

1:35 000 000

COPYRIGHT PHILIP'S

Projection: Bonne

7 ■ MÉXICO Capital Cities 8

1:35 000 000

West from Greenwich

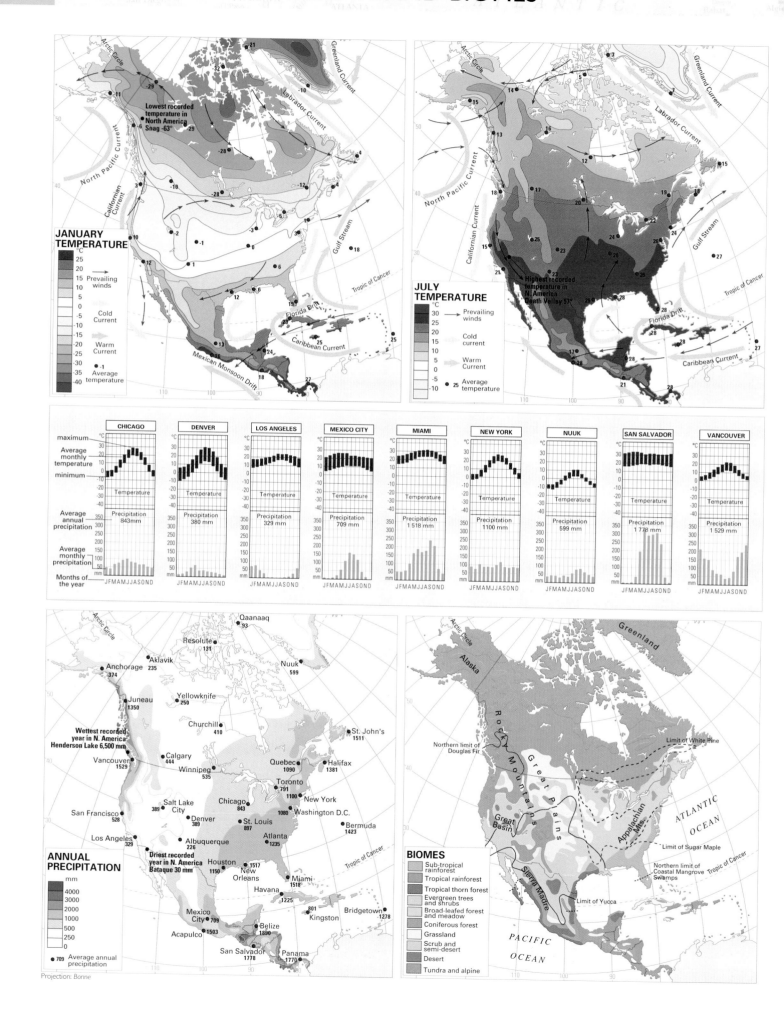

JANUARY TEMPERATURE

Lowest recorded temperature in North America Snag -63°

°C
25
20 → Prevailing winds
15
10
5
0
-5
-10 Cold Current
-15
-20
-25 → Warm Current
-30
-35
-40 -1 Average temperature

JULY TEMPERATURE

Highest recorded temperature in N. America Death Valley 57°

°C
30 → Prevailing winds
25
20
15 Cold current
10
5
0 → Warm Current
-5
-10 • 25 Average temperature

CHICAGO

maximum
Average monthly temperature
minimum

°C
30
20
10
0
-10
-20
-30
-40
Temperature

Average annual precipitation
Precipitation 843mm
350
300
250
200
150
100
50
mm
Average monthly precipitation
Months of the year JFMAMJJASOND

DENVER
Temperature
Precipitation 380 mm

LOS ANGELES
Temperature
Precipitation 329 mm

MEXICO CITY
Temperature
Precipitation 709 mm

MIAMI
Temperature
Precipitation 1 518 mm

NEW YORK
Temperature
Precipitation 1100 mm

NUUK
Temperature
Precipitation 599 mm

SAN SALVADOR
Temperature
Precipitation 1 778 mm

VANCOUVER
Temperature
Precipitation 1 529 mm

Qaanaaq 93
Resolute 131
Aklavik 235
Anchorage 374
Juneau 1350
Yellowknife 250
Nuuk 599
Churchill 410
St. John's 1511
Wettest recorded year in N. America Henderson Lake 6,500 mm
Calgary 444
Vancouver 1529
Winnipeg 535
Quebec 1090
Halifax 1381
Toronto 791
San Francisco 528
Salt Lake City 389
Chicago 843
New York 1100
Denver 389
Washington D.C. 1080
St. Louis 897
Bermuda 1423
Los Angeles 329
Atlanta 1235
Albuquerque 226
Driest recorded year in N. America Bataque 30 mm
Houston 1150
New Orleans 1517
Havana 1225
Miami 1518
Kingston 801
Bridgetown 1278
Mexico City 709
Acapulco 1503
Belize 1890
San Salvador 1778
Panama 1770

ANNUAL PRECIPITATION

mm
4000
3000
2000
1000
500
250
0
• 709 Average annual precipitation

Projection: Bonne

Northern limit of Douglas Fir
Limit of White Pine
Limit of Sugar Maple
Northern limit of Coastal Mangrove Swamps
Limit of Yucca

BIOMES
Sub-tropical rainforest
Tropical rainforest
Tropical thorn forest
Evergreen trees and shrubs
Broad-leafed forest and meadow
Coniferous forest
Grassland
Scrub and semi-desert
Desert
Tundra and alpine

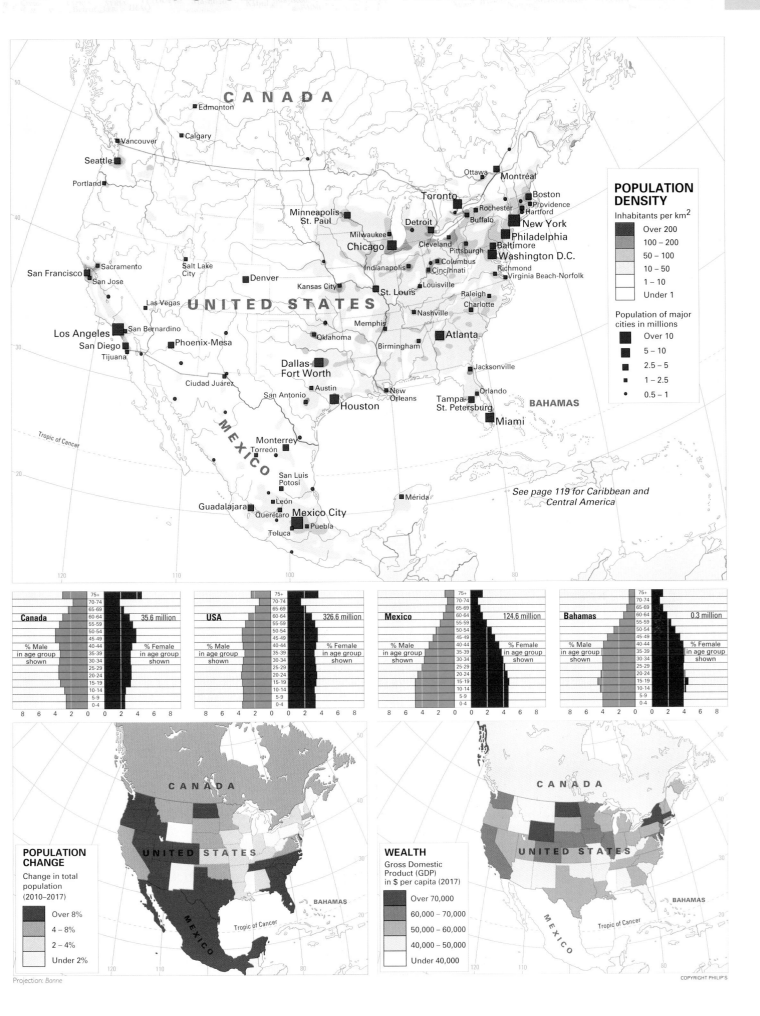

CANADA

Edmonton
Calgary
Vancouver
Seattle
Portland

UNITED STATES

Minneapolis-St. Paul
Milwaukee
Chicago
Detroit
Cleveland
Pittsburgh
Columbus
Indianapolis
Cincinnati
Louisville
Nashville
Memphis
Birmingham
Atlanta

Ottawa
Montréal
Toronto
Rochester
Buffalo
Boston
Providence
Hartford
New York
Philadelphia
Baltimore
Washington D.C.
Richmond
Virginia Beach-Norfolk
Raleigh
Charlotte

Sacramento
San Jose
San Francisco
Salt Lake City
Denver
Kansas City
St. Louis
Las Vegas
Los Angeles
San Bernardino
San Diego
Phoenix-Mesa
Tijuana
Oklahoma

Dallas-Fort Worth
Ciudad Juárez
San Antonio
Austin
Houston
New Orleans
Jacksonville
Orlando
Tampa-St. Petersburg
Miami

BAHAMAS

MEXICO

Monterrey
Torreón
San Luis Potosí
Guadalajara
León
Querétaro
Toluca
Mexico City
Puebla
Mérida

Tropic of Cancer

See page 119 for Caribbean and Central America

POPULATION DENSITY

Inhabitants per km²

	Over 200
	100 – 200
	50 – 100
	10 – 50
	1 – 10
	Under 1

Population of major cities in millions

■	Over 10
■	5 – 10
■	2.5 – 5
▪	1 – 2.5
•	0.5 – 1

Canada 35.6 million
% Male in age group shown / % Female in age group shown

USA 326.6 million
% Male in age group shown / % Female in age group shown

Mexico 124.6 million
% Male in age group shown / % Female in age group shown

Bahamas 0.3 million
% Male in age group shown / % Female in age group shown

Age groups: 75+, 70-74, 65-69, 60-64, 55-59, 50-54, 45-49, 40-44, 35-39, 30-34, 25-29, 20-24, 15-19, 10-14, 5-9, 0-4
Scale: 8 6 4 2 0 0 2 4 6 8

CANADA

UNITED STATES

MEXICO

Tropic of Cancer

BAHAMAS

POPULATION CHANGE

Change in total population (2010–2017)

	Over 8%
	4 – 8%
	2 – 4%
	Under 2%

CANADA

UNITED STATES

MEXICO

Tropic of Cancer

BAHAMAS

WEALTH

Gross Domestic Product (GDP) in $ per capita (2017)

	Over 70,000
	60,000 – 70,000
	50,000 – 60,000
	40,000 – 50,000
	Under 40,000

Projection: Bonne

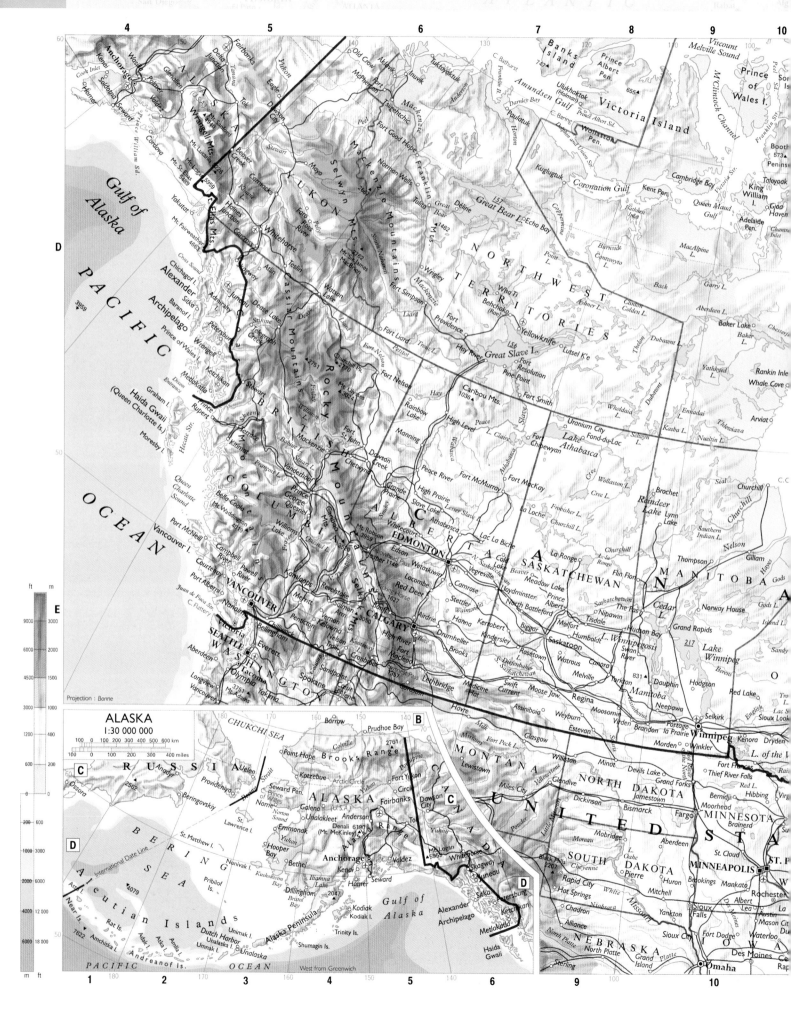

CANADA

ALASKA
1:30 000 000

NORTHERN CANADA

Continuation northwards on same scale as main map

1:15 000 000

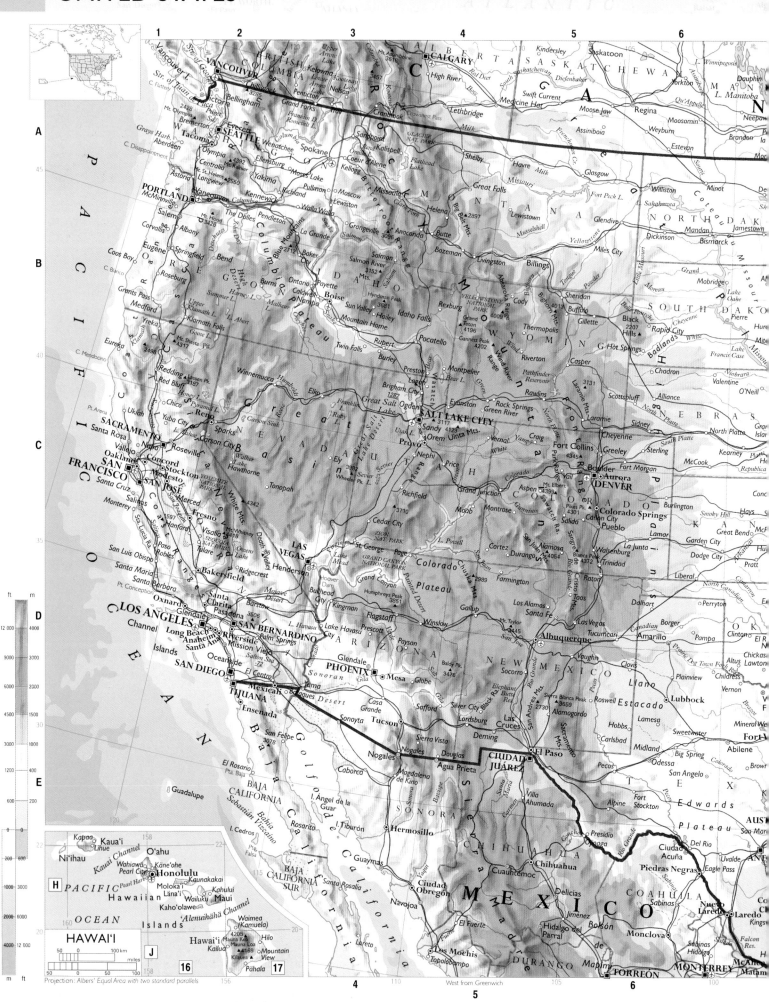

HAWAI'I

Projection: Albers' Equal Area with two standard parallels

West from Greenwich

See page 108 for map of Alaska

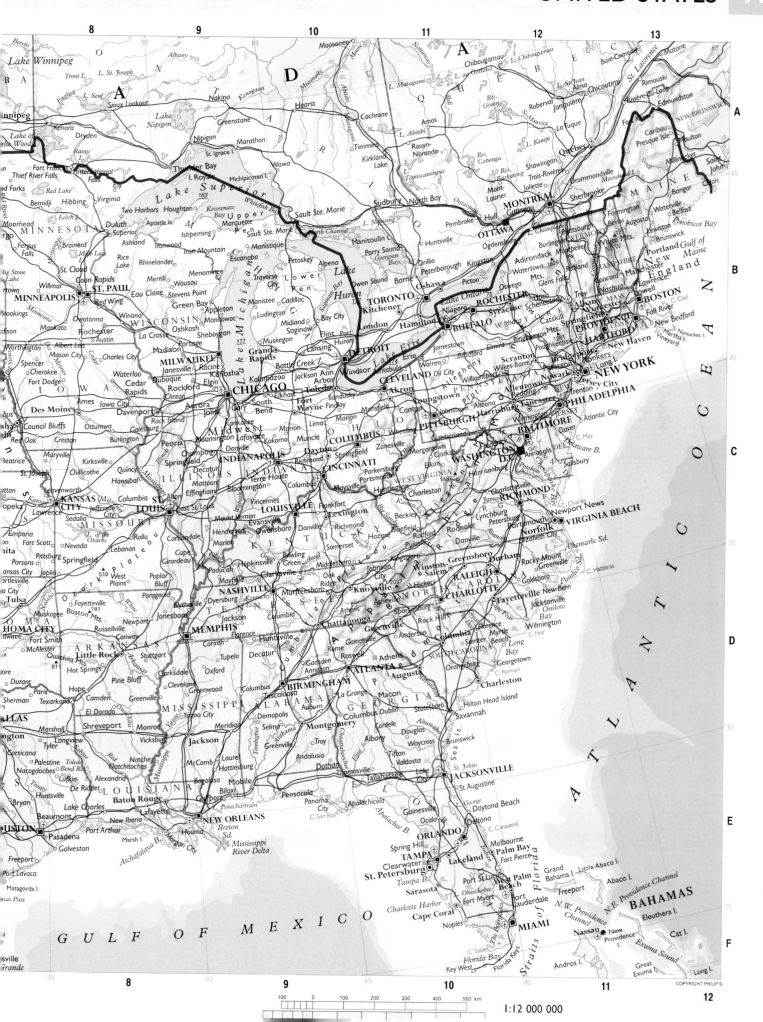

GULF OF MEXICO

ATLANTIC OCEAN

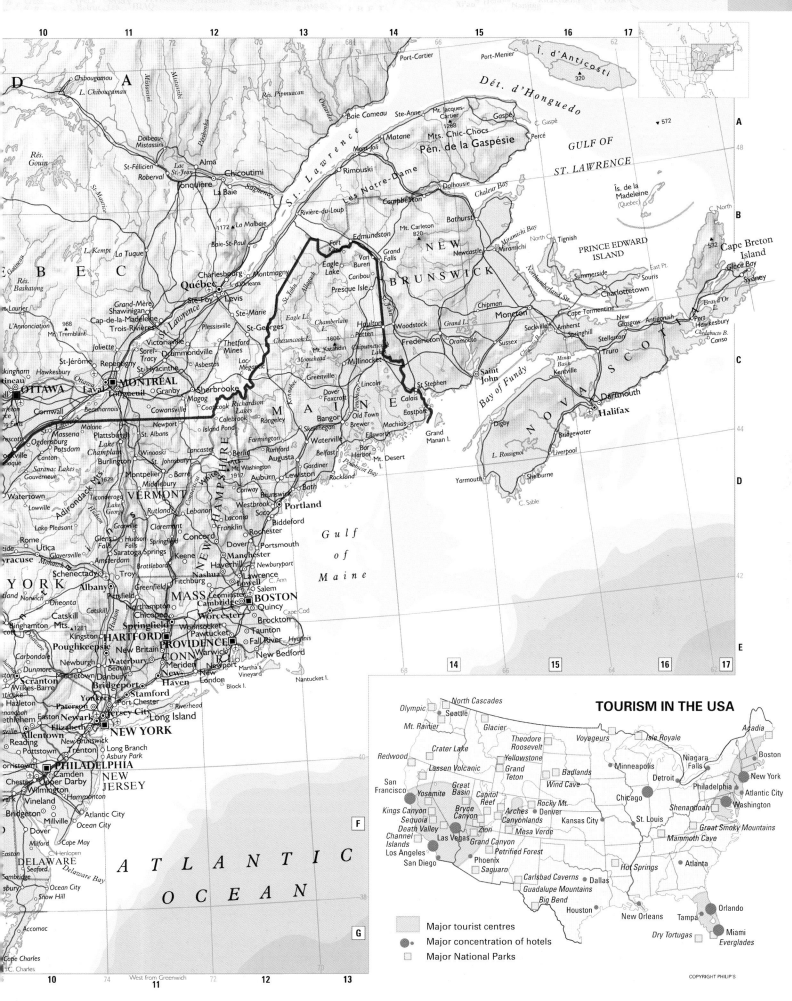

TOURISM IN THE USA

Major tourist centres

● Major concentration of hotels

□ Major National Parks

COPYRIGHT PHILIP'S

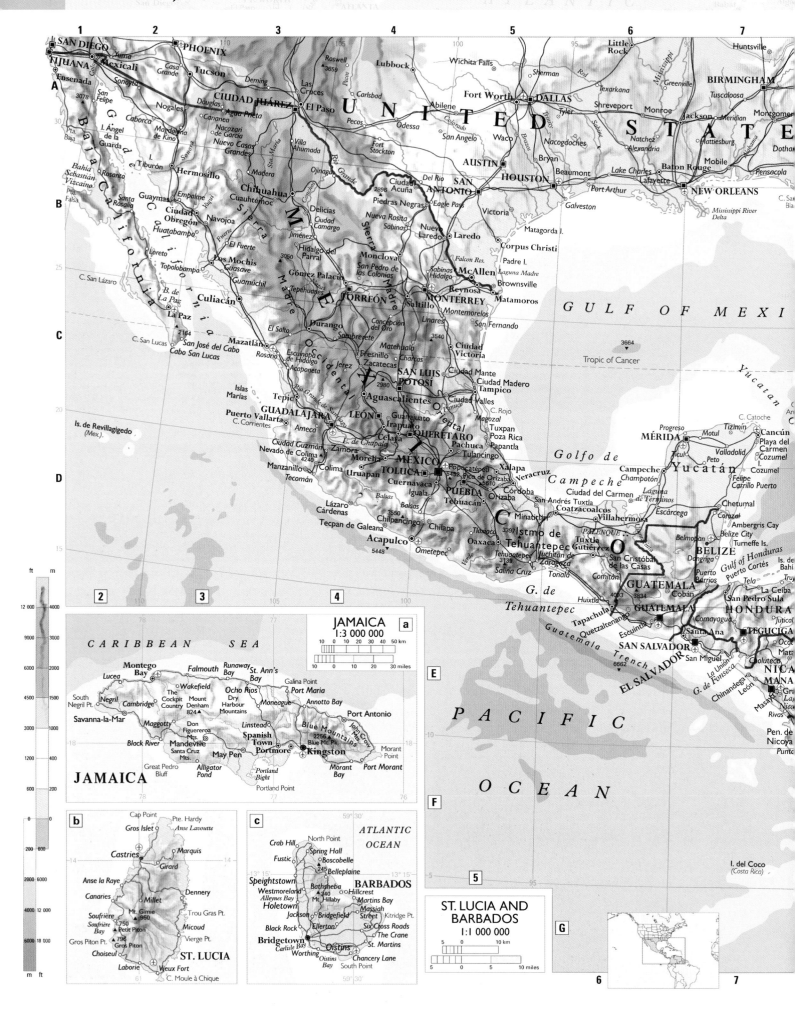

MEXICO, CENTRAL AMERICA AND THE CARIBBEAN

UNITED STATES

San Diego, Tijuana, Ensenada, Mexicali, Yuma, Phoenix, Tucson, Nogales, Hermosillo, Guaymas, Ciudad Obregón, Navojoa, Huatabampo, Los Mochis, Guasave, Guamúchil, Culiacán, La Paz, Cabo San Lucas, Cabo San Lucas, Mazatlán, Durango, Chihuahua, Ciudad Juárez, El Paso, Ciudad Camargo, Ciudad Jiménez, Hidalgo del Parral, Gómez Palacio, Torreón, Saltillo, Monterrey, Monclova, Piedras Negras, Nuevo Laredo, Laredo, Reynosa, Matamoros, Brownsville, McAllen

Dallas, Fort Worth, Houston, San Antonio, Austin, New Orleans, Birmingham, Little Rock

GULF OF MEXICO

Tropic of Cancer

San Luis Potosí, Aguascalientes, Zacatecas, Guadalajara, Tepic, Puerto Vallarta, León, Guanajuato, Irapuato, Celaya, Querétaro, Morelia, Colima, Manzanillo, Uruapan, Toluca, MEXICO, Cuernavaca, Puebla, Tehuacán, Oaxaca, Acapulco, Chilpancingo, Veracruz, Xalapa, Córdoba, Orizaba, Coatzacoalcos, Villahermosa, Minatitlán

Tampico, Ciudad Victoria, Ciudad Valles

Yucatán
Mérida, Progreso, Cancún, Cozumel, Campeche, Chetumal, Escárcega

Golfo de Campeche

BELIZE
Belize City, Belmopan

GUATEMALA
Guatemala, Quetzaltenango, Cobán

HONDURAS
Tegucigalpa, San Pedro Sula, Santa Ana

EL SALVADOR
San Salvador, San Miguel

NICARAGUA
Managua, León

PACIFIC OCEAN

a — JAMAICA 1:3 000 000
CARIBBEAN SEA
Montego Bay, Lucea, Falmouth, Runaway Bay, St. Ann's Bay, Ocho Rios, Port Maria, Annotto Bay, Port Antonio, Negril, South Negril Pt., Cambridge, Wakefield, The Cockpit Country, Mount Denham 824, Dry Harbour Mountains, Moneague, Galina Point, Savanna-la-Mar, Maggotty, Don Figueroa Mts., Black River, Mandeville, Santa Cruz Mts., Linstead, Spanish Town, Portmore, Blue Mountains 2256, Blue Mt. Pk., John Crow Mts., Kingston, May Pen, Great Pedro Bluff, Alligator Pond, Portland Bight, Portland Point, Morant Bay, Morant Point, Port Morant
JAMAICA

b — ST. LUCIA
Cap Point, Gros Islet, Pte. Hardy, Anse Lavoutte, Castries, Marquis, Girard, Anse la Raye, Canaries, Dennery, Millet, Soufrière, Mt. Gimie 950, Trou Gras Pt., Soufrière Bay, Petit Piton 750, Micoud, Gros Piton Pt., Gros Piton 798, Vierge Pt., Choiseul, Vieux Fort, Laborie, C. Moule à Chique

c — BARBADOS
ATLANTIC OCEAN
Cap Point, North Point, Crab Hill, Spring Hall, Fustic, Boscobelle, Belleplaine, Speightstown, Bathsheba, Martins Bay, Westmoreland, Alleynes Bay, Mt. Hillaby 340, Massiah Street, Holetown, Hillcrest, Jackson, Bridgefield, Kitridge Pt., Black Rock, Ellerton, Six Cross Roads, The Crane, Bridgetown, St. Martins, Carlisle Bay, Oistins, Worthing, Oistins Bay, Chancery Lane, South Point
BARBADOS

ST. LUCIA AND BARBADOS 1:1 000 000

Haiti Earthquake
- 12 January 2010
- Magnitude 7.0
- 230,000 killed
- 1,000,000 homeless

NORTH AMERICAN PLATE

Septentrional-Orient Fault

Puerto Rico Trench

GONÂVE MICROPLATE

Port-au-Prince 1946, 2010

Samana 1946

Aguadilla 1918

HISPANIOLA MICROPLATE

Cayman Trench

Walton Fault

Kingston 1692, 1907

Enriquillo-Plantain Garden Fault Zone

Soufrière Hills 1995–7

La Soufrière 1836

Leeward Is. 1843

CARIBBEAN PLATE

Mont Pelée 1902

Soufrière 1979

Kick-em Jenny

Lesser Antilles Trench

El Salvador, 2001

San Cristobal Momotombo Telica, 1987

Cerro Negro Masaya

Managua 1931, 1972

Rincon de la Vieja

Guatemala Trench

Arenal 1991

Poás 1991

Irzu 1991

Cartago 1910

Baru

PANAMA PLATE

NORTH ANDES PLATE

NASCA PLATE

Caracas, 1967

HAITI EARTHQUAKE   1:20 000 000

Plate boundary	Ocean trench
Direction of plate movement	Major fault line
Constructive plate boundary (plates moving apart)	Major active volcano
Destructive plate boundary or subduction zone (plates colliding)	Other active volcano
Conservative or transform plate boundary (plates sliding past each other)	Epicentre of 2010 earthquake
	Epicentre of other major earthquakes

Columbia

Wilmington

LANTA

C. Fear

Augusta

Long Bay

Macon

C. Romain

Charleston

Savannah

Altamaha

JACKSONVILLE

Daytona Beach

ORLANDO

MPA

C. Canaveral

St. Petersburg

Melbourne

rasota

West Palm Beach

L. Okeechobee

Grand Bahama

Cape Coral

MIAMI

Fort Lauderdale

Freeport

Abaco I.

C. Sable

Bimini Is.

New Providence I.

Key West

Nassau

Eleuthera I.

Straits of Florida

Andros I.

Cat I.

BAHAMAS

San Salvador I.

Matanzas

Cárdenas

HABANA (Havana)

Santa Clara

Sagua la Grande

Great Exuma I.

Long I.

G. de Batabanó

Güines

Placetas

Crooked I.

Cienfuegos

Morón

CUBA

Camagüey

Mayaguana I.

I. de la Juventud

Trinidad

Sancti Spiritus

Ciego de Ávila

Nuevitas

Acklins

Great Inagua

Turks & Caicos Is.

Las Tunas

Holguín

Greater

Cockburn Town (U.K.)

Banes

Manzanillo

Baracoa

Port-de-Paix

Monte Cristi

Puerto Plata

Milwaukee Deep 9605

Puerto Rico Trench

1972

GUANTÁNAMO BAY (U.S.A.)

Bayamo

Santiago de Cuba

Gonaïves

St-Marc

Cap-Haïtien

Santiago de los Caballeros

San Francisco de Macorís

Mona Passage

Arecibo

SAN JUAN

Virgin Is.

Anguilla (U.K.)

St-Martin (Fr.-Neth.)

ST. KITTS & NEVIS

Cayman Is.

Grand Cayman

George Town (U.K.)

Pico Duarte 3175

DOMINICAN REP.

La Vega

La Romana

Charlotte Amalie

ANTIGUA & BARBUDA

Cayman Trench 7680

Montego Bay

Jérémie

HAITI

San Juan

Barahona

Baní

San Pedro de Macorís

Ponce

Mayagüez

St. Croix

1156

Basseterre

St. John's

914

Montserrat (U.K.)

GUADELOUPE (Fr.)

1467 Pointe-à-Pitre

2256

Mandeville

Spanish Town

Kingston

Les Cayes

Jacmel

PORT-AU-PRINCE

Hispaniola

SANTO DOMINGO

PUERTO RICO (U.S.A.)

Leeward Islands

Basse-Terre

1447 DOMINICA

Roseau

JAMAICA

Antilles

Lesser

Mt. Pelée 1397

MARTINIQUE (Fr.)

Fort-de-France

Is. Santanilla (Honduras)

Castries

ST. LUCIA

CARIBBEAN SEA

Antilles

ST. VINCENT & THE GRENADINES

1234 Kingstown

Bridgetown

BARBADOS

L. de Caratasca

Windward

Islands

GRENADA

C. Gracias a Dios

St. George's

Puerto Cabezas

ABC Islands (Neth.)

I. de Providencia (Colombia)

Aruba

Curaçao

Willemstad

Bonaire

I. Blanquilla (Ven.)

Tobago

I. de San Andrés (Colombia)

Pen. de la Guajira

Pta. Gallinas

G. de Venezuela

Punto Fijo

Coro

Puerto Cabello

Maiquetía

I. de Margarita

Porlamar

Carúpano

Güiria

Port of Spain

Bluefields

Ríohacha

San Felipe

MARACAY

La Tortuga

Cumaná

Puerto La Cruz

San Fernando

G. de Paria

TRINIDAD & TOBAGO

Santa Marta

Sierra Nevada de Santa Marta 5775

MARACAIBO

Cabimas

CARACAS

Barcelona

2640

Maturín

BARRANQUILLA

Soledad

VALENCIA

BARQUISIMETO

COSTA RICA

CARTAGENA

Calamar

Valledupar

L. de Maracaibo

Acarigua

El Tigre

Ciudad Guayana

Irazú 432

Limón

G. de los Mosquitos

Sincelejo

Mompós

Mérida

Barinas

San Fernando de Apure

Orinoco

Ciudad Bolívar

Embalse de Guri

Cartago

Colón

Panama Canal

G. del Darién

Montería

Valera

Apure

Caicara

Tumereno

PANAMÁ

Volcán Barú 3475

PANAMA

Chitré

Arch. de las Perlas

La Palma

El Real

Riosucio

3960

Yarumal

Barrancabermeja

Puerto Wilches

BUCARAMANGA

Cúcuta

San Cristóbal

Pamplona

Arauca

VENEZUELA

San Fernando de Apure

Georgetown

Bartica

New Amsterdam

Linden

David

Santiago

ermuelles

Puerto

Jaqué

Pen. de Azuero

G. de Panamá

Antioquia

4981 Pico Bolívar

Puerto Carreño

GUYANA

I. de Coiba

Quibdó

Bello

MEDELLÍN

Sogamoso

Meta

Puerto Ayacucho

Angel Falls

Mt. Roraima 2810

Isthmus of Panama

C. Corrientes

COLOMBIA

Tunja

Vichada

Caura

Ventuari

SURINAME

Manizales

Pereira

Tolima 5215

BOGOTÁ

Villavicencio

Guaviare

Sierra Pacaraima

I. de Malpelo (Colombia)

Armenia

Ibagué

Girardot

Puerto Inírida

Orinoco

Boa Vista

Buenaventura

Palmira

Guaviare

Casiquiare

CALI

Huila 5750

Neiva

Popayán

BRAZIL

Volcán Puracé 4646

Equator

1:15 000 000

100   0   100   200   300   400   500   600 km

100   0   100   200   300   400 miles

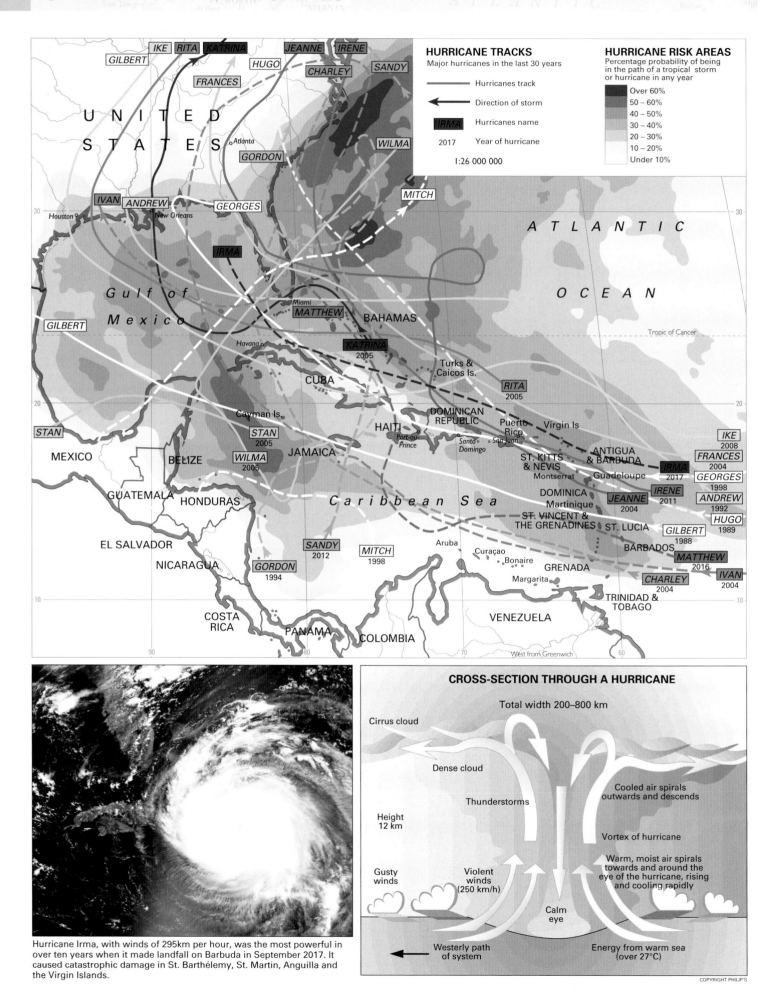

HURRICANE TRACKS
Major hurricanes in the last 30 years

——— Hurricanes track

←——— Direction of storm

IRMA   Hurricanes name

2017   Year of hurricane

1:26 000 000

HURRICANE RISK AREAS
Percentage probability of being in the path of a tropical storm or hurricane in any year

Over 60%
50 – 60%
40 – 50%
30 – 40%
20 – 30%
10 – 20%
Under 10%

IKE RITA KATRINA
GILBERT
JEANNE IRENE
HUGO
FRANCES
CHARLEY
SANDY
WILMA
GORDON
IVAN ANDREW
GEORGES
MITCH
IRMA
MATTHEW
BAHAMAS
KATRINA 2005
Turks & Caicos Is.
RITA 2005
STAN
GILBERT
CUBA
Cayman Is.
STAN 2005
HAITI
DOMINICAN REPUBLIC
Puerto Rico
Virgin Is
IKE 2008
WILMA 2005
JAMAICA
ST. KITTS & NEVIS
ANTIGUA & BARBUDA
IRMA 2017
FRANCES 2004
GEORGES 1998
MEXICO
BELIZE
Montserrat
Guadeloupe
DOMINICA
IRENE 2011
ANDREW 1992
GUATEMALA
HONDURAS
Caribbean Sea
Martinique
JEANNE 2004
HUGO 1989
SANDY 2012
MITCH 1998
ST. VINCENT & THE GRENADINES
ST. LUCIA
GILBERT 1988
EL SALVADOR
Aruba
Curaçao
Bonaire
GRENADA
BARBADOS
MATTHEW 2016
NICARAGUA
GORDON 1994
Margarita
CHARLEY 2004
IVAN 2004
COSTA RICA
PANAMA
COLOMBIA
VENEZUELA
TRINIDAD & TOBAGO

UNITED STATES
Houston
New Orleans
Atlanta
Miami
Havana
Port-au-Prince
Santo Domingo
San Juan
ATLANTIC OCEAN
Tropic of Cancer
Gulf of Mexico
West from Greenwich

Hurricane Irma, with winds of 295km per hour, was the most powerful in over ten years when it made landfall on Barbuda in September 2017. It caused catastrophic damage in St. Barthélemy, St. Martin, Anguilla and the Virgin Islands.

CROSS-SECTION THROUGH A HURRICANE

Total width 200–800 km

Cirrus cloud

Dense cloud

Thunderstorms

Cooled air spirals outwards and descends

Height 12 km

Vortex of hurricane

Warm, moist air spirals towards and around the eye of the hurricane, rising and cooling rapidly

Gusty winds

Violent winds (250 km/h)

Calm eye

Energy from warm sea (over 27°C)

Westerly path of system

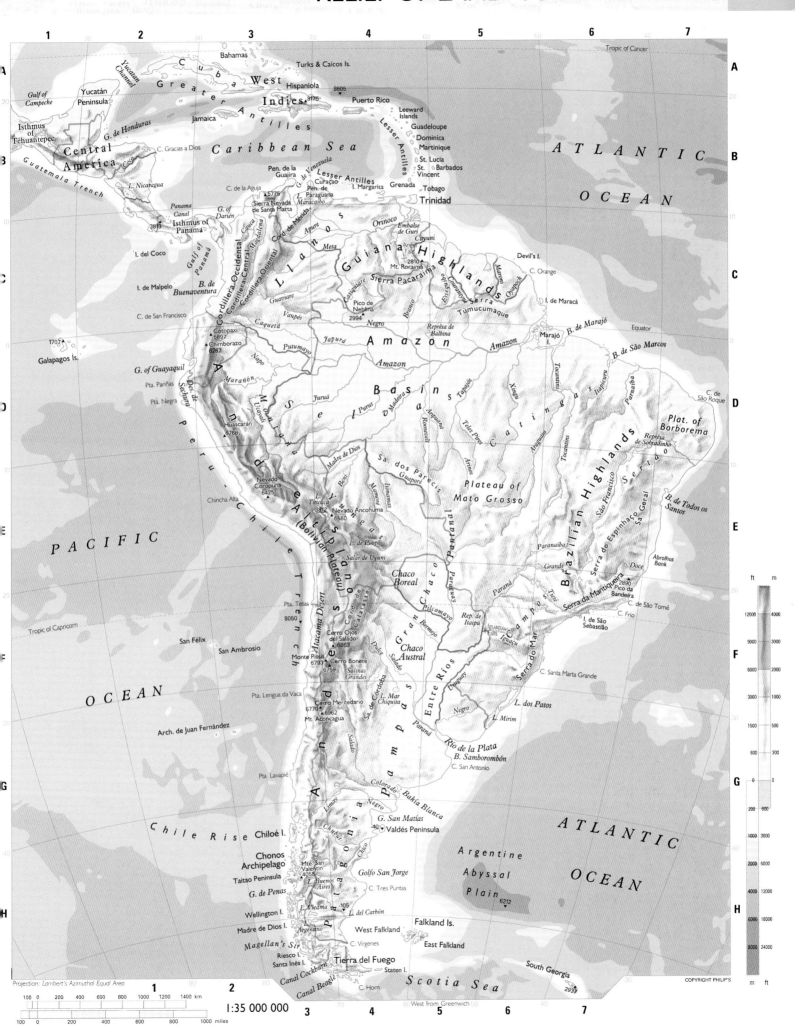

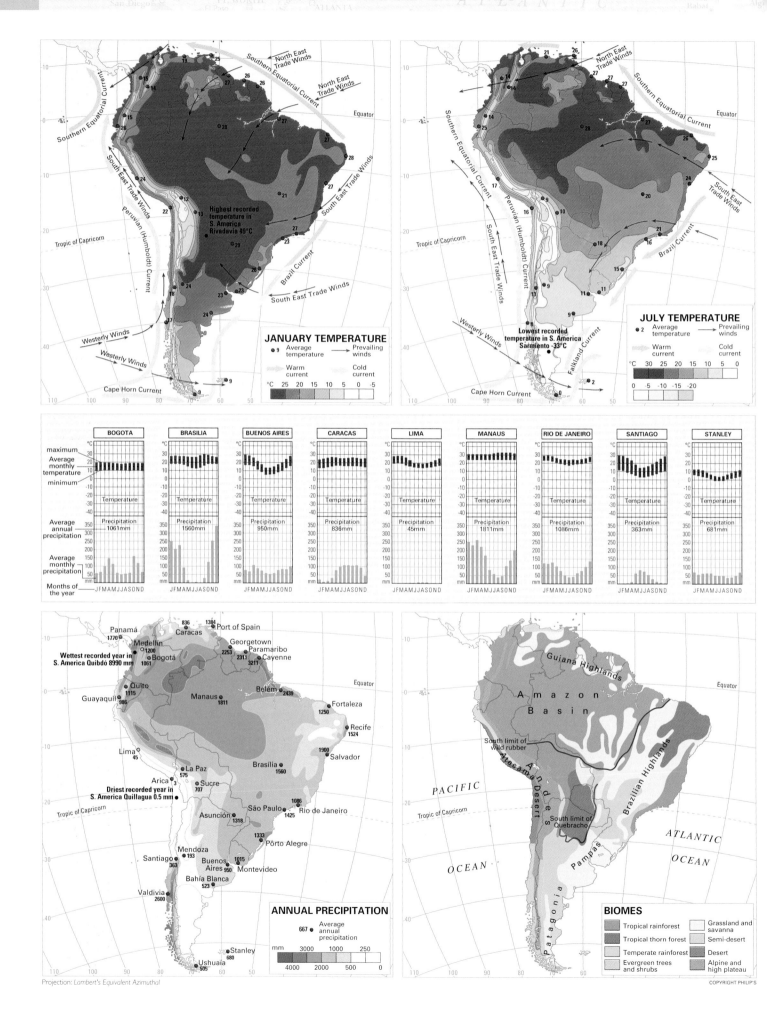

JANUARY TEMPERATURE

- 9 Average temperature
- → Prevailing winds
- Warm current
- Cold current

°C 25 20 15 10 5 0 -5

Highest recorded temperature in S. America Rivadavia 49°C

North East Trade Winds
Southern Equatorial Current
Equator
South East Trade Winds
Brazil Current
Southern Equatorial Current
South East Trade Winds
Peruvian (Humboldt) Current
Tropic of Capricorn
Westerly Winds
Westerly Winds
Cape Horn Current

JULY TEMPERATURE

- 2 Average temperature
- → Prevailing winds
- Warm current
- Cold current

°C 30 25 20 15 10 5 0

0 -5 -10 -15 -20

North East Trade Winds
Southern Equatorial Current
Equator
South East Trade Winds
Brazil Current
Southern Equatorial Current
South East Trade Winds
Peruvian (Humboldt) Current
Tropic of Capricorn
Westerly Winds
Lowest recorded temperature in S. America Sarmiento -33°C
Falkland Current
Cape Horn Current

Climate graphs

BOGOTA — Temperature / Precipitation 1061mm

BRASILIA — Temperature / Precipitation 1560mm

BUENOS AIRES — Temperature / Precipitation 950mm

CARACAS — Temperature / Precipitation 836mm

LIMA — Temperature / Precipitation 45mm

MANAUS — Temperature / Precipitation 1811mm

RIO DE JANEIRO — Temperature / Precipitation 1086mm

SANTIAGO — Temperature / Precipitation 363mm

STANLEY — Temperature / Precipitation 681mm

maximum
Average monthly temperature
minimum
Average annual precipitation
Average monthly precipitation
Months of the year

JFMAMJJASOND

ANNUAL PRECIPITATION

- 667 Average annual precipitation

mm 3000 1000 250
4000 2000 500 0

Panamá 1770
Caracas 836
Port of Spain 1384
Medellín 1200
Bogotá 1061
Wettest recorded year in S. America Quibdó 8990 mm
Georgetown 2253
Paramaribo 2311
Cayenne 3211
Quito 1115
Guayaquil 986
Manaus 1811
Belém 2439
Equator
Fortaleza 1250
Recife 1524
Lima 45
Salvador 1900
La Paz 575
Brasília 1560
Arica 3
Sucre 707
Driest recorded year in S. America Quillagua 0.5 mm
São Paulo 1425
Rio de Janeiro 1086
Asunción 1318
Tropic of Capricorn
Pôrto Alegre 1333
Mendoza 193
Santiago 363
Buenos Aires 950
Montevideo 1015
Bahía Blanca 523
Valdivia 2600
Stanley 680
Ushuaia 505

Projection: Lambert's Equivalent Azimuthal

BIOMES

- Tropical rainforest
- Tropical thorn forest
- Temperate rainforest
- Evergreen trees and shrubs
- Grassland and savanna
- Semi-desert
- Desert
- Alpine and high plateau

Guiana Highlands
Amazon Basin
Equator
South limit of wild rubber
Andes
Atacama Desert
Brazilian Highlands
PACIFIC OCEAN
South limit of Quebracho
Tropic of Capricorn
Pampas
ATLANTIC OCEAN
Patagonia

COPYRIGHT PHILIP'S

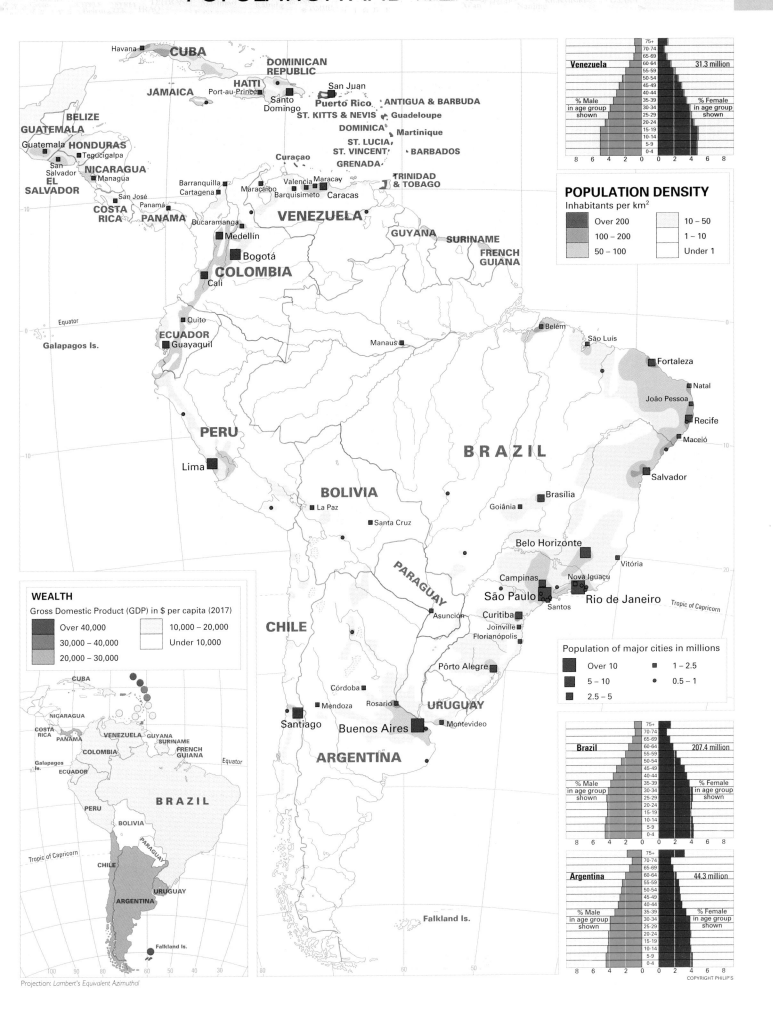

Venezuela — 31.3 million

% Male in age group shown / % Female in age group shown

POPULATION DENSITY

Inhabitants per km²

- Over 200
- 100 – 200
- 50 – 100
- 10 – 50
- 1 – 10
- Under 1

WEALTH

Gross Domestic Product (GDP) in $ per capita (2017)

- Over 40,000
- 30,000 – 40,000
- 20,000 – 30,000
- 10,000 – 20,000
- Under 10,000

Population of major cities in millions

- Over 10
- 5 – 10
- 2.5 – 5
- 1 – 2.5
- 0.5 – 1

Brazil — 207.4 million

% Male in age group shown / % Female in age group shown

Argentina — 44.3 million

% Male in age group shown / % Female in age group shown

Projection: Lambert's Equivalent Azimuthal

COPYRIGHT PHILIP'S

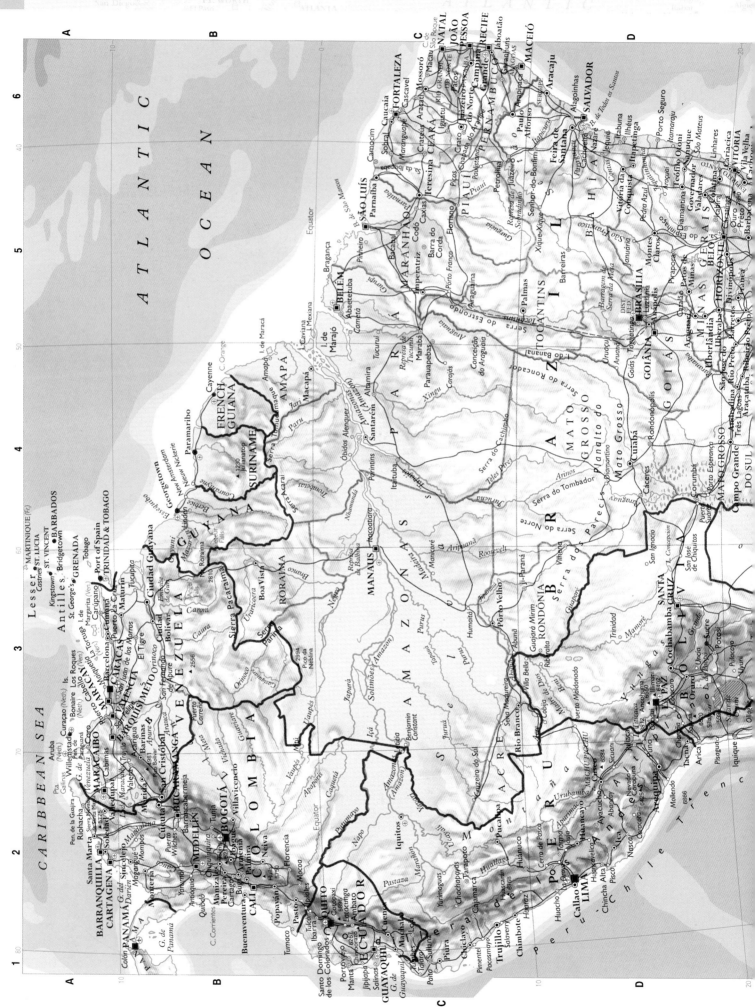

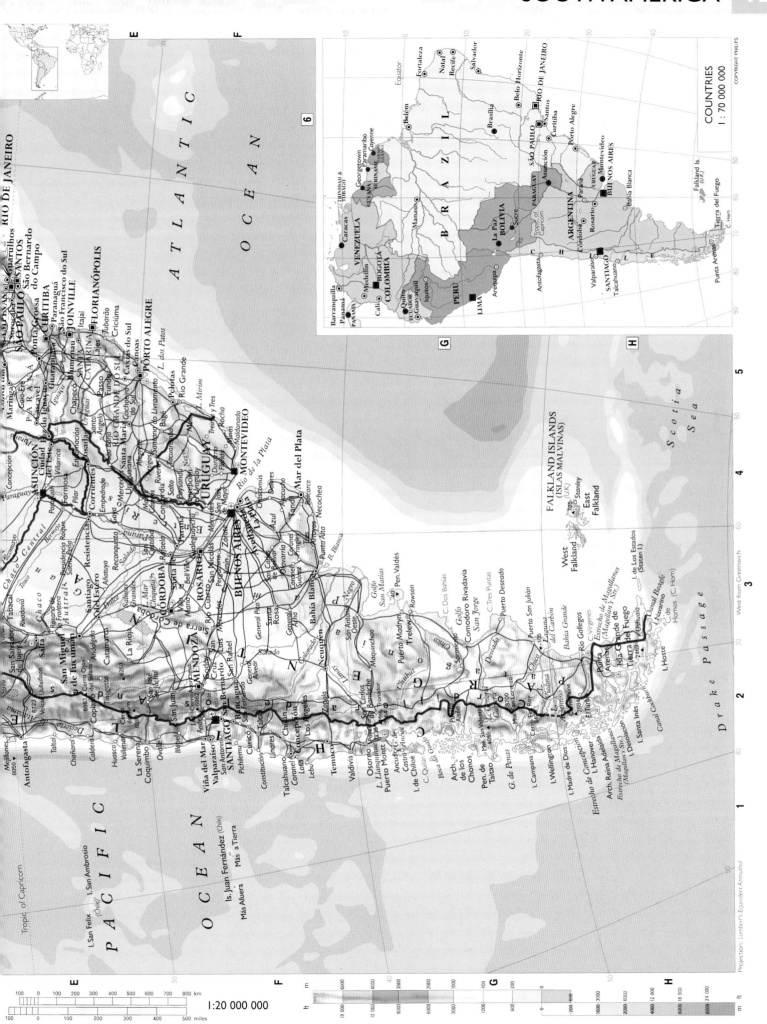

COUNTRIES
1 : 70 000 000

ATLANTIC OCEAN

PACIFIC OCEAN

Scotia Sea

Drake Passage

FALKLAND ISLANDS (ISLAS MALVINAS) (U.K.)
West Falkland
East Falkland
Stanley

1 : 20 000 000

100   0   100   200   300   400   500   600   700   800 km

100   0   100   200   300   400   500 miles

Projection: Lambert's Equivalent Azimuthal

West from Greenwich

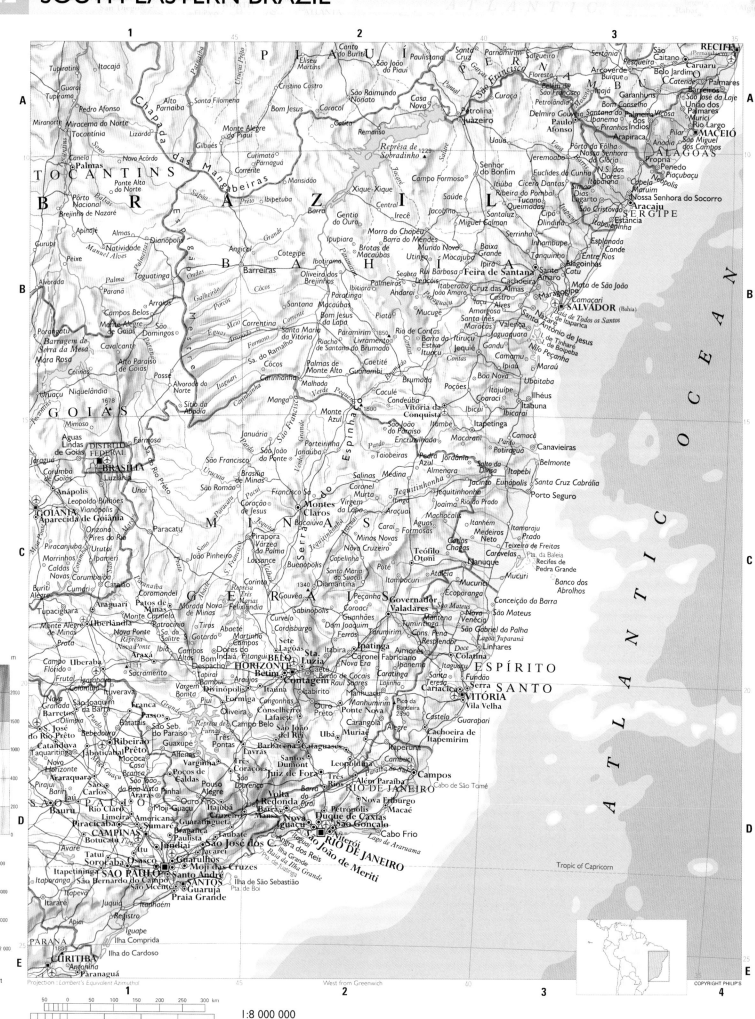

1:8 000 000

Projection : Lambert's Equivalent Azimuthal

West from Greenwich

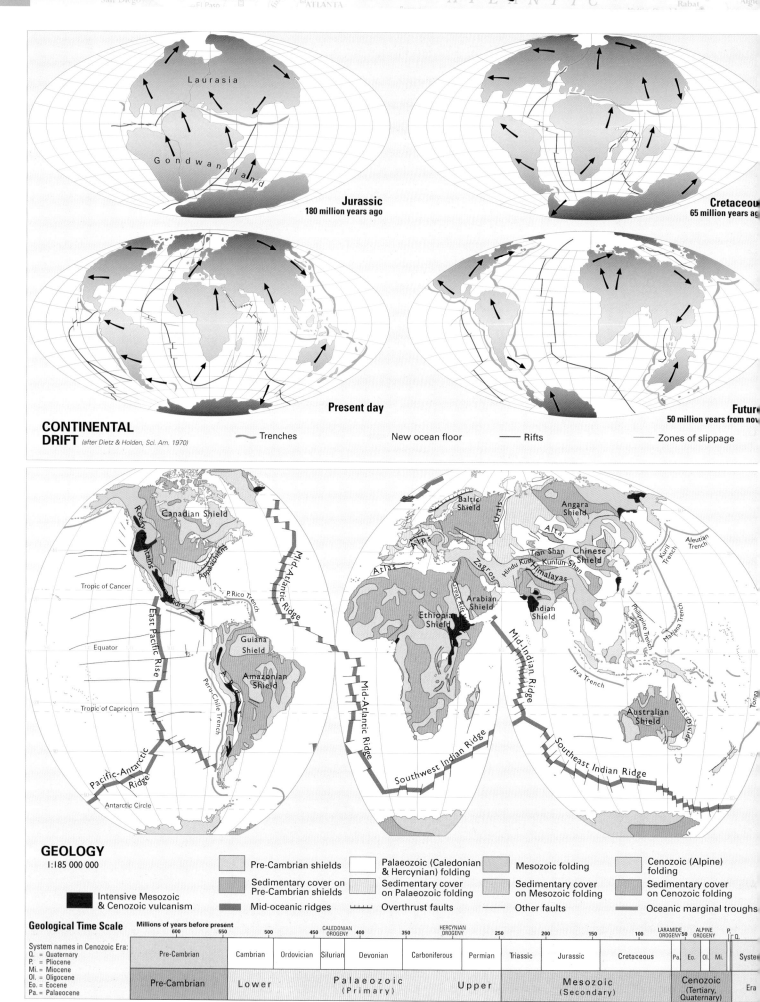

CONTINENTAL DRIFT *(after Dietz & Holden, Sci. Am. 1970)*

Laurasia

Gondwanaland

Jurassic
180 million years ago

Cretaceous
65 million years ago

Present day

Future
50 million years from now

—— Trenches   —— New ocean floor   —— Rifts   —— Zones of slippage

GEOLOGY
1:185 000 000

Canadian Shield
Rocky Mountains
Appalachians
Tropic of Cancer
P. Rico Trench
East Pacific Rise
Sierra Madre
Equator
Guiana Shield
Amazonian Shield
Andes
Peru-Chile Trench
Tropic of Capricorn
Mid-Atlantic Ridge
Pacific-Antarctic Ridge
Antarctic Circle

Baltic Shield
Urals
Angara Shield
Altai
Alps
Atlas
Tian Shan
Chinese Shield
Kunlun Shan
Hindu Kush
Zagros
Himalayas
Great Rift
Arabian Shield
Ethiopian Shield
Indian Shield
Mid-Indian Ridge
Southwest Indian Ridge
Southeast Indian Ridge
Australian Shield
Great Dividing Range
Aleutian Trench
Kuril Trench
Philippine Trench
Mariana Trench
Java Trench
Tonga
Mid-Atlantic Ridge

■ Intensive Mesozoic & Cenozoic vulcanism

Pre-Cambrian shields	Palaeozoic (Caledonian & Hercynian) folding
Sedimentary cover on Pre-Cambrian shields	Sedimentary cover on Palaeozoic folding
Mid-oceanic ridges	Overthrust faults

Mesozoic folding	Cenozoic (Alpine) folding
Sedimentary cover on Mesozoic folding	Sedimentary cover on Cenozoic folding
Other faults	Oceanic marginal troughs

Geological Time Scale

System names in Cenozoic Era:
Q. = Quaternary
P. = Pliocene
Mi. = Miocene
Ol. = Oligocene
Eo. = Eocene
Pa. = Palaeocene

Millions of years before present

600	550	500	450	400	350	250	200	150	100	50				
			CALEDONIAN OROGENY			HERCYNIAN OROGENY				LARAMIDE OROGENY	ALPINE OROGENY			

Pre-Cambrian	Cambrian	Ordovician	Silurian	Devonian	Carboniferous	Permian	Triassic	Jurassic	Cretaceous	Pa.	Eo.	Ol.	Mi.	System
Pre-Cambrian	Lower			Palaeozoic (Primary)		Upper		Mesozoic (Secondary)			Cenozoic (Tertiary, Quaternary)			Era

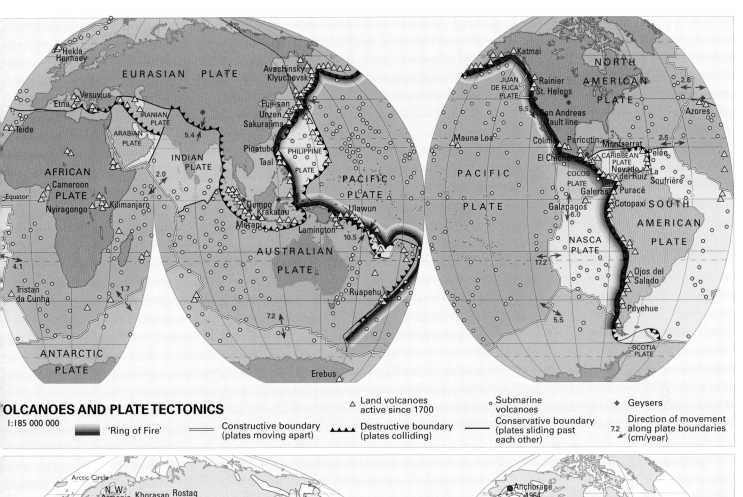

VOLCANOES AND PLATE TECTONICS

1:185 000 000

▰ 'Ring of Fire'	△ Land volcanoes active since 1700
═══ Constructive boundary (plates moving apart)	▲▲▲ Destructive boundary (plates colliding)
○ Submarine volcanoes	✦ Geysers
━━ Conservative boundary (plates sliding past each other)	7.2↗ Direction of movement along plate boundaries ↙ (cm/year)

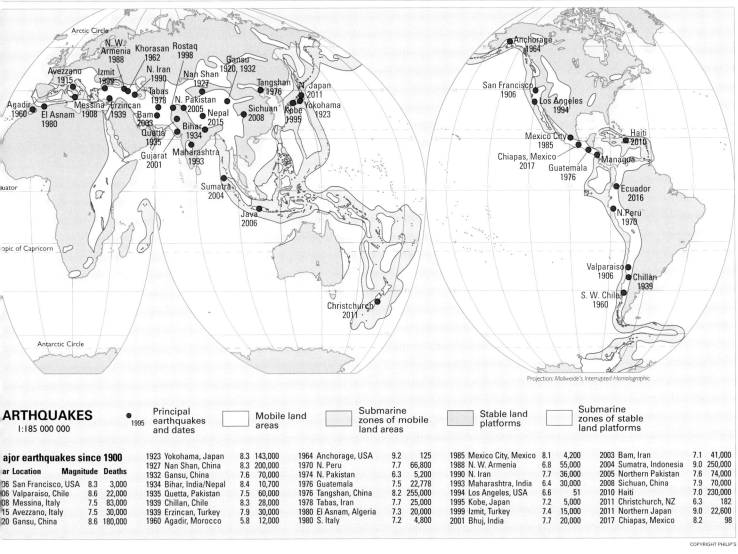

Projection: Mollweide's Interrupted Homolographic

EARTHQUAKES

1:185 000 000

● 1995 Principal earthquakes and dates	▢ Mobile land areas
▢ Submarine zones of mobile land areas	▢ Stable land platforms
▢ Submarine zones of stable land platforms	

Major earthquakes since 1900

Year Location	Magnitude	Deaths										
1906 San Francisco, USA	8.3	3,000	1923 Yokohama, Japan	8.3	143,000	1964 Anchorage, USA	9.2	125	1985 Mexico City, Mexico	8.1	4,200	2003 Bam, Iran	7.1	41,000
1906 Valparaiso, Chile	8.6	22,000	1927 Nan Shan, China	8.3	200,000	1970 N. Peru	7.7	66,800	1988 N. W. Armenia	6.8	55,000	2004 Sumatra, Indonesia	9.0	250,000
1908 Messina, Italy	7.5	83,000	1932 Gansu, China	7.6	70,000	1974 N. Pakistan	6.3	5,200	1990 N. Iran	7.7	36,000	2005 Northern Pakistan	7.6	74,000
1915 Avezzano, Italy	7.5	30,000	1934 Bihar, India/Nepal	8.4	10,700	1976 Guatemala	7.5	22,778	1993 Maharashtra, India	6.4	30,000	2008 Sichuan, China	7.9	70,000
1920 Gansu, China	8.6	180,000	1935 Quetta, Pakistan	7.5	60,000	1976 Tangshan, China	8.2	255,000	1994 Los Angeles, USA	6.6	51	2010 Haiti	7.0	230,000
			1939 Chillan, Chile	8.3	28,000	1978 Tabas, Iran	7.7	25,000	1995 Kobe, Japan	7.2	5,000	2011 Christchurch, NZ	6.3	182
			1939 Erzincan, Turkey	7.9	30,000	1980 El Asnam, Algeria	7.3	20,000	1999 Izmit, Turkey	7.4	15,000	2011 Northern Japan	9.0	22,600
			1960 Agadir, Morocco	5.8	12,000	1980 S. Italy	7.2	4,800	2001 Bhuj, India	7.7	20,000	2017 Chiapas, Mexico	8.2	98

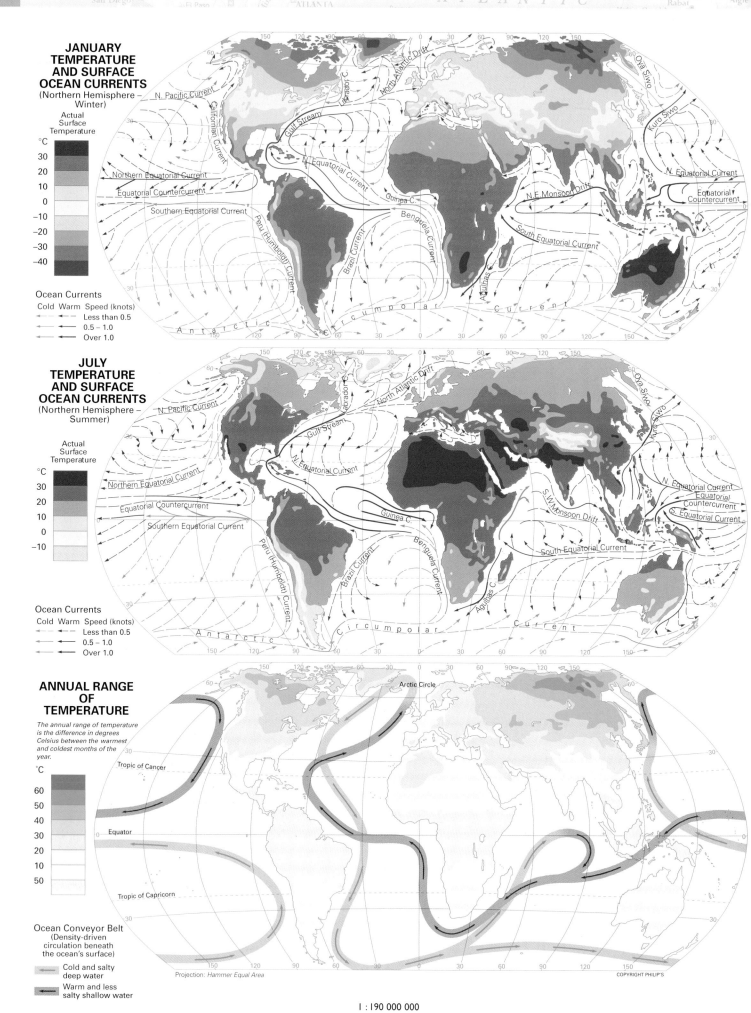

JANUARY TEMPERATURE AND SURFACE OCEAN CURRENTS
(Northern Hemisphere – Winter)

Actual Surface Temperature

°C
30
20
10
0
−10
−20
−30
−40

Ocean Currents
Cold Warm Speed (knots)
Less than 0.5
0.5 – 1.0
Over 1.0

JULY TEMPERATURE AND SURFACE OCEAN CURRENTS
(Northern Hemisphere – Summer)

Actual Surface Temperature

°C
30
20
10
0
−10

Ocean Currents
Cold Warm Speed (knots)
Less than 0.5
0.5 – 1.0
Over 1.0

ANNUAL RANGE OF TEMPERATURE

The annual range of temperature is the difference in degrees Celsius between the warmest and coldest months of the year.

°C
60
50
40
30
20
10
50

Ocean Conveyor Belt
(Density-driven circulation beneath the ocean's surface)

Cold and salty deep water

Warm and less salty shallow water

Projection: *Hammer Equal Area*

COPYRIGHT PHILIP'S

1 : 190 000 000

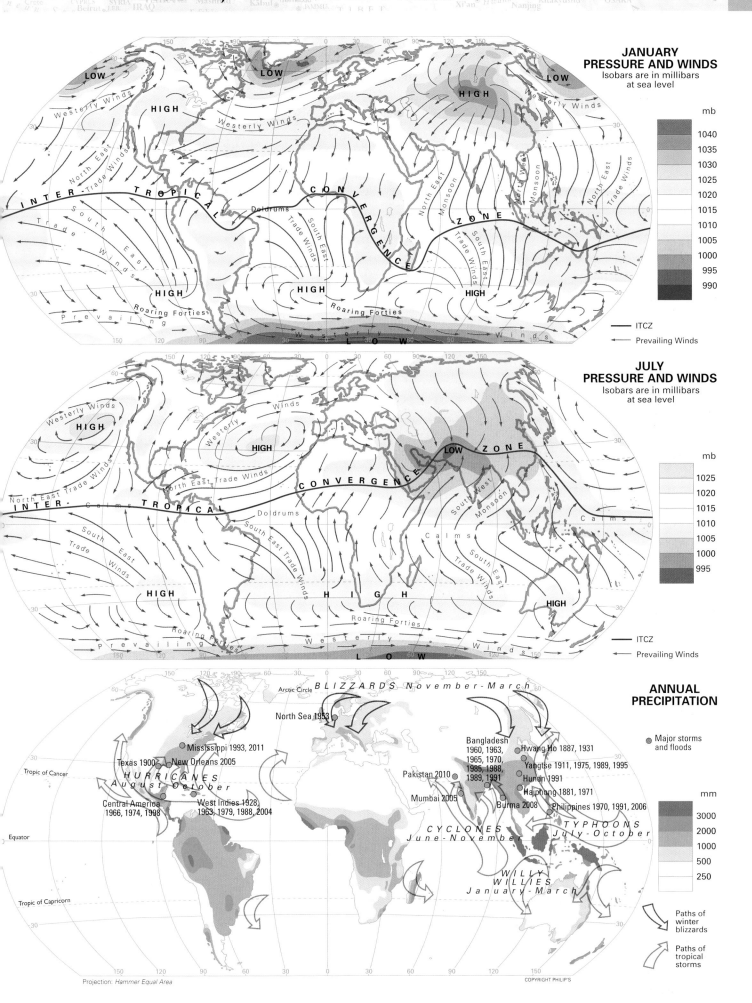

JANUARY PRESSURE AND WINDS
Isobars are in millibars at sea level

mb
1040
1035
1030
1025
1020
1015
1010
1005
1000
995
990

—— ITCZ
←— Prevailing Winds

JULY PRESSURE AND WINDS
Isobars are in millibars at sea level

mb
1025
1020
1015
1010
1005
1000
995

—— ITCZ
←— Prevailing Winds

ANNUAL PRECIPITATION

● Major storms and floods

mm
3000
2000
1000
500
250

Paths of winter blizzards

Paths of tropical storms

BLIZZARDS November–March

North Sea 1953

Bangladesh 1960, 1963, 1965, 1970, 1985, 1988, 1989, 1991

Hwang Ho 1887, 1931

Yangtse 1911, 1975, 1989, 1995

Pakistan 2010

Hunan 1991

Mumbai 2005

Haiphong 1881, 1971

Burma 2008

Philippines 1970, 1991, 2006

Mississippi 1993, 2011

Texas 1900

New Orleans 2005

HURRICANES August–October

Central America 1966, 1974, 1998

West Indies 1928, 1963, 1979, 1988, 2004

CYCLONES June–November

TYPHOONS July–October

WILLY WILLIES January–March

Arctic Circle

Tropic of Cancer

Equator

Tropic of Capricorn

Projection: Hammer Equal Area

COPYRIGHT PHILIP'S

KEY TO CLIMATE REGIONS MAP

Climate group	Climate	Temperature	Rainfall
A TROPICAL RAINY CLIMATES	**Af** RAIN FOREST CLIMATE / **Am** MONSOON CLIMATE / **Aw** SAVANNA CLIMATE	All mean monthly temperatures above 18°C	(rainfall graph: Af, Aw, Am; Annual rainfall mm 0–3000; Rainfall during the driest month mm)
B DRY CLIMATES	**BS** STEPPE CLIMATE / **BW** DESERT CLIMATE	Mean annual temperature; h = above 18°C; k = below 18°C	(graph: BW/BS boundary, BS/Wet Climates Boundary, Wet Climates A,C,D; Annual rainfall mm 0–600; summer rainfall / winter rainfall / rainfall evenly distributed)
C WARM TEMPERATE RAINY CLIMATES	**Cw** DRY WINTER CLIMATE / **Cs** DRY SUMMER CLIMATE (Mediterranean) / **Cf** CLIMATE WITH NO DRY SEASON	Mean temperature of the coldest month between –3°C to 18°C	a Mean temperature of hottest month above 22°C, and with more than 4 months of over 10°C; b Mean temperature of hottest month below 22°C and with more than 4 months of over 10°C; w dry winter: Rainfall of the driest month of the cold season is one-tenth or less of the rainfall of the wettest month of the hot season; s dry summer: Rainfall of the driest month of the hot season is less than one-third of the rainfall of the wettest month of the cold season and less than 40mm
D COLD TEMPERATE RAINY CLIMATES	**Dw** DRY WINTER CLIMATE / **Df** CLIMATE WITH NO DRY SEASON	Mean temperature of the coldest month below –3°C	c Mean temperature of hottest month below 22°C, but with less than 4 months of over 10°C; d Mean temperature of hottest month below 22°C, and of the coldest month below –38°C; f with no dry season: Rainfall does not correspond to w or s climates
E POLAR CLIMATES	**ET** TUNDRA CLIMATE / **EF** PERPETUAL FROST	Mean temperature of the hottest month between 0°C and 10°C; Mean temperature of the hottest month below 0°C	H More than 1500m above sea level

CLIMATE RECORDS

Highest recorded temperature: Death Valley, California, USA, 56.7°C, 10 July 1913.

Lowest recorded temperature (outside poles): Verkhoyansk, Siberia, –68°C, 7 February 1892. Verkhoyansk also registered the greatest annual range of temperature: –68°C to 37°C.

Highest barometric pressure: Agata, Siberia, 1,083.8 mb at altitude 262 m, 31 December 1968.

Lowest barometric pressure: Typhoon Tip, 480 km west of Guam, Pacific Ocean, 870 mb, 12 October 1979.

Driest place: Quillagua, N. Chile, 0.5 mm, 1964–2001.

Wettest place (12 months): Cherrapunji, Meghalaya, N.E. India: 26,461 mm, August 1860 to August 1861. Cherrapunji also holds the record for rainfall in one month: 2930 mm, July 1861.

Highest recorded wind speed: Mt Washington, New Hampshire, USA, 371 km/h, 12 April 1934. This is three times as strong as hurricane force on the Beaufort Scale.

Windiest place: Commonwealth Bay, George V Coast, Antarctica, where gales frequently reach over 320 km/h.

Projection: Interrupted Mollweide's Homolographic

WINDCHILL FACTOR

In sub-zero weather, even moderate winds significantly reduce effective temperatures. The chart below shows the windchill effect across a range of speeds.

	Wind speed in kilometres per hour				
	16	32	48	64	80
0°C	–8	–14	–17	–19	–20
–5°C	–14	–21	–25	–27	–28
–10°C	–20	–28	–33	–35	–36
–15°C	–26	–36	–40	–43	–44
–20°C	–32	–42	–48	–51	–52
–25°C	–38	–49	–56	–59	–60
–30°C	–44	–57	–63	–66	–68
–35°C	–51	–64	–72	–74	–76
–40°C	–57	–71	–78	–82	–84
–45°C	–63	–78	–86	–90	–92
–50°C	–69	–85	–94	–98	–100

ITCZ AND ATMOSPHERIC CIRCULATION

The Trade Winds converge on the Earth's surface at the Inter-Tropical Convergence Zone (ITCZ), where the hot and moist air rises rapidly to the upper limit of the Earth's troposphere to be carried by the Hadley Cell towards the mid-latitudes where it descends as dry air. Two lesser circulation cells – the Ferrel Cell and the Polar Cell carry the air further towards the Poles. The pattern of this circulation may vary from year to year and may affect the huge Pacific Cell, resulting in El Niño or La Niña events – see diagrams opposite.

High pressure / Low pressure / Warm air / Cold air / Surface winds / Clouds

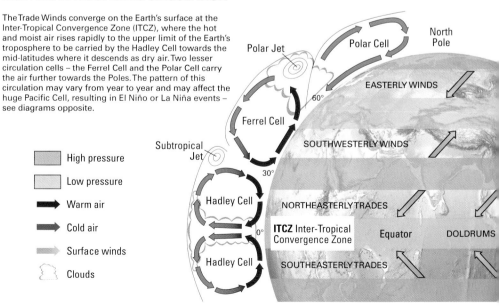

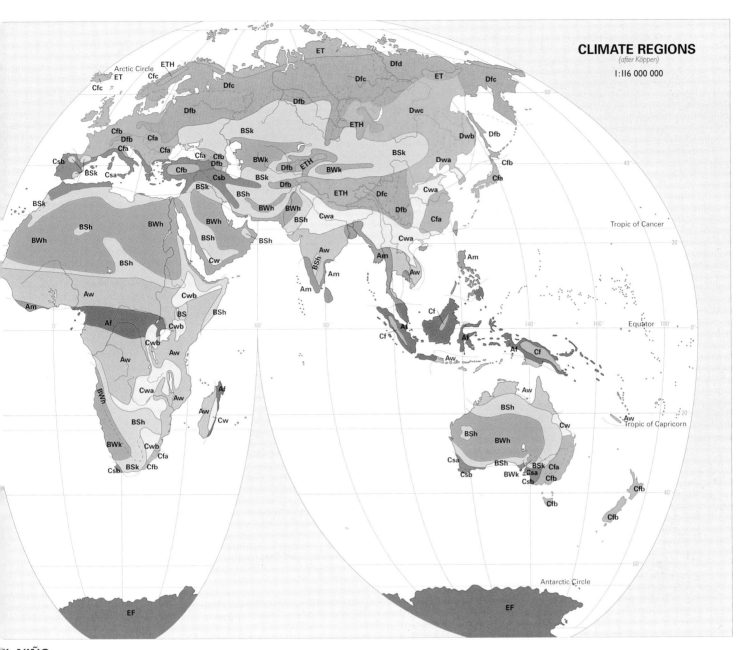

CLIMATE REGIONS
(after Köppen)
1:116 000 000

EL NIÑO

Niño, 'The Little Boy' in Spanish, was the name given by local fishermen to the warm current that can appear off the Pacific coast of South America. In a normal year, south-easterly trade winds drive surface waters westwards off the coast of South America, rawing cold, nutrient-rich water up from below. In an El Niño year, warm water from the est Pacific suppresses upwelling in the east, depriving the region of nutrients and driving e fish away. The water is warmed by as much as 7°C, disturbing the circulation of the Pacific ell. During an intense El Niño, the south-east trade winds change direction and become quatorial westerlies, resulting in climatic extremes in many regions of the world, such as rought in parts of Australia and India, and heavy rainfall in the SE USA.

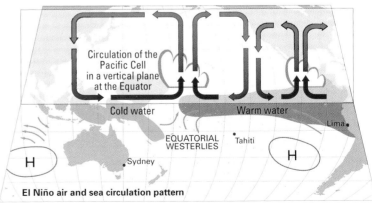

El Niño air and sea circulation pattern

El Niño events occur about every 4 to 7 years and typically last for around 12 to 18 months. El Niño usually results in reduced rainfall across northern and eastern Australia. This can lead to widespread and severe drought, as well as increased temperatures and bushfire risk. However, each El Niño event is unique in terms of its strength as well as its impact. It is measured by the Southern Oscillation Index (SOI) and the changes in ocean temperatures.

La Niña, or 'The Little Girl', is associated with cooler waters in the central and eastern Pacific. A La Niña year can result in cooler land temperatures across the tropics and subtropics and more storms in the North Atlantic.

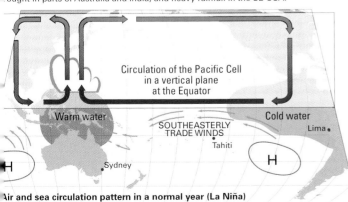

Air and sea circulation pattern in a normal year (La Niña)

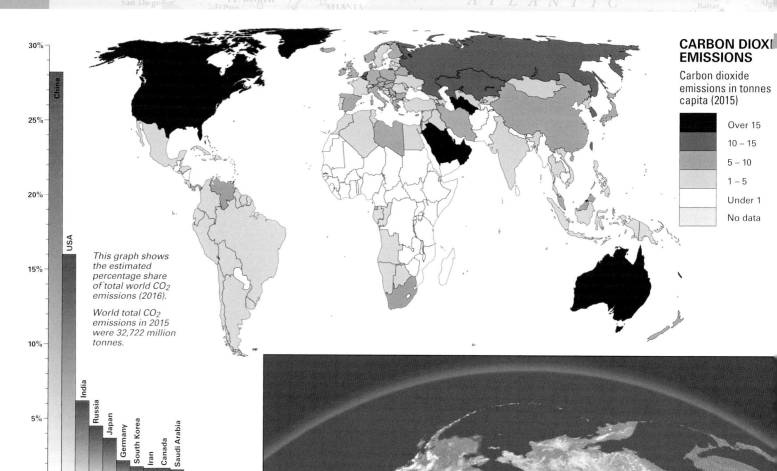

CARBON DIOXIDE EMISSIONS

Carbon dioxide emissions in tonnes capita (2015)

- Over 15
- 10 – 15
- 5 – 10
- 1 – 5
- Under 1
- No data

This graph shows the estimated percentage share of total world CO_2 emissions (2016).

World total CO_2 emissions in 2015 were 32,722 million tonnes.

Bar chart categories (left to right): China, USA, India, Russia, Japan, Germany, South Korea, Iran, Canada, Saudi Arabia

Arctic Ice Cap

This image shows the extent of sea-ice in the Arctic in September 2012. The sea-ice area expands and contracts seasonally and September, at the end of the northern hemisphere summer, represents its smallest extent. The year 2012 showed the biggest reduction in sea-ice since satellite surveillance began in 1979 and this is believed to be related to climate change and global warming. Although dramatic, the sea-ice itself is thought to be quite thin, on average about 3 m (10 ft) thick. Even large reductions would not in themselves involve any sea-level change since the ice is floating and displaces the sea water. One by-product of this is the opening-up of clear sea. This would enable shipping in the northern hemisphere to move between the Atlantic and Pacific Oceans using the much shorter routes around the north coasts of Canada and of Russia, rather than heading south to do this.

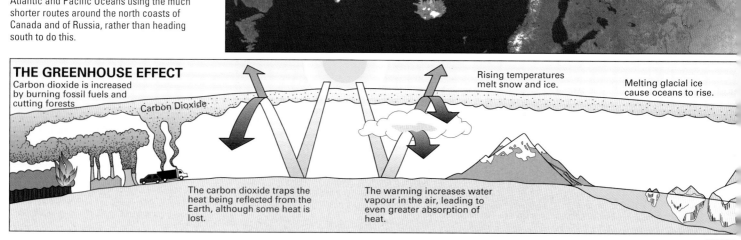

THE GREENHOUSE EFFECT

Carbon dioxide is increased by burning fossil fuels and cutting forests

Carbon Dioxide

Rising temperatures melt snow and ice.

Melting glacial ice cause oceans to rise.

The carbon dioxide traps the heat being reflected from the Earth, although some heat is lost.

The warming increases water vapour in the air, leading to even greater absorption of heat.

PREDICTED CHANGE IN TEMPERATURE

The difference between actual annual average surface air temperature, 1960–90, and predicted annual average surface air temperature, 2070–2100. This map shows the predicted increase, assuming a 'medium growth' of the global economy and assuming that no measures to combat the emission of greenhouse gases are taken.

- 5 – 10°C warmer
- 3 – 5°C warmer
- 2 – 3°C warmer
- 1 – 2°C warmer
- 0 – 1°C warmer

Source: The Hadley Centre of Climate Prediction and Research, The Met. Office.

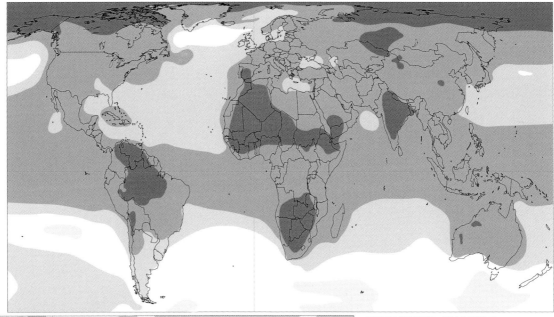

PREDICTED CHANGE IN PRECIPITATION

The difference between actual annual average precipitation, 1960–90, and predicted annual average precipitation, 2070–2100. It should be noted that these predicted annual mean changes mask quite significant seasonal detail.

- Over 2 mm more rain per day
- 1 – 2 mm more rain per day
- 0.5 – 1 mm more rain per day
- 0.2 – 0.5 mm more rain per day
- No change
- 0.2 – 0.5 mm less rain per day
- 0.5 – 1 mm less rain per day
- 1 – 2 mm less rain per day
- Over 2 mm less rain per day

DESERTIFICATION AND DEFORESTATION

- Existing deserts and dry areas
- Areas with a high risk of desertification
- Areas with a moderate risk of desertification
- Former extent of rainforest
- Existing rainforest

Deforestation 1990–2015

	Total forest cover in 1000sq km 1990	Total forest cover in 1000sq km 2015	% change 1990-2015
ezuela	520	148	-71.5
	7	2	-71.4
ria	172	70	-59.3
nda	48	21	-56.3
stan	25	15	-40.0
h Korea	82	50	-39.0
an	307	192	-37.8
abwe	222	141	-36.5
ragua	45	31	-31.1
r-Leste	10	7	-30.0
guay	212	153	-27.8
nmar	385	290	-24.7

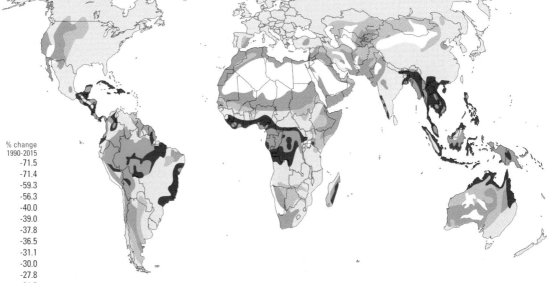

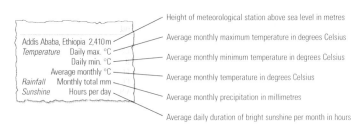

Addis Ababa, Ethiopia 2,410 m
Temperature Daily max. °C — Average monthly maximum temperature in degrees Celsius
Daily min. °C — Average monthly minimum temperature in degrees Celsius
Average monthly °C — Average monthly temperature in degrees Celsius
Rainfall Monthly total mm — Average monthly precipitation in millimetres
Sunshine Hours per day — Average daily duration of bright sunshine per month in hours
(2,410 m) — Height of meteorological station above sea level in metres

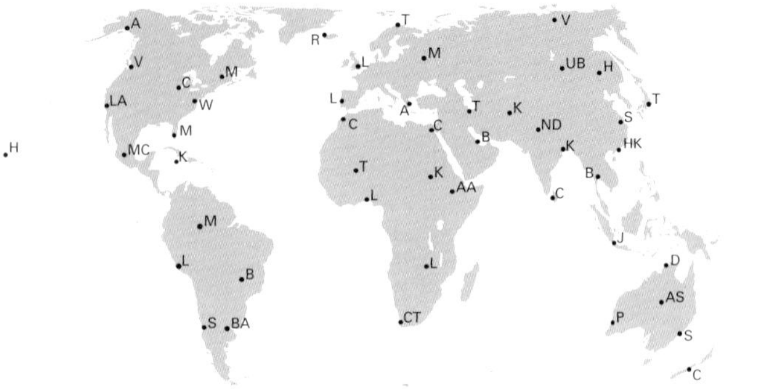

Addis Ababa, Ethiopia 2,410 m	Jan	Feb	Mar	Apr	May	June	July	Aug	Sept	Oct	Nov	Dec	Year
Temperature Daily max. °C	23	24	25	24	25	23	20	20	21	22	23	22	23
Daily min. °C	6	7	9	10	9	10	11	11	10	7	5	5	8
Average monthly °C	14	15	17	17	17	16	16	15	15	15	14	14	15
Rainfall Monthly total mm	13	35	67	91	81	117	247	255	167	29	8	5	1,115
Sunshine Hours per day	8.7	8.2	7.6	8.1	6.5	4.8	2.8	3.2	5.2	7.6	6.7	7	6.4

Alice Springs, Australia 580 m	Jan	Feb	Mar	Apr	May	June	July	Aug	Sept	Oct	Nov	Dec	Year
Temperature Daily max. °C	35	35	32	27	23	19	19	23	27	31	33	35	28
Daily min. °C	21	20	17	12	8	5	4	6	10	15	18	20	13
Average monthly °C	28	27	25	20	15	12	12	14	18	23	25	27	21
Rainfall Monthly total mm	44	33	27	10	15	13	7	8	7	18	29	38	249
Sunshine Hours per day	10.3	10.4	9.3	9.2	8	8	8.9	9.8	10	9.7	10.1	10	9.5

Anchorage, USA 183 m	Jan	Feb	Mar	Apr	May	June	July	Aug	Sept	Oct	Nov	Dec	Year
Temperature Daily max. °C	−7	−3	0	7	13	18	19	17	13	6	−2	−6	−6
Daily min. °C	−15	−12	−9	−2	4	8	10	9	5	−2	−9	−14	−2
Average monthly °C	−11	−7	−4	3	9	13	15	13	9	2	−5	−10	−4
Rainfall Monthly total mm	20	18	13	11	13	25	47	64	64	47	28	24	374
Sunshine Hours per day	2.4	4.1	6.6	8.3	8.3	9.2	8.5	6	4.4	3.1	2.6	1.6	5.4

Athens, Greece 107 m	Jan	Feb	Mar	Apr	May	June	July	Aug	Sept	Oct	Nov	Dec	Year
Temperature Daily max. °C	13	14	16	20	25	30	33	33	29	24	19	15	23
Daily min. °C	6	7	8	11	16	20	23	23	19	15	12	8	14
Average monthly °C	10	10	12	16	20	25	28	28	24	20	15	11	18
Rainfall Monthly total mm	62	37	37	23	23	14	6	7	15	51	56	71	402
Sunshine Hours per day	3.9	5.2	5.8	7.7	8.9	10.7	11.9	11.5	9.4	6.8	4.8	3.8	7.3

Bahrain City, Bahrain 2 m	Jan	Feb	Mar	Apr	May	June	July	Aug	Sept	Oct	Nov	Dec	Year
Temperature Daily max. °C	20	21	25	29	33	36	37	38	36	32	27	22	30
Daily min. °C	14	15	18	22	25	29	31	32	29	25	22	16	23
Average monthly °C	17	18	21	25	29	32	34	35	32	29	25	19	26
Rainfall Monthly total mm	18	12	10	9	2	0	0	0	0	0.4	3	16	70
Sunshine Hours per day	5.9	6.9	7.9	8.8	10.6	13.2	12.1	12	12	10.3	7.7	6.4	9.5

Bangkok, Thailand 10 m	Jan	Feb	Mar	Apr	May	June	July	Aug	Sept	Oct	Nov	Dec	Year
Temperature Daily max. °C	32	33	34	35	34	33	32	32	32	31	31	31	33
Daily min. °C	20	23	24	26	25	25	25	24	24	24	23	20	24
Average monthly °C	26	28	29	30	30	29	28	28	28	28	27	26	28
Rainfall Monthly total mm	9	30	36	82	165	153	168	183	310	239	55	8	1,438
Sunshine Hours per day	8.2	8	8	10	7.5	6.1	4.7	5.2	5.2	6.1	7.3	7.8	7

Brasilia, Brazil 910 m	Jan	Feb	Mar	Apr	May	June	July	Aug	Sept	Oct	Nov	Dec	Year
Temperature Daily max. °C	28	28	28	28	27	27	27	29	30	29	28	27	28
Daily min. °C	18	18	18	17	15	13	13	14	16	18	18	18	16
Average monthly °C	23	23	23	22	21	20	20	21	23	24	23	22	22
Rainfall Monthly total mm	252	204	227	93	17	3	6	3	30	127	255	343	1,560
Sunshine Hours per day	5.8	5.7	6	7.4	8.7	9.3	9.6	9.8	7.9	6.5	4.8	4.4	7.2

Buenos Aires, Argentina 25 m	Jan	Feb	Mar	Apr	May	June	July	Aug	Sept	Oct	Nov	Dec	Year
Temperature Daily max. °C	30	29	26	22	18	14	14	16	18	21	25	28	22
Daily min. °C	17	17	16	12	9	5	6	6	8	10	14	16	11
Average monthly °C	23	23	21	17	13	10	10	11	13	15	19	22	16
Rainfall Monthly total mm	79	71	109	89	76	61	56	61	79	86	84	99	950
Sunshine Hours per day	9.2	8.5	7.5	6.8	4.9	3.5	3.8	5.2	6	6.8	8.1	8.5	6.6

Cairo, Egypt 75 m	Jan	Feb	Mar	Apr	May	June	July	Aug	Sept	Oct	Nov	Dec	Year
Temperature Daily max. °C	19	21	24	28	32	35	35	35	33	30	26	21	28
Daily min. °C	9	9	12	14	18	20	22	22	20	18	14	10	16
Average monthly °C	14	15	18	21	25	28	29	28	26	24	20	16	22
Rainfall Monthly total mm	4	4	3	1	2	1	0	0	1	1	3	7	27
Sunshine Hours per day	6.9	8.4	8.7	9.7	10.5	11.9	11.7	11.3	10.4	9.4	8.3	6.4	9.5

Cape Town, South Africa 44 m	Jan	Feb	Mar	Apr	May	June	July	Aug	Sept	Oct	Nov	Dec	Year
Temperature Daily max. °C	26	26	25	23	20	18	17	18	19	21	24	25	22
Daily min. °C	15	15	14	11	9	7	7	7	8	10	13	15	11
Average monthly °C	21	20	20	17	14	13	12	12	14	16	18	20	16
Rainfall Monthly total mm	12	19	17	42	67	98	68	76	36	45	12	13	505
Sunshine Hours per day	11.4	10.2	9.4	7.7	6.1	5.7	6.4	6.6	7.6	8.6	10.2	10.9	8.4

Casablanca, Morocco 59 m	Jan	Feb	Mar	Apr	May	June	July	Aug	Sept	Oct	Nov	Dec	Year
Temperature Daily max. °C	17	18	20	21	22	24	26	26	26	24	21	18	22
Daily min. °C	8	9	11	12	15	18	19	20	18	15	12	10	14
Average monthly °C	13	13	15	16	18	21	23	23	22	20	17	14	18
Rainfall Monthly total mm	78	61	54	37	20	3	0	1	6	28	58	94	440
Sunshine Hours per day	5.2	6.3	7.3	9	9.4	9.7	10.2	9.7	9.1	7.4	5.9	5.3	7.9

Chicago, USA 186 m	Jan	Feb	Mar	Apr	May	June	July	Aug	Sept	Oct	Nov	Dec	Year
Temperature Daily max. °C	1	2	6	14	21	26	29	28	24	17	8	2	15
Daily min. °C	−7	−6	−2	5	11	16	20	19	14	8	0	−5	−6
Average monthly °C	−3	−2	2	9	16	21	24	23	19	13	4	−2	4
Rainfall Monthly total mm	47	41	70	77	96	103	86	80	69	71	56	48	844
Sunshine Hours per day	4	5	6.6	6.9	8.9	10.2	10	9.2	8.2	6.9	4.5	3.7	7

Christchurch, New Zealand 5 m	Jan	Feb	Mar	Apr	May	June	July	Aug	Sept	Oct	Nov	Dec	Year
Temperature Daily max. °C	21	21	19	17	13	11	10	11	14	17	19	21	16
Daily min. °C	12	12	10	7	4	2	1	3	5	7	8	11	7
Average monthly °C	16	16	15	12	9	6	6	7	9	12	13	16	11
Rainfall Monthly total mm	56	46	43	46	76	69	61	58	51	51	51	61	669
Sunshine Hours per day	7	6.5	5.6	4.7	4.3	3.9	4.1	4.7	5.6	6.1	6.9	6.3	5.5

Colombo, Sri Lanka 10 m	Jan	Feb	Mar	Apr	May	June	July	Aug	Sept	Oct	Nov	Dec	Year
Temperature Daily max. °C	30	31	31	31	30	30	29	29	30	29	29	30	30
Daily min. °C	22	22	23	24	25	25	25	25	25	24	23	22	24
Average monthly °C	26	26	27	28	28	27	27	27	27	27	26	26	27
Rainfall Monthly total mm	101	66	118	230	394	220	140	102	174	348	333	142	2,368
Sunshine Hours per day	7.9	9	8.1	7.2	6.4	5.4	6.1	6.3	6.2	6.5	6.4	7.8	6.9

Darwin, Australia 30 m	Jan	Feb	Mar	Apr	May	June	July	Aug	Sept	Oct	Nov	Dec	Year
Temperature Daily max. °C	32	32	33	33	33	31	31	32	33	34	34	33	33
Daily min. °C	25	25	25	24	23	21	19	21	23	25	26	26	24
Average monthly °C	29	29	29	29	28	26	25	26	28	29	30	29	28
Rainfall Monthly total mm	405	309	279	77	8	2	0	1	15	48	108	214	1,466
Sunshine Hours per day	5.8	5.8	6.6	9.8	9.3	10	9.9	10.4	10.1	9.4	9.6	6.8	8.6

Harbin, China 175 m	Jan	Feb	Mar	Apr	May	June	July	Aug	Sept	Oct	Nov	Dec	Year
Temperature Daily max. °C	−14	−9	0	12	21	26	29	27	20	12	−1	−11	9
Daily min. °C	−26	−23	−12	−1	7	14	18	16	8	0	−12	−22	−3
Average monthly °C	−20	−16	−6	6	14	20	23	22	14	6	−7	−17	3
Rainfall Monthly total mm	4	6	17	23	44	92	167	119	52	36	12	5	577
Sunshine Hours per day	6.4	7.8	8	7.8	8.3	8.6	8.6	8.2	7.2	6.9	6.1	5.7	7.5

Hong Kong, China 35 m	Jan	Feb	Mar	Apr	May	June	July	Aug	Sept	Oct	Nov	Dec	Year
Temperature Daily max. °C	18	18	20	24	28	30	31	31	30	27	24	20	25
Daily min. °C	13	13	16	19	23	26	26	26	25	23	19	15	20
Average monthly °C	16	15	18	22	25	28	28	28	27	25	21	17	23
Rainfall Monthly total mm	30	60	70	133	332	479	286	415	364	33	46	17	2,265
Sunshine Hours per day	4.7	3.5	3.1	3.8	5	5.4	6.8	6.5	6.6	7	6.2	5.5	5.3

Honolulu, Hawaii 5 m	Jan	Feb	Mar	Apr	May	June	July	Aug	Sept	Oct	Nov	Dec	Year
Temperature Daily max. °C	26	26	26	27	28	29	29	29	30	29	28	26	28
Daily min. °C	19	19	19	20	21	22	23	23	23	22	21	20	21
Average monthly °C	23	22	23	23	24	26	26	26	26	26	24	23	24
Rainfall Monthly total mm	96	84	73	33	25	8	11	23	25	47	55	76	556
Sunshine Hours per day	7.3	7.7	8.3	8.6	8.8	9.1	9.4	9.3	9.2	8.3	7.5	6.2	8.3

Jakarta, Indonesia 10 m	Jan	Feb	Mar	Apr	May	June	July	Aug	Sept	Oct	Nov	Dec	Year
Temperature Daily max. °C	29	29	30	31	31	31	31	31	31	31	30	29	30
Daily min. °C	23	23	23	24	24	23	23	23	23	23	23	23	23
Average monthly °C	26	26	27	27	27	27	27	27	27	27	27	26	27
Rainfall Monthly total mm	300	300	211	147	114	97	64	43	66	112	142	203	1,799
Sunshine Hours per day	6.1	6.5	7.7	8.5	8.4	8.5	9.1	9.5	9.6	9	7.7	7.1	8.1

Kabul, Afghanistan 1,791 m	Jan	Feb	Mar	Apr	May	June	July	Aug	Sept	Oct	Nov	Dec	Year
Temperature Daily max. °C	2	4	12	19	26	31	33	33	30	22	17	8	20
Daily min. °C	−8	−6	1	6	11	13	16	15	11	6	1	−3	5
Average monthly °C	−3	−1	6	13	18	22	25	24	20	14	9	3	12
Rainfall Monthly total mm	28	61	72	117	33	1	7	1	0	1	37	14	372
Sunshine Hours per day	5.9	6	5.7	6.8	10.1	11.5	11.4	11.2	9.8	9.4	7.8	6.1	8.5

Khartoum, Sudan 380 m	Jan	Feb	Mar	Apr	May	June	July	Aug	Sept	Oct	Nov	Dec	Year
Temperature Daily max. °C	32	33	37	40	42	41	38	36	38	39	35	32	37
Daily min. °C	16	17	20	23	26	27	26	25	25	25	21	17	22
Average monthly °C	24	25	28	32	34	34	32	30	32	32	28	25	30
Rainfall Monthly total mm	0	0	0	1	7	5	56	80	28	2	0	0	179
Sunshine Hours per day	10.6	11.2	10.4	10.8	10.4	10.1	8.6	8.6	9.6	10.3	10.8	10.6	10.2

Kingston, Jamaica 35 m	Jan	Feb	Mar	Apr	May	June	July	Aug	Sept	Oct	Nov	Dec	Year
Temperature Daily max. °C	30	30	30	31	31	32	32	32	32	31	31	31	31
Daily min. °C	20	20	20	21	22	24	23	23	23	23	22	21	22
Average monthly °C	25	25	25	26	26	28	28	28	27	27	26	26	26
Rainfall Monthly total mm	23	15	23	31	102	89	38	91	99	180	74	36	801
Sunshine Hours per day	8.3	8.8	8.7	8.7	8.3	7.8	8.5	8.5	7.6	7.3	8.3	7.7	8.2

		Jan	Feb	Mar	Apr	May	June	July	Aug	Sept	Oct	Nov	Dec	Year
Kolkata (Calcutta), India 5 m														
Temperature	Daily max. °C	27	29	34	36	35	34	32	32	32	32	29	26	31
	Daily min. °C	13	15	21	24	25	26	26	26	26	23	18	13	21
	Average monthly °C	20	22	27	30	30	30	29	29	29	28	23	20	26
Rainfall	Monthly total mm	10	30	34	44	140	297	325	332	253	114	20	5	1,604
Sunshine	Hours per day	8.6	8.7	8.9	9	8.7	5.4	4.1	4.1	5.1	6.5	8.3	8.4	7.1
Lagos, Nigeria 40 m														
Temperature	Daily max. °C	32	33	33	32	31	29	28	28	29	30	31	32	31
	Daily min. °C	22	23	23	23	23	22	22	21	22	22	23	22	22
	Average monthly °C	27	28	28	28	27	26	25	24	25	26	27	27	26
Rainfall	Monthly total mm	28	41	99	99	203	300	180	56	180	190	63	25	1,464
Sunshine	Hours per day	5.9	6.8	6.3	6.1	5.6	3.8	2.8	3.3	3	5.1	6.6	6.5	5.2
Lima, Peru 120 m														
Temperature	Daily max. °C	28	29	29	27	24	20	20	19	20	22	24	26	24
	Daily min. °C	19	20	19	17	16	15	14	14	14	15	16	17	16
	Average monthly °C	24	24	24	22	20	17	17	16	17	18	20	21	20
Rainfall	Monthly total mm	1	1	1	1	5	5	8	8	8	3	3	1	45
Sunshine	Hours per day	6.3	6.8	6.9	6.7	4	1.4	1.1	1	1.1	2.5	4.1	5	3.9
Lisbon, Portugal 77 m														
Temperature	Daily max. °C	14	15	17	20	21	25	27	28	26	22	17	15	21
	Daily min. °C	8	8	10	12	13	15	17	17	17	14	11	9	13
	Average monthly °C	11	12	14	16	17	20	22	23	21	18	14	12	17
Rainfall	Monthly total mm	111	76	109	54	44	16	3	4	33	62	93	103	708
Sunshine	Hours per day	4.7	5.9	6	8.3	9.1	10.6	11.4	10.7	8.4	6.7	5.2	4.6	7.7
London (Kew), UK 5 m														
Temperature	Daily max. °C	6	7	10	13	17	20	22	21	19	14	10	7	14
	Daily min. °C	2	2	3	6	8	12	14	13	11	8	5	4	7
	Average monthly °C	4	5	7	9	12	16	18	17	15	11	8	5	11
Rainfall	Monthly total mm	54	40	37	37	46	45	57	59	49	57	64	48	593
Sunshine	Hours per day	1.7	2.3	3.5	5.7	6.7	7	6.6	6	5	3.3	1.9	1.4	4.3
Los Angeles, USA 30 m														
Temperature	Daily max. °C	18	18	18	19	20	22	24	24	24	23	22	19	21
	Daily min. °C	7	8	9	11	13	15	17	17	16	14	11	9	12
	Average monthly °C	12	13	14	15	17	18	21	21	20	18	16	14	17
Rainfall	Monthly total mm	69	74	46	28	3	3	0	0	5	10	28	61	327
Sunshine	Hours per day	6.9	8.2	8.9	8.8	9.5	10.3	11.7	11	10.1	8.6	8.2	7.6	9.2
Lusaka, Zambia 1,154 m														
Temperature	Daily max. °C	26	26	26	27	25	23	23	26	29	31	29	27	27
	Daily min. °C	17	17	16	15	12	10	9	11	15	18	18	17	15
	Average monthly °C	22	22	21	21	18	17	16	19	22	25	23	22	21
Rainfall	Monthly total mm	224	173	90	19	3	1	0	1	1	17	85	196	810
Sunshine	Hours per day	5.1	5.4	6.9	8.9	9	9	9.1	9.6	9.5	9	7	5.5	7.8
Manaus, Brazil 45 m														
Temperature	Daily max. °C	31	31	31	31	31	31	32	33	34	34	33	32	32
	Daily min. °C	24	24	24	24	24	24	24	24	24	25	25	24	24
	Average monthly °C	28	28	28	27	28	28	28	29	29	29	29	28	28
Rainfall	Monthly total mm	278	278	300	287	193	99	61	41	62	112	165	220	2,096
Sunshine	Hours per day	3.9	4	3.6	3.9	5.4	6.9	7.9	8.2	7.5	6.6	5.9	4.9	5.7
Mexico City, Mexico 2,309 m														
Temperature	Daily max. °C	21	23	26	27	26	25	23	24	23	22	21	21	24
	Daily min. °C	5	6	7	9	10	11	11	11	11	9	6	5	8
	Average monthly °C	13	15	16	18	18	18	17	17	17	16	14	13	16
Rainfall	Monthly total mm	8	4	9	23	57	111	160	149	119	46	16	7	709
Sunshine	Hours per day	7.3	8.1	8.5	8.1	7.8	7	6.2	6.4	5.6	6.3	7	7.3	7.1
Miami, USA 2 m														
Temperature	Daily max. °C	24	25	27	28	30	31	32	32	31	29	27	25	28
	Daily min. °C	14	15	16	19	21	23	24	24	24	22	18	15	20
	Average monthly °C	19	20	21	23	25	27	28	28	27	25	22	20	24
Rainfall	Monthly total mm	51	48	58	99	163	188	170	178	241	208	71	43	1,518
Sunshine	Hours per day	7.7	8.3	8.7	9.4	8.9	8.5	8.7	8.4	7.1	6.5	7.5	7.1	8.1
Montreal, Canada 57 m														
Temperature	Daily max. °C	–6	–4	2	11	18	23	26	25	20	14	5	–3	11
	Daily min. °C	–13	–11	–5	2	9	14	17	16	11	6	0	–9	3
	Average monthly °C	–9	–8	–2	6	13	19	22	20	16	10	3	–6	7
Rainfall	Monthly total mm	87	76	86	83	81	91	98	87	96	84	89	89	1,047
Sunshine	Hours per day	2.8	3.4	4.5	5.2	6.7	7.7	8.2	7.7	5.6	4.3	2.4	2.2	5.1
Moscow, Russia 156 m														
Temperature	Daily max. °C	–6	–4	1	9	18	22	24	22	17	10	1	–5	9
	Daily min. °C	–14	–16	–11	–1	5	9	12	9	4	–2	–6	–12	–2
	Average monthly °C	–10	–10	–5	4	12	15	18	16	10	4	–2	–8	4
Rainfall	Monthly total mm	31	28	33	35	52	67	74	74	58	51	36	36	575
Sunshine	Hours per day	1	1.9	3.7	5.2	7.8	8.3	8.4	7.1	4.4	2.4	1	0.6	4.4
New Delhi, India 220 m														
Temperature	Daily max. °C	21	24	29	36	41	39	35	34	34	34	28	23	32
	Daily min. °C	6	10	14	20	26	28	27	26	24	17	11	7	18
	Average monthly °C	14	17	22	28	33	34	31	30	29	26	20	15	25
Rainfall	Monthly total mm	25	21	13	8	13	77	178	184	123	10	2	11	665
Sunshine	Hours per day	7.7	8.2	8.2	8.7	9.2	7.9	6	6.3	6.9	9.4	8.7	8.3	8

		Jan	Feb	Mar	Apr	May	June	July	Aug	Sept	Oct	Nov	Dec	Year
Perth, Australia 60 m														
Temperature	Daily max. °C	29	30	27	25	21	18	17	18	19	21	25	27	23
	Daily min. °C	17	18	16	14	12	10	9	9	10	11	14	16	13
	Average monthly °C	23	24	22	19	16	14	13	13	15	16	19	22	18
Rainfall	Monthly total mm	8	13	22	44	128	189	177	145	84	58	19	13	900
Sunshine	Hours per day	10.4	9.8	8.8	7.5	5.7	4.8	5.4	6	7.2	8.1	9.6	10.4	7.8
Reykjavik, Iceland 18 m														
Temperature	Daily max. °C	2	3	5	6	10	13	15	14	12	8	5	4	8
	Daily min. °C	–3	–3	–1	1	4	7	9	8	6	3	0	–2	3
	Average monthly °C	0	0	2	4	7	10	12	11	9	5	3	1	5
Rainfall	Monthly total mm	89	64	62	56	42	42	50	56	67	94	78	79	779
Sunshine	Hours per day	0.8	2	3.6	4.5	5.9	6.1	5.8	5.4	3.5	2.3	1.1	0.3	3.7
Santiago, Chile 520 m														
Temperature	Daily max. °C	30	29	27	24	19	15	15	17	19	22	26	29	23
	Daily min. °C	12	11	10	7	5	3	3	4	6	7	9	11	7
	Average monthly °C	21	20	18	15	12	9	9	10	12	15	17	20	15
Rainfall	Monthly total mm	3	3	5	13	64	84	76	56	31	15	8	5	363
Sunshine	Hours per day	10.8	8.9	8.5	5.5	3.6	3.3	3.3	3.6	4.8	6.1	8.7	10.1	6.4
Shanghai, China 5 m														
Temperature	Daily max. °C	8	8	13	19	24	28	32	32	27	23	17	10	20
	Daily min. °C	–1	0	4	9	14	19	23	23	19	13	7	2	11
	Average monthly °C	3	4	8	14	19	23	27	27	23	18	12	6	15
Rainfall	Monthly total mm	48	59	84	94	94	180	147	142	130	71	51	36	1,136
Sunshine	Hours per day	4	3.7	4.4	4.8	5.4	4.7	6.9	7.5	5.3	5.6	4.7	4.5	5.1
Sydney, Australia 40 m														
Temperature	Daily max. °C	26	26	25	22	19	17	17	18	20	22	24	25	22
	Daily min. °C	18	19	17	14	11	9	8	9	11	13	16	17	14
	Average monthly °C	22	22	21	18	15	13	12	13	16	18	20	21	18
Rainfall	Monthly total mm	89	101	127	135	127	117	117	76	74	71	74	74	1,182
Sunshine	Hours per day	7.5	7	6.4	6.1	5.7	5.3	6.1	7	7.3	7.5	7.5	7.5	6.8
Tehran, Iran 1,191 m														
Temperature	Daily max. °C	9	11	16	21	29	30	37	36	29	24	16	11	22
	Daily min. °C	–1	1	4	10	16	20	23	23	18	12	6	1	11
	Average monthly °C	4	6	10	15	22	25	30	29	23	18	11	6	17
Rainfall	Monthly total mm	37	23	36	31	14	2	1	1	1	5	29	27	207
Sunshine	Hours per day	5.9	6.7	7.5	7.4	8.6	11.6	11.2	11	10.1	7.6	6.9	6.3	8.4
Timbuktu, Mali 269 m														
Temperature	Daily max. °C	31	35	38	41	43	42	38	35	38	40	37	31	37
	Daily min. °C	13	16	18	22	26	27	25	24	24	23	18	14	21
	Average monthly °C	22	25	28	31	34	34	32	30	31	31	28	23	29
Rainfall	Monthly total mm	0	0	0	1	4	20	54	93	31	3	0	0	206
Sunshine	Hours per day	9.1	9.6	9.6	9.7	9.8	9.4	9.6	9	9.3	9.5	9.5	8.9	9.4
Tokyo, Japan 5 m														
Temperature	Daily max. °C	9	9	12	18	22	25	29	30	27	20	16	11	19
	Daily min. °C	–1	–1	3	4	13	17	22	23	19	13	7	1	10
	Average monthly °C	4	4	8	11	18	21	25	26	23	17	11	6	14
Rainfall	Monthly total mm	48	73	101	135	131	182	146	147	217	220	101	61	1,562
Sunshine	Hours per day	6	5.9	5.7	6	6.2	5	5.8	6.6	4.5	4.4	4.8	5.4	5.5
Tromsø, Norway 100 m														
Temperature	Daily max. °C	–2	–2	0	3	7	12	16	14	10	5	2	0	5
	Daily min. °C	–6	–6	–5	–2	1	6	9	8	5	1	–2	–4	0
	Average monthly °C	–4	–4	–3	0	4	9	13	11	7	3	0	–2	3
Rainfall	Monthly total mm	96	79	91	65	61	59	56	80	109	115	88	95	994
Sunshine	Hours per day	0.1	1.6	2.9	6.1	5.7	6.9	7.9	4.8	3.5	1.7	0.3	0	3.5
Ulan Bator, Mongolia 1,305 m														
Temperature	Daily max. °C	–19	–13	–4	7	13	21	22	21	14	6	–6	–16	4
	Daily min. °C	–32	–29	–22	–8	–2	7	11	8	2	–8	–20	–28	–11
	Average monthly °C	–26	–21	–13	–1	6	14	16	14	8	–1	–13	–22	–4
Rainfall	Monthly total mm	1	1	2	5	10	28	76	51	23	5	5	2	209
Sunshine	Hours per day	6.4	7.8	8	7.8	8.3	8.6	8.6	8.2	7.2	6.9	6.1	5.7	7.5
Vancouver, Canada 5 m														
Temperature	Daily max. °C	6	7	10	14	17	20	23	22	19	14	9	7	14
	Daily min. °C	0	1	3	5	8	11	13	12	10	7	3	2	6
	Average monthly °C	3	4	6	9	13	16	18	17	14	10	6	4	10
Rainfall	Monthly total mm	214	161	151	90	69	65	39	44	83	172	198	243	1,529
Sunshine	Hours per day	1.6	3	3.8	5.9	7.5	7.4	9.5	8.2	6	3.7	2	1.4	5
Verkhoyansk, Russia 137 m														
Temperature	Daily max. °C	–47	–40	–20	–1	11	21	24	21	12	–8	–33	–42	–8
	Daily min. °C	–51	–48	–40	–25	–7	4	6	1	–6	–20	–39	–50	–23
	Average monthly °C	–49	–44	–30	–13	2	12	15	11	3	–14	–36	–46	–16
Rainfall	Monthly total mm	7	5	5	4	5	25	33	30	13	11	10	7	155
Sunshine	Hours per day	0	2.6	6.9	9.6	9.7	10	9.7	7.5	4.1	2.4	0.6	0	5.4
Washington, D.C., USA 22 m														
Temperature	Daily max. °C	7	8	12	19	25	29	31	30	26	20	14	8	19
	Daily min. °C	–1	–1	2	8	13	18	21	20	16	10	4	–1	9
	Average monthly °C	3	3	7	13	19	24	26	25	21	15	9	4	14
Rainfall	Monthly total mm	84	68	96	85	103	88	108	120	100	78	75	75	1,080
Sunshine	Hours per day	4.4	5.7	6.7	7.4	8.2	8.8	8.6	8.2	7.5	6.5	5.3	4.5	6.8

Tropical Rain Forest

Tall broadleaved evergreen forest, trees 30–50m high with climbers and epiphytes forming continuous canopies. Associated with wet climate, 2–3000mm precipitation per year and high temperatures 24–28°C. High diversity of species, typically 100 per ha, including lianas, bamboo, palms, rubber, mahogany. Mangrove swamps form in coastal areas.

This diagram shows the highly stratified nature of the tropical rain forest. Crowns of trees form numerous layers at different heights and the dense shade limits undergrowth.

Temperate Deciduous and Coniferous Forest

A transition zone between broadleaves and conifers. Broadleaves are better suited to the warmer, damper and flatter locations.

Coniferous Forest (Taiga or Boreal)

Forming a large continuous belt across Northern America and Eurasia with a uniformity in tree species. Characteristically trees are tall, conical with short branches and wax-covered needle-shaped leaves to retain moisture. Cold climate with prolonged harsh winters and cool summers where average temperatures are under 0°C for more than six months of the year. Undergrowth is sparse with mosses and lichens. Tree species include pine, fir, spruce, larch, tamarisk.

Mountainous Forest, mainly Coniferous

Mild winters, high humidity and high levels of rainfall throughout the year provide habitat for dense needle-leaf evergreen forests and the largest trees in the world, up to 100m, including the Douglas fir, redwood and giant sequoia.

High Plateau Steppe and Tundra

Similar to arctic tundra with frozen ground for the majority of the year. Very sparse ground coverage of low, shallow-rooted herbs, small shrubs, mosses, lichens and heather interspersed with bare soil.

Arctic Tundra

Average temperatures are 0°C, precipitation is mainly snowfall and the ground remains frozen for 10 months of the year. Vegetation flourishes when the shallow surface layer melts in the long summer days. Underlying permafrost remains frozen and surface water cannot drain away, making conditions marshy. Consists of sedges, snow lichen, arctic meadow grass, cotton grasses and dwarf willow.

Polar and Mountainous Ice Desert

Areas of bare rock and ice with patches of rock-strewn lithosols, low in organic matter and low water content. In sheltered patches only a few mosses, lichens and low shrubs can grow, including woolly moss and purple saxifrage.

Subtropical and Temperate Rain Forest

Precipitation, which is less than in the Tropical Rain Forest, falls in the long wet season interspersed with a season of reduced rainfall and lower temperatures. As a result there are fewer species, thinner canopies, fewer lianas and denser ground level foliage. Vegetation consists of evergreen oak, laurel, bamboo, magnolia and tree ferns.

Monsoon Woodland and Open Jungle

Mostly deciduous trees, because of the long dry season and lower temperatu Trees can reach 30m but are sparser than in the rain forests. There is le competition for light and thick jungle vegetation grows at lower levels. H species diversity includes lianas, bamboo, teak, sandalwood, sal and banya

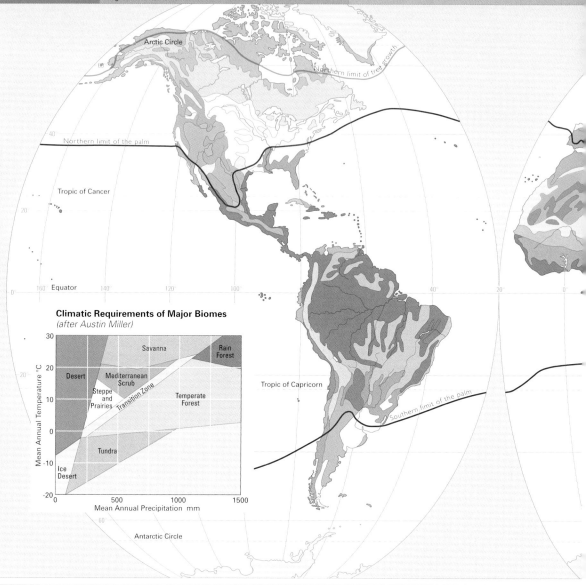

Climatic Requirements of Major Biomes
(after Austin Miller)

SOIL REGIONS

1:220 000 000

- Tundra soil
- Podzols
- Brown forest soil
- Lightly leached dry forest soil
- Red and yellow subtropical forest soil
- Reddish savanna soil and tropical red earths
- Laterites
- Chernozem
- Degraded chernozem
- Black savanna soil
- Chestnut steppe soil
- Desertic (arid) soil
- Alluvium
- Mountain and high plateau soils
- Oases soil
- Tropical and mangrove swamp

(after Glinka, Stremme, Marbut, and others)

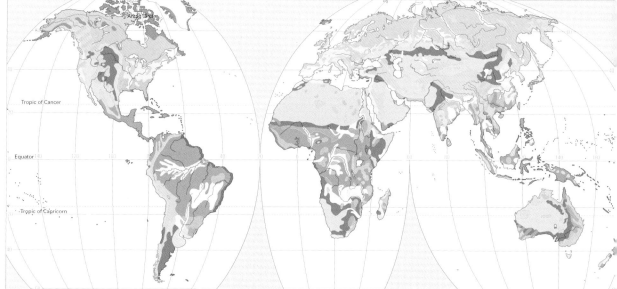

Projection: Interrupted Mollweide's Homolographic

btropical and Temperate Woodland, Scrub and Bush
st clearings with woody shrubs and tall grasses. Trees are fire-resistant and
er deciduous or xerophytic because of long dry periods. Species include
alyptus, acacia, mimosa and euphorbia.

Tropical Savanna with Low Trees and Bush
Tall, coarse grass with enough precipitation to support a scattering of short
deciduous trees and thorn scrub. Vegetation consists of elephant grass, acacia,
palms and baobab and is limited by aridity, grazing animals and periodic fires;
trees have developed thick, woody bark, small leaves or thorns.

Tropical Savanna and Grassland
Areas with a hot climate and long dry season. Extensive areas of tall grasses
often reach 3.5m with scattered fire and drought resistant bushes, low trees
and thickets of elephant grass. Shrubs include acacia, baobab and palms.

BIOMES
Classified by Climax Vegetation
1:116 000 000

Dry Semi-desert with Shrub and Grass
Xerophytic shrubs with thin grass cover and few trees, limited by a long dry season and short, hot, rainy period. Sagebrush, bunch grass and acacia shrubs are common.

Desert Shrub
Scattered xerophytic plants able to withstand daytime extremes in temperature and long periods of drought. There is a large diversity of desert flora such as cacti, yucca, tamarisk, hard grass and artemisia.

Desert
Precipitation less than 250mm per year. Vegetation is very sparse, mainly bare rock, sand dunes and salt flats. Vegetation comprises a few xerophytic shrubs and ephemeral flowers.

Dry Steppe and Shrub
Semi-arid with cold, dry winters and hot summers. Bare soil with sparsely distributed short grasses and scattered shrubs and short trees. Species include acacia, artemisia, saksaul and tamarisk.

Temperate Grasslands, Prairie and Steppe
Continuous, tall, dense and deep-rooted swards of ancient grasslands, considered to be natural climax vegetation as determined by soil and climate. Average precipitation 250–750mm, with a long dry season, limits growth of trees and shrubs. Includes Stipa grass, buffalo grass, blue stems and loco weed.

Mediterranean Hardwood Forest and Scrub
Areas with hot and arid summers. Sparse evergreen trees are short and twisted with thick bark, interspersed with areas of scrub land. Trees have waxy leaves or thorns and deep root systems to resist drought. Many of the hardwood forests have been cleared by man, resulting in extensive scrub formation – maquis and chaparral. Species found are evergreen oak, stone pine, cork, olive and myrtle.

Temperate Deciduous Forest and Meadow
Areas of relatively high, well-distributed rainfall and temperature favourable for forest growth. The Tall broadleaved trees form a canopy in the summer, but shed their leaves in the winter. The undergrowth is sparse and poorly developed, but in the spring, herbs and flowers develop quickly. Diverse species, with up to 20 per ha, including oak, beech, birch, maple, ash, elm, chestnut and hornbeam. Many of these forests have been cleared for urbanization and farming.

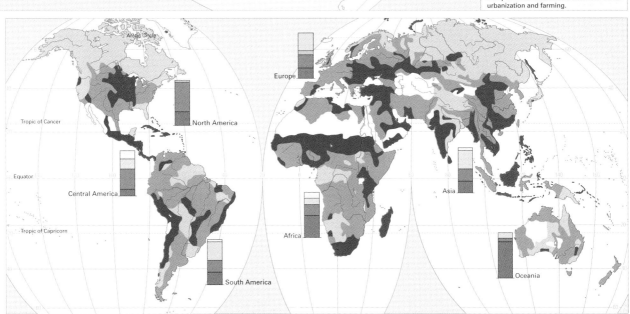

OIL DEGRADATION
1:220 000 000

Areas of Concern
- Areas of serious concern
- Areas of some concern
- Stable terrain
- Non-vegetated land

Causes of soil degradation (by region)
- Grazing practices
- Other agricultural practices
- Industrialization
- Deforestation
- Fuelwood collection

(after Wageningen)

COPYRIGHT PHILIP'S

AGRICULTURAL PRODUCTION

Crops

Wheat
China 17.6% | India 12.5% | Russia 9.8% | USA 8.4% | Canada 4.1% | France 3.9% | Ukraine 3.5%

World total (2016): 749,460,077 tonnes

Rice
China 28.6% | India 21.2% | Indonesia 9.6% | Bangladesh 6.1% | Vietnam 5.3% | Myanmar (Burma) 4.7% | Thailand 4.6%

World total (2016): 740,961,445 tonnes

Cassava
Nigeria 20.6% | Thailand 11.2% | Brazil 7.6% | Indonesia 7.5% | Ghana 6.4% | Congo (D.R.) 5.3%

World total (2016): 277,102,564 tonnes

Barley
Russia 12.7% | Germany 7.6% | France 7.3% | Australia 6.4% | Canada 6.2% | Spain 5.6%

World total (2016): 141,277,993 tonnes

Maize
USA 36.3% | China 21.9% | Brazil 6.1%

World total (2016): 1,060,107,470 tonnes

Potatoes
China 26.3% | India 11.6% | Russia 8.3% | Ukraine 5.9% | USA 5.3%

World total (2016): 376,826,967 tonnes

Soybeans
USA 35.0% | Brazil 28.8% | Argentina 17.6% | India 4.2%

World total (2016): 334,894,085 tonnes

Millet
India 36.3% | Niger 13.7% | China 7.0% | Mali 6.4% | Nigeria 5.2%

World total (2016): 28,357,451 tonnes

Sugar Cane
Brazil 38.2% | India 17.3% | China 12.2% | Thailand 4.3% | Pakistan 3.3% | Mexico 2.8%

World total (2016): 2,013,721,491 tonnes

Sugar Beet
Russia 18.5% | France 12.2% | USA 12.1% | Germany 9.2% | Turkey 7.0% | Ukraine 5.1% | Poland 4.9% | Egypt 4.8%

World total (2016): 277,230,790 tonnes

Animal Products

Milk
India 20.0% | USA 12.1% | China 5.3% | Pakistan 5.0% | Brazil 4.2% | Russia 3.9%

World total (2016): 798,476,318 tonnes

Eggs
China 36.3% | USA 8.2% | India 6.2% | Japan 3.5%

World total (2016): 73,889,905 tonnes

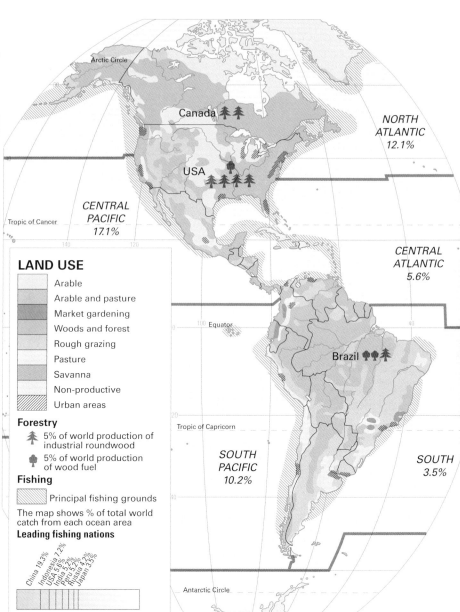

LAND USE

- Arable
- Arable and pasture
- Market gardening
- Woods and forest
- Rough grazing
- Pasture
- Savanna
- Non-productive
- Urban areas

Forestry

🌲 5% of world production of industrial roundwood

🌳 5% of world production of wood fuel

Fishing

Principal fishing grounds

The map shows % of total world catch from each ocean area

Leading fishing nations
China 19.3% | Indonesia 7.2% | USA 5.6% | India 5.2% | Peru 5.2% | Russia 4.2% | Japan 3.5%

World total (2016): 90,900,000 tonnes

Projection: Interrupted Mollweide's Homolographic

(Map labels: Arctic Circle; Canada; USA; Brazil; NORTH ATLANTIC 12.1%; CENTRAL PACIFIC 17.1%; CENTRAL ATLANTIC 5.6%; SOUTH PACIFIC 10.2%; SOUTH 3.5%; Tropic of Cancer; Equator; Tropic of Capricorn; Antarctic Circle)

This aerial photo shows shrimp farms, near Mahajanga, in north-western Madagascar. Shrimp farming is being used to stimulate the country's economy.

WILL THE WORLD RUN OUT OF FOOD?

At present-day rates, the world's population is predicted to reach at least 9 billion people by 2050. To sustain this population there will have to be a 70% increase in food production.

Currently, many people struggle to achieve the minimum food intake to sustain life. Globally, about 1 billion people are malnourished compared with 1 billion who are overweight.

Over 30% of the world's grain is fed to livestock because more and more people like to eat meat. But animals (and humans) are very inefficient in their utilization of nutrients; generally less than 20% of the nitrogen in their food is used; the rest is excreted, causing air and water pollution.

Meat is also very expensive in terms of water consumption: 0.5 kg of beef requires 8,442 litres of water to produce it. By 2030 there will be a 30% increase in water demand. Over 71% of the Earth's surface is covered in water but less than 3% of this is fresh water, of which over two-thirds is frozen in ice-caps and glaciers. Its over-exploitation in developed areas and availability in regions where it is scarce are major problems. For example, China currently has 20% of the world's population, but only 11% of its water.

How can we feed 9 billion people adequately and sustainably? The Royal Society has said that we need 'Sustainable Intensification', that is, to produce more using less and with less of an impact on the environment through good soil management, maintaining or enhancing crop genetic diversity, and introducing pest and disease resistance, as well as better fertiliser use.

Some, however, reject technological approaches and advocate extensive systems described as 'organic', 'bio-dynamic' or 'ecological', objecting to the reliance on chemical fertilisers and pesticides.

We need to reduce the 30% of the world's crop yield lost to pests, diseases and weeds; protect the fertile soil that irregularly covers only 11% of the global land surface and is a non-renewable asset; and cut back on food waste. In the UK it is estimated that 8.3 million tonnes of food worth £20 billion is sent to landfill each year. Some people now live on the food thrown away by shops – called 'skipping'.

If we adopt appropriate techniques and modify our behaviour, we stand a good chance of feeding the future, predominantly urban, population.

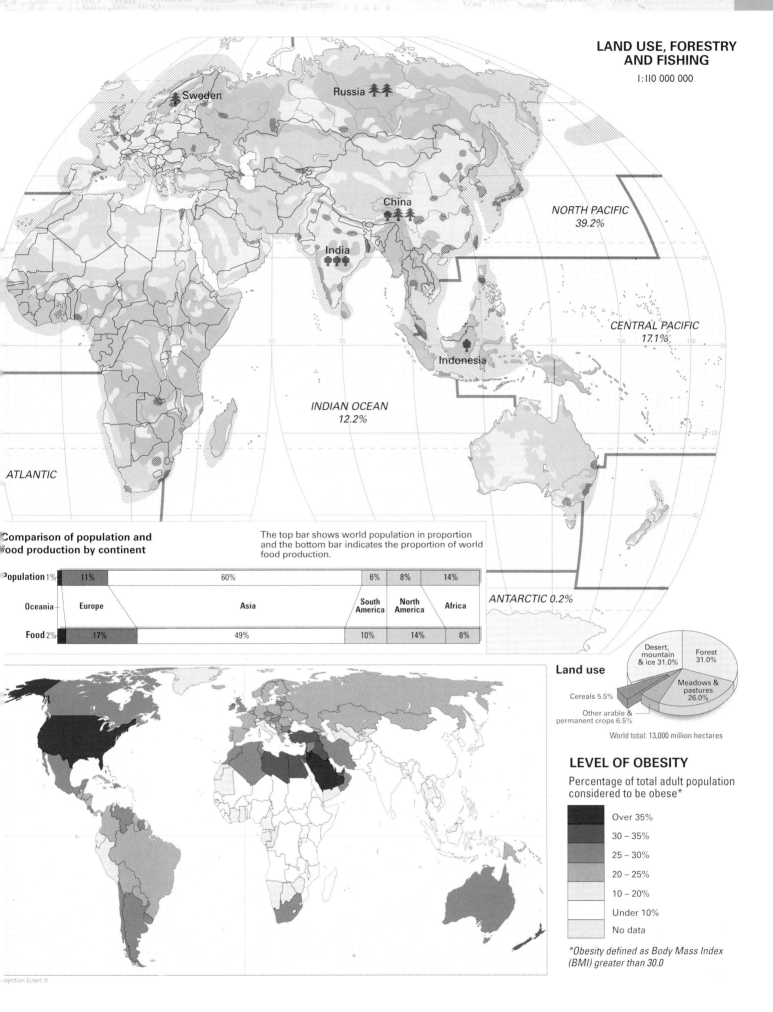

LAND USE, FORESTRY AND FISHING

1:110 000 000

Sweden

Russia

China

India

Indonesia

NORTH PACIFIC
39.2%

CENTRAL PACIFIC
17.1%

INDIAN OCEAN
12.2%

ATLANTIC

ANTARCTIC 0.2%

Comparison of population and food production by continent

The top bar shows world population in proportion and the bottom bar indicates the proportion of world food production.

Oceania	Europe	Asia	South America	North America	Africa
Population 1%	11%	60%	6%	8%	14%
Food 2%	17%	49%	10%	14%	8%

Land use

- Desert, mountain & ice 31.0%
- Forest 31.0%
- Meadows & pastures 26.0%
- Cereals 5.5%
- Other arable & permanent crops 6.5%

World total: 13,000 million hectares

LEVEL OF OBESITY

Percentage of total adult population considered to be obese*

- Over 35%
- 30 – 35%
- 25 – 30%
- 20 – 25%
- 10 – 20%
- Under 10%
- No data

*Obesity defined as Body Mass Index (BMI) greater than 30.0

Projection: Eckert IV

ENERGY BALANCE

Difference between primary energy production and consumption in millions of tonnes of oil equivalent (MtOe)

- Over 35 surplus
- 1 – 35 surplus
- 1 deficit – 1 surplus (approx. balance)
- 1 – 35 deficit
- Over 35 deficit

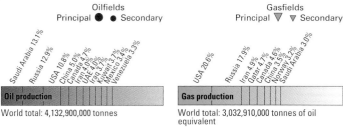

Projection: Eck

OIL RESERVES

World oil reserves by region and country, billion tonnes (2017)

World total 239 billion tonnes

Al:	Algeria	Ni:	Nigeria
Au:	Australia	No:	Norway
Br:	Brazil	Ru:	Russia
Cn:	China	SA:	Saudi Arabia
Col:	Colombia	S Af:	South Africa
Ge:	Germany	UAE:	United Arab Emirates
In:	Indonesia	Uk:	Ukraine
Iq:	Iraq	USA:	United States of America
Ka:	Kazakhstan		
Li:	Libya	Ve:	Venezuela

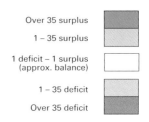

Fossil fuel production

Oilfields — Principal ● Secondary ●
Gasfields — Principal ▽ Secondary ▽
Coalfields — Principal △ Second △

Oil production: Saudi Arabia 13.1%, Russia 12.9%, USA 10.8%, China 5.0%, Canada 4.7%, Iran 4.0%, UAE 4.0%, Iraq 3.9%, Kuwait 3.7%, Mexico 3.4%, Venezuela 3.3%
World total: 4,132,900,000 tonnes

Gas production: USA 20.6%, Russia 17.9%, Iran 4.9%, Qatar 4.7%, Canada 4.6%, Norway 3.2%, Saudi Arabia 3.0%
World total: 3,032,910,000 tonnes of oil equivalent

Coal production: China 47.4%, USA 12.9%, Australia 6.9%, Indonesia 6.7%, India 5.9%, Russia 4.3%, South
World total: 3,881,400,000 tonnes of oil equivalent

GAS RESERVES

World natural gas reserves by region and country, billion tonnes of oil equivalent (2017)

World total 174 billion tonnes of oil equivalent

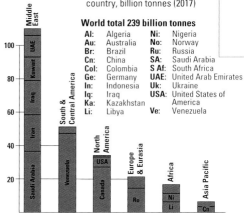

ENERGY PRODUCTION BY REGION

Each symbol represents 1% of world primary energy production

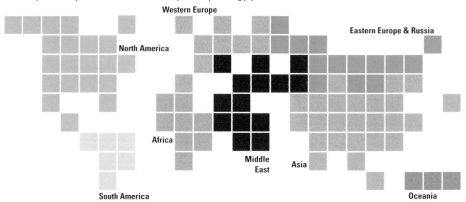

COAL RESERVES

World coal reserves (including lignite) by region and country, billion tonnes (2017)

World total 1,139 billion tonnes

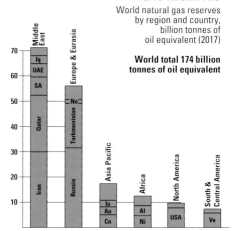

ENERGY CONSUMPTION BY REGION

Each symbol represents 1% of world primary energy consumption

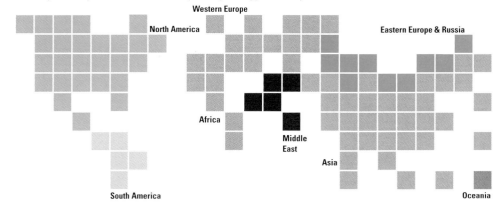

ELECTRICITY GENERATION
Percentage of electricity generated by source (latest available data)

- Over 75% from thermal
- 50 – 75% from thermal
- Over 75% from hydro
- 50 – 75% from hydro
- Over 50% from nuclear
- No dominant source
- No data
- selected geothermal plants ●
- selected hydroelectric plants ◆

WORLD ENERGY CONSUMPTION

Legend: Oil | Gas | Coal | Nuclear | Hydro | Renewables

- Africa
- South and Central America
- Middle East
- North America
- Europe and Eurasia
- Asia Pacific

million tonnes of oil equivalent

Source: BP Statistical Review of World Energy 2018

MINERAL PRODUCTION

Diamonds — Congo (DRI) 30.6%, Russia 29.0%, Australia 22.6%, Botswana 9.7%
World total (2017): 62,000,000 carats

Gold — China 14.0%, Australia 9.5%, Russia 8.1%, USA 7.8%, Canada 5.7%, Peru 4.9%
World total (2017): 3,150,000 kg

Silver — Mexico 22.4%, Peru 18.0%, China 10.0%, Russia 6.4%, Poland 5.6%, Chile 4.8%, Australia 4.8%, Bolivia 4.8%
World total (2017): 25,000 tonnes

Phosphate fertilizer — China 53.2%, USA 10.5%, Morocco 10.3%, Russia 4.8%
World total (2017): 263,000,000 tonnes

Iron ore — Australia 36.7%, Brazil 18.3%, China 14.2%, India 7.9%, Russia 4.2%
World total (2017): 2,400,000,000 tonnes

Copper — Chile 27.1%, Peru 12.1%, China 9.4%, USA 6.4%, Australia 4.7%, Congo (DRI) 4.3%
World total (2017): 19,700,000 tonnes

Lead — China 51.1%, Australia 9.6%, USA 6.7%, Peru 6.4%, Russia 5.3%
World total (2017): 4,700,000 tonnes

Zinc — China 38.6%, Peru 10.6%, India 9.8%, Australia 7.6%, USA 5.5%, Mexico 5.2%
World total (2017): 13,200,000 tonnes

Bauxite — Australia 27.7%, China 22.7%, Guinea 15.0%, Brazil 12.0%, India 9.0%
World total (2017): 300,000,000 tonnes

Nickel ore — Indonesia 19.0%, Philippines 11.0%, Canada 10.0%, New Caledonia 10.0%, Australia 9.0%, Russia 8.6%, Brazil 6.1%, China 4.7%
World total (2017): 2,100,000 tonnes

Chromium — S. Africa 48.4%, Kazakhstan 17.4%, India 10.3%, Turkey 9.0%
World total (2017): 31,000,000 tonnes

Precious metals
- ◇ Diamonds
- ○ Gold
- ◉ Silver

Iron and ferro-alloys
- ◇ Iron ore
- ◇ Nickel ore
- ◇ Chromium

Non-ferrous metals
- ◈ Bauxite
- ◇ Copper
- ◆ Lead
- ◇ Zinc
- △ Phosphates

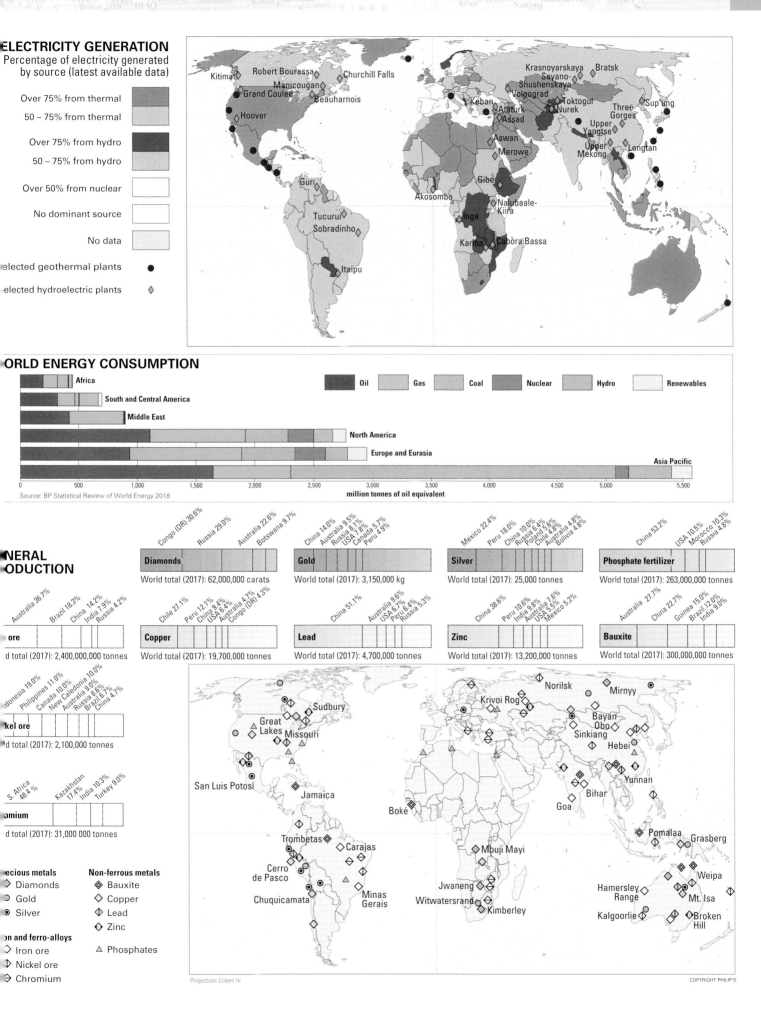

COPYRIGHT PHILIP'S

SHARE OF WORLD TRADE

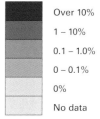

Percentage share of total world exports by value (2017)

- Over 10%
- 1 – 10%
- 0.1 – 1.0%
- 0 – 0.1%
- 0%
- No data

Countries with the largest share of world trade (2017)

China	12.4%	France	3.1%
USA	9.1%	Netherlands	3.0%
Germany	8.1%	Italy	2.9%
Japan	3.9%	UK	2.5%
South Korea	3.2%	Canada	2.5%

MAIN TRADING NATIONS

The imports and exports of the top ten trading nations as a percentage of world trade (2017). Each country's trade in manufactured goods is shown in dark blue.

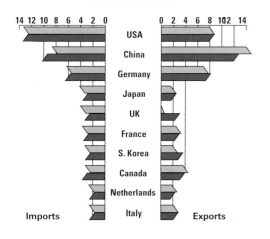

Imports — Exports

USA, China, Germany, Japan, UK, France, S. Korea, Canada, Netherlands, Italy

MAJOR EXPORTS   Leading manufactured items and their exporters

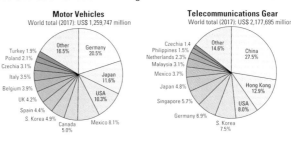

Motor Vehicles
World total (2017): US$ 1,259,747 million
Germany 20.5%, Japan 11.6%, USA 10.3%, Mexico 8.1%, Canada 5.0%, S. Korea 4.9%, Spain 4.4%, UK 4.2%, Belgium 3.9%, Italy 3.5%, Czechia 3.1%, Poland 2.1%, Turkey 1.9%, Other 16.5%

Telecommunications Gear
World total (2017): US$ 2,177,695 million
China 27.5%, Hong Kong 12.9%, USA 8.0%, S. Korea 7.5%, Germany 6.9%, Singapore 5.7%, Japan 4.8%, Mexico 3.7%, Malaysia 3.1%, Netherlands 2.3%, Philippines 1.5%, Czechia 1.4, Other 14.6%

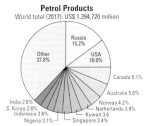

Petrol Products
World total (2017): US$ 1,394,720 million
Russia 15.2%, USA 10.0%, Canada 6.1%, Australia 5.0%, Norway 4.2%, Netherlands 3.9%, Kuwait 3.6, Singapore 3.4%, Nigeria 3.1%, Indonesia 2.6%, S. Korea 2.6%, India 2.6%, Other 37.8%

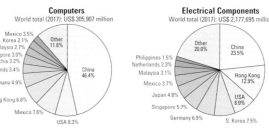

Computers
World total (2017): US$ 305,907 million
China 46.4%, USA 8.3%, Mexico 7.6%, Hong Kong 6.8%, Germany 4.9%, Netherlands 3.4%, Czechia 3.2%, Singapore 3.0%, Malaysia 2.7%, S. Korea 2.1%, Mexico 3.5%, Other 11.6%

Electrical Components
World total (2017): US$ 2,177,695 million
China 23.5%, Hong Kong 12.9%, USA 8.0%, S. Korea 7.5%, Germany 6.9%, Singapore 5.7%, Japan 4.8%, Mexico 3.7%, Malaysia 3.1%, Netherlands 2.3%, Philippines 1.5%, Other 20.0%

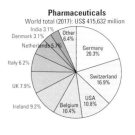

Pharmaceuticals
World total (2017): US$ 415,632 million
Germany 20.3%, Switzerland 16.9%, USA 10.8%, Belgium 10.4%, Ireland 9.2%, UK 7.9%, Italy 6.2%, Netherlands 5.7%, Denmark 3.1%, India 3.1%, Other 6.4%

BALANCE OF TRADE

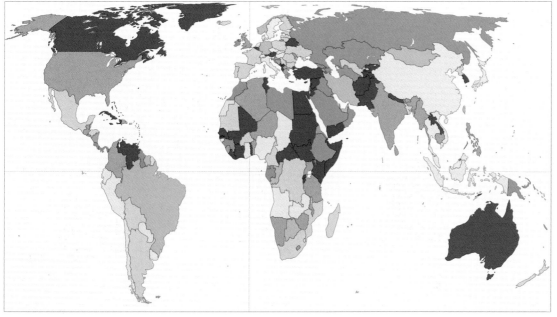

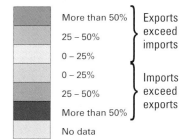

Value of exports in proportion to the value of imports (2017)

- More than 50% } Exports exceed imports
- 25 – 50%
- 0 – 25%
- 0 – 25% } Imports exceed exports
- 25 – 50%
- More than 50%
- No data

The total world trade balance should amount to zero since exports must equal imports on a global scale. In practice, at least $100 billion in exports go unrecorded, leaving the world with an apparent deficit and many countries in a better position than public accounting reveals. However, a favourable trade balance is not necessarily a sign of prosperity: many poorer countries must maintain a high surplus in order to service debt, and do so by restricting imports below the levels needed to sustain successful economies.

INDUSTRY AND TRADE

Manufactured exports as a percentage of total exports (2016)

- Over 75%
- 50 – 75%
- 25 – 50%
- 10 – 25%
- 0 – 10%
- No data

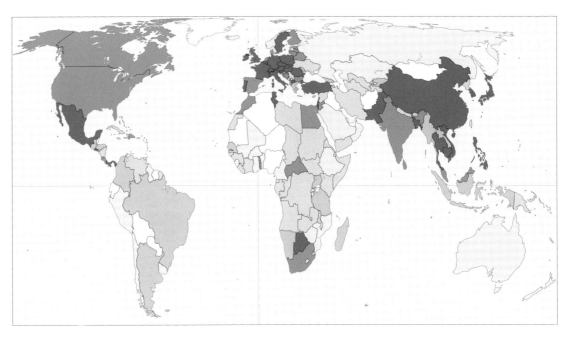

Countries most dependent on the export of manufactured goods (2016)

Botswana	94%
Israel	93%
China	94%
Switzerland	91%
Cambodia	93%
Czechia	90%

MERCHANT FLEETS

Merchant fleets by gross registered tonnage (millions) (2017). Although a large number of vessels are registered in Liberia and Panama, they are not part of the national fleet.

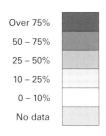

USA
India
South Korea
Bermuda
Indonesia
United Kingdom
Norway
Italy
Denmark
Cyprus
Japan
Greece
China
Bahamas
Malta
Singapore
Hong Kong
Liberia
Marshall Islands
Panama (216)

0 20 30 40 50 60 70 80 90 100 110 120 130 140

Top Ten Container Ports

Total container traffic, in million TEU (2016) ('TEU' stands for Twenty-foot Equivalent Unit, the equivalent of a standard container)

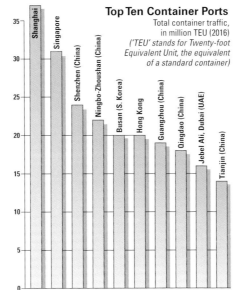

Shanghai
Singapore
Shenzhen (China)
Ningbo-Zhoushan (China)
Busan (S. Korea)
Hong Kong
Guangzhou (China)
Qingdao (China)
Jebel Ali, Dubai (UAE)
Tianjin (China)

Types of Vessels

World fleet by type of vessel (2017)

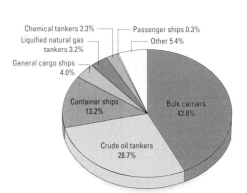

- Chemical tankers 2.3%
- Liquified natural gas tankers 3.2%
- General cargo ships 4.0%
- Container ships 13.2%
- Crude oil tankers 28.7%
- Bulk carriers 42.8%
- Passenger ships 0.3%
- Other 5.4%

SERVICE SECTOR

Percentage of GDP from services (2017)

- Over 70%
- 60 – 70%
- 50 – 60%
- 40 – 50%
- Under 40%
- No data

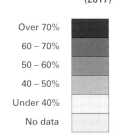

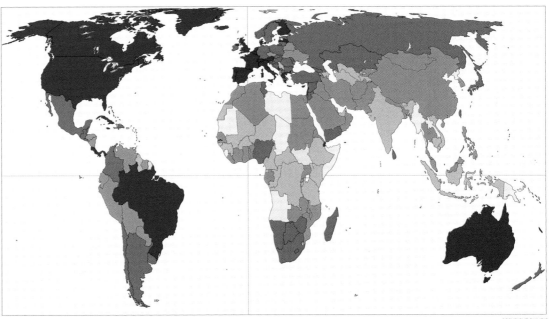

Countries with the highest and lowest percentage of GDP from services (2017)

Highest		Lowest	
Bahamas	90%	Timor-Leste	14%
Malta	88%	Chad	27%
Luxembourg	88%	Angola	28%
Barbados	87%	Somalia	33%
Cyprus	87%	Sierra Leone	33%

Projection: Eckert IV

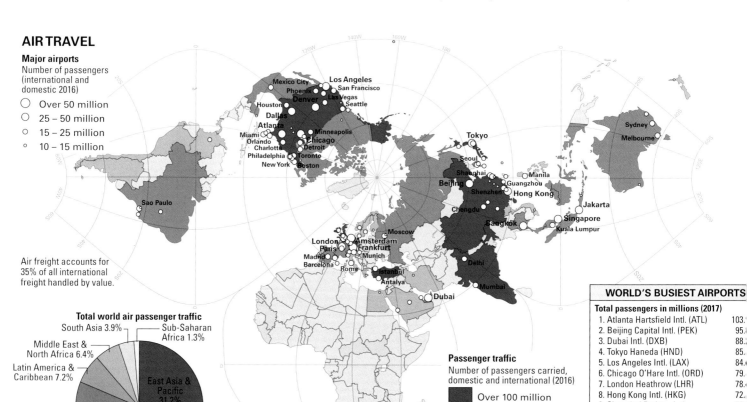

TIME ZONES

Zones using UT (Universal Time)	
Zones behind UT (Universal Time)	
Zones ahead of UT (Universal Time)	
Half-hour zones	
10	Hours behind or ahead of UT (Universal Time)

International boundaries
Time zone boundaries

International Date Line and Prime Meridian

Actual solar time, when it is noon at Greenwich, is shown at the top of the map.

Note: Certain time zones are affected by the incidence of daylight saving time in countries where it is adopted. UT (Universal Time) has replaced GMT (Greenwich Mean T

AIR TRAVEL

Major airports
Number of passengers (international and domestic 2016)

- ◯ Over 50 million
- ◯ 25 – 50 million
- ◦ 15 – 25 million
- ∘ 10 – 15 million

Air freight accounts for 35% of all international freight handled by value.

Total world air passenger traffic

- South Asia 3.9%
- Sub-Saharan Africa 1.3%
- Middle East & North Africa 6.4%
- Latin America & Caribbean 7.2%
- East Asia & Pacific 31.2%
- North America 24.6%
- Europe & Central Asia 25.5%

Total air passenger traffic (2016) 3,696,000,000

Passenger traffic
Number of passengers carried, domestic and international (2016)

- Over 100 million
- 50 – 100 million
- 10 – 50 million
- Under 10 million
- No data available

WORLD'S BUSIEST AIRPORTS

Total passengers in millions (2017)

	Airport	
1.	Atlanta Hartsfield Intl. (ATL)	103.
2.	Beijing Capital Intl. (PEK)	95.
3.	Dubai Intl. (DXB)	88.
4.	Tokyo Haneda (HND)	85.
5.	Los Angeles Intl. (LAX)	84.
6.	Chicago O'Hare Intl. (ORD)	79.
7.	London Heathrow (LHR)	78.
8.	Hong Kong Intl. (HKG)	72.
9.	Shanghai Pudong Intl.	70.
10.	Paris Charles de Gaulle (CDG)	69.

Dubai International handles the most international passengers (83.1 million), followed by London's Heathrow (71.0 million).

Projection: Peirce

UNESCO WORLD HERITAGE SITES 2017

Total sites = 1,073 (832 cultural, 206 natural and 35 mixed)

Region	Cultural sites	Natural sites	Mixed sites
Africa	51	37	5
Arab States	74	5	3
Asia & Pacific	177	64	12
Europe & North America	434	62	10
Latin America & Caribbean	96	38	5

Some sites are trans-boundary, therefore the total figures may not add up

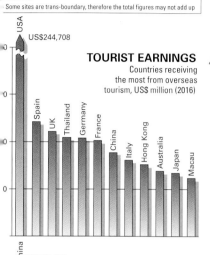

TOURIST EARNINGS

Countries receiving the most from overseas tourism, US$ million (2016)

USA US$244,708

Spain, UK, Thailand, Germany, France, China, Italy, Hong Kong, Australia, Japan, Macau

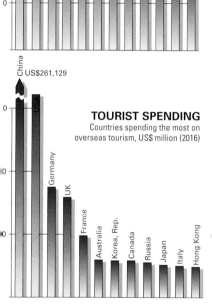

TOURIST SPENDING

Countries spending the most on overseas tourism, US$ million (2016)

China US$261,129

USA, Germany, UK, France, Australia, Korea, Rep., Canada, Russia, Japan, Italy, Hong Kong

Europe at larger scale

Fjords, Saimaa, St. Petersburg, Oland, Edinburgh, Dublin, Copenhagen, London, Amsterdam, Disneyland, Paris, Prague, Brittany, Paris, Vienna, Tatra, Budapest, Lourdes, Alps, Black Sea Coast, Costa Brava, Venice, Florence, Rome, Pyrenees, Lisbon, Barcelona, Côte d'Azur, Istanbul, Algarve, Balearic Islands, Costa del Sol, Costa Blanca, Ionian Islands, Aegean Is., Athens, Crete, Rhodes

Destinations

- ■ Cultural & historical centres
- ☐ Coastal resorts
- ☐ Ski resorts
- ▨ Centres of entertainment
- ▨ Places of pilgrimage
- ▨ Places of great natural beauty
- ☐ Other tourist destinations

Movement of tourists

- ⟶ More than 10 million
- ⟶ 5 – 10 million
- ⟶ 3 – 5 million
- ⟶ Less than 3 million

TOURIST DESTINATIONS

Projection: Peirce

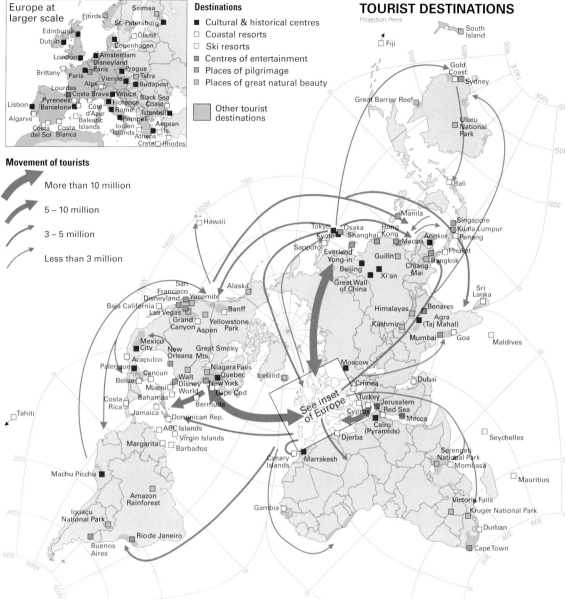

IMPORTANCE OF TOURISM

Tourism receipts as a percentage of Gross National Income (2016)

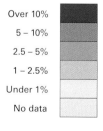

- ■ Over 10%
- ▨ 5 – 10%
- ▨ 2.5 – 5%
- ▨ 1 – 2.5%
- ☐ Under 1%
- ☐ No data

Tourist arrivals in millions (2016)

France	82.6
USA	75.6
Spain	75.6
China	59.3
Italy	52.4
UK	35.8

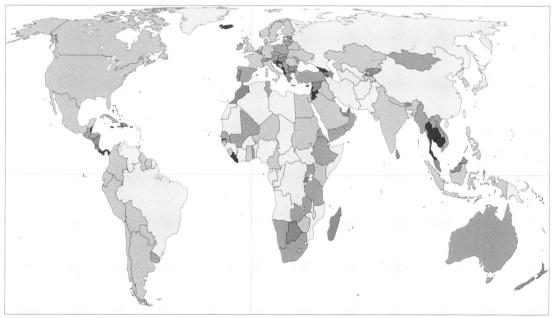

Projection: Eckert IV

WEALTH

The value of total production divided by the population (the Gross National Income per capita in 2017)

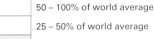

- Over 400% of world average
- 200 – 400% of world average
- 100 – 200% of world average

World average US$10,366

- 50 – 100% of world average
- 25 – 50% of world average
- 10 – 25% of world average
- Under 10% of world average
- No data

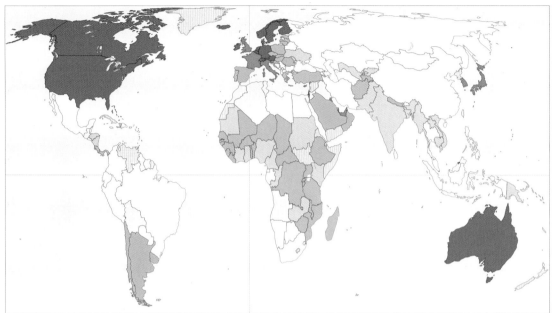

Wealthiest countries		Poorest countries	
Switz.	$80,560	Burundi	$290
Norway	$75,990	Malawi	$320
Lux.	$70,260	Niger	$360

UK $40,530

WATER SUPPLY

The percentage of total population with access to safe drinking water (2015)

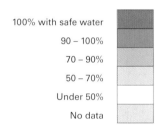

- 100% with safe water
- 90 – 100%
- 70 – 90%
- 50 – 70%
- Under 50%
- No data

Least well-provided countries

Somalia	32%
Papua New Guinea	40%
Equatorial Guinea	48%
Angola	49%

One person in eight in the world has no access to a safe water supply.

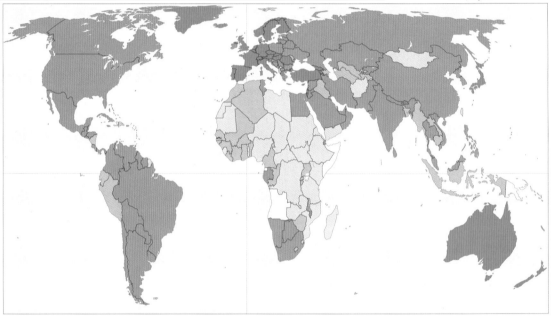

HUMAN DEVELOPMENT INDEX

The Human Development Index (HDI), calculated by the UN Development Programme (UNDP), gives a value to countries using indicators of life expectancy, education and standards of living in 2017 . Higher values show more developed countries.

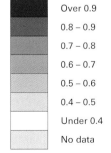

- Over 0.9
- 0.8 – 0.9
- 0.7 – 0.8
- 0.6 – 0.7
- 0.5 – 0.6
- 0.4 – 0.5
- Under 0.4
- No data

Highest values		Lowest values	
Norway	0.953	Niger	0.354
Switzerland	0.944	CAR	0.367
Australia	0.939	South Sudan	0.388

UK 0.922

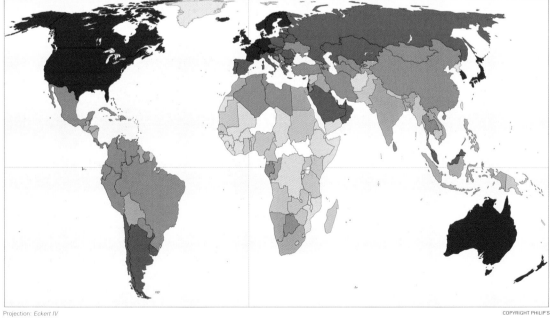

Projection: *Eckert IV*

COPYRIGHT PHILIP'S

HEALTH CARE

Expenditure on health as percantage of GDP (2015)

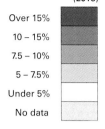

- Over 15%
- 10 – 15%
- 7.5 – 10%
- 5 – 7.5%
- Under 5%
- No data

Countries spending the most and least on health care (% of GDP)

Most		Least	
Marshall Is.	22.1%	Monaco	2.0%
Sierra Leone	18.3%	South Sudan	2.5%
USA	16.8%	Brunei	2.6%
Liberia	15.2%	Bangladesh	2.6%
Tuvalu	15.0%	Pakistan	2.7%
		UK 9.9%	

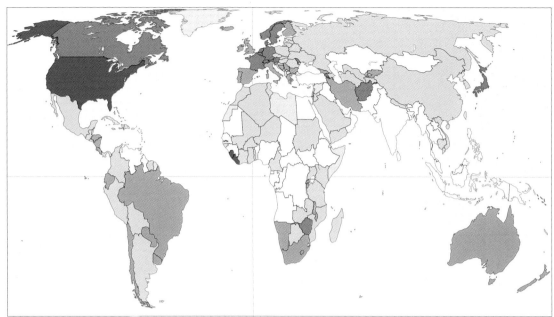

ILLITERACY

Percentage of adult total population unable to read or write (2015)

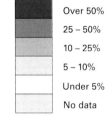

- Over 50%
- 25 – 50%
- 10 – 25%
- 5 – 10%
- Under 5%
- No data

Countries with the highest illiteracy rates (%)

Niger	81	Burkina Faso	64
Chad	78	CAR	63
South Sudan	73	Afghanistan	62
Guinea	70	Benin	62
Mali	67	Liberia	52

GENDER INEQUALITY INDEX

The Gender Inequality Index (GII) is a composite measure reflecting inequality in achievements between women and men in three categories: reproductive health, empowerment and the labour market. It varies between 0, when women and men fare equally, and 1, when women or men fare poorly compared to the other in all categories (2017).

- Over 0.65
- 0.5 – 0.65
- 0.25 – 0.5
- Under 0.25
- No data

Most equal		Least equal	
Switzerland	0.039	Yemen	0.835
Denmark	0.040	PNG	0.741
Sweden	0.044	Chad	0.708
		UK 0.116	

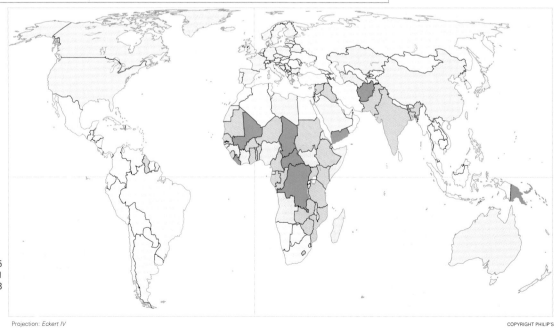

Projection: *Eckert IV*

AGE DISTRIBUTION PYRAMIDS

The bars represent the percentage of the total population (males plus females) in each age group. More Economically Developed Countries (MEDCs), such as New Zealand, have populations spread evenly across age groups and usually a growing percentage of elderly people. Less Economically Developed Countries (LEDCs), such as Kenya, have the great majority of their people in the younger age groups, about to enter their most fertile years.

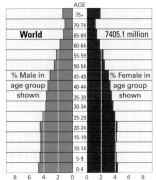

World — 7405.1 million

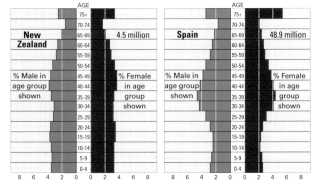

New Zealand — 4.5 million

Spain — 48.9 million

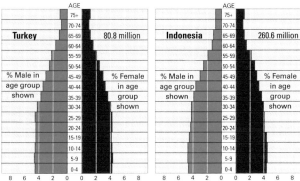

Turkey — 80.8 million

Indonesia — 260.6 million

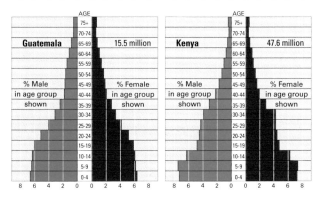

Guatemala — 15.5 million

Kenya — 47.6 million

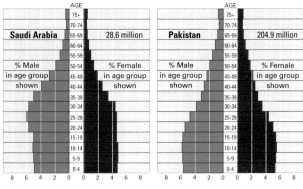

Saudi Arabia — 28.6 million

Pakistan — 204.9 million

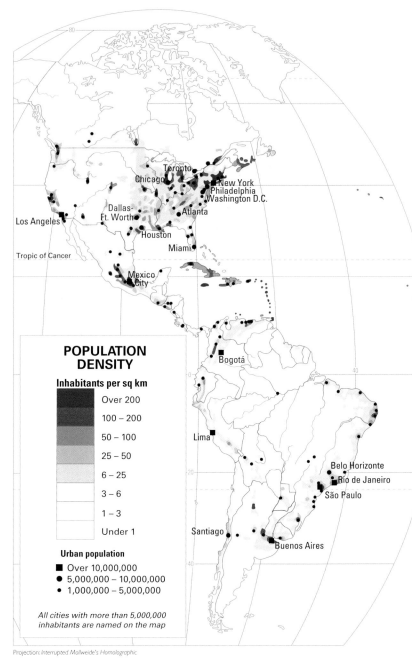

POPULATION DENSITY

Inhabitants per sq km

- Over 200
- 100 – 200
- 50 – 100
- 25 – 50
- 6 – 25
- 3 – 6
- 1 – 3
- Under 1

Urban population

- ■ Over 10,000,000
- ● 5,000,000 – 10,000,000
- • 1,000,000 – 5,000,000

All cities with more than 5,000,000 inhabitants are named on the map

Projection: *Interrupted Mollweide's Homolographic*

POPULATION CHANGE 1930–2020   Population totals are in millions

Figures in italics represent the percentage average annual increase for the period shown

	1930	1930–1960	1960	1960–1990	1990	1990–2020	2020
World	2,013	*1.4%*	3,019	*1.9%*	5,292	*1.2%*	7,631
Africa	155	*2.0%*	281	*2.9%*	648	*2.5%*	1,286
North America	135	*1.3%*	199	*1.1%*	276	*1.0%*	370
Latin America*	129	*1.8%*	218	*2.4%*	448	*1.3%*	647
Asia	1,073	*1.5%*	1,669	*2.1%*	3,108	*1.3%*	4,542
Europe	355	*0.6%*	425	*0.6%*	508	*0.3%*	549
Oceania	10	*1.4%*	16	*1.8%*	27	*1.3%*	39
CIS†	176	*0.7%*	214	*1.0%*	281	*0.1%*	285

* South America plus Central America, Mexico and the West Indies
† Commonwealth of Independent States, formerly the USSR

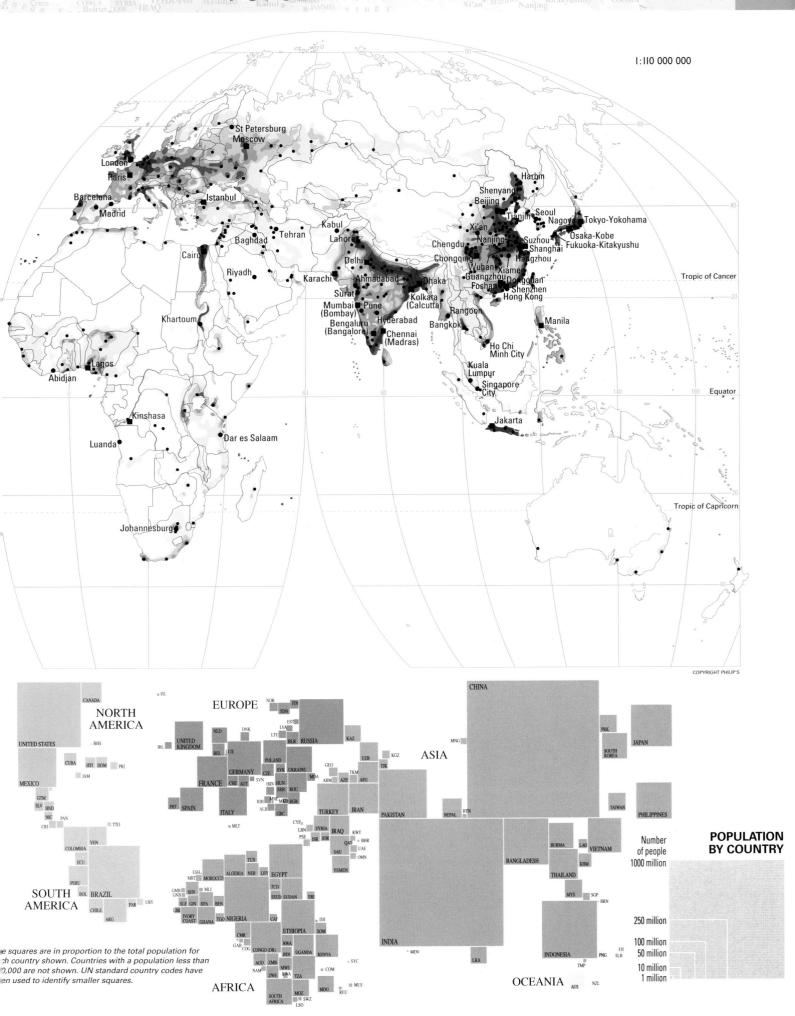

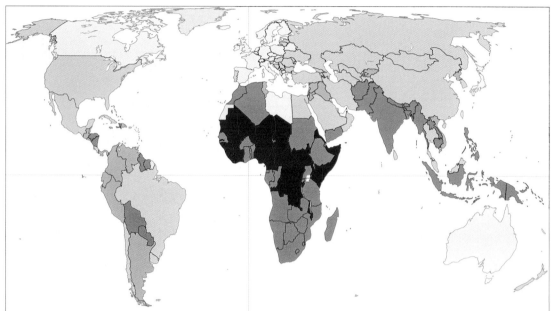

MATERNAL MORTALITY

The number of mothers who died
per 100,000 live births (2015)

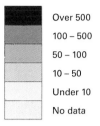

■	Over 500
■	100 – 500
■	50 – 100
▨	10 – 50
□	Under 10
□	No data

Countries with the highest and lowest
maternal mortality

Highest		Lowest	
Sierra Leone	1,360	Greece	3
CAR	882	Poland	3
Chad	856	Iceland	3
Nigeria	814	Finland	3
South Sudan	789	Italy	4

UK 9 mothers

POPULATION CHANGE

The projected population change
for the years 2004–2050

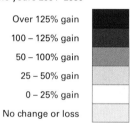

Over 125% gain	■
100 – 125% gain	■
50 – 100% gain	■
25 – 50% gain	▨
0 – 25% gain	□
No change or loss	□

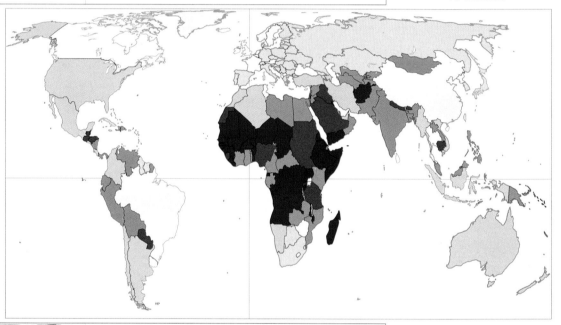

Based on estimates for the year 2050,
the ten most populous nations in the
world will be, in millions:

India	1,657	Pakistan	291
China	1,304	Bangladesh	250
USA	400	Brazil	232
Indonesia	300	Ethiopia	228
Nigeria	391	Philippines	172

UK (2050) 71 million

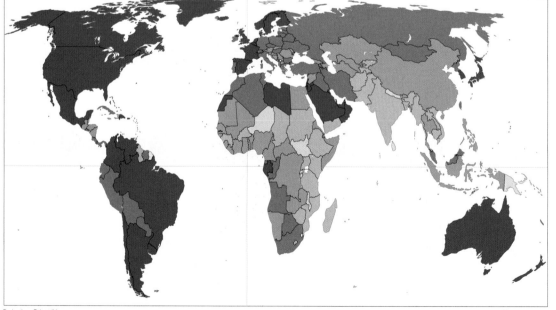

URBAN POPULATION

Percentage of total population
living in towns and cities (2018)

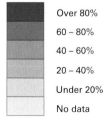

■	Over 80%
■	60 – 80%
■	40 – 60%
▨	20 – 40%
□	Under 20%
□	No data

Countries that are the most
and least urbanized (%)

Most urbanized		Least urbanized	
Singapore	100	Burundi	13
Kuwait	100	Papua New Guinea	13
Monaco	100	Niger	16

UK 83% urban

*In 2008, for the first time in history,
more than half the world's population
lived in urban areas.*

Projection: *Eckert IV*

COPYRIGHT PHILIP'S

INFANT MORTALITY

Number of babies who died under the age of one, per 1,000 live births
(2017)

Over 75	
50 – 75	
25 – 50	
10 – 25	
Under 10	
No data	

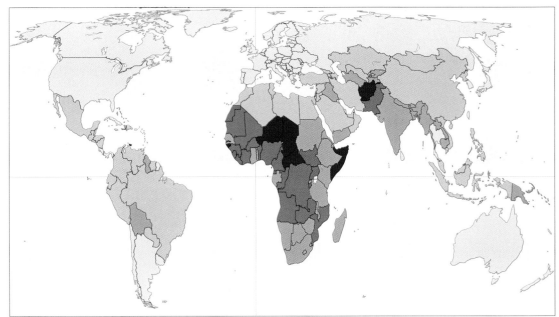

Countries with the highest and lowest child mortality

Highest		Lowest	
Afghanistan	111	Monaco	1.8
Somalia	95	Japan	2.0
CAR	86	Norway	2.1

UK 4 babies

LIFE EXPECTANCY

The average expected lifespan of babies born in 2017

Over 80	
70 – 80	
60 – 70	
Under 60	
No data	

Countries with the highest and lowest life expectancy at birth in years

Highest		Lowest	
Monaco	89	Chad	50
Japan	85	Guinea-Bissau	51
Singapore	85	Afghanistan	52
Iceland	83	Gabon	52
Switzerland	83	Eswatini	52

UK 81 years

FAMILY SIZE

Children born per woman (2017)

More than 5	
4 – 5	
3 – 4	
2 – 3	
Less than 2	
No data	

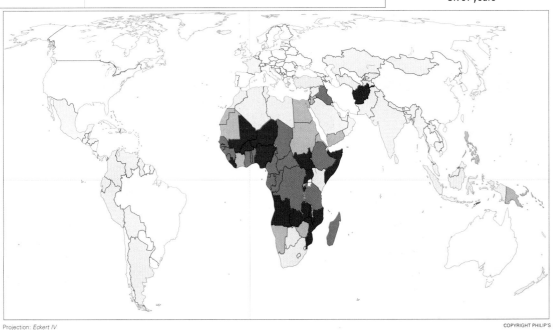

Countries with the largest and smallest family size

Largest		Smallest	
Niger	6.5	Singapore	0.8
Angola	6.2	Taiwan	1.1
Mali	6.0	South Korea	1.3
Burundi	6.0	Bosnia-Herz.	1.3
Somalia	5.8	Romania	1.4

UK 1.9 children

Projection: *Eckert IV*

COPYRIGHT PHILIP'S

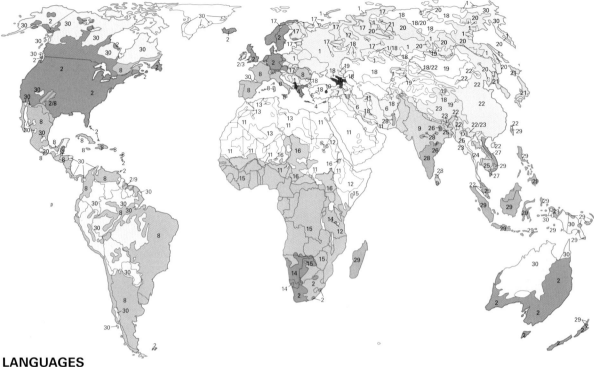

Languages of the World

Language can be classified by ancestry and structure. For example, the Romance and Germanic groups are both derived from an Indo-European language believed to have been spoken 5,000 years ago.

First-language speakers in millions

Mandarin Chinese 850, Spanish 430, English 340, Hindi 260, Arabic 240, Portuguese 215, Bengali 190, Russian 160, Japanese 130, Javanese 84, French 80, German 78, Wu Chinese 77, Korean 77, Telugu 74, Marathi Tamil 69, Vietnamese 68, Italian 64, Punjabi 63.

Distribution of living languages

The figures refer to the number of languages currently in use in the regions shown

Asia 2,303
Africa 2,146
Pacific 1,312
The Americas 1,060
Europe 285

LANGUAGES

INDO-EUROPEAN FAMILY

1	Balto-Slavic group (incl. Russian, Ukrainian)
2	Germanic group (incl. English, German)
3	Celtic group
4	Greek
8	Albanian
6	Iranian group
7	Armenian
8	Romance group (incl. Spanish, Portuguese, French, Italian)
9	Indo-Aryan group (incl. Hindi, Bengali, Urdu, Punjabi, Marathi)
10	CAUCASIAN FAMILY

AFRO-ASIATIC FAMILY

111	Semitic group (incl. Arabic)
21	Kushitic group
3	Berber group
14	KHOISAN FAMILY
15	NIGER-CONGO FAMILY
16	NILO-SAHARAN FAMILY
17	URALIC FAMILY

ALTAIC FAMILY

181	Turkic group (incl. Turkish)
92	Mongolian group
02	Tungus-Manchu group
1	Japanese and Korean

SINO-TIBETAN FAMILY

22	Sinitic (Chinese) languages (incl. Mandarin, Wu, Yue)
23	Tibetic-Burmic languages
24	TAI FAMILY

AUSTRO-ASIATIC FAMILY

25	Mon-Khmer group
26	Munda group
27	Vietnamese
28	DRAVIDIAN FAMILY (incl. Telugu, Tamil)
29	AUSTRONESIAN FAMILY (incl. Malay-Indonesian, Javanese)
30	OTHER LANGUAGES

RELIGIONS

- ▲ Roman Catholicism
- Orthodox and other Eastern Churches
- • Protestantism
- Sunni Islam
- Shiite Islam
- Buddhism
- Hinduism
- Confucianism
- ✱ Judaism
- Shintoism
- Tribal Religions

Religious Adherents

Religious adherents in millions

Christianity	2,000	Hinduism	900
Roman Catholic	*1,500*	Chinese folk	394
Orthodox	*225*	Buddhism	360
Anglican	*70*	Sikhism	23
Lutheran	*66*	Taoism	20
Methodist	*8*	Judaism	14
Others	*131*	Mormonism	12
Islam	1,300	Spiritualism	11
Sunni	*940*	Baha'i	6
Shi'ite	*120*	Confucianism	5
Others	*240*	Jainism	4
Non-religious/ Agnostic/Atheist	1,100	Shintoism	4

United Nations

Created in 1945 to promote peace and co-operation, and based in New York, the United Nations is the world's largest international organization, with 193 members and a budget for 2018–19 of US \$5.4 billion. Each member of the General Assembly has one vote, while the five permanent members of the 15-nation Security Council – China, France, Russia, the UK and the USA – hold a veto. The Secretariat is the UN's principal administrative arm. The 54 members of the Economic and Social Council are responsible for economic, social, cultural, educational, health and related matters. The UN has 16 specialized agencies – based in Canada, France, Switzerland and Italy, as well as the USA – which help members in fields such as education (UNESCO), agriculture (FAO), medicine (WHO) and finance (IFC). By the end of 1994, all the original 11 trust territories of the Trusteeship Council had become independent.

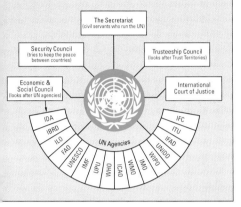

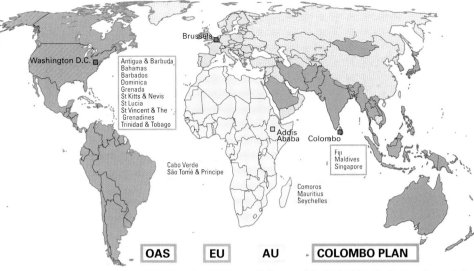

OAS EU AU COLOMBO PLAN

AU The African Union was set up in 2002, taking over from the Organization of African Unity (1963). It has 55 members. Working languages are Arabic, English, French and Portuguese.

COLOMBO PLAN (formed in 1951) Its 27 members aim to promote economic and social development in Asia and the Pacific.

OAS Organization of American States (formed in 1948). It aims to promote social and economic co-operation between countries in the developed North America and developing Latin America.

EU European Union (evolved from the European Community in 1993). Cyprus, Czechia, Estonia, Hungary, Latvia, Lithuania, Malta, Poland, Slovakia and Slovenia joined the EU in May 2004, Bulgaria and Romania joined in 2007,Croatia joined in 2013. The other 15 members of the EU are Austria, Belgium, Denmark, Finland, France, Germany, Greece,Ireland, Italy, Luxembourg, Netherlands, Portugal, Spain, Sweden and the UK. Together, the 28 members aim to integrate economies, co-ordinate social developments and bring about political union. Its member states have set up common institutions to which they delegate some of their sovereignty so that decisions on specific matters of joint interest can be made democratically at European level. The UK is scheduled to leave the EU in 2019.

ACP African-Caribbean-Pacific (formed in 1963). Members enjoy economic ties with the EU.

APEC Asia-Pacific Economic Co-operation (formed in 1989). It aims to enhance economic growth and prosperity for the region and to strengthen the Asia-Pacific community. APEC is the only intergovernmental grouping in the world operating on the basis of non-binding commitments, open dialogue, and equal respect for the views of all participants. There are 21 member economies.

G7 Group of seven leading industrialized nations, comprising Canada, France, Germany, Italy, Japan, the UK and the USA. Periodic meetings are held to discuss major world issues, such as world recessions.

OECD Organization for Economic Co-operation and Development (formed in 1961). It comprises 35 major free-market economies. The 'G7' is its 'inner group' of leading industrial nations, comprising Canada, France, Germany, Italy, Japan, the UK and the USA.

OPEC Organization of Petroleum Exporting Countries (formed in 1960). It controls about three-quarters of the world's oil supply. Gabon rejoined in 2016.

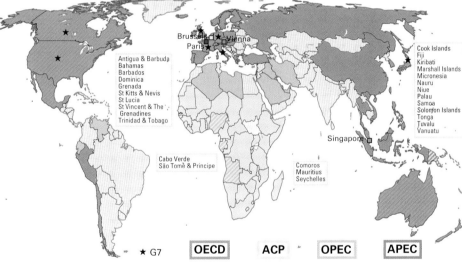

★ G7 OECD ACP OPEC APEC

ARAB LEAGUE (1945) Aims to promote economic, social, political and military co-operation. There are 22 member nations.

ASEAN Association of South-east Asian Nations (formed in 1967). Cambodia joined in 1999.

BRICS This acronym refers to the five largest and fastest growing developing economies, Brazil, Russia, India, China and South Africa.

COMMONWEALTH The Commonwealth of Nations evolved from the British Empire. Pakistan was suspended in 1999, but reinstated in 2004. Zimbabwe was suspended in 2002 and, in response to its continued suspension, left the Commonwealth in 2003. Rwanda joined the Commonwealth in 2009, as the 54th member state, becoming only the second country which was not formerly a British colony to be admitted to the group. The Gambia left in 2013.

LAIA The Latin American Integration Association (formed in 1980) superceded the Latin American Free Trade Association formed in 1961. Its aim is to promote freer regional trade.

NATO North Atlantic Treaty Organization (formed in 1949). It continues despite the winding-up of the Warsaw Pact in 1991. Bulgaria, Estonia, Latvia, Lithuania, Romania, Slovakia and Slovenia became members in 2004 and Albania and Croatia in 2009. Montenegro joined in 2017.

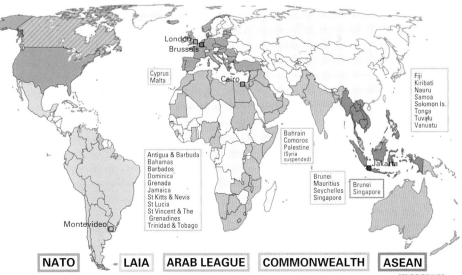

NATO LAIA ARAB LEAGUE COMMONWEALTH ASEAN

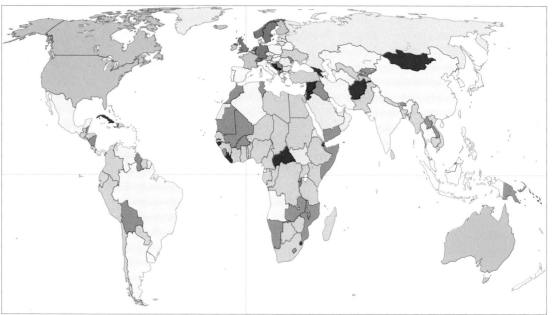

INTERNATIONAL AID

Official Development Assistance (OD,
provided & received, per capita (2016

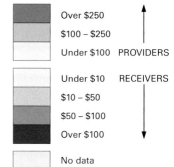

Over $250	
$100 – $250	
Under $100	PROVIDERS
Under $10	RECEIVERS
$10 – $50	
$50 – $100	
Over $100	
No data	

MONEY SENT HOME BY MIGRANTS

Remittances as a percentage
share of GDP (2016)

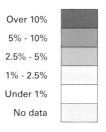

Over 10%	
5% - 10%	
2.5% - 5%	
1% - 2.5%	
Under 1%	
No data	

Most money sent home

Nepal	31.3%	Moldova	21.7%
Kyrgyzstan	30.5%	The Gambia	21.5%
Haiti	29.4%	Comoros	21.2%
Tajikistan	26.9%	Tonga	20.0%
Liberia	26.1%	Honduras	18.0%

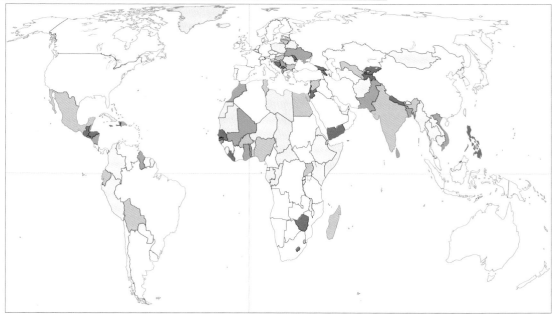

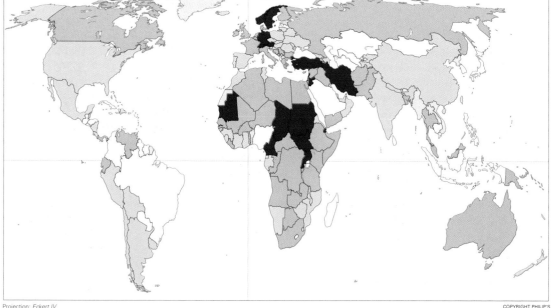

REFUGEES

Total refugees* as a percentage
of the population (2017)

Over 1%	
0.10% - 1%	
0.01% - 0.10%	
Under 0.01%	
No data	

*includes people in a refugee-like
situation

Largest percentage of refugees

Lebanon	16.1%	Sweden	2.4%
Jordan	6.8%	Djibouti	2.1%
Turkey	4.0%	South Sudan	2.1%
Chad	3.3%	Mauritania	2.1%
Uganda	3.2%	Malta	2.0%

Projection: *Eckert IV*

ARMED CONFLICTS

Current military and civilian deaths
countries with conflict, per year (2017)

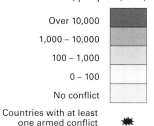

- Over 10,000
- 1,000 – 10,000
- 100 – 1,000
- 0 – 100
- No conflict

Countries with at least
one armed conflict
between 1994 and 2017

Leading arms exporting countries (US $ million)		Leading recipients of arms deliveries (US $ million)	
USA	$12,394	Saudi Arabia	$4,111
Russia	$6,148	India	$3,358
France	$2,163	Egypt	$2,355
Germany	$1,653	Australia	$1,806
Israel	$1,263	China	$1,117

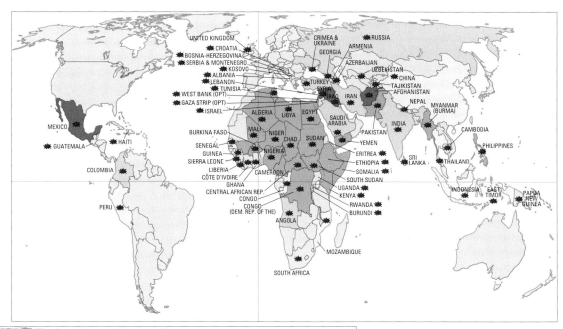

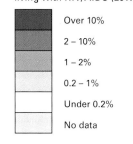

SPREAD OF HIV/AIDS

Percentage of the population
living with HIV/AIDS (2017)

- Over 10%
- 2 – 10%
- 1 – 2%
- 0.2 – 1%
- Under 0.2%
- No data

Caribbean 310,000 — Total number of adults and children living with HIV/AIDS by region (2017)

Human Immunodeficiency Virus (HIV) is passed
from one person to another and attacks the
body's defence against illness. It develops into
the Acquired Immunodeficiency Syndrome
(AIDS) when a particularly severe illness, such as
cancer, takes hold. The pandemic started about
30 years ago and by 2017 37 millon people were
living with HIV or AIDS.

TRAFFIC IN DRUGS

Countries producing illegal drugs

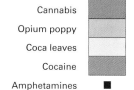

- Cannabis
- Opium poppy
- Coca leaves
- Cocaine
- Amphetamines ■

Major routes of drug trafficking

- Opium
- Coca leaves
- Cocaine
- Heroin
- Cannabis
- Amphetamines (usually used within producing countries)
- Conflicts relating to drug trafficking

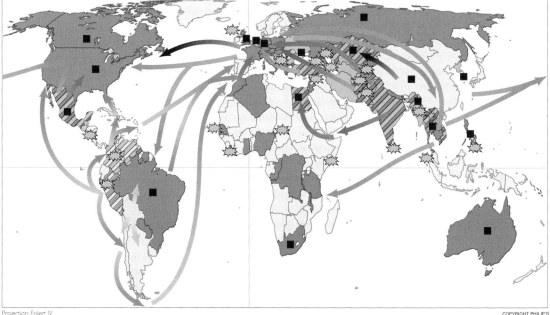

Projection: Eckert IV

	POPULATION						WEALTH						TRADE		
	Total population (millions 2017)	Population density (persons per km², 2017)	Population change (average annual % 2017)	Birth rate (births per thousand people 2017)	Death rate (deaths per thousand people 2017)	Urban population (% of total 2018)	Gross National income (million US$ 2017)	Gross National Income per capita (PPP US$ 2017)	GDP growth rate (percentage 2017)	GDP from agriculture (% of GDP 2017)	GDP from industry (% of GDP 2017)	GDP from services (% of GDP 2017)	Imports (% of GDP 2017)	Exports (% of GDP 2017)	Tourism receipts (US$ per capita 2016)
Afghanistan	34.1	52	2.4	38	13	26	20,182	2,000	2.5	23.0	21.1	55.9	–	–	0
Albania	3.0	106	0.3	13	7	60	12,416	12,120	3.9	22.6	23.8	53.7	47	32	15
Algeria	41.0	17	1.7	22	4	73	163,519	15,050	2.0	13.2	36.1	50.7	36	24	0
Angola	19.1	23.9	3.5	44	9	66	99,112	6,060	0.7	10.2	61.4	28.4	28	30	0
Argentina	44.3	16	0.9	17	7	92	577,147	20,270	2.9	10.9	28.2	60.9	14	11	
Armenia	3.0	102	–0.2	13	9	63	11,713	10,060	7.5	17.7	27.8	54.5	50	38	2
Australia	23.2	3	1.0	12	7	86	1,263,489	47,160	2.3	3.6	26.1	70.4	21	21	2
Austria	8.8	104	0.4	9	10	58	400,262	52,500	2.9	1.2	28.4	69.8	51	54	2
Azerbaijan	10.0	115	0.9	16	7	56	40,203	16,650	0.1	6.2	49.1	44.7	42	49	6
Bahamas	0.3	24	0.8	15	7	83	11,533	29,790	1.3	2.3	7.7	90.0	42	33	25
Bahrain	1.4	2,045	2.3	13	3	89	30,211	42,930	3.2	0.3	38.2	61.5	–	–	6
Bangladesh	157.8	1,096	1.0	19	5	37	242,753	4,040	7.1	14.2	29.2	56.5	20	15	0
Barbados	0.3	679	0.3	12	8	31	4,439	17,830	0.9	1.3	4.8	93.8	44	37	–
Belarus	9.5	46	–0.2	10	13	79	50,223	18,140	2.4	8.3	40.6	51.1	67	67	1
Belgium	11.5	377	0.7	11	10	98	475,204	48,240	1.7	0.7	21.8	77.5	84	85	2
Belize	0.4	16	1.8	24	6	46	1,643	7,890	0.8	9.7	13.8	62.2	61	52	24
Benin	11.0	98	2.7	35	8	47	8,981	2,260	5.6	25.6	23.1	51.3	48	31	–
Bhutan	0.8	16	1.1	17	6	41	2,200	8,850	6.0	15.7	42.6	41.7	48	26	8
Bolivia	11.1	10	1.5	22	6	69	34568	7,330	4.2	13.0	37.4	50.0	32	25	2
Bosnia-Herzegovina	3.9	75	–0.2	9	10	48	17,311	12,880	2.7	7.8	26.8	65.4	51	36	4
Botswana	2.2	4	1.5	22	10	69	15,625	16,990	2.2	1.7	29.2	69.1	–	–	7
Brazil	207.4	24	0.7	14	7	87	1,796,487	15,160	1.0	6.2	21.0	72.8	12	13	2
Brunei	0.4	77	1.6	17	4	78	12,684	83,760	0.5	1.2	56.6	42.3	37	50	0
Bulgaria	7.1	64	–0.6	9	14	75	54,875	20,500	3.6	4.3	28.0	67.7	65	66	2
Burkina Faso	20.1	63	3.1	41	11	29	11,695	1,810	6.4	31.9	22.0	46.1	34	50	1
Burundi	11.5	412	3.0	41	9	13	3,119	770	0.0	40.0	16.0	44.1	–	–	0
Cabo Verde	0.6	140	1.3	20	6	66	1,633	6,570	4.0	7.9	17.9	74.2	64	39	25
Cambodia	16.2	90	1.5	23	8	23	19,729	3,760	6.9	25.3	32.8	41.9	22	61	19
Cameroon	25.0	53	2.6	35	10	56	32,744	3,640	3.2	23.1	28.0	48.9	20	17	0
Canada	35.6	4	0.7	10	9	81	1,573,429	46,070	3.0	1.7	28.1	70.2	33	31	2
Central African Rep.	5.6	9	2.1	34	13	41	1,805	730	4.0	42.9	15.9	41.2	31	13	0
Chad	12.1	9	1.9	36	14	23	9,407	1,920	–3.1	59.0	14.1	27.0	40	34	0
Chile	17.8	23	0.8	14	6	88	245,748	23,670	1.5	4.4	31.4	63.3	27	29	1
China	1,379.3	144	0.4	12	8	59	12,042,906	16,760	6.9	8.3	39.5	52.2	18	20	2
Colombia	47.7	42	1.0	16	5	81	286,066	14,170	1.8	7.4	31.3	61.4	20	15	1
Comoros	0.8	367	1.6	26	7	29	618	1,570	2.5	49.5	11.8	38.7	44	18	2
Congo	5.0	14	2.1	34	10	67	7,170	4,880	–4.6	8.9	50.8	40.3	59	80	0
Congo (Dem. Rep.)	83.3	36	2.4	34	10	45	36,525	870	3.4	21.1	33.0	45.9	39	36	0
Costa Rica	4.9	96	1.1	16	5	79	54,145	16,100	3.2	5.5	21.0	73.5	39	34	6
Côte d'Ivoire	24.2	75	1.8	28	9	51	37,488	3,820	7.8	17.4	28.8	53.8	19	29	0
Croatia	4.3	76	–0.5	9	12	57	51,289	24,700	2.8	3.3	34.3	62.9	49	51	19
Cuba	11.1	100	–0.3	11	9	77			1.6	3.9	21.5	74.2	–	–	
Cyprus	1.2	131	1.1	11	7	67	20,351	33,610	3.9	2.3	11.0	86.8	68	64	17
Czechia	10.7	135	0.1	9	10	74	192,337	34,450	4.3	2.5	37.8	59.7	72	79	1
Denmark	5.6	130	0.2	10	10	88	318,623	52,390	2.1	1.1	23.7	75.2	48	55	1
Djibouti	0.9	37	2.1	23	8	77	1,789	–	6.7	2.8	21.0	76.1	75	34	–
Dominican Republic	10.7	221	1.1	18	5	81	71,428	15,290	4.6	5.5	33.8	60.8	28	25	5
Ecuador	16.3	57	1.3	18	5	64	97,842	11,350	2.7	7.7	35.2	56.9	21	21	1
Egypt	97.0	97	1.5	30	5	43	293,380	11,360	4.2	11.9	33.1	55.7	28	16	1
El Salvador	6.2	294	0.3	16	6	72	22,723	7,540	2.4	10.6	24.6	64.9	45	27	1
Equatorial Guinea	0.8	28	2.4	32	8	72	8,947	19,380	–4.4	2.5	56.5	41.0	38	57	0
Eritrea	5.9	50	0.9	30	7	40	–	–	5.0	11.7	29.6	58.7	–	–	0
Estonia	1.3	28	–0.6	10	13	69	23,923	31,100	4.9	3.4	27.8	68.8	74	78	12
Eswatini	1.5	84	1.1	24	13	–	4,050	–	0.2	6.5	45.0	48.6	–	–	1
Ethiopia	105.4	95	2.9	37	8	21	77,341	1,890	10.9	35.8	22.2	42.0	24	8	1
Fiji	0.9	50	0.7	19	6	57	4,501	9,090	3.8	10.6	17.9	71.5	–	–	23
Finland	5.5	16	0.4	11	10	85	245,678	45,400	3.0	2.7	27.8	69.5	22	39	1
France	67.1	122	0.4	12	9	80	2,548,256	37,580	1.8	2.0	21.1	77.9	13	31	2
Gabon	1.8	7	1.9	34	13	89	113,385	17,010	0.8	4.5	44.0	51.5	27	44	0
Gambia, The	2.1	182	2.0	29	7	61	946	1,670	3.5	20.4	14.2	65.4	40	21	1
Gaza Strip (OPT)*	1.8	4,986	2.3	31	3	76	–	–	–15.2	3.0	21.1	75.0	–	–	
Georgia	4.9	71	–0.0	12	11	59	14,080	10,120	4.8	9.6	23.4	66.2	62	50	19
Germany	80.6	226	–0.2	9	12	77	3,596,609	44,540	2.5	0.6	30.1	69.3	40	47	2
Ghana	27.5	115	2.2	31	7	56	42,919	4,490	8.4	18.3	24.5	57.2	51	40	0
Greece	10.8	82	–0.1	8	11	79	194,658	27,620	1.4	4.0	16.0	80.0	16	33	1

	ENERGY		LAND & AGRICULTURE					SOCIAL INDICATORS							
	Energy consumed (% of world total 2017)	Renewable energy consumption (% of world total 2017)	CO_2 emissions (tonnes per capita 2015)	Land area (thousand km²)	Arable and Permanent crops (% of land area)	Permanent pasture (% of land area)	Forest (% of land area)	Human Development Index (HDI) value 2017	Life expectancy (years 2014)	Level of obesity (% of adults 2016)	Adults living with HIV/AIDS (percentage 2017)	Gender Inequality Index (GII value 2017)	Adult illiteracy rate (percentage 2016)	Passenger cars (per thousand people 2017)	Internet users (% of population 2017)
ghanistan	–	–	0.68	652	21	79	2	0.498	52	5.5	–1.0	0.635	68	28	15.7
bania	–	–	1.42	28.7	59	40	28	0.785	78	21.7	0.1	0.238	3	124	65.8
geria	0.4	–	3.55	2,382	20	79	1	0.754	77	27.4	0.1	0.442	25	114	44.2
gola	–	–	1.67	1,247	9	79	47	0.581	60	8.2	1.9	–	34	38	19.3
gentina	0.6	0.1	4.36	2,780	17	39	11	0.825	78	28.3	0.4	0.358	2	314	93.1
menia	–	–	1.74	29.8	18	42	9	0.755	75	20.2	0.2	0.262	0	167	72.5
stralia	1.0	1.2	16.32	7,741	12	88	16	0.939	82	29.0	0.1	0.109	–	717	87.8
stria	0.3	0.6	7.24	83.9	17	21	47	0.908	82	20.1	0.1	0.071	–	578	87.9
erbaijan	0.1	–	3.85	86.6	25	32	11	0.757	73	19.9	0.1	0.318	0	101	80.6
hamas	–	–	10.74	13.9	1	0	51	0.807	73	31.6	1.9	0.340	–	–	83.4
hrain	–	–	27.41	0.69	6	5	1	0.846	79	29.8	0.1	0.222	5	379	98.0
ngladesh	0.2	–	0.42	144	65	5	11	0.608	73	3.6	0.1	0.542	27	3	48.4
rbados	–	–	6.69	0.43	28	5	19	0.800	75	23.1	1.6	0.284	–	469	79.9
larus	0.2	–	6.03	208	28	16	43	0.808	73	24.5	0.4	0.130	0	362	71.7
lgium	0.5	0.7	11.94	30.5	28	16	22	0.916	81	22.1	–1.0	0.048	–	559	94.4
lize	–	–	1.44	23	5	2	61	0.708	69	24.1	1.9	0.386	–	174	52.3
nin	–	–	0.58	113	26	5	40	0.515	62	9.6	1.0	0.611	67	22	33.1
utan	–	–	0.70	47	4	11	85	0.612	71	6.4	–1.0	0.476	43	57	45.3
livia	–	–	1.55	1,099	4	30	52	0.693	69	20.2	0.3	0.450	7	68	78.6
snia-Herzegovina	–	–	1.28	51.2	21	20	43	0.768	77	17.9	–1.0	0.166	3	214	80.7
tswana	–	–	2.65	582	0	45	20	0.717	63	18.9	22.8	0.434	–	113	39.6
azil	2.2	4.6	2.65	8,514	9	23	62	0.757	74	22.1	0.6	0.407	8	249	70.7
unei	–	–	22.76	5.8	2	1	72	0.852	77	14.1	–1.0	0.236	4	510	–
lgaria	–	–	7.53	111	31	16	38	0.813	74	25.0	0.1	0.217	2	443	66.3
rkina Faso	–	–	0.17	274	21	22	21	0.432	56	5.6	0.8	0.610	65	12	18.8
rundi	–	–	0.02	27.8	55	19	7	0.417	61	5.4	1.1	0.471	38	6	5.5
bo Verde	–	–	1.59	4	12	6	21	0.654	72	11.8	0.6	–	13	101	48.1
mbodia	–	–	0.30	181	24	9	51	0.582	65	3.9	0.5	0.473	26	21	49.3
meroon	–	–	0.41	475	15	4	41	0.556	59	11.4	3.7	0.569	28	14	0.0
nada	2.6	2.1	17.09	9,971	5	2	34	0.926	82	29.4	–1.0	0.092	–	662	89.9
entral African Rep.	–	–	0.09	623	3	5	36	0.367	53	7.5	4.0	0.637	63	4	5.4
had	–	–	0.03	1,284	4	36	9	0.404	51	6.1	1.3	0.319	77	6	5.0
ile	0.3	0.6	3.98	757	2	19	22	0.843	79	28.0	0.6	0.319	4	184	77.5
ina	23.2	21.9	6.48	9,597	13	42	22	0.752	76	6.2	–1.0	0.152	5	231	54.6
lombia	0.3	0.1	1.55	1,139	3	35	55	0.747	76	22.3	0.5	0.383	6	71	63.2
moros	–	–	0.24	2.2	77	8	1	0.503	65	7.8	0.1	–	50	33	15.7
ngo	–	–	1.48	342	2	29	66	0.606	60	–1.0	3.1	0.578	20	26	12.0
ngo (Dem. Rep.)	–	–	0.04	2,345	3	8	68	0.457	58	6.7	0.7	0.652	23	5	6.1
sta Rica	–	–	1.46	51.1	12	25	1	0.794	79	25.7	0.4	0.300	3	177	87.7
te d'Ivoire	–	–	0.42	322	23	42	33	0.492	59	10.3	2.8	0.663	56	20	26.3
oatia	–	–	3.91	56.5	17	6	34	0.831	76	24.4	–1.0	0.124	1	380	90.0
ba	–	–	2.91	111	38	23	27	0.777	79	24.6	0.4	0.301	0	38	40.3
prus	–	–	6.06	9.3	13	0	19	0.896	79	21.8	0.1	0.085	1	595	81.7
echia	0.3	0.4	8.94	78.9	42	13	34	0.888	79	26.0	0.1	0.124	–	502	87.7
nmark	–	–	6.06	43.1	59	4	13	0.929	79	19.7	0.1	0.040	–	480	96.9
ibouti	–	–	1.17	23.2	0	73	0	0.476	64	13.5	1.3	–	–	28	18.5
ominican Republic	–	–	1.98	48.5	27	25	41	0.736	78	27.6	0.9	0.451	8	128	61.1
uador	0.1	–	2.41	284	10	20	39	0.752	77	19.9	0.3	0.385	6	71	79.9
ypt	0.7	0.1	2.43	1,001	3	0	0	0.696	73	32.0	0.1	0.449	25	45	49.5
Salvador	–	–	1.09	21	44	31	14	0.674	75	24.6	0.6	0.392	12	94	57.7
uatorial Guinea	–	–	6.17	28.1	6	4	57	0.591	65	8.0	6.5	–	0	13	23.5
itrea	–	–	0.08	118	7	68	15	0.440	65	5.0	0.7	–	35	11	1.4
tonia	–	–	3.89	45.1	14	7	52	0.871	77	21.2	1.2	0.122	0	486	97.7
watini	–	–	0.67	17.4	11	58	32	0.588	52	16.5	27.4	0.569	–	51	32.1
hiopia	–	–	0.09	1,104	16	20	12	0.463	63	4.5	0.9	0.502	61	8	15.3
i	–	–	2.49	18.3	14	10	55	0.741	73	30.2	–1.0	0.352	–	179	54.9
nland	0.2	0.8	7.48	338	7	0	73	0.920	81	22.2	–1.0	0.058	–	604	94.3
ance	1.8	1.9	4.97	552	35	18	29	0.901	82	21.6	0.5	0.083	–	578	92.6
bon	–	–	3.76	268	2	17	81	0.702	52	15.0	4.2	0.534	18	14	47.7
ambia, The	–	–	0.27	11.3	40	26	48	0.460	65	10.3	1.6	0.623	58	7	18.1
aza Strip (OPT)*	–	–	1.01	0.4	–	–	–	–	74	–1.0	–1.0	–	–	28	–
eorgia	–	–	1.17	69.7	8	28	40	0.780	76	21.7	0.4	0.350	0	115	68.0
ermany	2.5	9.2	9.18	357	35	14	32	0.936	81	22.3	0.2	0.072	–	572	96.2
hana	–	–	0.52	239	33	37	21	0.592	67	10.9	1.7	0.538	29	30	34.3
reece	0.2	0.5	6.51	132	29	35	30	0.870	81	24.9	0.2	0.120	3	624	70.1

	POPULATION						WEALTH						TRADE		
	Total population (millions 2017)	Population density (persons per km² 2017)	Population change (average annual % 2017)	Birth rate (births per thousand people 2017)	Death rate (deaths per thousand people 2017)	Urban population (% of total 2018)	Gross National Income (million US$ 2017)	Gross National Income per capita (PPP US$ 2017)	GDP growth rate (percentage 2017)	GDP from agriculture (% of GDP 2017)	GDP from industry (% of GDP 2017)	GDP from services (% of GDP 2017)	Imports (% of GDP 2017)	Exports (% of GDP 2017)	Tourism receipts (US$ per capita 2016)
Guatemala	15.5	142	1.8	24	5	51	68,596	8,000	2.8	13.2	23.6	63.2	27	19	
Guinea	12.4	50	2.6	35	9	36	10,151	2,270	6.7	19.5	46.5	30.5	104	43	
Guinea-Bissau	1.8	50	1.9	33	14	43	1,235	1,700	5.5	44.1	12.9	43.0	32	27	
Guyana	0.7	3	0.3	15	7	27	3,466	8,120	2.1	17.5	37.8	44.7	57	44	
Haiti	10.6	383	1.3	23	8	55	8,380	1,830	1.2	21.9	20.8	57.3	56	19	
Honduras	9.0	81	1.6	22	5	57	20,845	4,630	4.8	13.8	28.4	57.8	59	44	
Hungary	9.9	106	−0.2	9	13	71	125,864	26,960	4.0	4.4	30.9	64.7	82	90	
Iceland	0.3	3	1.1	14	6	94	20,760	53,280	3.6	5.8	19.8	74.4	43	47	1
India	1,281.9	390	1.2	19	7	34	2,430,836	7,060	6.7	15.4	23.0	61.5	22	19	
Indonesia	260.6	137	0.9	16	6	55	934,365	11,900	5.1	13.9	40.3	45.9	19	20	
Iran	82.0	50	1.2	18	5	75	438,368	21,010	4.3	9.8	35.9	54.3	22	24	
Iraq	39.2	89	2.6	30	4	71	182,579	17,010	−0.8	4.8	40.6	54.6	36	38	
Ireland	5.0	71	1.2	14	7	63	266,160	61,910	7.8	1.0	38.2	60.7	88	120	
Israel	8.3	403	1.5	18	5	92	324,677	37,810	3.3	2.3	38.2	69.5	–	–	
Italy	62.1	206	0.2	9	10	70	1,878,329	39,640	1.5	2.1	24.0	73.9	28	31	
Jamaica	3.0	272	0.7	18	7	56	13,732	8,690	1.0	7.6	23.2	69.2	45	32	1
Japan	126.5	335	−0.2	8	10	92	4,888,123	44,850	1.7	1.0	29.7	69.2	–	–	
Jordan	10.2	115	2.0	24	4	91	38,660	9,110	2.3	4.3	28.9	66.8	57	36	1
Kazakhstan	18.6	7	1.0	18	8	57	142,274	23,440	4.0	4.8	34.4	60.8	–	–	
Kenya	47.6	82	1.7	24	7	27	71,4210	3,250	4.8	35.3	17.2	47.9	25	14	
Korea, North	25.2	209	0.5	15	9	62	–	–	−1.1	25.4	41.0	33.5	–	–	–
Korea, South	47.6	515	0.5	8	6	82	1,460,491	–	3.1	2.2	39.3	58.3	–	43	
Kosovo	1.9	174	–	–	–	–	7,122	11,050	4.1	11.9	17.7	70.4	53	27	
Kuwait	2.9	162	1.5	19	2	100	130,026	83,310	−2.5	0.4	58.7	40.9	–	–	
Kyrgyzstan	5.8	29	1.0	22	7	36	6,990	3,620	4.5	14.3	32.5	53.2	67	35	
Laos	7.1	30	1.5	24	7	35	15,595	6,650	6.8	20.9	33.2	45.9	41	34	
Latvia	1.9	30	−1.1	10	14	68	28,603	27,400	4.5	3.2	21.6	75.2	62	60	
Lebanon	6.2	599	−1.1	14	5	89	50,523	14,690	1.2	5.7	21.0	73.2	46	24	1
Lesotho	2.0	64	0.3	25	15	28	2,8481	3,510	3.1	5.3	34.6	60.1	–	–	
Liberia	4.7	42	2.5	38	8	51	1,792	710	2.5	36.1	10.5	53.4	–	–	
Libya	6.7	4	1.6	18	4	80	77,140	19,940	70.8	1.3	63.8	34.9	–	–	
Lithuania	2.8	43	−1.1	10	15	68	42,983	31,030	3.8	3.3	28.5	68.3	79	81	
Luxembourg	0.6	228	2.0	12	7	91	42,115	72,690	3.5	0.2	11.9	87.9	194	230	1
Macedonia (FYROM)	2.1	82	0.2	11	9	58	10,170	14,590	0.0	10.0	30.0	60.0	69	55	
Madagascar	25.1	43	2.5	32	7	37	10,305	1,510	4.1	23.7	16..0	60.0	39	35	
Malawi	19.2	163	3.3	41	8	17	5,978	1,180	4.0	28.1	15.8	56.1	36	29	
Malaysia	31.4	95	1.4	19	5	76	305,051	28,650	5.9	8.4	36.9	54.7	64	71	
Maldives	0.4	1.310	−0.1	16	4	40	4,175	15,350	4.8	3.0	16.0	81.0	78	73	1
Mali	17.9	14	3.0	44	10	42	14,283	2,160	5.3	40.9	18.9	40.2	41	221	
Malta	0.4	1,300	0.3	10	9	95	11,078	36,740	6.6	1.3	10.6	88.1	–	–	1
Mauritania	3.8	4	2.2	30	8	54	4,877	3,900	3.2	22.5	37.8	39.7	66	43	
Mauritius	1.4	678	0.6	13	7	41	12,822	22,570	3.9	4.0	21.8	74.2	55	42	1
Mexico	124.6	64	1.2	18	5	80	1,112,529	17,740	2.0	3.9	31.6	64.0	40	38	
Moldova	3.5	102	−1.0	12	13	43	7,753	6,060	4.0	12.2	14.6	73.2	71	43	
Mongolia	3.1	2	1.2	19	6	68	10,199	11,170	5.1	13.2	36.1	50.7	57	59	
Montenegro	0.6	46	−0.3	11	10	67	4,573	19,150	4.2	7.5	15.9	76.6	65	41	2
Morocco	34.0	76	1.0	18	5	100	103,910	8,060	4.2	14.8	29.1	56.0	47	37	
Mozambique	26.6	33	2.5	38	12	36	12,339	1,200	3.0	22.3	23.0	54.7	71	38	
Myanmar	55.1	81	0.9	18	7	31	63,475	5,830	6.7	24.8	35.4	39.9	–	–	
Namibia	2.5	3	2.0	27	8	50	11,645	10,320	−1.2	6.6	25.8	67.6	47	37	
Nepal	29.4	200	1.2	20	6	20	23,274	2,710	7.5	27.0	13.5	51.5	42	10	
Netherlands	17.1	412	0.4	11	9	92	791,270	52,200	3.1	1.6	17.9	70.2	75	86	
New Zealand	4.5	17	0.8	13	7	87	186,841	39,740	3.0	3.9	26.2	69.9	–	–	
Nicaragua	6.0	46	1.0	18	5	59	13,221	5,680	4.9	15.5	24.4	50.8	55	41	
Niger	19.2	15	3.2	44	12	16	7,723	990	5.2	41.5	18.1	40.1	32	17	
Nigeria	190.6	206	2.4	37	12	50	397,524	5,680	0.8	21.6	18.3	60.1	–	–	
Norway	5.3	16	1.0	12	8	82	401,390	63,980	1.8	2.4	31.1	66.5	33	37	
Oman	3.4	11	2.0	24	3	85	66,935	40,240	−0.3	1.7	45.2	53.0	–	–	
Pakistan	204.9	257	1.4	22	6	37	311,666	5,830	5.3	24.7	19.1	56.3	18	8	
Panama	3.8	50	1.3	18	5	68	41,328	21,890	5.4	2.4	15.7	82.0	–	–	1
Papua New Guinea	6.9	15	1.7	24	7	13	19,848	4,040	2.5	21.1	42.9	35.0	–	–	
Paraguay	6.9	17	1.2	17	5	61	26,679	9,180	4.3	17.9	27.7	35.0	43	42	
Peru	31.0	24	1.0	18	6	78	191,887	12,890	2.5	7.5	36.3	56.1	23	24	
Philippines	104.3	348	1.6	24	5	47	321,296	10,030	6.7	9.6	30.6	59.8	40	31	
Poland	38.5	119	−0.1	10	10	60	482,525	27,920	4.6	2.4	40.2	57.4	49	53	

	ENERGY			LAND & AGRICULTURE				SOCIAL INDICATORS							
	Energy consumed (% of world total 2017)	Renewable energy consumption (% of world total 2017)	CO₂ emissions (tonnes per capita 2015)	Land area (thousand km²)	Arable and Permanent crops (% of land area)	Permanent pasture (% of land area)	Forest (% of land area)	Human Development Index (HDI value 2017)	Life expectancy (years 2014)	Level of obesity (% of adults 2016)	Adults living with HIV/AIDS (percentage 2017)	Gender Inequality Index (GII value 2017)	Adult illiteracy rate (percentage 2016)	Passenger cars (per thousand people 2017)	Internet users (% of population 2017)
atemala	–	–	0.91	109	23	18	34	0.650	73	21.2	0.4	0.493	19	68	42.1
inea	–	–	0.21	246	15	44	27	0.459	61	7.7	1.5	–	68	5	12.3
inea-Bissau	–	–	0.23	36.1	15	30	55	0.455	51	9.5	3.4	–	54	33	6.3
yana	–	–	2.70	215	2	6	77	0.654	69	20.2	1.7	0.504	14	95	–
iti	–	–	0.28	27.8	48	18	4	0.498	64	22.7	1.9	0.601	51	12	18.0
nduras	–	–	1.00	112	13	16	45	0.617	71	21.4	0.3	0.461	11	95	38.2
ngary	0.2	0.2	5.00	93	50	8	22	0.838	76	26.4	0.1	0.259	–	345	88.6
land	–	–	8.98	103	1	17	0	0.935	83	21.9	–1.0	0.062	–	745	99.0
ia	5.6	4.5	1.51	3,287	57	3	23	0.640	69	3.9	0.2	0.524	30	50	34.1
onesia	1.3	0.6	1.96	1,905	25	6	52	0.694	73	6.9	0.4	0.453	5	60	53.7
n	2.0	–	7.99	1,648	12	18	7	0.798	74	25.5	0.1	0.461	15	200	69.1
q	0.4	–	3.84	438	9	9	2	0.685	75	30.4	0.1	0.542	56	50	48.3
and	–	–	7.17	70.3	16	50	11	0.938	81	25.4	0.2	0.109	–	513	92.7
ael	0.2	0.1	8.74	20.6	18	6	7	0.903	82	26.1	–1.0	0.098	–	384	79.7
y	1.2	3.2	5.68	301	31	16	31	0.880	82	19.9	0.2	0.087	1	679	92.4
naica	–	–	2.91	11	20	21	31	0.732	74	24.7	1.8	0.412	–	188	54.5
an	3.4	4.6	8.87	378	12	0	68	0.909	85	4.3	0.1	0.103	–	591	93.3
dan	–	–	2.85	89.3	3	8	1	0.735	75	35.5	–1.0	0.460	2	165	87.7
zakhstan	0.5	–	10.98	2,725	9	69	1	0.800	71	21.0	0.2	0.197	0	219	76.4
nya	–	–	0.36	580	10	37	6	0.590	64	7.1	4.8	0.547	21	24	85.0
rea, North	–	–	1.36	121	22	0	46	–	71	6.8	–1.0	–	0	–	–
rea, South	2.2	0.7	13.12	99.3	17	1	64	0.903	82	4.7	–1.0	0.063	–	284	92.6
sovo	–	–	3.84	10.9	29	23	42	–	69	–1.0	–1.0	–	–	–	80.4
wait	0.3	–	36.80	17.8	1	8	0	0.803	78	37.9	0.1	0.270	4	527	97.8
rgyzstan	–	–	1.74	200	7	48	5	0.672	71	16.6	0.2	0.392	1	63	40.7
os	–	–	0.15	237	7	4	68	0.601	65	5.3	0.3	0.461	41	20	35.0
via	–	–	4.03	64.6	19	10	54	0.847	78	23.6	–1.0	0.196	0	319	86.2
banon	–	–	3.71	10.4	24	39	13	0.757	78	32.0	0.1	0.381	9	343	91.0
sotho	–	–	0.38	30.4	10	66	1	0.520	53	16.6	23.8	0.544	23	4	27.7
eria	–	–	0.24	111	7	21	45	0.435	63	9.9	1.4	0.656	57	3	8.1
ya	–	–	8.34	1,760	1	8	0	0.706	77	32.5	–1.0	0.170	–	290	58.7
huania	–	–	4.28	65.2	35	9	35	0.858	75	26.3	0.2	0.123	0	560	90.4
xembourg	–	–	17.84	2.6	25	26	33	0.904	82	22.6	0.3	0.066	–	739	96.4
cedonia (FYROM)	–	–	3.38	25.7	19	26	40	0.732	76	22.4	–1.0	–	–	152	75.9
dagascar	–	–	0.13	587	7	64	22	0.519	66	5.3	0.3	–	28	26	7.2
lawi	–	–	0.07	118	39	20	34	0.477	61	5.8	9.6	0.619	38	8	9.5
laysia	0.7	0.1	6.71	330	22	1	62	0.802	75	15.6	0.4	0.287	7	361	78.3
dives	–	–	4.39	0.3	20	3	3	0.717	76	8.6	–1.0	0.343	1	28	76.5
li	–	–	0.07	1,240	4	28	10	0.427	60	8.6	1.2	0.678	67	14	65.3
lta	–	–	16.68	0.3	32	0	1	0.878	80	28.9	–1.0	0.216	7	693	83.3
uritania	–	–	0.58	1,026	0	38	0	0.520	63	12.7	0.3	0.617	54	5	17.8
uritius	–	–	4.13	2	40	3	17	0.790	76	10.8	–1.0	0.373	7	175	63.4
xico	1.4	0.9	3.72	1,958	13	42	33	0.774	76	28.9	0.3	0.343	6	275	65.0
ldova	–	–	2.07	33.9	64	11	12	0.700	71	18.9	0.6	0.226	1	156	71.2
ngolia	–	–	4.74	1,567	1	73	7	0.741	70	20.6	0.1	0.301	2	72	64.1
ntenegro	–	–	3.61	14	14	24	40	0.814	75	23.3	0.1	0.123	2	326	69.9
rocco	0.1	0.2	1.57	447	24	47	11	0.667	77	26.1	0.1	0.482	31	70	62.4
zambique	–	–	0.27	802	6	50	44	0.437	54	7.2	12.5	0.552	49	12	17.3
anmar	–	–	0.25	677	19	0	48	0.578	68	5.8	0.7	0.456	24	6	33.4
mibia	–	–	1.59	824	1	46	9	0.647	64	17.2	12.1	0.472	12	107	30.8
pal	–	–	0.16	147	16	12	25	0.574	71	4.1	0.2	0.479	40	5	54.7
therlands	0.6	0.8	13.72	41.5	31	24	11	0.931	81	20.4	0.2	0.044	–	528	95.9
w Zealand	0.2	0.5	8.51	271	2	41	31	0.917	81	30.8	0.1	0.136	–	774	88.1
caragua	–	–	0.80	130	15	27	25	0.614	73	23.7	0.2	0.456	–	57	43.0
ger	–	–	0.13	1,267	12	23	1	0.354	56	5.5	0.3	0.649	84	7	4.3
geria	–	–	0.54	924	45	33	10	0.532	54	8.9	2.8	–	51	31	99.2
rway	0.4	0.1	7.92	324	2	1	28	0.953	82	23.1	–1.0	0.048	–	584	50.2
man	0.2	–	21.13	310	0	5	0	0.821	76	27.0	–1.0	0.264	7	215	68.5
kistan	0.6	0.2	0.75	796	29	7	2	0.537	68	8.6	0.1	0.541	43	18	22.2
nama	–	–	6.43	75.5	10	21	44	0.789	79	22.7	1.0	0.461	6	132	69.7
ua New Guinea	–	–	1.03	463	2	0	64	0.544	67	21.3	0.9	0.741	–	13	10.8
raguay	–	–	0.86	407	11	43	44	0.702	77	20.3	0.5	0.467	5	54	89.6
ru	0.2	0.1	1.81	1,285	4	15	53	0.750	74	19.7	0.5	0.368	6	73	67.6
lippines	0.3	0.6	1.00	300	36	5	26	0.699	69	6.4	0.1	0.427	4	30	62.9
and	0.6	1.0	7.31	323	37	11	31	0.865	78	23.1	–1.0	0.132	–	537	78.1

	POPULATION						WEALTH						TRADE		
	Total population (millions 2017)	Population density (persons per km² 2017)	Population change (average annual % 2017)	Birth rate (births per thousand people 2017)	Death rate (deaths per thousand people 2017)	Urban population (% of total 2018)	Gross National Income (million US$ 2017)	Gross National Income per capita (PPP US$ 2017)	GDP growth rate (percentage 2017)	GDP from agriculture (% of GDP 2017)	GDP from industry (% of GDP 2017)	GDP from services (% of GDP 2017)	Imports (% of GDP 2017)	Exports (% of GDP 2017)	Tourism receipts (US$ per capita 2016)
Portugal	10.8	122	0.0	9	11	65	203,997	30,920	2.7	2.2	22.1	75.7	42	43	8
Qatar	2.2	210	2.3	10	2	99	161,182	128,060	2.1	0.2	50.3	49.5	29	–	
Romania	21.5	90	–0.3	9	12	54	195,182	18,060	7.0	4.2	32.4	62.3	44	41	
Russia	142.3	8	–0.1	11	13	74	1,355,592	25,150	1.5	4.7	37.5	58.3	21	26	
Rwanda	11.9	453	2.5	31	6	17	8,800	1,990	6.1	30.9	17.6	51.5	33	18	
Saudi Arabia	28.6	13	1.5	18	3	84	661,494	54,770	–0.7	2.6	44.2	53.2	28	34	
Senegal	14.7	74	2.4	33	8	47	15,058	2,620	7.2	16.9	24.3	58.8	43	27	
Serbia	7.1	92	–0.5	9	14	56	36,382	14,040	1.8	9.8	41.1	49.1	61	52	
Sierra Leone	6.2	86	2.4	36	10	42	3,827	1,480	3.5	60.7	6.5	32.9	–	–	
Singapore	5.9	8,660	1.8	9	3	100	306,047	90,570	3.6	0.0	24.8	75.2	149	173	
Slovakia	5.4	111	0.0	10	10	54	90,338	30,880	3.4	3.8	35.0	61.2	93	96	
Slovenia	2.0	97	–0.3	8	12	55	45,473	33,980	5.0	1.8	32.2	65.9	73	82	
Solomon Is.	0.6	22	2.0	25	4	24	1,172	2,270	3.2	34.3	7.6	58.1			
Somalia	11.0	17	2.0	40	13	45	–		1.8	60.2	7.4	32.5	64	13	
South Africa	54.8	45	1.0	20	9	66	308,189	13,090	1.3	2.8	29.7	67.4	28	30	
Spain	49.0	98	0.8	9	9	80	1,265,880	37,990	3.1	2.6	23.2	74.2	31	34	
Sri Lanka	22.4	342	0.8	15	6	19	82,425	12,470	3.1	7.8	30.5	61.7	29	22	
Sudan	37.3	20	1.6	28	7	35	–	4,480	3.2	39.6	2.6	57.8	12	10	
Sudan, South	13.0	21	3.8	36	8	20	–	–	–	–	–	–	–	–	
Suriname	0.6	4	1.0	16	6	66	4,994	14,290	0.0	11.6	31.1	57.4	61	69	
Sweden	10.0	22	0.8	12	9	87	529,459	50,980	2.4	1.6	33.0	66.8	41	45	
Switzerland	8.2	199	0.7	10	8	74	682,059	65,610	1.1	0.7	25.6	73.7	54	65	
Syria	18.0	97	–	21	4	54	–	–	–	20.0	19.6	60.4	–	–	
Taiwan	23.5	653	0.2	8	7	78	–	–	2.8	1.8	36.0	62.1	–	–	
Tajikistan	8.5	59	1.6	23	6	27	8,846	3,670	7.1	28.6	25.5	45.9	41	16	
Tanzania	54.0	57	2.8	36	8	34	50,360	2,920	6.0	23.4	28.6	47.6	–	–	
Thailand	68.4	133	0.3	11	8	50	411,731	17,090	3.9	8.2	36.2	55.6	–	–	
Timor-Leste	1.3	87	2.4	33	6	–	2,320	6,330	–0.5	9.4	57.8	32.6	–	–	
Togo	8.0	140	2.6	33	7	42	4,744	1,620	4.4	28.1	21.6	50.3	60	40	
Trinidad & Tobago	1.2	239	–0.2	13	9	53	21,022	30,520	–2.6	0.4	48.8	50.8	–	–	
Tunisia	11.4	70	1.0	18	6	69	40,352	11,490	1.9	9.9	25.6	64.0	56	44	
Turkey	80.8	104	0.5	16	6	75	882,852	26,160	7.0	6.7	31.8	61.4	29	25	
Turkmenistan	5.4	11	1.1	19	6	52	38,266	17,320	6.5	7.5	44.9	47.7	–	–	
Uganda	39.6	164	3.2	43	10	24	25,644	1,820	4.5	25.8	23.2	51.0	26	19	
Ukraine	44.0	73	–0.4	10	14	69	101,457	8,900	2.5	14.0	27.8	58.6	54	48	
United Arab Emirates	5.9	71	2.4	15	2	87	367,820	74,410	0.5	0.9	49.8	49.2	72	100	
United Kingdom	64.8	268	0.5	12	9	83	2,675,928	42,560	1.8	0.6	19.0	80.4	32	31	
USA	326.6	34	0.8	13	8	82	18,980,258	60,200	2.3	0.9	18.9	80.2	–	–	
Uruguay	3.4	19	0.3	13	9	95	52,727	21,870	3.1	6.2	25.0	68.8	18	22	
Uzbekistan	29.7	67	0.9	17	5	51	64,236	7,130	5.3	18.5	34.4	47.0	30	29	
Vanuatu	0.3	23	2.0	24	4	25	806	3,170	4.2	27.0	9.1	63.9	–	–	
Venezuela	31.3	34	1.3	19	5	88	–	–	–14.0	4.4	38.2	57.4	–	–	
Vietnam	96.2	290	1.0	16	6	36	206,882	6,450	6.8	15.3	33.3	41.3	99	102	
West Bank (OPT)*	2.7	466	1.9	26	4	76	15,665	–	5.3	3.0	21.1	75.0	56	19	
Yemen	28.0	53	2.3	28	6	37	–	–	–13.8	24.1	14.3	61.6	–	–	
Zambia	16.0	21	3.0	41	12	44	22,263	3,920	3.6	5.4	35.6	59.0	36	35	
Zimbabwe	13.8	35	1.6	34	10	32	15,085	1,850	3.0	12.5	26.9	60.6	37	24	

NOTES
The tables list information for the main states and territories of the world using the latest available data in each category.

OPT*
Occupied Palestinian Territory.

POPULATION TOTAL
These are estimates of the mid-year total in 2017.

POPULATION DENSITY
The total population divided by the land area (both are recorded in the table above).

BIRTH/DEATH RATES
These are 2017 estimates from the CIA World Factbook.

URBAN POPULATION
The urban population shows the percentage of the total population living in towns and cities (each country will differ with regard to the size or type of town that is defined as an urban area).

GNI
Gross National Income is a good indication of a country's wealth. It is the income in US dollars from goods and services in a country for one year, including income from overseas.

GNI PER CAPITA
The GNI (see note) divided by the total population by using the PPP method (see note).

PER CAPITA
An amount divided by the total population of a country or the amount per person.

PPP
Purchasing Power Parity (PPP) is a method used to enable real comparisons to be made between countries when measuring wealth. The UN International Comparison Programme gives estimates of the PPP for each country, so it can be used as an indicator of real price levels for goods and services rather than using currency exchange rates (see GNI and GNI per capita).

AGRICULTURE, INDUSTRY AND SERVICES
The percentage contributions that each of these three sectors makes to a country's Gross Domestic Product (GDP).

IMPORTS AND EXPORTS
The value of goods and services imported into a country and exported to other countries, given as a percentage of a country's Gross Domestic Product (GDP).

TOURISM RECEIPTS
The amount of income generated from tourism in US dollars per capita.

ENERGY CONSUMED
The total amount of commercial energy consumed in a country given as a percentage of the world total.

	ENERGY		CO² emissions (tonnes per capita 2015)	LAND & AGRICULTURE				SOCIAL INDICATORS							
	Energy consumed (% of world total 2017)	Renewable energy consumption (% of world total 2017)		Land area (thousand km²)	Arable and permanent crops (% of land area)	Permanent pasture (% of land area)	Forest (% of land area)	Human Development Index (HDI value 2017)	Life expectancy (years 2014)	Level of obesity (% of adults 2016)	Adults living with HIV/AIDS (percentage 2017)	Gender Inequality Index (GII value 2017)	Adult illiteracy rate (percentage 2016)	Passenger cars (per thousand people 2016)	Internet users (% of population 2017)
ortugal	0.2	0.8	4.77	88.8	20	20	38	0.847	79	20.8	0.6	0.088	6	548	77.9
atar	0.4	–	52.44	11	1	4	0	0.856	79	35.1	0.1	0.206	2	532	98.1
omania	0.3	0.5	3.10	238	41	19	28	0.811	75	22.5	0.1	0.311	1	235	73.5
ussia	5.2	0.1	11.84	17,075	7	6	49	0.816	71	23.1	1.2	0.257	–	369	76.1
wanda	–	–	0.07	26.3	57	17	18	0.524	64	5.8	2.7	0.381	32	5	29.8
udi Arabia	2.0	–	21.82	2,150	2	79	0	0.853	75	35.4	–1.0	0.234	6	336	90.2
negal	–	–	0.53	197	17	29	44	0.505	62	8.8	0.4	0.515	57	22	59.8
rbia	–	–	7.48	77.5	41	16	32	0.787	76	21.5	0.1	0.181	1	291	72.2
erra Leone	–	–	0.19	71.7	26	30	38	0.419	58	8.7	1.4	0.645	68	6	11.7
ngapore	2.2	0.1	40.73	0.7	1	0	3	0.932	85	6.1	0.2	0.067	3	149	83.6
ovakia	–	–	5.74	49	29	11	40	0.855	77	20.5	0.1	0.180	–	364	85.0
ovenia	–	–	5.96	20.3	10	13	62	0.896	78	20.2	0.1	0.054	–	567	79.9
olomon Is.	–	–	0.39	28.9	3	0	79	0.546	76	22.4	–1.0	–	–	3	12.1
omalia	–	–	0.08	638	2	69	11	–	53	8.3	0.1	–	–	3	7.9
uth Africa	0.9	0.4	7.56	1,221	13	69	8	0.699	64	28.3	18.8	0.389	6	165	53.7
ain	1.0	3.2	5.64	498	35	21	36	0.891	82	23.8	0.4	0.080	2	593	92.6
i Lanka	0.1	–	0.84	65.6	37	7	29	0.770	77	5.2	0.1	0.354	9	76	32.0
dan	–	–	0.43	1,886	16	84	0	0.502	64	6.6	0.2	0.564	46	27	28.5
dan, South	–	–	0.13	620	–	–	–	0.388	57	6.6	2.4	–	73	27	17.3
riname	–	–	4.51	163	0	0	95	0.720	72	26.4	1.3	0.441	7	291	0.0
veden	0.4	1.4	4.77	450	6	1	69	0.933	82	20.6	–1.0	0.044	–	520	96.7
vitzerland	0.2	0.2	4.84	41.3	11	28	31	0.944	83	16.5	–1.0	0.039	–	566	91.0
ria	–	–1	1.96	185	31	45	3	0.536	75	27.8	–1.0	–	–	73	33.0
iwan	0.9	0.2	12.62	36	23	–	58	–	80	–1.0	–1.0	–	–	324	87.9
jikistan	–	–	0.42	143	7	28	3	0.650	68	14.2	0.3	0.317	–	38	33.1
nzania	–	–	0.26	945	17	27	37	0.538	63	8.4	4.5	0.537	22	7	38.9
ailand	1.0	0.7	4.66	513	40	2	37	0.755	75	10.0	1.1	0.393	7	206	82.4
mor-Leste	–	–	0.67	14.9	15	10	49	0.625	68	3.8	–1.0	–	42	–	31.0
go	–	–	0.26	56.8	48	18	6	0.503	65	8.4	2.1	0.567	36	2	11.3
inidad & Tobago	0.1	–	44.02	5.1	9	1	44	0.784	73	18.6	1.1	0.324	–	353	73.1
nisia	–	–	2.04	164	3	31	7	0.735	76	26.9	0.1	0.298	21	125	67.7
rkey	1.2	1.4	4.15	775	31	19	14	0.791	75	32.1	–1.0	0.317	4	144	68.4
rkmenistan	0.2	–	20.73	488	4	68	9	0.706	70	18.6	–1.0	–	–	106	17.9
ganda	–	–	0.11	241	45	26	15	0.516	56	5.3	5.9	0.523	27	8	42.9
raine	0.6	0.1	3.89	604	57	14	17	0.751	72	24.1	0.9	0.285	–	173	93.0
nited Arab Emirates	0.8	–	40.96	83.6	1	4	4	0.863	78	31.7	–1.0	0.232	–	313	98.4
nited Kingdom	1.4	4.3	6.70	242	25	46	12	0.922	81	27.8	–1.0	0.116	–	519	94.7
SA	16.5	19.5	16.39	9,629	17	27	33	0.924	80	36.2	–1.0	0.189	–	910	95.6
ruguay	–	–	2.63	175	10	77	10	0.804	77	27.9	0.6	0.270	2	200	88.2
zbekistan	0.3	–	3.68	447	11	52	8	0.710	74	16.6	0.3	0.273	1	37	47.7
nuatu	–	–	0.54	12.2	12	3	36	0.603	74	25.2	–1.0	–	–	54	29.3
nezuela	0.5	–	5.89	912	4	20	53	0.761	76	25.6	–1.0	0.454	3	147	53.1
etnam	0.6	–	1.67	332	32	2	45	0.694	74	2.1	0.3	0.304	7	23	66.3
est Bank (OPT)*	–	–	0.68	5.9	18	25	2	–	75	–1.0	–1.0	–	–	28	–
men	–	–	0.68	528	3	42	1	0.452	66	17.1	–1.0	0.834	–	35	24.3
mbia	–	–	0.19	753	5	27	66	0.561	53	8.1	11.5	0.517	17	21	41.2
mbabwe	–	–	0.71	391	11	31	40	0.535	60	15.5	13.3	0.534	11	114	40.2

NEWABLE ENERGY
nsumption of energy generated from
main renewable sources given as a
centage of the world total.

RBON DIOXIDE EMISSIONS
e amount of carbon dioxide that each
ntry produces per capita.

ND AREA
s is the total land area of a country,
the area of major lakes and rivers,
quare kilometres.

ABLE AND PERMANENT CROPS
ese figures give a percentage of the
al land area that is used for crops and
t (including temporary fallow land or
dows).

PERMANENT PASTURE
This is the percentage of land area that
has permanent forage crops for cattle or
horses, cultivated or wild. Some land may
be classified both as permanent pasture
or as forest.

FOREST
Natural/planted trees including cleared
land that will be reforested in the near
future as a percentage of the land area.

HUMAN DEVELOPMENT INDEX (HDI)
Produced by the UN Development
Programme using indicators of life
expectancy, knowledge and standards
of living to give a value between 0 and 1
for each country. A high value shows a
higher human development.

LIFE EXPECTANCY
The average age that a child born today
is expected to live to, if mortality levels
of today last throughout its lifetime. It is a
measure of the overall quality of life.

LEVEL OF OBESITY
Percentage of the total adult population
considered to be obese, defined as having
a Body Mass Index (BMI) greater than
30.0.

ADULTS LIVING WITH HIV/AIDS
The percentage of all adults (aged 15–49)
who have the Human Immuno-deficiency
Virus or the Acquired Immunodeficiency
Syndrome. The total number of adults
and children with HIV/AIDS in 2017
was 37 million.

GENDER INEQUALITY INDEX
Like the HDI (see note), the GII uses the
same UNDP indicators but gives a value
between 0 and 1 to measure the social
and economic differences between men
and women. The higher the value, the
more equality exists between men and
women.

ILLITERACY
The percentage of all adults (over
15 years) who cannot read or write
simple sentences. High rates of illiteracy
can impede economic development.

PASSENGER CARS AND
INTERNET USERS
These are good indicators of a country's
development wealth.

Each topic list is divided into continents and within a continent the items are listed in order of size. The bottom part of many of the lists is selective in order to give examples from as many different countries as possible. The figures are rounded as appropriate.

WORLD, CONTINENTS, OCEANS

	km²	miles²	%
The World	509,450,000	196,672,000	–
Land	149,450,000	57,688,000	29.3
Water	360,000,000	138,984,000	70.7
Asia	44,500,000	17,177,000	29.8
Africa	30,302,000	11,697,000	20.3
North America	24,241,000	9,357,000	16.2
South America	17,793,000	6,868,000	11.9
Antarctica	14,100,000	5,443,000	9.4
Europe	9,957,000	3,843,000	6.7
Australia & Oceania	8,557,000	3,303,000	5.7
Pacific Ocean	155,557,000	60,061,000	46.4
Atlantic Ocean	76,762,000	29,638,000	22.9
Indian Ocean	68,556,000	26,470,000	20.4
Southern Ocean	20,327,000	7,848,000	6.1
Arctic Ocean	14,056,000	5,427,000	4.2

OCEAN DEPTHS

Atlantic Ocean	m	ft
Puerto Rico (Milwaukee) Deep	8,605	28,232
Cayman Trench	7,680	25,197
Gulf of Mexico	5,203	17,070
Mediterranean Sea	5,121	16,801
Black Sea	2,211	7,254
North Sea	660	2,165
Indian Ocean	**m**	**ft**
Java Trench	7,450	24,442
Red Sea	2,635	8,454
Pacific Ocean	**m**	**ft**
Mariana Trench	11,022	36,161
Tonga Trench	10,882	35,702
Japan Trench	10,554	34,626
Kuril Trench	10,542	34,587
Arctic Ocean	**m**	**ft**
Molloy Deep	5,608	18,399
Southern Ocean	**m**	**ft**
South Sandwich Trench	7,235	23,737

MOUNTAINS

Europe		m	ft
Elbrus	*Russia*	5,642	18,510
Dykh-Tau	*Russia*	5,205	17,076
Shkhara	*Russia/Georgia*	5,201	17,064
Koshtan-Tau	*Russia*	5,152	16,903
Kazbek	*Russia/Georgia*	5,047	16,558
Pushkin	*Russia/Georgia*	5,033	16,512
Katyn-Tau	*Russia/Georgia*	4,979	16,335
Shota Rustaveli	*Russia/Georgia*	4,860	15,945
Mont Blanc	*France/Italy*	4,808	15,774
Monte Rosa	*Italy/Switzerland*	4,634	15,203
Dom	*Switzerland*	4,545	14,911
Liskamm	*Switzerland*	4,527	14,852
Weisshorn	*Switzerland*	4,505	14,780
Taschorn	*Switzerland*	4,490	14,730
Matterhorn/Cervino	*Italy/Switzerland*	4,478	14,691
Grossglockner	*Austria*	3,797	12,457
Mulhacén	*Spain*	3,478	11,411
Zugspitze	*Germany*	2,962	9,718
Olympus	*Greece*	2,917	9,570
Galdhøpiggen	*Norway*	2,469	8,100
Kebnekaise	*Sweden*	2,117	6,946
Ben Nevis	*UK*	1,345	4,413
Asia		**m**	**ft**
Everest	*China/Nepal*	8,850	29,035
K2 (Godwin Austen)	*China/Kashmir*	8,611	28,251
Kanchenjunga	*India/Nepal*	8,598	28,208
Lhotse	*China/Nepal*	8,516	27,939
Makalu	*China/Nepal*	8,481	27,824
Cho Oyu	*China/Nepal*	8,201	26,906
Dhaulagiri	*Nepal*	8,167	26,795
Manaslu	*Nepal*	8,156	26,758
Nanga Parbat	*Kashmir*	8,126	26,660
Annapurna	*Nepal*	8,078	26,502
Gasherbrum	*China/Kashmir*	8,068	26,469
Broad Peak	*China/Kashmir*	8,051	26,414
Xixabangma	*China*	8,012	26,286
Kangbachen	*Nepal*	7,858	25,781
Trivor	*Pakistan*	7,720	25,328
Pik Imeni Ismail Samani	*Tajikistan*	7,495	24,590
Demavend	*Iran*	5,604	18,386
Ararat	*Turkey*	5,165	16,945
Gunong Kinabalu	*Malaysia (Borneo)*	4,101	13,455
Fuji-San	*Japan*	3,776	12,388
Africa m ft			
Kilimanjaro	*Tanzania*	5,895	19,340
Mt Kenya	*Kenya*	5,199	17,057
Ruwenzori	*Uganda/Congo (D.R.)*	5,109	16,762
Meru	*Tanzania*	4,565	14,977
Ras Dashen	*Ethiopia*	4,553	14,937
Karisimbi	*Rwanda/Congo (D.R.)*	4,507	14,787
Mt Elgon	*Kenya/Uganda*	4,321	14,176
Batu	*Ethiopia*	4,307	14,130
Toubkal	*Morocco*	4,165	13,665
Mt Cameroun	*Cameroon*	4,070	13,353
Oceania		**m**	**ft**
Puncak Jaya	*Indonesia*	4,884	16,024
Puncak Trikora	*Indonesia*	4,730	15,518
Puncak Mandala	*Indonesia*	4,702	15,427
Mt Wilhelm	*Papua New Guinea*	4,508	14,790
Mauna Kea	*USA (Hawaii)*	4,205	13,796
Mauna Loa	*USA (Hawaii)*	4,169	13,678
Aoraki Mt Cook	*New Zealand*	3,724	12,218
Mt Kosciuszko	*Australia*	2,228	7,310
North America		**m**	**ft**
De nali (Mt M cKinley)	*USA (Alaska)*	6,190	20,310
Mt Logan	*Canada*	5,959	19,551
Pico de Orizaba	*Mexico*	5,610	18,405
Mt St Elias	*USA/Canada*	5,489	18,008
Popocatépetl	*Mexico*	5,452	17,887
Mt Foraker	*USA (Alaska)*	5,304	17,401
Iztaccihuatl	*Mexico*	5,286	17,342
Lucania	*Canada*	5,226	17,146
Mt Steele	*Canada*	5,073	16,644
Mt Bona	*USA (Alaska)*	5,005	16,420
Mt Whitney	*USA*	4,418	14,495
Tajumulco	*Guatemala*	4,220	13,845
Chirripó	*Grande Costa Rica*	3,837	12,589
Pico Duarte	*Dominican Rep.*	3,175	10,417
South America		**m**	**ft**
Aconcagua	*Argentina*	6,962	22,841
Ojos del Salado	*Argentina/Chile*	6,863	22,516
Pissis	*Argentina*	6,793	22,288
Mercedario	*Argentina/Chile*	6,770	22,211
Huascarán	*Peru*	6,768	22,204
Bonete	*Argentina*	6,759	22,176
Llullaillaco	*Argentina/Chile*	6,723	22,057
Nevado de Cachi	*Argentina*	6,720	22,047
Yerupaja	*Peru*	6,632	21,758
Sajama	*Bolivia*	6,520	21,391
Chimborazo	Ecuador	6,267	20,561
Pico Cristóbal Colón	*Colombia*	5,775	18,948
Pico Bolivar	*Venezuela*	4,981	16,343
Antarctica		**m**	**ft**
Vinson Massif		4,897	16,066
Mt Kirkpatrick		4,528	14,855

RIVERS

Europe		km	miles
Volga	*Caspian Sea*	3,700	2,300
Danube	*Black Sea*	2,850	1,770
Ural	*Caspian Sea*	2,535	1,575
Dnieper	*Black Sea*	2,285	1,420
Kama	*Volga*	2,030	1,260
Don	*Black Sea*	1,990	1,240
Petchora	*Arctic Ocean*	1,790	1,110
Oka	*Volga*	1,480	920
Dniester	*Black Sea*	1,400	870
Vyatka	*Kama*	1,370	850
Rhine	*North Sea*	1,320	820
North Dvina	*Arctic Ocean*	1,290	800
Elbe	*North Sea*	1,145	710
Asia		**km**	**miles**
Yangtse	*Pacific Ocean*	6,380	3,960
Yenisey–Angara	*Arctic Ocean*	5,550	3,445
Huang He	*Pacific Ocean*	5,464	3,395
Ob–Irtysh	*Arctic Ocean*	5,410	3,360
Mekong	*Pacific Ocean*	4,500	2,795
Amur	*Pacific Ocean*	4,442	2,760
Lena	*Arctic Ocean*	4,402	2,735
Irtysh	*Ob*	4,250	2,640
Yenisey	*Arctic Ocean*	4,090	2,540
Ob	*Arctic Ocean*	3,680	2,285
Indus	*Indian Ocean*	3,100	1,925
Brahmaputra	*Indian Ocean*	2,900	1,800
Syrdarya	*Aralkum Desert*	2,860	1,775
Salween	*Indian Ocean*	2,800	1,740
Euphrates	*Indian Ocean*	2,700	1,675
Amudarya	*Aralkum Desert*	2,540	1,575
Africa		**km**	**miles**
Nile	*Mediterranean*	6,695	4,160
Congo	*Atlantic Ocean*	4,670	2,900
Niger	*Atlantic Ocean*	4,180	2,595
Zambezi	*Indian Ocean*	3,540	2,200
Oubangi/Uele	*Congo (Dem. Rep.)*	2,250	1,400
Kasai	*Congo (Dem. Rep.)*	1,950	1,210
Shaballe	*Indian Ocean*	1,930	1,200
Orange	*Atlantic Ocean*	1,860	1,155
Cubango	*Okavango Delta*	1,800	1,120
Limpopo	*Indian Ocean*	1,770	1,100
Senegal	*Atlantic Ocean*	1,640	1,020
Australia		**km**	**miles**
Murray–Darling	*Southern Ocean*	3,750	2,330
Darling	*Murray*	3,070	1,905
Murray	*Southern Ocean*	2,575	1,600
Murrumbidgee	*Murray*	1,690	1,050
North America		**km**	**miles**
Mississippi–Missouri	*Gulf of Mexico*	5,971	3,710
Mackenzie	*Arctic Ocean*	4,240	2,630
Missouri	*Mississippi*	4,088	2,540
Mississippi	*Gulf of Mexico*	3,782	2,350
Yukon	*Pacific Ocean*	3,185	1,980
Rio Grande	*Gulf of Mexico*	3,030	1,880
		km	**miles**
Arkansas	*Mississippi*	2,340	1,450
Colorado	*Pacific Ocean*	2,330	1,445
Red	*Mississippi*	2,040	1,270
Columbia	*Pacific Ocean*	1,950	1,210
Saskatchewan	*Lake Winnipeg*	1,940	1,205
South America		**km**	**miles**
Amazon	*Atlantic Ocean*	6,450	4,010
Paraná–Plate	*Atlantic Ocean*	4,500	2,800
Purus	*Amazon*	3,350	2,080
Madeira	*Amazon*	3,200	1,990
São Francisco	*Atlantic Ocean*	2,900	1,800
Paraná	*Plate*	2,800	1,740
Tocantins	*Atlantic Ocean*	2,750	1,710
Orinoco	*Atlantic Ocean*	2,740	1,700
Paraguay	*Paraná*	2,550	1,580
Pilcomayo	*Paraná*	2,500	1,550
Araguaia	*Tocantins*	2,250	1,400

LAKES

Europe		km²	miles²
Lake Ladoga	*Russia*	17,700	6,800
Lake Onega	*Russia*	9,700	3,700
Saimaa system	*Finland*	8,000	3,100
Vänern	*Sweden*	5,500	2,100
Asia		**km²**	**miles²**
Caspian Sea	*Asia*	371,000	143,000
Lake Baikal	*Russia*	30,500	11,780
Tonlé Sap	*Cambodia*	20,000	7,700
Lake Balqash	*Kazakhstan*	18,500	7,100
Aral Sea	*Kazakhstan/Uzbekistan*	17,160	6,625
Africa		**km²**	**miles²**
Lake Victoria	*East Africa*	68,000	26,000
Lake Tanganyika	*Central Africa*	33,000	13,000
Lake Malawi/Nyasa	*East Africa*	29,600	11,430
Lake Chad	*Central Africa*	25,000	9,700
Lake Turkana	*Ethiopia/Kenya*	8,500	3,290
Lake Volta	*Ghana*	8,480	3,270
Australia		**km²**	**miles²**
Kati-Thanda-Lake Eyre	*Australia*	8,900	3,400
Lake Torrens	*Australia*	5,800	2,200
Lake Gairdner	*Australia*	4,800	1,900
North America		**km²**	**miles²**
Lake Superior	*Canada/USA*	82,350	31,800
Lake Huron	*Canada/USA*	59,600	23,010
Lake Michigan	*USA*	58,000	22,400
Great Bear Lake	*Canada*	31,800	12,280
Great Slave Lake	*Canada*	28,500	11,000
Lake Erie	*Canada/USA*	25,700	9,900
Lake Winnipeg	*Canada*	24,400	9,400
Lake Ontario	*Canada/USA*	19,500	7,500
Lake Nicaragua	*Nicaragua*	8,200	3,200
South America		**km²**	**miles²**
Lake Titicaca	*Bolivia/Peru*	8,300	3,200
Lake Poopo	*Bolivia*	2,800	1,100

ISLANDS

Europe		km²	miles²
Great Britain	*UK*	229,880	88,700
Iceland	*Atlantic Ocean*	103,000	39,800
Ireland	*Ireland/UK*	84,400	32,600
Novaya Zemlya (N.)	*Russia*	48,200	18,600
Sicily	*Italy*	25,500	9,800
Asia		**km²**	**miles²**
Borneo	*South-east Asia*	744,360	287,400
Sumatra	*Indonesia*	473,600	182,860
Honshu	*Japan*	230,500	88,980
Celebes	*Indonesia*	189,000	73,000
Java	*Indonesia*	126,700	48,900
Luzon	*Philippines*	104,700	40,400
Hokkaido	*Japan*	78,400	30,300
Africa		**km²**	**miles²**
Madagascar	*Indian Ocean*	587,040	226,660
Socotra	*Indian Ocean*	3,600	1,400
Réunion	*Indian Ocean*	2,500	965
Oceania		**km²**	**miles²**
New Guinea	*Indonesia/Papua NG*	821,030	317,000
New Zealand (S.)	*Pacific Ocean*	150,500	58,100
New Zealand (N.)	*Pacific Ocean*	114,700	44,300
Tasmania	*Australia*	67,800	26,200
New Caledonia	*Pacific Ocean*	16,650	6,470
North Americakm²	**miles²**		
Greenland	*Atlantic Ocean*	2,175,600	839,800
Baffin I.	*Canada*	508,000	196,100
Victoria I.	*Canada*	212,200	81,900
Ellesmere I.	*Canada*	212,000	81,800
Cuba	*Caribbean Sea*	110,860	42,800
Hispaniola	*Dominican Rep./Haiti*	76,200	29,400
Jamaica	*Caribbean Sea*	11,400	4,400
Puerto Rico	*Atlantic Ocean*	8,900	3,400
South America km²	**miles²**		
Tierra del Fuego	*Argentina/Chile*	47,000	18,100
Chiloé	*Chile*	8,480	3,275
Falkland I. (E.)	*Atlantic Ocean*	6,800	2,600

How to use the Index

The index contains the names of all the principal places and features shown on the maps. Each name is followed by an additional entry in italics giving the country or region within which it is located. The alphabetical order of names composed of two or more words is governed primarily by the first word and then by the second. This is an example of the rule:

Albert, L. *Africa* 1°30N 31°0E **96** D6
Albert Lea *U.S.A.* 43°39N 93°22W **111** B8
Albert Nile → *Uganda* 3°36N 32°2E **96** D6
Alberta □ *Canada* 54°40N 115°0W **108** D8
Albertville *France* 45°40N 6°22E **66** D7

Physical features composed of a proper name (Erie) and a description (Lake) are positioned alphabetically by the proper name. The description is positioned after the proper name and is usually abbreviated:

Erie, L. *N. Amer.* 42°15N 81°0W **112** D7

Where a description forms part of a settlement or administrative name, however, it is always written in full and put in its true alphabetical position:

Mount Isa *Australia* 20°42S 139°26E **98** E6

Names beginning with M' and Mc are indexed as if they were spelled Mac. Names beginning St. are alphabetized under Saint, but Santa and San are spelled in full and are alphabetized accordingly. If the same place name occurs two or more times in the index and all are in the same country, each is followed by the name of the administrative subdivision in which it is located.

The geographical co-ordinates that follow each name in the index give the latitude and longitude of each place. The first co-ordinate indicates latitude – the distance north or south of the Equator. The second co-ordinate indicates longitude – the distance east or west of the Greenwich Meridian. Both latitude and longitude are measured in degrees and minutes (there are 60 minutes in a degree).

The latitude is followed by N(orth) or S(outh) and the longitude by E(ast) or W(est).

The number in bold type that follows the geographical co-ordinates refers to the number of the map page where that feature or place will be found. This is usually the largest scale at which the place or feature appears.

The letter and figure that are immediately after the page number give the grid square on the map page, within which the feature is situated. The letter represents the latitude and the figure the longitude. A lower-case letter immediately after the page number refers to an inset map on that page.

In some cases the feature itself may fall within the specified square, while the name is outside. This is usually the case only with features that are larger than a grid square.

Rivers are indexed to their mouths or confluences, and carry the symbol → after their names. The following symbols are also used in the index: ■ country, ⊠ overseas territory or dependency, □ first-order administrative area, △ national park, ✈ (LHR) principal airport (and location identifier).

Abbreviations used in the Index

Afghan. – Afghanistan
Ala. – Alabama
Alta. – Alberta
Amer. – America(n)
Arch. – Archipelago
Ariz. – Arizona
Ark. – Arkansas
Atl. Oc. – Atlantic Ocean
B. – Baie, Bahía, Bay, Bucht, Bugt
B.C. – British Columbia
Bangla. – Bangladesh
C. – Cabo, Cap, Cape, Coast
C.A.R. – Central African Republic
Calif. – California
Cent. – Central
Chan. – Channel
Colo. – Colorado
Conn. – Connecticut
Cord. – Cordillera
Cr. – Creek
D.C. – District of Columbia
Del. – Delaware
Dom. Rep. – Dominican Republic
E. – East
El Salv. – El Salvador
Eq. Guin. – Equatorial Guinea
Fla. – Florida
Falk. Is. – Falkland Is.
G. – Golfe, Golfo, Gulf
Ga. – Georgia
Hd. – Head
Hts. – Heights
I.(s). – Île, Ilha, Insel, Isla, Island, Isle(s)
Ill. – Illinois
Ind. – Indiana
Ind. Oc. – Indian Ocean
Ivory C. – Ivory Coast
Kans. – Kansas
Ky. – Kentucky
L. – Lac, Lacul, Lago, Lagoa, Lake, Limni, Loch, Lough
La. – Louisiana
Lux. – Luxembourg
Madag. – Madagascar
Man. – Manitoba
Mass. – Massachusetts
Md. – Maryland
Me. – Maine
Mich. – Michigan
Minn. – Minnesota
Miss. – Mississippi
Mo. – Missouri
Mont. – Montana
Mozam. – Mozambique
Mt.(s) – Mont, Monte, Monti, Montaña, Mountain
N. – Nord, Norte, North, Northern,
N.B. – New Brunswick
N.C. – North Carolina
N. Cal. – New Caledonia
N. Dak. – North Dakota
N.H. – New Hampshire
N.J. – New Jersey
N. Mex. – New Mexico
N.S. – Nova Scotia
N.S.W. – New South Wales
N.W.T. – North West Territory
N.Y. – New York
N.Z. – New Zealand
Nat. Park – National Park
Nebr. – Nebraska
Neths. – Netherlands
Nev. – Nevada
Nfld. – Newfoundland and Labrador
Nic. – Nicaragua
Okla. – Oklahoma
Ont. – Ontario
Oreg. – Oregon
P.E.I. – Prince Edward Island
Pa. – Pennsylvania
Pac. Oc. – Pacific Ocean
Papua N.G. – Papua New Guinea
Pen. – Peninsula, Péninsule
Phil. – Philippines
Pk. – Peak
Plat. – Plateau
Prov. – Province, Provincial
Pt. – Point
Pta. – Ponta, Punta
Pte. – Pointe
Qué. – Québec
Queens. – Queensland
R. – Rio, River
R.I. – Rhode Island
Ra.(s) – Range(s)
Reg. – Region
Rep. – Republic
Res. – Reserve, Reservoir
S. – San, South
Si. Arabia – Saudi Arabia
S.C. – South Carolina
S. Dak. – South Dakota
Sa. – Serra, Sierra
Sask. – Saskatchewan
Scot. – Scotland
Sd. – Sound
Sib. – Siberia
St. – Saint, Sankt, Sint
Str. – Strait, Stretto
Switz. – Switzerland
Tas. – Tasmania
Tenn. – Tennessee
Tex. – Texas
Trin. & Tob.. – Trinidad & Tobago
U.A.E. – United Arab Emirates
U.K. – United Kingdom
U.S.A. – United States of America
Va. – Virginia
Vic. – Victoria
Vol. – Volcano
Vt. – Vermont
W. – West
W. Va. – West Virginia
Wash. – Washington
Wis. – Wisconsin

A

Aachen *Germany* 50°45N 6°6E **64** C4
Aalborg *Denmark* 57°2N 9°54E **63** F5
Aarau *Switz.* 47°23N 8°4E **64** E5
Aare → *Switz.* 47°33N 8°14E **64** E5
Aarhus *Denmark* 56°8N 10°11E **63** F6
Aba *Nigeria* 5°10N 7°19E **94** G7
Abaco I. *Bahamas* 26°25N 77°10W **115** B9
Ābādān *Iran* 30°22N 48°20E **86** D7
Abaetetuba *Brazil* 1°40S 48°50W **120** C5
Abakan *Russia* 53°40N 91°10E **77** D10
Abancay *Peru* 13°35S 72°55W **120** D2
Abariringa *Kiribati* 2°50S 171°40W **99** A16
Abaya, L. *Ethiopia* 6°30N 37°50E **89** F2
Abbé, L. *Ethiopia* 11°8N 41°47E **89** E3
Abbeville *France* 50°6N 1°49E **66** A4
Abbey Town *U.K.* 54°51N 3°17W **26** C2
Abbot Ice Shelf *Antarctica* 73°0S 92°0W **55** D16
Abbots Bromley *U.K.* 52°50N 1°52W **27** G5
Abbotsbury *U.K.* 50°40N 2°37W **30** E3
ABC Islands *W. Indies* 12°15N 69°0W **115** E11
Abéché *Chad* 13°50N 20°35E **95** F10
Abeokuta *Nigeria* 7°3N 3°19E **94** G6
Aberaeron *U.K.* 52°15N 4°15W **28** C5
Aberchirder *U.K.* 57°34N 2°37W **23** G12
Aberdare *U.K.* 51°43N 3°27W **28** D7
Aberdaugleddau = Milford Haven *U.K.* 51°42N 5°7W **28** D3
Aberdeen *China* 22°14N 114°8E **79** a
Aberdeen *U.K.* 57°9N 2°5W **23** H13
Aberdeen *S. Dak., U.S.A.* 45°28N 98°29W **110** A7
Aberdeen *Wash., U.S.A.* 46°59N 123°50W **110** A2
Aberdeenshire □ *U.K.* 57°17N 2°36W **23** H12
Aberdovey = Aberdyfi *U.K.* 52°33N 4°3W **28** B5
Aberdyfi *U.K.* 52°33N 4°3W **28** B5
Aberfeldy *U.K.* 56°37N 3°51W **25** A8
Aberfoyle *U.K.* 56°11N 4°23W **24** B7
Abergavenny *U.K.* 51°49N 3°1W **28** D7
Abergele *U.K.* 53°17N 3°35W **28** A6
Abergwaun = Fishguard *U.K.* 52°0N 4°58W **28** D4
Aberhonddu = Brecon *U.K.* 51°57N 3°23W **28** D7
Abermaw = Barmouth *U.K.* 52°44N 4°4W **28** B5
Aberpennar = Mountain Ash *U.K.* 51°40N 3°23W **28** D7
Aberporth *U.K.* 52°8N 4°33W **28** C4
Abersoch *U.K.* 52°49N 4°30W **28** B5
Abersychan *U.K.* 51°44N 3°3W **28** D7
Abert, L. *U.S.A.* 42°38N 120°14W **110** B2
Abertawe = Swansea *U.K.* 51°37N 3°57W **29** D6
Aberteifi = Cardigan *U.K.* 52°5N 4°40W **28** C4
Abertillery *U.K.* 51°44N 3°8W **28** D7
Aberystwyth *U.K.* 52°25N 4°5W **28** C5
Abhā *Si. Arabia* 18°0N 42°34E **89** D3
Abidjan *Côte d'Ivoire* 5°26N 3°58W **94** G5
Abilene *U.S.A.* 32°28N 99°43W **110** D7
Abingdon-on-Thames *U.K.* 51°40N 1°17W **30** C6
Abitibi, L. *Canada* 48°40N 79°40W **109** E12
Abkhazia □ *Georgia* 43°12N 41°5E **71** F7
Abomey *Benin* 7°10N 2°5E **94** G6
Aboyne *U.K.* 57°4N 2°47W **23** H12
Abrolhos, Banco dos *Brazil* 18°0S 38°0W **122** C3
Absaroka Range *U.S.A.* 44°45N 109°50W **110** B5
Abu Dhabi *U.A.E.* 24°28N 54°22E **87** E8
Abu Hamed *Sudan* 19°32N 33°13E **95** E12
Abuja *Nigeria* 9°5N 7°32E **94** G7
Abunã *Brazil* 9°40S 65°20W **120** C3
Abunã → *Brazil* 9°41S 65°20W **120** C3
Abyei ⊠ *Sudan* 9°30N 28°30E **95** G11
Acaponeta *Mexico* 22°30N 105°22W **114** C3
Acapulco *Mexico* 16°51N 99°55W **114** D5
Acarai Mts. *Brazil* 1°50N 57°50W **120** B4
Acarigua *Venezuela* 9°33N 69°12W **120** B3
Accomac *U.S.A.* 37°43N 75°40W **113** G10
Accra *Ghana* 5°35N 0°6W **94** G5
Accrington *U.K.* 53°45N 2°22W **27** E4
Aceh □ *Indonesia* 4°15N 97°30E **82** D1
Acharnes *Greece* 38°5N 23°44E **69** E10
Acheloos → *Greece* 38°19N 21°7E **69** E9
Achill Hd. *Ireland* 53°58N 10°15W **18** D1
Achill I. *Ireland* 53°58N 10°1W **18** D1
Acklins I. *Bahamas* 22°30N 74°0W **115** C10
Acle *U.K.* 52°39N 1°33E **31** A12
Aconcagua, Cerro *Argentina* 32°39S 70°0W **121** F3
Acre □ *Brazil* 9°1S 71°0W **120** C2
Acre → *Brazil* 8°45S 67°22W **120** C3
Acton Burnell *U.K.* 52°37N 2°41W **27** G3
Ad Dammām *Si. Arabia* 26°20N 50°5E **86** E7
Ad Dīwānīyah *Iraq* 32°0N 45°0E **86** D6
Adair, C. *Canada* 71°30N 71°34W **109** B12
Adak I. *U.S.A.* 51°45N 176°45W **108** D2
Adamaoua, Massif de l' *Cameroon* 7°20N 12°20E **95** G8
Adam's Bridge *Sri Lanka* 9°15N 79°40E **84** Q11
Adana *Turkey* 37°0N 35°16E **71** G6
Adare, C. *Antarctica* 71°0S 171°0E **55** D11
Addis Ababa *Ethiopia* 9°2N 38°42E **89** F2
Adelaide *Australia* 34°52S 138°30E **98** G6
Adelaide I. *Antarctica* 67°15S 68°30W **55** C17
Adelaide Pen. *Canada* 68°15N 97°30W **108** C10
Adélie, Terre *Antarctica* 68°0S 140°0E **55** C10
Aden *Yemen* 12°45N 45°0E **89** E4
Aden, G. of *Ind. Oc.* 12°30N 47°30E **89** E4
Adige → *Italy* 45°9N 12°20E **68** B5
Adigrat *Ethiopia* 14°20N 39°26E **89** E2
Adirondack Mts. *U.S.A.* 44°0N 74°0W **113** D10
Admiralty Is. *Papua N. G.* 2°0S 147°0E **102** H6
Adour → *France* 43°32N 1°32W **66** E3
Adrar *Mauritania* 20°30N 7°30W **94** D3
Adrian *U.S.A.* 41°54N 84°2W **112** E5
Adriatic Sea *Medit. S.* 43°0N 16°0E **68** C6
Adwa *Ethiopia* 14°15N 38°52E **89** E2
Adwick le Street *U.K.* 53°34N 1°10W **27** E6
Adygea □ *Russia* 45°0N 40°0E **71** F7
Ægean Sea *Medit. S.* 38°30N 25°0E **69** E11
Afghanistan ■ *Asia* 33°0N 65°0E **87** C11
Africa 10°0N 20°0E **90** E6
Afyon *Turkey* 38°45N 30°33E **71** G5
Agadez *Niger* 16°58N 7°59E **94** E7
Agadir *Morocco* 30°28N 9°55W **94** B4
Agartala *India* 23°50N 91°23E **85** H17
Agen *France* 44°12N 0°38E **66** D4
Agra *India* 27°17N 77°58E **84** F10
Ağri *Turkey* 39°44N 43°3E **71** G7
Agrigento *Italy* 37°19N 13°34E **68** F5
Agua Prieta *Mexico* 31°18N 109°34W **114** A3
Aguascalientes *Mexico* 21°53N 102°18W **114** C4
Aguja, C. de la *Colombia* 11°18N 74°12W **117** B3
Agulhas, C. *S. Africa* 34°52S 20°0E **97** L4
Ahaggar *Algeria* 23°0N 6°30E **94** D7
Ahmadabad *India* 23°0N 72°40E **84** H8
Ahmadnagar *India* 19°7N 74°46E **84** K9
Ahmadpur East *Pakistan* 29°12N 71°10E **84** E7
Ahvāz *Iran* 31°20N 48°40E **86** D7
Ahvenanmaa *Finland* 60°15N 20°0E **63** E8
Aḩwar *Yemen* 13°30N 46°40E **89** E4
Ailsa Craig *U.K.* 55°15N 5°6W **24** D5
Aimorés *Brazil* 19°30S 41°4W **122** C2
Aïn Témouchent *Algeria* 35°16N 1°8W **94** A5
Ainsdale *U.K.* 53°37N 3°2W **27** E2
Aïr *Niger* 18°30N 8°0E **94** E7
Air Force I. *Canada* 67°58N 74°5W **109** C12
Aird, The *U.K.* 57°25N 4°33W **23** H8
Airdrie *Canada* 51°18N 114°2W **108** D8
Airdrie *U.K.* 55°52N 3°57W **25** C8
Aire → *U.K.* 53°43N 0°55W **27** E7
Aisgill *U.K.* 54°23N 2°21W **26** D4
Aisne → *France* 49°26N 2°50E **66** B5
Aix-en-Provence *France* 43°32N 5°27E **66** E6
Aix-les-Bains *France* 45°41N 5°53E **66** D6
Aizawl *India* 23°40N 92°44E **85** H18
Aizuwakamatsu *Japan* 37°30N 139°56E **81** E6
Ajaccio *France* 41°55N 8°40E **66** F8
Ajanta Ra. *India* 20°28N 75°50E **84** J9
Ajaria □ *Georgia* 41°30N 42°0E **71** F7
Ajdābiyā *Libya* 30°54N 20°4E **95** B10
'Ajmān *U.A.E.* 25°25N 55°30E **87** E8
Ajmer *India* 26°28N 74°37E **84** F9
Aketi *Dem. Rep. of the Congo* 2°38N 23°47E **96** D4
Akhisar *Turkey* 38°56N 27°48E **71** G4
Akimiski I. *Canada* 52°50N 81°30W **109** D11
Akita *Japan* 39°45N 140°7E **81** D7
'Akko *Israel* 32°55N 35°4E **86** C3
Aklavik *Canada* 68°12N 135°0W **108** C6
Akola *India* 20°42N 77°2E **84** J10
Akpatok I. *Canada* 60°25N 68°8W **109** C13
Akranes *Iceland* 64°19N 22°5W **63** B1
Akron *U.S.A.* 41°5N 81°31W **112** E7
Aksai Chin *China* 35°15N 79°55E **84** B11
Aksaray *Turkey* 38°25N 34°2E **71** G5
Akşehir Gölü *Turkey* 38°30N 31°25E **71** G5
Aksu *China* 41°5N 80°10E **78** C5
Aksum *Ethiopia* 14°5N 38°40E **89** E2
Akure *Nigeria* 7°15N 5°5E **94** G7
Akureyri *Iceland* 65°40N 18°6W **63** A2
Al 'Amārah *Iraq* 31°55N 47°15E **86** D6
Al 'Aqabah *Jordan* 29°31N 35°0E **86** D3
Al 'Aramah *Si. Arabia* 25°30N 46°0E **86** E6
Al 'Ayn *U.A.E.* 24°15N 55°45E **87** E8
Al 'Azīzīyah *Libya* 32°30N 13°1E **95** B8
Al Bayḑā *Libya* 32°50N 21°44E **95** B10
Al Fallūjah *Iraq* 33°20N 43°55E **86** C5
Al Fāw *Iraq* 30°0N 48°30E **86** D7
Al Ḩadīthah *Iraq* 34°0N 41°13E **86** C5
Al Ḩasakah *Syria* 36°35N 40°45E **86** B5
Al Ḩillah *Iraq* 32°30N 44°25E **86** C6
Al Hoceïma *Morocco* 35°8N 3°58W **94** A5
Al Ḩudaydah *Yemen* 14°50N 43°0E **89** E3
Al Hufūf *Si. Arabia* 25°25N 49°45E **86** E7
Al Jahrah *Kuwait* 29°25N 47°40E **86** D6
Al Jawf *Libya* 24°10N 23°24E **95** D10
Al Jubayl *Si. Arabia* 27°0N 49°50E **86** E7
Al Khalīl *West Bank* 31°32N 35°6E **86** D3
Al Khums *Libya* 32°40N 14°17E **95** B8
Al Kufrah *Libya* 24°17N 23°15E **95** D10
Al Kūt *Iraq* 32°30N 46°0E **86** C6
Al Manāmah *Bahrain* 26°10N 50°30E **87** E7
Al Mubarraz *Si. Arabia* 25°30N 49°40E **86** E7
Al Mukallā *Yemen* 14°33N 49°2E **89** E4
Al Musayyib *Iraq* 32°49N 44°20E **86** C6
Al Qāmishlī *Syria* 37°2N 41°14E **86** B5
Al Qaţīf *Si. Arabia* 26°35N 50°0E **86** E7
Al Qunfudhah *Si. Arabia* 19°3N 41°4E **89** D3
Al Qurayyāt *Si. Arabia* 31°20N 37°20E **86** D4
Ala Tau *Asia* 45°30N 80°40E **78** B5
Alabama □ *U.S.A.* 33°0N 87°0W **111** D9
Alabama → *U.S.A.* 31°8N 87°57W **111** D9
Alagoas □ *Brazil* 9°0S 36°0W **122** A3
Alagoinhas *Brazil* 12°7S 38°20W **122** B3
Alai Range *Asia* 39°45N 72°0E **87** B13
Alamogordo *U.S.A.* 32°54N 105°57W **110** D5
Alamosa *U.S.A.* 37°28N 105°52W **110** C5
Åland = Ahvenanmaa *Finland* 60°15N 20°0E **63** E8
Alanya *Turkey* 36°38N 32°0E **71** G5
Alappuzha *India* 9°30N 76°28E **84** Q10
Alaşehir *Turkey* 38°23N 28°30E **71** G4
Alaska □ *U.S.A.* 64°0N 154°0W **108** C5
Alaska, G. of *Pac. Oc.* 58°0N 145°0W **108** D5
Alaska Peninsula *U.S.A.* 56°0N 159°0W **108** D4
Alaska Range *U.S.A.* 62°50N 151°0W **108** C4
Alba-Iulia *Romania* 46°8N 23°39E **65** E12
Albacete *Spain* 39°0N 1°50W **67** C5
Albanel, L. *Canada* 50°55N 73°12W **109** D12
Albania ■ *Europe* 41°0N 20°0E **69** D9
Albany *Australia* 35°1S 117°58E **98** H2
Albany *Ga., U.S.A.* 31°35N 84°10W **111** D10
Albany *N.Y., U.S.A.* 42°39N 73°45W **113** D11
Albany *Oreg., U.S.A.* 44°38N 123°6W **110** B2
Albany → *Canada* 52°17N 81°31W **109** D11
Albemarle Sd. *U.S.A.* 36°5N 76°0W **111** C11
Albert, L. *Africa* 1°30N 31°0E **96** D6
Albert Lea *U.S.A.* 43°39N 93°22W **111** B8
Albert Nile → *Uganda* 3°36N 32°2E **96** D6
Alberta □ *Canada* 54°40N 115°0W **108** D8
Albertville *France* 45°40N 6°22E **66** D7
Albi *France* 43°56N 2°9E **66** E5
Albion *U.S.A.* 42°15N 84°45W **112** D5
Alboran Sea *Medit. S.* 36°0N 3°30W **67** E3
Albrighton *U.K.* 52°38N 2°16W **27** G4
Albuquerque *U.S.A.* 35°5N 106°39W **110** C5
Albury *Australia* 36°3S 146°56E **98** H8
Alcalá de Henares *Spain* 40°28N 3°22W **67** B4
Alcester *U.K.* 52°14N 1°52W **30** B5
Alchevsk *Ukraine* 48°30N 38°45E **71** E6

Alcoy   Āzarbāyjān

Alcoy Spain 38°43N 0°30W 67 C5
Aldabra Is. Seychelles 9°22S 46°28E 91 G8
Aldan Russia 58°40N 125°30E 77 D13
Aldan → Russia 63°28N 129°35E 77 C13
Aldborough U.K. 54°5N 1°22W 26 D6
Aldbourne U.K. 51°29N 1°37W 30 D5
Aldbrough U.K. 53°49N 0°6W 27 E8
Aldeburgh U.K. 52°10N 1°37E 31 B12
Alderley Edge U.K. 53°18N 2°13W 27 F4
Alderney U.K. 49°42N 2°11W 29 H9
Aldershot U.K. 51°15N 0°44W 31 D7
Aledo U.S.A. 41°12N 90°45W 112 E2
Alegrete Brazil 29°40S 56°0W 121 E4
Além Paraíba Brazil 21°52S 42°41W 122 D2
Alençon France 48°27N 0°4E 66 B4
Alenquer Brazil 1°56S 54°46W 120 C4
'Alenuihähä Channel U.S.A. 20°30N 156°0W 110 H17
Aleppo Syria 36°10N 37°15E 86 B4
Alert Canada 83°2N 60°0W 109 A13
Alès France 44°9N 4°5E 66 D6
Alessándria Italy 44°54N 8°37E 68 B3
Ålesund Norway 62°28N 6°12E 63 E5
Aleutian Is. Pac. Oc. 52°0N 175°0W 102 B10
Aleutian Trench Pac. Oc. 48°0N 180°0E 102 C10
Alexander Arch. U.S.A. 56°0N 136°0W 108 D6
Alexander I. Antarctica 69°0S 70°0W 55 C17
Alexandria Egypt 31°13N 29°58E 95 B11
Alexandria U.S.A. 55°59N 4°35W 24 C6
Alexandria La., U.S.A. 31°18N 92°27W 111 D8
Alexandria Va., U.S.A. 38°49N 77°5W 112 F9
Alford Aberds., U.K. 57°14N 2°41W 23 H12
Alford Lincs., U.K. 53°15N 0°10E 27 F9
Alfreton U.K. 53°6N 1°24W 27 F6
Alfriston U.K. 50°48N 0°10E 31 E9
Algarve Portugal 36°58N 8°20W 67 D1
Algeciras Spain 36°9N 5°28W 67 D3
Algeria ■ Africa 28°30N 2°0E 94 C6
Algiers Algeria 36°42N 3°8E 94 A6
Algoa B. S. Africa 33°50S 25°45E 90 K6
Alicante Spain 38°23N 0°30W 67 C5
Alice Springs Australia 23°40S 133°50E 98 E5
Aligarh India 27°55N 78°10E 84 F11
Alipur Duar India 26°30N 89°35E 85 F16
Aliquippa U.S.A. 40°37N 80°15W 112 E7
Aliwal North S. Africa 30°45S 26°45E 97 L5
Alkmaar Neths. 52°37N 4°45E 64 B3
Allahabad India 25°25N 81°58E 85 G12
Allegan U.S.A. 42°32N 85°51W 112 D5
Allegheny → U.S.A. 40°27N 80°1W 112 E8
Allegheny Mts. U.S.A. 38°15N 80°10W 111 C11
Allen → U.K. 54°58N 2°18W 26 C4
Allen, Bog of Ireland 53°15N 7°0W 21 B9
Allen, L. Ireland 54°8N 8°4W 18 C5
Allendale Town U.K. 54°53N 2°14W 26 C4
Allenheads U.K. 54°49N 2°12W 26 C4
Allentown U.S.A. 40°37N 75°29W 113 E10
Alleynes B. Barbados 13°13N 59°39W 114 c
Alliance U.S.A. 42°6N 102°52W 110 B6
Allier → France 46°57N 3°4E 66 C5
Alligator Pond Jamaica 17°52N 77°34W 114 a
Alloa U.K. 56°7N 3°47W 25 B8
Allonby U.K. 54°46N 3°26W 26 C2
Alma U.S.A. 43°23N 84°39W 112 D5
Alma Ata Kazakhstan 43°15N 76°57E 76 E8
Almada Portugal 38°41N 9°9W 67 C1
Almelo Neths. 52°22N 6°42E 64 B4
Almería Spain 36°52N 2°27W 67 D4
Almondsbury U.K. 51°32N 2°34W 30 C3
Aln → U.K. 55°24N 1°37W 26 B5
Alness U.K. 57°41N 4°16W 23 G9
Alnmouth U.K. 55°24N 1°37W 26 B5
Alnwick U.K. 55°24N 1°42W 26 B5
Alor Indonesia 8°15S 124°30E 83 F6
Alor Setar Malaysia 6°7N 100°22E 82 C2
Alpena U.S.A. 45°4N 83°27W 112 C6
Alpes Maritimes Europe 44°10N 7°10E 66 D7
Alphington U.K. 50°42N 3°31W 29 F6
Alpine U.S.A. 30°22N 103°40W 110 D6
Alps Europe 46°30N 9°30E 64 E5
Alrewas U.K. 52°44N 1°44W 27 G5
Alsace France 48°15N 7°25E 66 B7
Alsager U.K. 53°6N 2°18W 27 F4
Alston U.K. 54°49N 2°25W 26 C4
Altai Mongolia 46°40N 92°45E 78 B7
Altamira Brazil 3°12S 52°10W 120 C4
Altamura Italy 40°49N 16°33E 68 D7
Altarnun U.K. 50°35N 4°32W 29 F4
Altay China 47°48N 88°10E 78 B6
Altay Mongolia 46°22N 96°15E 78 B8
Altiplano Bolivia 17°0S 68°0W 120 D3
Alton U.K. 51°9N 0°59W 31 D7
Alton U.S.A. 38°53N 90°11W 112 F12
Alton Towers U.K. 52°59N 1°52W 27 G5
Altoona U.S.A. 40°31N 78°24W 112 E8
Altrincham U.K. 53°24N 2°21W 27 F4
Altun Shan China 38°30N 88°0E 78 D6
Altus U.S.A. 34°38N 99°20W 110 D7
Alucra Turkey 40°22N 38°47E 71 F6
Alvechurch U.K. 52°21N 1°57W 30 B5
Alwar India 27°38N 76°34E 84 F10
Alwinton U.K. 55°21N 2°7W 26 B4
Alxa Zuoqi China 38°50N 105°40E 78 D10
Alyth U.K. 56°38N 3°13W 23 J11
Amadjuak L. Canada 65°0N 71°8W 109 C12
Amagasaki Japan 34°42N 135°23E 81 F4
Amapá Brazil 2°5N 50°50W 120 B4
Amapá □ Brazil 1°40N 52°0W 120 B4
Amarillo U.S.A. 35°13N 101°50W 110 C6
Amasya Turkey 40°40N 35°50E 71 F6
Amazon = Amazonas → S. Amer. 0°5S 50°0W 120 C4
Amazonas □ Brazil 5°0S 65°0W 120 C3
Amazonas → S. Amer. 0°5S 50°0W 120 C4
Ambala India 30°23N 76°56E 84 D10
Ambato Ecuador 1°5S 78°42W 120 C2
Ambergris Cay Belize 18°0N 87°55W 114 D7
Ambikapur India 23°15N 83°15E 85 H13
Ambilobé Madag. 13°10S 49°3E 97 G9

Amble U.K. 55°20N 1°36W 26 B5
Ambleside U.K. 54°26N 2°58W 26 D3
Ambon Indonesia 3°43S 128°12E 83 E7
Amchitka I. U.S.A. 51°32N 179°0E 108 D1
Amderma Russia 69°45N 61°30E 76 C7
Amdo China 32°20N 91°40E 78 E7
Ameca Mexico 20°33N 104°2W 114 C4
Ameland Neths. 53°27N 5°45E 64 B3
American Highland Antarctica 73°0S 75°0E 55 D6
American Samoa ☑ Pac. Oc. 14°20S 170°0W 99 C16
Americana Brazil 22°45S 47°20W 122 D1
Amersham U.K. 51°40N 0°36W 31 C7
Ames U.S.A. 42°2N 93°37W 111 B8
Amesbury U.K. 51°10N 1°46W 30 D5
Amherst Canada 45°48N 64°8W 109 E13
Amiens France 49°54N 2°16E 66 B5
Amirante Is. Seychelles 6°0S 53°0E 72 J7
Amli I. India 52°4N 173°30W 108 D2
Amlwch U.K. 53°24N 4°20W 28 A3
'Ammān Jordan 31°57N 35°52E 86 D3
Ammanford U.K. 51°48N 3°59W 28 D6
Amos Canada 48°35N 78°5W 109 E12
Ampleforth U.K. 54°13N 1°6W 26 D6
Ampthill U.K. 52°2N 0°30W 31 B8
Amravati India 20°55N 77°45E 84 J10
Amreli India 21°35N 71°17E 84 J7
Amritsar India 31°35N 74°57E 84 D9
Amroha India 28°53N 78°30E 84 E11
Amsterdam Neths. 52°23N 4°54E 64 B3
Amsterdam U.S.A. 42°56N 74°11W 113 D10
Amsterdam I. Ind. Oc. 38°30S 77°30E 53 F13
Amudarya → Uzbekistan 43°58N 59°34E 87 A9
Amund Ringnes I. Canada 78°20N 96°25W 109 B10
Amundsen Gulf Canada 71°0N 124°0W 108 B7
Amundsen Sea Antarctica 72°0S 115°0W 55 D15
Amuntai Indonesia 2°28S 115°25E 82 E5
Amur → Russia 52°56N 141°10E 77 D15
An Najaf Iraq 32°3N 44°15E 86 C6
Anaconda U.S.A. 46°8N 112°57W 110 A4
Anadyr Russia 64°35N 177°20E 77 C18
Anadyr, G. of Russia 64°0N 180°0E 77 C19
Anaheim U.S.A. 33°50N 117°55W 110 D3
Anambas, Kepulauan Indonesia 3°20N 106°30E 82 D3
Anamur Turkey 36°8N 32°58E 71 G5
Anantapur India 14°39N 77°42E 84 M10
Anápolis Brazil 16°15S 48°50W 122 C1
Anār Iran 30°55N 55°13E 87 D8
Anatolia Turkey 39°0N 30°0E 71 G5
Añatuya Argentina 28°20S 62°50W 121 E3
Ancaster U.K. 52°59N 0°32W 27 G7
Ancholme → U.K. 53°40N 0°32W 27 E7
Anchorage U.S.A. 61°13N 149°54W 108 C5
Anci China 39°20N 116°40E 79 D12
Ancohuma Bolivia 16°0S 68°50W 120 D3
Ancona Italy 43°38N 13°30E 68 C5
Ancrum U.K. 55°31N 2°35W 25 C10
Ancud Chile 42°0S 73°50W 121 G2
Ancud, G. de Chile 42°0S 73°0W 121 G2
Anda China 46°24N 125°19E 79 B14
Andalgalá Argentina 27°40S 66°30W 121 E3
Andalucía □ Spain 37°35N 5°0W 67 D3
Andalusia U.S.A. 31°18N 86°29W 111 D9
Andaman Is. Ind. Oc. 12°30N 92°45E 53 D14
Anderson Alaska, U.S.A. 64°25N 149°15W 108 C5
Anderson Ind., U.S.A. 40°10N 85°41W 112 E5
Anderson S.C., U.S.A. 34°31N 82°39W 111 D10
Anderson → Canada 69°42N 129°0W 108 C7
Andes, Cord. de los S. Amer. 20°0S 68°0W 121 E3
Andhra Pradesh □ India 18°0N 79°0E 84 L11
Andijon Uzbekistan 41°10N 72°15E 87 A13
Andorra ■ Europe 42°30N 1°30E 66 E4
Andorra La Vella Andorra 42°31N 1°32E 66 E4
Andover U.K. 51°12N 1°29W 30 D6
Andradina Brazil 20°54S 51°23W 120 E4
Andreanof Is. U.S.A. 51°30N 176°0W 108 D2
Ándria Italy 41°13N 16°17E 68 D7
Andros Greece 37°50N 24°57E 69 F11
Andros I. Bahamas 24°30N 78°0W 115 C9
Aneityum Vanuatu 20°12S 169°45E 99 E12
Angara → Russia 58°5N 94°20E 77 D10
Angarsk Russia 52°30N 104°0E 77 D11
Ånge Sweden 62°31N 15°35E 63 E7
Angel Falls Venezuela 5°57N 62°30W 120 B3
Angeles Phil. 15°9N 120°33E 83 A6
Ångermanälven → Sweden 63°0N 17°20E 63 E7
Angers France 47°30N 0°35W 66 C3
Anglesey □ U.K. 53°16N 4°18W 28 A5
Angoche Mozam. 16°8S 39°55E 97 H7
Angola ■ Africa 12°0S 18°0E 97 G3
Angoulême France 45°39N 0°10E 66 D4
Angoumois France 45°50N 0°25E 66 D4
Angra dos Reis Brazil 23°0S 44°10W 122 D2
Angren Uzbekistan 41°1N 70°12E 87 A12
Anguilla ☑ W. Indies 18°14N 63°5W 115 D12
Angus □ U.K. 56°46N 2°56W 23 J11
Angus, Braes of U.K. 56°51N 3°10W 23 J11
Anhui □ China 32°0N 117°0E 79 E12
Anjou France 47°20N 0°15W 66 C3
Ankang China 32°40N 109°1E 79 E10
Ankara Turkey 39°57N 32°54E 71 G5
Ann, C. U.S.A. 42°38N 70°35W 113 D12
Ann Arbor U.S.A. 42°17N 83°45W 112 D6
Annaba Algeria 36°50N 7°46E 94 A7
Annalee → Ireland 54°2N 7°24W 18 C7
Annan U.K. 54°59N 3°16W 25 D9
Annan → U.K. 54°58N 3°16W 25 D9
Annandale U.K. 55°10N 3°25W 25 D9
Annapolis U.S.A. 38°59N 76°30W 112 F9
Annapurna Nepal 28°34N 83°50E 85 E14
Annecy France 45°55N 6°8E 66 D7
Annfield Plain U.K. 54°52N 1°44W 26 C5
Anniston U.S.A. 33°39N 85°50W 111 D9
Annobón Atl. Oc. 1°25S 5°36E 90 G4
Annotto B. Jamaica 18°17N 76°45W 114 a
Anqing China 30°30N 117°3E 79 E12
Anshan China 41°5N 122°58E 79 C13
Anshun China 26°18N 105°57E 78 F10
Anstey U.K. 52°41N 1°12W 27 G6

Anstruther U.K. 56°14N 2°41W 25 B10
Antalaha Madag. 14°57S 50°20E 97 G10
Antalya Turkey 36°52N 30°45E 71 G5
Antalya Körfezi Turkey 36°15N 31°30E 71 G5
Antananarivo Madag. 18°55S 47°31E 97 H9
Antarctic Pen. Antarctica 67°0S 60°0W 55 C18
Antarctica 90°0S 0°0 55 E3
Anti Atlas Morocco 30°0N 8°30W 94 C4
Antibes France 43°34N 7°6E 66 E7
Anticosti, Î. d' Canada 49°30N 63°0W 109 E13
Antigo U.S.A. 45°9N 89°9W 112 C3
Antigonish Canada 45°38N 61°58W 109 E13
Antigua & Barbuda ■ W. Indies 17°20N 61°48W 115 D12
Antilles Cent. Amer. 15°0N 65°0W 115 E12
Antioch = Hatay Turkey 36°14N 36°10E 71 G6
Antioquia Colombia 6°40N 75°55W 120 B2
Antipodes Is. Pac. Oc. 49°45S 178°40E 102 M9
Antofagasta Chile 23°50S 70°30W 121 E2
Antrim U.K. 54°43N 6°14W 19 B9
Antrim, Mts. of U.K. 55°3N 6°14W 19 A9
Antrim & Newtownabbey □ U.K. 54°40N 6°11W 19 B9
Antsirabe Madag. 19°55S 47°2E 97 H9
Antsiranana Madag. 12°25S 49°20E 97 G9
Antwerp Belgium 51°13N 4°25E 64 C3
Anuradhapura Sri Lanka 8°22N 80°28E 84 Q12
Anxi China 40°30N 95°43E 78 C8
Anyang China 36°5N 114°21E 79 D11
Anzhero-Sudzhensk Russia 56°10N 86°0E 76 D9
Ánzio Italy 41°27N 12°37E 68 D5
Aomori Japan 40°45N 140°45E 81 C7
Aoraki Mount Cook N.Z. 43°36S 170°9E 99 J13
Aosta Italy 45°45N 7°20E 68 B2
Aozou Strip Chad 22°0N 19°0E 95 D9
Apalachee B. U.S.A. 30°0N 84°0W 111 E10
Apaporis → Colombia 1°23S 69°25W 120 C3
Aparecida de Goiânia Brazil 16°49S 49°14W 122 C1
Apatity Russia 67°34N 33°22E 70 A5
Apeldoorn Neths. 52°13N 5°57E 64 B3
Apia Samoa 13°50S 171°50W 99 C16
Apostle Is. U.S.A. 47°0N 90°40W 112 B2
Appalachian Mts. U.S.A. 38°0N 80°0W 112 G7
Appennini Italy 44°30N 10°0E 68 B4
Appleby-in-Westmorland U.K. 54°35N 2°29W 26 C4
Applecross Forest U.K. 57°27N 5°40W 22 H6
Appledore Devon, U.K. 51°3N 4°13W 29 E5
Appledore Kent, U.K. 51°1N 0°47E 31 D10
Appleton U.S.A. 44°16N 88°25W 112 C3
Apure → Venezuela 7°37N 66°25W 120 B3
Apurímac → Peru 12°17S 73°56W 120 D2
Aqaba, G. of Red Sea 29°0N 34°40E 86 D3
Aqtaū Kazakhstan 43°39N 51°12E 71 F9
Aqtöbe Kazakhstan 50°17N 57°10E 71 D10
Aquitain, Bassin France 44°0N 0°30W 66 D3
Ar Ramādī Iraq 33°25N 43°20E 86 C5
Ar Raqqah Syria 35°59N 39°8E 86 B4
Ara India 25°35N 84°32E 85 G14
'Arab, Bahr el → South Sudan 9°0N 29°30E 95 G11
Arab, Shatt al → Asia 29°57N 48°34E 86 D7
Arabia Asia 25°0N 45°0E 72 F6
Arabian Sea Ind. Oc. 16°0N 65°0E 72 G8
Aracaju Brazil 10°55S 37°4W 122 B3
Aracati Brazil 4°30S 37°44W 120 C6
Araçatuba Brazil 21°10S 50°30W 120 E4
Araçuaí Brazil 16°52S 42°4W 122 C2
Arad Romania 46°10N 21°20E 65 E11
Arafura Sea E. Indies 9°0S 135°0E 98 B5
Aragón □ Spain 41°25N 0°40W 67 B5
Araguacema Brazil 8°50S 49°20W 120 C5
Araguaia → Brazil 5°21S 48°41W 120 C5
Araguari Brazil 18°38S 48°11W 122 C1
Arāk Iran 34°0N 49°40E 86 C7
Arakan Coast Myanmar 19°0N 94°0E 85 K19
Arakan Yoma Myanmar 20°0N 94°40E 85 K19
Aral Kazakhstan 46°41N 61°45E 76 E7
Aral Sea Asia 45°0N 58°20E 76 E6
Aran I. = Arranmore Ireland 55°0N 8°30W 18 B4
Aran Is. Ireland 53°6N 9°38W 20 B2
Aransas Pass U.S.A. 27°55N 97°9W 111 E7
Arapiraca Brazil 9°45S 36°39W 122 A3
Ar'ar Si. Arabia 30°59N 41°2E 86 D5
Araraquara Brazil 21°50S 48°0W 122 D1
Araras Brazil 22°22S 47°23W 122 D1
Ararat Turkey 39°50N 44°15E 71 G7
Araripe, Chapada do Brazil 7°20S 40°0W 120 C6
Aras, Rūd-e → Asia 40°5N 48°29E 86 A7
Arauca → Venezuela 7°24N 66°35W 120 B3
Araxá Brazil 19°35S 46°55W 122 C1
Arbroath U.K. 56°34N 2°35W 25 A10
Arcachon France 44°40N 1°10W 66 D3
Arctic Bay Canada 73°1N 85°7W 109 B11
Arctic Ocean Arctic 78°0N 160°0W 54 B18
Ardabīl Iran 38°15N 48°18E 86 B7
Ardee Ireland 53°52N 6°33W 19 D8
Ardennes Belgium 49°50N 5°5E 64 D3
Arderin Ireland 53°2N 7°39W 21 B7
Ardgour U.K. 56°45N 5°25W 22 J7
Ardingly U.K. 51°3N 0°4W 31 D8
Ardivachar Pt. U.K. 57°23N 7°26E 22 H3
Ardmore U.S.A. 34°10N 97°8W 111 D7
Ardnamurchan U.K. 56°43N 6°0W 22 J5
Ardnamurchan, Pt. of U.K. 56°43N 6°14W 22 J5
Ardnave Pt. U.K. 55°53N 6°20W 24 C6
Ardrossan U.K. 55°39N 4°49W 24 C6
Ards & North Down □ U.K. 54°35N 5°30W 19 B10
Ards Pen. U.K. 54°33N 5°34W 19 B10
Arecibo Puerto Rico 18°29N 66°43W 115 D11
Arena, Pt. U.S.A. 38°57N 123°44W 110 C2
Arendal Norway 58°28N 8°46E 63 F5
Arequipa Peru 16°20S 71°30W 120 D2
Arezzo Italy 43°25N 11°53E 68 C4
Argentan France 48°45N 0°1W 66 B3
Argentina ■ S. Amer. 35°0S 66°0W 121 F3
Argentino, L. Argentina 50°10S 73°0W 121 H2
Argostoli Greece 38°11N 20°29E 69 E9
Argun → Russia 53°20N 121°28E 79 A13
Argyle, L. Australia 16°20S 128°40E 98 D4
Argyll U.K. 56°10N 5°20W 24 B5

Argyll & Bute □ U.K. 56°13N 5°28W 24 B4
Ariana, L' Tunisia 36°52N 10°12E 95 A8
Arica Chile 18°32S 70°20W 120 D2
Arinos → Brazil 10°25S 58°20W 120 D4
Aripuanã → Brazil 5°7S 60°25W 120 C3
Arisaig U.K. 56°55N 5°51W 22 J7
Arizona □ U.S.A. 34°0N 112°0W 110 D4
Arkaig, L. U.K. 56°59N 5°10W 22 J7
Arkansas □ U.S.A. 35°0N 92°30W 111 D8
Arkansas → U.S.A. 33°47N 91°4W 111 D8
Arkansas City U.S.A. 37°4N 97°2W 111 C7
Arkhangelsk Russia 64°38N 40°36E 70 B7
Arklow Ireland 52°48N 6°10W 21 C10
Arkle → U.K. 54°24N 1°56W 26 D5
Arklow Ireland 52°48N 6°10W 21 C10
Arles France 43°41N 4°40E 66 E6
Arlington U.S.A. 38°53N 77°7W 112 F9
Arlon Belgium 49°42N 5°49E 64 D3
Armagh U.K. 54°21N 6°39W 19 C8
Armagh, Banbridge & Craigavon □ U.K. 54°20N 6°28W 19 C8
Armavir Russia 45°2N 41°7E 71 E7
Armenia Colombia 4°35N 75°45W 120 B2
Armenia ■ Asia 40°20N 45°0E 71 F7
Arnaud → Canada 59°59N 69°46W 109 D13
Arnhem Neths. 51°58N 5°55E 64 C3
Arnhem, C. Australia 12°20S 137°30E 98 C6
Arnhem Land Australia 13°10S 134°30E 98 C5
Arno → Italy 43°41N 10°17E 68 C4
Arnold U.K. 53°1N 1°7W 27 F6
Arnprior Canada 45°26N 76°21W 112 C9
Arnside U.K. 54°12N 2°49W 26 D3
Arra Mts. Ireland 52°50N 8°22W 20 C6
Arran U.K. 55°34N 5°12W 24 C5
Arranmore Ireland 55°0N 8°30W 18 B4
Arras France 50°17N 2°46E 66 A5
Arrecife Canary Is. 28°57N 13°37W 94 C3
Arrow, L. Ireland 54°3N 8°19W 18 C5
Artemivsk Ukraine 48°35N 38°0E 71 E6
Artigas Uruguay 30°20S 56°30W 121 F4
Artois France 50°20N 2°30E 66 A5
Artux China 39°40N 76°10E 78 D4
Artvin Turkey 41°14N 41°44E 71 F7
Aru, Kepulauan Indonesia 6°0S 134°30E 83 F8
Arua Uganda 3°1N 30°58E 96 D6
Aruanã Brazil 14°54S 51°10W 120 D4
Aruba ☑ W. Indies 12°30N 70°0W 115 E11
Arun → U.K. 50°49N 0°33W 31 E7
Arunachal Pradesh □ India 28°0N 95°0E 85 F19
Arundel U.K. 50°51N 0°33W 31 E7
Arusha Tanzania 3°20S 36°40E 96 E7
Aruwimi → Dem. Rep. of the Congo 1°13N 23°36E 96 D4
Arvayheer Mongolia 46°15N 102°48E 78 B9
Arviat Canada 61°6N 93°59W 108 C10
Arxan China 47°11N 119°57E 79 B12
Arzamas Russia 55°27N 43°55E 70 C7
As Sulaymānīyah Iraq 35°35N 45°29E 86 C6
As Sulaymānīyah Si. Arabia 24°9N 47°18E 86 E6
As Suwayq Oman 23°51N 57°26E 89 C6
Aş Şuwayrah Iraq 32°55N 45°0E 86 C6
Asahigawa Japan 43°46N 142°22E 81 B8
Asama-Yama Japan 36°24N 138°31E 81 E6
Asamankese Ghana 5°50N 0°40W 94 G5
Asansol India 23°40N 87°1E 85 H15
Asbestos Canada 45°47N 71°58W 113 C12
Asbury Park U.S.A. 40°13N 74°1W 113 E10
Ascension I. Atl. Oc. 7°57S 14°23W 52 E9
Áscoli Piceno Italy 42°51N 13°34E 68 C5
Ascot U.K. 51°25N 0°40W 31 D7
Aseb Eritrea 13°0N 42°40E 89 E3
Asenovgrad Bulgaria 42°1N 24°51E 69 C11
Asfordby U.K. 52°47N 0°57W 27 G7
Ash Kent, U.K. 51°16N 1°17E 31 D11
Ash Surrey, U.K. 51°15N 0°43W 31 D7
Ashbourne U.K. 53°2N 1°43W 27 F5
Ashburton U.K. 50°30N 3°46W 29 F6
Ashby-de-la-Zouch U.K. 52°46N 1°29W 27 G6
Ashchurch U.K. 52°0N 2°5W 30 C4
Ashdown Forest U.K. 51°3N 0°5E 31 D9
Asheville U.S.A. 35°36N 82°33W 111 C10
Ashford Derby, U.K. 53°14N 1°42W 27 F5
Ashford Kent, U.K. 51°8N 0°53E 31 D10
Ashington U.K. 55°11N 1°33W 26 B5
Ashkhabad Turkmenistan 37°58N 58°24E 87 B9
Ashland Ky., U.S.A. 38°28N 82°38W 112 F6
Ashland Ohio, U.S.A. 40°52N 82°19W 112 E6
Ashland Wis., U.S.A. 46°35N 90°53W 111 A8
Ashqelon Israel 31°42N 34°35E 86 D3
Ashtabula U.S.A. 41°52N 80°47W 112 E7
Ashton-in-Makerfield U.K. 53°30N 2°40W 27 F3
Ashton-under-Lyne U.K. 53°29N 2°6W 27 F4
Ashuanipi, L. Canada 52°45N 66°15W 109 D13
Ashwater U.K. 50°43N 4°19W 29 F5
Ashwick U.K. 51°13N 2°31W 30 D3
Asia 45°0N 75°0E 72 E9
Asinara Italy 41°4N 8°16E 68 D3
'Asīr Si. Arabia 18°40N 42°30E 89 D3
Asir, Ras Somalia 11°55N 51°10E 89 E5
Askrigg U.K. 54°19N 2°6W 26 D4
Aslackby U.K. 52°53N 0°24W 27 G8
Asmera Eritrea 15°19N 38°55E 89 D2
Aspatria U.K. 54°47N 3°19W 26 C2
Aspen U.S.A. 39°11N 106°49W 110 C5
Assal, L. Djibouti 11°40N 42°26E 89 E3
Assam □ India 26°0N 93°0E 85 G18
Assen Neths. 53°0N 6°35E 64 B4
Assiniboia Canada 49°40N 105°59W 108 E9
Assiniboine → Canada 49°53N 97°8W 108 E10
Assisi Italy 43°4N 12°37E 68 C5
Assynt U.K. 58°12N 5°12W 22 F7
Assynt, L. U.K. 58°11N 5°3W 22 F7
Astana Kazakhstan 51°10N 71°30E 76 D8
Asti Italy 44°54N 8°12E 68 B3
Astipálaia Greece 36°32N 26°22E 69 F12
Astoria U.S.A. 46°11N 123°50W 110 A2
Astrakhan Russia 46°25N 48°5E 71 E8
Asturias □ Spain 43°15N 6°0W 67 A3
Asunción Paraguay 25°10S 57°30W 121 E4
Aswân Egypt 24°4N 32°57E 95 D12

Aswan High Dam Egypt 23°54N 32°54E 95 D12
Asyût Egypt 27°11N 31°4E 95 C12
Aţ Ţā'if Si. Arabia 21°5N 40°27E 89 C3
Atacama, Desierto de Chile 24°0S 69°20W 121 E3
Atatürk Barajı Turkey 37°28N 38°30E 71 G6
Atbara Sudan 17°42N 33°59E 95 E12
Atbara → Sudan 17°40N 33°56E 95 E12
Atchafalaya B. U.S.A. 29°25N 91°25W 111 E8
Athabasca Canada 54°45N 113°20W 108 D8
Athabasca → Canada 58°40N 110°50W 108 D8
Athabasca, L. Canada 59°15N 109°15W 108 D9
Athboy Ireland 53°36N 6°56W 19 D8
Athenry Ireland 53°18N 8°44W 20 B5
Athens Greece 37°58N 23°43E 69 F10
Athens Ga., U.S.A. 33°57N 83°23W 111 D10
Athens Ohio, U.S.A. 39°20N 82°6W 112 F6
Atherstone U.K. 52°35N 1°33W 27 G5
Atherton U.K. 53°32N 2°30W 27 E4
Athlone Ireland 53°25N 7°56W 20 B7
Atholl, Forest of U.K. 56°51N 3°50W 23 J10
Athos Greece 40°9N 24°22E 69 D11
Athy Ireland 53°0N 7°0W 21 B8
Atikokan Canada 48°45N 91°37W 112 A2
Atka I. U.S.A. 52°7N 174°30W 108 D2
Atlanta U.S.A. 33°45N 84°23W 111 D10
Atlantic City U.S.A. 39°21N 74°27W 113 F10
Atlantic Ocean 0°0 20°0W 50 D8
Atlas Saharien Algeria 33°30N 1°0E 94 B6
Atlin Canada 59°31N 133°41W 108 D6
Attawapiskat Canada 52°56N 82°24W 109 D11
Attawapiskat → Canada 52°57N 82°18W 109 D11
Attleborough U.K. 52°32N 1°1E 31 A11
Attu I. U.S.A. 52°55N 172°55E 108 D1
Atyraū Kazakhstan 47°5N 52°0E 71 E9
Au Sable → U.S.A. 44°25N 83°20W 112 C6
Aube → France 48°34N 3°43E 66 B5
Auburn Ind., U.S.A. 41°22N 85°4W 112 E5
Auburn N.Y., U.S.A. 42°56N 76°34W 112 D9
Aubusson France 45°57N 2°11E 66 D5
Auch France 43°39N 0°36E 66 E4
Auchterarder U.K. 56°18N 3°41W 25 B8
Auchtermuchty U.K. 56°18N 3°13W 25 B8
Auckland N.Z. 36°52S 174°46E 99 H13
Auckland Is. Pac. Oc. 50°40S 166°5E 102 N8
Aude → France 43°13N 3°14E 66 E5
Audlem U.K. 52°59N 2°30W 27 G4
Aughnacloy U.K. 54°25N 6°59W 19 C8
Augsburg Germany 48°25N 10°52E 64 D6
Augusta Australia 34°19S 115°9E 98 G2
Augusta U.S.A. 33°28N 81°58W 111 D10
Aunis France 46°5N 0°50W 66 C3
Aurangabad Bihar, India 24°45N 84°18E 85 G14
Aurangabad Maharashtra, India 19°50N 75°23E 84 K9
Aurillac France 44°55N 2°26E 66 D5
Aurora Colo., U.S.A. 39°43N 104°49W 110 C6
Aurora Ill., U.S.A. 41°45N 88°19W 112 E3
Austin U.S.A. 30°17N 97°45W 110 D7
Australia ■ Oceania 23°0S 135°0E 98 E3
Australian Capital Territory □ Australia 35°30S 149°0E 98 H8
Austria ■ Europe 47°0N 14°0E 64 E8
Autun France 46°58N 4°17E 66 C6
Auvergne France 45°20N 3°15E 66 D5
Auvergne, Mts. d' France 45°20N 2°55E 66 D5
Auxerre France 47°48N 3°32E 66 C5
Avallon France 47°30N 3°53E 66 C5
Avaré Brazil 23°4S 48°58W 122 D1
Avebury U.K. 51°26N 1°50W 30 D5
Avellaneda Argentina 34°40S 58°22W 121 F4
Avellino Italy 40°54N 14°47E 68 D6
Aversa Italy 40°58N 14°12E 68 D6
Aveton Gifford U.K. 50°18N 3°50W 29 G6
Aveyron → France 44°5N 1°16E 66 D4
Aviemore U.K. 57°12N 3°50W 23 H10
Avignon France 43°57N 4°50E 66 E6
Avila Spain 40°39N 4°43W 67 B3
Avilés Spain 43°35N 5°57W 67 A3
Avoca → Ireland 52°48N 6°10W 21 C10
Avon → Bristol, U.K. 51°29N 2°41W 30 C4
Avon → Dorset, U.K. 50°44N 1°46W 30 E5
Avon → Warks., U.K. 52°0N 2°8W 30 B4
Avonmouth U.K. 51°30N 2°42W 30 C3
Avranches France 48°40N 1°20W 66 B3
Awasa Ethiopia 7°2N 38°28E 89 F2
Awash Ethiopia 9°1N 40°10E 89 F3
Awbārī, Idehan Libya 27°10N 11°30E 95 C8
Awe, L. U.K. 56°17N 5°16W 24 B5
Axbridge U.K. 51°17N 2°49W 30 D3
Axe → U.K. 50°42N 3°4W 29 E8
Axe Edge U.K. 53°14N 1°57W 27 F5
Axel Heiberg I. Canada 80°0N 90°0W 109 B11
Axholme, Isle of U.K. 53°32N 0°50W 27 E7
Axios → Greece 40°57N 22°35E 69 D10
Axminster U.K. 50°46N 3°0W 29 F8
Axmouth U.K. 50°42N 3°3W 29 F7
Ayacucho Argentina 37°5S 58°20W 121 F4
Ayacucho Peru 13°0S 74°0W 120 D2
Ayakkum Hu China 37°30N 89°20E 78 D6
Aydın Turkey 37°51N 27°51E 71 G4
Aydingkol Hu China 42°40N 89°15E 78 C6
Ayers Rock = Uluru Australia 25°23S 131°5E 98 F5
Ayeyawadi → Myanmar 15°50N 95°6E 85 M19
Aylesbury U.K. 51°49N 0°49W 31 C7
Aylesford U.K. 51°18N 0°30E 31 D10
Aylmer, L. Canada 64°5N 108°30W 108 C8
Aylsham U.K. 52°48N 1°15E 31 A11
Aynho U.K. 52°0N 1°15W 30 C6
Ayr U.K. 55°28N 4°38W 24 D6
Ayr → U.K. 55°28N 4°38W 24 D6
Aysgarth U.K. 54°18N 2°1W 26 D5
Ayton Borders, U.K. 55°51N 2°6W 25 C11
Ayton N. Yorks., U.K. 54°15N 0°28W 26 D8
Ayutthaya Thailand 14°25N 100°30E 82 B2
Ayvalık Turkey 39°20N 26°46E 71 G4
Az Zarqā Jordan 32°5N 36°4E 86 C4
Az Zāwiyah Libya 32°52N 12°56E 95 B8
Azad Kashmir □ Pakistan 33°50N 73°50E 84 B8
Azamgarh India 26°5N 83°13E 85 F13
Āzarbāyjān □ Iran 37°0N 44°30E 86 B6

Azare

Biarritz

Azare *Nigeria* 11°55N 10°10E **94** F8
Azerbaijan ■ *Asia* 40°20N 48°00E **71** F8
Azores *Atl. Oc.* 38°00N 27°00W **91** C1
Azov *Russia* 47°3N 39°25E **71** E6
Azov, Sea of *Europe* 46°0N 36°30E **71** E6
Azuero, Pen. de *Panama* 7°30N 80°30W **115** F8
Azul *Argentina* 36°42S 59°43W **121** F4

B

Bab el Mandeb *Red Sea* 12°35N 43°25E **89** E3
Bābā, Koh-i- *Afghan.* 34°30N 67°0E **84** B5
Babine L. *Canada* 54°48N 126°0W **108** D7
Bābol *Iran* 36°40N 52°50E **87** B8
Babruysk *Belarus* 53°10N 29°15E **65** B15
Babuyan Chan. *Phil.* 18°40N 121°30E **83** A6
Babylon *Iraq* 32°34N 44°22E **86** C6
Bac Lieu *Vietnam* 9°17N 105°43E **82** C3
Bacabal *Brazil* 4°15S 44°45W **120** C5
Bacău *Romania* 46°35N 26°55E **65** E14
Back → *Canada* 65°10N 104°0W **108** C9
Bacolod *Phil.* 10°40N 122°57E **83** B6
Bacton *U.K.* 52°52N 1°27E **31** A11
Bacup *U.K.* 53°42N 2°11W **27** E4
Bad Axe *U.S.A.* 43°48N 83°0W **112** D6
Badain Jaran Desert *China* 40°23N 102°0E **78** C9
Badajoz *Spain* 38°50N 6°59W **67** C2
Badakhshān □ *Afghan.* 36°30N 71°0E **87** B12
Badalona *Spain* 41°26N 2°15E **67** B7
Baden-Württemberg □
Germany 48°20N 8°40E **64** D5
Badenoch *U.K.* 56°59N 4°15W **23** J9
Badlands *U.S.A.* 43°55N 102°30W **110** B6
Baffin B. *N. Amer.* 72°0N 64°0W **109** B13
Baffin I. *Canada* 68°0N 75°0W **109** C12
Bafoulabé *Mali* 13°50N 10°55W **94** F3
Bafoussam *Cameroon* 5°28N 10°25E **96** C2
Bafra *Turkey* 41°34N 35°54E **71** F6
Bafwasende *Tanzania* 6°28S 38°55E **96** F7
Bagé *Brazil* 31°20S 54°15W **121** F4
Bagenalstown *Ireland* 52°42N 6°58W **21** C9
Baggy Pt. *U.K.* 51°8N 4°16W **29** E5
Baghdād *Iraq* 33°20N 44°23E **86** C6
Baghlān *Afghan.* 32°12N 68°46E **87** B12
Bagshot *U.K.* 51°22N 0°41W **31** D7
Baguio *Phil.* 16°26N 120°34E **83** A6
Bahamas ■ *N. Amer.* 24°0N 75°0W **115** C10
Baharampur *India* 24°2N 88°27E **85** G16
Bahawalpur *Pakistan* 29°24N 71°40E **84** E7
Bahia = Salvador *Brazil* 13°0S 38°30W **122** B3
Bahia □ *Brazil* 12°0S 42°0W **122** B2
Bahía Blanca *Argentina* 38°35S 62°13W **121** F3
Bahir Dar *Ethiopia* 11°37N 37°10E **89** E2
Bahr el Ghazal □ *South Sudan* 7°30N 25°30E **95** G11
Bahraich *India* 27°38N 81°37E **85** F12
Bahrain ■ *Asia* 26°0N 50°35E **87** E7
Baia Mare *Romania* 47°40N 23°35E **65** E12
Baicheng *China* 45°38N 122°42E **79** B13
Baie-Comeau *Canada* 49°12N 68°10W **109** E13
Baie-St-Paul *Canada* 47°28N 70°32W **113** B12
Baie Verte *Canada* 49°55N 56°12W **109** E14
Ba'iji *Iraq* 35°0N 43°30E **86** C5
Baikal, L. *Russia* 53°0N 108°0E **77** D11
Baildon *U.K.* 53°51N 1°46W **27** E4
Baile Sear = Baleshare *U.K.* 57°31N 7°22W **22** G3
Bain → *U.K.* 53°6N 0°12W **27** F8
Bainbridge *U.K.* 54°18N 2°6W **26** D4
Baja, Pta. *Mexico* 29°58N 115°49W **114** B1
Baja California *Mexico* 31°10N 115°12W **114** A1
Baker, L. *Canada* 64°0N 96°0W **108** C10
Baker City *U.S.A.* 44°47N 117°50W **110** B3
Baker I. *Pac. Oc.* 0°10N 176°35W **99** A15
Baker Lake *Canada* 64°20N 96°3W **108** C10
Bakers Dozen Is. *Canada* 56°45N 78°45W **109** D12
Bakersfield *U.S.A.* 35°23N 119°1W **110** C3
Bakewell *U.K.* 53°13N 1°40W **27** F5
Baku *Azerbaijan* 40°29N 49°56E **71** F8
Bala *U.K.* 52°54N 3°36W **28** B6
Bala, L. *U.K.* 52°53N 3°37W **28** B6
Balabac Str. *E. Indies* 7°53N 117°5E **82** C5
Balaghat Ra. *India* 18°50N 76°30E **84** K10
Balaklava *Ukraine* 44°30N 33°30E **71** F5
Balakovo *Russia* 52°4N 47°55E **70** D8
Balashov *Russia* 51°30N 43°10E **71** D7
Balaton *Hungary* 46°50N 17°40E **65** E9
Balbi, Mt. *Papua N. G.* 5°55S 154°58E **99** B10
Balbina, Represa de *Brazil* 2°0S 59°30W **120** C4
Balbriggan *Ireland* 53°37N 6°11W **19** D9
Balcarce *Argentina* 38°0S 58°10W **121** F4
Balderton *U.K.* 53°3N 0°47W **27** F7
Baldock *U.K.* 52°0N 0°11W **31** C8
Baldoyle *Ireland* 53°24N 6°8W **21** B10
Baldwin *U.S.A.* 43°54N 85°51W **112** D5
Baldy Peak *U.S.A.* 33°54N 109°34W **110** D5
Balearic Is. *Spain* 39°30N 3°0E **67** C7
Baleine → *Canada* 58°15N 67°40W **109** D13
Baleshare *U.K.* 57°31N 7°22W **22** G3
Baleshwar *India* 21°35N 87°3E **85** J15
Bali *Indonesia* 8°20S 115°0E **82** F4
Balıkesir *Turkey* 39°39N 27°53E **71** G4
Balikpapan *Indonesia* 1°10S 116°55E **82** E5
Balkan Mts. *Bulgaria* 43°15N 23°0E **69** C10
Balkanabat *Turkmenistan* 39°30N 54°22E **87** B8
Balkhash, L. *Kazakhstan* 46°0N 74°50E **76** E8
Ballachulish *U.K.* 56°41N 5°8W **22** J7
Ballaghadereen *Ireland* 53°55N 8°34W **18** D4
Ballantrae *U.K.* 55°6N 4°59W **24** D6
Ballarat *Australia* 37°33S 143°50E **98** H7
Ballari *India* 15°10N 76°56E **84** M10
Ballater *U.K.* 57°3N 3°3W **23** H11
Ballenas, B. de *Mexico* 26°45N 113°26W **114** B2
Balleny Is. *Antarctica* 66°30S 163°0E **55** C11
Ballina *Ireland* 54°7N 9°9W **18** C3
Ballinasloe *Ireland* 53°20N 8°13W **20** B6
Ballincollig *Ireland* 51°53N 8°35W **20** E5
Ballinrobe *Ireland* 53°38N 9°13W **20** B3
Ballinskelligs B. *Ireland* 51°48N 10°13W **20** E2
Ballybunion *Ireland* 52°31N 9°40W **20** C3
Ballycastle *U.K.* 55°12N 6°15W **19** A9
Ballyclare *U.K.* 54°46N 6°0W **19** B10
Ballycroy △ *Ireland* 54°5N 9°50W **18** C2

Ballycummin *Ireland* 52°38N 8°38W **20** C5
Ballyhaunis *Ireland* 53°46N 8°46W **18** D4
Ballyhoura Mts. *Ireland* 52°18N 8°33W **20** D5
Ballymena *U.K.* 54°52N 6°17W **19** B9
Ballymoney *U.K.* 55°5N 6°31W **19** A8
Ballymote *Ireland* 54°5N 8°31W **18** C4
Ballynahinch *U.K.* 54°24N 5°54W **19** C10
Ballyquintin Pt. *U.K.* 54°20N 5°30W **19** C11
Ballyshannon *Ireland* 54°30N 8°11W **18** B5
Balmoral Forest *U.K.* 57°0N 3°15W **23** J11
Balrampur *India* 27°30N 82°20E **85** F13
Balsas → *Mexico* 17°55N 102°10W **114** D4
Baltic Sea *Europe* 57°0N 19°0E **63** F7
Baltimore *Ireland* 51°29N 9°22W **20** F4
Baltimore *U.S.A.* 39°17N 76°36W **112** F9
Baluchistan □ *Pakistan* 27°30N 65°0E **84** F4
Bam *Iran* 29°7N 58°14E **87** D9
Bamako *Mali* 12°34N 7°55W **94** F4
Bambari *C.A.R.* 5°40N 20°35E **96** C4
Bamberg *Germany* 49°54N 10°54E **64** D6
Bamburgh *U.K.* 55°37N 1°43W **26** A5
Bamford *U.K.* 53°22N 1°41W **27** F5
Bampton *Devon, U.K.* 50°59N 3°29W **29** F7
Bampton *Oxon., U.K.* 51°44N 1°32W **30** C5
Banaba *Kiribati* 0°45S 169°50E **102** H8
Bananal, I. do *Brazil* 11°30S 50°30W **120** D4
Banbridge *U.K.* 54°22N 6°16W **19** C9
Banbury *U.K.* 52°4N 1°20W **30** B6
Banchory *U.K.* 57°3N 2°29W **23** H13
Bancroft *Canada* 45°3N 77°51W **112** C9
Banda *India* 25°30N 80°26E **84** G12
Banda, Kepulauan *Indonesia* 4°37S 129°50E **83** E7
Banda Aceh *Indonesia* 5°35N 95°20E **82** C1
Banda Sea *Indonesia* 6°0S 130°0E **83** F7
Bandar-e Abbās *Iran* 27°15N 56°15E **87** E9
Bandar-e Anzalī *Iran* 37°30N 49°30E **86** B7
Bandar-e Ma'shur *Iran* 30°35N 49°10E **86** D7
Bandar-e Torkeman *Iran* 37°0N 54°10E **87** B8
Bandar Lampung *Indonesia* 5°20S 105°10E **82** F3
Bandar Seri Begawan *Brunei* 4°52N 115°0E **82** C4
Bandeira, Pico da *Brazil* 20°26S 41°47W **122** D2
Bandırma *Turkey* 40°20N 28°0E **71** F4
Bandon *Ireland* 51°44N 8°44W **20** E5
Bandon → *Ireland* 51°43N 8°37W **20** E5
Bandundu
Dem. Rep. of the Congo 3°15S 17°22E **96** E3
Bandung *Indonesia* 6°54S 107°36E **82** F3
Banes *Cuba* 21°0N 75°42W **115** C9
Banff *Canada* 51°10N 115°34W **108** D8
Banff *U.K.* 57°40N 2°33W **23** G12
Bangalore = Bengaluru
India 12°59N 77°40E **84** N10
Bangassou *C.A.R.* 4°55N 23°7E **96** D4
Banggai, Kepulauan *Indonesia* 1°40S 123°30E **83** E6
Bangka *Indonesia* 2°0S 105°50E **82** E3
Bangkok *Thailand* 13°45N 100°35E **82** B2
Bangladesh ■ *Asia* 24°0N 90°0E **85** H17
Bangor *Down, U.K.* 54°40N 5°40W **19** B10
Bangor *Gwynedd, U.K.* 53°14N 4°8W **28** A5
Bangui *C.A.R.* 4°23N 18°35E **96** D3
Bangweulu, L. *Zambia* 11°0S 30°0E **96** G6
Banham *U.K.* 52°27N 1°2E **31** B11
Banja Luka *Bos.-H.* 44°49N 17°11E **68** B7
Banjarmasin *Indonesia* 3°20S 114°35E **82** E4
Banjul *Gambia* 13°28N 16°40W **94** F2
Bankend *U.K.* 55°1N 3°33W **25** D8
Banks I. *Canada* 73°15N 121°30W **108** B7
Banks Is. *Vanuatu* 13°50S 167°30E **99** C12
Bann → *U.K.* 55°8N 6°41W **19** A8
Bannockburn *U.K.* 56°5N 3°55W **25** B8
Bannu *Pakistan* 33°0N 70°18E **84** C7
Banská Bystrica *Slovakia* 48°46N 19°14E **65** D10
Bantry *Ireland* 51°41N 9°27W **20** E4
Bantry B. *Ireland* 51°37N 9°44W **20** E3
Banwell *U.K.* 51°19N 2°52W **30** D3
Banyak, Kepulauan *Indonesia* 2°10N 97°10E **82** D1
Banyuwangi *Indonesia* 8°13S 114°21E **82** F4
Bao'an *China* 22°34N 113°52E **79** a
Baoding *China* 38°50N 115°28E **79** C12
Baoji *China* 34°20N 107°5E **78** E10
Baoshan *China* 25°10N 99°5E **78** F8
Baotou *China* 40°32N 110°2E **78** C11
Ba'qūbah *Iraq* 33°45N 44°50E **86** C6
Bar Harbor *U.S.A.* 44°23N 68°13W **113** C13
Bar-le-Duc *France* 48°47N 5°10E **66** B6
Baraboo *U.S.A.* 43°28N 89°45W **112** D3
Baracoa *Cuba* 20°20N 74°30W **115** C10
Barahona *Dom. Rep.* 18°13N 71°7W **115** D10
Barail Range *India* 25°15N 93°20E **85** G18
Barakaldo *Spain* 43°18N 2°59W **67** A4
Baranof I. *U.S.A.* 57°0N 135°0W **108** D6
Barbacena *Brazil* 21°15S 43°56W **122** D2
Barbados ■ *W. Indies* 13°10N 59°30W **114** c
Barberton *U.S.A.* 41°1N 81°39W **112** E7
Barcelona *Spain* 41°22N 2°10E **67** B7
Barcelona *Venezuela* 10°10N 64°40W **120** A3
Barddhaman *India* 23°14N 87°39E **85** H15
Bardiyah *Libya* 31°45N 25°5E **95** B10
Bardney *U.K.* 53°13N 0°19W **27** F8
Bardsey I. *U.K.* 52°45N 4°47W **28** B4
Bardstown *U.S.A.* 37°49N 85°28W **112** G5
Bareilly *India* 28°22N 79°27E **84** E11
Barents Sea *Arctic* 73°0N 39°0E **54** B9
Barford *U.K.* 52°16N 1°35W **30** B5
Bargoed *U.K.* 51°42N 3°15W **28** D5
Barham *U.K.* 51°12N 1°11E **31** D11
Bari *Italy* 41°8N 16°51E **68** D7
Bari Doab *Pakistan* 30°20N 73°0E **84** D8
Barīm *Yemen* 12°39N 43°25E **90** E8
Barinas *Venezuela* 8°36N 70°15W **120** B2
Baring, C. *Canada* 70°0N 117°30W **108** C8
Barisal *Bangla.* 22°45N 90°20E **85** H17
Barking and Dagenham □
U.K. 51°32N 0°10E **31** C9
Barkly Tableland *Australia* 17°50S 136°40E **98** D6
Barlborough *U.K.* 53°17N 1°17W **27** F6
Barlby *U.K.* 53°48N 1°2W **27** E6

Barlee, L. *Australia* 29°15S 119°30E **98** F2
Barletta *Italy* 41°19N 16°17E **68** D7
Barmby Moor *U.K.* 53°56N 0°49W **27** E7
Barmer *India* 25°45N 71°20E **84** G7
Barmer Castle *U.K.* 55°39N 1°59W **26** A5
Barmouth *U.K.* 52°44N 4°4W **28** B5
Barnard Castle *U.K.* 54°33N 1°55W **26** C5
Barnaul *Russia* 53°20N 83°40E **76** D9
Barnetby le Wold *U.K.* 53°34N 0°24W **27** E8
Barnoldswick *U.K.* 53°55N 2°11W **27** E4
Barnsley *U.K.* 53°34N 1°27W **27** E6
Barnstaple *U.K.* 51°5N 4°4W **29** E5
Barnstaple Bay = Bideford Bay
U.K. 51°5N 4°20W **29** E5
Barotseland *Zambia* 15°0S 24°0E **97** H4
Barques, Pt. Aux *U.S.A.* 44°4N 82°58W **112** C6
Barquisimeto *Venezuela* 10°4N 69°19W **120** A3
Barra *Brazil* 11°5S 43°10W **122** B2
Barra *U.K.* 57°0N 7°29W **22** J2
Barra, Sd. of *U.K.* 57°4N 7°25W **22** J2
Barra do Corda *Brazil* 5°30S 45°10W **120** C5
Barra do Pirai *Brazil* 22°30S 43°50W **122** D2
Barra Hd. *U.K.* 56°47N 7°40W **22** J2
Barra Mansa *Brazil* 22°35S 44°12W **122** D2
Barrancabermeja *Colombia* 7°0N 73°50W **120** B2
Barranquilla *Colombia* 11°0N 74°50W **120** A2
Barre *U.S.A.* 44°12N 72°30W **113** C11
Barreiras *Brazil* 12°8S 45°0W **122** B2
Barreiro *Portugal* 38°39N 9°5W **67** C1
Barreiros *Brazil* 8°49S 35°12W **122** A3
Barretos *Brazil* 20°30S 48°35W **122** D1
Barrhead *U.K.* 55°48N 4°23W **24** C7
Barrie *Canada* 44°24N 79°40W **109** E12
Barrow *U.S.A.* 71°18N 156°47W **108** B4
Barrow → *Ireland* 52°25N 6°58W **21** D9
Barrow-in-Furness *U.K.* 54°7N 3°14W **26** D2
Barrow upon Humber *U.K.* 53°41N 0°23W **27** E8
Barrowford *U.K.* 53°51N 2°14W **27** E4
Barry *U.K.* 51°24N 3°16W **29** E7
Barry I. *U.K.* 51°23N 3°16W **29** E7
Barry's Bay *Canada* 45°29N 77°41W **112** C9
Barstow *U.S.A.* 34°54N 117°1W **110** D3
Bartlesville *U.S.A.* 36°45N 95°59W **111** C7
Barton *U.K.* 54°29N 1°38W **26** D5
Barton-upon-Humber *U.K.* 53°41N 0°25W **27** E8
Barú, Volcan *Panama* 8°55N 82°35W **115** F8
Baruun-Urt *Mongolia* 46°46N 113°15E **79** B11
Barwell *U.K.* 52°35N 1°21W **27** G6
Barysaw *Belarus* 54°17N 28°28E **65** A15
Bashkortostan □ *Russia* 54°0N 57°0E **70** D10
Basilan I. *Phil.* 6°35N 122°0E **83** C6
Basildon *U.K.* 51°34N 0°28E **31** C9
Basingstoke *U.K.* 51°15N 1°5W **30** D5
Baskatong, Rés. *Canada* 46°46N 75°50W **113** B10
Basle *Switz.* 47°35N 7°35E **64** E4
Basque Provinces = País Vasco □
Spain 42°50N 2°45W **67** A4
Basra *Iraq* 30°30N 47°50E **86** D6
Bass Rock *U.K.* 56°5N 2°38W **25** B10
Bass Str. *Australia* 39°15S 146°30E **98** H8
Bassas da India *Ind. Oc.* 22°0S 39°0E **97** J7
Basse-Terre *Guadeloupe* 16°0N 61°44W **115** D12
Bassenthwaite L. *U.K.* 54°40N 3°14W **26** C2
Basseterre *St. Kitts & Nevis* 17°17N 62°43W **115** D12
Basti *India* 26°52N 82°55E **85** F13
Bastia *France* 42°40N 9°30E **66** E8
Baston *U.K.* 52°43N 0°21W **27** G8
Bata *Eq. Guin.* 1°57N 9°50E **96** D1
Batabanó, G. de *Cuba* 22°30N 82°30W **115** C8
Batangas *Phil.* 13°35N 121°10E **83** B6
Batatais *Brazil* 20°54S 47°37W **122** D1
Batavia *U.S.A.* 43°0N 78°11W **112** D8
Bataysk *Russia* 47°3N 39°45E **71** E6
Batdambang *Cambodia* 13°7N 103°12E **82** B2
Bath *U.K.* 51°23N 2°22W **30** D4
Bath *Maine, U.S.A.* 43°55N 69°49W **113** D13
Bath *N.Y., U.S.A.* 42°20N 77°19W **112** D9
Bathford *U.K.* 51°24N 2°18W **30** D4
Bathgate *U.K.* 55°54N 3°39W **25** C8
Bathsheba *Barbados* 13°13N 59°32W **114** c
Bathurst *Australia* 33°25S 149°31E **98** G8
Bathurst *Canada* 47°37N 65°43W **109** E13
Bathurst, C. *Canada* 70°34N 128°0W **108** B7
Bathurst Inlet *Canada* 66°50N 108°1W **108** C9
Batley *U.K.* 53°43N 1°38W **27** E5
Batman *Turkey* 37°55N 41°5E **71** G7
Batna *Algeria* 35°34N 6°15E **94** A7
Baton Rouge *U.S.A.* 30°27N 91°11W **111** D8
Batticaloa *Sri Lanka* 7°43N 81°45E **84** R12
Battle *U.K.* 50°55N 0°30E **31** E9
Battle Creek *U.S.A.* 42°19N 85°11W **112** D5
Battu, Kepulauan *Indonesia* 0°30S 98°25E **82** E1
Batu Pahat *Malaysia* 1°50N 102°56E **82** D2
Batumi *Georgia* 41°39N 41°44E **71** F7
Bauld, C. *Canada* 51°38N 55°26W **109** D14
Bauru *Brazil* 22°10S 49°0W **122** D1
Bavaria = Bayern □ *Germany* 48°50N 12°0E **64** D6
Bawdsey *U.K.* 52°1N 1°27E **31** B11
Bawtry *U.K.* 53°26N 1°2W **27** F6
Bay City *U.S.A.* 43°36N 83°54W **112** D6
Bay Is. *Honduras* 16°45N 86°15W **114** D7
Bayamo *Cuba* 20°20N 76°40W **115** C9
Bayan Har Shan *China* 34°0N 98°0E **78** E8
Bayan Obo *China* 41°52N 109°59E **78** C10
Baydhabo *Somalia* 3°8N 43°30E **89** G3
Bayern □ *Germany* 48°50N 12°0E **64** D6
Bayeux *France* 49°17N 0°42W **66** B3
Bayonne *France* 43°30N 1°28W **66** E3
Beachley *U.K.* 51°37N 2°39W **30** C4
Beachy Hd. *U.K.* 50°44N 0°15E **31** E9
Beacon *U.S.A.* 41°30N 73°58W **113** E11
Beaconsfield *U.K.* 51°36N 0°38W **31** C7
Beadnell *U.K.* 55°33N 1°38W **26** A5
Beagle, Canal *S. Amer.* 55°0S 68°30W **121** H3
Beaminster *U.K.* 50°48N 2°44W **30** E3
Bear → *U.S.A.* 41°30N 112°8W **110** B4
Bear I. *Arctic* 74°30N 19°0E **54** B8
Bear I. *Ireland* 51°38N 9°50W **20** E2
Bear L. *U.S.A.* 41°59N 111°21W **110** B4
Beardmore Glacier *Antarctica* 84°30S 170°0E **55** E11

Beardstown *U.S.A.* 40°1N 90°26W **112** E2
Béarn *France* 43°20N 0°30W **66** E3
Bearsden *U.K.* 55°55N 4°21W **24** C7
Bearsted *U.K.* 51°16N 0°35E **31** D10
Beatrice *U.S.A.* 40°16N 96°45W **111** B7
Beattock *U.K.* 55°20N 3°28W **25** D9
Beattock Summit *U.K.* 55°25N 3°32W **25** D8
Beauce, Plaine de la *France* 48°10N 1°45E **66** B4
Beaufort Sea *Arctic* 72°0N 140°0W **54** B1
Beaufort West *S. Africa* 32°18S 22°36E **97** L4
Beauharnois *Canada* 45°20N 73°52W **113** C11
Beaulieu *U.K.* 50°48N 1°27W **30** E6
Beauly *U.K.* 57°30N 4°28W **23** H9
Beauly → *U.K.* 57°29N 4°27W **23** H9
Beauly Firth *U.K.* 57°30N 4°20W **23** H9
Beaumaris *U.K.* 53°16N 4°6W **28** A5
Beaumont *U.S.A.* 30°5N 94°6W **111** D8
Beaune *France* 47°2N 4°50E **66** C6
Beauvais *France* 49°25N 2°8E **66** B5
Beaver → *Canada* 55°26N 107°45W **108** D9
Beaver Creek *Canada* 63°0N 141°0W **108** C5
Beaver Dam *U.S.A.* 43°28N 88°50W **112** D3
Beaver Falls *U.S.A.* 40°46N 80°20W **112** E7
Beaver I. *U.S.A.* 45°40N 85°33W **112** C5
Beawar *India* 26°3N 74°18E **84** F9
Bebedouro *Brazil* 21°0S 48°25W **122** D1
Bebington *U.K.* 53°22N 3°0W **27** F3
Beccles *U.K.* 52°27N 1°35E **31** B12
Béchar *Algeria* 31°38N 2°18W **94** B5
Beckermet *U.K.* 54°27N 3°30W **26** D1
Beckfoot *U.K.* 54°50N 3°24W **26** C2
Beckingham *U.K.* 53°24N 0°50W **27** F7
Beckley *U.S.A.* 37°47N 81°11W **112** G7
Bedale *U.K.* 54°18N 1°36W **26** D5
Beddgelert *U.K.* 53°1N 4°6W **28** A5
Bedford *U.K.* 52°8N 0°28W **31** B8
Bedford *Ind., U.S.A.* 38°52N 86°29W **112** F4
Bedford *Va., U.S.A.* 37°20N 79°31W **112** G8
Bedford Level *U.K.* 52°32N 0°7W **31** A8
Bedlington *U.K.* 55°8N 1°35W **26** B5
Bedworth *U.K.* 52°29N 1°28W **30** B6
Beeford *U.K.* 53°58N 0°17W **27** E8
Beer *U.K.* 50°41N 3°6W **29** F7
Be'er Sheva *Israel* 31°15N 34°48E **86** D3
Beeston *U.K.* 52°56N 1°14W **27** G6
Beeville *U.S.A.* 28°24N 97°45W **110** E7
Behchoko *Canada* 62°50N 116°3W **108** C8
Bei Jiang → *China* 23°2N 112°58E **79** G11
Bei Shan *China* 41°30N 96°0E **78** C8
Bei'an *China* 48°10N 126°20E **79** B14
Beighton *U.K.* 53°21N 1°20W **27** F6
Beihai *China* 21°28N 109°6E **78** G10
Beijing *China* 39°53N 116°21E **79** D12
Beinn na Faoghla = Benbecula
U.K. 57°26N 7°21W **22** H3
Beira *Mozam.* 19°50S 34°52E **97** H6
Beirut *Lebanon* 33°53N 35°31E **86** C3
Beitbridge *Zimbabwe* 22°12S 30°0E **97** J6
Beith *U.K.* 55°45N 4°38W **24** C6
Béja *Tunisia* 36°43N 9°12E **95** A7
Bejaïa *Algeria* 36°42N 5°2E **94** A7
Békéscsaba *Hungary* 46°40N 21°5E **65** E11
Bela *Pakistan* 26°12N 66°20E **84** F5
Belagavi *India* 15°55N 74°35E **84** M9
Bela-Bela *S. Africa* 24°51S 28°19E **97** J5
Belarus ■ *Europe* 53°30N 27°0E **70** D4
Belau = Palau ■ *Palau* 7°30N 134°30E **102** G5
Belbroughton *U.K.* 52°24N 2°7W **30** B4
Belcher Chan. *Canada* 77°15N 95°0W **109** B10
Belcher Is. *Canada* 56°15N 78°45W **109** D12
Beledweyne *Somalia* 4°30N 45°5E **89** G4
Belém *Brazil* 1°20S 48°30W **120** C5
Belep, Îs. *N. Cal.* 19°45S 163°40E **99** D11
Belfast *S. Africa* 25°42S 30°2E **97** K6
Belfast *U.K.* 54°37N 5°56W **19** B10
Belfast *Maine, U.S.A.* 44°26N 69°1W **113** C13
Belfast L. *U.K.* 54°40N 5°50W **19** B10
Belford *U.K.* 55°36N 1°49W **26** A5
Belfort *France* 47°38N 6°50E **66** C7
Belgium ■ *Europe* 50°30N 5°0E **64** C3
Belgorod *Russia* 50°35N 36°35E **71** D6
Belgrade *Serbia* 44°50N 20°37E **69** B9
Belitung *Indonesia* 3°10S 107°50E **82** E3
Belize ■ *Cent. Amer.* 17°0N 88°30W **114** D7
Belize City *Belize* 17°25N 88°10W **114** D7
Bell Peninsula *Canada* 63°50N 82°0W **109** C11
Bell Ville *Argentina* 32°40S 62°40W **121** F3
Bella Coola *Canada* 52°25N 126°40W **108** D7
Bellaire *U.S.A.* 40°1N 80°45E **112** E7
Belle Fourche → *U.S.A.* 44°26N 102°18W **110** B6
Belle-Île *France* 47°20N 3°10W **66** C2
Belle Isle *Canada* 51°57N 55°25W **109** D14
Belle Isle, Str. of *Canada* 51°30N 56°30W **109** D14
Bellefontaine *U.S.A.* 40°22N 83°46W **112** E6
Bellefontaine *Barbados* 13°15N 59°34W **114** c
Belleville *Canada* 44°10N 77°23W **109** E12
Belleville *U.S.A.* 38°31N 89°59W **112** F3
Bellingham *U.K.* 55°9N 2°16W **26** B4
Bellingham *U.S.A.* 48°46N 122°29W **110** A2
Bellingshausen Sea *Antarctica* 66°0S 80°0W **55** C17
Bellinzona *Switz.* 46°11N 9°1E **64** E5
Belmonte *Brazil* 16°0S 39°0W **122** C3
Belmopan *Belize* 17°18N 88°30W **114** D7
Belmullet *Ireland* 54°14N 9°58W **18** C2
Belo Horizonte *Brazil* 19°55S 43°56W **122** C2
Belo Jardim *Brazil* 8°20S 36°26W **122** A3
Belogorsk *Russia* 51°0N 128°20E **77** D13
Beloit *U.S.A.* 42°31N 89°2W **112** D3
Belomorsk *Russia* 64°35N 34°54E **70** B5
Beloretsk *Russia* 53°58N 58°24E **70** D10
Beloye, L. *Russia* 60°10N 37°35E **70** B6
Belsay *U.K.* 55°6N 1°51W **26** B5
Belton *N. Lincs., U.K.* 53°33N 0°48W **27** E7
Belton *Norfolk, U.K.* 52°35N 1°40E **31** A12
Beltsy *Moldova* 47°48N 27°58E **65** E14
Belturbet *Ireland* 54°6N 7°26W **18** C7
Belvidere *U.S.A.* 42°15N 88°50W **112** D3
Bembridge *U.K.* 50°41N 1°5W **30** E6
Bemidji *U.S.A.* 47°28N 94°53W **111** A8
Ben Cruachan *U.K.* 56°26N 5°8W **24** B5
Ben Dearg *U.K.* 57°47N 4°56W **23** G8
Ben Hope *U.K.* 58°25N 4°36W **23** F8

Ben Lawers *U.K.* 56°32N 4°14W **24** A7
Ben Lomond *U.K.* 56°11N 4°38W **24** B6
Ben Macdhui *U.K.* 57°4N 3°40W **23** H10
Ben Mhor *U.K.* 57°15N 7°18W **22** H3
Ben More *Argyll & Bute, U.K.* 56°26N 6°1W **24** B3
Ben More *Stirling, U.K.* 56°23N 4°32W **24** B6
Ben More Assynt *U.K.* 58°8N 4°52W **23** F8
Ben Nevis *U.K.* 56°48N 5°1W **22** J7
Ben Vorlich *U.K.* 56°21N 4°14W **24** B7
Ben Wyvis *U.K.* 57°40N 4°35W **23** G8
Benares = Varanasi *India* 25°22N 83°0E **85** G13
Benbecula *U.K.* 57°26N 7°21W **22** H3
Bend *U.S.A.* 44°4N 121°19W **110** B2
Benderloch *U.K.* 56°30N 5°22W **24** A5
Bendery *Moldova* 46°50N 29°30E **65** E15
Bendigo *Australia* 36°40S 144°15E **98** H7
Benevento *Italy* 41°8N 14°45E **68** D6
Bengal, Bay of *Ind. Oc.* 15°0N 90°0E **85** M17
Bengaluru *India* 12°59N 77°40E **84** N10
Bengbu *China* 32°58N 117°20E **79** E12
Benghazi *Libya* 32°11N 20°3E **95** B10
Bengkulu *Indonesia* 3°50S 102°12E **82** E2
Benguela *Angola* 12°37S 13°25E **97** G2
Beni → *Bolivia* 10°23S 65°24W **120** D3
Beni Mellal *Morocco* 32°21N 6°21W **94** B4
Beni Suef *Egypt* 29°5N 31°6E **95** C12
Benidorm *Spain* 38°33N 0°9W **67** C5
Benin ■ *Africa* 10°0N 2°0E **94** G6
Benin, Bight of *W. Afr.* 5°0N 3°0E **94** H6
Benin City *Nigeria* 6°20N 5°31E **94** G7
Benington *U.K.* 53°0N 0°5E **27** F9
Benjamin Constant *Brazil* 4°40S 70°15W **120** C2
Benoni *S. Africa* 26°11S 28°18E **97** K5
Benson *U.K.* 51°37N 1°6W **30** C6
Bentley *Hants., U.K.* 51°12N 0°52W **31** D7
Bentley *S. Yorks., U.K.* 53°33N 1°8W **27** E6
Bentley Subglacial Trench
Antarctica 80°0S 115°0W **55** E14
Benton *U.S.A.* 38°0N 88°55W **112** G3
Benton Harbor *U.S.A.* 42°6N 86°27W **112** D4
Benue → *Nigeria* 7°48N 6°46E **94** G7
Benxi *China* 41°20N 123°48E **79** C13
Beppu *Japan* 33°15N 131°30E **81** G2
Berber *Sudan* 18°0N 34°0E **95** E12
Berbera *Somalia* 10°30N 45°2E **89** E4
Berbérati *C.A.R.* 4°15N 15°40E **96** D3
Berbice → *Guyana* 6°20N 57°32W **120** B4
Berdyansk *Ukraine* 46°45N 36°50E **71** E6
Berdychiv *Ukraine* 49°57N 28°30E **71** E4
Bere Alston *U.K.* 50°29N 4°13W **29** G4
Bere Regis *U.K.* 50°45N 2°14W **30** E4
Berea *U.S.A.* 37°34N 84°17W **112** G5
Berens → *Canada* 52°25N 97°2W **108** D10
Berezina → *Belarus* 52°33N 30°14E **70** D5
Bereznik *Russia* 62°51N 42°40E **70** B7
Berezniki *Russia* 59°24N 56°46E **70** C10
Bérgamo *Italy* 45°41N 9°43E **68** B3
Bergen *Norway* 60°20N 5°20E **63** E5
Bergerac *France* 44°51N 0°30E **66** D4
Bering Sea *Pac. Oc.* 58°0N 171°0W **102** B10
Bering Strait *Pac. Oc.* 65°30N 169°0W **108** C3
Berkeley *U.S.A.* 51°41N 2°27W **30** C4
Berkhamsted *U.K.* 51°45N 0°33W **31** C7
Berkner I. *Antarctica* 79°30S 50°0W **55** D18
Berkshire Downs *U.K.* 51°33N 1°29W **30** C6
Berlin *Germany* 52°31N 13°23E **64** B7
Berlin *U.S.A.* 44°28N 71°11W **113** C12
Bermejo → *Argentina* 26°51S 58°23W **121** E4
Bermuda ☑ *Atl. Oc.* 32°18N 64°45W **52** C6
Bern *Switz.* 46°57N 7°28E **64** E4
Berneray *U.K.* 57°43N 7°11W **22** G3
Berry *France* 46°50N 2°0E **66** C5
Berry Hd. *U.K.* 50°24N 3°29W **29** G7
Bertraghboy B. *Ireland* 53°22N 9°54W **20** B3
Berwick *U.S.A.* 41°3N 76°14W **112** E9
Berwick-upon-Tweed *U.K.* 55°46N 2°0W **26** A5
Berwyn Mts. *U.K.* 52°54N 3°26W **28** B5
Besançon *France* 47°15N 6°2E **66** C7
Bessarabiya *Moldova* 47°0N 28°10E **65** E15
Bessemer *U.S.A.* 46°29N 90°3W **112** B2
Bethel *U.S.A.* 60°48N 161°45W **108** C3
Bethesda *U.K.* 53°10N 4°3W **28** A5
Bethlehem *S. Africa* 28°14S 28°18E **97** K5
Bethlehem *U.S.A.* 40°37N 75°23W **113** E10
Béthune *France* 50°30N 2°38E **66** A5
Betim *Brazil* 19°58S 44°7W **122** C2
Bettiah *India* 26°48N 84°33E **85** F14
Betul *India* 21°58N 77°59E **84** J10
Betws-y-Coed *U.K.* 53°5N 3°48W **28** A6
Beverley *U.K.* 53°51N 0°26W **27** E8
Bewdley *U.K.* 52°23N 2°19W **30** B4
Bexhill *U.K.* 50°51N 0°29E **31** E9
Bexley □ *U.K.* 51°27N 0°9E **31** D9
Beyneu *Kazakhstan* 45°18N 55°9E **71** E10
Beypazarı *Turkey* 40°10N 31°56E **71** F5
Beyşehir Gölü *Turkey* 37°41N 31°33E **71** G5
Béziers *France* 43°20N 3°12E **66** E5
Bhagalpur *India* 25°10N 87°0E **85** G15
Bhaktapur *Nepal* 27°38N 85°24E **85** F14
Bhanrer Ra. *India* 23°40N 79°45E **84** H11
Bharatpur *India* 27°15N 77°30E **84** F10
Bharraig = Barra *U.K.* 57°0N 7°29W **22** J2
Bharuch *India* 21°47N 73°0E **84** J8
Bhatarsaigh = Vatersay *U.K.* 56°55N 7°32W **22** J2
Bhatpara *India* 22°50N 88°25E **85** H16
Bhavnagar *India* 21°45N 72°10E **84** J8
Bhearnaraigh = Berneray
U.K. 57°43N 7°11W **22** G3
Bhilainagar-Durg *India* 21°13N 81°26E **85** J12
Bhilwara *India* 25°25N 74°38E **84** G9
Bhima → *India* 16°25N 77°17E **84** L10
Bhiwandi *India* 19°20N 73°0E **84** K8
Bhiwani *India* 28°50N 76°9E **84** E10
Bhopal *India* 23°20N 77°30E **84** H10
Bhubaneshwar *India* 20°15N 85°50E **85** J14
Bhuj *India* 23°15N 69°49E **84** H6
Bhusawal *India* 21°3N 75°46E **84** J9
Bhutan ■ *Asia* 27°25N 90°30E **85** F17
Biala Podlaska *Poland* 52°4N 23°6E **65** B12
Bialystok *Poland* 53°10N 23°10E **65** B12
Biarritz *France* 43°29N 1°33W **66** E3

Bibury U.K. 51°45N 1°49W 30 C5
Bicester U.K. 51°54N 1°9W 30 C6
Bicton U.K. 52°44N 2°48W 27 G3
Bida Nigeria 9°3N 5°58E 94 G7
Biddeford U.S.A. 43°30N 70°28W 113 D12
Biddenden U.K. 51°7N 0°40E 31 D10
Biddulph U.K. 53°7N 2°10W 27 F4
Bideford U.K. 51°1N 4°13W 29 E5
Bideford Bay U.K. 51°5N 4°20W 29 E5
Bidford-on-Avon U.K. 52°11N 1°50W 30 B5
Bié Plateau Angola 12°0S 16°0E 97 G3
Biel Switz. 47°8N 7°14E 64 E4
Bielefeld Germany 52°1N 8°33E 64 B5
Biella Italy 45°34N 8°3E 68 B3
Bielsko-Biala Poland 49°50N 19°2E 65 D10
Bien Hoa Vietnam 10°57N 106°49E 82 B3
Bienville, L. Canada 55°5N 72°40W 109 D12
Big Belt Mts. U.S.A. 46°30N 111°25W 110 A4
Big Rapids U.S.A. 43°42N 85°29W 112 D5
Big Sioux → U.S.A. 42°29N 96°27W 111 B7
Big Spring U.S.A. 32°15N 101°28W 110 D6
Big Trout L. Canada 53°40N 90°0W 109 D11
Bigbury U.K. 50°18N 3°53W 29 G6
Bigbury B. U.K. 50°16N 3°54W 29 G6
Biggar Canada 52°4N 108°0W 108 D9
Biggar U.K. 55°38N 3°32W 25 C8
Biggleswade U.K. 52°5N 0°14W 31 B8
Bighorn → U.S.A. 46°10N 107°28W 110 A5
Bighorn Mts. U.S.A. 44°25N 107°0W 110 B5
Bihar India 25°5N 85°40E 85 G14
Bihar □ India 25°0N 86°0E 85 G15
Bijagós, Arquipélago dos
  Guinea-Biss. 11°15N 16°10W 94 F2
Bikaner India 28°2N 73°18E 84 E8
Bikini Atoll Marshall Is. 12°0N 167°30E 102 F8
Bila Tserkva Ukraine 49°45N 30°10E 65 D16
Bilaspur India 22°2N 82°15E 85 H13
Bilbao Spain 43°16N 2°56W 67 A4
Bilecik Turkey 40°5N 30°5E 71 F5
Bilhorod-Dnistrovskyy
  Ukraine 46°11N 30°23E 71 E5
Billericay U.K. 51°38N 0°26E 31 C9
Billesdon U.K. 52°38N 0°54W 27 G7
Billingham U.K. 54°36N 1°17W 26 C6
Billinghay U.K. 53°5N 0°15W 27 F8
Billings U.S.A. 45°47N 108°30W 110 A5
Billingshurst U.K. 51°2N 0°27W 31 D8
Bilma Niger 18°50N 13°30E 95 E8
Bilma, Grand Erg de Niger 18°30N 14°0E 95 E8
Biloxi U.S.A. 30°24N 88°53W 111 D9
Bilston U.K. 52°34N 2°4W 27 G4
Bimini Is. Bahamas 25°42N 79°25N 115 B9
Binbrook U.K. 53°26N 0°10W 27 F8
Bingham U.K. 52°57N 0°58W 27 F7
Binghamton U.S.A. 42°6N 75°55W 113 D10
Bingley U.K. 53°51N 1°50W 27 E5
Bioko Eq. Guin. 3°30N 8°40E 96 D1
Biratnagar Nepal 26°27N 87°17E 85 F15
Birchington U.K. 51°22N 1°19E 31 D11
Birdlip U.K. 51°50N 2°5W 30 C4
Birkdale U.K. 53°38N 3°1W 27 E2
Birkenhead U.K. 53°23N 3°2W 27 F2
Birmingham U.K. 52°29N 1°52W 27 H5
Birmingham U.S.A. 33°31N 86°48W 111 D9
Birmingham Int. ✈ (BHX)
  U.K. 52°26N 1°45W 27 H5
Birnin Kebbi Nigeria 12°32N 4°12E 94 F6
Birobidzhan Russia 48°50N 132°50E 77 E14
Birr Ireland 53°6N 7°54W 20 B7
Birtley Northumberland, U.K. 55°6N 2°12W 26 C4
Birtley Tyne & W., U.K. 54°54N 1°34W 26 C5
Biscay, B. of Atl. Oc. 45°0N 2°0W 66 D1
Bishkek Kyrgyzstan 42°54N 74°46E 76 E8
Bishop Auckland U.K. 54°39N 1°40W 26 C5
Bishop's Castle U.K. 52°30N 2°59W 27 H3
Bishop's Cleeve U.K. 51°57N 2°3W 30 C4
Bishop's Frome U.K. 52°8N 2°29W 30 B4
Bishop's Nympton U.K. 51°0N 3°47W 29 F6
Bishop's Stortford U.K. 51°52N 0°10E 31 C9
Bishop's Waltham U.K. 50°57N 1°11W 30 E6
Bishopsteignton U.K. 50°33N 3°33W 29 F6
Bishopstoke U.K. 50°58N 1°19W 30 E6
Biskra Algeria 34°50N 5°44E 94 B7
Bismarck U.S.A. 46°48N 100°47W 110 A6
Bismarck Arch. Papua N. G. 2°30S 150°0E 98 A9
Bissau Guinea-Biss. 11°45N 15°45W 94 F2
Bitolj Macedonia 41°1N 21°20E 69 D9
Bitterfontein S. Africa 31°1S 18°32E 97 L3
Bitterroot Range U.S.A. 46°0N 114°20W 110 A4
Bitton U.K. 51°25N 2°27W 30 C4
Biu Nigeria 10°40N 12°3E 95 F8
Biwa-Ko Japan 35°15N 136°10E 81 F5
Biysk Russia 52°40N 85°0E 76 D9
Bizerte Tunisia 37°15N 9°50E 95 A7
Blaby U.K. 52°35N 1°10W 27 G6
Black Combe U.K. 54°16N 3°20W 26 D2
Black Esk → U.K. 55°12N 3°11W 25 D9
Black Forest = Schwarzwald
  Germany 48°30N 8°20E 64 D5
Black Hd. Ireland 53°9N 9°16W 20 B4
Black Hd. U.K. 50°0N 5°7W 29 H3
Black Hills U.S.A. 44°0N 103°45W 110 B6
Black Isle U.K. 57°35N 4°16W 23 G9
Black Mt. = Mynydd Du U.K. 51°52N 3°50W 28 D6
Black Mts. U.K. 51°55N 3°7W 28 D7
Black Range U.S.A. 33°15N 107°50W 110 D5
Black River Jamaica 18°0N 77°50W 114 a
Black River Falls U.S.A. 44°18N 90°51W 112 C2
Black Rock Barbados 13°7N 59°37W 114 c
Black Sea Eurasia 43°30N 35°0E 71 F6
Blackburn U.K. 53°45N 2°29W 27 E4
Blackdown Hills U.K. 50°57N 3°15W 30 E2
Blackmoor Vale U.K. 50°54N 2°28W 30 E4
Blackpool U.K. 53°49N 3°3W 27 E4
Blackrock Ireland 53°18N 6°11W 21 B10
Blacksburg U.S.A. 37°14N 80°25W 112 G8
Blacksod B. Ireland 54°6N 10°0W 18 C1
Blackwater → Meath, Ireland 53°39N 6°41W 19 D8
Blackwater → Waterford,
  Ireland 52°4N 7°52W 20 D7
Blackwater → Essex, U.K. 51°44N 0°53E 31 C10

Blackwater → N. Ireland, U.K. 54°31N 6°35W 19 B8
Blaenau Ffestiniog U.K. 53°0N 3°56W 28 B6
Blaenavon U.K. 51°46N 3°5W 28 D7
Blagdon U.K. 51°20N 2°43W 30 D3
Blagoevgrad Bulgaria 42°2N 23°5E 69 C10
Blagoveshchensk Russia 50°20N 127°30E 77 D13
Blair Atholl U.K. 56°46N 3°50W 23 J10
Blairgowrie U.K. 56°35N 3°21W 25 A9
Blakeney Glouce., U.K. 51°46N 2°28W 30 C4
Blakeney Norfolk, U.K. 52°58N 1°1E 31 A11
Blanc, Mont Europe 45°48N 6°50E 66 D7
Blanca, B. Argentina 39°10S 61°30W 121 F3
Blanca, Costa Spain 38°25N 0°10W 67 C5
Blanca Peak U.S.A. 37°35N 105°29W 110 C5
Blanchardstown Ireland 53°23N 6°23W 21 B10
Blanco, C. U.S.A. 42°51N 124°34W 110 B2
Blandford Forum U.K. 50°51N 2°9W 30 E4
Blanquilla, I. Venezuela 11°51N 64°37W 115 E12
Blantyre Malawi 15°45S 35°0E 97 H6
Blarney Ireland 51°56N 8°33W 20 E5
Blaydon U.K. 54°58N 1°42W 26 C5
Blean U.K. 51°18N 1°3E 31 D11
Bleasdale Moors U.K. 53°55N 2°35W 27 E3
Blenheim N.Z. 41°38S 173°57E 99 J13
Bletchingdon U.K. 51°51N 1°15W 30 C6
Bletchley U.K. 51°59N 0°44W 31 C7
Blida Algeria 36°30N 2°49E 94 A6
Blisworth U.K. 52°10N 0°56W 31 B7
Blitar Indonesia 8°5S 112°11E 82 F4
Blockley U.K. 52°1N 1°44W 30 B5
Bloemfontein S. Africa 29°6S 26°7E 97 K5
Blofield U.K. 52°38N 1°26E 31 A11
Blois France 47°35N 1°20E 66 C4
Bloody Foreland Ireland 55°10N 8°17W 18 A5
Bloomington Ill., U.S.A. 40°28N 89°0W 112 E3
Bloomington Ind., U.S.A. 39°10N 86°32W 112 F4
Bloomsburg U.S.A. 41°0N 76°27W 112 E9
Bloxham U.K. 52°1N 1°21W 30 B6
Blue Mountain Pk. Jamaica 18°3N 76°36W 114 a
Blue Mt. U.S.A. 40°30N 76°30W 112 E9
Blue Mts. Jamaica 18°3N 76°36W 114 a
Blue Mts. U.S.A. 45°0N 118°20W 110 A3
Blue Nile → Sudan 15°38N 32°31E 95 E12
Blue Ridge U.S.A. 36°40N 80°50W 111 C10
Blue Stack Mts. Ireland 54°44N 8°12W 18 B5
Bluefield U.S.A. 37°15N 81°17W 112 G7
Bluefields Nic. 12°20N 83°50W 115 E8
Blumenau Brazil 27°0S 49°0W 121 E5
Blundeston U.K. 52°31N 1°42E 31 A12
Blyth Northumberland, U.K. 55°8N 1°31W 26 B5
Blyth Notts., U.K. 53°22N 1°3W 27 F6
Blyth → U.K. 55°8N 1°33W 26 B5
Blyth Bridge U.K. 55°42N 3°22W 25 C9
Blyton U.K. 53°27N 0°42W 27 F7
Bo S. Leone 7°55N 11°50W 94 G3
Bo Hai China 39°0N 119°0E 79 D12
Boa Vista Brazil 2°48N 60°30W 120 B3
Bobcaygeon Canada 44°33N 78°33W 112 C8
Bobo-Dioulasso Burkina Faso 11°8N 4°13W 94 F5
Bôbr → Poland 52°4N 15°4E 64 B8
Bochum Germany 51°28N 7°13E 64 C4
Boddam U.K. 59°56N 1°17W 22 C15
Boden Sweden 65°50N 21°42E 63 D8
Bodiam U.K. 51°0N 0°34E 31 D10
Bodinnick U.K. 50°20N 4°38W 29 G4
Bodmin U.K. 50°28N 4°43W 29 G4
Bodmin Moor U.K. 50°33N 4°36W 29 F4
Bodø Norway 67°17N 14°24E 63 D6
Bodrog → Hungary 48°11N 21°22E 65 D11
Bodrum Turkey 37°3N 27°30E 71 G4
Bogalusa U.S.A. 30°47N 89°52W 111 D9
Bogda Shan China 43°35N 89°40E 78 C6
Boggeragh Mts. Ireland 52°2N 8°55W 20 D5
Bognor Regis U.K. 50°47N 0°40W 31 E7
Bogor Indonesia 6°36S 106°48E 82 F3
Bogotá Colombia 4°34N 74°0W 120 B2
Bogra Bangla. 24°51N 89°22E 85 G16
Böhmerwald Germany 49°8N 13°14E 64 D7
Bohol Sea Phil. 9°0N 124°0E 83 C6
Boise U.S.A. 43°37N 116°13W 110 B3
Bole China 44°55N 81°37E 78 C5
Bolívar, Pico Venezuela 8°32N 71°2W 115 F10
Bolivia ■ S. Amer. 17°6S 64°0W 120 D3
Bollington U.K. 53°18N 2°6W 27 F4
Bolney U.K. 50°59N 0°12W 31 E8
Bologna Italy 44°29N 11°20E 68 B4
Bologoye Russia 57°55N 34°5E 70 C5
Bolsena, L. di Italy 42°36N 11°56E 68 C4
Bolsover U.K. 53°14N 1°16W 27 F6
Bolt Head U.K. 50°12N 3°48W 29 G6
Bolt Tail U.K. 50°14N 3°52W 29 G6
Bolton U.K. 53°35N 2°26W 27 E4
Bolton Abbey U.K. 53°59N 1°53W 27 E5
Bolton by Bowland U.K. 53°56N 2°20W 27 E4
Bolton-le-Sands U.K. 54°6N 2°48W 26 D3
Bolu Turkey 40°45N 31°35E 71 F5
Bolvadin Turkey 38°45N 31°4E 71 G5
Bolzano Italy 46°31N 11°22E 68 A4
Bom Despacho Brazil 19°43S 45°15W 122 C1
Bom Jesus da Lapa Brazil 13°15S 43°25W 122 B2
Boma Dem. Rep. of the Congo 5°50S 13°4E 96 F2
Bombala Australia 36°56S 149°15E 98 H8
Bombay = Mumbai India 18°56N 72°50E 84 K8
Bomi China 29°50N 95°45E 78 F8
Bomu → C.A.R. 4°40N 22°30E 96 D4
Bon, C. Tunisia 37°1N 11°2E 90 C5
Bonaire W. Indies 12°10N 68°15W 115 E11
Bonar Bridge U.K. 57°54N 4°20W 23 G9
Bonavista Canada 48°40N 53°5W 109 E14
Bonchester Bridge U.K. 55°24N 2°39W 25 D10
Bonchurch U.K. 50°37N 1°11W 30 E6
Bo'ness U.K. 56°1N 3°37W 25 B8
Bongor Chad 10°35N 15°20E 95 F9
Bongos, Massif des C.A.R. 8°40N 22°25E 96 C4
Bonifacio France 41°24N 9°10E 66 F8
Bonn Germany 50°46N 7°6E 64 C4
Bonny, Bight of Africa 3°30N 9°20E 96 D1
Bonnyrigg U.K. 55°53N 3°6W 25 C9
Böön Tsagaan Nuur Mongolia 45°35N 99°9E 78 B8
Boonville U.S.A. 38°3N 87°16W 112 F4
Boosaaso Somalia 11°12N 49°18E 89 E4

Boot U.K. 54°24N 3°13W 26 D2
Boothia, Gulf of Canada 71°0N 90°0W 109 B11
Boothia Pen. Canada 71°0N 94°0W 108 B10
Bootle Cumb., U.K. 54°18N 3°22W 26 D2
Bootle Mersey., U.K. 53°28N 3°1W 27 F2
Borås Sweden 57°43N 12°56E 63 F6
Borborema, Planalto da Brazil 7°0S 37°0W 117 D7
Bordeaux France 44°50N 0°36W 66 D3
Borden I. Canada 78°30N 111°30W 109 B8
Borden Pen. Canada 73°0N 83°0W 109 B11
Borders = Scottish Borders □
  U.K. 55°35N 2°50W 25 C10
Bordon U.K. 51°8N 0°52W 31 D7
Borehamwood U.K. 51°40N 0°15W 31 C8
Boreland U.K. 55°13N 3°17W 25 D9
Borger U.S.A. 35°39N 101°24W 110 C6
Borhoyn Tal Mongolia 43°50N 111°58E 79 C11
Borisoglebsk Russia 51°27N 42°5E 71 D7
Borkou Chad 18°15N 18°50E 95 E9
Borneo E. Indies 1°0N 115°0E 82 D5
Bornholm Denmark 55°10N 15°0E 63 F7
Borohoro Shan China 44°6N 83°10E 78 C5
Boroughbridge U.K. 54°6N 1°24W 26 D6
Borovichi Russia 58°25N 33°55E 70 C5
Borrowdale U.K. 54°31N 3°10W 26 C2
Borth U.K. 52°29N 4°2W 28 C5
Borüjerd Iran 33°55N 48°50E 86 C7
Bosbury U.K. 52°5N 2°26W 30 B4
Boscastle U.K. 50°41N 4°42W 29 F4
Boscobelle Barbados 13°17N 59°35W 114 c
Bose China 23°53N 106°35E 78 G10
Bosham U.K. 50°49N 0°51W 31 E7
Bosnia-Herzegovina ■ Europe 44°0N 18°0E 69 B7
Bosporus Turkey 41°5N 29°3E 71 F4
Bossangoa C.A.R. 6°35N 17°30E 96 C3
Bosten Hu China 41°55N 87°40E 78 C6
Boston U.K. 52°59N 0°2W 27 G8
Boston U.S.A. 42°22N 71°3W 113 D12
Bothel U.K. 54°45N 3°15W 26 C2
Bothnia, G. of Europe 62°0N 20°0E 63 E8
Botletle → Botswana 20°10S 23°15E 97 J4
Botoşani Romania 47°42N 26°41E 65 E14
Botswana ■ Africa 22°0S 24°0E 97 J4
Bottesford U.K. 52°57N 0°47W 27 G7
Botucatu Brazil 22°55S 48°30W 122 D1
Bou Saâda Algeria 35°11N 4°9E 94 A6
Bouaké Côte d'Ivoire 7°40N 5°2W 94 G4
Bouar C.A.R. 6°0N 15°40E 96 C3
Bouârfa Morocco 32°32N 1°58W 94 B5
Bougainville I. Papua N. G. 6°0S 155°0E 99 B10
Boulder U.S.A. 40°1N 105°17W 110 B5
Boulogne-sur-Mer France 50°42N 1°36E 66 A4
Bounty Is. Pac. Oc. 48°0S 178°30E 102 M9
Bourbonnais France 46°28N 3°0E 66 C5
Bourg-en-Bresse France 46°13N 5°12E 66 C6
Bourges France 47°9N 2°25E 66 C5
Bourgogne France 47°0N 4°50E 66 C6
Bourke Australia 30°8S 145°55E 98 G8
Bourne U.K. 52°47N 0°22W 27 G8
Bournemouth U.K. 50°43N 1°52W 30 E5
Bourton-on-the-Water U.K. 51°52N 1°45W 30 C5
Bouvet I. Antarctica 54°26S 3°24E 52 G10
Bovey Tracey U.K. 50°36N 3°41W 29 F6
Bow → Canada 49°57N 111°41W 108 D8
Bowes U.K. 54°32N 1°59W 26 C5
Bowland, Forest of U.K. 54°0N 2°30W 27 E3
Bowling Green Ky., U.S.A. 36°59N 86°27W 112 G4
Bowling Green Ohio, U.S.A. 41°23N 83°39W 112 E6
Bowmore U.K. 55°45N 6°17W 24 C3
Bowness-on-Solway U.K. 54°57N 3°12W 26 C2
Bowness-on-Windermere
  U.K. 54°22N 2°55W 26 D3
Box U.K. 51°25N 2°15W 30 D4
Box Hill U.K. 51°15N 0°16W 31 D8
Boyle Ireland 53°59N 8°18W 18 D5
Boyne → Ireland 53°43N 6°15W 19 D9
Boyoma, Chutes
  Dem. Rep. of the Congo 0°35N 25°23E 90 F6
Bozeat U.K. 52°14N 0°40W 31 B7
Bozeman U.S.A. 45°41N 111°2W 110 A4
Bozoum C.A.R. 6°25N 16°35E 96 C3
Brač Croatia 43°20N 16°40E 68 C7
Bracadale, L. U.K. 57°20N 6°30W 22 H4
Bracebridge Canada 45°2N 79°19W 112 C8
Bracebridge Heath U.K. 53°12N 0°32W 27 F7
Bräcke Sweden 62°45N 15°26E 63 E7
Brackley U.K. 52°2N 1°8W 30 B6
Bracknell U.K. 51°25N 0°43W 31 D7
Bradford U.K. 53°47N 1°45W 27 E5
Bradford U.S.A. 41°58N 78°38W 112 E8
Bradford on Avon U.K. 51°21N 2°14W 30 D4
Brading U.K. 50°41N 1°8W 30 E6
Bradwell-on-Sea U.K. 51°43N 0°56E 31 C10
Bradworthy U.K. 50°53N 4°24W 29 F5
Braemar U.K. 57°2N 3°26W 23 H11
Braga Portugal 41°35N 8°25W 67 B1
Bragança Brazil 1°0S 47°2W 120 C5
Bragança Paulista Brazil 22°55S 46°32W 122 D1
Brahmanbaria Bangla. 23°58N 91°15E 85 H17
Brahmani → India 20°39N 86°46E 85 J15
Brahmapur India 19°15N 84°54E 85 K14
Brahmaputra → Asia 23°40N 90°35E 85 H16
Braich-y-pwll U.K. 52°47N 4°46E 28 B4
Brăila Romania 45°19N 27°59E 65 F14
Brailsford U.K. 52°58N 1°35W 27 G5
Brainerd U.S.A. 46°22N 94°12W 111 A8
Braintree U.K. 51°53N 0°34E 31 C10
Bramford U.K. 52°4N 1°7E 31 B11
Brampton Canada 43°45N 79°45W 112 D8
Brampton Cambs., U.K. 52°20N 0°14W 31 B8
Brampton Cumb., U.K. 54°57N 2°44W 26 C3
Brancaster U.K. 52°58N 0°38E 31 A10
Branco → Brazil 1°20S 61°50W 120 C3
Brandenburg Germany 52°25N 12°33E 64 B7
Brandenburg □ Germany 52°50N 13°0E 64 B7
Brandon Canada 49°50N 99°57W 108 E10
Brandon Durham, U.K. 54°46N 1°37W 26 C5
Brandon Suffolk, U.K. 52°27N 0°37E 31 B10
Brandon B. Ireland 52°17N 10°8W 20 D2
Brandon Mt. Ireland 52°15N 10°15W 20 D2

Branston U.K. 53°12N 0°27W 27 F8
Brantford Canada 43°10N 80°15W 112 D7
Bras d'Or L. Canada 45°50N 60°50W 113 C17
Brasília Brazil 15°47S 47°55W 122 C1
Braşov Romania 45°38N 25°35E 65 F13
Bratislava Slovakia 48°10N 17°7E 65 D9
Bratsk Russia 56°10N 101°30E 77 D11
Bratsk Res. Russia 56°15N 101°45E 77 D11
Brattleboro U.S.A. 42°51N 72°34W 113 D11
Braunschweig Germany 52°15N 10°31E 64 B6
Braunton U.K. 51°7N 4°10W 29 E5
Brava, Costa Spain 41°30N 3°0E 67 B7
Bray Ireland 53°13N 6°7W 21 B10
Bray U.K. 51°30N 0°41W 31 D7
Brazil U.S.A. 39°32N 87°8W 112 F4
Brazil ■ S. Amer. 12°0S 50°0W 120 D4
Brazilian Highlands Brazil 18°0S 46°30W 117 E6
Brazos → U.S.A. 28°53N 95°23W 111 E7
Brazzaville Congo 4°9S 15°12E 96 E3
Breadalbane U.K. 56°30N 4°15W 24 A7
Breage U.K. 50°6N 5°20W 29 G3
Breamish → U.K. 55°35N 2°2W 26 A4
Brechin U.K. 56°44N 2°39W 23 J12
Breckland U.K. 52°30N 0°40E 31 B10
Brecon U.K. 51°57N 3°23W 28 D7
Brecon Beacons △ U.K. 51°50N 3°30W 28 D7
Breda Neths. 51°35N 4°45E 64 C3
Brede U.K. 50°56N 0°36E 31 E10
Bredon Hill U.K. 52°3N 2°2W 30 B4
Bregenz Austria 47°30N 9°45E 64 E5
Breiðafjörður Iceland 65°15N 23°15W 63 A1
Bremen Germany 53°4N 8°47E 64 B5
Bremerhaven Germany 53°33N 8°36E 64 B5
Bremerton U.S.A. 47°34N 122°37W 110 A2
Brendon Hills U.K. 51°6N 3°25W 30 D2
Brennerpass Austria 47°2N 11°30E 64 E6
Brent □ U.K. 51°33N 0°16W 31 C8
Brentwood U.K. 51°37N 0°19E 31 C9
Bréscia Italy 45°33N 10°15E 68 B4
Bressay U.K. 60°9N 1°6W 22 B15
Brest Belarus 52°10N 23°40E 65 B12
Brest France 48°24N 4°31W 66 B1
Bretagne □ France 48°10N 3°0W 66 B2
Breton Sd. U.S.A. 29°35N 89°15W 111 E9
Brewer U.S.A. 44°48N 68°46W 113 C13
Brewood U.K. 52°41N 2°9W 27 G4
Briançon France 44°54N 6°39E 66 D7
Bridestowe U.K. 50°41N 4°7W 29 F5
Bridge U.K. 51°15N 1°8E 31 D11
Bridgefield Barbados 13°9N 59°36W 114 c
Bridgend U.K. 51°30N 3°34W 29 D6
Bridgeport U.S.A. 41°11N 73°12W 113 E11
Bridgeton U.S.A. 39°26N 75°14W 113 F10
Bridgetown Barbados 13°6N 59°37W 114 c
Bridgewater Canada 44°25N 64°31W 109 E13
Bridgnorth U.K. 52°32N 2°25W 27 G4
Bridgwater U.K. 51°8N 2°59W 30 D3
Bridgwater B. U.K. 51°15N 3°15W 30 D2
Bridlington U.K. 54°5N 0°12W 26 D8
Bridlington B. U.K. 54°4N 0°10W 27 D8
Bridport U.K. 50°44N 2°45W 30 E3
Brierfield U.K. 53°49N 2°14W 27 E4
Brierley Hill U.K. 52°29N 2°6W 27 H4
Brig Switz. 46°18N 7°59E 64 E4
Brigg U.K. 53°34N 0°28W 27 E8
Brigham City U.S.A. 41°31N 112°1W 110 B4
Brighouse U.K. 53°42N 1°46W 27 E5
Brighstone U.K. 50°38N 1°23W 30 E6
Brightlingsea U.K. 51°49N 1°2E 31 C11
Brighton U.K. 50°49N 0°7W 31 E8
Brigstock U.K. 52°27N 0°36W 31 B7
Brill U.K. 51°49N 1°1W 30 C6
Brimfield U.K. 52°18N 2°41W 30 B3
Brindisi Italy 40°39N 17°55E 69 D7
Brinklow U.K. 52°25N 1°22W 30 B6
Brinkworth U.K. 51°33N 1°59W 30 C5
Brisbane Australia 27°25S 153°2E 98 F9
Bristol U.K. 51°26N 2°35W 30 D3
Bristol U.S.A. 58°0N 160°0W 108 D4
Bristol Channel U.K. 51°18N 4°30W 29 E5
Briston U.K. 52°51N 1°4E 31 A11
British Columbia □ Canada 55°0N 125°15W 108 D7
British Isles Europe 54°0N 4°0W 62 D5
British Virgin Is. ☑
  W. Indies 18°30N 64°30W 115 D12
Brittany = Bretagne □ France 48°10N 3°0W 66 B2
Brive-la-Gaillarde France 45°10N 1°32E 66 D4
Brixham U.K. 50°23N 3°31W 29 G6
Brixworth U.K. 52°20N 0°54W 31 B7
Brize Norton U.K. 51°46N 1°34W 30 C5
Brno Czechia 49°10N 16°35E 65 D9
Broad B. U.K. 58°14N 6°18W 22 F5
Broad Chalke U.K. 51°2N 1°56W 30 D5
Broad Haven Ireland 54°20N 9°55W 18 C2
Broad Law U.K. 55°30N 3°21W 25 C9
Broad Sd. U.K. 49°55N 6°21W 29 H1
Broadclyst U.K. 50°46N 3°27W 29 F7
Broadhembury U.K. 50°49N 3°18W 29 F7
Broadstairs U.K. 51°21N 1°27E 31 D11
Broadway U.K. 52°2N 1°50W 30 B5
Broadwindsor U.K. 50°48N 2°47W 30 E3
Brochet Canada 57°53N 101°40W 108 D9
Brock I. Canada 77°52N 114°19W 109 B8
Brocken Germany 51°47N 10°37E 64 C6
Brockenhurst U.K. 50°49N 1°34W 30 E5
Brockville Canada 44°35N 75°41W 113 C10
Brockworth U.K. 51°51N 2°9W 30 C4
Brodeur Pen. Canada 72°30N 88°10W 109 B11
Brodick U.K. 55°35N 5°9W 24 C5
Broken Hill Australia 31°58S 141°29E 98 G7
Bromfield U.K. 52°24N 2°45W 27 H3
Bromham U.K. 51°23N 2°1W 30 D4
Bromley □ U.K. 51°24N 0°2E 31 D9
Brompton U.K. 54°21N 1°25W 26 D6
Bromsgrove U.K. 52°21N 2°2W 30 B4
Bromyard U.K. 52°11N 2°30W 30 B4
Brookings U.S.A. 44°19N 96°48W 111 B7
Brooks Canada 50°35N 111°55W 108 D8
Brooks Range U.S.A. 68°0N 152°0W 108 C5
Broom, L. U.K. 57°55N 5°15W 22 G7
Broome Australia 18°0S 122°15E 98 D3
Broomhill U.K. 55°18N 1°36W 26 B5

Brora U.K. 58°0N 3°52W 23 F10
Brora → U.K. 58°0N 3°51W 23 F10
Broseley U.K. 52°37N 2°29W 27 G4
Brosna → Ireland 53°14N 7°58W 20 B7
Brothertoft U.K. 53°0N 0°7W 27 F8
Brotton U.K. 54°35N 0°56W 26 C7
Broughton Borders, U.K. 55°37N 3°24W 25 C9
Broughton N. Lincs., U.K. 53°34N 0°34W 27 E7
Broughton Northants., U.K. 52°22N 0°46W 31 B7
Broughton-in-Furness U.K. 54°17N 3°13W 26 D2
Broughty Ferry U.K. 56°29N 2°51W 25 B10
Brown Willy U.K. 50°35N 4°37W 29 F4
Brownhills U.K. 52°39N 1°54W 27 G5
Brownsville U.S.A. 25°54N 97°30W 111 F7
Brownwood U.S.A. 31°43N 98°59W 110 D7
Broxburn U.K. 55°56N 3°28W 25 C9
Bruay-la-Buissière France 50°29N 2°33E 66 A5
Bruce, Mt. Australia 22°37S 118°8E 98 E2
Brue → U.K. 51°13N 2°59W 30 D3
Brugge Belgium 51°13N 3°13E 64 C2
Brumado Brazil 14°14S 41°40W 122 B2
Brunei ■ Asia 4°50N 115°0E 82 D4
Brunswick Ga., U.S.A. 31°10N 81°30W 111 D10
Brunswick Maine, U.S.A. 43°55N 69°58W 113 D13
Brunton U.K. 55°2N 2°6W 26 B4
Brussels Belgium 50°51N 4°21E 64 C3
Bruton U.K. 51°7N 2°27W 30 D4
Bryan Ohio, U.S.A. 41°28N 84°33W 112 E5
Bryan Tex., U.S.A. 30°40N 96°22W 111 D7
Bryansk Russia 53°13N 34°25E 70 D5
Bryher U.K. 49°57N 6°22W 29 H1
Brynamman U.K. 51°49N 3°51W 28 D6
Brynmawr U.K. 51°48N 3°10W 28 D7
Bucaramanga Colombia 7°0N 73°0W 120 B2
Buchan U.K. 57°32N 2°21W 23 G13
Buchan Ness U.K. 57°29N 1°46W 23 H14
Buchanan Liberia 5°57N 10°2W 94 G3
Bucharest Romania 44°27N 26°10E 65 F14
Buckden U.K. 52°18N 0°14W 31 B8
Buckfastleigh U.K. 50°28N 3°48W 29 G6
Buckhannon U.S.A. 39°0N 80°8W 112 F7
Buckhaven U.K. 56°11N 3°3W 25 B9
Buckie U.K. 57°41N 2°58W 23 G12
Buckingham Canada 45°37N 75°24W 113 C10
Buckingham U.K. 51°59N 0°57W 31 C7
Buckinghamshire □ U.K. 51°53N 0°55W 31 C7
Buckland Brewer U.K. 50°58N 4°15W 29 F5
Buckland Newton U.K. 50°50N 2°26W 30 E4
Buckley U.K. 53°10N 3°5W 28 A7
Budapest Hungary 47°29N 19°3E 65 E10
Bude U.K. 50°49N 4°34W 29 F4
Bude B. U.K. 50°51N 4°35W 29 F4
Budle B. U.K. 55°37N 1°45W 26 A5
Budleigh Salterton U.K. 50°37N 3°19W 29 F7
Buena Vista U.S.A. 37°44N 79°21W 112 G8
Buenaventura Colombia 3°53N 77°4W 120 B2
Buenos Aires Argentina 34°36S 58°22W 121 F4
Buffalo N.Y., U.S.A. 42°53N 78°53W 112 D8
Buffalo Wyo., U.S.A. 44°21N 106°42W 110 B5
Bug → Poland 52°31N 21°5E 65 B11
Bug → Ukraine 46°59N 31°58E 71 E5
Bugle U.K. 50°24N 4°47W 29 G4
Bugulma Russia 54°33N 52°48E 70 D9
Buguruslan Russia 53°39N 52°26E 70 D9
Builth Wells U.K. 52°9N 3°25W 28 C7
Buir Nur Mongolia 47°50N 117°42E 79 B12
Buji China 22°37N 114°5E 79 a
Bujumbura Burundi 3°16S 29°18E 96 E5
Bukavu Dem. Rep. of the Congo 2°20S 28°52E 96 E5
Bukhara Uzbekistan 39°48N 64°25E 87 B11
Bukittinggi Indonesia 0°20S 100°20E 82 E2
Bulawayo Zimbabwe 20°7S 28°32E 97 J5
Bulford U.K. 51°11N 1°45W 30 D5
Bulgaria ■ Europe 42°35N 25°30E 69 C11
Bullhead City U.S.A. 35°8N 114°32W 110 C4
Bunbury Australia 33°20S 115°35E 98 G2
Bunclody Ireland 52°39N 6°40W 21 C9
Buncrana Ireland 55°8N 7°27W 18 A7
Bundaberg Australia 24°54S 152°22E 98 E9
Bundi India 25°30N 75°35E 84 G9
Bundoran Ireland 54°28N 8°18W 18 C5
Bungay U.K. 52°27N 1°28E 31 B11
Buntingford U.K. 51°56N 0°0 31 C9
Bunwell U.K. 52°30N 1°9E 31 A11
Buon Ma Thuot Vietnam 12°40N 108°3E 82 B3
Bûr Safâga Egypt 26°43N 33°57E 95 C12
Buraydah Si. Arabia 26°20N 43°59E 86 E5
Burbage Derby, U.K. 53°15N 1°55W 27 F5
Burbage Leics., U.K. 52°32N 1°21W 27 G6
Burbage Wilts., U.K. 51°21N 1°39W 30 D5
Burco Somalia 9°32N 45°32E 89 F4
Burdur Turkey 37°45N 30°17E 71 G5
Bure → U.K. 52°38N 1°43E 31 A12
Burford U.K. 51°49N 1°38W 30 C5
Burgas Bulgaria 42°33N 27°29E 69 C12
Burgess Hill U.K. 50°58N 0°6W 31 E8
Burgh le Marsh U.K. 53°9N 0°15E 27 F9
Burghead U.K. 57°43N 3°33W 23 G11
Burgos Spain 42°21N 3°41W 67 A4
Burgundy = Bourgogne France 47°0N 4°50E 66 C6
Burhanpur India 21°18N 76°14E 84 J10
Burkina Faso ■ Africa 12°0N 1°0W 94 F5
Burley U.K. 50°49N 1°43W 30 E5
Burley U.S.A. 42°32N 113°48W 110 B4
Burley in Wharfedale U.K. 53°54N 1°45W 27 E5
Burlington Colo., U.S.A. 39°18N 102°16W 110 C6
Burlington Iowa, U.S.A. 40°49N 91°14W 111 B8
Burlington N.C., U.S.A. 44°29N 73°12W 113 C11
Burlington Vt., U.S.A. 44°29N 73°12W 113 C11
Burma = Myanmar ■ Asia 21°0N 96°30E 85 J20
Burnham-on-Crouch U.K. 51°38N 0°49E 31 C10
Burnham-on-Sea U.K. 51°14N 3°0W 30 D2
Burnie Australia 41°4S 145°56E 98 J8
Burnley U.K. 53°47N 2°14W 27 E4
Burnmouth U.K. 55°50N 2°4W 25 C11
Burns U.S.A. 43°35N 119°3W 110 B3
Burnside → Canada 66°51N 108°4W 108 C9

Burntisland   Chesil Beach

Burntisland U.K. 56°4N 3°13W 25 B9
Burqin China 47°43N 87°0E 78 B6
Burray U.K. 58°51N 2°54W 23 E12
Burren △ Ireland 53°9N 9°5W 20 B4
Burrow Hd. U.K. 54°41N 4°24W 24 E7
Burry Port U.K. 51°41N 4°15W 28 D5
Bursa Turkey 40°15N 29°5E 71 F4
Burstwick U.K. 53°44N 0°8W 27 E8
Burton U.K. 54°11N 2°43W 26 D3
Burton Agnes U.K. 54°4N 0°18W 26 D8
Burton Bradstock U.K. 50°42N 2°43W 30 E3
Burton Fleming U.K. 54°8N 0°20W 26 D8
Burton Latimer U.K. 52°22N 0°41W 31 B7
Burton upon Stather U.K. 53°39N 0°41W 27 E7
Burton upon Trent U.K. 52°48N 1°38W 27 G5
Buru Indonesia 3°30S 126°30E 83 E7
Burundi ■ Africa 3°15S 30°0E 96 E5
Burwash U.K. 50°59N 0°23E 31 E9
Burwell U.K. 52°17N 0°20E 31 B9
Burwick U.K. 58°45N 2°58W 23 E12
Bury U.K. 53°35N 2°17W 27 E4
Bury St. Edmunds U.K. 52°15N 0°43E 31 B10
Buryatia □ Russia 53°0N 110°0E 77 D11
Busan S. Korea 35°5N 129°0E 79 D14
Büshehr Iran 28°55N 50°55E 87 D7
Bushey U.K. 51°38N 0°22W 31 C8
Busto Arsizio Italy 45°37N 8°51E 68 B3
Buta Dem. Rep. of the Congo 2°50N 24°53E 96 D4
Butare Rwanda 2°31S 29°52E 96 E5
Butaritari Kiribati 3°30N 174°0E 102 G9
Bute U.K. 55°48N 5°2W 24 C5
Bute, Kyles of U.K. 55°55N 5°10W 24 C5
Butembo Dem. Rep. of the Congo 0°9N 29°18E 96 D5
Butler U.S.A. 40°52N 79°54W 112 E8
Buton Indonesia 5°0S 122°45E 83 E6
Butte U.S.A. 46°0N 112°32W 110 A4
Buttermere U.K. 54°32N 3°16W 26 C2
Butterworth Malaysia 5°24N 100°23E 82 C2
Buttevant Ireland 52°14N 8°40W 20 D5
Butuan Phil. 8°57N 125°33E 83 C7
Buurhakaba Somalia 3°12N 44°20E 89 G3
Buxton U.K. 53°16N 1°54W 27 F6
Buyant-Uhaa Mongolia 44°55N 110°11E 79 C11
Buzău Romania 45°10N 26°50E 65 F14
Buzuluk Russia 52°48N 52°12E 70 D9
Byfield U.K. 52°10N 1°14W 30 B6
Bylot I. Canada 73°13N 78°34W 109 B12
Byrranga Ra. Russia 75°0N 100°0E 77 B11
Bytom Poland 50°25N 18°54E 65 C10

C

Ca Mau Vietnam 9°7N 105°8E 82 C3
Cabanatuan Phil. 15°30N 120°58E 83 A6
Cabedelo Brazil 7°0S 34°50W 120 C6
Cabimas Venezuela 10°23N 71°25W 120 A2
Cabinda Angola 5°33S 12°11E 96 F2
Cabinda □ Angola 5°0S 12°30E 96 F2
Cabo Frio Brazil 22°51S 42°3W 122 D2
Cabo San Lucas Mexico 22°53N 109°54W 114 C3
Cabo Verde ■ Atl. Oc. 16°0N 24°0W 91 E1
Cabonga, Réservoir Canada 47°20N 76°40W 109 E12
Cabora Bassa Dam Mozam. 15°20S 32°50E 97 H6
Cabot Str. Canada 47°15N 59°40W 109 E14
Čačak Serbia 43°54N 20°20E 69 C9
Cáceres Brazil 16°5S 57°40W 120 D4
Cáceres Spain 39°26N 6°23W 67 C2
Cachimbo, Serra do Brazil 9°30S 55°30W 120 C4
Cachoeira Brazil 12°30S 39°0W 122 B3
Cachoeira do Sul Brazil 30°3S 52°53W 121 F4
Cachoeiro de Itapemirim Brazil 20°51S 41°7W 122 D2
Cader Idris U.K. 52°42N 3°53W 28 B6
Cadillac U.S.A. 44°15N 85°24W 112 C5
Cádiz Spain 36°30N 6°20W 67 D2
Cádiz, G. de Spain 36°40N 7°0W 67 D2
Caen France 49°10N 0°22W 66 B3
Caenby Corner U.K. 53°24N 0°33W 27 F7
Caerdydd = Cardiff U.K. 51°29N 3°10W 29 F7
Caerfyrddin = Carmarthen U.K. 51°52N 4°19W 28 D5
Caergybi = Holyhead U.K. 53°18N 4°38W 28 A4
Caernarfon U.K. 53°8N 4°16W 28 A5
Caernarfon B. U.K. 53°4N 4°40W 28 A4
Caerphilly U.K. 51°35N 3°13W 29 F7
Caersws U.K. 52°31N 3°26W 28 B7
Caeté Brazil 19°55S 43°40W 122 D2
Caetité Brazil 13°50S 42°32W 122 B2
Cagayan de Oro Phil. 8°30N 124°40E 83 C6
Cágliari Italy 39°13N 9°7E 68 E3
Caguas Puerto Rico 18°14N 66°2W 115 D11
Caha Mts. Ireland 51°45N 9°40W 20 E3
Caherciveen Ireland 51°56N 10°14W 20 E2
Cahir Ireland 52°22N 7°56W 20 D7
Cahore Pt. Ireland 52°33N 6°12W 21 C10
Cahors France 44°27N 1°27E 66 D4
Cairn Gorm U.K. 57°7N 3°39W 23 H10
Cairngorm Mts. U.K. 57°6N 3°42W 23 H10
Cairngorms △ U.K. 57°10N 3°50W 23 H10
Cairnryan U.K. 54°59N 5°1W 24 E5
Cairns Australia 16°57S 145°45E 98 D8
Cairnsmore of Fleet U.K. 54°59N 4°20W 24 E7
Cairo Egypt 30°2N 31°13E 95 B12
Cairo U.S.A. 37°0N 89°11W 112 G3
Caister-on-Sea U.K. 52°40N 1°43E 31 A12
Caistor U.K. 53°30N 0°18W 27 F8
Caithness U.K. 58°25N 3°35W 23 F10
Caithness, Ord of U.K. 58°8N 3°36W 23 F10
Cajamarca Peru 7°5S 78°28W 120 C2
Calabar Nigeria 4°57N 8°20E 94 H7
Calábria □ Italy 39°0N 16°30E 68 E7
Calais France 50°57N 1°56E 66 A4
Calais U.S.A. 45°11N 67°17W 113 C14
Calama Chile 22°30S 68°55W 121 E3
Calamian Group Phil. 11°50N 119°55E 83 B5
Calanscio, Sarir Libya 27°30N 22°30E 95 C10
Calapan Phil. 13°25N 121°7E 83 B6
Calbayog Phil. 12°4N 124°38E 83 B6
Calcutta = Kolkata India 22°34N 88°21E 85 H16
Caldbeck U.K. 54°45N 3°3W 26 C2

Calder → U.K. 53°44N 1°22W 27 E6
Calder Bridge U.K. 54°27N 3°29W 26 D2
Caldera Chile 27°5S 70°55W 121 E2
Caldew → U.K. 54°54N 2°56W 26 C3
Caldwell U.S.A. 43°40N 116°41W 110 B3
Caledonian Canal U.K. 57°29N 4°15W 23 H9
Calgary Canada 51°0N 114°10W 108 D6
Cali Colombia 3°25N 76°35W 120 B2
Cálida, Costa Spain 37°30N 1°30W 67 D5
California □ U.S.A. 37°30N 119°30W 110 C2
California, G. de Mexico 27°0N 111°0W 114 B2
Callan Ireland 52°32N 7°24W 21 C8
Callander U.K. 56°15N 4°13W 24 B7
Callao Peru 12°3S 77°8W 120 D2
Calne U.K. 51°26N 2°0W 30 D5
Calshot U.K. 50°48N 1°19W 30 E6
Calstock U.K. 50°30N 4°13W 29 F3
Caltanissetta Italy 37°29N 14°4E 68 F6
Calvi France 42°34N 8°45E 66 E8
Calvinia S. Africa 31°28S 19°45E 97 L3
Cam → U.K. 52°21N 0°16E 31 B9
Cam Ranh Vietnam 11°54N 109°12E 82 B3
Camagüey Cuba 21°20N 77°55W 115 C9
Camargue France 43°34N 4°34E 66 E6
Camberley U.K. 51°20N 0°44W 31 D7
Cambo U.K. 55°10N 1°57W 26 B5
Cambodia ■ Asia 12°15N 105°0E 82 B3
Camborne U.K. 50°12N 5°19W 29 G3
Cambrai France 50°11N 3°14E 66 A5
Cambrian Mts. U.K. 52°3N 3°57W 28 C6
Cambridge Jamaica 18°18N 77°54W 114 a
Cambridge U.K. 52°12N 0°8E 31 B9
Cambridge Mass., U.S.A. 42°23N 71°7W 113 D12
Cambridge Md., U.S.A. 38°34N 76°5W 113 F9
Cambridge Ohio, U.S.A. 40°2N 81°35W 112 E7
Cambridge Bay Canada 69°10N 105°0W 108 C9
Cambridgeshire □ U.K. 52°25N 0°7W 31 B8
Camden Ark., U.S.A. 33°35N 92°50W 111 D8
Camden N.J., U.S.A. 39°55N 75°7W 113 F10
Camden □ U.K. 51°32N 0°8W 31 C8
Camel → U.K. 50°31N 4°51W 29 F4
Camelford U.K. 50°37N 4°42W 29 F4
Cameroon ■ Africa 6°0N 12°30E 96 C2
Cameroun, Mt. Cameroon 4°13N 9°10E 96 D1
Cametá Brazil 2°12S 49°30W 120 C5
Camocim Brazil 2°55S 40°50W 120 C5
Campana, I. Chile 48°20S 75°20W 121 G2
Campánia □ Italy 41°0N 14°30E 68 D6
Campbell I. Pac. Oc. 52°30S 169°0E 102 N8
Campbell River Canada 50°5N 125°20W 108 D7
Campbellsville U.S.A. 37°21N 85°20W 112 G5
Campbellton Canada 47°57N 66°43W 109 E13
Campbeltown U.K. 55°26N 5°36W 24 D4
Campeche Mexico 19°51N 90°32W 114 D6
Campeche, Golfo de Mexico 19°30N 93°0W 114 D6
Campina Grande Brazil 7°20S 35°47W 120 C6
Campinas Brazil 22°50S 47°0W 122 D1
Campo Belo Brazil 20°52S 45°16W 122 D1
Campo Grande Brazil 20°25S 54°40W 120 E4
Campobasso Italy 41°34N 14°39E 68 D6
Campos Brazil 21°50S 41°20W 122 D2
Campos Belos Brazil 13°10S 47°3W 122 B1
Camrose Canada 53°0N 112°50W 108 D8
Can Tho Vietnam 10°2N 105°46E 82 B3
Canada ■ N. Amer. 60°0N 100°0W 108 C10
Canadian → U.S.A. 35°28N 95°3W 111 C7
Canadian Shield Canada 53°0N 75°0W 104 C9
Çanakkale Turkey 40°8N 26°24E 71 F4
Canandaigua U.S.A. 42°54N 77°17W 112 D9
Cananea Mexico 31°0N 110°18W 114 A2
Canaries St. Lucia 13°55N 61°4W 114 b
Canary Is. Atl. Oc. 28°30N 16°0W 94 C2
Canaveral, C. U.S.A. 28°27N 80°32W 111 E10
Canavieiras Brazil 15°39S 39°0W 122 C3
Canberra Australia 35°15S 149°8E 98 H8
Cancún Mexico 21°8N 86°44W 114 C7
Cangzhou China 38°19N 116°52E 79 D12
Caniapiscau → Canada 56°40N 69°30W 109 D13
Caniapiscau, L. Canada 54°10N 69°55W 109 D13
Çankırı Turkey 40°40N 33°37E 71 F5
Canna U.K. 57°3N 6°33W 22 H4
Canna, Sd. of U.K. 57°1N 6°30W 22 H5
Cannes France 43°32N 7°1E 66 E7
Cannington U.K. 51°9N 3°4W 30 D2
Cannock U.K. 52°41N 2°1W 27 G4
Cannock Chase U.K. 52°44N 2°4W 27 G4
Canoas Brazil 29°56S 51°11W 121 E4
Cañon City U.S.A. 38°27N 105°14W 110 C5
Canonbie U.K. 55°5N 2°58W 25 D10
Canora Canada 51°40N 102°30W 108 D9
Canso Canada 45°20N 61°0W 113 C17
Cantabria □ Spain 43°10N 4°0W 67 A4
Cantábrica, Cordillera Spain 43°0N 5°10W 67 A3
Canterbury U.K. 51°16N 1°6E 31 D11
Canton = Guangzhou China 23°6N 113°13E 79 G11
Canton Ill., U.S.A. 40°33N 90°2W 112 E2
Canton N.Y., U.S.A. 44°36N 75°10W 113 C10
Canton Ohio, U.S.A. 40°48N 81°23W 112 E7
Canvey Island U.K. 51°31N 0°37E 31 C10
Cap-de-la-Madeleine Canada 46°22N 72°31W 113 B11
Cap-Haïtien Haiti 19°40N 72°20W 115 D10
Cap Pt. St. Lucia 14°7N 60°57W 114 b
Cape Breton I. Canada 46°0N 60°30W 113 C17
Cape Charles U.S.A. 37°16N 76°1W 113 G10
Cape Coast Ghana 5°5N 1°15W 94 G5
Cape Fear → U.S.A. 33°53N 78°1W 111 D11
Cape Girardeau U.S.A. 37°19N 89°32W 112 G3
Cape May U.S.A. 38°56N 74°56W 113 F10
Cape Town S. Africa 33°55S 18°22E 97 L3
Cape York Peninsula Australia 12°0S 142°30E 98 C7
Capela Brazil 10°30S 37°0W 122 B3
Capreol Canada 46°43N 80°56W 112 B7
Capri Italy 40°33N 14°14E 68 D6
Caprivi Strip Namibia 18°0S 23°0E 97 H4
Caquetá → Colombia 1°15S 69°15W 120 C3
Caracal Romania 44°8N 24°22E 65 F13
Caracas Venezuela 10°30N 66°55W 120 A3
Caracol Brazil 9°15S 43°22W 122 A2
Carangola Brazil 20°44S 42°5W 122 D2

Caratasca, L. de Honduras 15°20N 83°40W 115 D8
Caratinga Brazil 19°50S 42°10W 122 C2
Caravelas Brazil 17°45S 39°15W 122 C3
Carbón, L. del Argentina 49°35S 68°21W 121 G3
Carbondale Ill., U.S.A. 37°44N 89°13W 112 G3
Carbondale Pa., U.S.A. 41°35N 75°30W 113 E10
Carbonear Canada 47°42N 53°13W 109 E14
Cardamon Hills India 9°30N 77°15E 84 Q10
Cárdenas Cuba 23°0N 81°30W 115 C8
Cardiff U.K. 51°29N 3°10W 29 F7
Cardigan U.K. 52°5N 4°40W 28 C4
Cardigan B. U.K. 52°30N 4°30W 28 B4
Cardington U.K. 52°6N 0°25W 31 B8
Cardston Canada 49°15N 113°20W 108 E8
Cariacica Brazil 20°16S 40°25W 122 D2
Caribbean Sea W. Indies 15°0N 75°0W 115 E10
Cariboo Mts. Canada 53°0N 121°0W 108 D7
Caribou U.S.A. 46°52N 68°1W 113 B13
Caribou Mts. Canada 59°12N 115°40W 108 D8
Carinhanha Brazil 14°15S 44°46W 122 B2
Carinhanha → Brazil 14°20S 43°47W 122 B2
Carinthia = Kärnten □ Austria 46°52N 13°30E 64 E8
Carisbrooke U.K. 50°41N 1°19W 30 E6
Cark U.K. 54°11N 2°58W 26 D3
Carleton Place Canada 45°8N 76°9W 113 C9
Carleton Rode U.K. 52°30N 1°7E 31 A11
Carlingford L. U.K. 54°3N 6°9W 19 B5
Carlinville U.S.A. 39°17N 89°53W 112 F3
Carlisle U.K. 54°54N 2°56W 26 C4
Carlisle U.S.A. 40°12N 77°12W 112 E9
Carlisle B. Barbados 13°5N 59°37W 114 c
Carlops U.K. 55°47N 3°20W 25 D9
Carlow Ireland 52°50N 6°56W 21 C9
Carlow □ Ireland 52°43N 6°50W 21 C9
Carlsbad U.S.A. 32°25N 104°14W 110 D6
Carlton U.K. 52°59N 1°5W 27 G6
Carlton Colville U.K. 52°27N 1°43E 31 B12
Carlton Miniott U.K. 54°12N 1°22W 26 D6
Carluke U.K. 55°45N 3°50W 25 C8
Carmacks Canada 62°5N 136°16W 108 C6
Carman Canada 49°30N 98°0W 108 E10
Carmarthen U.K. 51°52N 4°19W 28 D5
Carmarthen B. U.K. 51°40N 4°30W 28 D4
Carmarthenshire □ U.K. 51°55N 4°13W 28 D5
Carmaux France 44°3N 2°10E 66 D5
Carn Ban U.K. 57°7N 4°15W 23 H9
Carn Eige U.K. 57°17N 5°8W 22 H7
Carnarvon Australia 24°51S 113°42E 98 E1
Carnarvon S. Africa 30°56S 22°8E 97 L4
Carndonagh Ireland 55°16N 7°15W 19 A7
Carnegie, L. Australia 26°5S 122°30E 98 F3
Carno U.K. 52°34N 3°30W 28 B6
Carnoustie U.K. 56°30N 2°42W 25 A10
Carnsore Pt. Ireland 52°10N 6°22W 21 D10
Caro U.S.A. 43°29N 83°24W 112 D6
Caroline I. Kiribati 9°58S 150°13W 103 H12
Caroline Is. Micronesia 8°0N 150°0E 102 G6
Carondelet Reef Kiribati 5°33S 173°50W 99 B16
Caroní → Venezuela 8°21N 62°43W 120 B3
Carpathians Europe 49°30N 21°0E 65 D11
Carpentaria, G. of Australia 14°0S 139°0E 98 C6
Carpentras France 44°3N 5°2E 66 D6
Carpi Italy 44°47N 10°53E 68 B4
Carrantuohill Ireland 52°0N 9°45W 20 E3
Carrick-on-Shannon Ireland 53°57N 8°7W 18 C6
Carrick-on-Suir Ireland 52°21N 7°24W 21 D8
Carrickfergus U.K. 54°43N 5°49W 19 B10
Carrickmacross Ireland 53°59N 6°43W 19 C8
Carrigaline Ireland 51°48N 8°23W 20 E6
Carrollton U.S.A. 39°18N 90°24W 112 F2
Carron → U.K. 57°53N 4°22W 23 H9
Carron, L. U.K. 57°22N 5°35W 22 H6
Carson City U.S.A. 39°10N 119°46W 110 C3
Carson Sink U.S.A. 39°50N 118°25W 110 C3
Cartagena Colombia 10°25N 75°33W 120 A2
Cartagena Spain 37°38N 0°59W 67 D5
Cartago Colombia 4°45N 75°55W 120 B2
Carter Bar U.K. 55°21N 2°29W 25 D10
Carthage Tunisia 36°52N 10°20E 95 A8
Cartmel U.K. 54°12N 2°57W 26 D3
Cartwright Canada 53°41N 56°58W 109 D14
Caruaru Brazil 8°15S 35°55W 122 A3
Carúpano Venezuela 10°39N 63°15W 120 A3
Casa Grande U.S.A. 32°53N 111°45W 110 D4
Casa Nova Brazil 9°25S 41°5W 122 A2
Casablanca Morocco 33°36N 7°36W 94 B4
Cascade Ra. U.S.A. 47°0N 121°30W 110 A2
Cascavel Ceará, Brazil 4°7S 38°14W 120 C6
Cascavel Paraná, Brazil 24°57S 53°28W 121 E4
Caserta Italy 41°4N 14°20E 68 D6
Cashel Ireland 52°30N 7°53W 20 D7
Casiquiare → Venezuela 2°1N 67°7W 120 B3
Casnewydd = Newport U.K. 51°35N 3°0W 29 F8
Casper U.S.A. 42°51N 106°19W 110 B5
Caspian Depression Eurasia 47°0N 48°0E 71 E8
Caspian Sea Eurasia 43°0N 50°0E 71 F9
Cassiar Mts. Canada 59°30N 130°30W 108 D6
Castell-Nedd = Neath U.K. 51°39N 3°48W 28 D6
Castellammare di Stábia Italy 40°42N 14°29E 68 D6
Castelló de la Plana Spain 39°58N 0°3W 67 C5
Castelsarrasin France 44°2N 1°7E 66 E4
Castilla-La Mancha □ Spain 39°30N 3°30W 67 C4
Castilla y Leon □ Spain 42°0N 5°0W 67 B3
Castle Acre U.K. 52°42N 0°42E 31 A10
Castle Cary U.K. 51°6N 2°31W 30 D3
Castle Donington U.K. 52°51N 1°20W 27 G6
Castle Douglas U.K. 54°56N 3°56W 25 E8
Castlebar Ireland 53°52N 9°18W 18 C2
Castlebay U.K. 56°57N 7°31W 22 J2
Castleblayney Ireland 54°7N 6°44W 19 C8
Castlederg U.K. 54°43N 7°35W 18 B6
Castleford U.K. 53°43N 1°21W 27 E6
Castlemaine Harbour Ireland 52°8N 9°50W 20 D3
Castlepollard Ireland 53°41N 7°19W 18 D7
Castlerea Ireland 53°46N 8°29W 18 D5

Castleside U.K. 54°50N 1°52W 26 C5
Castleton Derby, U.K. 53°22N 1°46W 27 F5
Castleton N. Yorks., U.K. 54°28N 0°57W 26 D7
Castletown I. of Man 54°5N 4°38W 19 C12
Castletown Bearhaven Ireland 51°39N 9°55W 20 E3
Castres France 43°37N 2°13E 66 E5
Castries St. Lucia 14°2N 60°58W 114 b
Castro Chile 42°30S 73°50W 121 G2
Castro Alves Brazil 12°46S 39°33W 122 B3
Cataguases Brazil 21°23S 42°39W 122 D2
Catalão Brazil 18°10S 47°57W 122 C1
Cataluña □ Spain 41°40N 1°15E 67 B6
Catamarca Argentina 28°30S 65°50W 121 E3
Catanduanes Phil. 13°50N 124°20E 83 B6
Catanduva Brazil 21°5S 48°58W 122 D1
Catánia Italy 37°30N 15°6E 68 F6
Catanzaro Italy 38°54N 16°35E 68 E7
Catcleugh U.K. 55°20N 2°24W 26 B4
Caterham U.K. 51°15N 0°4W 31 D8
Catoche, C. Mexico 21°35N 87°5W 114 C7
Caton U.K. 54°5N 2°35W 26 D4
Catskill U.S.A. 42°14N 73°52W 113 D11
Catskill Mts. U.S.A. 42°10N 74°25W 113 D10
Catterick U.K. 54°23N 1°37W 26 D5
Catterick Garrison U.K. 54°22N 1°42W 26 D5
Catton U.K. 54°55N 2°15W 26 C4
Cauca → Colombia 8°54N 74°28W 120 B2
Caucaia Brazil 3°40S 38°35W 120 C6
Caucasus Mountains Eurasia 42°50N 44°0E 71 F7
Caulkerbush U.K. 54°54N 3°41W 25 E9
Caura → Venezuela 7°38N 64°53W 120 B3
Causeway Coast & Glens □ U.K. 55°5N 6°33W 19 A8
Cauvery → India 11°9N 78°52E 84 P11
Cavan Ireland 54°0N 7°22W 18 D7
Cavan □ Ireland 54°1N 7°16W 19 C7
Caviana, I. Brazil 0°10N 50°10W 120 B4
Cawood U.K. 53°50N 1°8W 27 E6
Cawston U.K. 52°47N 1°9E 31 A11
Caxias Brazil 4°55S 43°20W 120 C5
Caxias do Sul Brazil 29°10S 51°10W 121 E4
Cayenne Fr. Guiana 5°5N 52°18W 120 B4
Cayman Is. ☑ W. Indies 19°40N 80°30W 115 D8
Cayman Trench Caribbean 17°0N 83°0W 115 D8
Cayuga L. U.S.A. 42°41N 76°41W 112 D9
Ceará □ Brazil 5°0S 40°0W 120 C6
Cebu Phil. 10°18N 123°54E 83 B6
Cedar → U.S.A. 41°17N 91°21W 112 E2
Cedar City U.S.A. 37°41N 113°4W 110 C4
Cedar L. Canada 53°10N 100°0W 108 D9
Cedar Rapids U.S.A. 41°59N 91°40W 111 B8
Cefalù Italy 38°2N 14°1E 68 E6
Cegléd Hungary 47°11N 19°47E 65 E10
Celaya Mexico 20°31N 100°37W 114 C4
Celebes Sea Indonesia 3°0N 123°0E 83 D6
Celina U.S.A. 40°33N 84°35W 112 E5
Cellar Hd. U.K. 58°25N 6°11W 22 F5
Celtic Sea Atl. Oc. 50°9N 9°34W 62 F4
Cemaes U.K. 53°24N 4°27W 28 A5
Central, Cordillera Colombia 5°0N 75°0W 117 C3
Central African Rep. ■ Africa 7°0N 20°0E 96 C4
Central Bedfordshire □ U.K. 52°5N 0°20W 31 B8
Central Makran Range Pakistan 26°30N 64°15E 84 F4
Central Russian Uplands Europe 54°0N 36°0E 56 E13
Central Siberian Plateau Russia 65°0N 105°0E 72 B12
Centralia Ill., U.S.A. 38°32N 89°8W 112 F3
Centralia Wash., U.S.A. 46°43N 122°58W 110 A2
Cephalonia = Kefalonia Greece 38°15N 20°30E 69 E9
Ceredigion □ U.K. 52°16N 4°15W 28 C5
Cerignola Italy 41°17N 15°53E 68 D6
Cerne Abbas U.K. 50°49N 2°29W 30 E4
Cerrigydrudion U.K. 53°1N 3°35W 28 A6
Cerro de Pasco Peru 10°45S 76°10W 120 D2
Cesena Italy 44°8N 12°15E 68 B5
České Budějovice Czechia 48°55N 14°25E 64 D8
Çeşme Turkey 38°20N 26°23E 71 G4
Ceuta N. Afr. 35°52N 5°18W 67 E3
Ceve-i-Ra Fiji 21°46S 174°31E 99 E13
Cévennes France 44°10N 3°50E 66 D5
Chacewater U.K. 50°15N 5°11W 29 G3
Chachapoyas Peru 6°15S 77°50W 120 C2
Chaco Austral S. Amer. 27°0S 61°30W 121 E3
Chaco Boreal S. Amer. 22°0S 60°0W 120 E4
Chaco Central S. Amer. 24°0S 61°0W 121 E4
Chad ■ Africa 15°0N 17°15E 95 F8
Chad, L. Chad 13°30N 14°30E 95 F8
Chadron U.S.A. 42°50N 103°0W 110 B6
Chagford U.K. 50°40N 3°50W 29 F6
Chaghcharān Afghan. 34°31N 65°15E 87 C11
Chagos Arch. ☑ Ind. Oc. 6°0S 72°0E 53 E13
Chāh Gay Hills Afghan. 29°30N 64°0E 87 D10
Chakradharpur India 22°45N 85°40E 85 H14
Chaleur B. Canada 47°55N 65°30W 113 B15
Chalisgaon India 20°30N 75°10E 84 J9
Challenger Deep Pac. Oc. 11°30N 142°0E 102 F6
Chalon-sur-Saône France 46°48N 4°50E 66 C6
Châlons-en-Champagne France 48°58N 4°20E 66 B6
Chambal → India 26°29N 79°15E 84 F11
Chambersburg U.S.A. 39°56N 77°40W 112 F9
Chambéry France 45°34N 5°55E 66 D6
Chamonix-Mont Blanc France 45°55N 6°51E 66 D7
Champagne France 48°40N 4°20E 66 B6
Champaign U.S.A. 40°7N 88°15W 112 E3
Champlain, L. U.S.A. 44°40N 73°20W 113 C11
Chañaral Chile 26°23S 70°40W 121 E2
Chancery Lane Barbados 13°3N 59°30W 114 c
Chandigarh India 30°43N 76°47E 84 D10
Chandler's Ford U.K. 50°59N 1°22W 30 E6
Chandpur Bangla. 23°8N 90°45E 85 H17
Chandrapur India 19°57N 79°25E 84 K11
Changbai Shan China 42°20N 129°0E 79 C14
Changchun China 43°57N 125°17E 79 C14
Changde China 29°4N 111°35E 79 F11
Changhua Taiwan 24°2N 120°30E 79 G13
Changji China 44°1N 87°19E 78 C6

Changsha China 28°12N 113°0E 79 F11
Changzhi China 36°10N 113°6E 79 D11
Changzhou China 31°47N 119°58E 79 E12
Chania Greece 35°30N 24°4E 69 G11
Channel Is. U.K. 49°19N 2°24W 29 J9
Channel-Port aux Basques Canada 47°30N 59°9W 109 E14
Chantrey Inlet Canada 67°48N 96°20W 108 C10
Chaoyang China 41°35N 120°22E 79 C13
Chaozhou China 23°42N 116°32E 79 G12
Chapala, L. de Mexico 20°15N 103°0W 114 C4
Chapayevsk Russia 53°0N 49°40E 70 D8
Chapel-en-le-Frith U.K. 53°20N 1°54W 27 F5
Chapel St. Leonards U.K. 53°13N 0°20E 27 F9
Chapleau Canada 47°50N 83°24W 109 E11
Charaña Bolivia 17°30S 69°25W 120 D3
Chard U.K. 50°52N 2°58W 30 E3
Chari → Chad 12°58N 14°31E 95 F8
Chārīkār Afghan. 35°0N 69°10E 87 C12
Charing U.K. 51°12N 0°49E 31 D10
Charlbury U.K. 51°53N 1°28W 30 C6
Charleroi Belgium 50°24N 4°27E 64 C3
Charles, C. U.S.A. 37°7N 75°58W 113 G10
Charles City U.S.A. 43°4N 92°41W 111 B8
Charleston Ill., U.S.A. 39°30N 88°10W 112 F3
Charleston Mo., U.S.A. 36°55N 89°21W 112 G3
Charleston S.C., U.S.A. 32°46N 79°56W 111 D11
Charleston W. Va., U.S.A. 38°21N 81°38W 112 F7
Charlestown Ireland 53°58N 8°48W 18 D4
Charlestown of Aberlour U.K. 57°28N 3°14W 23 H11
Charleville Australia 26°24S 146°15E 98 F8
Charleville Ireland 52°21N 8°40W 20 D5
Charleville-Mézières France 49°44N 4°40E 66 B6
Charlevoix U.S.A. 45°19N 85°16W 112 C5
Charlotte Mich., U.S.A. 42°34N 84°50W 112 D5
Charlotte N.C., U.S.A. 35°13N 80°50W 111 C10
Charlotte Amalie U.S. Virgin Is. 18°21N 64°56W 115 D12
Charlotte Harbor U.S.A. 26°57N 82°4W 111 E10
Charlottesville U.S.A. 38°2N 78°30W 112 F8
Charlottetown Canada 46°14N 63°8W 113 B16
Charlton I. Canada 52°0N 79°20W 109 D12
Charlton Kings U.K. 51°53N 2°3W 30 C4
Charlwood U.K. 51°9N 0°13W 31 D8
Charminster U.K. 50°44N 2°28W 30 E4
Charmouth U.K. 50°44N 2°54W 30 E3
Charnwood Forest U.K. 52°44N 1°17W 27 G6
Charolles France 46°27N 4°16E 66 C6
Charters Towers Australia 20°5S 146°13E 98 E8
Chartham U.K. 51°14N 1°1E 31 D11
Chartres France 48°29N 1°30E 66 B4
Chascomús Argentina 35°30S 58°0W 121 F4
Châteaubriant France 47°43N 1°23W 66 C3
Châteaulin France 48°11N 4°8W 66 B1
Châteauroux France 46°50N 1°40E 66 C4
Châtellerault France 46°50N 0°30E 66 C4
Chatham = Miramichi Canada 47°2N 65°28W 109 E13
Chatham Canada 42°24N 82°11W 112 D6
Chatham U.K. 51°22N 0°32E 31 D10
Chatham Is. Pac. Oc. 44°0S 176°40W 99 J15
Chatsworth U.K. 53°13N 1°36W 27 F5
Chattanooga U.S.A. 35°3N 85°19W 111 C9
Chatteris U.K. 52°28N 0°2E 31 B9
Chatton U.K. 55°35N 2°0W 26 A5
Chaumont France 48°7N 5°8E 66 B6
Chaykovskiy Russia 56°47N 54°9E 70 C9
Cheadle Gt. Man., U.K. 53°23N 2°12W 27 F4
Cheadle Staffs., U.K. 52°59N 1°58W 27 G5
Cheb Czechia 50°9N 12°28E 64 C7
Cheboksary Russia 56°8N 47°12E 70 C8
Cheboygan U.S.A. 45°39N 84°29W 112 C5
Chech, Erg Africa 25°0N 2°15W 94 D5
Chechenia □ Russia 43°30N 45°29E 71 F8
Chedabucto B. Canada 45°25N 61°8W 113 C17
Cheddar U.K. 51°17N 2°46W 30 D3
Cheddleton U.K. 53°4N 2°2W 27 F4
Cheduba I. Myanmar 18°45N 93°40E 85 K18
Chegutu Zimbabwe 18°10S 30°14E 97 H6
Chek Lap Kok China 22°18N 113°56E 79 a
Chelm Poland 51°8N 23°30E 65 C12
Chelmer → U.K. 51°44N 0°30E 31 C10
Chelmsford U.K. 51°44N 0°29E 31 C10
Cheltenham U.K. 51°54N 2°4W 30 C4
Chelyabinsk Russia 55°10N 61°24E 76 D7
Chelyuskin, C. Russia 77°30N 103°0E 77 B11
Chemnitz Germany 50°51N 12°54E 64 C7
Chenab → Pakistan 30°23N 71°2E 84 D7
Chengde China 40°59N 117°58E 79 C12
Chengdu China 30°38N 104°2E 78 E9
Chennai India 13°8N 80°19E 84 N12
Cheo, Eilean a' = Skye U.K. 57°15N 6°10W 22 H5
Chepstow U.K. 51°38N 2°41W 28 D8
Cher → France 47°21N 0°29E 66 C4
Cherbourg-Octeville France 49°39N 1°40W 66 B3
Cheremkhovo Russia 53°8N 103°1E 78 A9
Cherepovets Russia 59°5N 37°55E 70 C6
Chergui, Chott ech Algeria 34°21N 0°25E 94 B6
Cheriton U.K. 51°3N 1°8W 30 D6
Cheriton Fitzpaine U.K. 50°51N 3°35W 29 F6
Cherkasy Ukraine 49°27N 32°4E 71 E5
Cherkessk Russia 44°15N 42°5E 71 F7
Chernihiv Ukraine 51°28N 31°20E 70 D5
Chernivtsi Ukraine 48°15N 25°52E 65 D13
Chernobyl Ukraine 51°20N 30°15E 65 C16
Cherokee U.S.A. 42°45N 95°33W 111 B7
Cherrapunji India 25°17N 91°47E 85 G17
Cherski Ra. Russia 65°0N 143°0E 77 C15
Chertsey U.K. 51°23N 0°30W 31 D7
Chervonohrad Ukraine 50°25N 24°10E 71 D3
Cherwell → U.K. 51°44N 1°14W 30 C6
Chesapeake B. U.S.A. 38°0N 76°10W 112 F9
Chesha B. Russia 67°20N 47°0E 70 A8
Chesham U.K. 51°43N 0°36W 31 C7
Cheshire East □ U.K. 53°15N 2°15W 27 F4
Cheshire West and Chester □ U.K. 53°15N 2°40W 27 F3
Cheshunt U.K. 51°43N 0°1W 31 C8
Chesil Beach U.K. 50°37N 2°33W 30 E3

Chester   Cumberland Pen.

Chester *U.K.* 53°12N 2°53W 27 F3
Chester *U.S.A.* 39°51N 75°22W 113 F10
Chester-le-Street *U.K.* 54°51N 1°34W 26 C5
Chesterfield *U.K.* 53°15N 1°25W 27 F6
Chesterfield, Îs. *N. Cal.* 19°52S 158°15E 99 D10
Chesterfield Inlet *Canada* 63°30N 90°45W 108 C10
Chesuncook L. *U.S.A.* 46°0N 69°21W 113 B13
Chetumal *Mexico* 18°30N 88°20W 114 D7
Chetwynd *Canada* 55°45N 121°36W 108 D7
Cheviot, The *U.K.* 55°29N 2°9W 26 B4
Cheviot Hills *U.K.* 55°20N 2°30W 26 B3
Chew Bahir *Ethiopia* 4°40N 36°50E 89 G2
Chew Magna *U.K.* 51°22N 2°37W 30 D3
Cheyenne *U.S.A.* 41°8N 104°49W 110 B6
Cheyenne → *U.S.A.* 44°41N 101°18W 110 B6
Chhapra *India* 25°48N 84°44E 85 G14
Chhattisgarh □ *India* 22°0N 82°0E 85 J12
Chi → *Thailand* 15°11N 104°43E 82 A3
Chiai *Taiwan* 23°29N 120°25E 79 G13
Chiávari *Italy* 44°19N 9°19E 68 B3
Chiba *Japan* 35°30N 140°7E 81 F7
Chibougamau *Canada* 49°56N 74°24W 109 E12
Chibougamau, L. *Canada* 49°50N 74°20W 113 A10
Chic-Chocs, Mts. *Canada* 48°55N 66°0W 113 A14
Chicago *U.S.A.* 41°52N 87°38W 112 E4
Chichagof I. *U.S.A.* 57°30N 135°30W 108 D6
Chichester *U.K.* 50°50N 0°47W 31 E7
Chickasha *U.S.A.* 35°3N 97°58W 110 C7
Chiclayo *Peru* 6°42S 79°50W 120 C2
Chico *U.S.A.* 39°44N 121°50W 110 C2
Chico → *Chubut, Argentina* 44°0S 67°0W 121 G3
Chico → *Santa Cruz, Argentina* 50°0S 68°30W 121 G3
Chicopee *U.S.A.* 42°9N 72°37W 113 D11
Chicoutimi *Canada* 48°28N 71°5W 113 A12
Chiddingfold *U.K.* 51°7N 0°37W 31 D7
Chidley, C. *Canada* 60°23N 64°26W 109 C13
Chieti *Italy* 42°21N 14°10E 68 C6
Chifeng *China* 42°18N 118°58E 79 C12
Chihuahua *Mexico* 28°38N 106°5W 114 B3
Chilapa *Mexico* 17°36N 99°10W 114 D5
Chilaw *Sri Lanka* 7°30N 79°50E 84 R11
Childress *U.S.A.* 34°25N 100°13W 110 D6
Chile ■ *S. Amer.* 35°0S 72°0W 121 F2
Chililabombwe *Zambia* 12°18S 27°43E 97 G5
Chilka L. *India* 19°40N 85°25E 85 K14
Chillán *Chile* 36°40S 72°10W 121 F2
Chillicothe Ill., *U.S.A.* 40°55N 89°29W 112 E3
Chillicothe Ohio, *U.S.A.* 39°20N 82°59W 112 F6
Chilliwack *Canada* 49°10N 121°54W 108 E7
Chiloé, I. de *Chile* 42°30S 73°50W 121 G2
Chilpancingo *Mexico* 17°33N 99°30W 114 D5
Chiltern Hills *U.K.* 51°40N 0°53W 31 C7
Chilton *U.S.A.* 44°2N 88°10W 112 D3
Chilung *Taiwan* 25°3N 121°45E 79 F13
Chilwa, L. *Malawi* 15°15S 35°40E 97 H7
Chimborazo *Ecuador* 1°29S 78°55W 120 C2
Chimbote *Peru* 9°0S 78°35W 120 C2
Chimoio *Mozam.* 19°4S 33°30E 97 H6
Chin □ *Myanmar* 22°0N 93°0E 85 J18
Chin Hills *Myanmar* 22°30N 93°30E 85 H18
China ■ *Asia* 30°0N 110°0E 79 E11
China, Great Plain of *Asia* 35°0N 115°0E 72 E13
Chinandega *Nic.* 12°35N 87°12W 114 E7
Chincha Alta *Peru* 13°25S 76°7W 120 D2
Chindwin → *Myanmar* 21°26N 95°15E 85 J19
Chingola *Zambia* 12°31S 27°53E 97 G5
Chinhoyi *Zimbabwe* 17°20S 30°8E 97 H6
Chiniot *Pakistan* 31°45N 73°0E 84 D8
Chinmen Tao *Taiwan* 24°26N 118°22E 79 G12
Chinon *France* 47°10N 0°15E 66 C4
Chióggia *Italy* 45°13N 12°17E 68 B5
Chipata *Zambia* 13°38S 32°28E 97 G6
Chipman *Canada* 46°6N 65°53W 113 B15
Chippenham *U.K.* 51°27N 2°6W 30 D4
Chippewa Falls *U.S.A.* 44°56N 91°24W 112 C2
Chipping Campden *U.K.* 52°3N 1°45W 30 B5
Chipping Norton *U.K.* 51°56N 1°32W 30 C5
Chipping Ongar *U.K.* 51°42N 0°15E 31 C9
Chipping Sodbury *U.K.* 51°33N 2°23W 30 C4
Chiquinquira *Colombia* 5°37N 73°50W 120 B2
Chirbury *U.K.* 52°35N 3°4W 27 G2
Chirchiq *Uzbekistan* 41°29N 69°35E 87 A12
Chiredzi *Zimbabwe* 21°0S 31°38E 97 J6
Chirnside *U.K.* 55°48N 2°12W 25 C11
Chiseldon *U.K.* 51°31N 1°44W 30 C5
Chistopol *Russia* 55°25N 50°38E 70 C9
Chita *Russia* 52°0N 113°35E 77 D12
Chitral *Pakistan* 35°50N 71°56E 84 B7
Chittagong *Bangla.* 22°19N 91°48E 85 H17
Chitungwiza *Zimbabwe* 18°0S 31°6E 97 H6
Choiseul *St. Lucia* 13°47N 61°3W 114 b
Choiseul *Solomon Is.* 7°0S 156°40E 99 B10
Chōkai-San *Japan* 39°6N 140°3E 81 D7
Cholet *France* 47°4N 0°52W 66 C3
Chollerton *U.K.* 55°4N 2°7W 26 B4
Cholsey *U.K.* 51°35N 1°8W 30 C6
Choluteca *Honduras* 13°20N 87°14W 114 E7
Chon Buri *Thailand* 13°21N 101°1E 82 B2
Ch'ŏngjin *N. Korea* 41°47N 129°50E 79 C14
Chongqing *China* 29°35N 106°25E 78 F10
Chongqing Shi □ *China* 30°0N 108°0E 78 F10
Chonos, Arch. de los *Chile* 45°0S 75°0W 121 G2
Chorley *U.K.* 53°39N 2°38W 27 F4
Chorzów *Poland* 50°18N 18°57E 65 C10
Choybalsan *Mongolia* 48°4N 114°30E 79 B11
Choyr *Mongolia* 46°24N 108°2E 79 B10
Christchurch *N.Z.* 43°33S 172°47E 99 J13
Christchurch *U.K.* 50°44N 1°47W 30 E5
Christmas I. *Ind. Oc.* 10°30S 105°40E 102 J2
Chubut → *Argentina* 43°20S 65°5W 121 G3
Chudleigh *U.K.* 50°36N 3°36W 29 F6
Chudskoye, L. *Russia* 58°13N 27°30E 70 C4
Chukchi Sea *Russia* 68°0N 175°0W 77 C19
Chukot Ra. *Russia* 68°0N 175°0E 77 C18
Chulmleigh *U.K.* 50°54N 3°51W 29 F6
Chunchon *S. Korea* 37°58N 127°44E 79 D14
Chuquicamata *Chile* 22°15S 69°0W 121 E3
Chur *Switz.* 46°52N 9°32E 64 E5
Church Stretton *U.K.* 52°32N 2°48W 27 G3

Churchdown *U.K.* 51°52N 2°10W 30 C4
Churchill *Canada* 58°47N 94°11W 108 D10
Churchill → *Man., Canada* 58°47N 94°12W 108 D10
Churchill → *Nfld. & L., Canada* 53°19N 60°10W 109 D13
Churchill, C. *Canada* 58°46N 93°12W 108 D10
Churchill Falls *Canada* 53°36N 64°19W 109 D13
Churchill L. *Canada* 55°55N 108°20W 108 D9
Churchill Pk. *Canada* 58°10N 125°10W 108 D7
Churu *India* 28°20N 74°50E 84 E9
Chuska Mts. *U.S.A.* 36°15N 108°50W 110 C5
Chusovoy *Russia* 58°22N 57°50E 70 C10
Chuvashia □ *Russia* 55°30N 47°0E 70 C8
Chuxiong *China* 25°2N 101°28E 78 F9
Cicero *U.S.A.* 41°51N 87°44W 112 E4
Ciechanów *Poland* 52°52N 20°38E 65 B11
Ciego de Ávila *Cuba* 21°50N 78°50W 115 C9
Cienfuegos *Cuba* 22°10N 80°30W 115 C8
Cilo Daği *Turkey* 37°28N 43°55E 71 G7
Cimarron → *U.S.A.* 36°10N 96°16W 111 C7
Cincinnati *U.S.A.* 39°9N 84°27W 112 F5
Cinderford *U.K.* 51°49N 2°30W 30 C3
Cinto, Mte. *France* 42°24N 8°54E 66 E8
Circle *U.S.A.* 65°50N 144°4W 108 C5
Circleville *U.S.A.* 39°36N 82°57W 112 F6
Cirebon *Indonesia* 6°45S 108°32E 82 F3
Cirencester *U.K.* 51°43N 1°57W 30 C5
Ciudad Acuña *Mexico* 29°18N 100°55W 114 B4
Ciudad Bolívar *Venezuela* 8°5N 63°36W 120 B3
Ciudad del Carmen *Mexico* 18°38N 91°50W 114 D6
Ciudad del Este *Paraguay* 25°30S 54°50W 121 E4
Ciudad Guayana *Venezuela* 8°0N 62°30W 120 B3
Ciudad Guzmán *Mexico* 19°41N 103°29W 114 D4
Ciudad Juárez *Mexico* 31°44N 106°29W 114 A3
Ciudad Madero *Mexico* 22°19N 97°50W 114 C5
Ciudad Mante *Mexico* 22°44N 98°59W 114 C5
Ciudad Obregón *Mexico* 27°29N 109°56W 114 B3
Ciudad Real *Spain* 38°59N 3°55W 67 C4
Ciudad Valles *Mexico* 21°59N 99°1W 114 C5
Ciudad Victoria *Mexico* 23°44N 99°8W 114 C5
Civitavécchia *Italy* 42°6N 11°48E 68 C4
Cizre *Turkey* 37°19N 42°10E 71 G7
Clackmannan *U.K.* 56°7N 3°45W 25 B8
Clacton-on-Sea *U.K.* 51°47N 1°11E 31 C11
Claire, L. *Canada* 58°35N 112°5W 108 D8
Clara *Ireland* 53°21N 7°37W 18 E6
Clare *U.K.* 52°4N 0°34E 31 B10
Clare □ *Ireland* 52°45N 9°0W 20 D4
Clare → *Ireland* 53°20N 9°2W 18 E3
Clare I. *Ireland* 53°49N 10°0W 18 D1
Claremont *U.S.A.* 43°23N 72°20W 113 D11
Clark Fork → *U.S.A.* 48°9N 116°15W 110 A3
Clarksburg *U.S.A.* 39°17N 80°30W 112 F7
Clarksdale *U.S.A.* 34°12N 90°35W 111 D8
Clarksville *U.S.A.* 36°32N 87°21W 111 C9
Claverley *U.K.* 52°32N 2°18W 27 G4
Clay Cross *U.K.* 53°10N 1°25W 27 F6
Claydon *U.K.* 52°7N 1°8E 31 B11
Clear, C. *Ireland* 51°25N 9°32W 20 F3
Clear I. *Ireland* 51°26N 9°30W 20 F3
Clearfield *U.S.A.* 41°2N 78°27W 112 E8
Clearwater *U.S.A.* 27°59N 82°48W 111 E10
Cleator Moor *U.K.* 54°32N 3°30W 26 C2
Clee Hills *U.K.* 52°26N 2°35W 27 H3
Cleethorpes *U.K.* 53°33N 0°3W 27 E8
Cleeve Cloud *U.K.* 51°56N 2°0W 30 C5
Clent Hills *U.K.* 52°25N 2°4W 30 B4
Cleobury Mortimer *U.K.* 52°22N 2°28W 27 H4
Clermont-Ferrand *France* 45°46N 3°4E 66 D5
Clevedon *U.K.* 51°26N 2°52W 30 D3
Cleveland Miss., *U.S.A.* 33°45N 90°43W 111 D8
Cleveland Ohio, *U.S.A.* 41°29N 81°41W 112 E7
Cleveland Hills *U.K.* 54°25N 1°11W 26 D6
Clew B. *Ireland* 53°50N 9°49W 18 D2
Cley *U.K.* 52°57N 1°2E 31 A11
Clifden *Ireland* 53°29N 10°1W 18 E1
Cliffe *U.K.* 51°28N 0°31E 31 C10
Clifford *U.K.* 52°7N 3°6W 30 B2
Clinton Iowa, *U.S.A.* 41°51N 90°12W 112 E2
Clinton Okla., *U.S.A.* 35°31N 98°58W 110 C7
Clinton Colden L. *Canada* 63°58N 107°27W 108 C9
Clipperton, Î. *Pac. Oc.* 10°18N 109°13W 103 F17
Clipston *U.K.* 52°27N 0°58W 31 B7
Clitheroe *U.K.* 53°53N 2°22W 27 E4
Cloghaneely *Ireland* 55°8N 8°5W 18 A5
Clogher Hd. *Ireland* 53°48N 6°14W 19 D9
Cloghran *Ireland* 53°27N 6°14W 21 B10
Clonakilty *Ireland* 51°37N 8°53W 20 E5
Clonakilty B. *Ireland* 51°35N 8°51W 20 E5
Cloncurry → *Australia* 18°37S 140°40E 98 E7
Clondalkin *Ireland* 53°19N 6°25W 21 B10
Clones *Ireland* 54°11N 7°15W 19 C7
Clonmel *Ireland* 52°21N 7°42W 21 D7
Clontarf *Ireland* 53°22N 6°11W 21 B10
Cloughton *U.K.* 54°20N 0°26W 26 D8
Clovelly *U.K.* 51°0N 4°25W 29 F5
Clovis *U.S.A.* 34°24N 103°12W 110 D6
Clowne *U.K.* 53°16N 1°17W 27 F6
Cluj-Napoca *Romania* 46°47N 23°38E 65 E12
Clun Forest *U.K.* 52°27N 3°7W 27 H2
Clunbury *U.K.* 52°25N 2°55W 27 H3
Clwyd → *U.K.* 53°19N 3°31W 28 A6
Clyde → *U.K.* 55°55N 4°30W 24 D5
Clyde River *Canada* 70°30N 68°30W 109 B13
Clydebank *U.K.* 55°54N 4°23W 24 C7
Clydesdale *U.K.* 55°43N 3°51W 25 C8
Coalbrookdale *U.K.* 52°39N 2°30E 27 G4
Coalisland *U.K.* 54°33N 6°42W 19 B8
Coalville *U.K.* 52°44N 1°23W 27 G6
Coast Mts. *Canada* 55°0N 129°20W 108 D7
Coast Ranges *U.S.A.* 39°0N 123°0W 110 B2
Coatbridge *U.K.* 55°52N 4°6W 24 C7
Coaticook *Canada* 45°10N 71°46W 113 C12
Coats I. *Canada* 62°30N 83°0W 109 C11
Coats Land *Antarctica* 77°0S 25°0W 55 D1
Coatzacoalcos *Mexico* 18°7N 94°25W 114 D6
Cobán *Guatemala* 15°30N 90°21W 114 D6
Cobar *Australia* 31°27S 145°48E 98 G8
Cobh *Ireland* 51°51N 8°17W 20 E6
Cobija *Bolivia* 11°0S 68°50W 120 D3

Cobourg *Canada* 43°58N 78°10W 112 D8
Cochabamba *Bolivia* 17°26S 66°10W 120 D3
Cochrane *Canada* 49°0N 81°0W 109 E11
Cockburn, Canal *Chile* 54°30S 72°0W 121 H2
Cockburn I. *Canada* 45°55N 83°22W 112 C6
Cockburn Town *Bahamas* 24°2N 74°31W 115 C10
Cockerham *U.K.* 53°58N 2°49W 27 E3
Cockermouth *U.K.* 54°40N 3°22W 26 C2
Cockfield *U.K.* 52°10N 0°48E 31 B10
Cockpit Country, The *Jamaica* 18°15N 77°45W 114 a
Coco → *Cent. Amer.* 15°0N 83°8W 115 E8
Cocos I. *Pac. Oc.* 5°25N 87°55W 114 F7
Cocos Is. *Ind. Oc.* 12°10S 96°55E 102 J1
Cod, C. *U.S.A.* 42°5N 70°10W 113 D12
Coddenham *U.K.* 52°9N 1°8E 31 B11
Codó *Brazil* 4°30S 43°55W 120 C5
Cody *U.S.A.* 44°32N 109°3W 110 B5
Coeur d'Alene *U.S.A.* 47°41N 116°46W 110 A3
Coggeshall *U.K.* 51°52N 0°42E 31 C10
Cognac *France* 45°41N 0°20W 66 D3
Coigach *U.K.* 57°59N 5°14W 22 G7
Coigeach, Rubha *U.K.* 58°6N 5°26W 22 F7
Coimbatore *India* 11°2N 76°59E 84 P10
Coimbra *Brazil* 19°32S 40°37W 122 C2
Coimbra *Portugal* 40°15N 8°27W 67 B1
Colatina *Brazil* 19°32S 40°37W 122 C2
Colchester *U.S.A.* 51°54N 0°55E 31 C10
Cold Fell *U.K.* 54°53N 2°36W 26 C3
Coldstream *U.K.* 55°39N 2°15W 25 C11
Colebrook *U.S.A.* 44°54N 71°30W 113 C12
Colebrooke *U.K.* 50°47N 3°44W 29 F6
Coleford *U.K.* 51°47N 2°36W 30 C3
Coleraine *U.K.* 55°8N 6°41W 19 A8
Coleshill *U.K.* 52°30N 1°41W 27 G5
Colgrave Sd. *U.K.* 60°36N 0°58E 22 A16
Colima *Mexico* 19°14N 103°43W 114 D4
Colima, Nevado de *Mexico* 19°33N 103°38W 114 D4
Coll *U.K.* 56°39N 6°34W 24 J4
Collier Law *U.K.* 54°47N 1°59W 26 C5
Collin *U.K.* 55°4N 3°35W 25 D8
Collingbourne Kingston *U.K.* 51°18N 1°40W 30 D5
Collingham *U.K.* 53°8N 0°46W 27 F7
Collingwood *Canada* 44°29N 80°13W 112 C7
Collooney *Ireland* 54°11N 8°29W 18 C5
Colmar *France* 48°5N 7°20E 66 B7
Colne *U.K.* 53°51N 2°9W 27 E4
Colne → *Bucks., U.K.* 51°27N 0°32W 31 D7
Colne → *Essex, U.K.* 51°51N 0°58E 31 C10
Cologne *Germany* 50°56N 6°57E 64 C4
Colombia ■ *S. Amer.* 3°45N 73°0W 120 B2
Colombo *Sri Lanka* 6°56N 79°58E 84 R11
Colonsay *U.K.* 56°5N 6°12W 24 B3
Colorado □ *U.S.A.* 39°30N 105°30W 110 C5
Colorado → *Argentina* 39°50S 62°8W 121 F3
Colorado → *N. Amer.* 31°45N 114°40W 110 D4
Colorado → *U.S.A.* 28°36N 95°59W 111 E7
Colorado Plateau *U.S.A.* 37°0N 111°0W 110 C4
Colorado Springs *U.S.A.* 38°50N 104°49W 110 C6
Colsterworth *U.K.* 52°49N 0°37W 27 G7
Coltishall *U.K.* 52°44N 1°21E 31 A11
Columbia Mo., *U.S.A.* 38°57N 92°20W 111 F8
Columbia S.C., *U.S.A.* 34°0N 81°2W 111 D10
Columbia Tenn., *U.S.A.* 35°37N 87°2W 111 C9
Columbia → *N. Amer.* 46°15N 124°5W 110 A2
Columbia, District of □ *U.S.A.* 38°55N 77°0W 112 F9
Columbia Plateau *U.S.A.* 44°0N 117°30W 110 B3
Columbus Ga., *U.S.A.* 32°28N 84°59W 111 D10
Columbus Ind., *U.S.A.* 39°13N 85°55W 112 F5
Columbus Miss., *U.S.A.* 33°30N 88°25W 111 D9
Columbus Nebr., *U.S.A.* 41°26N 97°22W 111 E7
Columbus Ohio, *U.S.A.* 39°58N 83°0W 112 F6
Colville → *U.S.A.* 70°25N 150°30W 108 B4
Colville, C. *N.Z.* 36°29N 175°21E 99 H14
Colwell *U.K.* 55°5N 2°4W 26 B4
Colwich *U.K.* 52°48N 1°58W 27 G5
Colwyn Bay *U.K.* 53°18N 3°44W 28 A6
Colyton *U.K.* 50°44N 3°5W 29 F7
Comayagua *Honduras* 14°25N 87°37W 114 E7
Combe Martin *U.K.* 51°12N 4°3W 29 E5
Comber *U.K.* 54°33N 5°45W 19 B10
Comeragh Mts. *Ireland* 52°18N 7°34W 21 D7
Comilla *Bangla.* 23°28N 91°10E 85 H17
Comitán *Mexico* 16°15N 92°8W 114 D6
Committee B. *Canada* 68°30N 86°30W 109 C11
Como *Italy* 45°47N 9°5E 68 B3
Como, L. di *Italy* 46°0N 9°11E 68 B3
Comodoro Rivadavia *Argentina* 45°50S 67°40W 121 G3
Comoros ■ *Ind. Oc.* 12°10S 44°15E 91 H8
Compass Mt. *S. Africa* 31°45S 24°32E 90 K6
Compiègne *France* 49°24N 2°50E 66 B5
Conakry *Guinea* 9°29N 13°49W 94 G3
Conceição da Barra *Brazil* 18°35S 39°45W 122 C3
Concepción *Chile* 36°50S 73°0W 121 F2
Concepción *Paraguay* 23°22S 57°26W 121 E4
Concepción, Est. de *Chile* 50°30S 74°55W 121 H2
Concepción del Oro *Mexico* 24°38N 101°25W 114 C4
Concepción del Uruguay *Argentina* 32°35S 58°20W 121 F4
Conception, Pt. *U.S.A.* 34°27N 120°28W 110 D2
Conchos → *Mexico* 29°35N 104°25W 114 B4
Concord Calif., *U.S.A.* 37°59N 122°2W 110 C2
Concord N.H., *U.S.A.* 43°12N 71°32W 113 D12
Concordia *Argentina* 31°20S 58°2W 121 F4
Concordia *U.S.A.* 39°34N 97°40W 110 C7
Condeúba *Brazil* 14°52S 42°0W 122 B2
Condover *U.K.* 52°39N 2°44W 27 G3
Congleton *U.K.* 53°10N 2°13W 27 F4
Congo ■ *Africa* 1°0S 16°0E 96 E3
Congo → *Africa* 6°4S 12°24E 96 F2
Congo, Dem. Rep. of the ■ *Africa* 3°0S 23°0E 96 E4
Congo Basin *Africa* 0°10S 24°30E 96 E4
Congresbury *U.K.* 51°22N 2°48W 30 D3
Coningsby *U.K.* 53°7N 0°10W 27 F8
Conisbrough *U.K.* 53°29N 1°14W 27 F6
Coniston *Canada* 46°29N 80°51W 112 B7
Coniston *U.K.* 54°22N 3°5W 26 D2
Coniston Water *U.K.* 54°20N 3°5W 26 D2
Conn, L. *Ireland* 54°3N 9°15W 18 C3
Connah's Quay *U.K.* 53°13N 3°4W 28 A5
Connaught □ *Ireland* 53°43N 9°12W 18 D3
Conneaut *U.S.A.* 41°57N 80°34W 112 E7

Connecticut □ *U.S.A.* 41°30N 72°45W 113 E11
Connecticut → *U.S.A.* 41°16N 72°20W 113 E11
Connellsville *U.S.A.* 40°1N 79°35W 112 E8
Connemara *Ireland* 53°29N 9°45W 18 E2
Connemara △ *Ireland* 53°32N 9°52W 18 D2
Consett *U.K.* 54°51N 1°50W 26 C5
Conselheiro Lafaiete *Brazil* 20°40S 43°48W 122 D2
Constance, L. *Europe* 47°35N 9°25E 64 E5
Constanţa *Romania* 44°14N 28°38E 65 F15
Constantine *Algeria* 36°25N 6°42E 94 A7
Constitución *Chile* 35°20S 72°30W 121 F2
Contagem *Brazil* 19°56S 44°3W 122 C2
Contas → *Brazil* 14°17S 39°1W 122 B3
Contwoyto L. *Canada* 65°42N 110°50W 108 C8
Conway Ark., *U.S.A.* 35°5N 92°26W 111 C8
Conway N.H., *U.S.A.* 43°59N 71°7W 113 D12
Conwy *U.K.* 53°10N 3°50W 28 A6
Conwy □ *U.K.* 53°10N 3°44W 28 A6
Conwy → *U.K.* 53°17N 3°50W 28 A6
Coober Pedy *Australia* 29°1S 134°43E 98 F6
Cook Inlet *U.S.A.* 60°0N 152°0W 108 D4
Cook Is. ☑ *Pac. Oc.* 17°0S 160°0W 103 J12
Cook Strait *N.Z.* 41°15S 174°29E 99 J13
Cookstown *U.K.* 54°38N 6°45W 19 B8
Cooktown *Australia* 15°30S 145°16E 98 D8
Coondapoor *India* 13°42N 74°40E 84 N9
Coos Bay *U.S.A.* 43°22N 124°13W 110 B2
Cootehill *Ireland* 54°4N 7°5W 19 C7
Copenhagen *Denmark* 55°40N 12°26E 63 F6
Copiapó *Chile* 27°30S 70°20W 121 E2
Copper Harbor *U.S.A.* 47°28N 87°53W 112 B4
Coppermine → *Canada* 67°49N 116°4W 108 C8
Coquet → *U.K.* 55°20N 1°32W 26 B5
Coquet I. *U.K.* 55°20N 1°36W 26 B5
Coquimbo *Chile* 30°0S 71°20W 121 E2
Coracora *Peru* 15°5S 73°45W 120 D2
Coral Harbour *Canada* 64°8N 83°10W 109 C11
Coral Sea *Pac. Oc.* 15°0S 150°0E 98 C9
Coralbridge *U.K.* 54°58N 2°0W 26 C5
Corby *U.K.* 52°30N 0°41W 31 A7
Corby Glen *U.K.* 52°49N 0°30W 27 G7
Cordele *U.S.A.* 31°58N 83°47W 111 D10
Córdoba *Argentina* 31°20S 64°10W 121 F3
Córdoba *Mexico* 18°53N 96°56W 114 D5
Córdoba *Spain* 37°50N 4°50W 67 D3
Córdoba, Sierra de *Argentina* 31°10S 64°25W 121 F3
Cordova *U.S.A.* 60°33N 145°45W 108 C5
Corfe Castle *U.K.* 50°38N 2°3W 30 E4
Corfe Mullen *U.K.* 50°46N 2°1W 30 E4
Corfu *Greece* 39°38N 19°50E 69 E8
Corinth *Greece* 37°56N 22°55E 69 F10
Corinth *U.S.A.* 34°56N 88°31W 111 D9
Corinto *Brazil* 18°20S 44°30W 122 C2
Cork *Ireland* 51°54N 8°29W 20 E6
Cork □ *Ireland* 51°57N 8°40W 20 E6
Cork Harbour *Ireland* 51°47N 8°16W 20 E6
Corner Brook *Canada* 48°57N 57°58W 109 E14
Corning *U.S.A.* 42°9N 77°3W 112 D9
Cornwall *Canada* 45°2N 74°44W 113 C10
Cornwall □ *U.K.* 50°26N 4°40W 29 G4
Cornwall, C. *U.K.* 50°8N 5°43W 29 G2
Cornwall I. *Canada* 77°37N 94°38W 109 B10
Cornwallis I. *Canada* 75°8N 95°0W 109 B10
Coro *Venezuela* 11°25N 69°41W 120 A3
Corocoro *Bolivia* 17°15S 68°28W 120 D3
Coromandel Coast *India* 12°30N 81°0E 84 N12
Coronation Gulf *Canada* 68°25N 110°0W 108 B8
Coronel *Chile* 37°0S 73°10W 121 F2
Coronel Fabriciano *Brazil* 19°31S 42°38W 122 C2
Coronel Pringles *Argentina* 38°0S 61°30W 121 F3
Coronel Suárez *Argentina* 37°30S 61°52W 121 F3
Coropuna, Nevado *Peru* 15°30S 72°41W 120 D2
Corpus Christi *U.S.A.* 27°47N 97°24W 110 E7
Corraun Pen. *Ireland* 53°54N 9°54W 18 D2
Corrib, L. *Ireland* 53°27N 9°16W 20 B4
Corrientes *Argentina* 27°30S 58°45W 121 E4
Corrientes, C. *Colombia* 5°30N 77°34W 120 B2
Corrientes, C. *Mexico* 20°25N 105°42W 114 C3
Corringham *U.K.* 53°25N 0°41W 27 F7
Corry *U.S.A.* 41°55N 79°39W 112 E8
Corse, C. *France* 43°1N 9°25E 66 E8
Corsham *U.K.* 51°27N 2°10W 30 D4
Corsica □ *France* 42°0N 9°0E 66 F8
Corsicana *U.S.A.* 32°6N 96°28W 111 D7
Corsley *U.K.* 51°13N 2°14W 30 D4
Corte *France* 42°19N 9°11E 66 E8
Cortez *U.S.A.* 37°21N 108°35W 110 C5
Cortland *U.S.A.* 42°36N 76°11W 112 D9
Corton *U.K.* 52°31N 1°45E 31 A12
Çorum *Turkey* 40°30N 34°57E 71 F5
Corumbá *Brazil* 19°0S 57°30W 120 D4
Corunna = La Coruña *Spain* 43°20N 8°25W 67 A1
Corvallis *U.S.A.* 44°34N 123°16W 110 B2
Corve → *U.K.* 52°22N 2°43W 27 H3
Coseley *U.K.* 52°33N 2°5W 27 G4
Cosenza *Italy* 39°18N 16°15E 68 E7
Cosham *U.K.* 50°51N 1°2W 30 E6
Coshocton *U.S.A.* 40°16N 81°51W 112 E7
Costa Brava *Spain* 36°15N 5°58W 67 D2
Costa del Azahar *Spain* 39°39N 0°13W 67 B6
Costa Rica ■ *Cent. Amer.* 10°0N 84°0W 115 F8
Costa Verde *Spain* 43°22N 4°14W 67 A3
Costessey *U.K.* 52°40N 1°13E 31 A11
Cotabato *Phil.* 7°14N 124°15E 83 C6
Côte d'Azur *France* 43°25N 7°10E 66 E7
Côte-d'Ivoire ■ *Africa* 7°30N 5°0W 94 G4
Coteau du Missouri *U.S.A.* 47°0N 100°0W 110 A6
Cotentin *France* 49°15N 1°30W 66 B3
Cotherstone *U.K.* 54°35N 1°59W 26 C5
Cotonou *Benin* 6°20N 2°25E 94 G6
Cotopaxi *Ecuador* 0°40S 78°30W 120 C2
Cotswold Hills *U.K.* 51°42N 2°10W 30 C4
Cottbus *Germany* 51°45N 14°20E 64 C8
Cottenham *U.K.* 52°18N 0°9E 31 B9
Coudersport *U.S.A.* 41°46N 78°1W 112 E8
Council Bluffs *U.S.A.* 41°16N 95°52W 111 B7
Courantyne → *S. Amer.* 5°55N 57°5W 120 B4
Courtenay *Canada* 49°45N 125°0W 108 E7
Cove *U.K.* 56°0N 4°51W 24 B6

Coventry *U.K.* 52°25N 1°28W 30 B6
Cover → *U.K.* 54°17N 1°47W 26 D5
Coverack *U.K.* 50°1N 5°7W 29 G3
Covington *U.S.A.* 39°5N 84°30W 112 F5
Cowal *U.K.* 56°5N 5°8W 24 B5
Cowbridge *U.K.* 51°27N 3°27W 29 D8
Cowdenbeath *U.K.* 56°7N 3°21W 25 B9
Cowes *U.K.* 50°45N 1°18W 30 E6
Cowfold *U.K.* 50°59N 0°16W 31 E8
Cowpen *U.K.* 55°8N 1°32W 26 B5
Cox's Bazar *Bangla.* 21°26N 91°59E 85 J17
Cozumel, Isla *Mexico* 20°30N 86°40W 114 C7
Crab Hill *Barbados* 13°19N 59°38W 114 c
Cradock *S. Africa* 32°8S 25°36E 97 L5
Craig *U.S.A.* 40°31N 107°33W 110 B5
Craigavon *U.K.* 54°27N 6°23W 19 C9
Crail *U.K.* 56°16N 2°37W 25 B10
Craiova *Romania* 44°21N 23°48E 65 F12
Cramlington *U.K.* 55°6N 1°34W 26 B5
Cranborne *U.K.* 50°55N 1°54W 30 E5
Cranborne Chase *U.K.* 50°56N 2°6W 30 E4
Cranbrook *Canada* 49°30N 115°46W 108 E8
Cranbrook *U.K.* 51°6N 0°34E 31 D10
Crandon *U.S.A.* 45°34N 88°54W 112 C3
Crane, The *Barbados* 13°6N 59°27W 114 c
Cranleigh *U.K.* 51°8N 0°28W 31 D8
Cranwell *U.K.* 53°3N 0°27W 27 F8
Cratéus *Brazil* 5°10S 40°39W 120 C5
Crato *Brazil* 7°10S 39°25W 120 C6
Craven Arms *U.K.* 52°26N 2°50W 27 H3
Crawfordsville *U.S.A.* 40°2N 86°54W 112 E4
Crawley *U.K.* 51°7N 0°11W 31 D8
Credenhill *U.K.* 52°5N 2°48W 30 B3
Crediton *U.K.* 50°47N 3°40W 29 F6
Cree → *Canada* 58°57N 105°47W 108 D9
Cree → *U.K.* 54°55N 4°25W 24 E7
Cree L. *Canada* 57°30N 106°30W 108 D9
Cremona *Italy* 45°7N 10°2E 68 B4
Cres *Croatia* 44°58N 14°25E 68 B6
Crete *Greece* 35°15N 25°0E 69 G11
Créteil *France* 48°47N 2°27E 66 B5
Creuse → *France* 47°0N 0°34E 66 C4
Crewe *U.K.* 53°6N 2°26W 27 F4
Crewkerne *U.K.* 50°53N 2°48W 30 E3
Crianlarich *U.K.* 56°24N 4°37W 24 B6
Criccieth *U.K.* 52°55N 4°13W 28 B5
Crick *U.K.* 52°22N 1°8W 30 B6
Crickhowell *U.K.* 51°52N 3°8W 28 D7
Cricklade *U.K.* 51°38N 1°50W 30 C5
Crieff *U.K.* 56°22N 3°50W 25 B8
Criffell *U.K.* 54°56N 3°39W 25 E9
Crimea ☑ *Ukraine* 45°30N 33°10E 71 E5
Crimean Pen. *Ukraine* 45°0N 34°0E 71 F5
Crişul Alb → *Romania* 46°42N 21°17E 65 E11
Crişul Negru → *Romania* 46°42N 21°16E 65 E11
Croagh Patrick *Ireland* 53°46N 9°40W 18 D2
Croaghan *Ireland* 53°59N 10°10W 18 D1
Croatia ■ *Europe* 45°20N 16°0E 68 B7
Croglin *U.K.* 54°50N 2°39W 26 C3
Crohy Hd. *Ireland* 54°55N 8°26W 18 B5
Croker, C. *Australia* 10°58S 132°35E 98 C5
Cromarty *U.K.* 57°40N 4°2W 23 G9
Cromarty Firth *U.K.* 57°40N 4°15W 23 G9
Cromdale, Hills of *U.K.* 57°20N 3°34W 23 H11
Cromer *U.K.* 52°56N 1°17E 31 A11
Crondall *U.K.* 51°14N 0°51W 31 D7
Crook *U.K.* 54°43N 1°45W 26 C5
Crooked I. *Bahamas* 22°50N 74°10W 115 C10
Crooklands *U.K.* 54°16N 2°42W 26 D3
Crosby Cumb., *U.K.* 54°45N 3°25W 26 C2
Crosby Mersey., *U.K.* 53°30N 3°3W 27 F2
Crosby Ravensworth *U.K.* 54°33N 2°35W 26 C3
Cross Fell *U.K.* 54°43N 2°28W 26 C4
Cross Sound *U.S.A.* 58°0N 135°0W 108 D6
Crosshaven *Ireland* 51°47N 8°17W 20 E6
Crossmaglen *U.K.* 54°5N 6°36W 19 C8
Crotone *Italy* 39°5N 17°8E 68 E7
Crouch → *U.K.* 51°37N 0°53E 31 C10
Crow Hd. *Ireland* 51°35N 10°9W 20 E2
Crow Sound *U.K.* 49°56N 6°16W 29 H1
Crowborough *U.K.* 51°3N 0°11E 31 D9
Crowland *U.K.* 52°41N 0°10W 27 G8
Crowle *U.K.* 53°36N 0°49W 27 E7
Crowsnest Pass *Canada* 49°40N 114°40W 108 E8
Croyde *U.K.* 51°7N 4°14W 29 E5
Croydon □ *U.K.* 51°22N 0°5W 31 D8
Crozet, Îs. *Ind. Oc.* 46°27S 52°0E 53 G12
Cruden Bay *U.K.* 57°25N 1°52W 23 H14
Crudgington *U.K.* 52°46N 2°32W 27 G3
Crummock Water *U.K.* 54°33N 3°18W 26 C2
Cruz das Almas *Brazil* 12°0S 39°6W 122 B3
Cruzeiro *Brazil* 22°33S 45°0W 122 D1
Cruzeiro do Sul *Brazil* 7°35S 72°35W 120 C2
Crystal Falls *U.S.A.* 46°5N 88°20W 112 B3
Cuando → *Angola* 17°30S 23°15E 97 H4
Cuango → *Dem. Rep. of the Congo* 3°14S 17°22E 96 E3
Cuanza → *Angola* 9°21S 13°9E 96 F2
Cuauhtémoc *Mexico* 28°25N 106°52W 114 B3
Cuba ■ *W. Indies* 22°0N 79°0W 115 C9
Cubango → *Africa* 18°50S 22°25E 97 H4
Cuckfield *U.K.* 51°1N 0°8W 31 D8
Cúcuta *Colombia* 7°54N 72°31W 120 B2
Cuddalore *India* 11°46N 79°45E 84 P11
Cuddapah *India* 14°30N 78°47E 84 M11
Cuenca *Ecuador* 2°50S 79°9W 120 C2
Cuenca *Spain* 40°5N 2°10W 67 B4
Cuernavaca *Mexico* 18°55N 99°15W 114 D5
Cuiabá *Brazil* 15°30S 56°0W 120 D4
Cuihangcun *China* 22°27N 113°32E 79 a
Cuillin Hills *U.K.* 57°13N 6°15W 22 H5
Cuillin Sd. *U.K.* 57°4N 6°20W 22 H5
Cuito → *Angola* 18°1S 20°48E 97 H4
Culiacán *Mexico* 24°50N 107°23W 114 C3
Cullen *U.K.* 57°42N 2°49W 23 G12
Cullompton *U.K.* 50°51N 3°24W 29 F7
Culm → *U.K.* 50°46N 3°31W 29 F7
Culpeper *U.S.A.* 38°30N 78°0W 112 F9
Cumaná *Venezuela* 10°30N 64°5W 120 A3
Cumberland → *U.S.A.* 37°9N 88°25W 111 C9
Cumberland Pen. *Canada* 67°0N 64°0W 109 C13

Cumberland Plateau

Eastern Group

Cumberland Plateau U.S.A. 36°0N 85°0W **111** C10
Cumberland Sd. Canada 65°30N 66°0W **109** C13
Cumbernauld U.K. 55°57N 3°58W **25** C8
Cumbrae Is. U.K. 55°46N 4°54W **24** C6
Cumbria □ U.K. 54°42N 2°52W **26** C3
Cumbrian Mts. U.K. 54°30N 3°0W **26** D2
Cummertrees U.K. 54°59N 3°20W **25** E9
Cumnock U.K. 55°28N 4°17W **24** D7
Cumnor U.K. 51°44N 1°19W **30** C6
Cumwhinton U.K. 54°52N 2°50W **26** C3
Cunene → Angola 17°20S 11°50E **97** H2
Cúneo Italy 44°23N 7°32E **68** B2
Cunnamulla Australia 28°2S 145°38E **98** F8
Cunninghame U.K. 55°38N 4°35W **24** C6
Cupar U.K. 56°19N 3°1W **25** B9
Curaçao W. Indies 12°10N 69°0W **115** E11
Curicó Chile 34°55S 71°20W **121** F2
Curitiba Brazil 25°20S 49°10W **122** E1
Curlew Mts. Ireland 54°0N 8°20W **18** B3
Curry Rivel U.K. 51°1N 2°52W **30** D3
Curvelo Brazil 18°45S 44°27W **122** C2
Cusco Peru 13°32S 72°0W **120** D2
Cuttack India 20°25N 85°57E **85** J14
Cuxhaven Germany 53°51N 8°41E **64** B5
Cuyahoga Falls U.S.A. 41°8N 81°29W **112** E7
Cuyuni → Guyana 6°23N 58°41W **120** B4
Cwmbran U.K. 51°39N 3°2W **28** D7
Cyclades Greece 37°0N 24°30E **69** F7
Cynthiana U.S.A. 38°23N 84°18W **112** F5
Cyprus ■ Asia 35°0N 33°0E **86** C3
Cyrenaica Libya 27°0N 23°0E **95** C10
Czech Rep. = Czechia ■ Europe 50°0N 15°0E **64** D8
Czechia ■ Europe 50°0N 15°0E **64** D8
Częstochowa Poland 50°49N 19°7E **65** C10

D

Da Lat Vietnam 11°56N 108°25E **82** B3
Da Nang Vietnam 16°4N 108°13E **82** A3
Da Yunhe → Hopei, China 39°10N 117°10E **79** D12
Da Yunhe → Jiangsu, China 34°25N 120°5E **79** E13
Daba Shan China 32°0N 109°0E **79** E10
Dabie Shan China 31°20N 115°20E **79** E10
Dadra & Nagar Haveli □ India 20°5N 73°0E **84** J8
Dadu Pakistan 26°45N 67°45E **84** F5
Daegu S. Korea 35°50N 128°37E **79** D14
Daejeon S. Korea 36°20N 127°28E **79** D14
Dagupan Phil. 16°3N 120°20E **83** A6
Dahod India 22°50N 74°15E **84** H9
Dahongliutan China 35°45N 79°20E **78** D4
Daingean Ireland 53°18N 7°17W **21** B8
Dajarra Australia 21°42S 139°30E **98** D6
Dakar Senegal 14°34N 17°29W **94** F2
Dakhla W. Sahara 23°50N 15°53W **94** D2
Dakhla, El Wâhât el Egypt 25°30N 28°50E **95** C11
Dalandzadgad Mongolia 43°27N 104°30E **78** C9
Dalbeattie U.K. 54°56N 3°50W **25** E8
Dalhart U.S.A. 36°4N 102°31W **110** C6
Dalhousie Canada 48°5N 66°26W **113** A14
Dali China 25°40N 100°10E **78** F9
Dalian China 38°50N 121°40E **79** D13
Daliang Shan China 28°0N 102°45E **78** F9
Dalkeith U.K. 55°54N 3°4W **25** C9
Dalkey Ireland 53°16N 6°6W **21** B10
Dallas U.S.A. 32°47N 96°48W **111** D7
Dalles, The U.S.A. 45°36N 121°10W **110** A2
Dalmatia Croatia 43°20N 17°0E **68** C7
Dalmellington U.K. 55°19N 4°23W **24** D7
Daloa Côte d'Ivoire 7°0N 6°30W **94** G4
Dalry U.K. 55°42N 4°43W **24** C6
Dalrymple, L. Australia 20°40S 147°0E **98** E8
Dalton Dumf. & Gall., U.K. 55°4N 3°24W **25** D9
Dalton N. Yorks., U.K. 54°28N 1°32W **26** D5
Dalton-in-Furness U.K. 54°10N 3°11W **26** D2
Daly Waters Australia 16°15S 133°24E **98** D5
Daman India 20°25N 72°57E **84** J8
Damanhûr Egypt 31°0N 30°30E **95** B12
Damaraland Namibia 20°0S 15°0E **97** H2
Damascus Syria 33°30N 36°18E **86** C4
Damavand Iran 35°57N 52°7E **87** C8
Damerham U.K. 50°56N 1°51W **30** E5
Dampier Australia 20°41S 116°42E **98** E2
Danakil Desert Ethiopia 12°45N 41°0E **89** E3
Danbury U.S.A. 41°24N 73°28W **113** E11
Dandong China 40°10N 124°20E **79** C13
Danube → Europe 45°20N 29°40E **65** F15
Danville Ill., U.S.A. 40°8N 87°37W **112** E4
Danville Ky., U.S.A. 37°39N 84°46W **112** G5
Danville Va., U.S.A. 36°36N 79°23W **111** C11
Daqing China 46°35N 125°0E **79** B13
Dar Banda Africa 8°0N 23°0E **90** F6
Dar es Salaam Tanzania 6°50S 39°12E **96** F7
Darbhanga India 26°15N 85°55E **85** F14
Dardanelles Turkey 40°17N 26°32E **86** A1
Darent → U.K. 51°28N 0°14E **31** D9
Dârfûr Sudan 13°40N 24°0E **95** F10
Darhan Mongolia 49°37N 106°21E **78** B10
Darién, G. del Caribbean 9°0N 77°0W **120** B2
Darjiling India 27°3N 88°18E **85** F16
Darling → Australia 34°4S 141°54E **98** G7
Darling Ra. Australia 32°30S 116°20E **98** G2
Darlington U.K. 54°32N 1°33W **26** C5
Darmstadt Germany 49°51N 8°39E **64** D5
Darnah Libya 32°45N 22°45E **95** B10
Darnley, C. Antarctica 68°0S 69°0E **55** C6
Darnley B. Canada 69°30N 123°30W **108** C7
Dart → U.K. 50°24N 3°39W **29** G6
Dartford U.K. 51°26N 0°13E **31** D9
Dartington U.K. 50°27N 3°43W **29** G6
Dartmoor △ U.K. 50°37N 3°59W **29** F6
Dartmouth Canada 44°40N 63°30W **113** C16
Dartmouth U.K. 50°21N 3°36W **29** G6
Darton U.K. 53°35N 1°31W **27** E5
Darwen U.K. 53°42N 2°29W **27** E4
Darwin Australia 12°25S 130°51E **98** C5
Dashen, Ras Ethiopia 13°8N 38°26E **89** E2
Dasht → Pakistan 25°10N 61°40E **84** G2
Daşoguz Turkmenistan 41°49N 59°58E **87** A9
Datong China 40°6N 113°18E **79** C11
Daugava → Latvia 57°4N 24°3E **63** F9

Daugavpils Latvia 55°53N 26°32E **63** F9
Dauphin Canada 51°9N 100°5W **108** D9
Dauphiné France 45°15N 5°25E **66** D6
Daurada, Costa Spain 41°12N 1°15E **67** B6
Davangere India 14°25N 75°55E **84** M9
Davao Phil. 7°0N 125°40E **83** C7
Davenport U.S.A. 41°32N 90°35W **112** E2
Daventry U.K. 52°16N 1°10W **30** B6
David Panama 8°30N 82°30W **115** F8
Davis Str. N. Amer. 65°0N 58°0W **104** C14
Dawlish U.K. 50°35N 3°28W **29** F7
Dawmat al Jandal Si. Arabia 29°55N 39°40E **86** D4
Dawna Ra. Myanmar 16°30N 98°30E **85** L21
Dawros Hd. Ireland 54°50N 8°33W **18** B4
Dawson City Canada 64°10N 139°30W **108** C6
Dawson Creek Canada 55°45N 120°15W **108** D7
Dax France 43°44N 1°3W **66** E3
Daxian China 31°15N 107°23E **78** E10
Daxue Shan China 30°30N 101°30E **78** E9
Dayr az Zawr Syria 35°20N 40°5E **86** C5
Dayton U.S.A. 39°45N 84°12W **112** F5
Daytona Beach U.S.A. 29°13N 81°1W **111** E10
De Aar S. Africa 30°39S 24°0E **97** L4
De Pere U.S.A. 44°27N 88°4W **112** C3
Dead Sea Asia 31°30N 35°30E **86** D3
Deal U.K. 51°13N 1°25E **31** D11
Dean, Forest of U.K. 51°45N 2°33W **30** C3
Dease → Canada 54°44N 3°25W **26** C2
Dease → Canada 59°56N 128°32W **108** D7
Dease Lake Canada 58°25N 130°6W **108** D6
Death Valley U.S.A. 36°15N 116°50W **110** C3
Deben → U.K. 52°0N 1°25E **31** B11
Debenham U.K. 52°14N 1°12E **31** A11
Debre Markos Ethiopia 10°20N 37°40E **89** E2
Debre Tabor Ethiopia 11°50N 38°26E **89** E2
Debrecen Hungary 47°33N 21°42E **65** E11
Decatur Ala., U.S.A. 34°36N 86°59W **111** D9
Decatur Ill., U.S.A. 39°51N 88°57W **112** F3
Decatur Ind., U.S.A. 40°50N 84°56W **112** E5
Deccan India 18°0N 79°0E **84** L11
Deddington U.K. 51°59N 1°18W **30** C6
Dee → Aberds., U.K. 57°9N 2°5W **23** H13
Dee → Dumf. & Gall., U.K. 54°51N 4°3W **24** E7
Dee → Wales, U.K. 53°22N 3°17W **28** A7
Deeping Fen U.K. 52°45N 0°15W **27** G8
Deeping St. Nicholas U.K. 52°44N 0°12W **27** G8
Deer Lake Canada 49°11N 57°27W **109** E14
Defiance U.S.A. 41°17N 84°22W **112** E5
Dehra Dun India 30°20N 78°4E **84** D11
DeKalb U.S.A. 41°56N 88°46W **112** E3
Del Rio U.S.A. 29°22N 100°54W **110** E6
Delabole U.K. 50°37N 4°46W **29** F4
Delaware U.S.A. 40°18N 83°4W **112** E6
Delaware □ U.S.A. 39°0N 75°20W **113** F10
Delaware → U.S.A. 39°15N 75°20W **113** F10
Delaware B. U.S.A. 39°0N 75°10W **111** C12
Delgado, C. Mozam. 10°45S 40°40E **96** G8
Delhi India 28°39N 77°13E **84** E10
Delice Turkey 39°54N 34°2E **71** G5
Delicias Mexico 28°13N 105°28W **114** B3
Déline Canada 65°11N 123°25W **108** C7
Delphos U.S.A. 40°51N 84°21W **112** E5
Delta Junction U.S.A. 64°2N 145°44W **108** C5
Demanda, Sierra de la Spain 42°15N 3°0W **67** A4
Deming U.S.A. 32°16N 107°46W **110** D5
Demopolis U.S.A. 32°31N 87°50W **111** D9
Den Helder Neths. 52°57N 4°45E **64** B3
Denali U.S.A. 63°4N 151°0W **108** C4
Denbigh U.K. 53°12N 3°25W **28** A7
Denbighshire □ U.K. 53°8N 3°22W **28** A7
Denby Dale U.K. 53°34N 1°40W **27** E5
Denham, Mt. Jamaica 18°13N 77°32W **114** a
Denia Spain 38°49N 0°8E **67** C6
Denizli Turkey 37°42N 29°2E **71** G4
Denmark ■ Europe 55°45N 10°0E **63** F6
Denmark Str. Atl. Oc. 66°0N 30°0W **54** C6
Dennery St. Lucia 13°55N 60°54W **114** b
Denny U.K. 56°1N 3°55W **25** B8
Denpasar Indonesia 8°39S 115°13E **82** F5
Dent U.K. 54°17N 2°27W **26** D4
Denton Gt. Man., U.K. 53°27N 2°9W **27** F4
Denton Lincs., U.K. 52°53N 0°43W **27** G7
Denton U.S.A. 33°13N 97°8W **111** D7
D'Entrecasteaux Is. Papua N.G. 9°0S 151°0E **98** B9
Deoghar India 24°30N 86°42E **85** G15
Deolali India 19°58N 73°50E **84** K8
Deosai Mts. Pakistan 35°40N 75°0E **84** B9
Dera Ghazi Khan Pakistan 30°5N 70°43E **84** D7
Dera Ismail Khan Pakistan 31°50N 70°50E **84** D7
Derbent Russia 42°5N 48°15E **71** F8
Derby Australia 17°18S 123°38E **98** D3
Derby U.K. 52°56N 1°28W **27** G6
Derbyshire □ U.K. 53°11N 1°38W **27** F5
Dereham U.K. 52°41N 0°57E **31** A10
Derg → U.K. 54°44N 7°26W **18** B7
Derg, L. Ireland 53°0N 8°20W **20** C6
Derridder U.S.A. 30°51N 93°17W **111** D8
Derry = Londonderry U.K. 55°0N 7°20W **18** A7
Derry & Strabane □ U.K. 54°47N 7°22W **18** B6
Derrynasaggart Mts. Ireland 51°58N 9°15W **20** D4
Derryveagh Mts. Ireland 54°56N 8°11W **18** B5
Derwent → Derby, U.K. 52°57N 1°28W **27** G6
Derwent → N. Yorks., U.K. 53°45N 0°58W **27** E7
Derwent → Tyne & W., U.K. 54°58N 1°41W **26** C5
Derwent Water U.K. 54°35N 3°9W **26** C2
Des Moines U.S.A. 41°35N 93°37W **111** B8
Des Moines → U.S.A. 40°23N 91°25W **111** B8
Desborough U.K. 52°27N 0°49W **31** B7
Deschutes → U.S.A. 45°38N 120°55W **110** A2
Dese Ethiopia 11°5N 39°40E **89** E2
Deseado → Argentina 47°45S 65°54W **121** G3
Desford U.K. 52°37N 1°17W **27** G6
Desolación, I. Chile 53°0S 74°0W **121** H2
Dessau Germany 51°51N 12°14E **64** C7
Detour, Pt. U.S.A. 45°40N 86°40W **112** C4
Detroit U.S.A. 42°19N 83°12W **112** D6
Deutsche Bucht Germany 54°15N 8°0E **64** A5
Deventer Neths. 52°15N 6°10E **64** B4
Devils Lake U.S.A. 48°7N 98°52W **110** A7
Devizes U.K. 51°22N 1°58W **30** D5

Devon □ U.K. 50°50N 3°40W **29** F6
Devon I. Canada 75°10N 85°0W **109** B11
Devonport U.K. 50°22N 4°11W **29** G5
Dewsbury U.K. 53°42N 1°37W **27** E5
Dexter U.S.A. 36°48N 89°57W **112** G3
Deyang China 31°3N 104°27E **78** E9
Dezful Iran 32°20N 48°30E **86** C7
Dezhneva, C. Russia 66°5N 169°40W **77** C20
Dezhou China 37°26N 116°18E **79** D12
Dhahran Si. Arabia 26°10N 50°7E **86** E7
Dhaka Bangla. 23°43N 90°26E **85** H17
Dhaka □ Bangla. 23°30N 90°0E **85** G17
Dhamar Yemen 14°30N 44°20E **89** E3
Dhamtari India 20°42N 81°35E **85** J12
Dhanbad India 23°50N 86°30E **85** H15
Dharwad India 15°30N 75°4E **84** M9
Dhaulagiri Nepal 28°39N 83°28E **85** E13
Dhenkanal India 20°45N 85°35E **85** J14
Dhuburi India 26°2N 89°59E **85** F16
Dhule India 20°58N 74°50E **84** J9
Diamantina Brazil 18°17S 43°40W **122** C2
Diamantina → Australia 26°45S 139°10E **98** F6
Diamantino Brazil 14°30S 56°30W **120** D4
Dibrugarh India 27°29N 94°55E **85** F19
Dickinson U.S.A. 46°53N 102°47W **110** A6
Didcot U.K. 51°36N 1°14W **30** C6
Diefenbaker, L. Canada 51°0N 106°55W **108** D9
Dieppe France 49°54N 1°4E **66** B4
Digby Canada 44°38N 65°50W **109** E13
Digne-les-Bains France 44°5N 6°12E **66** D7
Dijon France 47°20N 5°3E **66** C6
Dikson Russia 73°40N 80°5E **76** B9
Dili E. Timor 8°39S 125°34E **83** F7
Dillingham U.S.A. 59°3N 158°28W **108** D4
Dimitrovgrad Bulgaria 42°5N 25°35E **69** C11
Dimitrovgrad Russia 54°14N 49°39E **70** D8
Dinajpur Bangla. 25°33N 88°43E **85** G16
Dinan France 48°28N 2°2W **66** B2
Dinant Belgium 50°16N 4°55E **64** C3
Dinaric Alps Croatia 44°0N 16°30E **68** C7
Dinbych = Denbigh U.K. 53°12N 3°25W **28** A7
Dinbych-y-Pysgod = Tenby U.K. 51°40N 4°42W **28** D4
Dingle Ireland 52°9N 10°17W **20** D2
Dingle B. Ireland 52°3N 10°20W **20** D2
Dingle Pen. Ireland 52°12N 10°5W **20** D2
Dingwall U.K. 57°36N 4°26W **23** G9
Dipolog Phil. 8°36N 123°20E **83** C6
Dire Dawa Ethiopia 9°35N 41°45E **89** F3
Dirranbandi Australia 28°33S 148°17E **98** F8
Disappointment, C. U.S.A. 46°18N 124°5W **110** A2
Disappointment, L. Australia 23°20S 122°40E **98** E3
Diss U.K. 52°23N 1°7E **31** B11
Distington U.K. 54°36N 3°32W **26** C1
Distrito Federal □ Brazil 15°45S 47°45W **122** C1
Ditchingham U.K. 52°28N 1°28E **31** B11
Ditchling Beacon U.K. 50°54N 0°6W **31** E8
Dittisham U.K. 50°22N 3°37W **29** G6
Ditton Priors U.K. 52°30N 2°34W **27** H3
Diu India 20°45N 70°58E **84** J7
Divinópolis Brazil 20°10S 44°54W **122** D2
Dixon U.S.A. 41°50N 89°29W **112** E3
Dixon Entrance U.S.A. 54°30N 132°0W **108** D6
Diyarbakır Turkey 37°55N 40°18E **71** G7
Dizzard Pt. U.K. 50°44N 4°40W **29** F4
Djerba, Î. de Tunisia 33°50N 10°48E **95** B8
Djerid, Chott Tunisia 33°42N 8°30E **94** B7
Djibouti Djibouti 11°30N 43°5E **89** E3
Djibouti ■ Africa 12°0N 43°0E **89** E3
Djourab, Erg du Chad 16°40N 18°50E **95** E9
Dmitri Laptev Str. Russia 73°0N 140°0E **77** B15
Dnepropetrovsk Ukraine 48°30N 35°0E **71** E6
Dnieper → Ukraine 46°30N 32°18E **71** E5
Dniester → Europe 46°18N 30°17E **65** E16
Dniprodzerzhynsk Ukraine 48°32N 34°37E **71** E5
Doba Chad 8°40N 16°50E **95** G9
Doberai, Jazirah Indonesia 1°25S 133°0E **83** E8
Dobrich Bulgaria 43°37N 27°49E **69** C12
Dobruja Europe 44°30N 28°15E **65** F15
Docking U.K. 52°54N 0°38E **31** A10
Doddington Cambs., U.K. 52°30N 0°3E **31** B9
Doddington Northumberland, U.K. 55°33N 1°54W **26** A5
Dodecanese Greece 36°35N 27°0E **69** F12
Dodge City U.S.A. 37°45N 100°1W **110** C6
Dodman Pt. U.K. 50°13N 4°48W **29** G4
Dodoma Tanzania 6°8S 35°45E **96** F7
Doha Qatar 25°15N 51°35E **87** E7
Dokdo = Liancourt Rocks Asia 37°15N 131°52E **81** E2
Dolbeau-Mistassini Canada 48°53N 72°14W **109** E12
Dole France 47°7N 5°31E **66** C6
Dolgarrog U.K. 53°11N 3°50W **28** A6
Dolgellau U.K. 52°45N 3°53W **28** B6
Dolo Ethiopia 4°11N 42°3E **89** G3
Dolomites Italy 46°23N 11°51E **68** A4
Dolores Argentina 36°20S 57°40W **121** F4
Dolphin and Union Str. Canada 69°5N 114°45W **108** C8
Dolphinton U.K. 55°42N 3°25W **25** C9
Dolton U.K. 50°53N 4°2W **29** F5
Dominica ■ W. Indies 15°20N 61°20W **115** D12
Dominican Rep. ■ W. Indies 19°0N 70°30W **115** D10
Don → Russia 47°4N 39°18E **71** E6
Don → Aberds., U.K. 57°11N 2°5W **23** H13
Don → S. Yorks., U.K. 53°41N 0°52W **27** E7
Don Figuereoa Mts. Jamaica 18°5N 77°36W **114** a
Donaghadee U.K. 54°39N 5°33W **19** B10
Doncaster U.K. 53°32N 1°6W **27** E6
Dondra Head Sri Lanka 5°55N 80°40E **84** S12
Donegal Ireland 54°39N 8°5W **18** B5
Donegal □ Ireland 54°53N 8°0W **18** B5
Donegal B. Ireland 54°31N 8°49W **18** B4
Donets → Russia 47°33N 40°55E **71** E7
Donetsk Ukraine 48°0N 37°45E **71** E6
Dong Hoi Vietnam 17°29N 106°36E **82** A3
Dongchuan China 26°8N 103°1E **78** F9
Dongguan China 22°58N 113°44E **79** a
Dongola Sudan 19°9N 30°22E **95** E12
Dongsha Dao S. China Sea 20°45N 116°43E **79** G12
Dongting Hu China 29°18N 112°45E **79** F11
Donhead U.K. 51°1N 2°7W **30** D4

Donington U.K. 52°54N 0°12W **27** G8
Donna Nook U.K. 53°29N 0°8E **27** F9
Donostia-San Sebastián Spain 43°17N 1°58W **67** A5
Doon → U.K. 55°27N 4°39W **24** D6
Dorchester Dorset, U.K. 50°42N 2°27W **30** E4
Dorchester Oxon., U.K. 51°39N 1°10W **30** C6
Dorchester, C. Canada 65°27N 77°27W **109** C12
Dordogne → France 45°2N 0°36W **66** D3
Dordrecht Neths. 51°48N 4°39E **64** C3
Dores do Indaiá Brazil 19°27S 45°36W **122** C1
Dorking U.K. 51°14N 0°19W **31** D8
Dornie U.K. 57°17N 5°31W **22** H6
Dornoch U.K. 57°53N 4°2W **23** G9
Dornoch Firth U.K. 57°51N 4°4W **23** G9
Döröö Nuur Mongolia 48°0N 93°0E **78** B7
Dorset □ U.K. 50°45N 2°26W **30** E4
Dorstone U.K. 52°3N 2°59W **30** B3
Dortmund Germany 51°30N 7°28E **64** C4
Dos Bahías, C. Argentina 44°58S 65°32W **121** G3
Dos Hermanas Spain 37°16N 5°55W **67** D3
Dothan U.S.A. 31°13N 85°24W **111** D9
Douai France 50°21N 3°4E **66** A5
Douala Cameroon 4°0N 9°45E **96** D1
Doubs → France 46°53N 5°1E **66** C6
Douglas Ireland 51°52N 8°25W **20** E6
Douglas I. of Man 54°10N 4°28W **19** C13
Douglas U.S.A. 31°21N 109°33W **110** D5
Dounreay U.K. 58°35N 3°44W **23** E10
Dourados Brazil 22°9S 54°50W **120** E4
Douro → Europe 41°8N 8°40W **67** B1
Dove → Derby, U.K. 52°51N 1°36W **27** G5
Dove → N. Yorks., U.K. 54°15N 0°55W **26** D7
Dove Dale U.K. 53°7N 1°46W **27** F5
Dover U.K. 51°7N 1°19E **31** D11
Dover Del., U.S.A. 39°10N 75°32W **113** F10
Dover N.H., U.S.A. 43°12N 70°56W **113** D12
Dover, Str. of Europe 51°0N 1°30E **62** F7
Dover-Foxcroft U.S.A. 45°11N 69°13W **113** C13
Doveridge U.K. 52°54N 1°49W **27** G5
Dovey = Dyfi → U.K. 52°32N 4°3W **28** B5
Dovrefjell Norway 62°15N 9°33E **63** E5
Downham U.K. 52°26N 0°14E **31** B9
Downham Market U.K. 52°37N 0°23E **31** A9
Downpatrick U.K. 54°20N 5°43W **19** B10
Downpatrick Hd. Ireland 54°20N 9°21W **18** C3
Downton U.K. 50°59N 1°44W **30** E5
Drâa, Oued → Morocco 28°40N 11°10W **94** C3
Draguignan France 43°32N 6°27E **66** E7
Drake Passage S. Ocean 58°0S 68°0W **55** B17
Drakensberg S. Africa 31°0S 28°0E **97** L5
Drammen Norway 59°42N 10°12E **63** F6
Drava → Croatia 45°33N 18°55E **69** B8
Dresden Germany 51°3N 13°44E **64** C7
Dreux France 48°44N 1°23E **66** B4
Driffield U.K. 54°0N 0°26W **27** D8
Drina → Bos.-H. 44°53N 19°21E **69** B8
Drobeta-Turnu Severin Romania 44°39N 22°41E **65** F12
Drogheda Ireland 53°43N 6°22W **19** C9
Drohobych Ukraine 49°20N 23°30E **71** E3
Droitwich U.K. 52°16N 2°8W **30** B4
Dromore U.K. 54°31N 7°28W **18** B7
Dromore West Ireland 54°15N 8°52W **18** C4
Dronfield U.K. 53°19N 1°27W **27** F6
Dronning Maud Land Antarctica 72°30S 12°0E **55** D3
Drum Hills Ireland 52°1N 7°45W **20** D7
Drumheller Canada 51°25N 112°40W **108** D8
Drummond I. U.S.A. 46°1N 83°39W **112** B5
Drummondville Canada 45°55N 72°25W **113** C11
Drumochter, Pass of U.K. 56°50N 4°15W **23** J9
Dry Harbour Mts. Jamaica 18°19N 77°24W **114** a
Dryden Canada 49°47N 92°50W **108** E10
Drygalski I. Antarctica 66°0S 92°0E **55** C7
Du Quoin U.S.A. 38°1N 89°14W **112** F3
Duarte, Pico Dom. Rep. 19°2N 70°59W **115** D10
Dubai U.A.E. 25°18N 55°20E **87** E8
Dubawnt → Canada 64°33N 100°6W **108** C9
Dubawnt L. Canada 63°8N 101°28W **108** C9
Dubbo Australia 32°11S 148°35E **98** G8
Dublin Ireland 53°21N 6°15W **21** B10
Dublin U.S.A. 32°32N 82°54W **111** D10
Dublin □ Ireland 53°24N 6°20W **21** B10
Dublin ✈ (DUB) Ireland 53°26N 6°15W **21** B10
DuBois U.S.A. 41°7N 78°46W **112** E8
Dubrovnik Croatia 42°39N 18°6E **69** C8
Dubuque U.S.A. 42°30N 90°41W **112** D2
Duddington U.K. 52°36N 0°32W **31** A7
Duddon → U.K. 54°12N 3°15W **26** D2
Dudinka Russia 69°30N 86°13E **77** C9
Dudley U.K. 52°31N 2°5W **27** G4
Duffield U.K. 52°59N 1°29W **27** G6
Dufftown U.K. 57°27N 3°8W **23** H11
Dugi Otok Croatia 44°0N 15°3E **68** C6
Duisburg Germany 51°26N 6°45E **64** C4
Dukinfield U.K. 53°28N 2°6W **27** F4
Dulce → Argentina 30°32S 62°33W **121** F3
Duluth U.S.A. 46°47N 92°6W **111** A8
Dulverton U.K. 51°2N 3°33W **29** E6
Dumaguete Phil. 9°17N 123°15E **83** C6
Dumbarton U.K. 55°57N 4°33W **24** C6
Dumfries U.K. 55°4N 3°37W **25** D8
Dumfries & Galloway □ U.K. 55°9N 3°58W **25** D8
Dumyât Egypt 31°24N 31°48E **95** B12
Dún Laoghaire Ireland 53°17N 6°8W **21** B10
Dunbar U.K. 56°0N 2°31W **25** B10
Dunblane U.K. 56°11N 3°58W **25** B8
Duncan U.S.A. 34°30N 97°57W **110** D7
Duncansby Head U.K. 58°38N 3°1W **23** E11
Dunchurch U.K. 52°21N 1°17W **30** B6
Dundalk Ireland 54°1N 6°24W **19** B9
Dundalk Bay Ireland 53°55N 6°15W **19** C9
Dundee U.K. 56°28N 2°59W **25** B10
Dundrum Ireland 53°18N 6°14W **21** B10
Dundrum U.K. 54°16N 5°52W **19** B10
Dundrum B. U.K. 54°13N 5°47W **19** B10
Dunedin N.Z. 45°50S 170°33E **99** K13
Dunfermline U.K. 56°5N 3°27W **25** B9
Dungannon U.K. 54°31N 6°46W **19** B8

Dungarvan Ireland 52°5N 7°37W **21** D7
Dungarvan Harbour Ireland 52°4N 7°35W **21** D7
Dungeness U.K. 50°54N 0°59E **31** E10
Dunhua China 43°20N 128°14E **79** C14
Dunhuang China 40°8N 94°36E **78** C7
Dunkeld U.K. 56°34N 3°35W **25** A8
Dunkerque France 51°2N 2°20E **66** A5
Dunkery Beacon U.K. 51°9N 3°36W **29** E6
Dunkirk U.S.A. 42°29N 79°20W **112** D8
Dunleer Ireland 53°50N 6°24W **19** C9
Dunmanway Ireland 51°43N 9°6W **20** E4
Dunmore U.S.A. 41°25N 75°38W **113** E10
Dunnet Hd. U.K. 58°40N 3°21W **23** E11
Dunoon U.K. 55°57N 4°56W **24** C6
Duns U.K. 55°47N 2°20W **25** C11
Dunsford U.K. 50°41N 3°42W **29** F6
Dunstable U.K. 51°53N 0°32W **31** C7
Dunster U.K. 51°11N 3°27W **30** D2
Dunston U.K. 52°46N 2°7W **27** G4
Dunvant U.K. 51°37N 4°5W **28** D4
Dunvegan U.K. 57°27N 6°35W **22** H4
Duolun China 42°12N 116°28E **79** C12
Duque de Caxias Brazil 22°46S 43°18W **122** D2
Durance → France 43°55N 4°45E **66** E6
Durango Mexico 24°3N 104°39W **114** C4
Durango U.S.A. 37°16N 107°53W **110** C5
Durant U.S.A. 33°59N 96°25W **111** D7
Durazno Uruguay 33°25S 56°31W **121** F4
Durban S. Africa 29°49S 31°1E **97** K6
Düren Germany 50°48N 6°29E **64** C4
Durgapur India 23°30N 87°20E **85** H15
Durham U.K. 54°47N 1°34W **26** C5
Durham U.S.A. 35°59N 78°54W **111** C11
Durham □ U.K. 54°42N 1°45W **26** C5
Durlston Hd. U.K. 50°36N 1°57W **30** E5
Durness U.K. 58°34N 4°45W **23** E8
Durrës Albania 41°19N 19°28E **69** D8
Durrington U.K. 51°12N 1°47W **30** D5
Durrow Ireland 52°51N 7°24W **21** C8
Dursey I. Ireland 51°36N 10°12W **20** E2
Dursley U.K. 51°40N 2°21W **30** C4
Dushanbe Tajikistan 38°33N 68°48E **87** B12
Düsseldorf Germany 51°14N 6°47E **64** C4
Dutch Harbor U.S.A. 53°53N 166°32W **108** D3
Duyun China 26°18N 107°29E **78** F10
Dvina, N. → Russia 64°32N 40°30E **70** B7
Dvina B. Russia 65°0N 39°0E **70** B6
Dwarka India 22°18N 69°8E **84** H6
Dyce U.K. 57°13N 2°12W **23** H13
Dyer, C. Canada 66°37N 61°16W **109** C13
Dyersburg U.S.A. 36°3N 89°23W **111** C9
Dyfi → U.K. 52°32N 4°3W **28** B5
Dymchurch U.K. 51°1N 1°0E **31** D11
Dymock U.K. 51°59N 2°26W **30** C4
Dzavhan Gol → Mongolia 48°54N 93°23E **78** B7
Dzerzhinsk Russia 56°14N 43°30E **70** C7
Dzhankoy Ukraine 45°40N 34°20E **71** E5
Dzhugdzhur Ra. Russia 57°30N 138°0E **77** D14
Dzungarian Basin China 44°30N 86°0E **78** C6
Dzungarian Gate Asia 45°10N 82°0E **78** B5
Dzüünmod Mongolia 47°45N 106°58E **78** B10

E

Eagle U.S.A. 64°47N 141°12W **108** C5
Eagle L. U.S.A. 46°20N 69°22W **113** B13
Eagle Pass U.S.A. 28°43N 100°30W **110** E6
Eagle River U.S.A. 47°25N 88°18W **112** B3
Eaglesfield U.K. 55°4N 3°12W **25** D9
Eakring U.K. 53°9N 0°58W **27** F7
Ealing □ U.K. 51°31N 0°20W **31** C8
Earby U.K. 53°55N 2°7W **27** E4
Eardisley U.K. 52°8N 3°1W **30** B2
Earith U.K. 52°22N 0°2E **31** B9
Earl Shilton U.K. 52°35N 1°18W **27** G6
Earl Soham U.K. 52°14N 1°18E **31** B11
Earls Barton U.K. 52°16N 0°45W **31** B7
Earl's Colne U.K. 51°56N 0°43E **31** C10
Earlston U.K. 55°39N 2°40W **25** C10
Earn → U.K. 56°21N 3°18W **25** B9
Earn, L. U.K. 56°23N 4°13W **24** B7
Earsdon U.K. 55°3N 1°29W **26** B6
Easebourne U.K. 51°0N 0°43W **31** E7
Easington Durham, U.K. 54°47N 1°21W **26** C6
Easington E. Riding, U.K. 53°39N 0°6E **27** E9
Easington Colliery U.K. 54°48N 1°19W **26** C6
Easingwold U.K. 54°8N 1°11W **26** D6
East Ayrshire □ U.K. 55°26N 4°11W **24** C7
East Bengal Bangla. 24°0N 90°0E **85** H17
East Bergholt U.K. 51°59N 1°3E **31** C11
East Beskids Europe 49°20N 22°0E **65** D11
East Brent U.K. 51°14N 2°55W **30** D3
East C. = Dezhneva, C. Russia 66°5N 169°40W **77** C20
East China Sea Asia 30°0N 126°0E **79** F14
East Cowes U.K. 50°45N 1°16W **30** E6
East Falkland Falk. Is. 51°30S 58°30W **121** H4
East Fen U.K. 53°4N 0°5E **27** F9
East Grinstead U.K. 51°7N 0°0 **31** D9
East Harling U.K. 52°26N 0°56E **31** B10
East Ilsley U.K. 51°31N 1°16W **30** C6
East Indies Asia 0°0 120°0E **72** J14
East Kilbride U.K. 55°47N 4°11W **24** C7
East Lansing U.S.A. 42°44N 84°29W **112** D5
East London S. Africa 33°0S 27°55E **97** L5
East Lothian □ U.K. 55°58N 2°44W **25** C10
East Markham U.K. 53°15N 0°53W **27** F7
East Moor U.K. 53°16N 1°34W **27** F5
East Pt. Canada 46°27N 61°58W **113** C17
East St. Louis U.S.A. 38°37N 90°9W **112** F2
East Sea = Japan, Sea of Asia 40°0N 135°0E **81** D4
East Siberian Sea Russia 73°0N 160°0E **77** B17
East Sussex □ U.K. 50°56N 0°19E **31** E9
East Timor = Timor-Leste ■ Asia 8°50S 126°0E **83** F7
East Wittering U.K. 50°46N 0°52W **31** E7
East Woodhay U.K. 51°21N 1°25W **30** D6
Eastbourne U.K. 50°46N 0°18E **31** E9
Eastchurch U.K. 51°24N 0°53E **31** D10
Eastern Desert Egypt 27°30N 32°30E **95** C12
Eastern Ghats India 14°0N 78°50E **84** N11
Eastern Group Fiji 17°0S 178°30W **99** D15

Eastleigh U.K. 50°58N 1°21W 30 E6
Eastmain Canada 52°10N 78°30W 109 D12
Eastmain → Canada 52°27N 78°26W 109 D12
Eastnor U.K. 52°2N 2°23W 30 B4
Easton Dorset, U.K. 50°33N 2°26W 30 E4
Easton Northants., U.K. 52°37N 0°31W 31 A7
Easton Md., U.S.A. 38°47N 76°5W 113 F9
Easton Pa., U.S.A. 40°41N 75°13W 113 E10
Easton-in-Gordano U.K. 51°28N 2°42W 30 D3
Eastport U.S.A. 44°56N 67°0W 113 C14
Eastry U.K. 51°14N 1°19E 31 D11
Eastwood U.K. 53°1N 1°18W 27 F6
Eaton U.K. 52°51N 0°49W 27 G7
Eaton Socon U.K. 52°14N 0°17W 31 B8
Eau Claire U.S.A. 44°49N 91°30W 112 C2
Eau Claire, L. à l' Canada 56°10N 74°25W 109 D12
Ebberston U.K. 54°14N 0°37W 26 D7
Ebbw Vale U.K. 51°46N 3°12W 28 D7
Eberswalde-Finow Germany 52°50N 13°49E 64 B7
Ebetsu Japan 43°7N 141°34E 81 B7
Ebinur Hu China 44°55N 82°55E 78 C5
Ebolowa Cameroon 2°55N 11°10E 96 D2
Ebro → Spain 40°43N 0°54E 67 B6
Ecclefechan U.K. 55°4N 3°16W 25 D9
Eccleshall U.K. 52°52N 2°15W 27 G4
Ech Chélif Algeria 36°10N 1°20E 94 A6
Echo Bay Canada 66°5N 117°55W 108 C8
Eckington U.K. 53°18N 1°22W 27 F6
Eclipse Sd. Canada 72°38N 79°0W 109 B12
Ecuador ■ S. Amer. 2°0S 78°0W 120 C2
Ed Damazin Sudan 11°46N 34°21E 95 F12
Eday U.K. 59°11N 2°47W 23 D12
Eddrachillis B. U.K. 58°17N 5°14W 22 F7
Eddystone U.K. 50°11N 4°16W 29 G5
Eden → U.K. 54°57N 3°1W 26 C2
Edenbridge U.K. 51°12N 0°5E 31 D9
Edenderry Ireland 53°21N 7°4W 21 B8
Edfu Egypt 24°55N 32°49E 95 D12
Edge Hill U.K. 52°8N 1°26W 30 B6
Edinburgh U.K. 55°57N 3°13W 25 C9
Edinburgh ✈ (EDI) U.K. 55°54N 3°22W 25 C9
Edington U.K. 51°17N 2°50W 30 D4
Edirne Turkey 41°40N 26°34E 71 F4
Edmonton Canada 53°30N 113°30W 108 D8
Edmundbyers U.K. 54°50N 1°58W 26 C5
Edmundston Canada 47°23N 68°20W 109 E13
Edremit Turkey 39°34N 27°0E 86 B1
Edson Canada 53°35N 116°28W 108 D8
Edward, L. Africa 0°25S 29°40E 96 E5
Edward VII Land Antarctica 80°0S 150°0W 55 E13
Edwards Plateau U.S.A. 30°45N 101°20W 110 D6
Effingham U.S.A. 39°7N 88°33W 112 F3
Égadi, Ísole Italy 37°55N 12°16E 68 F5
Eganville Canada 45°32N 77°5W 112 C9
Eger Hungary 47°53N 20°27E 65 E11
Egham U.K. 51°25N 0°32W 31 D7
Eglinton I. Canada 75°48N 118°30W 109 B8
Egremont U.K. 54°29N 3°32W 26 D1
Eğridir Turkey 37°52N 30°51E 71 G5
Eğridir Gölü Turkey 37°53N 30°50E 71 G5
Egton U.K. 54°28N 0°44W 26 D7
Egypt ■ Africa 28°0N 31°0E 95 C12
Eifel Germany 50°15N 6°50E 64 C4
Eigg U.K. 56°54N 6°10W 22 J5
Eil, L. U.K. 56°51N 5°16W 22 J7
Eilat Israel 29°30N 34°56E 86 D3
Eilean Siar □ U.K. 57°30N 7°10W 22 G3
Eindhoven Neths. 51°26N 5°28E 64 C3
Eire = Ireland ■ Europe 53°50N 7°52W 62 E2
Eiriosgaigh = Eriskay U.K. 57°4N 7°18W 22 H3
Eivissa Spain 38°54N 1°26E 67 C6
Ekaterinburg Russia 56°50N 60°30E 76 D7
Ekibastuz Kazakhstan 51°50N 75°10E 76 D8
El Aaiún W. Sahara 27°9N 13°12W 94 C3
El Alamein Egypt 30°48N 28°58E 95 B11
El Centro U.S.A. 32°48N 115°34W 110 D3
El Djouf Mauritania 21°25N 6°40W 94 D4
El Dorado U.S.A. 33°12N 92°40W 111 D8
El Faiyûm Egypt 29°19N 30°50E 95 C12
El Fâsher Sudan 13°33N 25°26E 95 F11
El Fuerte Mexico 26°25N 108°39W 114 B3
El Geneina Sudan 13°27N 22°45E 95 F10
El Gezira □ Sudan 15°0N 33°0E 95 F12
El Gîza Egypt 30°0N 31°12E 95 C12
El Istiwa'iya Sudan 5°0N 28°0E 95 G11
El Jadida Morocco 33°11N 8°17W 94 B4
El Khârga Egypt 25°30N 30°33E 95 C12
El Mahalla el Kubra Egypt 31°0N 31°0E 95 B12
El Mansûra Egypt 31°0N 31°19E 95 B12
El Minyâ Egypt 28°7N 30°33E 95 C12
El Obeid Sudan 13°8N 30°10E 95 F12
El Oued Algeria 33°20N 6°58E 94 B7
El Paso U.S.A. 31°45N 106°29W 110 D5
El Puerto de Santa Maria Spain 36°36N 6°13W 67 D2
El Reno U.S.A. 35°32N 97°57W 110 C7
El Salvador ■ Cent. Amer. 13°50N 89°0W 114 E7
El Tigre Venezuela 8°44N 64°15W 120 B3
El Uqsur Egypt 25°41N 32°38E 95 C12
Elazığ Turkey 38°37N 39°14E 71 G6
Elba Italy 42°46N 10°17E 68 C4
Elbasan Albania 41°9N 20°9E 69 D9
Elbe → Europe 53°50N 9°0E 64 B5
Elbert, Mt. U.S.A. 39°7N 106°27W 110 C5
Elbeuf France 49°17N 1°2E 66 B4
Elblag Poland 54°10N 19°25E 65 A10
Elbrus Russia 43°21N 42°30E 71 F7
Elburz Mts. Iran 36°0N 52°0E 87 B8
Elche Spain 38°15N 0°42W 67 C5
Elda Spain 38°29N 0°47W 67 C5
Eldoret Kenya 0°30N 35°17E 96 D7
Elektrostal Russia 55°41N 38°32E 70 C6
Elephant Butte Res. U.S.A. 33°9N 107°11W 110 D5
Elephant I. Antarctica 61°0S 55°0W 55 C18
Eleuthera I. Bahamas 25°0N 76°20W 115 C9
Elgin U.K. 57°39N 3°19W 23 G11
Elgin U.S.A. 42°2N 88°17W 112 D3
Elgon, Mt. Africa 1°10N 34°30E 96 D6
Elham U.K. 51°9N 1°8E 31 D11
Elishaw U.K. 55°15N 2°14W 26 B4
Elista Russia 46°16N 44°14E 71 E7

Elizabeth U.S.A. 40°39N 74°12W 113 E10
Elizabeth City U.S.A. 36°18N 76°14W 111 C11
Elizabethtown U.S.A. 37°42N 85°52W 112 G5
Elkhart U.S.A. 41°41N 85°58W 112 E5
Elkins U.S.A. 38°55N 79°51W 112 F8
Elko U.S.A. 40°50N 115°46W 110 B3
Elland U.K. 53°41N 1°50W 27 E5
Ellef Ringnes I. Canada 78°30N 102°2W 109 B9
Ellen → U.K. 54°44N 3°30W 26 C2
Ellensburg U.S.A. 46°59N 120°34W 110 A2
Ellerton Barbados 13°7N 59°33W 114 c
Ellesmere U.K. 52°55N 2°53W 27 G3
Ellesmere I. Canada 79°30N 80°0W 109 B12
Ellesmere Port U.K. 53°17N 2°54W 27 F3
Ellington U.K. 55°14N 1°33W 26 B5
Elliot Lake Canada 46°25N 82°35W 109 E11
Ellon U.K. 57°22N 2°4W 23 H13
Ellsworth Land Antarctica 76°0S 89°0W 55 D16
Elmalı Turkey 36°44N 29°56E 71 G4
Elmira U.S.A. 42°6N 76°48W 112 D9
Elmswell U.K. 52°15N 0°55E 31 B10
Eluru India 16°48N 81°8E 84 F6
Ely U.K. 52°24N 0°16E 31 B9
Ely U.S.A. 39°15N 114°54W 110 C4
Elyria U.S.A. 41°22N 82°7W 112 E6
eMalahleni S. Africa 25°51S 29°14E 97 K5
Emâmrûd Iran 36°30N 55°0E 87 B8
Embarcación Argentina 23°10S 64°0W 121 E3
Embleton U.K. 55°29N 1°38W 26 B5
Emden Germany 53°21N 7°12E 64 B4
Emerald Australia 37°56S 145°29E 98 E8
Emmen Neths. 52°48N 6°57E 64 B4
Emmonak U.S.A. 62°47N 164°31W 108 C3
Empalme Mexico 27°58N 110°51W 114 B2
Empangeni S. Africa 28°50S 31°52E 97 K6
Empedrado Argentina 28°0S 58°46W 121 E4
Emporia U.S.A. 38°25N 96°11W 111 C7
Emporium U.S.A. 41°31N 78°14W 112 E8
Empty Quarter = Rub' al Khālī Si. Arabia 19°0N 48°0E 89 D4
Ems → Germany 53°20N 7°12E 64 B4
En Nahud Sudan 12°45N 28°25E 95 F11
Enard B. U.K. 58°5N 5°20W 22 F7
Encarnación Paraguay 27°15S 55°50W 121 E4
Encounter B. Australia 35°45S 138°45E 98 H6
Ende Indonesia 8°45S 121°40E 83 F6
Enderbury Kiribati 3°8S 171°5W 102 H10
Enderby U.K. 52°36N 1°13W 27 G6
Enderby Land Antarctica 66°0S 53°0E 55 C5
Endicott U.S.A. 42°6N 76°4W 113 D9
Enewetak Atoll Marshall Is. 11°30N 162°15E 102 F8
Enez Turkey 40°45N 26°5E 71 F4
Enfield □ U.K. 51°38N 0°5W 31 C8
Engadin Switz. 46°45N 10°10E 64 E6
Engels Russia 51°28N 46°6E 71 D8
Enggano Indonesia 5°20S 102°40E 82 F2
England □ U.K. 53°0N 2°0W 62 E6
English → Canada 49°12N 91°5W 108 D10
English Channel Europe 50°0N 2°0W 62 F6
Enid U.S.A. 36°24N 97°53W 110 C7
Ennadai L. Canada 60°58N 101°20W 108 C9
Ennedi Chad 17°15N 22°0E 95 E10
Ennerdale Water U.K. 54°32N 3°24W 26 C2
Ennis Ireland 52°51N 8°59W 20 C5
Enniscorthy Ireland 52°30N 6°34W 21 D9
Enniskillen U.K. 54°21N 7°39W 18 C6
Ennistymon Ireland 52°57N 9°17W 20 C4
Enns → Austria 48°14N 14°32E 64 D8
Enschede Neths. 52°13N 6°53E 64 B4
Ensenada Mexico 31°52N 116°37W 114 A1
Enshi China 30°18N 109°29E 79 E10
Enstone U.K. 51°55N 1°27W 30 C6
Entebbe Uganda 0°4N 32°28E 96 D6
Entre Rios □ Argentina 30°30S 58°30W 121 F4
Enugu Nigeria 6°30N 7°30E 94 G7
Eólie, Ís. Italy 38°30N 14°57E 68 E6
Épernay France 49°3N 3°56E 66 B5
Épinal France 48°10N 6°27E 66 B7
Erfurt Germany 50°58N 11°2E 64 C6
Ergeni Lowlands Russia 47°0N 44°0E 71 E7
Eriboll, L. U.K. 58°30N 4°42W 23 E8
Erie U.S.A. 42°8N 80°5W 112 D7
Erie, L. N. Amer. 42°15N 81°0W 112 D7
Eriskay U.K. 57°4N 7°18W 22 H3
Eritrea ■ Africa 14°0N 38°30E 89 D2
Erlangen Germany 49°36N 11°0E 64 D6
Ermoupoli Greece 37°28N 24°57E 69 F11
Ernakulam India 9°59N 76°22E 84 Q10
Erne → Ireland 54°30N 8°16W 18 C5
Erne, Lower L. U.K. 54°28N 7°47W 18 C6
Erne, Upper L. U.K. 54°14N 7°32E 18 C6
Erode India 11°24N 77°45E 84 P10
Erramala Hills India 15°30N 78°15E 84 M11
Errigal Ireland 55°2N 8°6W 18 A5
Erris Hd. Ireland 54°17N 10°0W 18 B1
Erromango Vanuatu 18°45S 169°5E 99 D12
Erzgebirge Germany 50°27N 12°55E 64 C7
Erzincan Turkey 39°46N 39°30E 71 G6
Erzurum Turkey 39°57N 41°15E 71 G7
Esbjerg Denmark 55°29N 8°29E 63 F5
Escada Brazil 8°22S 35°8W 122 A3
Escanaba U.S.A. 45°45N 87°4W 112 C4
Esch-sur-Alzette Lux. 49°32N 6°0E 64 D3
Escrick U.K. 53°53N 1°2W 27 E6
Escuinapa de Hidalgo Mexico 22°50N 105°50W 114 C3
Escuintla Guatemala 14°20N 90°48W 114 E6

Esk → Dumf. & Gall., U.K. 54°58N 3°2W 25 E9
Esk → N. Yorks., U.K. 54°30N 0°37W 26 D7
Eskdale U.K. 55°12N 3°4W 25 D9
Esker Siding Canada 53°53N 66°25W 109 D13
Eskilstuna Sweden 59°22N 16°32E 63 F7
Eskişehir Turkey 39°50N 30°30E 71 G5
Eslāmābād-e Gharb Iran 34°10N 46°30E 86 C6
Esna Egypt 25°17N 32°30E 95 C12
Esperance Australia 33°45S 121°55E 98 G3
Espinhaço, Serra do Brazil 17°30S 43°30W 122 C2
Espírito Santo □ Brazil 20°0S 40°45W 122 C2
Espíritu Santo Vanuatu 15°15S 166°50E 99 D12
Espoo Finland 60°12N 24°40E 63 E8
Essaouira Morocco 31°32N 9°42W 94 B4
Essen Germany 51°28N 7°2E 64 C4
Essequibo → Guyana 6°50N 58°30W 120 B4
Essex □ U.K. 51°54N 0°27E 31 C10
Esslingen Germany 48°44N 9°18E 64 D5
Estados, I. de Los Argentina 54°40S 64°30W 121 H3
Estância Brazil 11°16S 37°26W 122 B3
Estevan Canada 49°10N 102°59W 108 E9
Eston U.K. 54°34N 1°8W 26 C6
Estonia ■ Europe 58°30N 25°30E 63 F8
Estrela, Serra da Portugal 40°10N 7°45W 67 B2
Estrondo, Serra do Brazil 7°20S 48°0W 120 C5
Eswatini ■ Africa 26°30S 31°30E 94 A6
Etawah India 26°48N 79°6E 84 F11
Etchingham U.K. 51°0N 0°26E 31 D9
Ethiopia ■ Africa 8°0N 40°0E 89 F3
Ethiopian Highlands Ethiopia 10°0N 37°0E 89 F2
Etive, L. U.K. 56°29N 5°10W 24 B5
Etna Italy 37°50N 14°55E 68 F6
Eton U.K. 51°30N 0°36W 31 C7
Etosha Pan Namibia 18°40S 16°30E 97 H3
Ettington U.K. 52°8N 1°35W 30 B5
Ettrick Forest U.K. 55°30N 3°0W 25 C9
Ettrick Water → U.K. 55°31N 2°55W 25 C10
Euclid U.S.A. 41°34N 81°32W 112 E7
Eugene U.S.A. 44°5N 123°4W 110 B2
Euphrates → Asia 31°0N 47°25E 86 D6
Eureka Canada 80°0N 85°56W 109 B11
Eureka U.S.A. 40°47N 124°9W 110 B2
Europa, Île d' Ind. Oc. 22°20S 40°22E 97 J8
Europa, Picos de Spain 43°10N 4°49W 67 A3
Europe 50°0N 20°0E 56 E10
Eurotunnel Terminal U.K. 51°6N 1°10E 31 D11
Euxton U.K. 53°41N 2°41W 27 E3
Evanston Ill., U.S.A. 42°3N 87°40W 112 D4
Evanston Wyo., U.S.A. 41°16N 110°58W 110 B4
Evansville U.S.A. 37°58N 87°35W 112 G4
Evercreech U.K. 51°9N 2°30W 30 D4
Everest, Mt. Nepal 28°5N 86°58E 85 E15
Everett U.S.A. 47°59N 122°12W 110 A2
Everglades, The U.S.A. 25°50N 81°0W 111 E10
Evesham U.K. 52°6N 1°56W 30 B5
Evia Greece 38°30N 24°0E 69 E11
Évora Portugal 38°33N 7°57W 67 C2
Évreux France 49°3N 1°8E 66 B4
Evros → Greece 41°40N 26°34E 69 D12
Ewe, L. U.K. 57°49N 5°38W 22 G6
Ewell U.K. 51°20N 0°14W 31 D8
Ewhurst U.K. 51°9N 0°25W 31 D8
Exe → U.K. 50°41N 3°29W 29 F7
Exeter U.K. 50°43N 3°31W 29 F6
Exminster U.K. 50°40N 3°29W 29 F7
Exmoor △ U.K. 51°8N 3°42W 29 E6
Exmouth U.K. 50°37N 3°25W 29 F7
Exton U.K. 52°42N 0°39W 31 B7
Extremadura □ Spain 39°30N 6°5W 67 C2
Eyam U.K. 53°17N 1°40W 27 F5
Eyasi, L. Tanzania 3°30S 35°0E 96 E6
Eye Cambs., U.K. 52°37N 0°11W 31 A8
Eye Suffolk, U.K. 52°19N 1°9E 31 B11
Eye Pen. U.K. 58°13N 6°10W 22 F5
Eyemouth U.K. 55°52N 2°5W 25 C11
Eyjafjallajökull Iceland 63°38N 19°36W 63 B2
Eynsham U.K. 51°47N 1°22W 30 C6
Eyre Pen. Australia 33°30S 136°17E 98 G6

F

F.Y.R.O.M. = Macedonia ■ Europe 41°53N 21°40E 69 D9
Faenza Italy 44°17N 11°53E 68 B4
Fair Hd. U.K. 55°14N 6°9W 19 A9
Fair Isle U.K. 59°32N 1°38W 22 C14
Fairbanks U.S.A. 64°51N 147°43W 108 C5
Fairfield U.S.A. 38°23N 88°22W 112 F3
Fairford U.K. 51°43N 1°46W 30 C5
Fairlight U.K. 50°52N 0°40E 31 E10
Fairmont U.S.A. 39°29N 80°9W 112 F7
Fairweather, Mt. U.S.A. 58°55N 137°32W 108 D6
Faisalabad Pakistan 31°30N 73°5E 84 D8
Faizabad India 26°45N 82°10E 85 F13
Fakenham U.K. 52°51N 0°51E 31 A10
Falcon Res. U.S.A. 26°34N 99°10W 110 E7
Faldingworth U.K. 53°21N 0°24W 27 F8
Falkirk U.K. 56°0N 3°47W 25 C8
Falkland U.K. 56°16N 3°12W 25 B9
Falkland Is. □ Atl. Oc. 51°30S 59°0W 121 H4
Fall River U.S.A. 41°43N 71°10W 113 E12
Falmouth Jamaica 18°30N 77°40W 114 a
Falmouth U.K. 50°9N 5°5W 29 G3
Falmouth B. U.K. 50°6N 5°5W 29 G3
Falstone U.K. 55°11N 2°26W 26 B4
Falun Sweden 60°37N 15°37E 63 E7
Famagusta Cyprus 35°8N 33°55E 86 C3
Fanad Ireland 55°7N 7°36W 18 A7
Fanad Hd. Ireland 55°17N 7°38W 18 A6
Fannich, L. U.K. 57°38N 4°59W 23 G8
Fano Italy 43°50N 13°1E 68 C5
Far East Asia 40°0N 130°0E 72 E14
Farāh Afghan. 32°20N 62°7E 87 C10
Farasān Si. Arabia 16°45N 41°55E 89 D3
Fareham U.K. 50°51N 1°11W 30 E6
Farewell, C. Greenland 59°48N 43°55W 54 D5
Fargo U.S.A. 46°53N 96°48W 111 A7
Farg'ona Uzbekistan 40°23N 71°19E 76 E7
Faridabad India 28°26N 77°19E 84 E10
Esfahān Iran 32°39N 51°43E 87 C7
Faringdon U.K. 51°39N 1°34W 30 C5
Farmington U.S.A. 36°44N 108°12W 110 C5

Farmville U.S.A. 37°18N 78°24W 112 G8
Farnborough U.K. 51°16N 0°45W 31 D7
Farne Is. U.K. 55°38N 1°37W 26 A5
Farnham U.K. 51°13N 0°47W 31 D7
Farnworth U.K. 53°34N 2°25W 27 E4
Faro Canada 62°11N 133°22W 108 C6
Faro Portugal 37°2N 7°55W 67 D2
Faroe Is. ☑ Atl. Oc. 62°0N 7°0W 57 C4
Färs □ Iran 29°30N 55°0E 87 D8
Faslane U.K. 56°5N 4°49W 24 B6
Fataka Solomon Is. 11°55S 170°12E 99 C12
Fatehgarh India 27°25N 79°35E 84 F11
Fatehpur Raj., India 28°0N 74°40E 84 F9
Fatehpur Ut. P., India 25°56N 81°13E 85 G12
Fauldhouse U.K. 55°50N 3°43W 25 C8
Faversham U.K. 51°19N 0°56E 31 D10
Fawley U.K. 50°50N 1°20W 30 E6
Fayetteville Ark., U.S.A. 36°4N 94°10W 111 C8
Fayetteville N.C., U.S.A. 35°3N 78°53W 111 D11
Fazeley U.K. 52°37N 1°40W 27 G5
Fazilka India 30°27N 74°2E 84 D9
Fdérik Mauritania 22°40N 12°45W 94 D3
Feale → Ireland 52°27N 9°37W 20 D3
Fear, C., U.S.A. 33°50N 77°58W 111 D11
Fécamp France 49°45N 0°22E 66 B4
Fehmarn Germany 54°27N 11°7E 64 A6
Feira de Santana Brazil 12°15S 38°57W 122 B3
Felipe Carrillo Puerto Mexico 19°38N 88°3W 114 D7
Felixstowe U.K. 51°58N 1°23E 31 C11
Felton U.K. 55°18N 1°42W 26 B5
Feltwell U.K. 52°30N 0°32E 31 B10
Fenny Bentley U.K. 53°3N 1°45W 27 F5
Fenny Compton U.K. 52°10N 1°23W 30 B6
Fenny Stratford U.K. 52°0N 0°44W 31 C7
Fens, The U.K. 52°38N 0°2W 31 A8
Fenyang China 37°18N 111°48E 79 D11
Feodosiya Ukraine 45°2N 35°16E 71 E6
Fergus Falls U.S.A. 46°17N 96°4W 111 A7
Ferkéssédougou Côte d'Ivoire 9°35N 5°6W 94 G4
Fermanagh & Omagh □ U.K. 54°34N 7°24W 18 C6
Fermoy Ireland 52°9N 8°16W 20 D6
Fernhurst U.K. 51°3N 0°43W 31 D7
Ferrara Italy 44°50N 11°35E 68 B4
Ferret, C. France 44°38N 1°15W 66 D3
Ferrol Spain 43°29N 8°15W 67 A1
Ferryhill U.K. 54°41N 1°33W 26 C5
Fès Morocco 34°0N 5°0W 94 B5
Fethiye Turkey 36°36N 29°6E 71 G4
Fetlar U.K. 60°36N 0°52W 22 A16
Feuilles → Canada 58°47N 70°4W 109 D12
Feyzābād Afghan. 37°7N 70°33E 87 B12
Fezzan Libya 27°0N 13°0E 95 C8
Ffestiniog U.K. 52°57N 3°55W 28 B6
Fianarantsoa Madag. 21°26S 47°5E 97 J9
Fife □ U.K. 56°16N 3°1W 25 B9
Fife Ness U.K. 56°17N 2°35W 25 B10
Figeac France 44°37N 2°2E 66 D5
Figueres Spain 42°18N 2°58E 67 A7
Fiji ■ Pac. Oc. 17°20S 179°0E 99 D14
Filby U.K. 52°40N 1°39E 31 A12
Filey U.K. 54°12N 0°18W 26 D8
Filey B. U.K. 54°12N 0°15W 26 D8
Filton U.K. 51°30N 2°34W 30 C4
Fincham U.K. 52°38N 0°30E 31 A9
Findhorn → U.K. 57°38N 3°38W 23 G10
Findlay U.S.A. 41°2N 83°39W 112 E6
Findon U.K. 52°21N 0°39W 31 B7
Fingal's Cave U.K. 56°27N 6°21W 24 B3
Finglas Ireland 53°23N 6°19W 21 B10
Finike Turkey 36°21N 30°10E 86 B2
Finland ■ Europe 63°0N 27°0E 63 E9
Finland, G. of Europe 60°0N 26°0E 63 F9
Finlay → Canada 57°0N 125°10W 108 D7
Finn → Ireland 54°51N 7°28W 18 B7
Firozabad India 27°10N 78°25E 84 F11
Firozpur India 30°55N 74°40E 84 D9
Fish → Namibia 28°7S 17°10E 97 K3
Fishguard U.K. 51°59N 4°58W 28 D3
Fishtoft U.K. 52°58N 0°1E 27 G9
Fisterra, C. Spain 42°50N 9°19W 67 A1
Fitchburg U.S.A. 42°35N 71°48W 113 D12
Flagstaff U.S.A. 35°12N 111°39W 110 C4
Flamborough U.K. 54°7N 0°7W 26 D8
Flamborough Hd. U.K. 54°7N 0°5W 26 D8
Flandre Europe 50°50N 2°30E 64 C2
Flathead L. U.S.A. 47°51N 114°8W 110 A4
Flattery, C. U.S.A. 48°23N 124°29W 110 A2
Fleet U.K. 51°17N 0°50W 31 D7
Fleetwood U.K. 53°55N 3°1W 27 E2
Flensburg Germany 54°47N 9°27E 64 A5
Flers France 48°47N 0°33W 66 B3
Flimby U.K. 54°42N 3°30W 26 C2
Flin Flon Canada 54°46N 101°53W 108 D9
Flinders → Australia 17°36S 140°36E 98 D7
Flinders I. Australia 40°0S 148°0E 98 H8
Flinders Ranges Australia 31°30S 138°30E 98 G6
Flint U.K. 53°15N 3°8W 28 A7
Flint U.S.A. 43°1N 83°41W 112 D6
Flint → U.S.A. 30°57N 84°34W 111 D10
Flint I. Kiribati 11°26S 151°48W 103 J12
Flintshire □ U.K. 53°17N 3°17W 28 A7
Flitwick U.K. 52°0N 0°30W 31 C8
Flodden U.K. 55°37N 2°8W 26 A4
Flora U.S.A. 38°40N 88°29W 112 F3
Florence Italy 43°46N 11°15E 68 C4
Florence U.S.A. 34°12N 79°46W 111 D11
Florencia Colombia 1°36N 75°36W 120 B2
Flores Indonesia 8°35S 121°0E 83 F6
Flores Sea Indonesia 6°30S 120°0E 83 F6
Florianópolis Brazil 27°30S 48°30W 121 E5
Florida Uruguay 34°7S 56°10W 121 F4
Florida □ U.S.A. 28°0N 82°0W 111 E10
Florida, Straits of U.S.A. 25°0N 80°0W 115 C9
Florida Keys U.S.A. 24°40N 81°0W 111 F10
Florø Norway 61°35N 5°1E 63 E5
Fly → Papua N. G. 8°25S 143°0E 98 B7
Fochabers U.K. 57°37N 3°6W 23 G11
Focșani Romania 45°41N 27°15E 65 F14
Fóggia Italy 41°27N 15°34E 68 D6
Foix France 42°58N 1°38E 66 E4

Foligno Italy 42°57N 12°42E 68 C5
Folkestone U.K. 51°5N 1°12E 31 D11
Fond-du-Lac Canada 59°19N 107°12W 108 D9
Fond du Lac U.S.A. 43°47N 88°27W 112 D3
Fongafale Tuvalu 8°31S 179°13E 99 B14
Fontainebleau France 48°24N 2°40E 66 B5
Fontenay-le-Comte France 46°28N 0°48W 66 C3
Fordham U.K. 52°19N 0°23E 31 B9
Fordingbridge U.K. 50°56N 1°47W 30 E5
Forel, Mt. Greenland 66°52N 36°55W 54 C6
Forest Row U.K. 51°5N 0°3E 31 D9
Forfar U.K. 56°39N 2°53W 23 J12
Forlì Italy 44°13N 12°3E 68 B5
Formartine U.K. 57°20N 2°15W 23 H13
Formby U.K. 53°34N 3°4W 27 E2
Formby Pt. U.K. 53°33N 3°6W 27 E2
Formentera Spain 38°43N 1°27E 67 C6
Formiga Brazil 20°27S 45°25W 122 D1
Formosa Argentina 26°15S 58°10W 121 E4
Formosa Brazil 15°32S 47°20W 122 C1
Forres U.K. 57°37N 3°37W 23 G10
Forsayth Australia 18°33S 143°34E 98 D7
Fort Albany Canada 52°15N 81°35W 109 D11
Fort Augustus U.K. 57°9N 4°42W 23 H8
Fort Chipewyan Canada 58°42N 111°8W 108 D8
Fort Collins U.S.A. 40°35N 105°5W 110 B5
Fort-Coulonge Canada 45°50N 76°45W 112 C9
Fort-de-France Martinique 14°36N 61°5W 115 E12
Fort Dodge U.S.A. 42°30N 94°11W 111 B8
Fort Good Hope Canada 66°14N 128°40W 108 C7
Fort Kent U.S.A. 47°15N 68°36W 113 B13
Fort Lauderdale U.S.A. 26°7N 80°8W 111 E10
Fort Liard Canada 60°14N 123°30W 108 C7
Fort MacKay Canada 57°12N 111°41W 108 D8
Fort Macleod Canada 49°45N 113°30W 108 E8
Fort McMurray Canada 56°44N 111°7W 108 D8
Fort McPherson Canada 67°30N 134°55W 108 C6
Fort Morgan U.S.A. 40°15N 103°48W 110 B6
Fort Myers U.S.A. 26°39N 81°52W 111 E10
Fort Nelson Canada 58°50N 122°44W 108 D7
Fort Nelson → Canada 59°32N 124°0W 108 D7
Fort Peck L. U.S.A. 48°0N 106°26W 110 A5
Fort Providence Canada 61°3N 117°40W 108 C8
Fort Resolution Canada 61°10N 113°40W 108 C8
Fort St. John Canada 56°15N 120°50W 108 D7
Fort Shevchenko Kazakhstan 44°35N 50°23E 71 F9
Fort Simpson Canada 61°45N 121°15W 108 C7
Fort Smith Canada 60°0N 111°51W 108 C8
Fort Smith U.S.A. 35°23N 94°25W 111 C8
Fort Stockton U.S.A. 30°53N 102°53W 110 D6
Fort Wayne U.S.A. 41°4N 85°9W 112 E5
Fort William U.K. 56°49N 5°7W 22 J7
Fort Worth U.S.A. 32°43N 97°19W 111 D7
Fort Yukon U.S.A. 66°34N 145°16W 108 C5
Fortaleza Brazil 3°45S 38°35W 120 C6
Forth → U.K. 56°9N 3°50W 25 B9
Forth, Firth of U.K. 56°5N 2°55W 25 B10
Fortrose U.K. 57°35N 4°9W 23 G9
Foshan China 23°3N 113°9E 79 G11
Fostoria U.S.A. 41°10N 83°25W 112 E6
Fothergill U.K. 54°43N 3°29W 26 C2
Fotheringhay U.K. 52°32N 0°27W 31 A8
Fougères France 48°21N 1°14W 66 B3
Foula U.K. 60°10N 2°5W 22 a
Foulness I. U.K. 51°36N 0°55E 31 C10
Foulness Pt. U.K. 51°37N 0°58E 31 C10
Foulsham U.K. 52°48N 0°59E 31 A10
Fountainhall U.K. 55°44N 2°53W 25 C10
Fouta Djallon Guinea 11°20N 12°10W 94 F3
Fovant U.K. 51°4N 2°0W 30 D5
Fowey U.K. 50°20N 4°39W 29 G4
Fownhope U.K. 52°0N 2°36W 30 B3
Foxe Basin Canada 66°0N 77°0W 109 C12
Foxe Chan. Canada 65°0N 80°0W 109 C11
Foxe Pen. Canada 65°0N 76°0W 109 C12
Foyle → U.K. 55°3N 7°15W 19 A7
Foyle, Lough U.K. 55°7N 7°4W 19 A7
Foynes Ireland 52°37N 9°7W 20 C4
Foz do Iguaçu Brazil 25°30S 54°30W 121 E4
Framlingham U.K. 52°14N 1°21E 31 B11
Franca Brazil 20°33S 47°30W 122 D1
France ■ Europe 47°0N 3°0E 66 C5
Franceville Gabon 1°40S 13°32E 96 E2
Franche-Comté France 46°50N 5°55E 66 C6
Francis Case, L. U.S.A. 43°4N 98°34W 110 B7
Francistown Botswana 21°7S 27°33E 97 J5
François L. Canada 54°0N 125°30W 108 D7
Frankfort Ind., U.S.A. 40°17N 86°31W 112 E4
Frankfort Ky., U.S.A. 38°12N 84°52W 112 F5
Frankfurt Brandenburg, Germany 52°20N 14°32E 64 B8
Frankfurt Hessen, Germany 50°7N 8°41E 64 C5
Fränkische Alb Germany 49°10N 11°23E 64 D6
Franklin N.H., U.S.A. 43°27N 71°39W 113 D12
Franklin Pa., U.S.A. 41°24N 79°50W 112 E8
Franklin B. Canada 69°45N 126°0W 108 C7
Franklin D. Roosevelt L. U.S.A. 48°18N 118°9W 110 A3
Franklin L. U.S.A. 40°25N 115°22W 110 B3
Franklin Mts. Canada 65°0N 125°0W 108 C7
Franklin Str. Canada 72°0N 96°0W 108 B10
Frant U.K. 51°5N 0°16E 31 D9
Franz Josef Land Arctic 82°0N 55°0E 54 A7
Fraser → Canada 49°7N 123°11W 108 E7
Fraserburgh U.K. 57°42N 2°1W 23 G13
Frederick U.S.A. 39°25N 77°25W 112 F9
Fredericksburg U.S.A. 38°18N 77°28W 112 F9
Fredericktown U.S.A. 37°34N 90°18W 112 G2
Fredericton Canada 45°57N 66°40W 113 C14
Frederikshavn Denmark 57°28N 10°31E 63 F6
Fredonia U.S.A. 42°26N 79°20W 112 D8
Fredrikstad Norway 59°13N 10°57E 63 F6
Free State □ S. Africa 28°30S 27°0E 97 K5
Freeport Bahamas 26°30N 78°47W 115 B9
Freeport Ill., U.S.A. 42°17N 89°36W 112 D3
Freeport Tex., U.S.A. 28°57N 95°21W 111 E7
Freetown S. Leone 8°30N 13°17W 94 G3
Freiburg Germany 47°59N 7°51E 64 E4
Fréjus France 43°25N 6°44E 66 E7

French Creek   Guarapuava

French Creek

French Creek → *U.S.A.* 41°24N 79°50W **112 E8**
French Guiana ☑ *S. Amer.* 4°0N 53°0W **120 B4**
French Polynesia ☑ *Pac. Oc.* 20°0S 145°0W **103 J13**
Frenchman Cr. →
  N. Amer. 48°31N 107°10W **110 A5**
Freshwater *U.K.* 50°41N 1°31W **30 E5**
Fresnillo *Mexico* 23°10N 102°53W **114 C4**
Fresno *U.S.A.* 36°44N 119°47W **110 C3**
Fria, C. *Namibia* 18°0S 12°0E **90 H5**
Fridaythorpe *U.K.* 54°2N 0°39W **27 D7**
Friedrichshafen *Germany* 47°39N 9°30E **64 E5**
Frimley *U.K.* 51°19N 0°44W **31 D7**
Frinton-on-Sea *U.K.* 51°49N 1°15E **31 C11**
Frio, C. *Brazil* 22°50S 41°50W **117 F6**
Frizington *U.K.* 54°33N 3°28W **26 C2**
Frobisher B. *Canada* 62°30N 66°0W **109 C13**
Frobisher L. *Canada* 56°20N 108°15W **108 D9**
Frodsham *U.K.* 53°18N 2°43W **27 F3**
Frome *U.K.* 51°14N 2°19W **30 D4**
Frome → *U.K.* 50°41N 2°6W **30 E4**
Front Range *U.S.A.* 40°25N 105°45W **110 B5**
Front Royal *U.S.A.* 38°55N 78°12W **112 F8**
Frutal *Brazil* 20°0S 49°0W **122 C1**
Frýdek-Místek *Czechia* 49°40N 18°20E **65 D10**
Fuchū *Japan* 34°34N 133°14E **81 F3**
Fuengirola *Spain* 36°32N 4°41W **67 D3**
Fuerte → *Mexico* 25°54N 109°22W **114 B3**
Fuerteventura *Canary Is.* 28°30N 14°0W **94 C3**
Fuidhaigh = Wiay *U.K.* 57°24N 7°13W **22 H3**
Fuji *Japan* 35°9N 138°39E **81 F6**
Fuji-San *Japan* 35°22N 138°44E **81 F6**
Fujian ☐ *China* 26°0N 118°0E **79 F12**
Fujin *China* 47°16N 132°1E **79 B15**
Fukui *Japan* 36°5N 136°10E **81 E5**
Fukuoka *Japan* 33°39N 130°21E **81 G2**
Fukushima *Japan* 37°44N 140°28E **81 E7**
Fukuyama *Japan* 34°35N 133°20E **81 F3**
Fulda *Germany* 50°32N 9°40E **64 C5**
Fulda → *Germany* 51°25N 9°39E **64 C5**
Fulton *U.S.A.* 43°19N 76°25W **112 D9**
Fulwood *U.K.* 53°47N 2°40W **27 E3**
Funabashi *Japan* 35°45N 140°0E **81 F7**
Funchal *Madeira* 32°38N 16°54W **94 B2**
Fundy, B. of *Canada* 45°0N 66°0W **113 C15**
Furnas, Represa de *Brazil* 20°50S 45°30W **122 D1**
Furneaux Group *Australia* 40°10S 147°50E **98 J8**
Fürth *Germany* 49°28N 10°59E **64 D6**
Fury and Hecla Str. *Canada* 69°56N 84°0W **109 C11**
Fushun *China* 41°50N 123°56E **79 C13**
Fustic *Barbados* 13°16N 59°38W **114 c**
Fuxin *China* 42°5N 121°48E **79 C13**
Fuyang *China* 33°0N 115°48E **79 E12**
Fuyong *China* 22°40N 113°49E **79 a**
Fuyu *Heilongjiang, China* 47°49N 124°27E **79 B13**
Fuyu *Jilin, China* 45°12N 124°43E **79 B13**
Fuyun *China* 47°0N 89°28E **78 B6**
Fuzhou *China* 26°5N 119°16E **79 F12**
Fylingdales Moor *U.K.* 54°25N 0°41W **26 D7**
Fyn *Denmark* 55°20N 10°30E **63 F6**
Fyne, L. *U.K.* 55°59N 5°23W **24 C5**

G

Gaalkacyo *Somalia* 6°30N 47°30E **89 F4**
Gabès *Tunisia* 33°53N 10°2E **95 B8**
Gabès, G. de *Tunisia* 34°0N 10°30E **95 B8**
Gabon ■ *Africa* 0°10S 10°0E **96 E2**
Gaborone *Botswana* 24°45S 25°57E **97 J5**
Gabrovo *Bulgaria* 42°52N 25°19E **69 C11**
Gachsārān *Iran* 30°15N 50°45E **87 D7**
Gadarwara *India* 22°50N 78°50E **84 H11**
Gadsden *U.S.A.* 34°1N 86°1W **111 D9**
Gafsa *Tunisia* 34°24N 8°43E **95 B7**
Găgăuzia ☐ *Moldova* 46°10N 28°40E **65 E15**
Gagnoa *Côte d'Ivoire* 6°56N 6°16W **94 G4**
Gagnon *Canada* 51°50N 68°5W **109 D13**
Gainesville *Fla., U.S.A.* 29°40N 82°20W **111 E10**
Gainesville *Ga., U.S.A.* 34°18N 83°50W **111 D10**
Gainford *U.K.* 54°34N 1°43W **26 C5**
Gainsborough *U.K.* 53°24N 0°46W **27 F7**
Gairdner, L. *Australia* 31°30S 136°0E **98 G6**
Gairloch *U.K.* 57°43N 5°41W **22 G6**
Gairloch, L. *U.K.* 57°43N 5°45W **22 G6**
Galapagos *Ecuador* 0°0 91°0W **117 D1**
Galashiels *U.K.* 55°37N 2°49W **25 C10**
Galați *Romania* 45°27N 28°2E **65 F15**
Galena *U.S.A.* 64°44N 156°56W **108 C4**
Galesburg *U.S.A.* 40°57N 90°22W **112 E2**
Galgate *U.K.* 53°59N 2°46W **27 E3**
Galicia ☐ *Spain* 42°43N 7°45W **67 A2**
Galilee, Sea of *Israel* 32°45N 35°35E **86 C3**
Galina Pt. *Jamaica* 18°24N 76°58W **114 a**
Gallan Hd. *U.K.* 58°15N 7°2W **22 F3**
Galle *Sri Lanka* 6°5N 80°10E **84 R12**
Galley Hd. *Ireland* 51°32N 8°55W **20 E5**
Gallinas, Pta. *Colombia* 12°28N 71°40W **120 A2**
Gallipoli *Italy* 38°49N 82°12W **112 F6**
Gállivare *Sweden* 67°9N 20°40E **63 D8**
Galloway *U.K.* 55°1N 4°29W **24 D7**
Galloway, Mull of *U.K.* 54°39N 4°52W **24 E6**
Gallup *U.S.A.* 35°32N 108°45W **110 C5**
Galmpton *U.K.* 50°23N 3°35W **29 G6**
Galmudug *Somalia* 6°30N 48°0E **89 F4**
Galston *U.K.* 55°36N 4°24W **24 C7**
Galty Mts. *Ireland* 52°22N 8°10W **20 D6**
Galtymore *Ireland* 52°21N 8°11W **20 D6**
Galveston *U.S.A.* 29°18N 94°48W **111 E8**
Galway *Ireland* 53°17N 9°3W **20 B4**
Galway ☐ *Ireland* 53°22N 9°1W **20 B4**
Galway B. *Ireland* 53°13N 9°10W **20 B4**
Gambia ■ *W. Afr.* 13°25N 16°0W **94 F2**
Gambia → *W. Afr.* 13°28N 16°34W **94 F2**
Gamlingay *U.K.* 52°10N 0°11W **31 B8**
Gan Jiang → *China* 29°15N 116°0E **79 F12**
Gananoque *Canada* 44°20N 76°10W **113 C9**
Gäncä *Azerbaijan* 40°45N 46°20E **71 F8**
Gand = Gent *Belgium* 51°2N 3°42E **64 C2**
Gand → *India* 20°0N 75°40E **85 G14**
Gandhi Sagar *India* 24°40N 75°40E **84 G9**

Gandia *Spain* 38°58N 0°9W **67 C5**
Ganganagar *India* 29°56N 73°56E **84 E8**
Gangdisê Shan *China* 31°20N 81°0E **78 E5**
Ganges → *India* 23°20N 90°30E **85 H17**
Gangneung *S. Korea* 37°45N 128°54E **79 D14**
Gangtok *India* 27°20N 88°37E **85 F16**
Gannett Peak *U.S.A.* 43°11N 109°39W **110 B5**
Gansu ☐ *China* 36°0N 104°0E **78 D9**
Ganzhou *China* 25°51N 114°56E **79 F11**
Gao *Mali* 16°15N 0°5W **94 E5**
Gap *France* 44°33N 6°5E **66 D7**
Gar *China* 32°10N 79°58E **78 E4**
Garanhuns *Brazil* 8°50S 36°30W **122 A3**
Garboldisham *U.K.* 52°23N 0°57E **31 B10**
Garda, L. di *Italy* 45°40N 10°41E **68 B4**
Garden City *U.S.A.* 37°58N 100°53W **110 C6**
Gardēz *Afghan.* 33°37N 69°9E **87 C12**
Gare L. *U.K.* 56°1N 4°50W **24 B6**
Garforth *U.K.* 53°47N 1°24W **27 E6**
Gargrave *U.K.* 53°59N 2°7W **27 E4**
Garioch *U.K.* 57°18N 2°40W **23 H12**
Garissa *Kenya* 0°25S 39°40E **96 E7**
Garoowe *Somalia* 8°25N 48°33E **89 F4**
Garoua *Cameroon* 9°19N 13°21E **95 G8**
Garron Pt. *U.K.* 55°3N 5°59W **19 A10**
Garry → *U.K.* 56°44N 3°47W **23 J10**
Garry, L. *Canada* 65°58N 100°18W **108 C9**
Garsdale Head *U.K.* 54°20N 2°20W **26 D4**
Garstang *U.K.* 53°55N 2°46W **27 E3**
Gary *U.S.A.* 41°36N 87°20W **112 E4**
Garzê *China* 31°38N 100°1E **78 E9**
Gascogne *France* 43°45N 0°20E **66 E4**
Gascogne, G. de *Europe* 44°0N 2°0W **66 D2**
Gashua *Nigeria* 12°54N 11°0E **95 F8**
Gaspé *Canada* 48°52N 64°30W **109 E13**
Gaspé, C. de *Canada* 48°48N 64°7W **113 A15**
Gaspésie, Pén. de la *Canada* 48°45N 65°40W **113 A15**
Gata, Sierra de *Spain* 40°20N 6°45W **67 B2**
Gatehouse of Fleet *U.K.* 54°53N 4°12W **24 E7**
Gateshead *U.K.* 54°57N 1°35W **26 C5**
Gatineau *Canada* 45°29N 75°39W **113 C10**
Gatineau → *Canada* 45°27N 75°42W **113 C10**
Gatley *U.K.* 53°24N 2°15W **27 F4**
Gävle *Sweden* 60°40N 17°9E **63 E7**
Gawilgarh Hills *India* 21°15N 76°45E **84 J10**
Gawthwaite *U.K.* 54°16N 3°8W **26 D2**
Gaxun Nur *China* 42°22N 100°30E **78 C9**
Gaya *India* 24°47N 85°4E **85 G14**
Gaylord *U.S.A.* 45°2N 84°41W **112 C5**
Gayton *U.K.* 52°45N 0°36E **31 A10**
Gaywood *U.K.* 52°46N 0°26E **31 A9**
Gaza *Gaza Strip* 31°30N 34°28E **86 D3**
Gaza Strip ☐ *Asia* 31°29N 34°25E **86 D3**
Gaziantep *Turkey* 37°6N 37°23E **71 G6**
Gdańsk *Poland* 54°22N 18°40E **65 A10**
Gdynia *Poland* 54°35N 18°33E **65 A10**
Gebze *Turkey* 40°47N 29°25E **71 F4**
Gedaref *Sudan* 14°2N 35°28E **95 F13**
Gedney *U.K.* 52°48N 0°4E **27 G9**
Gedser *Denmark* 54°35N 11°55E **63 G6**
Geelong *Australia* 38°10S 144°22E **98 H7**
Gejiu *China* 23°20N 103°10E **78 G9**
Gela *Italy* 37°4N 14°15E **68 F6**
Gelibolu *Turkey* 40°28N 26°43E **71 F4**
Gelsenkirchen *Germany* 51°32N 7°6E **64 C4**
General Acha *Argentina* 37°20S 64°38W **121 F3**
General Alvear *Argentina* 35°0S 67°40W **121 F3**
General Carrera, L. *S. Amer.* 46°35S 72°0W **121 G2**
General Pico *Argentina* 35°45S 63°50W **121 F3**
General Santos *Phil.* 6°5N 125°14E **83 C4**
Geneva *Switz.* 46°12N 6°9E **64 E4**
Geneva *U.S.A.* 42°52N 76°59W **112 D9**
Geneva, L. = Léman, L. *Europe* 46°26N 6°30E **64 E4**
Gennargentu, Mti. del *Italy* 40°1N 9°19E **68 D3**
Genoa *Italy* 44°25N 8°57E **68 D3**
Génova, G. di *Italy* 44°0N 9°0E **68 C3**
Gent *Belgium* 51°2N 3°42E **64 C2**
George *S. Africa* 33°58S 22°29E **97 L4**
George → *Canada* 58°49N 66°10W **109 D13**
George, L. *U.S.A.* 29°17N 81°36W **111 E10**
George Town *Cayman Is.* 19°20N 81°24W **114 D8**
George Town *Malaysia* 5°25N 100°20E **82 C2**
George V Land *Antarctica* 69°0S 148°0E **55 C10**
Georgetown *Guyana* 6°50N 58°12W **120 B4**
Georgetown *Ky., U.S.A.* 38°13N 84°33W **112 F5**
Georgetown *S.C., U.S.A.* 33°23N 79°17W **111 D11**
Georgia ☐ *U.S.A.* 32°50N 83°15W **111 D10**
Georgia ■ *Asia* 42°0N 43°0E **71 F7**
Georgian B. *Canada* 45°15N 81°0W **112 C7**
Georgiyevsk *Russia* 44°12N 43°28E **71 F7**
Gera *Germany* 50°53N 12°4E **64 C7**
Geraldton *Australia* 28°48S 114°32E **98 F1**
Germany ■ *Europe* 51°0N 10°0E **64 C6**
Germiston *S. Africa* 26°13S 28°10E **97 K5**
Gerrans B. *U.K.* 50°12N 4°57W **29 G4**
Gerrards Cross *U.K.* 51°35N 0°33W **31 C7**
Getafe *Spain* 40°18N 3°43W **67 B4**
Ghadāmis *Libya* 30°11N 9°29E **95 B8**
Ghaghara → *India* 25°45N 84°40E **85 G14**
Ghana ■ *W. Afr.* 8°0N 1°0W **94 G5**
Ghardaïa *Algeria* 32°20N 3°37E **94 B6**
Gharyān *Libya* 32°10N 13°0E **95 B8**
Ghats, Eastern *India* 14°0N 78°50E **84 N11**
Ghats, Western *India* 14°0N 75°0E **84 N9**
Ghazal, Bahr el → *Chad* 13°0N 15°47E **95 F9**
Ghazal, Bahr el →
  South Sudan 9°31N 30°25E **95 G12**
Ghaziabad *India* 28°42N 77°26E **84 E10**
Ghazipur *India* 25°38N 83°35E **85 G13**
Ghazni *Afghan.* 33°30N 68°28E **87 C12**
Ghent = Gent *Belgium* 51°2N 3°42E **64 C2**
Giant's Causeway *U.K.* 55°16N 6°29W **19 A9**
Gibraltar ☑ *Europe* 36°7N 5°22W **67 D3**
Gibraltar, Str. of *Medit. S.* 35°55N 5°40W **67 E3**
Gibraltar Pt. *U.K.* 53°6N 0°19E **27 F9**
Gibson Desert *Australia* 24°0S 126°0E **98 E4**
Gifu *Japan* 35°30N 136°45E **81 F5**
Gigglewick *U.K.* 54°5N 2°17W **26 D4**
Gigha *U.K.* 55°42N 5°44W **24 C4**
Gijón *Spain* 43°32N 5°42W **67 A3**

Gila → *U.S.A.* 32°43N 114°33W **110 D4**
Gīlān ☐ *Iran* 37°0N 50°0E **86 B7**
Gilbert Is. *Kiribati* 1°0N 172°0E **102 G9**
Gilgit *India* 35°50N 74°15E **84 B9**
Gilgit-Baltistan ☐ *Pakistan* 36°30N 73°0E **84 B9**
Gillam *Canada* 56°20N 94°40W **108 D10**
Gillingham *Dorset, U.K.* 51°2N 2°16E **30 D4**
Gillingham *Medway, U.K.* 51°23N 0°33E **31 D10**
Gilsland *U.K.* 55°0N 2°34W **26 C3**
Gimie, Mt. *St. Lucia* 13°54N 61°0W **114 b**
Girdle Ness *U.K.* 57°9N 2°3W **23 H13**
Giresun *Turkey* 40°55N 38°30E **71 F6**
Girga *Egypt* 26°17N 31°55E **95 C12**
Girona *Spain* 41°58N 2°46E **67 B7**
Gironde → *France* 45°32N 1°7W **66 D3**
Girvan *U.K.* 55°14N 4°51W **24 D6**
Gisborne *N.Z.* 38°39S 178°5E **99 H14**
Gisburn *U.K.* 53°56N 2°16W **27 E4**
Gitega *Burundi* 3°26S 29°56E **96 E5**
Gizhiga *Russia* 62°3N 160°30E **77 C17**
Gjoa Haven *Canada* 68°38N 95°53W **108 C10**
Glace Bay *Canada* 46°11N 59°58W **113 B18**
Glacier Nat. Park △ *U.S.A.* 48°42N 113°48W **110 A4**
Gladstone *Australia* 23°52S 151°16E **98 E9**
Gladstone *U.S.A.* 45°51N 87°1W **112 C4**
Gladwin *U.S.A.* 43°59N 84°29W **112 D5**
Glamorgan, Vale of ☐ *U.K.* 51°28N 3°25W **29 E7**
Glanaruddery Mts. *Ireland* 52°20N 9°27W **20 D3**
Glanton *U.K.* 55°26N 1°54W **26 B5**
Glasgow *U.K.* 55°51N 4°15W **24 C7**
Glasgow *Ky., U.S.A.* 37°0N 85°55W **112 G5**
Glasgow *Mont., U.S.A.* 48°12N 106°38W **110 A5**
Glasgow Int. ✈ (GLA) *U.K.* 55°51N 4°21W **24 C7**
Glastonbury *U.K.* 51°9N 2°43W **30 D3**
Glazov *Russia* 58°9N 52°40E **70 C9**
Glemsford *U.K.* 52°6N 0°40E **31 B10**
Glen → *U.K.* 52°51N 0°7W **27 G8**
Glen Affric *U.K.* 57°17N 5°1W **22 H7**
Glen Almond *U.K.* 56°28N 3°50W **25 B8**
Glen Coe *U.K.* 56°40N 5°0W **22 J7**
Glen Etive *U.K.* 56°37N 5°0W **24 A5**
Glen Garry *Highl., U.K.* 57°3N 5°7W **22 H6**
Glen Garry *Perth & Kinr., U.K.* 56°47N 4°5W **23 J9**
Glen Mor *U.K.* 57°9N 4°37W **23 H8**
Glen Moriston *U.K.* 57°11N 4°52W **23 H8**
Glen Orchy *U.K.* 56°27N 4°52W **24 B6**
Glen Orrin *U.K.* 57°31N 4°45W **23 G8**
Glen Oykel *U.K.* 58°5N 4°50W **23 F8**
Glen Roy *U.K.* 56°56N 4°50W **23 J8**
Glen Shee *U.K.* 56°50N 3°28W **23 J11**
Glen Shiel *U.K.* 57°9N 5°18W **22 H6**
Glen Spean *U.K.* 56°53N 4°40W **23 J8**
Glenamaddy *Ireland* 53°37N 8°33W **18 D4**
Glendale *Ariz., U.S.A.* 33°32N 112°11W **110 D4**
Glendale *Calif., U.S.A.* 34°9N 118°15W **110 D3**
Glendive *U.S.A.* 47°7N 104°43W **110 A6**
Gleneagles *U.K.* 56°17N 3°43W **25 B8**
Glenfinnan *U.K.* 56°53N 5°27W **22 J7**
Glengarriff *Ireland* 51°45N 9°34W **20 E3**
Glenkens, The *U.K.* 55°12N 4°12W **24 D7**
Glenluce *U.K.* 54°52N 4°48W **24 E6**
Glennallen *U.S.A.* 62°7N 145°33W **108 C5**
Glenrothes *U.K.* 56°12N 3°10W **25 B9**
Glens Falls *U.S.A.* 43°19N 73°39W **113 D11**
Glenties *Ireland* 54°48N 8°17W **18 B5**
Glenveagh △ *Ireland* 55°3N 7°54W **18 A6**
Gliwice *Poland* 50°22N 18°41E **65 C10**
Globe *U.S.A.* 33°24N 110°47W **110 D4**
Głogów *Poland* 51°37N 16°5E **64 C9**
Glomma → *Norway* 59°12N 10°57E **63 F6**
Glossop *U.K.* 53°27N 1°56W **27 F5**
Gloucester *U.K.* 51°53N 2°15W **30 C4**
Gloucestershire ☐ *U.K.* 51°46N 2°15W **30 C4**
Gloversville *U.S.A.* 43°3N 74°21W **113 D10**
Glyn Ebwy = Ebbw Vale *U.K.* 51°46N 3°12W **28 D7**
Gniezno *Poland* 52°30N 17°35E **65 B9**
Goa ☐ *India* 15°33N 73°59E **84 M8**
Goa *India* 15°33N 73°59E **84 M8**
Goat Fell *U.K.* 55°38N 5°11W **24 C5**
Gobi *Asia* 44°0N 110°0E **79 C10**
Godalming *U.K.* 51°11N 0°36W **31 D7**
Godavari → *India* 16°25N 82°18E **85 L13**
Goderich *Canada* 43°45N 81°41W **112 D7**
Godhra *India* 22°49N 73°40E **84 H8**
Godmanchester *U.K.* 52°20N 0°11W **31 B8**
Godoy Cruz *Argentina* 32°56S 68°52W **121 F3**
Gods → *Canada* 56°22N 92°51W **108 D10**
Gods L. *Canada* 54°40N 94°15W **108 D10**
Godshill *U.K.* 50°38N 1°15W **30 E6**
Gogama *Canada* 47°35N 81°43W **112 B7**
Goiânia *Brazil* 16°43S 49°20W **122 C1**
Goiás *Brazil* 15°55S 50°10W **120 D4**
Goiás ☐ *Brazil* 12°10S 48°0W **122 B1**
Goio-Erê *Brazil* 24°12S 53°1W **121 E4**
Gold Coast *Australia* 28°0S 153°25E **98 F9**
Gold Coast *W. Afr.* 4°0N 1°40W **94 H5**
Golden Vale *Ireland* 52°33N 8°17W **20 D6**
Goldsboro *U.S.A.* 35°23N 77°59W **111 C11**
Golestān ☐ *Iran* 37°20N 55°25E **87 B8**
Golmud *China* 36°25N 94°55E **78 C7**
Golspie *U.K.* 57°58N 3°59W **23 G10**
Goma *Dem. Rep. of the Congo* 1°37S 29°10E **96 E5**
Gomel *Belarus* 52°28N 31°0E **65 B16**
Gomera *Canary Is.* 28°7N 17°14W **94 C2**
Gómez Palacio *Mexico* 25°34N 103°30W **114 B4**
Gonābād *Iran* 34°15N 58°45E **87 C9**
Gonaïves *Haiti* 19°20N 72°42W **115 D10**
Gonda *India* 27°9N 81°58E **85 F12**
Gonder *Ethiopia* 12°39N 37°30E **89 E2**
Gongbei *China* 22°13N 113°32E **79 a**
Gongga Shan *China* 29°40N 101°55E **78 F9**
Good Hope, C. of *S. Africa* 34°24S 18°30E **97 L3**
Goodrich *U.K.* 51°52N 2°37W **30 C3**
Goodwood *U.K.* 50°53N 0°44W **31 E7**
Goole *U.K.* 53°42N 0°53W **27 E7**
Goose L. *U.S.A.* 41°56N 120°26W **110 B2**

Gorakhpur *India* 26°47N 83°23E **85 F13**
Gordon *U.K.* 55°41N 2°35W **25 C10**
Gore *Ethiopia* 8°12N 35°32E **89 F2**
Gorebridge *U.K.* 55°50N 3°2W **25 C9**
Gorey *Ireland* 52°41N 6°18W **21 C10**
Gorgān *Iran* 36°55N 54°30E **87 B8**
Goring *U.K.* 51°31N 1°7W **30 C6**
Goring-by-Sea *U.K.* 50°49N 0°24W **31 E8**
Gorleston-on-Sea *U.K.* 52°35N 1°44E **31 A12**
Görlitz *Germany* 51°9N 14°58E **64 C8**
Gorno-Altay ☐ *Russia* 51°0N 86°0E **76 D9**
Gorontalo *Indonesia* 0°35N 123°5E **83 D6**
Gort *Ireland* 53°3N 8°49W **20 B5**
Gorzów Wielkopolski *Poland* 52°43N 15°15E **64 B8**
Gosberton *U.K.* 52°53N 0°9W **27 G8**
Gosforth *U.K.* 54°26N 3°27W **26 D2**
Gosport *U.K.* 50°48N 1°9W **30 E6**
Göta kanal *Sweden* 58°30N 15°58E **63 F7**
Götaland *Sweden* 57°30N 14°30E **63 F6**
Göteborg *Sweden* 57°43N 11°59E **63 F6**
Gotha *Germany* 50°56N 10°42E **64 C6**
Gothenburg = Göteborg
  Sweden 57°43N 11°59E **63 F6**
Gotland *Sweden* 57°30N 18°33E **63 F7**
Gotō-Rettō *Japan* 32°55N 129°5E **81 G1**
Göttingen *Germany* 51°31N 9°55E **64 C5**
Gouda *Neths.* 52°1N 4°42E **64 B3**
Goudhurst *U.K.* 51°6N 0°29E **31 D9**
Gouin, Rés. *Canada* 48°35N 74°40W **113 A10**
Goulburn *Australia* 34°44S 149°44E **98 G8**
Goundam *Mali* 16°27N 3°40W **94 E5**
Gourock *U.K.* 55°57N 4°49W **24 C6**
Governador Valadares
  Brazil 18°15S 41°57W **122 C2**
Gower *U.K.* 51°35N 4°10W **29 D5**
Gowna, L. *Ireland* 53°51N 7°34W **18 D6**
Goya *Argentina* 29°10S 59°10W **121 E4**
Gozo *Malta* 36°3N 14°15E **68 a**
Graaff-Reinet *S. Africa* 32°13S 24°32E **97 L4**
Gracias a Dios, C. *Honduras* 15°0N 83°10W **115 E8**
Grafham Water *U.K.* 52°19N 0°18W **31 B8**
Grafton *Australia* 29°38S 152°58E **98 F9**
Grafton *U.S.A.* 48°25N 97°25W **111 A7**
Graham Land *Antarctica* 65°0S 64°0W **55 C17**
Grahamstown *S. Africa* 33°19S 26°31E **97 L5**
Grain L. *W. Afr.* 4°20N 10°0W **94 H3**
Grainthorpe *U.K.* 53°27N 0°5E **27 F9**
Grampian Mts. *U.K.* 56°50N 4°0W **23 J9**
Gran Canaria *Canary Is.* 27°55N 15°35W **94 C2**
Gran Chaco *S. Amer.* 25°0S 61°0W **121 E3**
Gran Sasso d'Itália *Italy* 42°27N 13°42E **68 C5**
Granada *Nic.* 11°58N 86°0W **114 E7**
Granada *Spain* 37°10N 3°35W **67 D4**
Granard *Ireland* 53°47N 7°30W **18 D6**
Granby *Canada* 45°25N 72°45W **113 C11**
Grand → *U.S.A.* 45°40N 100°45W **110 A6**
Grand Bahama I. *Bahamas* 26°40N 78°30W **115 B9**
Grand Canyon *U.S.A.* 36°3N 112°9W **110 C4**
Grand Canyon Nat. Park △
  U.S.A. 36°15N 112°30W **110 C4**
Grand Cayman *Cayman Is.* 19°20N 81°20W **115 D8**
Grand Falls *Canada* 47°3N 67°44W **109 E13**
Grand Falls-Windsor
  Canada 48°56N 55°40W **109 E14**
Grand Forks *U.S.A.* 47°55N 97°3W **111 A7**
Grand Haven *U.S.A.* 43°4N 86°13W **112 D4**
Grand Island *U.S.A.* 40°55N 98°21W **110 B7**
Grand Junction *U.S.A.* 39°4N 108°33W **110 C5**
Grand L. *Canada* 45°57N 66°7W **113 C14**
Grand Manan I. *Canada* 44°45N 66°52W **113 C14**
Grand-Mère *Canada* 46°36N 72°40W **113 B11**
Grand Rapids *Canada* 53°12N 99°19W **108 D10**
Grand Rapids *U.S.A.* 42°58N 85°40W **112 D4**
Grand St-Bernard, Col du
  Europe 45°50N 7°10E **64 F4**
Grand Teton *U.S.A.* 43°54N 110°50W **110 B4**
Grande → *Bolivia* 15°51S 64°39W **120 D3**
Grande → *Brazil* 11°30S 44°30W **122 B2**
Grande, B. *Argentina* 50°30S 68°20W **121 H3**
Grande, Rio → *N. Amer.* 25°58N 97°9W **111 E7**
Grande Baleine → *Canada* 55°16N 77°47W **109 D12**
Grande Prairie *Canada* 55°10N 118°50W **108 D8**
Grange-over-Sands *U.K.* 54°12N 2°54W **26 D3**
Grangemouth *U.K.* 56°1N 3°42W **25 B9**
Grangeville *U.S.A.* 45°56N 116°7W **110 A3**
Grantham *U.K.* 52°55N 0°38W **27 G7**
Grantown-on-Spey *U.K.* 57°20N 3°36W **23 H10**
Grants Pass *U.S.A.* 42°26N 123°19W **110 B2**
Granville *U.S.A.* 43°24N 73°16W **113 D11**
Grasmere *U.K.* 54°28N 3°1W **26 D2**
Grasse *France* 43°38N 6°56E **66 E7**
Grassington *U.K.* 54°5N 1°59W **26 D5**
Graulhet *France* 43°45N 1°59E **66 E4**
Gravesend *U.K.* 51°26N 0°22E **31 D9**
Grayling *U.S.A.* 44°40N 84°43W **112 C5**
Grayrigg *U.K.* 54°23N 2°39W **26 D3**
Grays *U.S.A.* 51°28N 0°21E **31 D9**
Graz *Austria* 47°4N 15°27E **64 E8**
Great Australian Bight
  Australia 33°30S 130°0E **98 G5**
Great Ayton *U.K.* 54°30N 1°8W **26 D6**
Great Baddow *U.K.* 51°43N 0°31E **31 C10**
Great Barrier Reef *Australia* 18°0S 146°50E **98 D8**
Great Basin *U.S.A.* 40°0N 117°0W **110 B3**
Great Bear → *Canada* 65°0N 126°0W **108 C7**
Great Bear L. *Canada* 65°30N 120°0W **108 B7**
Great Bend *U.S.A.* 38°22N 98°46W **110 C7**
Great Bentley *U.K.* 51°51N 1°4E **31 C11**
Great Blasket I. *Ireland* 52°6N 10°32W **20 D1**
Great Britain *Europe* 54°0N 2°15W **62 D5**
Great Broughton *U.K.* 54°26N 1°9W **26 D6**
Great Chesterford *U.K.* 52°4N 0°13E **31 B9**
Great Clifton *U.K.* 54°39N 3°29W **26 D2**
Great Dividing Ra. *Australia* 23°0S 146°0E **98 E8**
Great Dunmow *U.K.* 51°52N 0°23E **31 C9**
Great Exuma I. *Bahamas* 23°30N 75°50W **115 C9**
Great Falls *U.S.A.* 47°30N 111°17W **110 A4**
Great Glen = Glen Mor *U.K.* 57°9N 4°37W **23 H8**
Great Harwood *U.K.* 53°47N 2°24W **27 E4**
Great Inagua I. *Bahamas* 21°0N 73°20W **115 C10**

Great Karoo *S. Africa* 31°55S 21°0E **97 L4**
Great Khingan Mts. *China* 48°0N 121°0E **79 B13**
Great Malvern *U.K.* 52°7N 2°18W **30 B4**
Great Massingham *U.K.* 52°47N 0°40E **31 A10**
Great Missenden *U.K.* 51°42N 0°41W **31 C7**
Great Ormes Head *U.K.* 53°20N 3°52W **28 A6**
Great Ouse → *U.K.* 52°48N 0°21E **31 A9**
Great Pedro Bluff *Jamaica* 17°51N 77°44W **114 a**
Great Plains *N. Amer.* 47°0N 105°0W **110 A6**
Great Salt Desert *Iran* 34°30N 55°0E **87 C8**
Great Salt L. *U.S.A.* 41°15N 112°40W **110 B4**
Great Salt Lake Desert
  U.S.A. 40°50N 113°30W **110 B4**
Great Sandy Desert *Australia* 21°0S 124°0E **98 E3**
Great Sandy Desert *U.S.A.* 43°35N 120°15W **110 B2**
Great Shefford *U.K.* 51°28N 1°28W **30 D6**
Great Shelford *U.K.* 52°9N 0°8E **31 B9**
Great Shunner Fell *U.K.* 54°22N 2°14W **26 D4**
Great Skellig *Ireland* 51°47N 10°33W **20 E1**
Great Slave L. *Canada* 61°23N 115°38W **108 C8**
Great Snow Mt. *Canada* 57°26N 124°0W **108 D7**
Great Torrington *U.K.* 50°57N 4°9W **29 F5**
Great Victoria Desert
  Australia 29°30S 126°30E **98 F4**
Great Wall of China *China* 38°30N 109°30E **79 D10**
Great Waltham *U.K.* 51°47N 0°28E **31 C9**
Great Whernside *U.K.* 54°10N 1°58W **26 D5**
Great Yarmouth *U.K.* 52°37N 1°44E **31 A12**
Greater Antilles *W. Indies* 17°40N 74°0W **115 D10**
Greater London ☐ *U.K.* 51°31N 0°6W **31 C8**
Greater Manchester ☐ *U.K.* 53°30N 2°17W **27 F4**
Greater Sudbury *Canada* 46°30N 81°0W **112 B7**
Greater Sunda Is. *Indonesia* 7°0S 112°0E **82 F4**
Greatham *U.K.* 54°39N 1°14W **26 C6**
Greece ■ *Europe* 40°0N 23°0E **69 E9**
Greeley *U.S.A.* 40°25N 104°42W **110 B6**
Greely Fd. *Canada* 80°30N 85°0W **109 A11**
Green → *Ky., U.S.A.* 37°54N 87°30W **112 G4**
Green → *Utah, U.S.A.* 38°11N 109°53W **110 C5**
Green B. *U.S.A.* 45°0N 87°30W **112 C4**
Green Bay *U.S.A.* 44°31N 88°0W **112 C4**
Green Hammerton *U.K.* 54°1N 1°18W **27 D6**
Green River *U.S.A.* 41°32N 109°28W **110 B5**
Greencastle *U.S.A.* 39°38N 86°52W **112 F4**
Greenfield *Ind., U.S.A.* 39°47N 85°46W **112 F5**
Greenfield *Mass., U.S.A.* 42°35N 72°36W **113 D11**
Greenhead *U.K.* 54°59N 2°30W **26 C3**
Greenland ☑ *N. Amer.* 66°0N 45°0W **54 C5**
Greenland Sea *Arctic* 73°0N 10°0W **54 B7**
Greenlaw *U.K.* 55°43N 2°27W **25 C11**
Greenock *U.K.* 55°57N 4°46W **24 C6**
Greenodd *U.K.* 54°14N 3°4W **26 D2**
Greenore *Ireland* 54°1N 6°9W **19 B9**
Greenore Pt. *Ireland* 52°14N 6°19W **21 D10**
Greensboro *U.S.A.* 36°4N 79°48W **111 C11**
Greensburg *Ind., U.S.A.* 39°20N 85°29W **112 F5**
Greensburg *Pa., U.S.A.* 40°18N 79°33W **112 E8**
Greenstone Pt. *U.K.* 57°55N 5°37W **22 G6**
Greenville *Ala., U.S.A.* 31°50N 86°38W **111 D9**
Greenville *Maine, U.S.A.* 45°28N 69°35W **113 C13**
Greenville *Mich., U.S.A.* 43°11N 85°15W **112 D5**
Greenville *Miss., U.S.A.* 33°24N 91°4W **111 D8**
Greenville *Ohio, U.S.A.* 40°6N 84°38W **112 E5**
Greenville *S.C., U.S.A.* 34°51N 82°24W **111 D10**
Greenwich ☐ *U.K.* 51°29N 0°1E **31 D9**
Greenwood *U.S.A.* 33°31N 90°11W **111 D8**
Gremikha *Russia* 67°59N 39°47E **70 A6**
Grenada ■ *W. Indies* 12°10N 61°40W **115 E12**
Grenoble *France* 45°12N 5°42E **66 D6**
Greta → *U.K.* 54°9N 2°37W **26 D3**
Gretna *U.K.* 55°0N 3°3W **25 D9**
Gretna Green *U.K.* 55°1N 3°3W **25 D9**
Gretton *U.K.* 52°33N 0°40W **31 A7**
Grey Ra. *Australia* 27°0S 143°30E **98 F7**
Greymouth *N.Z.* 42°29S 171°13E **99 J13**
Greystoke *U.K.* 54°41N 2°51W **26 C3**
Greystones *Ireland* 53°9N 6°5W **21 B10**
Griffith *Australia* 34°18S 146°2E **98 G8**
Grimsay *U.K.* 57°29N 7°14W **22 H3**
Grimsby *U.K.* 53°34N 0°5W **27 E8**
Griomasaigh = Grimsay *U.K.* 57°29N 7°14W **22 H3**
Gris-Nez, C. *France* 50°52N 1°35E **66 A4**
Grise Fiord *Canada* 76°25N 82°57W **109 B11**
Grizebeck *U.K.* 54°16N 3°10W **26 D2**
Groningen *Neths.* 53°15N 6°35E **64 B4**
Groote Eylandt *Australia* 14°0S 136°40E **98 C6**
Gros Islet *St. Lucia* 14°5N 60°58W **114 b**
Gros Piton *St. Lucia* 13°49N 61°5W **114 b**
Gros Piton Pt. *St. Lucia* 13°49N 61°5W **114 b**
Grosseto *Italy* 42°46N 11°8E **68 C4**
Grossglockner *Austria* 47°5N 12°40E **64 E7**
Groundhog → *Canada* 48°45N 82°58W **112 A6**
Groznyy *Russia* 43°20N 45°45E **71 F8**
Grudziądz *Poland* 53°30N 18°47E **65 B10**
Gruinard B. *U.K.* 57°56N 5°35W **22 G6**
Guadalajara *Mexico* 20°40N 103°20W **114 C4**
Guadalajara *Spain* 40°37N 3°12W **67 B4**
Guadalcanal *Solomon Is.* 9°32S 160°12E **99 B11**
Guadalete → *Spain* 36°35N 6°13W **67 D2**
Guadalquivir → *Spain* 36°47N 6°22W **67 D2**
Guadarrama, Sierra de *Spain* 41°0N 4°0W **67 B4**
Guadeloupe ☑ *W. Indies* 16°15N 61°40W **115 D12**
Guadiana → *Portugal* 37°14N 7°22W **67 D2**
Guadix *Spain* 37°18N 3°11W **67 D4**
Guafo, Boca del *Chile* 43°35S 74°0W **121 G2**
Guajará-Mirim *Brazil* 10°50S 65°20W **120 D3**
Guajira, Pen. de la *Colombia* 12°0N 72°0W **120 A2**
Gualeguaychú *Argentina* 33°3S 59°31W **121 F4**
Guam ☑ *Pac. Oc.* 13°27N 144°45E **102 F6**
Guamúchil *Mexico* 25°28N 108°6W **114 B3**
Guanajuato *Mexico* 21°1N 101°15W **114 C4**
Guane *Cuba* 22°10N 84°7W **115 C8**
Guangdong ☐ *China* 23°0N 113°0E **79 G11**
Guangxi Zhuang ☐ *China* 24°0N 109°0E **79 G10**
Guangyuan *China* 32°26N 105°51E **78 E10**
Guangzhou *China* 23°6N 113°13E **79 G11**
Guantánamo *Cuba* 20°10N 75°14W **115 C9**
Guantánamo B. *Cuba* 19°59N 75°10W **115 D9**
Guaporé → *Brazil* 11°55S 65°4W **120 D3**
Guaqui *Bolivia* 16°41S 68°54W **120 D3**
Guarapuava *Brazil* 25°20S 51°30W **121 E4**

170 INDEX

Guaratinguetá Hungerford

Guaratinguetá Brazil 22°49S 45°9W 122 D1
Guarulhos Brazil 23°29S 46°33W 122 D1
Guatemala Guatemala 14°40N 90°22W 114 E6
Guatemala ■ Cent. Amer. 15°40N 90°30W 114 D6
Guaviare → Colombia 4°3N 67°44W 120 B3
Guaxupé Brazil 21°10S 47°5W 122 D1
Guayaquil Ecuador 2°15S 79°52W 120 C2
Guayaquil, G. de Ecuador 3°10S 81°0W 120 C1
Guaymas Mexico 27°56N 110°54W 114 B2
Gubkin Russia 51°17N 37°32E 71 D6
Guelmim Morocco 28°56N 10°0W 94 C3
Guelph Canada 43°35N 80°20W 112 D7
Guéret France 46°11N 1°51E 66 C4
Guernsey U.K. 49°26N 2°35W 29 J8
Guestling Green U.K. 50°53N 0°39E 31 E10
Guiana Highlands S. Amer. 5°10N 60°40W 117 C4
Guidónia-Montecélio Italy 42°1N 12°45E 68 C5
Guildford U.K. 51°14N 0°34W 31 D7
Guilin China 25°18N 110°15E 79 F11
Guinea ■ W. Afr. 10°20N 11°30W 94 F3
Guinea, Gulf of Atl. Oc. 3°0N 2°30E 90 F4
Guinea-Bissau ■ Africa 12°0N 15°0W 94 F3
Güines Cuba 22°50N 82°0W 115 C8
Guingamp France 48°34N 3°10W 66 B2
Guisborough U.K. 54°33N 1°4W 26 C6
Guiyang China 26°32N 106°40E 78 F10
Guizhou □ China 27°0N 107°0E 78 F10
Gujarat □ India 23°20N 71°0E 84 H7
Gujranwala Pakistan 32°10N 74°12E 84 C9
Gujrat Pakistan 32°40N 74°2E 84 C9
Gulf, The = Persian Gulf Asia 27°0N 50°0E 87 E7
Gulfport U.S.A. 30°22N 89°6W 111 D9
Gulian China 52°56N 122°21E 79 A13
Gulu Uganda 2°48N 32°17E 96 D6
Guna India 24°40N 77°19E 84 G10
Gunnison → U.S.A. 39°4N 108°35W 110 C5
Gunsan S. Korea 35°59N 126°45E 79 D14
Guntur India 16°23N 80°30E 85 L12
Gurbantünggüt Desert China 45°8N 87°20E 78 B6
Gurgueia → Brazil 6°50S 43°24W 120 C5
Guri, Embalse de Venezuela 7°50N 62°52W 120 B3
Gurkha Nepal 28°5N 84°40E 85 E14
Gurnard's Hd. U.K. 50°11N 5°37W 29 G2
Gürün Turkey 38°43N 37°15E 71 G6
Gurupi Brazil 11°43S 49°4W 122 B1
Gurupi → Brazil 1°13S 46°6W 120 C5
Gurvan Sayhan Uul Mongolia 43°50N 104°0E 78 C9
Gusau Nigeria 12°12N 6°40E 94 F7
Guwahati India 26°10N 91°45E 85 F17
Guyana ■ S. Amer. 5°0N 59°0W 120 B4
Guyenne France 44°30N 0°40E 66 D4
Gwādar Pakistan 25°10N 62°18E 84 G3
Gwalchmai U.K. 53°16N 4°25W 28 A5
Gwalior India 26°12N 78°10E 84 F11
Gwanda Zimbabwe 20°55S 29°0E 97 J5
Gwangju S. Korea 35°9N 126°54E 79 D14
Gweebarra B. Ireland 54°51N 8°23W 18 B5
Gweedore Ireland 55°3N 8°14W 18 A5
Gweek U.K. 50°5N 5°13W 29 G3
Gwennap U.K. 50°12N 5°11W 29 G3
Gweru Zimbabwe 19°28S 29°45E 97 H5
Gwynedd □ U.K. 52°52N 4°10W 28 B6
Gyaring Hu China 34°50N 97°40E 78 E8
Gydan Peninsula Russia 70°0N 78°0E 76 B8
Gympie Australia 26°11S 152°38E 98 F9
Győr Hungary 47°41N 17°40E 65 E9
Gyumri Armenia 40°47N 43°50E 71 F7

H

Ha'apai Group Tonga 19°47S 174°27W 99 D16
Haarlem Neths. 52°23N 4°39E 64 B3
Hachinohe Japan 40°30N 141°29E 81 C7
Hackney □ U.K. 51°33N 0°3W 31 C8
Hackthorpe U.K. 54°34N 2°42W 26 C3
Hadd, Ra's al Oman 22°35N 59°50E 87 F9
Haddenham U.K. 51°46N 0°55W 31 C7
Haddington U.K. 55°57N 2°47W 25 C10
Hadejia Nigeria 12°30N 10°5E 94 F7
Hadleigh U.K. 52°3N 0°58E 31 B10
Hadlow U.K. 51°13N 0°22E 31 D9
Hadramawt □ Yemen 15°30N 49°30E 89 D4
Hadrian's Wall U.K. 55°0N 2°30W 26 B4
Haeju N. Korea 38°3N 125°45E 79 D14
Hafizabad Pakistan 32°5N 73°40E 84 C8
Hagen Germany 51°21N 7°27E 64 C4
Hagerstown U.S.A. 39°39N 77°43W 112 F9
Hags Hd. Ireland 52°57N 9°28W 20 C4
Hague, C. de la France 49°44N 1°56W 66 B3
Hague, The Neths. 52°7N 4°17E 64 B3
Haguenau France 48°49N 7°47E 66 B7
Haida Gwaii Canada 53°20N 132°10W 108 D6
Haifa Israel 32°46N 35°0E 86 C3
Haikou China 20°1N 110°16E 79 G11
Ḥā'il Si. Arabia 27°28N 41°45E 86 E5
Hailar China 49°10N 119°38E 79 B12
Hailey U.S.A. 43°31N 114°19W 110 B4
Haileybury Canada 47°30N 79°38W 112 B8
Hailsham U.K. 50°52N 0°16E 31 E9
Hailun China 47°28N 126°50E 79 B14
Hainan □ China 19°0N 109°30E 79 H10
Hainan Dao China 19°0N 109°30E 79 H10
Hainan Str. China 20°10N 110°15E 79 G11
Haines Junction Canada 60°45N 137°30W 108 C6
Hainton U.K. 53°21N 0°14W 27 F8
Haiphong Vietnam 20°47N 106°41E 78 G10
Haiti ■ W. Indies 19°0N 72°30W 115 D10
Haji Ibrahim Iraq 36°40N 44°30E 86 B6
Ḥajjah Yemen 15°42N 43°36E 89 D3
Hakkoda-San Japan 40°39N 140°53E 81 C7
Hakodate Japan 41°45N 140°44E 81 C7
Haku-San Japan 36°9N 136°46E 81 E5
Halaib Triangle Africa 22°30N 35°20E 95 D12
Halberstadt Germany 51°54N 11°3E 64 C6
Halberton U.K. 50°54N 3°25W 29 F7
Halden Norway 59°9N 11°23E 63 F6
Haldia India 22°5N 88°3E 85 H16
Haldwani India 29°31N 79°30E 84 E11
Halesowen U.K. 52°27N 2°3W 27 H4
Halesworth U.K. 52°20N 1°31E 31 B12
Halifax Canada 44°38N 63°35W 113 C16
Halifax U.K. 53°43N 1°52W 27 E5
Halkirk U.K. 58°30N 3°29W 23 E11
Hall Beach Canada 68°46N 81°12W 109 C11
Hall Pen. Canada 63°30N 66°0W 109 C13
Halle Germany 51°30N 11°56E 64 C6
Hallow U.K. 52°14N 2°15W 30 B4
Halls Creek Australia 18°16S 127°38E 98 D4
Hallworthy U.K. 50°39N 4°35W 29 F4
Halmahera Indonesia 0°40N 128°0E 83 D7
Halmstad Sweden 56°41N 12°52E 63 F6
Halstead U.K. 51°57N 0°40E 31 C10
Haltwhistle U.K. 54°58N 2°26W 26 C4
Hamadān Iran 34°52N 48°32E 86 C7
Ḥamāh Syria 35°5N 36°40E 86 C4
Hamamatsu Japan 34°45N 137°45E 81 F5
Hamar Norway 60°48N 11°7E 63 E6
Hambantota Sri Lanka 6°10N 81°10E 84 R12
Hambledon U.K. 50°55N 1°5W 30 E6
Hambleton Hills U.K. 54°17N 1°12W 26 D6
Hamburg Germany 53°33N 9°59E 64 B5
Hämeenlinna Finland 61°0N 24°28E 63 E8
Hameln Germany 52°6N 9°21E 64 B5
Hamersley Ra. Australia 22°0S 117°45E 98 E2
Hamhŭng N. Korea 39°54N 127°30E 79 D14
Hami China 42°55N 93°25E 78 C7
Hamilton Canada 43°15N 79°50W 111 B11
Hamilton N.Z. 37°47S 175°19E 99 H14
Hamilton U.K. 55°46N 4°2W 24 C7
Hamilton U.S.A. 39°24N 84°34W 112 F5
Hamm Germany 51°40N 7°50E 64 C4
Hammerfest Norway 70°39N 23°41E 63 A8
Hammersmith and Fulham □ U.K. 51°30N 0°14W 31 D8
Hammond U.S.A. 41°38N 87°30W 112 E4
Hammonton U.S.A. 39°39N 74°48W 113 F10
Hampshire □ U.K. 51°7N 1°23W 30 D6
Hampshire Downs U.K. 51°15N 1°10W 30 D6
Hampton in Arden U.K. 52°26N 1°41W 27 H5
Han Shui → China 30°34N 114°17E 79 E11
Hancock U.S.A. 47°8N 88°35W 112 B3
Handan China 36°35N 114°28E 79 D11
Hanford U.S.A. 36°20N 119°39W 110 C3
Hangayn Nuruu Mongolia 47°30N 99°0E 78 B8
Hangzhou China 30°18N 120°11E 79 E13
Hangzhou Wan China 30°15N 120°45E 79 E13
Hankö Finland 59°50N 22°57E 63 F8
Hanna Canada 51°40N 111°54W 108 D8
Hannibal U.S.A. 39°42N 91°22W 111 C8
Hanningfield Res. U.K. 51°40N 0°31E 31 C10
Hannover Germany 52°22N 9°46E 64 B5
Hanoi Vietnam 21°5N 105°55E 78 G10
Hanover U.S.A. 39°48N 76°59W 112 F9
Hanover, I. Chile 51°0S 74°50W 121 H2
Hans I. Arctic 80°49N 66°38W 109 A13
Hanzhong China 33°10N 107°1E 78 E10
Haora India 22°34N 88°18E 85 H16
Haparanda Sweden 65°52N 24°8E 63 D8
Happy Valley-Goose Bay Canada 53°15N 60°20W 109 D13
Har Hu China 38°20N 97°38E 78 D8
Har Us Nuur Mongolia 48°0N 92°0E 78 B7
Ḥaraḍ Si. Arabia 24°22N 49°0E 86 E7
Harare Zimbabwe 17°43S 31°2E 97 H6
Harbin China 45°48N 126°40E 79 B14
Harbor Beach U.S.A. 43°51N 82°39W 112 D6
Hardangerfjorden Norway 60°5N 6°0E 63 E5
Hardy, Pte. St. Lucia 14°6N 60°56W 114 b
Harer Ethiopia 9°20N 42°8E 89 F3
Harewood U.K. 53°54N 1°30W 27 E6
Hargeisa Somalia 9°30N 44°2E 89 F3
Haridwar India 29°58N 78°9E 84 E11
Haringey □ U.K. 51°34N 0°5W 31 C8
Haringhata → Bangla. 22°0N 89°58E 85 J16
Harīrūd → Asia 37°24N 60°38E 87 B10
Harlech U.K. 52°52N 4°6W 28 B5
Harleston U.K. 52°24N 1°18E 31 B11
Harlingen U.S.A. 26°12N 97°42W 110 E7
Harlow U.K. 51°46N 0°8E 31 C9
Harney L. U.S.A. 43°14N 119°8W 110 B3
Härnösand Sweden 62°38N 17°55E 63 E7
Haroldswick U.K. 60°48N 0°50W 22 A16
Harpenden U.K. 51°49N 0°21W 31 C8
Harricana → Canada 50°56N 79°32W 109 D12
Harrietsham U.K. 51°14N 0°41E 31 D10
Harrington U.K. 54°37N 3°33W 26 C1
Harris U.K. 57°50N 6°55W 22 G4
Harris, Sd. of U.K. 57°44N 7°6W 22 G3
Harrisburg U.S.A. 40°16N 76°53W 112 E9
Harrison, C. Canada 54°55N 57°55W 109 D14
Harrisonburg U.S.A. 38°27N 78°52W 112 F8
Harrisville U.S.A. 44°39N 83°17W 112 C6
Harrogate U.K. 54°0N 1°33W 27 D5
Harrow □ U.K. 51°35N 0°21W 31 C8
Hart U.S.A. 43°42N 86°22W 112 D4
Hartest U.K. 52°8N 0°40E 31 B10
Hartford Conn., U.S.A. 41°46N 72°41W 113 E11
Hartford Ky., U.S.A. 37°27N 86°55W 112 G4
Hartford Wis., U.S.A. 43°19N 88°22W 112 D3
Hartland U.K. 50°59N 4°29W 29 F5
Hartland Pt. U.K. 51°1N 4°32W 29 E4
Hartlebury U.K. 52°20N 2°14W 30 B4
Hartlepool U.K. 54°42N 1°13W 26 C6
Hartley U.K. 55°5N 1°28W 26 B6
Hartpury U.K. 51°55N 2°17W 30 C4
Harvey U.S.A. 41°36N 87°50W 112 E4
Harwell U.K. 51°36N 1°17W 30 C6
Harwich U.K. 51°56N 1°17E 31 C11
Haryana □ India 29°0N 76°10E 84 E10
Harz Germany 51°38N 10°44E 64 C6
Hasa Si. Arabia 25°50N 49°0E 86 E7
Haskovo Bulgaria 41°56N 25°30E 69 D11
Haslemere U.K. 51°5N 0°43W 31 D7
Haslingden U.K. 53°42N 2°19W 27 E4
Hastings U.K. 50°51N 0°35E 31 E10
Hastings U.S.A. 40°35N 98°23W 110 B7
Hat Yai Thailand 7°1N 100°27E 82 C2
Hatay Turkey 36°14N 36°10E 71 G6
Hatfield U.K. 51°46N 0°13W 31 C8
Hatgal Mongolia 50°26N 100°9E 78 A9
Hatherleigh U.K. 50°49N 4°5W 29 F5
Hathersage U.K. 53°20N 1°39W 27 F5
Hathras India 27°36N 78°6E 84 F11
Hatia Bangla. 22°30N 91°5E 85 H17
Hatteras, C. U.S.A. 35°14N 75°32W 111 C11
Hattiesburg U.S.A. 31°20N 89°17W 111 D9
Haugesund Norway 59°23N 5°13E 63 F5
Haughley U.K. 52°14N 0°57E 31 B10
Haut Atlas Morocco 32°30N 5°0W 94 B4
Hauts Plateaux Algeria 35°0N 1°0E 94 B6
Havana = La Habana Cuba 23°8N 82°22W 115 C8
Havant U.K. 50°51N 0°58W 31 E7
Havasu, L. U.S.A. 34°18N 114°28W 110 D4
Havel → Germany 52°50N 12°3E 64 B7
Haverfordwest U.K. 51°48N 4°58W 28 D4
Haverhill U.K. 52°5N 0°28E 31 B9
Haverhill U.S.A. 42°47N 71°5W 113 D12
Haverigg U.K. 54°13N 3°17W 26 D2
Havering □ U.K. 51°34N 0°13E 31 C9
Havre U.S.A. 48°33N 109°41W 110 A5
Havre-St.-Pierre Canada 50°18N 63°33W 109 D13
Hawai'i U.S.A. 19°30N 155°30W 110 J17
Hawai'i □ U.S.A. 19°30N 156°30W 110 H16
Hawaiian Is. Pac. Oc. 20°30N 156°0W 103 E12
Hawes U.K. 54°19N 2°12W 26 D4
Haweswater U.K. 54°31N 2°47W 26 C3
Hawick U.K. 55°26N 2°47W 25 D10
Hawkchurch U.K. 50°48N 2°56W 30 E3
Hawkesbury Canada 45°37N 74°37W 113 C10
Hawkesbury Upton U.K. 51°35N 2°19W 30 C4
Hawkhurst U.K. 51°2N 0°32E 31 D10
Hawkshead U.K. 54°23N 2°59W 26 D3
Haworth U.K. 53°50N 1°58W 27 E5
Hawsker U.K. 54°27N 0°34W 26 D7
Haxby U.K. 54°1N 1°4W 27 D6
Hay Australia 34°30S 144°51E 98 G8
Hay → Canada 60°50N 116°26W 108 C8
Hay-on-Wye U.K. 52°5N 3°8W 28 C7
Hay River Canada 60°51N 115°44W 108 C8
Haydon Bridge U.K. 54°58N 2°14W 26 C4
Hayes → Canada 57°3N 92°12W 108 D10
Hayle U.K. 50°11N 5°26W 29 G3
Hays U.S.A. 38°53N 99°20W 110 C7
Hayton U.K. 54°55N 2°45W 26 C3
Hayward U.S.A. 46°1N 91°29W 112 B2
Haywards Heath U.K. 51°0N 0°5W 31 E8
Hazar Turkmenistan 39°34N 53°16E 71 G9
Hazard U.S.A. 37°15N 83°12W 112 G6
Hazaribag India 23°58N 85°26E 85 H14
Heacham U.K. 52°54N 0°29E 31 A9
Headcorn U.K. 51°10N 0°38E 31 D10
Heanor U.K. 53°1N 1°21W 27 F6
Heard I. Ind. Oc. 53°6S 72°36E 53 G13
Hearst Canada 49°40N 83°41W 109 E11
Heathfield U.K. 50°58N 0°16E 31 E9
Hebburn U.K. 54°59N 1°32W 26 C5
Hebden Bridge U.K. 53°45N 2°0W 27 E5
Hebei □ China 39°0N 116°0E 79 D12
Hebrides U.K. 57°30N 7°0W 56 D4
Hebrides, Sea of the U.K. 57°5N 7°0W 22 H4
Hebron Canada 58°5N 62°30W 109 D13
Hecate Str. Canada 53°10N 130°30W 108 D6
Hechi China 24°40N 108°2E 78 G10
Hechuan China 30°2N 106°12E 78 E10
Heckington U.K. 52°59N 0°17W 27 G8
Hednesford U.K. 52°43N 1°59W 27 G5
Hedon U.K. 53°44N 0°12W 27 E8
Heerlen Neths. 50°55N 5°58E 64 C3
Hefei China 31°52N 117°18E 79 E12
Hegang China 47°20N 130°19E 79 B15
Heidelberg Germany 49°24N 8°42E 64 D5
Heihe China 50°10N 127°30E 79 A14
Heilbronn Germany 49°9N 9°13E 64 D5
Heilongjiang □ China 48°0N 126°0E 79 B14
Heimaey Iceland 63°26N 20°17W 63 B1
Hekla Iceland 63°56N 19°35W 63 B2
Helena U.S.A. 46°36N 112°2W 110 A4
Helensburgh U.K. 56°1N 4°43W 24 B6
Helgoland Germany 54°10N 7°53E 64 A4
Hellifield U.K. 54°1N 2°12W 27 D4
Helmand → Afghan. 31°12N 61°34E 87 D10
Helmsdale U.K. 58°7N 3°39W 23 F10
Helmsley U.K. 54°15N 1°3W 26 D6
Helperby U.K. 54°8N 1°19W 26 D6
Helsby U.K. 53°17N 2°46W 27 F3
Helsingborg Sweden 56°3N 12°42E 63 F6
Helsinki Finland 60°10N 24°55E 63 E9
Helston U.K. 50°6N 5°17W 29 G3
Helvellyn U.K. 54°32N 3°1W 26 C2
Helwân Egypt 29°50N 31°20E 95 C12
Hemel Hempstead U.K. 51°44N 0°28W 31 C8
Hempton U.K. 52°50N 0°50E 31 A10
Hemsworth U.K. 53°37N 1°21W 27 E6
Hemyock U.K. 50°54N 3°15W 29 F7
Henan □ China 34°0N 114°0E 79 E11
Henderson Ky., U.S.A. 37°50N 87°35W 112 G4
Henderson Nev., U.S.A. 36°2N 114°58W 110 C3
Henfield U.K. 50°56N 0°16W 31 E8
Hengduan Shan China 28°30N 98°50E 78 F8
Henggang China 22°39N 114°12E 79 a
Hengyang China 26°59N 112°22E 79 F11
Henley-in-Arden U.K. 52°18N 1°46W 30 B5
Henley-on-Thames U.K. 51°32N 0°54W 31 C7
Henlopen, C. U.S.A. 38°48N 75°6W 113 F10
Henlow U.K. 52°2N 0°17W 31 B8
Henrietta Maria, C. Canada 55°9N 82°20W 109 D11
Henstridge U.K. 50°58N 2°24W 30 E4
Hentiyn Nuruu Mongolia 48°30N 108°30E 79 B10
Herāt Afghan. 34°20N 62°7E 87 C10
Hereford U.K. 52°4N 2°43W 30 B3
Herefordshire □ U.K. 52°8N 2°40W 30 B3
Herford Germany 52°7N 8°39E 64 B5
Herlen → Asia 48°48N 117°0E 79 B12
Herm U.K. 49°30N 2°28W 29 J9
Herma Ness U.K. 60°50N 0°54W 22 A16
Hermosillo Mexico 29°10N 111°0W 114 B2
Hernád → Hungary 47°56N 21°8E 65 D11
Herne Bay U.K. 51°21N 1°8E 31 D11
Herstmonceux U.K. 50°53N 0°20E 31 E9
Hertford U.K. 51°48N 0°4W 31 C8
Hertfordshire □ U.K. 51°51N 0°5W 31 C8
's-Hertogenbosch Neths. 51°42N 5°17E 64 C3
Hessen □ Germany 50°30N 9°0E 64 C5
Hessle U.K. 53°44N 0°24W 27 E8
Hethersett U.K. 52°36N 1°10E 31 A11
Hetton-le-Hole U.K. 54°50N 1°26W 26 C6
Hexham U.K. 54°58N 2°4W 26 C4
Heybridge U.K. 51°45N 0°42E 31 C10
Heysham U.K. 54°3N 2°53W 26 D3
Heytesbury U.K. 51°11N 2°6W 30 D4
Heywood U.K. 53°35N 2°12W 27 E4
Heze China 35°14N 115°20E 79 D12
Hibbing U.S.A. 47°25N 92°56W 111 A8
Hickman U.S.A. 36°34N 89°11W 112 G3
Hidalgo del Parral Mexico 26°56N 105°40W 114 B3
Hierro Canary Is. 27°44N 18°0W 94 C2
Higashiōsaka Japan 34°39N 135°37E 81 F4
High Bentham U.K. 54°7N 2°28W 26 D4
High Ercall U.K. 52°45N 2°35W 27 G3
High Hesket U.K. 54°48N 2°49W 26 C3
High Level Canada 58°31N 117°8W 108 D8
High Pike U.K. 54°43N 3°4W 26 C2
High Prairie Canada 55°30N 116°30W 108 D8
High River Canada 50°30N 113°50W 108 D8
High Veld Africa 27°0S 27°0E 90 J6
High Willhays U.K. 50°40N 4°0W 29 F5
High Wycombe U.K. 51°37N 0°45W 31 C7
Higham Ferrers U.K. 52°19N 0°35W 31 B7
Highbridge U.K. 51°13N 2°58W 30 D3
Highclere U.K. 51°20N 1°21W 30 D6
Highland □ U.K. 57°17N 4°21W 22 H7
Highley U.K. 52°27N 2°23W 27 H4
Hightae U.K. 55°6N 3°26W 25 D9
Highworth U.K. 51°37N 1°43W 30 C5
Hiiumaa Estonia 58°50N 22°45E 63 F8
Ḥijāz Si. Arabia 24°0N 40°0E 86 E4
Hildesheim Germany 52°9N 9°56E 64 B5
Hilgay U.K. 52°34N 0°24E 31 A9
Hillaby, Mt. Barbados 13°12N 59°35W 114 c
Hillcrest Barbados 13°13N 59°31W 114 c
Hillingdon □ U.K. 51°32N 0°27W 31 C8
Hillsborough U.K. 54°28N 6°5W 19 C9
Hillsdale U.S.A. 41°56N 84°38W 112 E5
Hilo U.S.A. 19°44N 155°5W 110 J17
Hilpsford Pt. U.K. 54°3N 3°12W 26 D2
Hilversum Neths. 52°14N 5°10E 64 B3
Himachal Pradesh □ India 31°30N 77°0E 84 D10
Himalaya Asia 29°0N 84°0E 85 E14
Himeji Japan 34°50N 134°40E 81 F4
Hinckley U.K. 52°33N 1°22W 27 G6
Hinderwell U.K. 54°32N 0°45W 26 C7
Hindhead U.K. 51°7N 0°43W 31 D7
Hindley U.K. 53°33N 2°35W 27 E3
Hindu Kush Asia 36°0N 71°0E 87 C12
Hingham U.K. 52°35N 1°0E 31 A10
Hingoli India 19°41N 77°15E 84 K10
Hinkley Pt. U.K. 51°12N 3°8W 30 D2
Hinstock U.K. 52°50N 2°27W 27 G4
Hinton U.S.A. 37°40N 80°54W 112 G7
Hios Greece 38°27N 26°9E 69 E12
Hirosaki Japan 40°34N 140°28E 81 C7
Hiroshima Japan 34°24N 132°30E 81 F3
Hisar India 29°12N 75°45E 84 E9
Hispaniola W. Indies 19°0N 71°0W 115 D10
Histon U.K. 52°16N 0°7E 31 B9
Hitachi Japan 36°36N 140°39E 81 E7
Hitchin U.K. 51°58N 0°16W 31 C8
Hjälmaren Sweden 59°18N 15°40E 63 F7
Hkakabo Razi Myanmar 28°25N 97°23E 85 E20
Ho Chi Minh City Vietnam 10°58N 106°40E 82 B3
Hoare B. Canada 65°17N 62°30W 109 C13
Hobart Australia 42°50S 147°21E 98 J8
Hobbs U.S.A. 32°42N 103°8W 110 D6
Hodder → U.K. 53°57N 2°27W 27 E4
Hoddesdon U.K. 51°45N 0°1W 31 C8
Hodge → U.K. 54°16N 0°56W 26 D7
Hodgson Canada 51°13N 97°36W 108 D10
Hódmezővásárhely Hungary 46°28N 20°22E 65 E11
Hodna, Chott el Algeria 35°26N 4°43E 94 A6
Hoek van Holland Neths. 52°0N 4°7E 64 B3
Hoff U.K. 54°34N 2°31W 26 C3
Hōfu Japan 34°3N 131°34E 81 F2
Hog's Back U.K. 51°13N 0°38W 31 D7
Hoh Xil Shan China 36°30N 89°0E 78 D6
Hoher Rhön Germany 50°24N 9°58E 64 C5
Hohhot China 40°52N 111°40E 79 C11
Hokkaidō □ Japan 43°30N 143°0E 81 B8
Holbeach U.K. 52°48N 0°1E 27 G9
Holbeach Marsh U.K. 52°52N 0°5E 27 G9
Holderness U.K. 53°45N 0°5W 27 E8
Holetown Barbados 13°11N 59°38W 114 c
Holguín Cuba 20°50N 76°20W 115 C9
Holkham U.K. 52°57N 0°48E 31 A10
Holland U.S.A. 42°47N 86°7W 112 D4
Holland Fen U.K. 53°0N 0°8W 27 G8
Holland on Sea U.K. 51°48N 1°13E 31 C11
Holme U.K. 53°50N 0°46W 27 E7
Holmes Chapel U.K. 53°12N 2°21W 27 F4
Holmfirth U.K. 53°35N 1°46W 27 E5
Holstebro Denmark 56°22N 8°37E 63 F5
Holsworthy U.K. 50°48N 4°22W 29 F5
Holt U.K. 52°55N 1°6E 31 A11
Holy I. Anglesey, U.K. 53°17N 4°37W 28 A4
Holy I. Northumberland, U.K. 55°40N 1°47W 26 A5
Holyhead U.K. 53°18N 4°38W 28 A4
Holywell U.K. 53°16N 3°14W 28 A7
Home B. Canada 68°40N 67°10W 109 C13
Homer U.S.A. 59°39N 151°33W 108 D4
Homs Syria 34°40N 36°45E 86 C4
Honduras ■ Cent. Amer. 14°40N 86°30W 114 E7
Honduras, G. of Caribbean 16°50N 87°0W 114 D7
Hønefoss Norway 60°10N 10°18E 63 E6
Honey L. U.S.A. 40°15N 120°19W 110 B2
Hong Kong □ China 22°11N 114°14E 79 a
Hong Kong Int. ✈ (HKG) China 22°19N 113°57E 79 a
Hongjiang China 27°7N 109°59E 79 F10
Hongshui He → China 23°48N 109°30E 79 G10
Hongze Hu China 33°15N 118°35E 79 E12
Honiara Solomon Is. 9°27S 159°57E 99 B10
Honington U.K. 52°59N 0°35W 27 G7
Honiton U.K. 50°47N 3°11W 29 F7
Honolulu U.S.A. 21°19N 157°52W 103 E12
Honshū Japan 36°0N 138°0E 81 F6
Hoo St. Werburgh U.K. 51°25N 0°35E 31 D10
Hood, Mt. U.S.A. 45°23N 121°42W 110 A2
Hook U.K. 51°17N 0°57W 31 D7
Hook Hd. Ireland 52°7N 6°56W 21 D9
Hooper Bay U.S.A. 61°32N 166°6W 108 C3
Hoopeston U.S.A. 40°28N 87°40W 112 E4
Hoorn Neths. 52°38N 5°4E 64 B3
Hoover Dam U.S.A. 36°1N 114°44W 110 C4
Hope U.S.A. 33°40N 93°36W 111 D8
Hopedale Canada 55°28N 60°13W 109 D13
Horden U.K. 54°46N 1°19W 26 C6
Horley U.K. 51°10N 0°10W 31 D8
Horlivka Ukraine 48°19N 38°5E 71 E6
Hormuz, Str. of The Gulf 26°30N 56°30E 87 E9
Horn, C. = Hornos, C. de Chile 55°50S 67°30W 121 H3
Horn, Is. Wall. & F. Is. 14°16S 178°6W 99 C15
Horn Head Ireland 55°14N 8°0W 18 A6
Hornavan Sweden 66°15N 17°30E 63 D7
Horncastle U.K. 53°13N 0°7W 27 F8
Horndean U.K. 50°55N 1°1W 30 E6
Hornell U.S.A. 42°20N 77°40W 112 D9
Hornepayne Canada 49°14N 84°48W 112 A5
Horningsham U.K. 51°10N 2°15W 30 D4
Hornos, C. de Chile 55°50S 67°30W 121 H3
Hornsea U.K. 53°55N 0°11W 27 E8
Horqin Youyi Qianqi China 46°5N 122°3E 79 B13
Horsforth U.K. 53°50N 1°39W 27 E5
Horsham Australia 36°44S 142°13E 98 H7
Horsham U.K. 51°4N 0°20W 31 D8
Horsham St. Faith U.K. 52°43N 1°14E 31 A11
Horsted Keynes U.K. 51°2N 0°1W 31 D8
Horton → Canada 69°56N 126°52W 108 C7
Horton in Ribblesdale U.K. 54°9N 2°17W 26 D4
Horwich U.K. 53°36N 2°33W 27 E3
Hoste, I. Chile 55°0S 69°0W 121 H3
Hot Springs Ark., U.S.A. 34°31N 93°3W 111 D8
Hot Springs S. Dak., U.S.A. 43°26N 103°29W 110 B6
Hotan China 37°25N 79°55E 78 D4
Hotan He → China 40°22N 80°56E 78 C5
Houghton U.S.A. 47°7N 88°34W 112 B3
Houghton L. U.S.A. 44°21N 84°44W 112 C5
Houghton-le-Spring U.K. 54°51N 1°28W 26 C6
Houghton Regis U.K. 51°54N 0°32W 31 C7
Houlton U.S.A. 46°8N 67°51W 113 B14
Houma U.S.A. 29°36N 90°43W 111 E8
Hounslow □ U.K. 51°28N 0°21W 31 D8
Hourn, L. U.K. 57°7N 5°35W 22 H6
Houston U.S.A. 29°45N 95°21W 111 E7
Hove U.K. 50°50N 0°10W 31 E8
Hoveton U.K. 52°43N 1°25E 31 A11
Hovingham U.K. 54°11N 0°58W 26 D7
Hövsgöl Nuur Mongolia 51°0N 100°30E 78 A9
Howden U.K. 53°45N 0°52W 27 E7
Howe, C. Australia 37°30S 150°0E 98 H9
Howell U.S.A. 42°36N 83°56W 112 D6
Howland I. Pac. Oc. 0°48N 176°38W 102 G10
Howth Ireland 53°23N 6°7W 21 B10
Howth Hd. Ireland 53°22N 6°4W 21 B10
Hoxne U.K. 52°21N 1°12E 31 B11
Hoy U.K. 58°50N 3°15W 23 E11
Høyanger Norway 61°13N 6°4E 63 E5
Hoylake U.K. 53°24N 3°10W 27 F2
Hradec Králové Czechia 50°15N 15°50E 64 C8
Hrodna Belarus 53°42N 23°52E 65 B12
Hron → Slovakia 47°49N 18°45E 65 E10
Hsinchu Taiwan 24°48N 120°58E 79 G13
Huacho Peru 11°10S 77°35W 120 D2
Huai He → China 33°0N 118°30E 79 E12
Huaibei China 34°0N 116°48E 79 E12
Huaihua China 27°32N 109°57E 79 F10
Huainan China 32°38N 116°58E 79 E12
Huallaga → Peru 5°15S 75°30W 120 C2
Huambo Angola 12°42S 15°54E 97 G3
Huancavelica Peru 12°50S 75°5W 120 D2
Huancayo Peru 12°5S 75°12W 120 D2
Huang He → China 37°55N 118°50E 79 D12
Huangshan China 29°42N 118°25E 79 F12
Huangshi China 30°10N 115°3E 79 E12
Huánuco Peru 9°55S 76°15W 120 C2
Huaraz Peru 9°30S 77°32W 120 C2
Huascarán, Nevado Peru 9°7S 77°37W 120 C2
Huasco Chile 28°30S 71°15W 121 E2
Huatabampo Mexico 26°50N 109°38W 114 B3
Hubballi India 15°22N 75°15E 84 M9
Hubei □ China 31°0N 112°0E 79 E11
Hucknall U.K. 53°3N 1°13W 27 F6
Huddersfield U.K. 53°39N 1°47W 27 E5
Hudiksvall Sweden 61°43N 17°10E 63 E7
Hudson → U.S.A. 40°42N 74°2W 113 E10
Hudson Bay Canada 60°0N 86°0W 109 D11
Hudson Falls U.S.A. 43°18N 73°35W 113 D11
Hudson Str. Canada 62°0N 70°0W 109 C13
Hue Vietnam 16°30N 107°35E 82 A3
Huelva Spain 37°18N 6°57W 67 D2
Huesca Spain 42°8N 0°25W 67 A5
Hugh Town U.K. 49°55N 6°19W 29 H1
Hughenden Australia 20°52S 144°10E 98 E7
Hugli → India 21°56N 88°4E 85 J16
Huila, Nevado del Colombia 3°0N 76°0W 120 B2
Hull = Kingston upon Hull U.K. 53°45N 0°21W 27 E8
Hull Canada 45°26N 75°43W 113 C10
Hull → U.K. 53°44N 0°20W 27 E8
Hullavington U.K. 51°32N 2°8W 30 C4
Hulme End U.K. 53°8N 1°50W 27 F5
Hulun Nur China 49°0N 117°30E 79 B12
Humaitá Brazil 7°35S 63°1W 120 C3
Humber → U.K. 53°42N 0°27W 27 E8
Humber, Mouth of the U.K. 53°32N 0°8E 27 E9
Humboldt Canada 52°15N 105°9W 108 D9
Humboldt → U.S.A. 39°59N 118°36W 110 B3
Humen China 22°50N 113°40E 79 a
Humphreys Peak U.S.A. 35°21N 111°41W 110 C4
Humshaugh U.K. 55°3N 2°8W 26 B4
Húnaflói Iceland 65°50N 20°50W 63 A1
Hunan □ China 27°30N 112°0E 79 F11
Hunchun China 42°52N 130°28E 79 C15
Hungary ■ Europe 47°20N 19°20E 65 E10
Hungary, Plain of Europe 47°0N 20°0E 56 F10
Hungerford U.K. 51°25N 1°31W 30 D5

Hŭngnam N. Korea 39°49N 127°45E 79 D14
Hunmanby U.K. 54°10N 0°20W 26 D8
Hunsrück Germany 49°56N 7°27E 64 D4
Hunstanton U.K. 52°56N 0°29E 31 A9
Huntingdon U.K. 52°20N 0°11W 31 B8
Huntington Ind., U.S.A. 40°53N 85°30W 112 E3
Huntington W. Va., U.S.A. 38°25N 82°27W 112 F6
Huntly U.K. 57°27N 2°47W 23 H12
Huntsville Canada 45°20N 79°14W 109 E12
Huntsville Ala., U.S.A. 34°44N 86°35W 111 D9
Huntsville Tex., U.S.A. 30°43N 95°33W 111 D7
Hurghada Egypt 27°15N 33°50E 95 C12
Hurley U.S.A. 46°27N 90°11W 112 B2
Huron U.S.A. 44°22N 98°13W 110 B7
Huron, L. U.S.A. 44°30N 82°40W 112 C6
Hursley U.K. 51°2N 1°23W 30 D6
Hurstbourne Tarrant U.K. 51°17N 1°26W 30 D6
Hurstpierpoint U.K. 50°56N 0°11W 31 E8
Húsavík Iceland 66°3N 17°21W 63 A2
Husband's Bosworth U.K. 52°28N 1°4W 27 H6
Hutchinson U.S.A. 38°5N 97°56W 110 C7
Huyton U.K. 53°25N 2°51W 27 F3
Huzhou China 30°51N 120°8E 79 E13
Hvar Croatia 43°11N 16°28E 68 C7
Hwang Ho = Huang He → China 37°55N 118°50E 79 D12
Hwange Zimbabwe 18°18S 26°30E 97 H5
Hwlffordd = Haverfordwest U.K. 51°48N 4°58W 28 D4
Hyargas Nuur Mongolia 49°0N 93°0E 78 B7
Hyde U.K. 53°27N 2°4W 27 F4
Hyderabad India 17°22N 78°29E 84 L11
Hyderabad Pakistan 25°23N 68°24E 84 G6
Hyères France 43°8N 6°9E 66 E7
Hyères, Îs. d' France 43°0N 6°20E 66 E7
Hyndman Peak U.S.A. 43°45N 114°8W 110 B4
Hythe U.K. 51°4N 1°5E 31 D11

I

Ialomiţa → Romania 44°42N 27°51E 65 F14
Iaşi Romania 47°10N 27°40E 65 E14
Ibadan Nigeria 7°22N 3°58E 94 G6
Ibagué Colombia 4°20N 75°20W 120 B2
Ibarra Ecuador 0°21N 78°7W 120 B2
Ibb Yemen 14°2N 44°10E 89 E3
Iberian Peninsula Europe 40°0N 5°0W 56 H5
Ibiá Brazil 19°30S 46°30W 122 C1
Ibiapaba, Sa. da Brazil 4°0S 41°30W 120 C5
Ibiza = Eivissa Spain 38°54N 1°26E 67 C6
Ibotirama Brazil 12°13S 43°12W 122 B2
Ibstock U.K. 52°42N 1°24W 27 G6
Ica Peru 14°0S 75°48W 120 D2
Içá → Brazil 2°55S 67°58W 120 C3
Iceland ■ Europe 64°45N 19°0W 63 B2
Ichihara Japan 35°28N 140°5E 81 F7
Ichinomiya Japan 35°18N 136°48E 81 F5
Idaho □ U.S.A. 45°0N 115°0W 110 B4
Idaho Falls U.S.A. 43°30N 112°2W 110 B4
Idar-Oberstein Germany 49°43N 7°16E 64 D4
Idle → U.K. 53°27N 0°49W 27 F7
Idlib Syria 35°55N 36°36E 86 C4
Idmiston U.K. 51°9N 1°42W 30 D5
Ife Nigeria 7°30N 4°31E 94 G6
Iforas, Adrar des Africa 19°40N 1°40E 94 C5
Igarapava Brazil 20°3S 47°47W 122 D1
Igarka Russia 67°30N 86°33E 79 C9
Iglésias Italy 39°19N 8°32E 68 E3
Iglulik Canada 69°20N 81°49W 109 C11
Ignace Canada 49°30N 91°40W 112 A2
Igoumenitsa Greece 39°32N 20°18E 69 E9
Iguaçu → Brazil 25°36S 54°36W 121 E4
Iguaçu, Cat. del Brazil 25°41S 54°26W 121 E4
Iguala Mexico 18°21N 99°32W 114 D5
Iguatu Brazil 6°20S 39°18W 120 C6
Iguidi, Erg Africa 27°0N 6°0W 94 C4
Iisalmi Finland 63°32N 27°10E 63 E9
Ijebu-Ode Nigeria 6°47N 3°58E 94 G6
IJsselmeer Neths. 52°45N 5°20E 64 B3
Ikare Nigeria 7°32N 5°40E 94 G7
Ikaría Greece 37°35N 26°10E 69 F12
Ikeda Japan 34°1N 133°48E 81 F3
Ilagan Phil. 17°7N 121°53E 83 A6
İlâm Iran 33°36N 46°36E 86 C6
Ilchester U.K. 51°0N 2°41W 30 D3
Île-de-France □ France 49°0N 2°20E 66 B5
Ilebo Dem. Rep. of the Congo 4°17S 20°55E 96 E4
Ilemi Triangle Africa 7°37N 4°40E 94 G6
Ilesha Nigeria 7°37N 4°40E 94 G6
Ilfracombe U.K. 51°12N 4°8W 29 E5
Ilhéus Brazil 14°49S 39°2W 122 B3
Ili → Kazakhstan 45°53N 77°10E 76 E8
Iliamna L. U.S.A. 59°30N 155°0W 108 D4
Iligan Phil. 8°12N 124°13E 83 C6
Ilkeston U.K. 52°58N 1°19W 27 G6
Ilkley U.K. 53°56N 1°48W 27 E5
Illapel Chile 32°0S 71°10W 121 F2
Iller → Germany 48°23N 9°58E 64 D6
Illimani Bolivia 16°30S 67°50W 120 D3
Illinois □ U.S.A. 40°15N 89°30W 111 B9
Illinois → U.S.A. 38°58N 90°28W 111 C8
Ilmen, L. Russia 58°15N 31°10E 70 C5
Ilminster U.K. 50°55N 2°55W 30 E3
Iloilo Phil. 10°45N 122°33E 83 B6
Ilorin Nigeria 8°30N 4°35E 94 G6
Imabari Japan 34°4N 133°0E 81 F3
Imandra, L. Russia 67°30N 33°0E 70 A5
Imatra Finland 61°12N 28°48E 63 E9
imeni Ismail Samani, Pik Tajikistan 39°0N 72°2E 87 B13
Immingham U.K. 53°37N 0°13W 27 E8
Ímola Italy 44°20N 11°42E 68 B4
Imperatriz Brazil 5°30S 47°29W 120 C5
Impéria Italy 43°53N 8°3E 68 C3
Imphal India 24°48N 93°56E 85 G18
In Salah Algeria 27°10N 2°32E 94 C6
Inari Finland 68°54N 27°1E 63 D9
Inarijärvi Finland 69°0N 28°0E 63 D9
İnce Burun Turkey 42°7N 34°56E 71 F5
Incheon S. Korea 37°27N 126°40E 79 D14

Incomáti → Mozam. 25°46S 32°43E 97 K6
Indalsälven → Sweden 62°36N 17°30E 63 E7
India ■ Asia 20°0N 78°0E 84 K11
Indian Ocean 5°0S 75°0E 53 E13
Indiana U.S.A. 40°37N 79°9W 112 E8
Indiana □ U.S.A. 40°0N 86°0W 112 E4
Indianapolis U.S.A. 39°46N 86°9W 112 F4
Indigirka → Russia 70°48N 148°54E 77 B15
Indira Gandhi Canal India 28°0N 72°0E 84 F8
Indo-China Asia 15°0N 102°0E 72 G12
Indonesia ■ Asia 5°0S 115°0E 82 F5
Indore India 22°42N 75°53E 84 H9
Indre → France 47°16N 0°11E 66 C4
Indus → Pakistan 24°20N 67°47E 84 G5
İnebolu Turkey 41°55N 33°40E 71 F5
Inga, Barrage d' Dem. Rep. of the Congo 5°39S 13°39E 96 F2
Ingatestone U.K. 51°40N 0°24E 31 C9
Ingleborough U.K. 54°10N 2°22W 26 D4
Ingleton U.K. 54°10N 2°27W 26 D4
Ingolstadt Germany 48°46N 11°26E 64 D6
Ingraj Bazar India 24°58N 88°10E 85 G16
Ingushetia □ Russia 43°20N 44°50E 71 F8
Inishbofin Ireland 53°37N 10°13W 18 D1
Inisheer Ireland 53°3N 9°32W 20 B3
Inishfree B. Ireland 55°4N 8°23W 18 A5
Inishkea North Ireland 54°9N 10°11W 18 C1
Inishkea South Ireland 54°7N 10°12W 18 C1
Inishmaan Ireland 53°5N 9°35W 20 B3
Inishmore Ireland 53°8N 9°45W 20 B3
Inishowen Pen. Ireland 55°14N 7°15W 19 A7
Inishshark Ireland 53°37N 10°16W 18 D1
Inishtrahull Ireland 55°26N 7°13W 19 A7
Inishturk Ireland 53°42N 10°7W 18 D1
Inishvickillane Ireland 52°3N 10°37W 20 D1
Inkberrow U.K. 52°13N 1°58W 30 B5
Inland Sea Japan 34°20N 133°30E 81 F3
Inn → Austria 48°35N 13°28E 64 D7
Inner Hebrides U.K. 57°0N 6°30W 22 J4
Inner Mongolia = Nei Mongol Zizhiqu □ China 42°0N 112°0E 79 C11
Inner Sound U.K. 57°30N 5°55W 22 H6
Innerleithen U.K. 55°37N 3°4W 25 C9
Innsbruck Austria 47°16N 11°23E 64 E6
Inowrocław Poland 52°50N 18°12E 65 B10
Insein Myanmar 16°50N 96°5E 85 L20
Inta Russia 66°5N 60°8E 70 A11
Interlaken Switz. 46°41N 7°50E 64 E4
Inukjuak Canada 58°25N 78°15W 109 D12
Inuvik Canada 68°16N 133°40W 108 C6
Inveraray U.K. 56°14N 5°5W 24 B5
Invercargill N.Z. 46°24S 168°24E 99 K12
Invergordon U.K. 57°41N 4°10W 23 G9
Inverkeithing U.K. 56°2N 3°24W 25 B9
Inverness U.K. 57°29N 4°13W 23 H9
Inverurie U.K. 57°17N 2°23W 23 H13
Ioánnina Greece 39°42N 20°47E 69 E9
Iona U.S.A. 42°59N 85°4W 112 D5
Ionian Is. Greece 38°40N 20°0E 69 E9
Ionian Sea Medit. S. 37°30N 17°30E 69 E7
Ios Greece 36°41N 25°20E 69 F11
Iowa □ U.S.A. 42°18N 93°30W 111 B8
Iowa City U.S.A. 41°40N 91°32W 111 B8
Ipameri Brazil 17°44S 48°9W 122 C1
Ipatinga Brazil 19°32S 42°30W 122 C2
Ipiales Colombia 0°50N 77°37W 120 B2
Ipoh Malaysia 4°35N 101°5E 82 D2
Ipswich Australia 27°35S 152°40E 98 F9
Ipswich U.K. 52°4N 1°10E 31 B11
Iqaluit Canada 63°44N 68°31W 109 C13
Iquique Chile 20°19S 70°5W 120 E2
Iquitos Peru 3°45S 73°10W 120 C2
Iráklio Greece 35°20N 25°12E 69 G11
Iran ■ Asia 33°0N 53°0E 87 C8
İranshahr Iran 27°15N 60°40E 87 E10
Irapuato Mexico 20°41N 101°28W 114 C4
Iraq ■ Asia 33°0N 44°0E 86 C5
Irazú, Volcan Costa Rica 9°59N 83°51W 115 E8
Irbil Iraq 36°15N 44°5E 86 B6
Irchester U.K. 52°18N 0°39W 31 B7
Ireland ■ Europe 53°50N 7°52W 62 E2
Ireland's Eye Ireland 53°24N 6°4W 21 B10
Iringa Tanzania 7°48S 35°43E 96 F7
Irish Sea Europe 53°38N 4°48W 62 E4
Irkutsk Russia 52°18N 104°20E 77 D11
Irlam U.K. 53°26N 2°26W 27 F4
Iron Gate Europe 44°44N 22°30E 65 F12
Iron Mountain U.S.A. 45°49N 88°4W 112 C3
Ironbridge U.K. 52°38N 2°30W 27 G3
Ironton U.S.A. 38°32N 82°41W 112 F6
Ironwood U.S.A. 46°27N 90°9W 112 B2
Irt → U.K. 54°23N 3°26W 26 D2
Irthlingborough U.K. 52°20N 0°37W 31 B7
Irtysh → Russia 61°4N 68°52E 76 C7
Irún Spain 43°20N 1°52W 67 A5
Irvine U.K. 55°37N 4°41W 24 C6
Irvinestown U.K. 54°28N 7°39W 18 C6
Isafjörður Iceland 66°5N 23°9W 63 A1
Isar → Germany 48°48N 12°57E 64 D7
Ischia Italy 40°44N 13°57E 68 D5
Isère → France 44°59N 4°51E 66 D6
Ishim → Russia 57°45N 71°10E 76 D8
Ishinomaki Japan 38°32N 141°20E 81 D7
Ishpeming U.S.A. 46°29N 87°40W 112 B4
Isiro Dem. Rep. of the Congo 2°53N 27°40E 96 D5
İskenderun Turkey 36°32N 36°10E 71 G6
Isla → U.K. 56°32N 3°20W 25 A9
Islamabad Pakistan 33°40N 73°10E 84 C8
Island L. Canada 53°47N 94°25W 108 D10
Island Pond U.S.A. 44°49N 71°53W 113 C12
Islay U.K. 55°46N 6°10W 24 C3
Isleham U.K. 52°21N 0°25E 31 B9
Islington U.K. 51°33N 0°5W 31 C8
Islip U.K. 51°50N 1°12W 30 C6
Ismâ'ilîya Egypt 30°37N 32°18E 95 B12
Isparta Turkey 37°47N 30°30E 71 G5
Israel ■ Asia 32°0N 34°50E 86 D5
Issoire France 45°32N 3°15E 66 D5
Issyk Kul Kyrgyzstan 42°25N 77°15E 72 D9

İstanbul Turkey 41°0N 28°58E 71 F4
Istres France 43°31N 4°59E 66 E6
Istria Croatia 45°10N 14°0E 68 B5
Itaberaba Brazil 12°32S 40°18W 122 B2
Itabira Brazil 19°37S 43°13W 122 C2
Itabuna Brazil 14°48S 39°16W 122 B3
Itacoatiara Brazil 3°8S 58°25W 120 C4
Itaipú, Represa de Brazil 25°30S 54°30W 117 F5
Itajaí Brazil 27°50S 48°39W 121 E5
Itajubá Brazil 22°24S 45°30W 122 D1
Italy ■ Europe 42°0N 13°0E 68 C5
Itaperuna Brazil 21°10S 41°54W 122 D2
Itapetinga Brazil 15°15S 40°15W 122 C2
Itapetininga Brazil 23°36S 48°7W 122 D1
Itapicuru → Brazil 11°47S 37°32W 122 B3
Itararé Brazil 24°6S 49°23W 122 D1
Itaúna Brazil 20°4S 44°34W 122 D2
Itchen → U.K. 50°55N 1°22W 30 E6
Ithaca U.S.A. 42°27N 76°30W 112 D9
Ittoqqortoormiit Greenland 70°20N 23°0W 54 B6
Itu Brazil 23°17S 47°15W 122 D1
Ivanava Belarus 52°7N 25°29E 65 B13
Ivano-Frankivsk Ukraine 48°40N 24°40E 65 D13
Ivanovo Russia 57°5N 41°0E 70 C7
Iveragh Pen. Ireland 51°52N 10°15W 20 D2
Ivinghoe U.K. 51°50N 0°37W 31 C7
Ivory Coast = Côte d'Ivoire ■ Africa 7°30N 5°0W 94 G4
Ivujivik Canada 62°24N 77°55W 109 C12
Ivybridge U.K. 50°23N 3°56W 29 G6
Iwaki Japan 37°3N 140°55E 81 E7
Iwakuni Japan 34°15N 132°8E 81 F3
Iwate-San Japan 39°51N 141°0E 81 D7
Iwo Nigeria 7°39N 4°9E 94 G6
Ixworth U.K. 52°18N 0°51E 31 B10
Izhevsk Russia 56°51N 53°14E 70 C9
Izmayil Ukraine 45°22N 28°46E 71 E4
İzmir Turkey 38°25N 27°8E 71 G4
İznik Gölü Turkey 40°27N 29°30E 71 F4
Izumi-Sano Japan 34°23N 135°18E 81 F4

J

Jabalpur India 23°9N 79°58E 84 H11
Jaboatão Brazil 8°7S 35°1W 122 A3
Jaboticabal Brazil 21°15S 48°17W 122 D1
Jacareí Brazil 23°20S 46°0W 122 D1
Jackson Barbados 13°7N 59°36W 114 c
Jackson Ky., U.S.A. 37°33N 83°23W 112 G6
Jackson Mich., U.S.A. 42°15N 84°24W 112 D5
Jackson Miss., U.S.A. 32°18N 90°12W 111 D8
Jackson Mo., U.S.A. 37°23N 89°40W 112 G3
Jackson Tenn., U.S.A. 35°37N 88°49W 111 C9
Jacksonville Fla., U.S.A. 30°20N 81°39W 111 D10
Jacksonville Ill., U.S.A. 39°44N 90°14W 112 F2
Jacmel Haiti 18°14N 72°32W 115 D10
Jacobabad Pakistan 28°20N 68°29E 84 E6
Jacobina Brazil 11°11S 40°30W 122 B2
Jade Mt. Taiwan 23°25N 120°52E 79 G13
Jaén Spain 37°44N 3°43W 67 D4
Jaffna Sri Lanka 9°45N 80°2E 84 Q12
Jahrom Iran 28°30N 53°31E 87 D8
Jaipur India 27°0N 75°50W 84 F9
Jakarta Indonesia 6°9S 106°52E 82 F3
Jalālābād Afghan. 34°30N 70°29E 87 C12
Jalandhar India 31°20N 75°40E 84 D9
Jalgaon India 21°0N 75°42E 84 J9
Jalna India 19°48N 75°38E 84 K9
Jalpaiguri India 26°32N 88°46E 85 F16
Jaluit I. Marshall Is. 6°0N 169°30E 102 G8
Jamaame Somalia 0°4N 42°44E 89 G3
Jamaica ■ W. Indies 18°10N 77°30W 114 a
Jalpur Bangla. 24°52N 89°56E 85 G16
Jalpur India 25°18N 86°28E 85 G15
Jambi Indonesia 1°38S 103°30E 82 E2
James → U.S.A. 42°52N 97°18W 111 B7
James B. Canada 54°0N 80°0W 109 D12
Jamestown N. Dak., U.S.A. 46°54N 98°42W 110 A7
Jamestown N.Y., U.S.A. 42°6N 79°14W 112 D8
Jammu India 32°43N 74°54W 84 C9
Jammu & Kashmir □ India 34°25N 77°0E 84 B10
Jamnagar India 22°30N 70°6E 84 H7
Jamshedpur India 22°44N 86°12E 85 H15
Jan Mayen Arctic 71°0N 9°0W 54 B7
Janaúba Brazil 15°48S 43°19W 122 C2
Janesville U.S.A. 42°41N 89°1W 112 D3
Janora India 23°40N 75°10E 84 H9
Japan ■ Asia 36°0N 136°0E 81 F5
Japan, Sea of Asia 40°0N 135°0E 81 D4
Japan Trench Pac. Oc. 32°0N 142°0E 102 D6
Japurá → Brazil 3°8S 65°46W 120 C3
Jari → Brazil 1°9S 51°54W 120 C4
Jarrow U.K. 54°59N 1°28W 26 C6
Jarvis I. Pac. Oc. 0°15S 160°5W 103 H12
Jāsk Iran 25°38N 57°45E 87 E9
Jasper Canada 52°55N 118°5W 108 D8
Jaú Brazil 22°10S 48°30W 122 D1
Jauja Peru 11°45S 75°15W 120 D2
Jaunpur India 25°46N 82°44E 85 G13
Java Indonesia 7°0S 110°0E 82 F3
Java Sea Indonesia 4°35S 107°15E 82 E3
Java Trench Ind. Oc. 9°0S 105°0E 82 F3
Jawhar Somalia 2°48N 45°30E 89 G4
Jaya, Puncak Indonesia 3°57S 137°17E 83 E9
Jebel, Bahr el → South Sudan 9°30N 30°25E 95 G12
Jedburgh U.K. 55°29N 2°33W 25 C10
Jedda Si. Arabia 21°29N 39°10E 86 F4
Jefferson City U.S.A. 38°17N 85°44W 112 F5
Jeju S. Korea 33°31N 126°32E 79 E14
Jelenia Góra Poland 50°50N 15°45E 64 C8
Jelgava Latvia 56°41N 23°49E 63 F8
Jena Germany 50°54N 11°35E 64 C6
Jeonju S. Korea 35°50N 127°4E 79 D14
Jequié Brazil 13°51S 40°5W 122 B2
Jequitinhonha Brazil 16°30S 41°0W 122 C2
Jequitinhonha → Brazil 15°51S 38°53W 122 C3
Jérémie Haiti 18°40N 74°10W 115 D10
Jerez de la Frontera Spain 36°41N 6°7W 67 D2
Jersey U.K. 49°11N 2°7W 29 J9
Jersey City U.S.A. 40°42N 74°4W 113 E10

Jerseyville U.S.A. 39°7N 90°20W 112 F2
Jerusalem Israel/West Bank 31°47N 35°10E 86 D3
Jervaulx U.K. 54°16N 1°43W 26 D5
Jessore Bangla. 23°10N 89°10E 85 H16
Jhang Maghiana Pakistan 31°15N 72°22E 84 D8
Jhansi India 25°30N 78°36E 84 G11
Jharkhand □ India 24°0N 85°50E 85 H14
Jhelum Pakistan 33°0N 73°45E 84 C8
Jhelum → Pakistan 31°20N 72°10E 84 D8
Jiamusi China 46°40N 130°26E 79 B15
Ji'an Jiangxi, China 27°6N 114°59E 79 F11
Ji'an Jilin, China 41°5N 126°10E 79 C14
Jiangsu □ China 33°0N 120°0E 79 E12
Jiangxi □ China 27°30N 116°0E 79 F12
Jiaxing China 30°49N 120°45E 79 E13
Jiayuguan China 39°49N 98°18E 78 D8
Jihlava → Czechia 48°55N 16°36E 65 D9
Jijiga Ethiopia 9°20N 42°50E 89 F3
Jilib Somalia 0°29N 42°46E 89 G3
Jilin China 43°44N 126°30E 79 C14
Jilin □ China 44°0N 127°0E 79 C14
Jima Ethiopia 7°40N 36°47E 89 F2
Jinan China 36°38N 117°1E 79 D12
Jinchang China 38°30N 102°10E 78 D9
Jincheng China 35°29N 112°50E 79 D11
Jinding China 22°22N 113°33E 79 a
Jingdezhen China 29°20N 117°11E 79 F12
Jingmen China 31°0N 112°10E 79 E11
Jinhua China 29°8N 119°38E 79 F12
Jining Nei Monggol Zizhiqu, China 41°5N 113°0E 79 C11
Jining Shandong, China 35°22N 116°34E 79 D12
Jinja Uganda 0°25N 33°12E 96 D6
Jinsha Jiang → China 28°50N 104°36E 78 F9
Jinxi China 40°52N 120°50E 79 C13
Jinzhong China 37°42N 112°46E 79 D11
Jinzhou China 41°5N 121°3E 79 C13
Jipijapa Ecuador 1°0S 80°40W 120 C1
Jishou China 28°21N 109°43E 79 F10
Jiujiang China 29°42N 115°58E 79 F12
Jiwani Pakistan 25°1N 61°44E 87 G10
Jixi China 45°20N 130°50E 79 B15
Jīzān Si. Arabia 17°0N 42°20E 89 D3
Jizzax Uzbekistan 40°6N 67°50E 87 A11
João Pessoa Brazil 7°10S 34°52W 120 C6
Jodhpur India 26°23N 73°8E 84 F8
Joensuu Finland 62°37N 29°49E 63 E9
Jōetsu Japan 37°12N 138°10E 81 E6
Johannesburg S. Africa 26°11S 28°2E 97 K5
John Crow Mts. Jamaica 18°5N 76°25W 114 a
John Day → U.S.A. 45°44N 120°39W 110 A2
John o' Groats U.K. 58°38N 3°4W 23 E11
Johnson City U.S.A. 36°19N 82°21W 111 C10
Johnston Atoll Pac. Oc. 17°10N 169°8W 103 F11
Johnstone U.K. 55°49N 4°31W 24 C6
Johnstown U.S.A. 40°20N 78°55W 112 E8
Johor Bahru Malaysia 1°28N 103°46E 82 D2
Joinville Brazil 26°15S 48°55W 121 E5
Joliet U.S.A. 41°32N 88°5W 112 E3
Joliette Canada 46°3N 73°24W 109 E12
Jolo Phil. 6°0N 121°0E 83 C6
Jones Sound Canada 76°0N 85°0W 109 B11
Jonesboro U.S.A. 35°50N 90°42W 111 C8
Jönköping Sweden 57°45N 14°8E 63 F6
Jonquière Canada 48°27N 71°14W 113 A12
Joplin U.S.A. 37°6N 94°31W 111 C8
Jordan ■ Asia 31°0N 36°0E 86 D4
Jordan → Asia 31°48N 35°32E 86 D3
Jos Nigeria 9°53N 8°51E 94 G7
Joseph Bonaparte G. Australia 14°35S 128°50E 98 C4
Jotunheimen Norway 61°35N 8°25E 63 E5
Juan de Fuca, Str. of N. Amer. 48°15N 124°0W 110 A2
Juan Fernández, Arch. de Pac. Oc. 33°50S 80°0W 103 L20
Juàzeiro Brazil 9°30S 40°30W 122 A2
Juàzeiro do Norte Brazil 7°10S 39°18W 120 C6
Juba South Sudan 4°50N 31°35E 95 H12
Juba → Somalia 1°30N 42°35E 89 G3
Juchitán de Zaragoza Mexico 16°26N 95°1W 114 D5
Juiz de Fora Brazil 21°43S 43°19W 122 D2
Juliaca Peru 15°25S 70°10W 120 D2
Julianatop Suriname 3°40N 56°30W 120 B4
Junagadh India 21°30N 70°30E 84 J7
Jundiaí Brazil 24°30S 47°0W 122 D1
Juneau U.S.A. 58°18N 134°25W 108 D6
Junín Argentina 34°33S 60°57W 121 F3
Jur → South Sudan 8°45N 29°15E 95 G11
Jura Europe 46°40N 6°5E 66 C6
Jura U.K. 56°0N 5°50W 24 C4
Jura, Sd. of U.K. 55°57N 5°45W 24 C4
Juruá → Brazil 2°37S 65°44W 120 C3
Juruena → Brazil 7°20S 58°3W 120 C4
Juticalpa Honduras 14°40N 86°12W 114 E7
Jutland Denmark 56°25N 9°30E 63 F5
Juventud, I. de la Cuba 21°40N 82°40W 115 C8
Jyväskylä Finland 62°14N 25°50E 63 E9

K

K2 Pakistan 35°58N 76°32E 84 B10
Kabardino-Balkaria □ Russia 43°30N 43°30E 71 F7
Kābul Afghan. 34°28N 69°11E 87 C12
Kabwe Zambia 14°30S 28°29E 97 G5
Kachchh, Gulf of India 22°50N 69°15E 84 H6
Kachchh, Rann of India 24°0N 70°0E 84 H7
Kachin □ Myanmar 26°0N 97°30E 85 G20
Kaçkar Turkey 40°45N 41°10E 71 F7
Kadavu Fiji 19°0S 178°15E 99 E14
Kade Ghana 6°7N 0°56W 94 G5
Kadoma Zimbabwe 18°20S 29°52E 97 H5
Kaduna Nigeria 10°30N 7°21E 94 F7
Kaesŏng N. Korea 37°58N 126°35E 79 D14
Kafue → Zambia 15°30S 29°0E 97 H5
Kaga Bandoro C.A.R. 7°0N 19°10E 96 C3
Kagera → Uganda 0°57S 31°47E 96 E6
Kagoshima Japan 31°35N 130°33E 81 H2
Kaho'olawe U.S.A. 20°33N 156°37W 110 H16
Kahramanmaraş Turkey 37°37N 36°53E 71 G6

Kai, Kepulauan Indonesia 5°55S 132°45E 83 F8
Kaidu He → China 41°46N 86°31E 78 C6
Kaieteur Falls Guyana 5°1N 59°10W 120 B4
Kaifeng China 34°48N 114°21E 79 E11
Kailua Kona U.S.A. 19°39N 155°59W 110 J17
Kaingaroa N.Z. 10°1N 4°40E 94 F6
Kaira India 35°45N 10°55E 95 A8
Kairouan Tunisia 35°45N 10°5E 95 A8
Kaiserslautern Germany 49°26N 7°45E 64 D4
Kaitaia N.Z. 35°8S 173°17E 99 H13
Kaiyuan China 23°40N 103°12E 78 G9
Kajaani Finland 64°17N 27°46E 63 E9
Kajabbi Australia 20°0S 140°1E 98 E7
Kakamega Kenya 0°20N 34°46E 96 D6
Kakhovka Res. Ukraine 47°5N 34°0E 71 E5
Kakinada India 16°57N 82°11E 85 L13
Kalaallit Nunaat = Greenland ☑ N. Amer. 66°0N 45°0W 54 C5
Kalaburagi India 17°20N 76°50E 84 L10
Kalahari Africa 24°0S 21°30E 97 J4
Kalamata Greece 37°3N 22°10E 69 F10
Kalamazoo U.S.A. 42°17N 85°35W 112 D5
Kalamazoo → U.S.A. 42°40N 86°10W 112 D4
Kalemie Dem. Rep. of the Congo 5°55S 29°9E 96 F5
Kalgoorlie-Boulder Australia 30°40S 121°22E 98 G3
Kalimantan Indonesia 0°0 114°0E 82 E4
Kálimnos Greece 37°0N 27°0E 69 F12
Kaliningrad Russia 54°42N 20°32E 63 G8
Kalispell U.S.A. 48°12N 114°19W 110 A4
Kalisz Poland 51°45N 18°8E 65 C10
Kalkaska U.S.A. 44°44N 85°11W 112 C5
Kallsjön Sweden 63°38N 13°0E 63 E6
Kalmar Sweden 56°40N 16°20E 63 F7
Kalmykia □ Russia 46°5N 46°1E 71 E8
Kaluga Russia 54°35N 36°10E 70 D6
Kalutara Sri Lanka 6°35N 80°0E 84 R12
Kalyan India 19°15N 73°9E 84 K8
Kama → Russia 55°45N 52°0E 70 C9
Kamchatka Pen. Russia 57°0N 160°0E 77 D16
Kamensk Uralskiy Russia 56°25N 62°2E 76 D7
Kamina Dem. Rep. of the Congo 8°45S 25°0E 96 F5
Kamloops Canada 50°40N 120°20W 108 D7
Kampala Uganda 0°20N 32°32E 96 D6
Kampong Cham Cambodia 12°0N 105°30E 82 B3
Kampong Saom Cambodia 10°38N 103°30E 82 B2
Kamyanets-Podilskyy Ukraine 48°45N 26°40E 65 D14
Kamyshin Russia 50°10N 45°24E 71 D8
Kananga Dem. Rep. of the Congo 5°55S 22°18E 96 F4
Kanash Russia 55°30N 47°32E 70 C8
Kanawha → U.S.A. 38°50N 82°9W 112 F6
Kanazawa Japan 36°30N 136°38E 81 E5
Kanchenjunga Nepal 27°50N 88°10E 85 F16
Kanchipuram India 12°52N 79°45E 84 N11
Kandahār Afghan. 31°32N 65°43E 87 D11
Kandalaksha Russia 67°9N 32°30E 70 A5
Kandalaksha, G. of Russia 66°0N 35°0E 70 A6
Kandi Benin 11°7N 2°55E 94 F6
Kandy Sri Lanka 7°18N 80°43E 84 R12
Kane U.S.A. 41°40N 78°49W 112 E8
Kāne'ohe U.S.A. 21°25N 157°48W 110 H16
Kangaroo I. Australia 35°45S 137°0E 98 H6
Kangiqsualujjuaq Canada 58°30N 65°59W 109 D13
Kangiqsujuaq Canada 61°30N 72°0W 109 C12
Kangirsuk Canada 60°0N 70°0W 109 D13
Kanin Pen. Russia 68°0N 45°0E 70 A8
Kankakee U.S.A. 41°7N 87°52W 112 E4
Kankakee → U.S.A. 41°23N 88°15W 112 E3
Kankan Guinea 10°23N 9°15W 94 F4
Kannur India 11°53N 75°27E 84 P9
Kannyakumari India 8°3N 77°40E 84 Q10
Kano Nigeria 12°2N 8°30E 94 F7
Kanpur India 26°28N 80°20E 84 F12
Kansas □ U.S.A. 38°30N 99°0W 110 C7
Kansas → U.S.A. 39°7N 94°37W 111 C8
Kansas City U.S.A. 39°6N 94°35W 111 C8
Kansk Russia 56°20N 95°37E 77 D10
Kanturk Ireland 52°11N 8°54W 20 D5
Kanye Botswana 24°55S 25°28E 97 J5
Kaohsiung Taiwan 22°35N 120°16E 79 G13
Kaolack Senegal 14°5N 16°8W 94 F2
Kapa'a U.S.A. 22°5N 159°19W 110 G15
Kapiri Mposhi Zambia 13°59S 28°43E 97 G5
Kaposvár Hungary 46°25N 17°47E 65 E9
Kaptai L. Bangla. 22°40N 92°20E 85 H18
Kapuas → Indonesia 0°25S 109°20E 82 E3
Kapuskasing Canada 49°25N 82°30W 112 A6
Kara Bogaz Gol Turkmenistan 41°0N 53°30E 87 A8
Kara Kum Turkmenistan 39°30N 60°0E 87 B9
Kara Sea Russia 75°0N 70°0E 76 B7
Karabük Turkey 41°12N 32°37E 71 F5
Karachey-Cherkessia □ Russia 43°40N 41°30E 71 F7
Karachi Pakistan 24°50N 67°0E 84 G5
Karaganda Kazakhstan 49°50N 73°10E 76 E8
Karagiye Depression Kazakhstan 43°27N 51°45E 71 F9
Karakalpakstan □ Uzbekistan 43°0N 58°0E 87 A9
Karaman Turkey 37°14N 33°13E 71 G5
Karatax Shan China 35°57N 81°0E 78 D5
Karayazı Turkey 39°41N 42°9E 71 G7
Karbalā' Iraq 32°36N 44°3E 86 C6
Karelia □ Russia 65°30N 32°30E 70 A5
Kariba, L. Zimbabwe 16°40S 28°25E 97 H5
Kariba Dam Zimbabwe 16°30S 28°35E 97 H5
Karimata, Str. of Indonesia 2°0S 108°40E 82 E3
Karlovac Croatia 45°31N 15°36E 68 B6
Karlskrona Sweden 56°10N 15°35E 63 F7
Karlsruhe Germany 49°0N 8°23E 64 D5
Karlstad Sweden 59°23N 13°30E 63 F6
Karnal India 29°42N 77°2E 84 E10
Kärnten □ Austria 46°52N 13°30E 64 E8
Karnataka □ India 13°15N 77°0E 84 N10
Karpathos Greece 35°37N 27°10E 69 G12
Kars Turkey 40°40N 43°5E 71 F7
Karwar India 14°55N 74°13E 84 M9
Kasai → Dem. Rep. of the Congo 3°30S 16°10E 96 E3
Kasaragod India 12°30N 74°58E 84 N9
Kasba L. Canada 60°20N 102°10W 108 C9

Kāshān   **Lake District**

Kāshān Iran 34°5N 51°30E 87 C7
Kashi China 39°30N 76°2E 78 D4
Kasongo Dem. Rep. of the Congo 4°30S 26°33E 96 E5
Kaspiysk Russia 42°52N 47°40E 71 F8
Kassalā Sudan 15°30N 36°0E 95 E13
Kassel Germany 51°18N 9°26E 64 C5
Kastamonu Turkey 41°25N 33°43E 71 F5
Kasur Pakistan 31°5N 74°25E 84 D9
Katanga Dem. Rep. of the Congo 8°0S 25°0E 96 F4
Kathiawar India 22°20N 71°0E 84 H7
Kathmandu Nepal 27°45N 85°20E 85 F14
Kati Thanda-Lake Eyre
Australia 29°30S 137°26E 98 F6
Katihar India 25°34N 87°36E 85 G15
Katima Mulilo Namibia 17°28S 24°13E 97 H4
Katiola Côte d'Ivoire 8°10N 5°10W 94 G4
Katowice Poland 50°17N 19°5E 65 C10
Katrine, L. U.K. 56°15N 4°30W 24 B7
Katsina Nigeria 13°0N 7°32E 94 F7
Kattegat Denmark 56°40N 11°20E 63 F6
Kaua'i U.S.A. 22°3N 159°30W 110 H15
Kauai Channel U.S.A. 21°45N 158°50W 110 H15
Kaukauna U.S.A. 44°17N 88°17W 112 C3
Kaunakakai U.S.A. 21°6N 157°1W 110 H16
Kaunas Lithuania 54°54N 23°54E 63 G8
Kavala Greece 40°57N 24°28E 69 D11
Kavieng Papua N. G. 2°36S 150°51E 98 A9
Kawagoe Japan 35°55N 139°29E 81 F6
Kawaguchi Japan 35°52N 139°45E 81 F6
Kawardha India 22°0N 81°17E 85 J12
Kawasaki Japan 35°31N 139°43E 81 F6
Kawawachikamach
Canada 54°48N 66°50W 109 D13
Kayes Mali 14°25N 11°30W 94 F3
Kayseri Turkey 38°45N 35°30E 71 G6
Kazan Russia 55°50N 49°10E 70 C8
Kazan-Rettō Pac. Oc. 25°0N 141°0E 102 E6
Kazanlak Bulgaria 42°38N 25°20E 69 C11
Kea U.K. 37°35N 24°22E 69 F11
Keady U.K. 54°15N 6°42W 19 C8
Kearney U.S.A. 40°42N 99°5W 110 B7
Keban Turkey 38°50N 38°50E 71 G6
Keban Baraji Turkey 38°41N 38°33E 71 G6
Kebnekaise Sweden 67°53N 18°33E 63 D7
Kebri Dehar Ethiopia 6°45N 44°17E 89 F3
Kebumen Indonesia 7°42S 109°40E 83 G13
Kecskemét Hungary 46°57N 19°42E 65 E10
Kediri Indonesia 7°51S 112°1E 82 F4
Keelby U.K. 53°35N 0°16W 27 E8
Keele U.K. 53°0N 2°17W 27 F4
Keene U.S.A. 42°56N 72°17W 113 D11
Keeper Hill Ireland 52°45N 8°16W 20 C6
Keetmanshoop Namibia 26°35S 18°8E 97 K3
Kefalonia Greece 38°15N 20°30E 69 E9
Keflavik Iceland 64°2N 22°35W 63 B1
Kegworth U.K. 52°50N 1°17W 27 G6
Keighley U.K. 53°52N 1°54W 27 E5
Keith U.K. 57°32N 2°57W 23 G12
Keld U.K. 54°24N 2°10W 26 D4
Kelkit → Turkey 40°45N 36°32E 71 F6
Kellett, C. Canada 72°0N 126°0W 109 B7
Kellogg U.S.A. 47°32N 116°7W 110 A3
Kells Ireland 53°44N 6°53W 19 D8
Kelowna Canada 49°50N 119°25W 108 E8
Kelsale U.K. 52°14N 1°31E 31 B12
Kelsall U.K. 53°13N 2°43W 27 F3
Kelso U.K. 55°36N 2°26W 25 C11
Kelvedon U.K. 51°50N 0°43E 31 C10
Kem Russia 65°0N 34°38E 70 B5
Kemble U.K. 51°40N 1°59W 30 C5
Kemerovo Russia 55°20N 86°5E 76 D9
Kemi Finland 65°44N 24°34E 63 D8
Kemijoki → Finland 65°47N 24°32E 63 D8
Kemp Land Antarctica 69°0S 55°0E 5 C5
Kempsey U.K. 52°8N 2°12W 30 B4
Kempston U.K. 52°7N 0°30W 31 B7
Kempten Germany 47°45N 10°17E 64 E6
Kenai U.S.A. 60°33N 151°16W 108 C4
Kendal U.K. 54°20N 2°44W 26 D3
Kendari Indonesia 3°50S 122°30E 83 E6
Kenema S. Leone 7°50N 11°14W 94 G3
Kenilworth U.K. 52°21N 1°34W 30 B5
Kenitra Morocco 34°15N 6°40W 94 B4
Kenmare Ireland 51°53N 9°36W 20 E3
Kenmare River → Ireland 51°48N 9°51W 20 E3
Kennet → U.K. 51°27N 0°57W 31 D7
Kennewick U.S.A. 46°12N 119°7W 110 A3
Kenninghall U.K. 52°26N 1°0E 31 B11
Kenogami → Canada 51°6N 84°28W 109 D11
Kenora Canada 49°47N 94°29W 108 E10
Kenosha U.S.A. 42°35N 87°49W 112 D4
Kent U.S.A. 41°9N 81°22W 112 E7
Kent □ U.K. 51°12N 0°40E 31 D10
Kent Pen. Canada 68°30N 107°0W 108 C9
Kentisbeare U.K. 50°51N 3°20W 29 F7
Kenton U.S.A. 40°39N 83°37W 112 E6
Kentucky □ U.S.A. 37°0N 84°0W 112 G5
Kentucky → U.S.A. 38°41N 85°11W 112 F5
Kentville Canada 45°6N 64°29W 109 E13
Kenya ■ Africa 1°0N 38°0E 96 D7
Kenya, Mt. Kenya 0°10S 37°18E 96 E7
Kerala □ India 11°0N 76°15E 84 P10
Kerch Ukraine 45°20N 36°20E 71 E6
Kerguelen Ind. Oc. 49°15S 69°10E 53 G13
Kericho Kenya 0°22S 35°15E 96 E7
Kerinci Indonesia 1°40S 101°15E 82 E2
Kermadec Is. Pac. Oc. 30°0S 178°15W 99 G15
Kermadec Trench Pac. Oc. 30°30S 176°0W 99 G15
Kermān Iran 30°15N 57°1E 87 D9
Kermānshāh Iran 34°23N 47°0E 86 C6
Kernow = Cornwall □ U.K. 50°26N 4°40W 29 G3
Kerrera U.K. 56°24N 5°33W 24 B4
Kerrobert Canada 51°56N 109°8W 108 D9
Kerry □ Ireland 52°7N 9°35W 20 D3
Kerry Hd. Ireland 52°25N 9°56W 20 D3
Kessingland U.K. 52°26N 1°43E 31 B12
Keswick U.K. 54°36N 3°8W 26 C2
Ketchikan U.S.A. 55°21N 131°39W 108 D6
Kettering U.K. 52°24N 0°43W 31 B7
Kettle Ness U.K. 54°33N 0°42W 26 C7

Kettlewell U.K. 54°9N 2°3W 26 D4
Kewaunee U.S.A. 44°27N 87°31W 112 C4
Keweenaw B. U.S.A. 47°0N 88°15W 112 B3
Keweenaw Pen. U.S.A. 47°15N 88°15W 112 B3
Keweenaw Pt. U.S.A. 47°25N 87°43W 112 B4
Kexby U.K. 53°22N 0°42W 27 E7
Key West U.S.A. 24°33N 81°48W 111 F10
Keyingham U.K. 53°43N 0°7W 27 E8
Keymer U.K. 50°55N 0°7W 31 E8
Keynsham U.K. 51°24N 2°29W 30 D4
Keyser U.S.A. 39°26N 78°59W 112 F8
Keyworth U.K. 52°52N 1°5W 27 G6
Khabarovsk Russia 48°30N 135°5E 77 E14
Khairpur Pakistan 27°32N 68°49E 84 F6
Khambhat India 22°23N 72°33E 84 H8
Khambhat, G. of India 20°45N 72°30E 84 J8
Khamis Mushayt Si. Arabia 18°18N 42°44E 89 D3
Khan Tengri, Pik Asia 42°12N 80°10E 78 C5
Khandyga Russia 62°42N 135°35E 77 C14
Khanewal Pakistan 30°20N 71°55E 84 D7
Khanka, L. Asia 45°0N 132°24E 79 C15
Kharagpur India 22°20N 87°25E 85 H15
Kharg Iran 29°15N 50°28E 86 D7
Khârga, El Wâhât el Egypt 25°10N 30°35E 95 C12
Kharkov Ukraine 49°58N 36°20E 71 E6
Khartoum Sudan 15°31N 32°35E 95 E12
Khasavyurt Russia 43°16N 46°40E 71 F8
Khatanga Russia 72°0N 102°20E 77 B11
Khemisset Morocco 33°50N 6°1W 94 B4
Khenchela Algeria 35°28N 7°11E 94 A7
Kherson Ukraine 46°35N 32°35E 71 E5
Khmelnytskyy Ukraine 49°23N 27°0E 65 D14
Khojak Pass Afghan. 30°51N 66°34E 87 D11
Kholm Afghan. 36°45N 67°40E 87 B11
Khon Kaen Thailand 16°30N 102°47E 82 A2
Khorāsān Iran 34°0N 58°0E 87 C9
Khorramābād Iran 33°30N 48°25E 86 C7
Khorramshahr Iran 30°29N 48°15E 86 D7
Khouribga Morocco 32°58N 6°57W 94 B4
Khūjand Tajikistan 40°17N 69°37E 87 B12
Khulna Bangla. 22°45N 89°34E 85 H16
Khunjerab Pass Asia 36°40N 75°25E 84 A9
Khushab Pakistan 32°20N 72°20E 84 C8
Khuzdar Pakistan 27°52N 66°30E 84 F5
Khūzestān □ Iran 31°0N 49°0E 86 D7
Khvoy Iran 38°35N 45°0E 86 B6
Khyber Pakhtunkhwa □
Pakistan 34°0N 72°0E 84 B8
Khyber Pass Afghan. 34°10N 71°8E 84 B7
Kibworth Beauchamp U.K. 52°33N 0°59W 27 G7
Kicking Horse Pass Canada 51°28N 116°16W 108 D8
Kidderminster U.K. 52°24N 2°15W 30 B4
Kidlington U.K. 51°50N 1°15W 30 C6
Kidsgrove U.K. 53°5N 2°14W 27 F4
Kidstones U.K. 54°13N 2°2W 26 D4
Kidwelly U.K. 51°44N 4°18W 28 D5
Kiel Germany 54°19N 10°8E 64 A6
Kiel Canal = Nord-Ostsee-Kanal
Germany 54°12N 9°32E 64 A5
Kielce Poland 50°52N 20°42E 65 C11
Kielder U.K. 55°14N 2°35W 26 B3
Kieler Bucht Germany 54°35N 10°25E 64 A6
Kiev = Kyiv Ukraine 50°30N 30°28E 65 C16
Kigali Rwanda 1°59S 30°4E 96 E6
Kigoma-Ujiji Tanzania 4°55S 29°36E 96 E5
Kikwit Dem. Rep. of the Congo 5°0S 18°45E 96 E3
Kīlauea U.S.A. 19°25N 155°17W 110 J17
Kilbirnie U.K. 55°46N 4°41W 24 C6
Kilbrannan Sd. U.K. 55°37N 5°26W 24 C5
Kildare Ireland 53°9N 6°55W 21 B9
Kildare □ Ireland 53°10N 6°50W 21 B9
Kilfinnane Ireland 52°21N 8°28W 20 D6
Kilham U.K. 54°4N 0°23W 26 D8
Kilifi Kenya 3°40S 39°48E 96 E7
Kilimanjaro Tanzania 3°7S 37°20E 96 E7
Kilindini Kenya 4°4S 39°40E 96 E7
Kilkee Ireland 52°41N 9°39W 20 C3
Kilkeel U.K. 54°7N 5°55W 19 C10
Kilkenny Ireland 52°39N 7°15N 21 C8
Kilkenny □ Ireland 52°35N 7°15N 21 C8
Kilkhampton U.K. 50°52N 4°31W 29 F4
Kilkieran B. Ireland 53°20N 9°41W 20 B3
Killala Ireland 54°13N 9°13W 18 C3
Killala B. Ireland 54°16N 9°8W 18 C3
Killaloe Ireland 52°48N 8°28W 20 C6
Killarney Ireland 52°4N 9°30W 20 D4
Killarney △ Ireland 52°0N 9°33W 20 D3
Killary Harbour Ireland 53°38N 9°52W 18 D2
Killeen U.S.A. 31°7N 97°44W 110 D7
Killin U.K. 56°28N 4°19W 24 B7
Killiney Ireland 53°15N 6°7W 21 B10
Killinghall U.K. 54°2N 1°33W 26 D5
Killorglin Ireland 52°6N 9°47W 20 D3
Killybegs Ireland 54°38N 8°26W 18 B5
Kilmarnock U.K. 55°37N 4°29W 24 C7
Kilrush Ireland 52°38N 9°29W 20 C4
Kilsby U.K. 52°20N 1°10W 30 B6
Kilsyth U.K. 55°59N 4°3W 24 C7
Kilwa Kivinje Tanzania 8°45S 39°25E 96 F7
Kilwinning U.K. 55°39N 4°43W 24 C6
Kimberley Australia 16°20S 127°0E 98 D4
Kimberley S. Africa 28°43S 24°46E 97 K4
Kimbolton U.K. 52°18N 0°24W 31 B8
Kimch'aek N. Korea 40°40N 129°10E 79 C14
Kimmirut Canada 62°50N 69°50W 109 C13
Kimry Russia 56°55N 37°15E 70 C6
Kinabalu, Gunung Malaysia 6°3N 116°14E 82 C5
Kincardine Aberds., U.K. 56°57N 2°25W 23 J13
Kincardine Fife, U.K. 56°4N 3°43W 25 B8
Kinder Scout U.K. 53°24N 1°52W 27 F5
Kindersley Canada 51°30N 109°10W 108 D9
Kindia Guinea 10°0N 12°52W 94 F3
Kindu Dem. Rep. of the Congo 2°55S 25°50E 96 E5
Kineshma Russia 57°30N 42°5E 70 C7
Kineton U.K. 52°10N 1°31W 30 B5
King George I. Antarctica 60°0S 60°0W 55 C18
King George Is. Canada 57°20N 80°30W 109 D11
King William I. Canada 69°10N 97°25W 108 C10
Kingman U.S.A. 35°12N 114°4W 110 C4

King's Lynn U.K. 52°45N 0°24E 31 A9
King's Sutton U.K. 52°2N 1°15W 30 B6
King's Worthy U.K. 51°6N 1°17W 30 D6
Kingsbridge U.K. 50°17N 3°47W 29 G6
Kingsbury U.K. 52°34N 1°40W 27 G5
Kingscourt Ireland 53°54N 6°48W 19 D8
Kingskerswell U.K. 50°29N 3°35W 29 G6
Kingsland U.K. 52°15N 2°48W 30 B3
Kingsteignton U.K. 50°33N 3°36W 29 F6
Kingston Canada 44°14N 76°30W 109 E12
Kingston Jamaica 17°55N 76°50W 114 a
Kingston N.Y., U.S.A. 41°56N 73°59W 113 E10
Kingston Pa., U.S.A. 41°16N 75°54W 113 E10
Kingston upon Hull U.K. 53°45N 0°21W 27 E8
Kingston-upon-Thames □
U.K. 51°24N 0°17W 31 D8
Kingstown St. Vincent 13°10N 61°10W 115 E12
Kingsville U.S.A. 27°31N 97°52W 110 E7
Kingswear U.K. 50°21N 3°35W 29 G6
Kingswood U.K. 51°27N 2°31W 30 D3
Kington U.K. 52°13N 3°1W 30 B2
Kingussie U.K. 57°6N 4°2W 23 H9
Kinlochleven U.K. 56°43N 5°0W 22 J7
Kinnairds Hd. U.K. 57°43N 2°1W 23 G13
Kinngait Canada 64°14N 76°32W 109 C12
Kinross U.K. 56°13N 3°25W 25 B9
Kinsale Ireland 51°42N 8°31W 20 E5
Kinsale, Old Hd. of Ireland 51°37N 8°33W 20 E5
Kinshasa Dem. Rep. of the Congo 4°20S 15°15E 96 E3
Kintore U.K. 57°14N 2°20W 23 H13
Kintyre U.K. 55°30N 5°35W 24 D4
Kintyre, Mull of U.K. 55°17N 5°47W 24 D4
Kippure Ireland 53°11N 6°21W 21 B10
Kirensk Russia 57°50N 107°55E 77 D11
Kirgiz Steppe Eurasia 50°0N 55°0E 71 E10
Kiribati ■ Pac. Oc. 3°0S 180°0E 102 H10
Kırıkkale Turkey 39°51N 33°32E 71 G5
Kiritimati Kiribati 1°58N 157°27W 103 G12
Kirkbean U.K. 54°55N 3°36W 25 E9
Kirkbride U.K. 54°54N 3°12W 26 C2
Kirkburton U.K. 53°37N 1°42W 27 E5
Kirkby U.K. 53°30N 2°54W 27 F3
Kirkby-in-Ashfield U.K. 53°6N 1°14W 27 F6
Kirkby Lonsdale U.K. 54°12N 2°36W 26 D3
Kirkby Malzeard U.K. 54°10N 1°37W 26 D5
Kirkby Stephen U.K. 54°29N 2°21W 26 D4
Kirkby Thore U.K. 54°37N 2°32W 26 C3
Kirkbymoorside U.K. 54°17N 0°56W 26 D7
Kirkcaldy U.K. 56°7N 3°9W 25 B9
Kirkcudbright U.K. 54°50N 4°2W 24 E7
Kirkham U.K. 53°47N 2°53W 27 E3
Kirkintilloch U.K. 55°56N 4°8W 24 C7
Kirkland Lake Canada 48°9N 80°2W 109 E11
Kirklareli Turkey 41°44N 27°15E 86 A1
Kirkoswald U.K. 54°46N 2°41W 26 C3
Kirksville U.S.A. 40°12N 92°35W 111 B8
Kirkūk Iraq 35°30N 44°21E 86 C6
Kirkwall U.K. 58°59N 2°58W 23 E12
Kirkwhelpington U.K. 55°9N 1°59W 26 B5
Kirov Russia 58°35N 49°40E 70 C8
Kirovohrad Ukraine 48°35N 32°20E 71 E5
Kirriemuir U.K. 56°41N 3°1W 23 J11
Kırşehir Turkey 39°14N 34°5E 71 G5
Kirthar Range Pakistan 27°0N 67°0E 84 F5
Kirtling U.K. 52°12N 0°28E 31 B9
Kirtlington U.K. 51°53N 1°15W 30 C6
Kirton U.K. 52°56N 0°3W 27 G8
Kirton in Lindsey U.K. 53°29N 0°34W 27 F7
Kiruna Sweden 67°52N 20°15E 63 D8
Kiryū Japan 36°24N 139°20E 81 E6
Kisangani
Dem. Rep. of the Congo 0°35N 25°15E 96 D5
Kiselevsk Russia 54°5N 86°39E 76 D9
Kishanganj India 26°3N 88°14E 85 F16
Kishinev Moldova 47°2N 28°50E 65 E15
Kisii Kenya 0°40S 34°45E 96 E6
Kislovodsk Russia 43°50N 42°45E 71 F7
Kismaayo Somalia 0°22S 42°32E 89 H3
Kisumu Kenya 0°3S 34°45E 96 E6
Kitakyūshū Japan 33°50N 130°50E 81 G2
Kitale Kenya 1°0N 35°0E 96 D7
Kitami Japan 43°48N 143°54E 81 B8
Kitchener Canada 43°27N 80°29W 112 D7
Kithnos Greece 37°26N 24°27E 69 F11
Kitimat Canada 54°3N 128°38W 108 D7
Kittanning U.S.A. 40°49N 79°31W 112 E8
Kitwe Zambia 12°54S 28°13E 97 G5
Kivu, L. Dem. Rep. of the Congo 1°48S 29°0E 96 E5
Kızıl Irmak → Turkey 41°44N 35°58E 71 F6
Kizlyar Russia 43°51N 46°40E 71 F8
Kladno Czechia 50°10N 14°7E 64 C8
Klagenfurt Austria 46°38N 14°20E 64 E8
Klaipėda Lithuania 55°43N 21°10E 63 F8
Klamath → U.S.A. 41°33N 124°5W 110 B2
Klamath Falls U.S.A. 42°13N 121°46W 110 B2
Klang Malaysia 3°2N 101°26E 82 D2
Klarälven → Sweden 59°23N 13°32E 63 F6
Klerksdorp S. Africa 26°53S 26°38E 97 K5
Kluang Malaysia 2°3N 103°18E 82 D2
Klyuchevskaya, Sopka
Russia 55°50N 160°30E 77 D17
Knaresborough U.K. 54°1N 1°28W 27 D6
Knebworth U.K. 51°52N 0°11W 31 C8
Knighton U.K. 52°21N 3°3W 28 C7
Knock Ireland 53°48N 8°55W 18 D4
Knockmealdown Mts. Ireland 52°14N 7°56W 20 D7
Knossos Greece 35°16N 25°10E 69 G11
Knottingley U.K. 53°43N 1°16W 27 E6
Knowle U.K. 52°23N 1°43W 30 B5
Knoxville U.S.A. 35°58N 83°55W 111 C10
Knutsford U.K. 53°18N 2°21W 27 F4
Kōbe Japan 34°45N 135°10E 81 F4
Koblenz Germany 50°21N 7°36E 64 C4
Kocaeli Turkey 40°45N 29°50E 71 F4
Koch Bihar India 26°22N 89°29E 85 F16
Kōchi India 9°58N 76°20E 84 Q10
Kōchi Japan 33°30N 133°35E 81 G3
Kodiak U.S.A. 57°47N 152°24W 108 D4
Kodiak I. U.S.A. 57°30N 152°45W 108 D4

Koforidua Ghana 6°3N 0°17W 94 G5
Kōfu Japan 35°40N 138°30E 81 F6
Kogalym Russia 62°16N 74°29E 76 C8
Kohat Pakistan 33°40N 71°29E 84 C7
Kohima India 25°35N 94°10E 85 G19
Kohtla-Järve Estonia 59°20N 27°20E 63 E9
Kokkola Finland 63°50N 23°8E 63 E8
Koko Kyunzu Myanmar 14°7N 93°22E 85 M18
Koko Nur China 36°40N 100°10E 78 D9
Kokomo U.S.A. 40°29N 86°8W 112 E4
Kokopo Papua N. G. 4°22S 152°19E 98 A9
Kökshetaū Kazakhstan 53°20N 69°25E 76 D7
Koksoak → Canada 58°30N 68°10W 109 D13
Kola Pen. Russia 67°30N 38°0E 70 A6
Kolar Gold Fields India 12°58N 78°16E 84 N11
Kolguyev Russia 69°20N 48°30E 70 A8
Kolhapur India 16°43N 74°15E 84 L9
Kolkata India 22°34N 88°21E 85 H16
Kollam India 8°50N 76°38E 84 Q10
Kolomna Russia 55°8N 38°45E 70 C6
Kolomyya Ukraine 48°31N 25°2E 71 E4
Kolpino Russia 59°44N 30°39E 70 C5
Kolwezi Dem. Rep. of the Congo 10°40S 25°25E 96 G5
Kolyma → Russia 69°30N 161°0E 77 C17
Kolyma Ra. Russia 63°0N 157°0E 77 C16
Komatsu Japan 36°25N 136°30E 81 E5
Komi □ Russia 64°0N 55°0E 70 B10
Komsomolsk-na-Amur
Russia 50°30N 137°0E 77 D14
Kondoz Afghan. 36°50N 68°50E 87 B12
Kongur Shan China 38°34N 75°18E 78 D4
Konin Poland 52°12N 18°15E 65 B10
Konosha Russia 61°0N 40°5E 70 B7
Konotop Ukraine 51°12N 33°7E 71 D5
Konqi He → China 40°45N 90°10E 78 C6
Konya Turkey 37°52N 32°35E 71 G5
Kootenay L. Canada 49°45N 116°50W 108 E8
Kopet Dagh Asia 38°0N 58°0E 87 B9
Korçë Albania 40°37N 20°50E 69 D9
Korčula Croatia 42°56N 16°57E 68 C7
Kordofân Sudan 13°0N 29°0E 95 F11
Korea Bay Korea 39°0N 124°0E 79 D13
Korea Strait Asia 34°0N 129°30E 79 E14
Korhogo Côte d'Ivoire 9°29N 5°28W 94 G4
Kōriyama Japan 37°24N 140°23E 81 E7
Korla China 41°45N 86°4E 78 C6
Koror Palau 7°20N 134°28E 102 G5
Körös → Hungary 46°43N 20°12E 65 E11
Korosten Ukraine 50°54N 28°36E 71 D4
Kortrijk Belgium 50°50N 3°17E 64 C2
Koryak Ra. Russia 61°0N 171°0E 77 C18
Kos Greece 36°50N 27°15E 69 F12
Kościuszko, Mt. Australia 36°27S 148°16E 98 H8
Košice Slovakia 48°42N 21°15E 65 D11
Kosovo ■ Europe 42°30N 21°0E 69 C9
Kôstî Sudan 13°8N 32°43E 95 F12
Kostroma Russia 57°50N 40°58E 70 C7
Koszalin Poland 54°11N 16°8E 64 A9
Kota India 25°14N 75°49E 84 G9
Kota Bharu Malaysia 6°7N 102°14E 82 C2
Kota Kinabalu Malaysia 6°0N 116°4E 82 C5
Kotabumi Indonesia 4°49S 104°54E 82 E2
Kotelnich Russia 58°22N 48°24E 70 C8
Kotka Finland 60°28N 26°58E 63 E9
Kotlas Russia 61°17N 46°43E 70 B8
Kotor Montenegro 42°25N 18°47E 69 C8
Kotri Pakistan 25°22N 68°22E 84 G6
Kotuy → Russia 71°54N 102°6E 77 B11
Kotzebue U.S.A. 66°53N 162°39W 108 C3
Koudougou Burkina Faso 12°10N 2°20W 94 F5
Koumra Chad 8°50N 17°35E 95 G9
Kovel Ukraine 51°11N 24°38E 70 D3
Kovrov Russia 56°25N 41°25E 70 C7
Kowloon China 22°19N 114°11E 79 G11
Kozhikode India 11°15N 75°43E 84 P9
Kpalimé Togo 6°57N 0°44E 94 G6
Kra, Isthmus of Thailand 10°15N 99°30E 82 B1
Kragujevac Serbia 44°2N 20°56E 69 B9
Krakatoa Indonesia 6°10S 105°20E 82 F3
Kraków Poland 50°4N 19°57E 65 C10
Kraljevo Serbia 43°44N 20°41E 69 C9
Kramatorsk Ukraine 48°50N 37°30E 71 E6
Krasnodar Russia 45°5N 39°0E 71 E6
Krasnokamensk Russia 50°3N 118°0E 77 D12
Krasnokamsk Russia 58°4N 55°48E 70 C10
Krasnoturinsk Russia 59°46N 60°12E 70 C11
Krasnoyarsk Russia 56°8N 93°0E 77 D10
Krasnyy Luch Ukraine 48°13N 39°0E 71 E6
Krefeld Germany 51°20N 6°33E 64 C4
Kremenchuk Ukraine 49°5N 33°25E 71 E5
Kribi Cameroon 2°57N 9°56E 96 D1
Krishna → India 15°57N 80°59E 85 M12
Kristiansand Norway 58°8N 8°1E 63 F5
Kristiansund Norway 63°7N 7°45E 63 E5
Krivoy Rog Ukraine 47°51N 33°20E 71 E5
Krk Croatia 45°8N 14°40E 68 B6
Kronshtadt Russia 59°57N 29°51E 70 B4
Kroonstad S. Africa 27°43S 27°19E 97 K5
Kropotkin Russia 45°28N 40°28E 71 E7
Krosno Poland 49°42N 21°46E 65 D11
Krugersdorp S. Africa 26°5S 27°46E 97 K5
Kruševac Serbia 43°35N 21°28E 69 C9
Ksar el Kebir Morocco 35°0N 6°0W 94 B4
Kuala Belait Malaysia 4°35N 114°11E 82 D4
Kuala Lumpur Malaysia 3°9N 101°41E 82 D2
Kuala Terengganu Malaysia 5°20N 103°8E 82 C2
Kuantan Malaysia 3°49N 103°20E 82 D2
Kuching Malaysia 1°33N 110°25E 82 D4
Kudymkar Russia 59°1N 54°39E 70 C9
Kuglugtuk Canada 67°50N 115°5W 108 C8
Kuito Angola 12°22S 16°55E 97 G3
Kūlob Tajikistan 37°55N 69°50E 87 B12
Kuma → Russia 44°55N 47°0E 71 F8
Kumagaya Japan 36°9N 139°22E 81 E6
Kumamoto Japan 32°45N 130°45E 81 G2
Kumanovo Macedonia 42°9N 21°42E 69 C9
Kumasi Ghana 6°41N 1°38W 94 G5
Kumba Cameroon 4°36N 9°24E 96 D1
Kumbakonam India 10°58N 79°25E 84 P11
Kumertau Russia 52°45N 55°57E 70 D10
Kumtag Desert China 39°40N 92°0E 78 D7

Kungur Russia 57°25N 56°57E 70 C10
Kunlun Shan Asia 36°0N 86°30E 78 D6
Kunming China 25°1N 102°41E 78 F9
Kuopio Finland 62°53N 27°35E 63 E9
Kupang Indonesia 10°19S 123°39E 83 F6
Kür → Azerbaijan 39°29N 49°15E 71 G8
Kurdistan Asia 37°20N 43°30E 86 B5
Kure Japan 34°14N 132°32E 81 F3
Kurgan Russia 55°26N 65°18E 76 D7
Kuril Is. Russia 45°0N 150°0E 77 E16
Kuril-Kamchatka Trench
Pac. Oc. 44°0N 153°0E 102 C7
Kurnool India 15°45N 78°0E 84 M11
Kursk Russia 51°42N 36°11E 70 D6
Kuruktag China 41°0N 89°0E 78 C6
Kurume Japan 33°15N 130°30E 81 G2
Kushiro Japan 43°0N 144°25E 81 B9
Kushtia Bangla. 23°55N 89°5E 85 H16
Kuskokwim B. U.S.A. 59°45N 162°25W 108 D3
Kütahya Turkey 39°30N 30°2E 71 G5
Kutaisi Georgia 42°19N 42°40E 71 F7
Kuujjuaq Canada 58°6N 68°15W 109 D13
Kuujjuarapik Canada 55°20N 77°35W 109 D12
Kuwait Kuwait 29°30N 48°0E 86 D7
Kuwait ■ Asia 29°30N 47°30E 86 D6
Kuybyshev Res. Russia 55°2N 49°30E 70 C8
Kuznetsk Russia 53°12N 46°40E 70 D8
Kuzomen Russia 66°22N 36°50E 70 A6
KwaMashu S. Africa 29°45S 30°58E 97 K6
KwaZulu Natal □ S. Africa 29°0S 30°0E 97 K6
Kwekwe Zimbabwe 18°58S 29°48E 97 H5
Kwun Tong China 22°19N 114°13E 79 a
Kyiv Ukraine 50°30N 30°28E 65 C16
Kyle of Lochalsh U.K. 57°17N 5°44W 22 H6
Kyoga, L. Uganda 1°35N 33°0E 96 D6
Kyōto Japan 35°0N 135°45E 81 F4
Kyrenia Cyprus 35°20N 33°20E 86 C3
Kyrgyzstan ■ Asia 42°0N 75°0E 76 E8
Kythira Greece 36°8N 23°0E 69 F10
Kyūshū Japan 33°0N 131°0E 81 G2
Kyustendil Bulgaria 42°16N 22°41E 69 C10
Kyzyl Russia 51°50N 94°30E 77 D10
Kyzyl Kum Uzbekistan 42°30N 65°0E 87 A10
Kyzyl-Orda Kazakhstan 44°48N 65°28E 76 E7

L

La Alcarria Spain 40°31N 2°45W 67 B4
La Barra Nic. 12°54N 83°33W 115 E8
La Ceiba Honduras 15°40N 86°50W 114 D7
La Coruña Spain 43°20N 8°25W 67 A1
La Crosse U.S.A. 43°48N 91°15W 112 D2
La Grande U.S.A. 45°20N 118°5W 110 A3
La Grande → Canada 53°50N 79°0W 109 D12
La Grange U.S.A. 33°2N 85°2W 111 D10
La Habana Cuba 23°8N 82°22E 115 C8
La Junta U.S.A. 37°59N 103°33W 110 C6
La Linea de la Concepción
Spain 36°15N 5°23W 67 D3
La Loche Canada 56°29N 109°26W 108 D9
La Mancha Spain 39°10N 2°54W 67 C4
La Oroya Peru 11°32S 75°54W 120 D2
La Palma Canary Is. 28°40N 17°50W 94 C2
La Paz Bolivia 16°20S 68°10W 120 D3
La Paz Mexico 24°10N 110°18W 114 C2
La Perouse Str. Asia 45°40N 142°0E 79 B17
La Plata Argentina 35°0S 57°55W 121 F4
La Quiaca Argentina 22°5S 65°35W 121 E3
La Rioja Argentina 29°20S 67°0W 121 E3
La Rioja □ Spain 42°20N 2°20W 67 A4
La Roche-sur-Yon France 46°40N 1°25W 66 C3
La Rochelle France 46°10N 1°9W 66 C3
La Romana Dom. Rep. 18°27N 68°57W 115 D11
La Ronge Canada 55°5N 105°20W 108 D9
La Sarre Canada 48°45N 79°15W 112 A8
La Serena Chile 29°55S 71°10W 121 E2
La Seyne-sur-Mer France 43°7N 5°52E 66 E6
La Spézia Italy 44°7N 9°50E 68 B3
La Tortuga, I. Venezuela 11°0N 65°22W 120 A3
La Tuque Canada 47°30N 72°50W 109 E12
La Vega Dom. Rep. 19°20N 70°30W 115 D10
Labé Guinea 11°24N 12°16W 94 F3
Labinsk Russia 44°40N 40°48E 71 F7
Laborie St. Lucia 13°45N 61°2W 114 b
Labrador Canada 53°20N 61°0W 109 D13
Labrador City Canada 52°57N 66°55W 109 D13
Labrador Sea Atl. Oc. 57°0N 54°0W 109 D14
Labuan Malaysia 5°21N 115°13E 82 C5
Lac La Biche Canada 54°45N 111°58W 108 D8
Lac-Mégantic Canada 45°35N 70°53W 113 C12
Laccadive Is. = Lakshadweep Is.
India 10°0N 72°30E 72 G9
Laceby U.K. 53°33N 0°10W 27 E8
Lacock U.K. 51°24N 2°7W 30 D4
Lacombe Canada 52°30N 113°44W 108 D8
Laconia U.S.A. 43°32N 71°28W 113 D12
Ladakh Ra. India 34°0N 78°0E 84 C11
Ladder Hills U.K. 57°13N 3°16W 23 H11
Ladock U.K. 50°19N 4°58W 29 G4
Ladoga, L. Russia 61°15N 30°30E 70 B5
Ladysmith S. Africa 28°32S 29°46E 97 K5
Ladysmith U.S.A. 45°28N 91°12W 112 C2
Lae Papua N. G. 6°40S 147°2E 98 B8
Lafayette Ind., U.S.A. 40°25N 86°54W 112 E4
Lafayette La., U.S.A. 30°14N 92°1W 111 D8
Lafia Nigeria 8°30N 8°34E 94 G7
Lagan → U.K. 54°36N 5°55W 19 B10
Lagarto Brazil 10°54S 37°41W 122 B3
Lagdo, L. de Cameroon 8°40N 14°0E 95 G8
Laghouat Algeria 33°50N 2°59E 94 B6
Lagos Nigeria 6°25N 3°27E 94 G6
Lagos Portugal 37°5N 8°41W 67 D1
Lahn → Germany 50°19N 7°37E 64 C4
Lahore Pakistan 31°32N 74°22E 84 D9
Lahti Finland 60°58N 25°40E 63 E9
Lairg U.K. 58°2N 4°24W 23 F8
Laizhou China 37°8N 119°57E 79 D12
Lake Charles U.S.A. 30°14N 93°13W 111 D8
Lake City U.S.A. 30°11N 82°38W 111 D10
Lake District △ U.K. 54°30N 3°21W 26 C2

Lake Havasu City   **Lyubertsy**

Lake Havasu City U.S.A. 34°27N 114°22W 110 D4
Lakeland U.S.A. 28°3N 81°57W 111 E10
Lakenheath U.K. 52°25N 0°32E 31 B10
Lakewood U.S.A. 41°28N 81°47W 112 E7
Lakshadweep Is. India 10°0N 72°30E 72 G9
Lamar U.S.A. 38°5N 102°37W 110 C6
Lambaréné Gabon 0°41S 10°12E 96 E2
Lambay I. Ireland 53°29N 6°1W 21 B10
Lamberhurst U.K. 51°5N 0°24E 31 D9
Lambeth □ U.K. 51°28N 0°6W 31 D8
Lambley U.K. 54°56N 2°30W 26 C4
Lambourn U.K. 51°30N 1°32W 30 C5
Lamesa U.S.A. 32°44N 101°58W 110 D6
Lamma I. China 22°12N 114°7E 79 a
Lammermuir U.K. 55°50N 2°25W 25 C11
Lammermuir Hills U.K. 55°50N 2°40W 25 C10
Lamon B. Phil. 14°30N 122°20E 83 B6
Lampedusa Medit. S. 35°36N 12°40E 68 G5
Lampeter U.K. 52°7N 4°4W 28 C5
Lamu Kenya 2°16S 40°55E 96 E8
Lanark U.K. 55°40N 3°47W 25 C8
Lancang Jiang → China 21°40N 101°10E 78 G9
Lancashire □ U.K. 53°50N 2°48W 27 E3
Lancaster U.K. 54°3N 2°48W 26 C4
Lancaster N.H., U.S.A. 44°29N 71°34W 113 C12
Lancaster Pa., U.S.A. 40°2N 76°19W 112 E9
Lancaster Wis., U.S.A. 42°51N 90°43W 112 D2
Lancaster Sd. Canada 74°13N 84°0W 109 B11
Lanchester U.K. 54°50N 1°44W 26 C5
Lancing U.K. 50°49N 0°19W 31 E8
Landes France 44°0N 1°0W 66 D3
Landkey U.K. 51°3N 4°0W 29 E6
Land's End U.K. 50°4N 5°44W 29 G2
Langholm U.K. 55°9N 3°0W 25 D10
Langport U.K. 51°2N 2°50W 30 D3
Langreo Spain 43°18N 5°40W 67 A3
Langres France 47°52N 5°20E 66 C6
Langres, Plateau de France 47°45N 5°3E 66 C6
Langsa Indonesia 4°30N 97°57E 82 D1
Langstrothdale Chase U.K. 54°14N 2°13W 26 D4
Langtoft U.K. 52°42N 0°20W 27 G8
Langtree U.K. 50°55N 4°13W 29 F5
Languedoc France 43°58N 3°55E 66 E5
Lannion France 48°46N 3°29W 66 B2
L'Annonciation Canada 46°25N 74°55W 113 B10
L'Anse U.S.A. 46°45N 88°27W 112 B3
Lansing U.S.A. 42°44N 84°33W 112 D5
Lantau I. China 22°15N 113°56E 79 a
Lanzarote Canary Is. 29°0N 13°40W 94 C3
Lanzhou China 36°1N 103°52E 78 D9
Laoag Phil. 18°7N 120°34E 83 A6
Laois □ Ireland 52°57N 7°27W 21 C7
Laon France 49°33N 3°35E 66 B5
Laos ■ Asia 17°45N 105°0E 82 A3
Lapeer U.S.A. 43°3N 83°19W 112 D6
Lapford U.K. 50°51N 3°48W 29 F6
Lapland Europe 68°7N 24°0E 63 D8
LaPorte U.S.A. 41°36N 86°43W 112 E4
Laptev Sea Russia 76°0N 125°0E 77 B13
L'Aquila Italy 42°22N 13°22E 68 C5
Laramie U.S.A. 41°19N 105°35W 110 B5
Laramie Mts. U.S.A. 42°0N 105°30W 110 B5
Laredo U.S.A. 27°30N 99°30W 110 E7
Largs U.K. 55°47N 4°52W 24 C6
Larisa Greece 39°36N 22°27E 69 E10
Larnaca Cyprus 34°55N 33°38E 86 C3
Larne U.K. 54°51N 5°51W 19 B10
Larne L. U.K. 54°50N 5°48W 19 B10
Larrimah Australia 15°35S 133°12E 98 D5
Larsen Ice Shelf Antarctica 67°0S 62°0W 55 C17
Larvik Norway 59°4N 10°2E 63 F6
Las Cruces U.S.A. 32°19N 106°47W 110 D5
Las Palmas de Gran Canaria Canary Is. 28°7N 15°26W 94 C2
Las Tunas Cuba 20°58N 76°59W 115 C9
Las Vegas N. Mex., U.S.A. 35°36N 105°13W 110 C5
Las Vegas Nev., U.S.A. 36°10N 115°8W 110 C3
Lashio Myanmar 22°56N 97°45E 85 H20
Lassen Pk. U.S.A. 40°29N 121°30W 110 B2
Lastoursville Gabon 0°55S 12°38E 96 E2
Latacunga Ecuador 0°50S 78°35W 120 C2
Latakia Syria 35°30N 35°45E 86 C3
Latina Italy 41°28N 12°52E 68 D5
Latvia ■ Europe 56°50N 24°0E 63 F8
Lauder U.K. 55°43N 2°43W 25 C10
Lauderdale U.K. 55°44N 2°41W 25 C10
Launceston Australia 41°24S 147°8E 98 J8
Launceston U.K. 50°38N 4°22W 29 F5
Laune → Ireland 52°7N 9°47W 20 D3
Laurel U.S.A. 31°41N 89°8W 111 D9
Laurencekirk U.K. 56°50N 2°28W 23 J13
Laurentian Plateau Canada 52°0N 70°0W 104 E12
Lausanne Switz. 46°32N 6°38E 64 E4
Lavagh More Ireland 54°46N 8°6W 18 B5
Laval Canada 45°33N 73°42W 113 C11
Laval France 48°4N 0°48W 66 B3
Lavendon U.K. 52°11N 0°39W 31 B7
Lavenham U.K. 52°6N 0°48E 31 B10
Lavras Brazil 21°20S 45°0W 122 D2
Lawrence Kans., U.S.A. 38°58N 95°14W 111 C7
Lawrence Mass., U.S.A. 42°43N 71°10W 113 D12
Lawton U.S.A. 34°37N 98°25W 110 D7
Laxey U.K. 54°14N 4°23W 19 C13
Laxfield U.K. 52°18N 1°22E 31 B11
Laxford, L. U.K. 58°24N 5°6W 22 F7
Lazio □ Italy 42°10N 12°30E 68 C5
Lazonby U.K. 54°46N 2°42W 26 C3
Le Creusot France 46°48N 4°24E 66 C6
Le Havre France 49°30N 0°5E 66 B4
Le Mans France 48°0N 0°10E 66 C4
Le Puy-en-Velay France 45°3N 3°52E 66 D5
Lea U.K. 53°22N 0°45W 27 F7
Lea → U.K. 51°31N 0°1E 31 C9
Leadenham U.K. 53°3N 0°35W 27 F7
Leamington Canada 42°3N 82°36W 112 D6
Leane, L. Ireland 52°2N 9°32W 20 D3
Leatherhead U.K. 51°18N 0°20W 31 D8
Leavenworth U.S.A. 39°19N 94°55W 111 C8
Lebanon Ind., U.S.A. 40°3N 86°28W 112 E4
Lebanon Ky., U.S.A. 37°34N 85°15W 112 G5
Lebanon Mo., U.S.A. 37°41N 92°40W 111 C8

Lebanon Pa., U.S.A. 40°20N 76°26W 112 E9
Lebanon ■ Asia 34°0N 36°0E 86 C3
Lebu Chile 37°40S 73°47W 121 F2
Lecce Italy 40°23N 18°11E 69 D8
Lechlade U.K. 51°42N 1°41W 30 C5
Ledbury U.K. 52°2N 2°25W 30 B4
Lee → Ireland 51°53N 8°56W 20 E5
Lee-on-the-Solent U.K. 50°48N 1°12W 30 E6
Leech L. U.S.A. 47°10N 94°24W 111 A8
Leeds U.K. 53°48N 1°33W 27 E5
Leek U.K. 53°7N 2°1W 27 F4
Leeuwarden Neths. 53°15N 5°48E 64 B3
Leeuwin, C. Australia 34°20S 115°9E 98 G2
Leeward Is. Atl. Oc. 16°30N 63°30W 115 D12
Lefkada Greece 38°40N 20°43E 69 E9
Leganés Spain 40°19N 3°45W 67 B4
Legazpi Phil. 13°10N 123°45E 83 B6
Legionowo Poland 52°25N 20°50E 65 B11
Legnica Poland 51°12N 16°10E 64 C9
Leicester U.K. 52°38N 1°8W 27 G6
Leicestershire □ U.K. 52°41N 1°17W 27 G6
Leiden Neths. 52°9N 4°30E 64 B3
Leigh Gt. Man., U.K. 53°30N 2°32W 27 E3
Leigh Hereford, U.K. 52°11N 2°20W 30 B4
Leighton Buzzard U.K. 51°54N 0°38W 31 C7
Leine → Germany 52°43N 9°36E 64 B5
Leinster □ Ireland 53°3N 7°8W 21 B8
Leinster, Mt. Ireland 52°37N 6°46W 21 C9
Leintwardine U.K. 52°22N 2°51W 30 B3
Leipzig Germany 51°18N 12°22E 64 C7
Leiston U.K. 52°12N 1°36E 31 B12
Leith U.K. 55°59N 3°11W 25 C9
Leith Hill U.K. 51°11N 0°22W 31 D8
Leitholm U.K. 55°41N 2°20W 25 C11
Leitrim Ireland 54°0N 8°5W 18 C5
Leitrim □ Ireland 54°8N 8°0W 18 C5
Leixlip Ireland 53°22N 6°30W 21 B9
Leizhou Pen. China 21°0N 110°0E 79 G11
Lelant U.K. 50°11N 5°28W 29 G3
Léman, L. Europe 46°26N 6°30E 64 E4
Lena → Russia 72°52N 126°40E 77 B13
Lenham U.K. 51°14N 0°44E 31 D10
Leninsk-Kuznetskiy Russia 54°44N 86°10E 76 D9
Lennox Hills U.K. 56°3N 4°12W 24 B7
Lens France 50°26N 2°50E 66 A5
Leodhais = Lewis U.K. 58°9N 6°40W 22 F4
Leominster U.K. 52°14N 2°43W 30 B3
Leominster U.S.A. 42°32N 71°46W 113 D12
León Mexico 21°6N 101°41W 114 C4
León Nic. 12°27N 86°51W 114 E7
León Spain 42°38N 5°34W 67 A3
Leonora Australia 28°49S 121°19E 98 F3
Leopoldina Brazil 21°28S 42°40W 122 D2
Lerwick U.K. 60°9N 1°9W 22 B15
Les Cayes Haiti 18°15N 73°46W 115 D10
Les Sables-d'Olonne France 46°30N 1°45W 66 C3
Lesbos Greece 39°10N 26°20E 69 E12
Lesbury U.K. 55°25N 1°36W 26 B5
Leshan China 29°33N 103°41E 78 F9
Leskovac Serbia 43°0N 21°58E 69 C10
Lesosibirsk Russia 58°14N 92°29E 77 D10
Lesotho ■ Africa 29°40S 28°0E 97 K5
Lesser Antilles W. Indies 15°0N 61°0W 115 E12
Lesser Slave L. Canada 55°30N 115°25W 108 D8
Lesser Sunda Is. Indonesia 8°0S 120°0E 83 F6
Leszno Poland 51°50N 16°30E 65 C9
Letchworth Garden City U.K. 51°59N 0°13W 31 C8
Lethbridge Canada 49°45N 112°45W 108 E8
Leti, Kepulauan Indonesia 8°10S 128°0E 83 F7
Leticia Colombia 4°9S 70°0W 120 C2
Letterkenny Ireland 54°57N 7°45W 18 B6
Leuchars U.K. 56°24N 2°53W 25 B10
Leuven Belgium 50°52N 4°42E 64 C3
Leven U.K. 53°53N 0°18W 27 E8
Leven Fife, U.K. 56°12N 3°0W 25 B10
Leven U.K. 54°31N 1°19W 26 C6
Leven, L. Highl., U.K. 56°42N 5°6W 22 J7
Leven, L. Perth & Kinr., U.K. 56°12N 3°22W 25 B9
Lévis Canada 46°48N 71°9W 113 B12
Lewes U.K. 50°52N 0°1E 31 E9
Lewis U.K. 58°9N 6°40W 22 F4
Lewis, Butt of U.K. 58°31N 6°16W 22 E5
Lewisham □ U.K. 51°27N 0°1W 31 D8
Lewisporte Canada 49°15N 55°3W 109 E14
Lewiston Idaho, U.S.A. 46°25N 117°1W 110 A3
Lewiston Maine, U.S.A. 44°6N 70°13W 113 C12
Lewistown Mont., U.S.A. 47°4N 109°26W 110 A5
Lewistown Pa., U.S.A. 40°36N 77°34W 112 E9
Lexington U.S.A. 38°3N 84°30W 112 F5
Lexington Park U.S.A. 38°16N 76°27W 112 F9
Leyburn U.K. 54°19N 1°48W 26 D5
Leyland U.K. 53°42N 2°43W 27 E3
Leysdown on Sea U.K. 51°24N 0°56E 31 D10
Leyte Phil. 11°0N 125°0E 83 B6
Lhasa China 29°25N 90°58E 78 F7
Lhazê China 29°5N 87°38E 78 F6
L'Hospitalet de Llobregat Spain 41°21N 2°6E 67 B7
Liancourt Rocks Asia 37°15N 131°52E 81 E2
Lianyungang China 34°40N 119°11E 79 E12
Liaodong Pen. China 40°0N 122°30E 79 D13
Liaoning □ China 41°40N 122°30E 79 C13
Liaotung, G. of China 40°20N 121°10E 79 C13
Liaoyang China 41°15N 122°58E 79 C13
Liaoyuan China 42°58N 125°2E 79 C14
Liard → Canada 61°51N 121°18W 108 C7
Liberal U.S.A. 37°3N 100°55W 110 C6
Liberec Czechia 50°47N 15°7E 64 C8
Liberia ■ W. Afr. 6°30N 9°30W 94 G4
Libourne France 44°55N 0°14W 66 D3
Libreville Gabon 0°25N 9°26E 96 D1
Libya ■ N. Afr. 27°0N 17°0E 95 C9
Libyan Desert Africa 25°0N 25°0E 95 C10
Libyan Plateau Egypt 30°40N 26°30E 95 B11
Lichfield U.K. 52°41N 1°49W 27 G5
Lichinga Mozam. 13°13S 35°11E 97 G7
Liddesdale U.K. 55°12N 2°50W 25 D10
Liechtenstein ■ Europe 47°8N 9°35E 64 E5
Liège Belgium 50°38N 5°35E 64 C3
Liepāja Latvia 56°30N 21°0E 63 F8
Liffey → Ireland 53°21N 6°13W 21 B10

Lifford Ireland 54°51N 7°29W 18 B7
Liguria □ Italy 44°30N 8°50E 68 B3
Ligurian Sea Medit. S. 43°20N 9°0E 68 C3
Lihu'e U.S.A. 21°59N 159°23W 110 H15
Lijiang China 26°55N 100°20E 78 F9
Likasi Dem. Rep. of the Congo 10°55S 26°48E 96 G5
Lille France 50°38N 3°3E 66 A5
Lillehammer Norway 61°8N 10°30E 63 E6
Lilleshall U.K. 52°44N 2°23W 27 G4
Lilongwe Malawi 14°0S 33°48E 97 G6
Lima Peru 12°3S 77°2W 120 D2
Lima U.S.A. 40°44N 84°6W 112 E5
Limassol Cyprus 34°42N 33°1E 86 C3
Limavady U.K. 55°3N 6°56W 19 A8
Limay → Argentina 39°0S 68°0W 121 F3
Limbe Cameroon 4°1N 9°10E 96 D1
Limeira Brazil 22°35S 47°28W 122 D1
Limerick Ireland 52°40N 8°37W 20 C5
Limerick □ Ireland 52°30N 8°50W 20 C5
Limfjorden Denmark 56°55N 9°0E 63 F5
Limnos Greece 39°50N 25°5E 69 E11
Limoges France 45°50N 1°15E 66 D4
Limón Costa Rica 10°0N 83°2W 115 F8
Limousin France 45°30N 1°30E 66 D4
Limoux France 43°4N 2°12E 66 E5
Limpopo → Africa 25°5S 33°30E 97 K6
Linares Chile 35°50S 71°40W 121 F2
Linares Mexico 24°52N 99°34W 114 C5
Linares Spain 38°10N 3°40W 67 C4
Linchuan China 27°57N 116°15E 79 F12
Lincoln U.K. 53°14N 0°32W 27 F7
Lincoln Maine, U.S.A. 45°22N 68°30W 113 C13
Lincoln Nebr., U.S.A. 40°49N 96°41W 111 B7
Lincoln Sea Arctic 84°0N 55°0W 54 A5
Lincolnshire □ U.K. 53°14N 0°32W 27 F7
Lincolnshire Wolds U.K. 53°26N 0°13W 27 F8
Lindale U.K. 54°14N 2°53W 26 D3
Lindesnes Norway 57°58N 7°3E 63 F5
Lindsay Canada 44°22N 78°43W 112 C8
Linfen China 36°3N 111°30E 79 D11
Lingfield U.K. 51°11N 0°1W 31 D8
Lingga, Kepulauan Indonesia 0°10S 104°30E 82 E2
Linhares Brazil 19°25S 40°4W 122 C2
Linhe China 40°48N 107°20E 78 C10
Linkinhorne U.K. 50°32N 4°24W 29 F5
Linköping Sweden 58°28N 15°36E 63 F7
Linnhe, L. U.K. 56°36N 5°25W 24 A5
Linslade U.K. 51°54N 0°41W 31 C7
Linstead Jamaica 18°8N 77°2W 114 a
Linton U.K. 52°6N 0°17E 31 B9
Linton U.S.A. 39°2N 87°10W 112 F4
Linxi China 43°36N 118°2E 79 C12
Linxia China 35°36N 103°10E 78 D9
Linyi China 35°5N 118°21E 79 D12
Linz Austria 48°18N 14°18E 64 D8
Lion, G. du France 43°10N 4°0E 66 E6
Lipa Phil. 13°57N 121°10E 83 B6
Lipari Italy 38°26N 14°58E 68 E6
Lipetsk Russia 52°37N 39°35E 70 C6
Lippe → Germany 51°39N 6°36E 64 C4
Lisbon Portugal 38°42N 9°8W 67 C1
Lisburn U.K. 54°31N 6°3W 19 B9
Lisburn & Castlereagh □ U.K. 54°30N 6°9W 19 B9
Liscannor B. Ireland 52°55N 9°24W 20 C4
Lisianski I. U.S.A. 26°2N 174°0W 102 E10
Lisieux France 49°10N 0°12E 66 B4
Liskeard U.K. 50°27N 4°29W 29 G5
Liski Russia 51°3N 39°30E 70 D6
Lismore Australia 28°44S 153°21E 98 F9
Lismore Ireland 52°8N 7°55W 20 D7
Liss U.K. 51°3N 0°54W 31 D7
Listowel Canada 43°44N 80°58W 112 D7
Listowel Ireland 52°27N 9°29W 20 D4
Litani → Lebanon 33°20N 35°15E 86 C3
Litcham U.K. 52°44N 0°47E 31 A10
Litchfield U.S.A. 39°11N 89°39W 112 F3
Lithuania ■ Europe 55°30N 24°0E 63 F8
Little Current Canada 45°55N 82°0W 112 C7
Little Khingan Mts. China 49°0N 127°0E 79 B14
Little Minch U.K. 57°35N 6°45W 22 G6
Little Missouri → U.S.A. 47°36N 102°25W 110 A6
Little Ouse → U.K. 52°22N 1°12E 31 B11
Little Rock U.S.A. 34°45N 92°17W 111 D8
Little Walsingham U.K. 52°54N 0°52E 31 A10
Littlehampton U.K. 50°49N 0°32W 31 E7
Littleport U.K. 52°27N 0°19E 31 B9
Littleton-on-Sea U.S.A. 50°58N 0°58E 31 E10
Liupanshui China 26°38N 104°48E 78 F9
Liuwa Plain Zambia 14°20S 22°30E 97 G4
Liuzhou China 24°22N 109°22E 79 G10
Liverpool Canada 44°5N 64°41W 109 E13
Liverpool U.K. 53°25N 3°0W 27 E3
Livingston U.K. 55°54N 3°30W 25 C9
Livingston U.S.A. 45°40N 110°34W 110 A4
Livingstone Zambia 17°46S 25°52E 97 H5
Livonia U.S.A. 42°23N 83°23W 112 D6
Livorno Italy 43°33N 10°19E 68 C4
Lizard U.K. 49°58N 5°13W 29 H3
Lizard Pt. U.K. 49°57N 5°13W 29 H3
Ljubljana Slovenia 46°4N 14°33E 64 E8
Llandeilo U.K. 51°53N 3°59W 28 D6
Llandovery U.K. 51°59N 3°48W 28 D6
Llandrindod Wells U.K. 52°14N 3°22W 28 C7
Llandudno U.K. 53°19N 3°50W 28 A6
Llanelli U.K. 51°41N 4°10W 28 D5
Llanerchymedd U.K. 53°20N 4°23W 28 A5
Llanfair Caereinion U.K. 52°39N 3°20E 28 B7
Llanfair Talhaiarn U.K. 53°13N 3°37W 28 A6
Llanfair-ym-Muallt = Builth Wells U.K. 52°9N 3°25W 28 C7
Llanfairfechan U.K. 53°15N 3°58W 28 A6
Llangefni U.K. 53°15N 4°18W 28 A5
Llangollen U.K. 52°58N 3°11W 28 B7
Llanidloes U.K. 52°27N 3°31W 28 C6
Llanllyfni U.K. 53°2N 4°17W 28 A5
Llano Estacado U.S.A. 33°30N 103°0W 110 D6
Llanos S. Amer. 5°0N 71°35W 120 B2
Llanquihue, L. Chile 41°10S 72°50W 121 G2

Llanrhystyd U.K. 52°19N 4°7W 28 C5
Llantrisant U.K. 51°32N 3°22W 29 D7
Llantwit Major U.K. 51°24N 3°29W 29 E7
Llanwrtyd Wells U.K. 52°7N 3°38W 28 C6
Llanybloldwel U.K. 52°48N 3°8W 28 B7
Llanymynech U.K. 52°47N 3°5W 28 B7
Lleida Spain 41°37N 0°39E 67 B6
Lleyn Peninsula U.K. 52°51N 4°36W 28 B5
Llobregat → Spain 41°19N 2°5E 67 B7
Lloret de Mar Spain 41°41N 2°53E 67 B7
Lloydminster Canada 53°17N 110°0W 108 D9
Llullaillaco, Volcán S. Amer. 24°43S 68°30W 121 E3
Lobatse Botswana 25°12S 25°40E 97 K5
Lobito Angola 12°18S 13°35E 97 G2
Loch Lomond and the Trossachs △ U.K. 56°10N 4°40W 24 B6
Lochaber U.K. 56°59N 5°1W 22 J7
Locharbriggs U.K. 55°7N 3°35W 25 D8
Lochboisdale U.K. 57°9N 7°20W 22 H3
Loches France 47°7N 1°0E 66 C4
Lochgelly U.K. 56°7N 3°19W 25 B9
Lochgilphead U.K. 56°2N 5°26W 24 B5
Lochinver U.K. 58°9N 5°14W 22 F7
Lochmaben U.K. 55°8N 3°27W 25 D9
Lochmaddy U.K. 57°36N 7°10W 22 G3
Lochnagar U.K. 56°57N 3°15W 23 J11
Lochy, L. U.K. 57°0N 4°53W 23 J8
Lock Haven U.S.A. 41°8N 77°28W 112 E9
Lockerbie U.K. 55°7N 3°21W 25 D9
Loddon U.K. 52°32N 1°31E 31 A12
Lodwar Kenya 3°7N 35°36E 96 D7
Łódź Poland 51°45N 19°27E 65 C10
Lofoten Norway 68°30N 13°59E 63 D6
Loftus U.K. 54°34N 0°53W 26 C7
Logan Ohio, U.S.A. 39°32N 82°25W 112 F6
Logan Utah, U.S.A. 41°44N 111°50W 110 B4
Logan W. Va., U.S.A. 37°51N 81°59W 112 G7
Logan, Mt. Canada 60°34N 140°23W 108 C5
Logansport U.S.A. 40°45N 86°22W 112 E4
Logroño Spain 42°28N 2°27E 67 A4
Lohardaga India 23°27N 84°45E 85 H14
Loir → France 47°33N 0°32W 66 C3
Loire → France 47°16N 2°10W 66 C2
Loja Ecuador 3°59S 79°16W 120 C2
Lomami → Dem. Rep. of the Congo 0°46N 24°16E 96 D4
Lombárdia □ Italy 45°40N 9°30E 68 B3
Lomblen Indonesia 8°30S 123°32E 83 F6
Lombok Indonesia 8°45S 116°30E 82 F5
Lomé Togo 6°9N 1°20E 94 G6
Lomela → Dem. Rep. of the Congo 0°15S 20°40E 96 E4
Lomond, L. U.K. 56°8N 4°38W 24 B6
Łomża Poland 53°10N 22°2E 65 B12
London Canada 42°59N 81°15W 112 D7
London U.K. 51°30N 0°3W 31 D8
London Gateway U.K. 51°31N 0°29E 31 C10
London Gatwick × (LGW) U.K. 51°10N 0°11W 31 D8
London Heathrow × (LHR) U.K. 51°28N 0°27W 31 D8
London Stansted × (STN) U.K. 51°54N 0°14E 31 C9
Londonderry U.K. 55°0N 7°20W 18 A7
Londonderry, C. Australia 13°45S 126°55E 98 C4
Londrina Brazil 23°18S 51°10W 121 E4
Long, L. U.K. 56°4N 4°50W 24 B6
Long Beach U.S.A. 33°46N 118°11W 110 D3
Long Bennington U.K. 52°59N 0°44W 27 G7
Long Branch U.S.A. 40°18N 74°0W 113 E11
Long Clawson U.K. 52°51N 0°56W 27 G7
Long Crendon U.K. 51°46N 0°59W 31 C7
Long Eaton U.K. 52°53N 1°15W 27 G6
Long I. Bahamas 23°20N 75°10W 115 C9
Long I. Ireland 51°30N 9°34W 20 E3
Long I. U.S.A. 40°45N 73°30W 113 E11
Long Itchington U.K. 52°16N 1°22W 30 B6
Long Melford U.K. 52°4N 0°45E 31 B10
Long Mynd, The U.K. 52°35N 2°50W 27 G3
Long Preston U.K. 54°2N 2°14W 27 D4
Long Sutton U.K. 52°48N 0°7E 27 G9
Long Xuyen Vietnam 10°19N 105°28E 82 B3
Longford Ireland 53°43N 7°49W 18 D6
Longford □ Ireland 53°42N 7°45W 18 D6
Longframlington U.K. 55°18N 1°47W 26 B5
Longhoughton U.K. 55°26N 1°37W 26 B5
Longhua China 22°39N 114°0E 79 a
Longlac Canada 49°45N 86°25W 112 A4
Longreach Australia 23°28S 144°14E 98 E7
Longridge U.K. 53°50N 2°35W 27 E3
Longton U.K. 52°58N 0°58E 31 B10
Longtown Cumb., U.K. 55°1N 2°58W 26 B3
Longtown Hereford, U.K. 51°58N 2°59W 30 C3
Longueuil Canada 45°31N 73°29W 113 C11
Longview Tex., U.S.A. 32°30N 94°44W 111 D8
Longview Wash., U.S.A. 46°8N 122°57W 110 A2
Longyan China 25°10N 117°0E 79 F12
Lons-le-Saunier France 46°40N 5°31E 66 C6
Looe U.K. 50°22N 4°28W 29 G5
Loop Hd. Ireland 52°34N 9°56W 20 C3
Lop China 37°3N 80°11E 78 D5
Lop Nur China 40°20N 90°10E 78 C7
Lopez, C. Gabon 0°47S 8°40E 90 G4
Lorain U.S.A. 41°28N 82°11W 112 E6
Loralai Pakistan 30°20N 68°41E 84 D6
Lorca Spain 37°41N 1°42W 67 D5
Lord Howe I. Pac. Oc. 31°33S 159°6E 99 L7
Lord Howe Rise Pac. Oc. 30°0S 162°30E 99 H12
Lordsburg U.S.A. 32°21N 108°43W 110 D5
Lorestān □ Iran 33°30N 48°40E 86 C7
Lorient France 47°45N 3°23W 66 C2
Lorn U.K. 56°26N 5°10W 24 B5
Lorn, Firth of U.K. 56°20N 5°40W 24 B4
Lorraine France 48°53N 6°0E 66 B7
Los Alamos U.S.A. 35°53N 106°19W 110 C5
Los Angeles Chile 37°28S 72°23W 121 F2
Los Angeles U.S.A. 34°4N 118°15W 110 D3
Los Mochis Mexico 25°45N 108°57W 114 B3
Los Roques, Is. Venezuela 11°50N 66°45W 120 A3

Lošinj Croatia 44°30N 14°30E 68 B6
Lossiemouth U.K. 57°42N 3°17W 23 G11
Lostwithiel U.K. 50°24N 4°41W 29 G4
Lot → France 44°18N 0°20E 66 D4
Lota Chile 37°5S 73°10W 121 F2
Loubomo Congo 4°9S 12°47E 96 E2
Loughborough U.K. 52°47N 1°11W 27 G6
Lougheed I. Canada 77°26N 105°6W 109 B9
Loughrea Ireland 53°12N 8°33W 20 B5
Loughros More B. Ireland 54°48N 8°32W 18 B4
Louis XIV, Pte. Canada 54°37N 79°45W 109 D12
Louisa U.S.A. 38°7N 82°36W 112 F6
Louisiade Arch. Papua N. G. 11°10S 153°0E 98 C9
Louisiana □ U.S.A. 30°50N 92°0W 111 D8
Louisville U.S.A. 38°15N 85°46W 112 F5
Lourdes France 43°6N 0°3W 66 E3
Louth Ireland 53°58N 6°32W 19 D8
Louth U.K. 53°22N 0°1W 27 F8
Louth □ Ireland 53°56N 6°34W 19 D8
Lovech Bulgaria 43°8N 24°42E 69 C11
Lowell U.S.A. 42°38N 71°19W 113 D12
Lower Beeding U.K. 51°2N 0°15W 31 D8
Lower Saxony = Niedersachsen □ Germany 52°50N 9°0E 64 B5
Lower Tunguska → Russia 65°48N 88°4E 77 C9
Lowestoft U.K. 52°29N 1°45E 31 B12
Lowick U.K. 55°39N 1°57W 26 A5
Lowther Hills U.K. 55°20N 3°40W 25 D8
Lowville U.S.A. 43°47N 75°29W 113 D10
Loyauté, Îs. N. Cal. 20°50S 166°30E 99 E12
Lu Wo China 22°33N 114°6E 79 a
Lualaba → Dem. Rep. of the Congo 0°26N 25°20E 96 D5
Lu'an China 31°45N 116°29E 79 E12
Luanda Angola 8°50S 13°15E 96 F2
Luangwa → Zambia 14°25S 30°25E 97 G6
Luanshya Zambia 13°3S 28°28E 97 G5
Luapula → Africa 9°26S 28°33E 96 F5
Lubango Angola 14°55S 13°30E 97 G2
Lubbock U.S.A. 33°35N 101°51W 110 D6
Lübeck Germany 53°52N 10°40E 64 B6
Lublin Poland 51°12N 22°38E 65 C12
Lubumbashi Dem. Rep. of the Congo 11°40S 27°28E 97 G5
Lucan Ireland 53°22N 6°28W 21 B10
Lucania, Mt. Canada 61°1N 140°27W 108 C5
Lucca Italy 43°50N 10°29E 68 C4
Luce Bay U.K. 54°45N 4°48W 24 E6
Lucea Jamaica 18°27N 78°10W 114 a
Lucena Phil. 13°56N 121°37E 83 B6
Lucknow India 26°50N 81°0E 85 F12
Lüda = Dalian China 38°50N 121°40E 79 D13
Lüderitz Namibia 26°41S 15°8E 97 K3
Ludgershall U.K. 51°15N 1°37W 30 D5
Ludgvan U.K. 50°9N 5°30W 29 G2
Ludhiana India 30°57N 75°56E 84 D9
Ludington U.S.A. 43°57N 86°27W 112 D4
Ludlow U.K. 52°22N 2°42W 27 H3
Ludwigsburg Germany 48°53N 9°11E 64 D5
Ludwigshafen Germany 49°29N 8°26E 64 D5
Lufkin U.S.A. 31°21N 94°44W 111 D8
Luga Russia 58°40N 29°55E 70 C4
Lugano Switz. 46°1N 8°57E 64 E5
Lugansk Ukraine 48°38N 39°15E 71 E6
Lugnaquilla Ireland 52°58N 6°28W 21 C10
Lugo Spain 43°2N 7°35W 67 A2
Lugwardine U.K. 52°4N 2°39W 30 B3
Luing U.K. 56°14N 5°39W 24 B4
Luleå Sweden 65°35N 22°10E 63 D8
Luleälven → Sweden 65°35N 22°10E 63 D8
Lundy U.K. 51°10N 4°41W 29 E4
Lune → U.K. 54°0N 2°51W 27 D3
Lüneburger Heide Germany 53°10N 10°12E 64 B6
Lunéville France 48°36N 6°30E 66 B7
Luni → India 24°41N 71°14E 84 G7
Luofu Dem. Rep. of the Congo 0°10S 29°15E 96 E5
Luoyang China 34°40N 112°26E 79 E11
Luray U.S.A. 38°40N 78°28W 112 F8
Lurgan U.K. 54°27N 6°20W 19 C9
Lusaka Zambia 15°28S 28°16E 97 H5
Lüt, Dasht-e Iran 31°30N 58°0E 87 D9
Lutherstadt Wittenberg Germany 51°53N 12°39E 64 C7
Luton U.K. 51°53N 0°24W 31 C8
Lutsel K'e Canada 62°24N 110°44W 108 C8
Lutsk Ukraine 50°50N 25°15E 65 C13
Lutterworth U.K. 52°28N 1°12W 27 H6
Luvua → Dem. Rep. of the Congo 6°50S 27°30E 96 F5
Luxembourg Lux. 49°37N 6°9E 64 D4
Luxembourg ■ Europe 49°45N 6°0E 64 D4
Luxor = El Uqsur Egypt 25°41N 32°38E 95 C12
Luzern Switz. 47°3N 8°18E 64 E5
Luzhou China 28°52N 105°20E 78 F10
Luziânia Brazil 16°20S 48°0W 122 C2
Luzon Phil. 16°0N 121°0E 83 A6
Lviv Ukraine 49°50N 24°0E 65 D13
Lyakhov Is. Russia 73°40N 141°0E 77 B15
Lybster U.K. 58°18N 3°15E 23 F11
Lydd U.K. 50°57N 0°55E 31 E10
Lydford U.K. 50°38N 4°8W 29 F5
Lydham U.K. 52°31N 2°58E 27 H3
Lyme B. U.K. 50°42N 2°53W 30 E3
Lyme Regis U.K. 50°43N 2°57W 30 E3
Lyminge U.K. 51°7N 1°6E 31 D11
Lymington U.K. 50°45N 1°32W 30 E5
Lymm U.K. 53°23N 2°29W 27 F4
Lympne U.K. 51°4N 1°2E 31 D11
Lyndhurst U.K. 50°52N 1°35W 30 E5
Lyneham U.K. 51°30N 1°58W 30 C5
Lynmouth U.K. 51°13N 3°49W 29 E6
Lynn Lake Canada 56°51N 101°3W 108 D9
Lynton U.K. 51°13N 3°50W 29 E6
Lyonnais France 45°45N 4°15E 66 D6
Lyon France 45°46N 4°50E 66 D6
Lysva Russia 58°7N 57°49E 70 C10
Lysychansk Ukraine 48°55N 38°30E 71 E6
Lytchett Minster U.K. 50°44N 2°4W 30 E4
Lytham St. Anne's U.K. 53°45N 3°0W 27 E2
Lythe U.K. 54°31N 0°41W 26 C7
Lyubertsy Russia 55°40N 37°51E 70 C6

174 INDEX

Ma'ān Mexicali

M

Ma'ān Jordan 30°12N 35°44E 86 D3
Maas → Neths. 51°45N 4°32E 64 C3
Maastricht Neths. 50°50N 5°40E 64 C3
Mablethorpe U.K. 53°20N 0°15E 27 F9
Macaé Brazil 22°20S 41°43W 122 D2
McAlester U.S.A. 34°56N 95°46W 111 D7
McAllen U.S.A. 26°12N 98°14W 110 E7
MacAlpine L. Canada 66°32N 102°45W 108 C9
Macapá Brazil 0°5N 51°4W 120 B4
Macau Brazil 5°15S 36°40W 120 C6
Macau China 22°12N 113°33E 79 a
Macclesfield U.K. 53°15N 2°8W 27 F4
M'Clintock Chan. Canada 72°0N 102°0W 108 B9
M'Clure Str. Canada 75°0N 119°0W 109 B8
McComb U.S.A. 31°15N 90°27W 111 D8
McCook U.S.A. 40°12N 100°38W 110 B6
McDonald Is. Ind. Oc. 53°0S 73°0E 53 G13
MacDonnell Ranges Australia 23°40S 133°0E 98 E5
Macduff U.K. 57°40N 2°31W 23 G12
Macedonia □ Greece 40°39N 22°0E 69 D10
Macedonia ■ Europe 41°53N 21°40E 69 D9
Maceió Brazil 9°40S 35°41W 122 A3
Macgillycuddy's Reeks Ireland 51°58N 9°45W 20 E3
Mach Pakistan 29°50N 67°20E 84 E5
Machakos Kenya 1°30S 37°15E 96 E7
Machala Ecuador 3°20S 79°57W 120 C2
Machars, The U.K. 54°46N 4°30W 24 E6
Machias U.S.A. 44°43N 67°28W 113 C14
Machilipatnam India 16°12N 81°8E 85 L12
Machrihanish U.K. 55°25N 5°43W 24 D4
Machu Picchu Peru 13°8S 72°30W 120 D2
Machynlleth U.K. 52°35N 3°50W 28 B6
Mackay Australia 21°8S 149°11E 98 E8
Mackay, L. Australia 22°30S 129°0E 98 E4
McKeesport U.S.A. 40°20N 79°51W 112 E8
Mackenzie Canada 55°20N 123°5W 108 D7
Mackenzie → Canada 69°10N 134°20W 108 C6
Mackenzie King I. Canada 77°45N 111°0W 109 B8
Mackenzie Mts. Canada 64°0N 130°0W 108 B6
Mackinaw City U.S.A. 45°47N 84°44W 112 C5
McKinley, Mt. = Denali U.S.A. 63°4N 151°0W 108 C4
McKinley Sea Arctic 82°0N 0°0 54 A7
McMinnville U.S.A. 45°13N 123°12W 110 A2
McMurdo Sd. Antarctica 77°0S 170°0E 55 D11
Macomb U.S.A. 40°27N 90°40W 112 E2
Mâcon France 46°19N 4°50E 66 C6
Macon U.S.A. 32°51N 83°38W 111 D10
McPherson U.S.A. 38°22N 97°40W 110 C7
Macquarie I. Pac. Oc. 54°36S 158°55E 102 N7
Macroom Ireland 51°54N 8°57W 20 E5
Madagascar ■ Africa 20°0S 47°0E 97 J9
Madang Papua N. G. 5°12S 145°49E 98 B8
Madeira Atl. Oc. 32°50N 17°0W 94 B2
Madeira → Brazil 3°22S 58°45W 120 C4
Madeleine, Îs. de la Canada 47°30N 61°40W 113 B17
Madeley U.K. 53°0N 2°20W 27 F4
Madhya Pradesh □ India 22°50N 78°0E 84 H11
Madison Ind., U.S.A. 38°44N 85°23W 112 F5
Madison S. Dak., U.S.A. 44°0N 97°7W 111 B7
Madison Wis., U.S.A. 43°4N 89°24W 112 D3
Madisonville U.S.A. 37°20N 87°30W 112 G4
Madiun Indonesia 7°38S 111°32E 82 F4
Madley U.K. 52°2N 2°51W 30 B3
Madras = Chennai India 13°8N 80°19E 84 N12
Madre de Dios → Bolivia 10°59S 66°8W 120 D3
Madre de Dios, I. Chile 50°20S 75°10W 121 H2
Madre Occidental, Sierra Mexico 27°0N 107°0W 114 B3
Madre Oriental, Sierra Mexico 25°0N 100°0W 114 C5
Madrid Spain 40°24N 3°42W 67 B4
Madura Indonesia 7°30S 114°0E 82 F4
Madurai India 9°55N 78°10E 84 Q11
Maebashi Japan 36°24N 139°4E 81 E6
Maesteg U.K. 51°36N 3°40W 29 D6
Mafeking S. Africa 25°50S 25°38E 97 K5
Mafia I. Tanzania 7°45S 39°50E 96 F7
Magadan Russia 59°38N 150°50E 77 D16
Magallanes, Estrecho de Chile 52°30S 75°0W 121 H2
Magangué Colombia 9°14N 74°45W 120 B2
Magdalena → Colombia 11°6N 74°51W 120 A2
Magdeburg Germany 52°7N 11°38E 64 B6
Magee Isle U.K. 54°48N 5°43W 19 B10
Magelang Indonesia 7°29S 110°13E 82 F4
Magellan's Str. = Magallanes, Estrecho de Chile 52°30S 75°0W 121 H2
Maggiore, L. Italy 45°57N 8°39E 68 B3
Maggotty Jamaica 18°9N 77°46W 114 a
Maghâgha Egypt 28°38N 30°50E 95 C12
Magherafelt U.K. 54°45N 6°37W 19 B8
Maghreb N. Afr. 32°0N 4°0W 90 C3
Maghull U.K. 53°31N 2°57W 27 E3
Magnetic Pole (North) Arctic 85°9N 149°0W 54 A2
Magnetic Pole (South) Antarctica 64°8S 138°8E 55 C9
Magnitogorsk Russia 53°27N 59°4E 70 D10
Magog Canada 45°18N 72°9W 113 C11
Magway Myanmar 20°10N 95°0E 85 J19
Mahābād Iran 36°50N 45°45E 86 B6
Mahajanga Madag. 15°40S 46°25E 97 H9
Mahakam → Indonesia 0°35S 117°17E 82 E5
Mahalapye Botswana 23°1S 26°51E 97 J5
Mahallāt Iran 33°55N 50°30E 87 C7
Mahanadi → India 20°20N 86°25E 85 J15
Maharashtra □ India 20°30N 75°30E 84 J9
Mahdia Tunisia 35°28N 11°0E 95 A8
Mahesana India 23°39N 72°26E 84 H8
Mahilyow Belarus 53°55N 30°18E 65 B16
Mai-Ndombe, L. Dem. Rep. of the Congo 2°0S 18°20E 96 E3
Maiden Bradley U.K. 51°9N 2°17W 30 D4
Maiden Newton U.K. 50°46N 2°34W 30 E3
Maidenhead U.K. 51°31N 0°42W 31 C7
Maidstone U.K. 51°16N 0°32E 31 D10
Maiduguri Nigeria 12°0N 13°20E 95 F8
Main → Germany 50°0N 8°18E 64 C5
Main → U.K. 54°48N 6°18W 19 B9
Maine France 48°20N 0°15W 66 C3
Maine □ U.S.A. 45°20N 69°0W 113 C13
Maine → Ireland 52°9N 9°45W 20 D3
Mainland Orkney, U.K. 58°59N 3°8W 23 E11
Mainland Shet., U.K. 60°15N 1°22W 22 B15
Mainz Germany 50°1N 8°14E 64 C5
Maiquetia Venezuela 10°36N 66°57W 120 A3
Majorca = Mallorca Spain 39°30N 3°0E 67 C7
Majuro Marshall Is. 7°9N 171°12E 102 G9
Makale Indonesia 3°6S 119°51E 83 E5
Makalu Nepal 27°55N 87°8E 78 F6
Makassar Indonesia 5°10S 119°20E 83 F5
Makassar, Str. of Indonesia 1°0S 118°20E 83 E5
Makgadikgadi Salt Pans Botswana 20°40S 25°45E 97 J5
Makhachkala Russia 43°0N 47°30E 71 F8
Makhado S. Africa 23°1S 29°43E 97 J5
Makran Coast Range Pakistan 25°40N 64°0E 84 G4
Makurdi Nigeria 7°43N 8°35E 94 G7
Mal B. Ireland 52°50N 9°30W 20 C4
Malabar Coast India 11°0N 75°0E 84 P9
Malacca, Straits of Indonesia 3°0N 101°0E 82 D2
Málaga Spain 36°43N 4°23W 67 D3
Malahide Ireland 53°26N 6°9W 21 B10
Malaita Solomon Is. 9°0S 161°0E 99 B11
Malakal South Sudan 9°33N 31°40E 95 G12
Malakula Vanuatu 16°15S 167°30E 99 D12
Malang Indonesia 7°59S 112°45E 82 F4
Malanje Angola 9°36S 16°17E 96 F3
Mälaren Sweden 59°30N 17°10E 63 F7
Malatya Turkey 38°25N 38°20E 71 G6
Malawi ■ Africa 11°55S 34°0E 97 G6
Malawi, L. Africa 12°30S 34°30E 97 G6
Malay Pen. Asia 7°25N 100°0E 72 H12
Malāyer Iran 34°19N 48°51E 86 C7
Malaysia ■ Asia 5°0N 110°0E 82 D4
Malden U.S.A. 36°34N 89°57W 112 G3
Malden I. Kiribati 4°3S 155°1W 103 H12
Maldives ■ Ind. Oc. 5°0N 73°0E 73 H9
Maldon U.K. 51°44N 0°42E 31 C10
Maldonado Uruguay 34°59S 55°0W 121 F4
Malegaon India 20°30N 74°38E 84 J9
Malham Tarn U.K. 54°6N 2°10W 26 D4
Malheur L. U.S.A. 43°20N 118°48W 110 B3
Mali ■ Africa 17°0N 3°0W 94 E5
Malin Hd. Ireland 55°23N 7°23W 18 A7
Malin Pen. Ireland 55°20N 7°17W 19 A7
Malindi Kenya 3°12S 40°5E 96 E8
Mallaig U.K. 57°0N 5°50W 22 H6
Mallawi Egypt 27°44N 30°44E 95 C12
Mallorca Spain 39°30N 3°0E 67 C7
Mallow Ireland 52°8N 8°39W 20 D5
Malmesbury U.K. 51°35N 2°5W 30 C4
Malmö Sweden 55°36N 12°59E 63 F6
Malone U.S.A. 44°51N 74°18W 113 C10
Malpas U.K. 53°1N 2°45W 27 F3
Malpelo, I. de Colombia 4°3N 81°35W 115 G8
Malta ■ Europe 35°55N 14°26E 68 a
Maltby U.K. 53°25N 1°12W 27 F6
Malton U.K. 54°8N 0°49W 26 D7
Malvinas, Is. = Falkland Is. ☒ Atl. Oc. 51°30S 59°0W 121 H4
Mamoré → Bolivia 10°23S 65°53W 120 D3
Mamoudzou Mayotte 12°48S 45°14E 91 H8
Man Côte d'Ivoire 7°30N 7°40W 94 G4
Man, I. of U.K. 54°15N 4°30W 19 C12
Manacles, The U.K. 50°2N 5°4W 29 G3
Manado Indonesia 1°29N 124°51E 83 D6
Managua Nic. 12°6N 86°20W 114 E7
Manaus Brazil 3°0S 60°0W 120 C3
Manby U.K. 53°21N 0°6E 27 F9
Manchester U.K. 53°29N 2°12W 27 F4
Manchester U.S.A. 42°59N 71°28W 113 D12
Manchester Int. ✕ (MAN) U.K. 53°21N 2°17W 27 F4
Manchuria China 45°0N 125°0E 79 C14
Manchurian Plain China 47°0N 124°0E 72 D14
Mandal Norway 58°2N 7°25E 63 F5
Mandalay Myanmar 22°0N 96°4E 85 J20
Mandan U.S.A. 46°50N 100°54W 110 A6
Mandaue Phil. 10°20N 123°56E 83 B6
Mandeville Jamaica 18°2N 77°31W 114 a
Mandla India 22°39N 80°30E 85 H12
Mandsaur India 24°3N 75°8E 84 G9
Mandvi India 22°51N 69°22E 84 H6
Manea U.K. 52°29N 0°10E 31 B9
Manfalût Egypt 27°20N 30°52E 95 C12
Manfredónia Italy 41°38N 15°55E 68 D6
Mangabeiras, Chapada das Brazil 10°0S 46°30W 122 B1
Mangaluru India 12°55N 74°47E 84 N9
Mangnai China 37°52N 91°43E 78 D7
Mangole Indonesia 1°50S 125°55E 83 E6
Mangotsfield U.K. 51°29N 2°30W 30 D4
Manhattan U.S.A. 39°11N 96°35W 111 C7
Manhuaçu Brazil 20°15S 42°2W 122 D2
Manica Mozam. 18°58S 32°59E 97 H6
Manicoré Brazil 5°48S 61°16W 120 C3
Manicouagan → Canada 49°30N 68°30W 109 E13
Manicouagan, Rés. Canada 51°5N 68°40W 109 D13
Manihiki Cook Is. 10°24S 161°1W 103 J11
Manila Phil. 14°35N 120°58E 83 B6
Manipur □ India 25°0N 94°0E 85 G19
Manisa Turkey 38°38N 27°30E 71 G4
Manistee U.S.A. 44°15N 86°19W 112 C4
Manistee → U.S.A. 44°15N 86°21W 112 C4
Manistique U.S.A. 45°57N 86°15W 112 C4
Manitoba □ Canada 53°30N 97°0W 108 D10
Manitoba, L. Canada 51°0N 98°45W 108 D10
Manitou Is. U.S.A. 45°8N 86°0W 112 C4
Manitoulin I. Canada 45°40N 82°30W 112 C6
Manitowoc U.S.A. 44°5N 87°40W 112 C4
Manizales Colombia 5°5N 75°32W 120 B2
Mankato U.S.A. 44°10N 94°0W 111 B8
Mannar Sri Lanka 9°1N 79°54E 84 Q11
Mannar, G. of Asia 8°30N 79°0E 84 Q11
Mannheim Germany 49°29N 8°29E 64 D5
Manning Canada 56°53N 117°39W 108 D8
Manningtree U.K. 51°56N 1°5E 31 C11
Manokwari Indonesia 0°54S 134°0E 83 E8
Manosque France 43°49N 5°47E 66 E6
Manresa Spain 41°48N 1°50E 67 B6
Mansel I. Canada 62°0N 80°0W 109 C12
Mansfield U.K. 53°9N 1°11W 27 F6
Mansfield U.S.A. 40°45N 82°31W 112 E6
Mansfield Woodhouse U.K. 53°11N 1°12W 27 F6
Manta Ecuador 1°0S 80°40W 120 C1
Mantes-la-Jolie France 48°58N 1°41E 66 B4
Mantiqueira, Serra da Brazil 22°0S 44°0W 117 F6
Manton U.K. 52°38N 0°41W 27 G7
Manton U.S.A. 44°25N 85°24W 112 C5
Mántova Italy 45°9N 10°48E 68 B4
Manuel Alves → Brazil 11°19S 48°28W 122 B1
Manzai Pakistan 32°12N 70°15E 84 C7
Manzanillo Cuba 20°20N 77°31W 115 C9
Manzanillo Mexico 19°3N 104°20W 114 D4
Manzouli China 49°35N 117°25E 79 B12
Maó Spain 39°53N 4°16E 67 C8
Maoming China 21°50N 110°54E 79 G11
Mapam Yumco China 30°45N 81°28E 78 E5
Maputo Mozam. 25°58S 32°32E 97 K6
Maputo B. Mozam. 25°50S 32°45E 90 J7
Maqên China 34°24N 100°6E 78 E9
Maqên Gangri China 34°55N 99°18E 78 E8
Maquinchao Argentina 41°15S 68°50W 121 G3
Maquoketa U.S.A. 42°4N 90°40W 112 D2
Mar U.K. 57°11N 2°53W 23 H12
Mar, Serra do Brazil 25°30S 49°0W 117 F6
Mar Chiquita, L. Argentina 30°40S 62°50W 121 F3
Mar del Plata Argentina 38°0S 57°30W 121 F4
Mara Rosa Brazil 14°1S 49°11W 122 B1
Marabá Brazil 5°20S 49°5W 120 C5
Maracá, I. de Brazil 2°10N 50°30W 120 B4
Maracaibo Venezuela 10°40N 71°37W 120 A2
Maracaibo, L. de Venezuela 9°40N 71°30W 120 B2
Maracay Venezuela 10°15N 67°28W 120 A3
Maradi Niger 13°29N 7°20E 94 F7
Maragogipe Brazil 12°46S 38°55W 122 B3
Marajo, I. de Brazil 1°0S 49°30W 120 C5
Maranguape Brazil 3°55S 38°50W 120 C6
Maranhão □ Brazil 5°0S 46°0W 120 C5
Marañón → Peru 4°30S 73°35W 120 C2
Marazion U.K. 50°7N 5°29W 29 G3
Marbella Spain 36°30N 4°57W 67 D3
March U.K. 52°33N 0°5E 31 A9
Marche France 46°5N 1°20E 66 C4
Marcus I. Pac. Oc. 24°20N 153°58E 102 E7
Mardan Pakistan 34°20N 72°0E 84 B8
Marden U.K. 52°7N 2°42W 30 B3
Mardin Turkey 37°20N 40°43E 71 G7
Maree, L. U.K. 57°40N 5°26W 22 G7
Mareham le Fen U.K. 53°8N 0°4W 27 F8
Marfleet U.K. 53°45N 0°17W 27 E8
Margarita, I. de Venezuela 11°0N 64°0W 120 A3
Margate U.K. 51°23N 1°23E 31 D11
Marg'ilon Uzbekistan 40°27N 71°42E 87 A12
Mārgow, Dasht-e Afghan. 30°40N 62°30E 87 D10
Mari El □ Russia 56°30N 48°0E 70 C8
Mariana Trench Pac. Oc. 13°0N 145°0E 102 F6
Marías, Is. Mexico 21°25N 106°28W 114 C3
Maribor Slovenia 46°36N 15°40E 64 E8
Marie Byrd Land Antarctica 79°30S 125°0W 55 D14
Mariental Namibia 24°36S 18°0E 97 J3
Marietta U.S.A. 39°25N 81°27W 112 F7
Marília Brazil 22°13S 50°0W 120 E4
Marinette U.S.A. 45°6N 87°38W 112 C4
Maringá Brazil 23°26S 52°2W 121 E4
Marion Ill., U.S.A. 37°44N 88°56W 112 G3
Marion Ind., U.S.A. 40°32N 85°40W 112 E5
Marion Ohio, U.S.A. 40°35N 83°8W 112 E6
Mariupol Ukraine 47°5N 37°31E 71 E6
Marka Somalia 1°48N 44°50E 89 G3
Markam China 29°42N 98°38E 78 F8
Market Bosworth U.K. 52°38N 1°24W 27 G6
Market Deeping U.K. 52°41N 0°19W 27 G8
Market Drayton U.K. 52°54N 2°29W 27 G4
Market Harborough U.K. 52°29N 0°55W 27 H7
Market Lavington U.K. 51°17N 1°58W 30 D5
Market Rasen U.K. 53°24N 0°20W 27 F8
Market Warsop U.K. 53°12N 1°9W 27 F6
Market Weighton U.K. 53°52N 0°40W 27 E7
Markfield U.K. 52°42N 1°17W 27 G6
Markham, Mt. Antarctica 83°0S 164°0E 55 E11
Marks Tey U.K. 51°52N 0°49E 31 C10
Marlborough U.K. 51°25N 1°43W 30 D5
Marlborough Downs U.K. 51°27N 1°53W 30 D5
Marlow U.K. 51°34N 0°46W 31 C7
Marmara, Sea of Turkey 40°45N 28°15E 71 F4
Marmaris Turkey 36°50N 28°14E 86 B2
Marmora Canada 44°28N 77°41W 112 C9
Marne → France 48°47N 2°29E 66 B5
Marnhull U.K. 50°57N 2°19W 30 E4
Maroua Cameroon 10°40N 14°20E 95 F8
Marple U.K. 53°24N 2°4W 27 F4
Marquette U.S.A. 46°33N 87°24W 112 B4
Marquis St. Lucia 14°2N 60°54W 114 b
Marquises, Îs. French Polynesia 9°30S 140°0W 103 H14
Marrakesh Morocco 31°9N 8°0W 94 B4
Marree Australia 29°39S 138°1E 98 F6
Marsá Matrûh Egypt 31°19N 27°9E 95 B11
Marsabit Kenya 2°18N 38°0E 96 D7
Marsala Italy 37°48N 12°26E 68 F5
Marseilles France 43°18N 5°23E 66 E6
Marsh I. U.S.A. 29°34N 91°53W 111 E8
Marshall U.S.A. 32°33N 94°23W 111 D8
Marshall Is. ■ Pac. Oc. 9°0N 171°0E 102 G9
Marshfield U.K. 51°28N 2°19W 30 D4
Marshfield U.S.A. 44°40N 90°10W 112 C2
Marske-by-the-Sea U.K. 54°36N 1°0W 26 C7
Marston Moor U.K. 53°58N 1°17W 27 E6
Martaban Myanmar 16°30N 97°35E 85 L20
Martapura Indonesia 3°22S 114°47E 82 E4
Martham U.K. 52°42N 1°37E 31 A12
Martha's Vineyard U.S.A. 41°25N 70°38W 113 E12
Martigues France 43°24N 5°4E 66 E6
Martinique ☒ W. Indies 14°40N 61°0W 115 E12
Martins Bay Barbados 13°12N 59°29W 114 c
Martinsburg U.S.A. 39°27N 77°58W 112 F9
Martinsville U.S.A. 39°26N 86°25W 112 F4
Martley U.K. 52°15N 2°21W 30 B4
Martock U.K. 50°58N 2°46W 30 E3
Marwar India 25°43N 73°45E 84 G8
Mary Turkmenistan 37°40N 61°50E 87 B10
Maryborough Australia 25°31S 152°37E 98 F9
Maryland □ U.S.A. 39°0N 76°30W 112 F9
Maryport U.K. 54°44N 3°28W 26 C2
Marystown Canada 47°10N 55°10W 109 E14
Marytavy U.K. 50°36N 4°7W 29 F5
Masai Steppe Tanzania 4°30S 36°30E 96 E7
Masan S. Korea 35°11N 128°32E 79 D14
Masandam, Ra's Oman 26°30N 56°30E 89 B6
Masaya Nic. 12°0N 86°7W 114 E7
Masbate Phil. 12°21N 123°36E 83 B6
Mascara Algeria 35°26N 0°6E 94 A6
Maseru Lesotho 29°18S 27°30E 97 K5
Masham U.K. 54°14N 1°39W 26 D5
Mashhad Iran 36°20N 59°35E 87 B9
Mashonaland Zimbabwe 16°30S 31°0E 97 H6
Maşīrah, Jazīrat Oman 21°0N 58°50E 89 C6
Masjed Soleyman Iran 31°55N 49°18E 86 D7
Mask, L. Ireland 53°36N 9°22W 18 D3
Mason City U.S.A. 43°9N 93°12W 111 B8
Massa Italy 44°1N 10°9E 68 B4
Massachusetts □ U.S.A. 42°30N 72°0W 113 D11
Massawa Eritrea 15°35N 39°25E 89 D2
Massena U.S.A. 44°56N 74°54W 113 C10
Massiah Street Barbados 13°9N 59°29W 114 c
Massif Central France 44°55N 3°0E 66 D5
Massillon U.S.A. 40°48N 81°32W 112 E7
Masurian Lakes Poland 53°50N 21°0E 65 B11
Masvingo Zimbabwe 20°8S 30°49E 97 J6
Mata-Utu Wall. & F. Is. 13°17S 176°8W 99 C15
Matabeleland Zimbabwe 18°0S 27°0E 97 H5
Matadi Dem. Rep. of the Congo 5°52S 13°31E 96 F2
Matagalpa Nic. 13°0N 85°58W 114 E7
Matagami Canada 49°45N 77°34W 109 E12
Matagami, L. Canada 49°50N 77°40W 109 E12
Matagorda I. U.S.A. 28°15N 96°30W 111 E7
Matamoros Coahuila, Mexico 25°32N 103°15W 114 B5
Matamoros Tamaulipas, Mexico 25°53N 97°30W 114 B5
Matane Canada 48°50N 67°33W 109 E13
Matanzas Cuba 23°0N 81°40W 115 C8
Matara Sri Lanka 5°58N 80°30E 84 S12
Mataró Spain 41°32N 2°29E 67 B7
Matehuala Mexico 23°39N 100°39W 114 C4
Mateke Hills Zimbabwe 21°48S 31°0E 97 J6
Matera Italy 40°40N 16°36E 68 D7
Mathura India 27°30N 77°40E 84 F10
Mati Phil. 6°55N 126°15E 83 C7
Matlock U.K. 53°9N 1°33W 27 F5
Mato Grosso □ Brazil 14°0S 55°0W 120 D4
Mato Grosso, Planalto do Brazil 15°0S 55°0W 120 D4
Mato Grosso do Sul □ Brazil 18°0S 55°0W 120 D4
Matola Mozam. 25°57S 32°27E 97 K6
Matopo Hills Zimbabwe 20°36S 28°20E 97 J5
Maṭruḥ Oman 23°37N 58°30E 87 F9
Matsu Tao Taiwan 26°8N 119°56E 79 F12
Matsue Japan 35°25N 133°10E 81 F3
Matsumoto Japan 36°15N 138°0E 81 E6
Matsusaka Japan 34°34N 136°32E 81 F5
Matsuyama Japan 33°45N 132°45E 81 G3
Mattagami → Canada 50°43N 81°29W 109 D11
Mattancheri India 9°50N 76°15E 84 Q10
Mattawa Canada 46°20N 78°45W 112 B8
Matterhorn Switz. 45°58N 7°39E 64 F4
Matthew, Î. N. Cal. 22°29S 171°15E 99 E13
Mattoon U.S.A. 39°29N 88°23W 112 F3
Maturín Venezuela 9°45N 63°11W 120 B3
Maubeuge France 50°17N 3°57E 66 A6
Maubin Myanmar 16°44N 95°39E 85 L19
Maudin Sun Myanmar 16°0N 94°30E 85 M19
Maui U.S.A. 20°48N 156°20W 110 H16
Maumee → U.S.A. 41°42N 83°28W 112 E6
Maumturk Mts. Ireland 53°32N 9°42W 18 D2
Maun Botswana 20°0S 23°26E 97 H4
Mauna Kea U.S.A. 19°50N 155°28W 110 J17
Mauna Loa U.S.A. 19°30N 155°35W 110 J17
Mauritania ■ Africa 20°50N 10°0W 94 E3
Mauritius ■ Ind. Oc. 20°0S 57°0E 91 J9
Mawgan U.K. 50°4N 5°13W 29 G3
Mawlamyine Myanmar 16°30N 97°40E 85 L20
Maxixe Mozam. 23°54S 35°17E 97 J7
Maxwellheugh U.K. 55°35N 2°26W 25 C11
May, I. of U.K. 56°11N 2°32W 25 B10
May Pen Jamaica 17°58N 77°15W 114 a
Mayaguana I. Bahamas 22°30N 72°44W 115 C10
Mayagüez Puerto Rico 18°12N 67°9W 115 D11
Maybole U.K. 55°21N 4°42W 24 D6
Mayfield E. Sussex, U.K. 51°1N 0°17E 31 D9
Mayfield Staffs., U.K. 53°1N 1°47W 27 F5
Mayfield U.S.A. 36°44N 88°38W 112 G3
Maykop Russia 44°35N 40°10E 71 F7
Maynooth Ireland 53°23N 6°34W 21 B9
Mayo Canada 63°38N 135°57W 108 C6
Mayo □ Ireland 53°53N 9°3W 18 D3
Mayon Volcano Phil. 13°15N 123°41E 83 B6
Mayotte ☒ Ind. Oc. 12°50S 45°10E 97 G9
Maysville U.S.A. 38°39N 83°46W 112 F6
Māzandarān □ Iran 36°30N 52°0E 87 B8
Mazar China 36°32N 77°1E 78 D4
Mazār-e Sharīf Afghan. 36°41N 67°0E 87 B11
Mazaruni → Guyana 6°25N 58°35W 120 B4
Mazatlán Mexico 23°13N 106°25W 114 C3
Mazyr Belarus 51°59N 29°15E 70 D4
Mbabane Eswatini 26°18S 31°6E 97 K6
Mbaïki C.A.R. 3°53N 18°1E 96 D3
Mbala Zambia 8°46S 31°24E 96 F6
Mbale Uganda 1°8N 34°12E 96 D6
Mbandaka Dem. Rep. of the Congo 0°1N 18°18E 96 D3
Mbanza Ngungu Dem. Rep. of the Congo 5°12S 14°53E 96 F2
Mbeya Tanzania 8°54S 33°29E 96 F6
Mbour Senegal 14°22N 16°54W 94 F2
Mbuji-Mayi Dem. Rep. of the Congo 6°9S 23°40E 96 F4
Mdantsane S. Africa 32°56S 27°46E 97 L5
Mead, L. U.S.A. 36°0N 114°44W 110 C4
Meadow Lake Canada 54°10N 108°26W 108 D9
Meadville U.S.A. 41°39N 80°9W 112 E7
Meaford Canada 44°36N 80°35W 112 C7
Mealsgate U.K. 54°47N 3°13W 26 C2
Mearns, Howe of the U.K. 56°52N 2°26W 23 J13
Measham U.K. 52°43N 1°31W 27 G5
Meath □ Ireland 53°40N 6°57W 19 D8
Meaux France 48°58N 2°50E 66 B5
Mecca Si. Arabia 21°30N 39°54E 86 F4
Mechelen Belgium 51°2N 4°29E 64 C3
Mecklenburg Germany 53°33N 11°40E 64 B7
Mecklenburger Bucht Germany 54°20N 11°40E 64 A6
Medan Indonesia 3°40N 98°38E 82 D1
Médéa Algeria 36°12N 2°50E 94 A6
Medellín Colombia 6°15N 75°35W 120 B2
Medford Oreg., U.S.A. 42°19N 122°52W 110 B2
Medford Wis., U.S.A. 45°9N 90°20W 112 C2
Medicine Hat Canada 50°0N 110°45W 108 E8
Medina Si. Arabia 24°35N 39°52E 86 E4
Mediterranean Sea Europe 35°0N 15°0E 90 C5
Médoc France 45°10N 0°50W 66 D3
Medstead U.K. 51°8N 1°3W 30 D6
Medvezhyegorsk Russia 63°0N 34°25E 70 B5
Medway → U.K. 51°27N 0°46E 31 D10
Meekatharra Australia 26°32S 118°29E 98 F2
Meerut India 29°1N 77°42E 84 E10
Meghalaya □ India 25°50N 91°0E 85 G17
Meghna → Bangla. 22°50N 90°50E 85 H17
Megisti Greece 36°8N 29°34E 86 B2
Meharry, Mt. Australia 22°59S 118°35E 98 D2
Meighen I. Canada 80°0N 99°30W 109 B10
Meiktila Myanmar 20°53N 95°54E 85 J19
Meizhou China 24°16N 116°6E 79 G12
Mejillones Chile 23°10S 70°30W 121 E2
Mekele Ethiopia 13°33N 39°30E 89 E2
Mekhtar Pakistan 30°30N 69°15E 84 D6
Meknès Morocco 33°57N 5°33W 94 B4
Mekong → Asia 9°30N 106°15E 82 C3
Melaka Malaysia 2°15N 102°15E 82 D2
Melanesia Pac. Oc. 4°0S 155°0E 102 H7
Melbourn U.K. 52°4N 0°0 31 B9
Melbourne Australia 37°48S 144°58E 98 H8
Melbourne U.K. 52°50N 1°25W 27 G6
Melekeok Palau 7°27N 134°38E 102 G5
Mélèzes → Canada 57°40N 69°29W 109 D13
Melfort Canada 52°50N 104°37W 108 D9
Melilla N. Afr. 35°21N 2°57W 67 E4
Melitopol Ukraine 46°50N 35°22E 71 E6
Melksham U.K. 51°23N 2°8W 30 D4
Melmerby U.K. 54°45N 2°35W 26 C3
Melrhir, Chott Algeria 34°13N 6°30E 94 B7
Melrose U.K. 55°36N 2°43W 25 C10
Melsonby U.K. 54°29N 1°42W 26 D5
Melton Constable U.K. 52°52N 1°2E 31 A11
Melton Mowbray U.K. 52°47N 0°54W 27 G7
Melun France 48°32N 2°39E 66 B5
Melville Canada 50°55N 102°50W 108 D9
Melville, L. Canada 53°30N 60°0W 109 D14
Melville I. Australia 11°30S 131°0E 98 C5
Melville I. Canada 75°30N 112°0W 109 B8
Melville Pen. Canada 68°0N 84°0W 109 C11
Memphis U.S.A. 35°8N 90°2W 111 C9
Menai Bridge U.K. 53°14N 4°10W 28 A5
Menai Strait U.K. 53°11N 4°13W 28 A5
Mende France 44°31N 3°30E 66 D5
Mendip Hills U.K. 51°17N 2°40W 30 D3
Mendlesham U.K. 52°16N 1°6E 31 B11
Mendocino, C. U.S.A. 40°26N 124°25W 110 B2
Mendota U.S.A. 41°33N 89°7W 112 E3
Mendoza Argentina 32°50S 68°52W 121 F3
Menominee U.S.A. 45°6N 87°37W 112 C4
Menominee → U.S.A. 45°6N 87°35W 112 C4
Menomonie U.S.A. 44°53N 91°55W 112 C2
Menorca Spain 40°0N 4°0E 67 C8
Mentawai, Kepulauan Indonesia 2°0S 99°0E 82 E1
Merced U.S.A. 37°18N 120°29W 110 C2
Mercedes Corrientes, Argentina 29°10S 58°5W 121 E4
Mercedes San Luis, Argentina 33°40S 65°21W 121 F3
Mercedes Uruguay 33°12S 58°0W 121 F4
Mercy, C. Canada 65°0N 63°30W 109 C13
Mere U.K. 51°6N 2°16W 30 D4
Mergui Myanmar 12°26N 98°34E 82 B1
Mérida Mexico 20°58N 89°37W 114 C7
Mérida Spain 38°55N 6°25W 67 C2
Mérida Venezuela 8°24N 71°8W 120 B2
Mérida, Cord. de Venezuela 9°0N 71°0W 117 C3
Meriden U.K. 52°26N 1°38W 27 H5
Meriden U.S.A. 41°32N 72°48W 113 E11
Meridian U.S.A. 32°22N 88°42W 111 D9
Merowe Dam Sudan 18°35N 31°56E 95 E12
Merrick U.K. 55°8N 4°28W 24 D7
Merrill U.S.A. 45°11N 89°41W 112 C3
Merritt Canada 50°10N 120°45W 108 D7
Merse U.K. 55°43N 2°16W 25 C11
Mersea I. U.K. 51°47N 0°58E 31 C10
Mersey → U.K. 53°25N 3°1W 27 F2
Merseyside □ U.K. 53°31N 3°2W 27 E2
Mersin Turkey 36°51N 34°36E 71 G5
Merthyr Tydfil U.K. 51°45N 3°22W 28 D7
Merton □ U.K. 51°25N 0°11W 31 D8
Meru Kenya 0°3N 37°40E 96 D7
Meru Tanzania 3°15S 36°46E 96 E7
Mesa U.S.A. 33°25N 111°50W 110 D4
Mesopotamia Iraq 33°30N 44°0E 86 C5
Messina Italy 38°11N 15°34E 68 E6
Messina, Str. di Italy 38°15N 15°35E 68 F6
Mestre, Espigão Brazil 12°30S 46°10W 122 B1
Meta → S. Amer. 6°12N 67°28W 120 B3
Meta Incognita Pen. Canada 62°45N 68°30W 109 C13
Metheringham U.K. 53°9N 0°23W 27 F8
Methwold U.K. 52°32N 0°33E 31 A10
Metlakatla U.S.A. 55°8N 131°35W 108 D6
Metropolis U.S.A. 37°9N 88°44W 112 G3
Metz France 49°8N 6°10E 66 B7
Meuse → Europe 50°45N 5°41E 64 C3
Mevagissey U.K. 50°16N 4°48W 29 G4
Mevagissey B. U.K. 50°17N 4°47W 29 G4
Mexborough U.K. 53°30N 1°15W 27 E6
Mexiana, I. Brazil 0°0 49°30W 120 B5
Mexicali Mexico 32°40N 115°30W 114 A1

México — Needles, The

México

México *Mexico* 19°24N 99°9W 114 D5
Mexico ■ *Cent. Amer.* 25°0N 105°0W 114 C4
Mexico, G. of *Cent. Amer.* 25°0N 90°0W 114 C7
Meymaneh *Afghan.* 35°53N 64°38E 87 C11
Mezen → *Russia* 65°44N 44°22E 70 A7
Mezhdurechensk *Russia* 53°41N 88°3E 76 D9
Mhonadh, Na h-Eileanan = Monach
  Is. *U.K.* 57°32N 7°40W 22 G2
Miami *U.S.A.* 25°46N 80°11W 111 E10
Mīāndowāb *Iran* 37°0N 46°5E 86 B6
Mīāneh *Iran* 37°30N 47°40E 86 B6
Mianwali *Pakistan* 32°38N 71°28E 84 C7
Mianyang *China* 31°22N 104°47E 78 E9
Miass *Russia* 54°59N 60°6E 70 D11
Micheldever *U.K.* 51°9N 1°14W 30 D6
Michigan □ *U.S.A.* 44°0N 85°0W 112 B4
Michigan, L. *U.S.A.* 44°0N 87°0W 112 D4
Michipicoten I. *Canada* 47°40N 85°40W 112 B5
Michurinsk *Russia* 52°58N 40°27E 70 D7
Mickle Fell *U.K.* 54°37N 2°18W 26 C4
Mickleover *U.K.* 52°55N 1°33W 27 G5
Mickleton *U.K.* 54°36N 2°2W 26 C5
Micoud *St. Lucia* 13°49N 60°54W 114 b
Micronesia *Pac. Oc.* 11°0N 160°0E 102 G7
Micronesia, Federated States of ■
  Pac. Oc. 9°0N 150°0E 102 G7
Mid & East Antrim □ *U.K.* 54°52N 6°14W 19 B9
Mid Ulster □ *U.K.* 54°36N 6°45W 19 B8
Middelburg *S. Africa* 31°30S 25°0E 97 L5
Middle East *Asia* 35°0N 40°0E 72 E5
Middleham *U.K.* 54°17N 1°48W 26 D5
Middlemarsh *U.K.* 50°51N 2°28W 30 E4
Middlesbrough *U.K.* 54°35N 1°13W 26 C6
Middleton Gt. Man., *U.K.* 53°33N 2°12W 27 E4
Middleton Norfolk, *U.K.* 52°43N 0°29E 31 A9
Middleton Cheney *U.K.* 52°5N 1°16W 30 B6
Middleton in Teesdale *U.K.* 54°38N 2°4W 26 C4
Middleton on the Wolds *U.K.* 53°56N 0°35W 27 E7
Middletown *U.K.* 54°17N 6°51W 19 C8
Middletown N.Y., *U.S.A.* 41°27N 74°25W 113 E10
Middletown Ohio, *U.S.A.* 39°31N 84°24W 112 F5
Middlewich *U.K.* 53°12N 2°28W 27 F4
Middlezoy *U.K.* 51°5N 2°54W 30 D3
Midhurst *U.K.* 50°59N 0°44W 31 E7
Midi, Canal du → *France* 43°45N 1°21E 66 E4
Midland *Canada* 44°45N 79°50W 112 C8
Midland Mich., *U.S.A.* 43°37N 84°14W 112 D5
Midland Tex., *U.S.A.* 32°0N 102°3W 110 D6
Midleton *Ireland* 51°55N 8°10W 20 E6
Midsomer Norton *U.K.* 51°17N 2°28W 30 D4
Midway Is. *Pac. Oc.* 28°13N 177°22W 102 E10
Midwest *U.S.A.* 42°0N 90°0W 111 C9
Mieres *Spain* 43°18N 5°48W 67 A3
Mikhaylovka *Russia* 50°3N 43°5E 71 D7
Milan *Italy* 45°28N 9°10E 68 B3
Milborne Port *U.K.* 50°58N 2°28W 30 E4
Mildenhall *U.K.* 52°21N 0°32E 31 B10
Mildura *Australia* 34°13S 142°9E 98 G7
Miles City *U.S.A.* 46°25N 105°51W 110 A6
Milford *U.S.A.* 38°55N 75°26W 113 F10
Milford Haven *U.K.* 51°42N 5°7W 28 D2
Milford on Sea *U.K.* 50°43N 1°35W 30 E5
Milh, Baḥr al *Iraq* 32°40N 43°35E 86 C5
Milk → *U.S.A.* 48°4N 106°19W 110 A5
Millau *France* 44°8N 3°4E 66 D5
Millbrook *U.K.* 50°20N 4°14W 29 G3
Millet *St. Lucia* 13°55N 60°59W 114 b
Millinocket *U.S.A.* 45°39N 68°43W 113 C13
Millom *U.K.* 54°13N 3°16W 26 D2
Millville *U.S.A.* 39°24N 75°2W 113 F10
Milngavie *U.K.* 55°56N 4°19W 24 C7
Milnthorpe *U.K.* 54°14N 2°46W 26 D3
Milos *Greece* 36°44N 24°25E 69 F11
Milton Abbot *U.K.* 50°35N 4°16W 29 F5
Milton Keynes *U.K.* 52°1N 0°44W 31 B7
Miltown Malbay *Ireland* 52°52N 9°24W 20 C4
Milverton *U.K.* 51°1N 3°16W 30 D2
Milwaukee *U.S.A.* 43°2N 87°54W 112 D4
Milwaukee Deep Atl. Oc. 19°50N 68°0W 115 D11
Min Jiang → Fujian, *China* 26°0N 119°35E 79 F12
Min Jiang → Sichuan, *China* 28°45N 104°40E 78 F9
Minas *Uruguay* 34°20S 55°10W 121 F4
Minas Gerais □ *Brazil* 18°50S 46°0W 122 C1
Minatitlán *Mexico* 17°59N 94°31W 114 D6
Minchinhampton *U.K.* 51°42N 2°11W 30 C4
Mindanao *Phil.* 8°0N 125°0E 83 C6
Mindoro *Phil.* 13°0N 121°0E 83 B6
Mindoro Str. *Phil.* 12°30N 120°30E 83 B6
Minehead *U.K.* 51°12N 3°29W 30 D2
Mineral Wells *U.S.A.* 32°48N 98°7W 110 D7
Minfeng *China* 37°4N 82°46E 78 D5
Minginish *U.K.* 57°14N 6°15W 22 H5
Mingulay *U.K.* 56°49N 7°39W 22 J2
Minna *Nigeria* 9°37N 6°30E 94 G7
Minneapolis *U.S.A.* 44°57N 93°16W 111 A8
Minnesota □ *U.S.A.* 46°0N 94°15W 111 A8
Minorca = Menorca *Spain* 40°0N 4°0E 67 C8
Minot *U.S.A.* 48°14N 101°18W 110 A6
Minsk *Belarus* 53°52N 27°30E 65 B14
Minster Kent, *U.K.* 51°20N 1°20E 31 D11
Minster Kent, *U.K.* 51°25N 0°50E 31 D10
Minsterley *U.K.* 52°39N 2°54W 27 G3
Minto, L. *Canada* 57°13N 75°0W 109 D12
Miramichi *Canada* 47°2N 65°28W 109 E13
Miramichi B. *Canada* 47°15N 65°0W 113 B15
Mirim, L. *S. Amer.* 32°45S 52°50W 121 F4
Mirnyy *Russia* 62°33N 113°53E 77 C12
Mirpur Khas *Pakistan* 25°30N 69°0E 84 G6
Mirs Bay *China* 22°33N 114°24E 79 a
Mirzapur *India* 25°10N 82°34E 85 G13
Mishawaka *U.S.A.* 41°40N 86°11W 112 E4
Miskolc *Hungary* 48°7N 20°50E 65 D11
Misool *Indonesia* 1°52S 130°10E 83 E8
Mişrātah *Libya* 32°24N 15°3E 95 B9
Mississinaibi → *Canada* 50°43N 81°29W 109 D11
Mississippi □ *U.S.A.* 33°0N 90°0W 111 D9
Mississippi → *U.S.A.* 29°9N 89°15W 111 E9
Mississippi River Delta
  U.S.A. 29°10N 89°15W 111 E9
Missoula *U.S.A.* 46°52N 114°1W 110 A4
Missouri □ *U.S.A.* 38°25N 92°30W 111 C8

Missouri → *U.S.A.* 38°49N 90°7W 111 C8
Mistassini, L. *Canada* 51°0N 73°30W 109 D12
Misterton Notts., *U.K.* 53°27N 0°50W 27 F7
Misterton Somst., *U.K.* 50°52N 2°47W 30 E3
Mitchaldean *U.K.* 51°51N 2°28W 30 C4
Mitchell *U.S.A.* 43°43N 98°2W 110 B7
Mitchell → *Australia* 15°12S 141°35E 98 D7
Mitchelstown *Ireland* 52°15N 8°16W 20 D6
Mito *Japan* 36°20N 140°30E 81 E7
Mitrovicë *Kosovo* 42°54N 20°52E 69 C9
Mitú *Colombia* 1°15N 70°13W 120 B2
Mitumba, Mts.
  Dem. Rep. of the Congo 7°0S 27°30E 96 F5
Miugh Laigh = Mingulay
  U.K. 56°49N 7°39W 22 J2
Miyakonojō *Japan* 31°40N 131°5E 81 H2
Miyazaki *Japan* 31°56N 131°30E 81 H2
Mizen Hd. Cork, *Ireland* 51°27N 9°50W 20 E3
Mizen Hd. Wicklow, *Ireland* 52°51N 6°4W 21 C10
Mizoram □ *India* 23°30N 92°40E 85 H18
Mjøsa *Norway* 60°40N 11°0E 63 E6
Mljet *Croatia* 42°43N 17°30E 68 C7
Mo i Rana *Norway* 66°20N 14°7E 63 D6
Moab *U.S.A.* 38°35N 109°33W 110 C5
Moate *Ireland* 53°24N 7°44W 18 E6
Mobaye *C.A.R.* 4°25N 21°5E 96 D4
Moberly *U.S.A.* 39°25N 92°26W 111 C8
Mobile *U.S.A.* 30°41N 88°3W 111 D9
Mobridge *U.S.A.* 45°32N 100°26W 110 A6
Moçambique *Mozam.* 15°3S 40°42E 97 H8
Mochudi *Botswana* 24°27S 26°7E 97 J5
Mocoa *Colombia* 1°7N 76°35W 120 B2
Mococa *Brazil* 21°28S 47°0W 122 D1
Mocuba *Mozam.* 16°54S 36°57E 97 H7
Modbury *U.K.* 50°21N 3°55W 29 G6
Módena *Italy* 44°40N 10°55E 68 B4
Modesto *U.S.A.* 37°39N 121°0W 110 C2
Moffat *U.K.* 55°21N 3°27W 25 D9
Mogadishu *Somalia* 2°2N 45°25E 89 G4
Mogi-Mirim *Brazil* 22°29S 47°0W 122 D1
Mohammedia *Morocco* 33°44N 7°21W 94 B4
Moher, Cliffs of *Ireland* 52°58N 9°27W 20 C4
Moidart *U.K.* 56°49N 5°41W 22 J6
Moidart, L. *U.K.* 56°47N 5°52W 22 J6
Moisie → *Canada* 50°14N 66°5W 109 D13
Mojave Desert *U.S.A.* 35°0N 116°30W 110 C3
Moji das Cruzes *Brazil* 23°31S 46°11W 122 D1
Mokpo *S. Korea* 34°50N 126°25E 79 E14
Mold *U.K.* 53°9N 3°8W 28 A7
Molde *Norway* 62°45N 7°9E 63 E5
Moldova ■ *Europe* 47°0N 28°0E 65 E15
Mole → *U.K.* 51°24N 0°21W 31 D8
Molepolole *Botswana* 24°28S 25°28E 97 J5
Mollendo *Peru* 17°0S 72°0W 120 D2
Moloka'i *U.S.A.* 21°8N 157°0W 110 H16
Molopo → *Africa* 28°30S 20°12E 97 K4
Molucca Sea *Indonesia* 0°0 125°0E 83 E6
Moluccas *Indonesia* 1°0S 127°0E 83 E7
Mombasa *Kenya* 4°3S 39°40E 96 E7
Mompós *Colombia* 9°14N 74°26W 120 B2
Mon □ *Myanmar* 16°0N 97°30E 85 L20
Mona Passage *W. Indies* 18°30N 67°45W 115 D11
Monach Is. *U.K.* 57°32N 7°40W 22 G2
Monaco ■ *Europe* 43°46N 7°23E 66 E7
Monadhliath Mts. *U.K.* 57°10N 4°4W 23 H9
Monaghan *Ireland* 54°15N 6°57W 19 C8
Monaghan □ *Ireland* 54°11N 6°56W 19 C8
Monar, L. *U.K.* 57°26N 5°8W 22 H7
Monar Forest *U.K.* 57°27N 5°10W 22 H7
Monasterevin *Ireland* 53°8N 7°4W 21 B8
Monavullagh Mts. *Ireland* 52°14N 7°35W 21 D7
Mönchengladbach *Germany* 51°11N 6°27E 64 C4
Monclova *Mexico* 26°54N 101°25W 114 B4
Moncton *Canada* 46°7N 64°51W 113 B15
Moneague *Jamaica* 18°16N 77°7W 114 a
Moneymore *U.K.* 54°41N 6°40W 19 B8
Mongolia ■ *Asia* 47°0N 103°0E 78 B9
Mongolia, Plateau of *Asia* 45°0N 105°0E 72 D12
Mongu *Zambia* 15°16S 23°12E 97 H4
Monifieth *U.K.* 56°30N 2°48W 25 B10
Monmouth *U.K.* 51°48N 2°42W 28 D8
Monmouth *U.S.A.* 40°55N 90°39W 112 E2
Monmouthshire □ *U.K.* 51°48N 2°54W 28 D8
Monnow → *U.K.* 51°49N 2°43W 30 C3
Monroe La., *U.S.A.* 32°30N 92°7W 111 D8
Monroe Mich., *U.S.A.* 41°55N 83°24W 112 E6
Monroe Wis., *U.S.A.* 42°36N 89°38W 112 D3
Monrovia *Liberia* 6°18N 10°47W 94 G3
Mons *Belgium* 50°27N 3°58E 64 C3
Mont-de-Marsan *France* 43°54N 0°31W 66 E3
Mont-Laurier *Canada* 46°35N 75°30W 109 E12
Montana *Bulgaria* 43°27N 23°16E 69 C10
Montaña *Peru* 6°0S 73°0W 120 C2
Montana □ *U.S.A.* 47°0N 110°0W 110 A5
Montargis *France* 47°59N 2°43E 66 C5
Montauban *France* 44°2N 1°21E 66 D4
Montbéliard *France* 47°31N 6°48E 66 C7
Montceau-les-Mines *France* 46°40N 4°23E 66 C6
Monte Azul *Brazil* 15°9S 42°53W 122 C2
Monte-Carlo *Monaco* 43°44N 7°25E 66 E7
Monte Caseros *Argentina* 30°10S 57°50W 121 F4
Monte Cristi *Dom. Rep.* 19°52N 71°39W 115 D10
Montego Bay *Jamaica* 18°28N 77°55W 114 a
Montélimar *France* 44°33N 4°45E 66 D6
Montello *U.S.A.* 43°48N 89°20W 112 D3
Montemorelos *Mexico* 25°12N 99°49W 114 B5
Montenegro ■ *Europe* 42°40N 19°20E 69 C8
Monteria *Colombia* 8°46N 75°53W 120 B2
Monterrey *Mexico* 25°40N 100°19W 114 B4
Montes Claros *Brazil* 16°30S 43°50W 122 C2
Montevideo *Uruguay* 34°50S 56°11W 121 F4
Montgomery *U.K.* 52°34N 3°8W 28 B7
Montgomery *U.S.A.* 32°23N 86°19W 111 D9
Monticello *U.S.A.* 40°45N 86°46W 112 E4
Montluçon *France* 46°22N 2°36E 66 C5
Montmagny *Canada* 46°58N 70°34W 113 B12
Montpelier Idaho, *U.S.A.* 42°19N 111°18W 110 B4
Montpelier Vt., *U.S.A.* 44°16N 72°35W 113 C11
Montpellier *France* 43°37N 3°52E 66 E5
Montréal *Canada* 45°30N 73°33W 113 C11

Montreux *Switz.* 46°26N 6°55E 64 E4
Montrose *U.K.* 56°44N 2°27W 23 J13
Montrose *U.S.A.* 38°29N 107°53W 110 C5
Montserrat ☑ *W. Indies* 16°40N 62°10W 115 D12
Monywa *Myanmar* 22°7N 95°11E 85 H19
Monza *Italy* 45°35N 9°16E 68 B3
Monze, C. *Pakistan* 24°47N 66°37E 84 G5
Moorfoot Hills *U.K.* 55°44N 3°8W 25 C9
Moorhead *U.S.A.* 46°53N 96°45W 111 A7
Moose Jaw *Canada* 50°24N 105°30W 108 D9
Moosehead L. *U.S.A.* 45°38N 69°40W 113 C13
Moosomin *Canada* 50°9N 101°40W 108 D9
Moosonee *Canada* 51°17N 80°39W 109 D11
Mopti *Mali* 14°30N 4°0W 94 F5
Mora, Na h-Eileanan = Shiant Is.
  U.K. 57°54N 6°22W 22 G5
Moradabad *India* 28°50N 78°50E 84 E11
Morant Bay *Jamaica* 17°53N 76°25W 114 a
Morant Pt. *Jamaica* 17°55N 76°12W 114 a
Morar, L. *U.K.* 56°57N 5°40W 22 J6
Moratuwa *Sri Lanka* 6°45N 79°55E 84 R11
Morava → *Serbia* 44°36N 21°4E 69 B9
Morava → *Slovakia* 48°10N 16°59E 65 D9
Moravian Hts. *Czechia* 49°30N 15°40E 56 F9
Moray □ *U.K.* 57°31N 3°18W 23 G11
Moray Firth *U.K.* 57°40N 3°52W 23 G10
Morden *Canada* 49°15N 98°10W 108 E10
Mordvinia □ *Russia* 54°20N 44°30E 70 D7
Moreau → *U.S.A.* 45°18N 100°43W 110 A6
Morebattle *U.K.* 55°31N 2°22W 25 C11
Morecambe *U.K.* 54°5N 2°52W 26 D3
Morecambe B. *U.K.* 54°7N 3°0W 26 D3
Moree *Australia* 29°28S 149°54E 98 F8
Morehead *U.S.A.* 38°11N 83°26W 112 F6
Morelia *Mexico* 19°42N 101°7W 114 D4
Morena, Sierra *Spain* 38°20N 4°0W 67 C3
Moresby I. *Canada* 52°30N 131°40W 108 D6
Moreton-in-Marsh *U.K.* 51°59N 1°41W 30 C5
Moretonhampstead *U.K.* 50°39N 3°46W 29 F6
Morgan City *U.S.A.* 29°42N 91°12W 111 E8
Morgantown *U.S.A.* 39°38N 79°57W 112 F8
Morioka *Japan* 39°45N 141°8E 81 D7
Morlaix *France* 48°36N 3°52W 66 B2
Morley *U.K.* 53°45N 1°36W 27 E5
Morocco ■ *N. Afr.* 32°0N 5°50W 94 B4
Morogoro *Tanzania* 6°50S 37°40E 96 F7
Morón *Cuba* 22°8N 78°39W 115 C9
Mörön *Mongolia* 49°38N 100°9E 78 B9
Morondava *Madag.* 20°17S 44°17E 97 J8
Moroni *Comoros Is.* 11°40S 43°16E 91 H8
Morotai *Indonesia* 2°10N 128°30E 83 D7
Morpeth *U.K.* 55°10N 1°41W 26 B5
Morphou *Cyprus* 35°12N 80°28E 85 H12
Morrinhos *Brazil* 17°45S 49°10W 122 C1
Morris *U.S.A.* 41°22N 88°26W 112 E3
Morte Bay *U.K.* 51°9N 4°14W 29 E5
Morte Pt. *U.K.* 51°11N 4°14W 29 E5
Mortehoe *U.K.* 51°11N 4°12W 29 E5
Mortimer's Cross *U.K.* 52°16N 2°50W 30 B3
Morton Fen *U.K.* 52°49N 0°20W 27 G8
Morvan *France* 47°5N 4°3E 66 C6
Morwenstow *U.K.* 50°54N 4°33W 29 F4
Moscos Is. *Myanmar* 14°0N 97°30E 85 N20
Moscow *Russia* 55°45N 37°37E 70 C6
Moscow *U.S.A.* 46°44N 117°0W 110 A3
Mosel → *Europe* 50°22N 7°36E 64 C4
Moses Lake *U.S.A.* 47°8N 119°17W 110 A3
Moshi *Tanzania* 3°22S 37°18E 96 E7
Mosjøen *Norway* 65°51N 13°12E 63 D6
Mosselbaai *S. Africa* 34°11S 22°8E 97 L4
Mossley *U.K.* 53°33N 2°1W 27 E4
Mossoró *Brazil* 5°10S 37°15W 120 C6
Most *Czechia* 50°31N 13°38E 64 C7
Mostaganem *Algeria* 35°54N 0°5E 94 A6
Mostar *Bos.-H.* 43°22N 17°50E 69 C7
Mosul *Iraq* 36°15N 43°5E 86 B5
Motcombe *U.K.* 51°1N 2°13W 30 D4
Motherwell *U.K.* 55°47N 3°58W 25 D8
Motihari *India* 26°30N 84°55E 85 F14
Motril *Spain* 36°31N 3°37W 67 D4
Mottama, G. of *Myanmar* 16°5N 96°30E 85 L20
Mottisfont *U.K.* 51°2N 1°32W 30 D5
Mouila *Gabon* 1°50S 11°0E 96 E2
Moule à Chique, C. *St. Lucia* 13°43N 60°57W 114 b
Moulins *France* 46°35N 3°19E 66 C5
Moulouya, O. → *Morocco* 35°5N 2°25W 94 B5
Moulton *U.K.* 52°17N 0°52W 31 B7
Moundou *Chad* 8°40N 16°10E 95 G9
Moundsville *U.S.A.* 39°55N 80°44W 112 F4
Mount Carmel *U.S.A.* 38°25N 87°46W 112 F4
Mount Desert I. *U.S.A.* 44°21N 68°20W 113 C13
Mount Gambier *Australia* 37°50S 140°46E 98 H7
Mount Hagen *Papua N. G.* 5°52S 144°16E 98 B7
Mount Isa *Australia* 20°42S 139°26E 98 E6
Mount Magnet *Australia* 28°2S 117°47E 98 F2
Mount Pleasant *U.S.A.* 43°36N 84°46W 112 D5
Mount Sterling *U.S.A.* 38°4N 83°56W 112 F6
Mount Vernon Ind., *U.S.A.* 37°56N 87°54W 112 F3
Mount Vernon Ohio, *U.S.A.* 40°23N 82°29W 112 E6
Mountain Ash *U.K.* 51°40N 3°23W 28 D7
Mountain Home *U.S.A.* 43°8N 115°41W 110 B3
Mountain View *U.S.A.* 19°33N 155°7W 110 J17
Mountmellick *Ireland* 53°7N 7°20W 21 B8
Mountrath *Ireland* 53°0N 7°28W 21 C8
Mount's Bay *U.K.* 50°5N 5°31W 29 G2
Mountsorrel *U.K.* 52°44N 1°8W 27 G6
Mourne → *U.K.* 54°52N 7°26W 18 B7
Mourne Mts. *U.K.* 54°10N 6°0W 19 C9
Moy → *Ireland* 54°8N 9°8W 18 B2
Moyen Atlas *Morocco* 33°0N 5°0W 94 B4
Mozambique ■ *Africa* 19°0S 35°0E 97 H7
Mozambique Chan. *Africa* 17°30S 42°30E 97 H8
Mozdok *Russia* 43°45N 44°48E 71 F7
Mpanda *Tanzania* 6°23S 31°1E 96 F6
Mpumalanga *S. Africa* 29°50S 30°33E 97 K6
Msaken *Tunisia* 35°49N 10°33E 95 A8
Mthatha *S. Africa* 31°36S 28°49E 97 L5
Mtwara-Mikindani *Tanzania* 10°20S 40°20E 96 G8
Muar *Malaysia* 2°3N 102°34E 82 D2

Mubi *Nigeria* 10°18N 13°16E 95 F8
Much Dewchurch *U.K.* 51°58N 2°45W 30 C3
Much Marcle *U.K.* 51°59N 2°29W 30 C4
Much Wenlock *U.K.* 52°35N 2°33W 27 G3
Muchinga Mts. *Zambia* 11°30S 31°30E 97 G6
Muck *U.K.* 56°50N 6°15W 22 J5
Muckle Flugga *U.K.* 60°51N 0°54W 22 A16
Muckle Roe *U.K.* 60°23N 1°27W 22 B15
Mucuri *Brazil* 18°0S 39°36W 122 C3
Mudanjiang *China* 44°38N 129°30E 79 C14
Mufulira *Zambia* 12°32S 28°15E 97 G5
Mugla *Turkey* 37°15N 28°22E 71 G4
Muir of Ord *U.K.* 57°32N 4°28W 23 G9
Muktsar *India* 30°30N 74°30E 84 D9
Mulanje, Mt. *Malawi* 16°2S 35°33E 97 H7
Mulde → *Germany* 51°53N 12°15E 64 C7
Mulhacén *Spain* 37°4N 3°20W 67 D4
Mulhouse *France* 47°40N 7°20E 66 C7
Mull *U.K.* 56°25N 5°56W 24 B4
Mullaghareirk Mts. *Ireland* 52°20N 9°10W 20 D4
Mullet Pen. *Ireland* 54°13N 10°2W 18 C1
Mullingar *Ireland* 53°31N 7°21W 18 D7
Mullion *U.K.* 50°1N 5°16W 29 G3
Mulroy B. *Ireland* 55°15N 7°46W 18 A6
Multan *Pakistan* 30°15N 71°36E 84 D7
Mumbai *India* 18°56N 72°50E 84 K8
Mumbles Hd. *U.K.* 51°34N 3°59W 29 D6
Muna *Indonesia* 5°0S 122°30E 83 F6
Muncie *U.S.A.* 40°12N 85°23W 112 E5
Mundesley *U.K.* 52°53N 1°25E 31 A11
Mundo Novo *Brazil* 11°50S 40°29W 122 B2
Munger *India* 25°23N 86°30E 85 G15
Munich *Germany* 48°8N 11°34E 64 D6
Munising *U.S.A.* 46°25N 86°40W 112 B4
Münster *Germany* 51°58N 7°37E 64 C4
Munster □ *Ireland* 52°18N 8°44W 20 D5
Murashi *Russia* 59°30N 49°0E 70 C8
Murat → *Turkey* 38°46N 40°0E 71 G7
Murcia *Spain* 38°5N 1°10W 67 D5
Murcia □ *Spain* 37°50N 1°30W 67 D5
Mureş → *Romania* 46°15N 20°13E 65 E11
Murfreesboro *U.S.A.* 35°51N 86°24W 111 C9
Muriaé *Brazil* 21°8S 42°23W 122 D2
Müritz *Germany* 53°25N 12°42E 64 B7
Murmansk *Russia* 68°57N 33°10E 70 A5
Murom *Russia* 55°35N 42°3E 70 C7
Muroran *Japan* 42°25N 141°0E 81 B7
Murray → *U.S.A.* 36°37N 88°19W 112 G3
Murray → *Australia* 35°20S 139°22E 98 H6
Murton *U.K.* 54°50N 1°22W 26 C6
Mururoa *French Polynesia* 21°52S 138°55W 103 K14
Murwara *India* 23°46N 80°28E 85 H12
Murzüq *Libya* 25°53N 13°57E 95 C8
Muş *Turkey* 38°45N 41°30E 71 G7
Mûsa, Gebel *Egypt* 28°33N 33°59E 86 D3
Muscat *Oman* 23°37N 58°36E 87 F9
Musgrave Ranges *Australia* 26°0S 132°0E 98 F5
Musina *S. Africa* 22°20S 30°5E 97 J6
Muskegon *U.S.A.* 43°14N 86°16W 112 D4
Muskegon → *U.S.A.* 43°14N 86°21W 112 D4
Muskogee *U.S.A.* 35°45N 95°22W 111 C7
Musselburgh *U.K.* 55°57N 3°2W 25 C9
Musselshell → *U.S.A.* 47°21N 107°57W 110 A5
Mutare *Zimbabwe* 18°58S 32°38E 97 H6
Mutton I. *Ireland* 52°49N 9°32W 20 C3
Müynoq *Uzbekistan* 43°44N 59°10E 87 A8
Muz Tag *China* 36°25N 87°25E 78 D6
Muzaffarabad *Pakistan* 34°25N 73°30E 84 B8
Muzaffarnagar *India* 29°26N 77°40E 84 E10
Muztagh-Ata *China* 38°17N 75°7E 78 D4
Mwanza *Tanzania* 2°30S 32°58E 96 E6
Mweelrea *Ireland* 53°39N 9°49W 18 D2
Mwene-Ditu
  Dem. Rep. of the Congo 6°35S 22°27E 96 F4
Mweru, L. *Zambia* 9°0S 28°40E 96 F5
My Tho *Vietnam* 10°29N 106°23E 82 B3
Myanmar ■ *Asia* 21°0N 96°30E 85 J20
Mycenae *Greece* 37°43N 22°46E 69 F10
Myddle *U.K.* 52°49N 2°47W 27 G3
Myingyan *Myanmar* 21°30N 95°20E 85 J19
Myitkyina *Myanmar* 25°24N 97°26E 85 G20
Mymensingh *Bangla.* 24°45N 90°24E 85 G17
Mynydd Du *U.K.* 51°52N 3°50W 28 D6
Mynydd Preseli *U.K.* 51°57N 4°48W 28 D4
Myrtoan Sea *Greece* 37°0N 23°20E 69 F10
Mysuru *India* 12°17N 76°41E 84 N10
Mytishchi *Russia* 55°50N 37°50E 70 C6

N

Na Hearadh = Harris *U.K.* 57°50N 6°55W 22 G4
Na Hearadh a Deas = South Harris
  U.K. 57°50N 7°0W 22 G4
Na Hearadh a Tuath = North Harris
  U.K. 57°50N 6°55W 22 G4
Naab → *Germany* 49°1N 12°2E 64 D6
Naas *Ireland* 53°12N 6°40W 21 B9
Naberezhnyye Chelny *Russia* 55°42N 52°19E 70 C9
Nabeul *Tunisia* 36°30N 10°44E 95 A8
Nābulus *West Bank* 32°14N 35°15E 86 C3
Nacala *Mozam.* 14°32S 40°34E 97 G8
Nacogdoches *U.S.A.* 31°36N 94°39W 111 D8
Nacozari de García *Mexico* 30°25N 109°38W 114 A3
Nadiad *India* 22°41N 72°56E 84 H8
Nador *Morocco* 35°14N 2°58W 94 B5
Nafferton *U.K.* 54°1N 0°23W 27 D8
Nafud Desert *Si. Arabia* 28°15N 41°0E 86 D5
Naga *Phil.* 13°38N 123°15E 83 B6
Nagaland □ *India* 26°0N 94°30E 85 G19
Nagano *Japan* 36°40N 138°10E 81 E6
Nagaoka *Japan* 37°27N 138°51E 81 E6
Nagappattinam *India* 10°46N 79°51E 84 P11
Nagasaki *Japan* 32°47N 129°50E 81 G1
Nagaur *India* 27°15N 73°45E 84 F8
Nagercoil *India* 8°12N 77°26E 84 Q10
Nagles Mts. *Ireland* 52°8N 8°30W 20 D6
Nagorno-Karabakh □
  Azerbaijan 39°55N 46°45E 71 F8
Nagoya *Japan* 35°10N 136°50E 81 F5

Nagpur *India* 21°8N 79°10E 84 J11
Nagqu *China* 31°29N 92°3E 78 E7
Naha *Japan* 26°13N 127°42E 79 F14
Nailsea *U.K.* 51°26N 2°44W 30 D3
Nailsworth *U.K.* 51°41N 2°14W 30 C4
Nain *Canada* 56°34N 61°40W 109 D13
Nairn *U.K.* 57°35N 3°53W 23 G10
Nairobi *Kenya* 1°17S 36°48E 96 E7
Naivasha *Kenya* 0°40S 36°30E 96 E7
Najafābād *Iran* 32°40N 51°15E 87 C7
Najd *Si. Arabia* 26°30N 42°0E 86 E5
Najibabad *India* 29°40N 78°20E 84 E11
Najin *N. Korea* 42°12N 130°15E 79 C15
Najrān *Si. Arabia* 17°34N 44°18E 89 D3
Nakhodka *Russia* 42°53N 132°54E 77 E14
Nakhon Ratchasima
  Thailand 14°59N 102°12E 82 B2
Nakhon Sawan *Thailand* 15°35N 100°10E 82 A2
Nakhon Si Thammarat
  Thailand 8°29N 100°0E 82 C2
Nakina *Canada* 50°10N 86°40W 109 D11
Nakuru *Kenya* 0°15S 36°4E 96 E7
Nalchik *Russia* 43°30N 43°33E 71 F7
Nallamalai Hills *India* 15°30N 78°50E 84 M11
Nam Co *China* 30°30N 90°45E 78 E7
Namak, Daryācheh-ye *Iran* 34°30N 52°0E 87 C8
Namaland *Namibia* 26°0S 17°0E 97 K3
Namangan *Uzbekistan* 41°0N 71°40E 87 A12
Namcha Barwa *China* 29°40N 95°10E 78 F8
Namib Desert *Namibia* 22°30S 15°0E 97 J3
Namibe *Angola* 15°7S 12°11E 97 H2
Namibia ■ *Africa* 22°0S 18°9E 97 J3
Nampa *U.S.A.* 43°34N 116°34W 110 B3
Namp'o *N. Korea* 38°52N 125°10E 79 D14
Nampula *Mozam.* 15°6S 39°15E 97 H7
Namumea *Tuvalu* 5°41S 176°9E 99 B14
Namur *Belgium* 50°27N 4°52E 64 C3
Nan Ling *China* 25°0N 112°30E 79 F11
Nanaimo *Canada* 49°10N 124°0W 108 E7
Nanchang *China* 28°42N 115°55E 79 F12
Nanchong *China* 30°43N 106°2E 78 E10
Nancy *France* 48°42N 6°12E 66 B7
Nanda Devi *India* 30°23N 79°59E 84 D11
Nanded *India* 19°10N 77°20E 84 K10
Nandurbar *India* 21°20N 74°15E 84 J9
Nanga Parbat *Pakistan* 35°10N 74°35E 84 B9
Nanjing *China* 32°2N 118°47E 79 E12
Nanning *China* 22°48N 108°20E 78 G10
Nanping *China* 26°38N 118°10E 79 F12
Nansen Sd. *Canada* 81°0N 91°0W 109 A10
Nantes *France* 47°12N 1°33W 66 C3
Nantong *China* 32°1N 120°52E 79 E13
Nantou *China* 22°32N 113°55E 79 a
Nantucket I. *U.S.A.* 41°16N 70°5W 113 E12
Nantwich *U.K.* 53°4N 2°31W 27 F3
Nanuque *Brazil* 17°50S 40°21W 122 C2
Nanyang *China* 33°11N 112°30E 79 E11
Nanyuki *Kenya* 0°2N 37°4E 96 D7
Napa *U.S.A.* 38°18N 122°17W 110 C2
Napier *N.Z.* 39°30S 176°56E 99 H14
Naples *Italy* 40°50N 14°15E 68 D6
Napo → *Peru* 3°20S 72°40W 120 C2
Nappa *U.K.* 53°58N 2°13W 27 E4
Narayanganj *Bangla.* 23°40N 90°33E 85 H17
Narberth *U.K.* 51°47N 4°44W 28 D4
Narbonne *France* 43°11N 3°0E 66 E5
Narborough *U.K.* 52°34N 1°13W 27 G6
Nares Str. *Arctic* 80°0N 70°0W 109 A13
Narmada → *India* 21°38N 72°36E 84 J8
Narodnaya *Russia* 65°5N 59°58E 70 A10
Narva *Estonia* 59°23N 28°12E 63 F9
Narvik *Norway* 68°28N 17°26E 63 D7
Naryan-Mar *Russia* 67°42N 53°12E 70 A9
Nasca *Peru* 14°50S 74°57W 120 D2
Naseby *U.K.* 52°24N 0°59W 31 B7
Nashua *U.S.A.* 42°45N 71°28W 113 D12
Nashville *U.S.A.* 36°10N 86°47W 111 C9
Nasik *India* 19°58N 73°50E 84 K8
Nasirabad *India* 26°15N 74°45E 84 F9
Nasiriyah *Iraq* 31°0N 46°15E 86 D6
Nassau *Bahamas* 25°5N 77°20W 115 B9
Nasser, L. *Egypt* 23°0N 32°30E 95 D12
Natal *Brazil* 5°47S 35°13W 120 C6
Natashquan *Canada* 50°14N 61°46W 109 D13
Natashquan → *Canada* 50°7N 61°50W 109 D13
Natchez *U.S.A.* 31°34N 91°24W 111 D8
Natchitoches *U.S.A.* 31°46N 93°5W 111 D8
Nathdwara *India* 24°55N 73°50E 84 G8
Natitingou *Benin* 10°20N 1°26E 94 F6
Natron, L. *Tanzania* 2°20S 36°0E 96 E7
Natuna Besar, Kepulauan
  Indonesia 4°0N 108°15E 82 D3
Nauru ■ *Pac. Oc.* 1°0S 166°0E 102 H8
Navan *Ireland* 53°39N 6°41W 19 D8
Navarino, I. *Chile* 55°0S 67°40W 121 H3
Navarra □ *Spain* 42°40N 1°40W 67 A5
Navenby *U.K.* 53°6N 0°31W 27 F7
Naver → *U.K.* 58°32N 4°14W 23 E9
Navoiy *Uzbekistan* 40°9N 65°22E 76 E7
Navojoa *Mexico* 27°6N 109°26W 114 B3
Navsari *India* 20°57N 72°59E 84 J8
Nawabshah *Pakistan* 26°15N 68°25E 84 F6
Naxçıvan □ *Azerbaijan* 39°25N 45°26E 71 G8
Naxos *Greece* 37°8N 25°25E 69 F11
Naypyidaw *Myanmar* 19°44N 96°12E 85 K20
Nazaré *Brazil* 13°2S 39°0W 122 B3
Nazas → *Mexico* 25°12N 104°12W 114 B4
Naze, The *U.K.* 51°53N 1°18E 31 C11
Nazret *Ethiopia* 8°32N 39°22E 89 F2
Ndjamena *Chad* 12°10N 15°0E 95 F8
Ndola *Zambia* 13°0S 28°34E 97 G5
Neagh, Lough *U.K.* 54°37N 6°25W 19 B9
Near Is. *U.S.A.* 52°30N 174°0E 108 D1
Neath *U.K.* 51°39N 3°48W 28 D6
Neblina, Pico da *Brazil* 0°48N 66°2W 120 B3
Nebraska □ *U.S.A.* 41°30N 99°30W 110 B7
Neckar → *Germany* 49°27N 8°29E 64 D5
Necochea *Argentina* 38°30S 58°50W 121 F4
Needham Market *U.K.* 52°9N 1°4E 31 B11
Needles, The *U.K.* 50°39N 1°35W 30 E5

Neenah   Oshakati

Neenah *U.S.A.* 44°11N 88°28W **112** C3
Neepawa *Canada* 50°15N 99°30W **108** D10
Neftekumsk *Russia* 44°46N 44°50E **71** F7
Nefteyugansk *Russia* 61°5N 72°42E **76** C8
Negaunee *U.S.A.* 46°30N 87°36W **112** B4
Negele *Ethiopia* 5°20N 39°36E **89** F2
Negombo *Sri Lanka* 7°12N 79°50E **84** R11
Negra, Pta. *Peru* 6°6S 81°10W **117** D2
Negril *Jamaica* 18°22N 78°20W **114** a
Negro → *Argentina* 41°2S 62°47W **121** G3
Negro → *Brazil* 3°0S 60°0W **120** C3
Negros *Phil.* 9°30N 122°40E **83** C6
Nei Mongol Zizhiqu □ *China* 42°0N 112°0E **79** C11
Neijiang *China* 29°35N 104°55E **78** F9
Neisse → *Europe* 52°4N 14°46E **64** B8
Neiva *Colombia* 2°56N 75°18W **120** B2
Nellore *India* 14°27N 79°59E **84** M11
Nelson *Canada* 49°30N 117°20W **108** E8
Nelson *N.Z.* 41°18S 173°16E **99** J13
Nelson *U.K.* 53°50N 2°13W **27** E4
Nelson → *Canada* 54°33N 98°2W **108** D10
Neman → *Lithuania* 55°25N 21°10E **63** F8
Nen Jiang → *China* 45°28N 124°30E **79** B13
Nenagh *Ireland* 52°52N 8°11W **20** C6
Nene → *U.K.* 52°49N 0°11E **31** A9
Nenjiang *China* 49°10N 125°10E **79** B14
Neosho → *U.S.A.* 36°48N 95°18W **111** C7
Nepal ■ *Asia* 28°0N 84°30E **85** F14
Nephi *U.S.A.* 39°43N 111°50W **110** C4
Nephin *Ireland* 54°1N 9°22W **18** C3
Nephin Beg Range *Ireland* 54°0N 9°40W **18** C2
Nerastro, Sarīr *Libya* 24°20N 20°37E **95** D10
Neryungri *Russia* 57°38N 124°28E **77** D13
Ness, L. *U.K.* 57°15N 4°32W **23** H8
Neston *U.K.* 53°17N 3°4W **27** F2
Netherbury *U.K.* 50°46N 2°45W **30** E3
Netherlands ■ *Europe* 52°0N 5°30E **64** B3
Netherlands Antilles = ABC Islands
 W. Indies 12°15N 69°0W **115** E11
Netley *U.K.* 50°52N 1°20W **30** E6
Nettilling L. *Canada* 66°30N 71°0W **109** C12
Nettlebed *U.K.* 51°34N 0°59W **31** C7
Nettleham *U.K.* 53°16N 0°29W **27** F8
Neuchâtel *Switz.* 47°0N 6°55E **64** E4
Neuchâtel, Lac de *Switz.* 46°53N 6°50E **64** E4
Neuquén *Argentina* 38°55S 68°0W **121** F3
Neusiedler See *Austria* 47°50N 16°47E **65** E9
Neva → *Russia* 59°56N 30°20E **70** C5
Nevada □ *U.S.A.* 39°0N 117°0W **110** C4
Nevers *France* 47°0N 3°9E **66** C5
Nevinnomyssk *Russia* 44°40N 42°0E **71** F7
New Abbey *U.K.* 54°59N 3°37W **25** E9
New Alresford *U.K.* 51°5N 1°8W **30** D6
New Amsterdam *Guyana* 6°15N 57°36W **120** B4
New Bedford *U.S.A.* 41°38N 70°56W **113** E12
New Britain *Papua N. G.* 5°50S 150°20E **98** B9
New Britain *U.S.A.* 41°40N 72°47W **113** E11
New Brunswick *U.S.A.* 40°30N 74°27W **113** E10
New Brunswick □ *Canada* 46°50N 66°30W **113** B14
New Caledonia ☑ *Pac. Oc.* 21°0S 165°0E **99** E12
New Castle *Ind., U.S.A.* 39°55N 85°22W **112** F5
New Castle *Pa., U.S.A.* 41°0N 80°21W **112** E7
New Delhi *India* 28°36N 77°11E **84** G10
New England *U.S.A.* 43°0N 71°0W **111** B12
New Forest △ *U.K.* 50°53N 1°34W **30** E5
New Galloway *U.K.* 55°5N 4°9W **24** D7
New Georgia Is. *Solomon Is.* 8°15S 157°30E **99** B10
New Glasgow *Canada* 45°35N 62°36W **109** E13
New Guinea *Oceania* 4°0S 136°0E **98** B7
New Hampshire □ *U.S.A.* 44°0N 71°30W **113** C12
New Haven *U.S.A.* 41°18N 72°55W **113** E11
New Hebrides = Vanuatu ■
 Pac. Oc. 15°0S 168°0E **99** D12
New Holland *U.K.* 53°42N 0°21W **27** E8
New Iberia *U.S.A.* 30°1N 91°49W **111** D8
New Ireland *Papua N. G.* 3°20S 151°50E **98** A9
New Jersey □ *U.S.A.* 40°0N 74°30W **113** E10
New Lexington *U.S.A.* 39°43N 82°13W **112** F6
New Liskeard *Canada* 47°31N 79°41W **109** E12
New London *U.S.A.* 41°22N 72°6W **113** E11
New Madrid *U.S.A.* 36°36N 89°32W **112** G3
New Mexico □ *U.S.A.* 34°30N 106°0W **110** D5
New Mills *U.K.* 53°23N 2°0W **27** F5
New Milton *U.K.* 50°45N 1°40W **30** E5
New Orleans *U.S.A.* 29°57N 90°4W **111** E8
New Philadelphia *U.S.A.* 40°30N 81°27W **112** E7
New Plymouth *N.Z.* 39°4S 174°5E **99** H13
New Providence *Bahamas* 25°25N 77°35W **115** B9
New Quay *U.K.* 52°13N 4°21W **28** C5
New Radnor *U.K.* 52°15N 3°9W **28** C7
New Romney *U.K.* 50°59N 0°57E **31** E10
New Ross *Ireland* 52°23N 6°57W **21** D9
New Rossington *U.K.* 53°29N 1°4W **27** F6
New Siberian Is. *Russia* 75°0N 142°0E **77** B15
New South Wales □ *Australia* 33°0S 146°0E **98** G8
New York *U.S.A.* 40°43N 74°0W **113** E11
New York □ *U.S.A.* 43°0N 75°0W **113** D9
New Zealand ■ *Oceania* 40°0S 176°0E **99** J14
Newark *Del., U.S.A.* 39°41N 75°46W **113** F10
Newark *N.J., U.S.A.* 40°44N 74°10W **113** E10
Newark *N.Y., U.S.A.* 43°3N 77°6W **112** D9
Newark *Ohio, U.S.A.* 40°3N 82°24W **112** E6
Newark-on-Trent *U.K.* 53°5N 0°48W **27** F7
Newberry *U.S.A.* 46°21N 85°30W **112** B5
Newbiggin-by-the-Sea *U.K.* 55°11N 1°31W **26** B5
Newbigging *U.K.* 55°42N 3°34W **25** C8
Newbridge *Ireland* 53°11N 6°48W **21** C9
Newburgh *U.S.A.* 41°30N 74°1W **113** E10
Newburn *U.K.* 54°59N 1°43W **26** C5
Newbury *U.K.* 51°24N 1°20W **30** D6
Newburyport *U.S.A.* 42°49N 70°53W **113** D12
Newby Bridge *U.K.* 54°17N 2°57W **26** D3
Newcastle *Australia* 33°0S 151°46E **98** G9
Newcastle *Canada* 47°1N 65°38W **113** B15
Newcastle *Ireland* 52°27N 9°3W **20** D4
Newcastle *S. Africa* 27°45S 29°58E **97** K6
Newcastle *U.K.* 54°13N 5°54W **19** C10
Newcastle Emlyn *U.K.* 52°2N 4°28W **28** C5
Newcastle-under-Lyme *U.K.* 53°1N 2°14W **27** F4
Newcastle-upon-Tyne *U.K.* 54°58N 1°36W **26** C5
Newcastleton *U.K.* 55°11N 2°49W **25** D10

Newent *U.K.* 51°56N 2°24W **30** C4
Newfoundland & Labrador □
 Canada 52°0N 58°0W **109** D14
Newham □ *U.K.* 51°31N 0°3E **31** C9
Newhaven *U.K.* 50°47N 0°3E **31** E9
Newington *Kent, U.K.* 51°6N 1°7E **31** D11
Newington *Kent, U.K.* 51°21N 0°41E **31** D10
Newlyn *U.K.* 50°6N 5°34W **29** G2
Newlyn East *U.K.* 50°22N 5°5W **29** G3
Newman *Australia* 23°18S 119°45E **98** E2
Newmarket *Ireland* 52°13N 9°0W **20** D5
Newmarket *U.K.* 52°15N 0°25E **31** B9
Newnham *U.K.* 51°48N 2°27W **30** C4
Newport *Ireland* 53°53N 9°33W **18** D2
Newport *Essex, U.K.* 51°59N 0°14E **31** C9
Newport *I. of W., U.K.* 50°42N 1°17W **30** E6
Newport *Newport, U.K.* 51°35N 3°0W **29** D8
Newport *Pembs., U.K.* 52°1N 4°51W **28** C4
Newport *Telford & Wrekin, U.K.* 52°46N 2°22W **27** G4
Newport *Ark., U.S.A.* 35°37N 91°16W **111** C8
Newport *Ky., U.S.A.* 39°5N 84°29W **112** F5
Newport *R.I., U.S.A.* 41°29N 71°19W **113** E12
Newport *Vt., U.S.A.* 44°56N 72°13W **113** C11
Newport News *U.S.A.* 36°58N 76°25W **111** C11
Newport Pagnell *U.K.* 52°5N 0°43W **31** B7
Newquay *U.K.* 50°25N 5°6W **29** G3
Newry *U.K.* 54°11N 6°21W **19** C9
Newry, Mourne & Down □
 U.K. 54°8N 6°3W **19** C10
Newton Abbot *U.K.* 50°32N 3°37W **29** F6
Newton Arlosh *U.K.* 54°53N 3°14W **26** C2
Newton Aycliffe *U.K.* 54°37N 1°34W **26** C5
Newton Ferrers *U.K.* 50°19N 4°3W **29** G5
Newton le Willows *U.K.* 53°28N 2°38W **27** F3
Newton St. Cyres *U.K.* 50°46N 3°36W **29** F6
Newton Stewart *U.K.* 54°57N 4°30W **24** E6
Newtonmore *U.K.* 57°4N 4°8W **23** H9
Newtown *U.K.* 52°31N 3°19W **28** B7
Newtown St. Boswells *U.K.* 55°34N 2°39W **25** C10
Newtownabbey *U.K.* 54°40N 5°56W **19** B10
Newtownabbey □ *U.K.* 54°36N 5°42W **19** B10
Newtownstewart *U.K.* 54°43N 7°23W **18** B7
Neyshābūr *Iran* 36°10N 58°50E **87** B9
Ngamring *China* 29°14N 87°10E **78** F6
Nganglong Kangri *China* 33°0N 81°0E **78** E5
Ngaoundéré *Cameroon* 7°15N 13°35E **96** C2
Ngoring Hu *China* 34°55N 97°5E **78** E8
Ngorongoro *Tanzania* 3°11S 35°32E **96** E7
Nguru *Nigeria* 12°56N 10°29E **95** F8
Nha Trang *Vietnam* 12°16N 109°10E **82** B3
Nhamundá → *Brazil* 2°12S 56°41W **120** C4
Niagara Falls *Canada* 43°7N 79°5W **109** E12
Niagara Falls *U.S.A.* 43°5N 79°4W **112** D8
Niamey *Niger* 13°27N 2°6E **94** F6
Nias *Indonesia* 1°0N 97°30E **82** D1
Nicaragua ■ *Cent. Amer.* 11°40N 85°30W **114** E7
Nicaragua, L. de *Nic.* 12°0N 85°30W **114** E7
Nice *France* 43°42N 7°14E **66** E7
Nicholasville *U.S.A.* 37°53N 84°34W **112** G5
Nicobar Is. *Ind. Oc.* 8°0N 93°30E **53** D14
Nicosia *Cyprus* 35°10N 33°25E **86** C3
Nicoya, Pen. de *Costa Rica* 9°45N 85°40W **114** F7
Nidd → *U.K.* 53°59N 1°23W **27** E6
Nidderdale *U.K.* 54°5N 1°46W **26** D5
Niedersachsen □ *Germany* 52°50N 9°0E **64** B5
Nieuw Nickerie *Surinam* 6°0N 56°59W **120** B4
Niğde *Turkey* 37°58N 34°40E **86** B3
Niger ■ *W. Afr.* 17°30N 10°0E **94** E7
Niger → *W. Afr.* 5°33N 6°33E **94** G7
Nigeria ■ *W. Afr.* 8°30N 8°0E **94** G7
Niigata *Japan* 37°58N 139°0E **81** E6
Ni'ihau *U.S.A.* 21°54N 160°9W **110** H14
Nijmegen *Neths.* 51°50N 5°52E **64** C3
Nikolayev *Ukraine* 46°58N 32°0E **71** E5
Nikolayevsk-na-Amur
 Russia 53°8N 140°44E **77** D15
Nikopol *Ukraine* 47°35N 34°25E **71** E5
Nikšić *Montenegro* 42°50N 18°57E **69** C8
Nile → *Africa* 30°10N 31°6E **95** B12
Nimach *India* 24°30N 74°56E **84** G9
Nîmes *France* 43°50N 4°23E **66** E6
Nineveh *Iraq* 36°25N 43°10E **86** B5
Ninfield *U.K.* 50°53N 0°26E **31** E9
Ningbo *China* 29°51N 121°28E **79** F13
Ningjing Shan *China* 31°0N 98°20E **78** E8
Ningxia Hui □ *China* 38°0N 106°0E **78** D10
Niobrara → *U.S.A.* 42°46N 98°3W **110** B7
Niort *France* 46°19N 0°29W **66** C3
Nipawin *Canada* 53°20N 104°0W **108** D9
Nipigon *Canada* 49°0N 88°17W **112** A3
Nipigon, L. *Canada* 49°50N 88°30W **109** E11
Nipissing, L. *Canada* 46°20N 80°0W **109** E12
Niquelândia *Brazil* 14°33S 48°23W **122** B1
Niš *Serbia* 43°19N 21°58E **69** C9
Niterói *Brazil* 22°53S 43°7W **122** D2
Nith → *U.K.* 55°14N 3°33W **25** D8
Niton *U.K.* 50°35N 1°17W **30** E6
Nitra *Slovakia* 48°19N 18°4E **65** D10
Nitra → *Slovakia* 47°46N 18°10E **65** E10
Niuafo'ou *Tonga* 15°30S 175°58W **99** D15
Niue ☑ *Pac. Oc.* 19°2S 169°54W **99** D17
Nivernais *France* 47°15N 3°30E **66** C5
Nizamabad *India* 18°45N 78°7E **84** K11
Nizhnekamsk *Russia* 55°38N 51°49E **70** C9
Nizhnevartovsk *Russia* 60°56N 76°38E **76** C8
Nizhniy Novgorod *Russia* 56°20N 44°0E **70** C7
Nizhniy Tagil *Russia* 57°55N 59°57E **70** C10
Nizhyn *Ukraine* 51°5N 31°55E **71** D5
Nizwá *Oman* 22°56N 57°32E **89** C6
Njombe *Tanzania* 9°20N 34°49W **96** F6
Nkawkaw *Ghana* 6°36N 0°49W **94** G5
Nkongsamba *Cameroon* 4°55N 9°55E **96** D1
Noakhali *Bangla.* 22°48N 91°10E **85** H17
Nobeoka *Japan* 32°36N 131°41E **81** G2
Noblesville *U.S.A.* 40°3N 86°1W **112** E5
Nogales *Mexico* 31°19N 110°56W **114** A2
Nogales *U.S.A.* 31°20N 110°56W **110** D4
Noirmoutier, Î. de *France* 46°58N 2°10W **66** C2
Nola *C.A.R.* 3°35N 16°4E **96** D3
Nome *U.S.A.* 64°30N 165°25W **108** C3
Nord-Ostsee-Kanal *Germany* 54°12N 9°32E **64** A5
Nordelph *U.K.* 52°35N 0°17E **31** A9

Norderstedt *Germany* 53°42N 10°1E **64** B5
Nordfriesische Inseln *Germany* 54°40N 8°20E **64** A5
Nordkapp *Norway* 71°10N 25°50E **63** C9
Nordrhein-Westfalen □
 Germany 51°45N 7°30E **64** C4
Nordvik *Russia* 74°2N 111°32E **77** B12
Nore → *Ireland* 52°25N 6°58W **21** D9
Norfolk *Nebr., U.S.A.* 42°2N 97°25W **111** B7
Norfolk *Va., U.S.A.* 36°50N 76°17W **111** C11
Norfolk □ *U.K.* 52°39N 0°54E **31** A10
Norfolk I. *Pac. Oc.* 28°58S 168°3E **99** F12
Norfolk Broads △ *U.K.* 52°45N 1°30E **31** A11
Norham *U.K.* 55°43N 2°9W **26** A4
Norilsk *Russia* 69°20N 88°6E **77** C9
Normal *U.S.A.* 40°31N 88°59W **112** E3
Norman *U.S.A.* 35°13N 97°26W **110** C7
Norman Wells *Canada* 65°17N 126°51W **108** C7
Normandie *France* 48°45N 0°10E **66** B4
Normanton *Australia* 17°40S 141°10E **98** D7
Normanton *U.K.* 53°42N 1°24W **27** E6
Norristown *U.S.A.* 40°7N 75°21W **113** E10
Norrköping *Sweden* 58°37N 16°11E **63** F7
Norrland *Sweden* 62°15N 15°45E **63** E7
Norseman *Australia* 32°8S 121°43E **98** G3
Norte, Serra do *Brazil* 11°20S 59°0W **120** D4
North, C. *Canada* 47°2N 60°20W **113** B17
North Ayrshire □ *U.K.* 55°45N 4°44W **24** C6
North Battleford *Canada* 52°50N 108°17W **108** D9
North Bay *Canada* 46°20N 79°30W **109** E12
North Berwick *U.K.* 56°4N 2°42W **25** B10
North C. *Canada* 47°5N 64°0W **113** B15
North C. *N.Z.* 34°23S 173°4E **99** G13
North Canadian → *U.S.A.* 35°22N 95°37W **110** C7
North Carolina □ *U.S.A.* 35°30N 80°0W **111** C11
North Cerney *U.K.* 51°45N 1°57W **30** C5
North Channel *Canada* 46°0N 83°0W **112** B6
North Channel *U.K.* 55°13N 5°52W **24** D4
North Dakota □ *U.S.A.* 47°30N 100°15W **110** A7
North Dorset Downs *U.K.* 50°51N 2°30W **30** E4
North Downs *U.K.* 51°19N 0°21E **31** D9
North Esk → *U.K.* 56°46N 2°24W **25** B10
North European Plain *Europe* 55°0N 25°0E **56** E10
North Foreland *U.K.* 51°22N 1°28E **31** D11
North Harris *U.K.* 58°0N 6°55W **22** F4
North Hill *U.K.* 50°33N 4°27W **29** F5
North Hykeham *U.K.* 53°11N 0°35W **27** F7
North I. *N.Z.* 38°0S 175°0E **99** H14
North Korea ■ *Asia* 40°0N 127°0E **79** D14
North Magnetic Pole *Arctic* 85°9N 149°0W **54** A2
North Minch *U.K.* 58°5N 5°55W **22** F6
North Molton *U.K.* 51°3N 3°49W **29** E6
North Ossetia-Alaniya □
 Russia 43°30N 44°30E **71** F7
North Petherton *U.K.* 51°5N 3°1W **30** D2
North Platte *U.S.A.* 41°8N 100°46W **110** B6
North Platte → *U.S.A.* 41°7N 100°42W **110** B6
North Pole *Arctic* 90°0N 0°0W **54** A
North Pt. *Barbados* 13°20N 59°37W **114** c
North Ronaldsay *U.K.* 59°22N 2°26W **23** D13
North Saskatchewan →
 Canada 53°15N 105°5W **108** D9
North Sea *Europe* 56°0N 4°0E **56** D6
North Sea Canal = Nord-Ostsee-Kanal
 Germany 54°12N 9°32E **64** A5
North Somercotes *U.K.* 53°27N 0°8E **27** F9
North Sunderland *U.K.* 55°34N 1°40W **26** A5
North Tawton *U.K.* 50°48N 3°54W **29** F6
North Thompson →
 Canada 50°40N 120°20W **108** D7
North Thoresby *U.K.* 53°28N 0°4W **27** F8
North Tidworth *U.K.* 51°15N 1°40W **30** D5
North Tyne → *U.K.* 55°0N 2°8W **26** C4
North Uist *U.K.* 57°40N 7°15W **22** G3
North Vernon *U.S.A.* 39°0N 85°38W **112** F5
North Walsham *U.K.* 52°50N 1°22E **31** A11
North West C. *Australia* 21°45S 114°9E **98** E1
North West Highlands *U.K.* 57°33N 4°58W **23** G8
North West River *Canada* 53°30N 60°10W **109** D13
North York Moors △ *U.K.* 54°27N 0°51W **26** D7
North Yorkshire □ *U.K.* 54°15N 1°25W **26** D6
Northallerton *U.K.* 54°20N 1°26W **26** D6
Northam *Australia* 31°35S 116°42E **98** G2
Northam *U.K.* 51°2N 4°13W **29** E5
Northampton *U.K.* 52°15N 0°53W **31** B7
Northampton *U.S.A.* 42°19N 72°38W **113** D11
Northamptonshire □ *U.K.* 52°16N 0°55W **31** B7
Northern Circars *India* 17°30N 82°30E **85** L13
Northern Ireland □ *U.K.* 54°45N 7°0W **19** B8
Northern Marianas ☑ *Pac. Oc.* 17°0N 145°0E **102** F6
Northern Sporades *Greece* 39°15N 23°30E **69** E10
Northern Territory □ *Australia* 20°0S 133°0E **98** E5
Northfleet *U.K.* 51°26N 0°20E **31** D9
Northiam *U.K.* 50°59N 0°36E **31** E10
Northleach *U.K.* 51°49N 1°50W **30** C5
Northrepps *U.K.* 52°54N 1°21E **31** A11
Northumberland □ *U.K.* 55°12N 2°0W **26** B4
Northumberland △ *Northumberland, U.K.* 55°15N 2°20W **26** B4
Northumberland Str.
 Canada 46°20N 64°0W **109** E13
Northwest Territories □
 Canada 63°0N 118°0W **108** C9
Northwich *U.K.* 53°15N 2°31W **27** F3
Northwold *U.K.* 52°33N 0°36E **31** A10
Norton *N. Yorks., U.K.* 54°8N 0°47W **26** D7
Norton *Suffolk, U.K.* 52°16N 0°52E **31** B10
Norton Fitzwarren *U.K.* 51°1N 3°8W **30** D2
Norton Sd. *U.S.A.* 63°50N 164°0W **108** C3
Norwalk *U.S.A.* 41°15N 82°37W **112** E6
Norway ■ *Europe* 63°0N 11°0E **63** E6
Norway House *Canada* 53°59N 97°50W **108** D10
Norwegian B. *Canada* 77°30N 90°0W **109** B11
Norwegian Sea *Atl. Oc.* 66°0N 1°0E **56** B6
Norwich *U.K.* 52°38N 1°18E **31** A11
Norwich *U.S.A.* 42°32N 75°32W **113** D10
Noss Hd. *U.K.* 58°28N 3°3W **23** F11
Nossa Senhora do Socorro
 Brazil 10°52S 37°7W **122** B3
Nossob → *S. Africa* 26°55S 20°45E **97** K4
Notre Dame B. *Canada* 49°45N 55°30W **109** E14
Nottaway → *Canada* 51°22N 78°55W **109** D12

Nottingham *U.K.* 52°58N 1°10W **27** G6
Nottingham I. *Canada* 63°20N 77°55W **109** C12
Nottinghamshire □ *U.K.* 53°10N 1°3W **27** F6
Nouâdhibou *Mauritania* 20°54N 17°0W **94** D2
Nouâdhibou, Râs *Mauritania* 20°50N 17°0W **94** D2
Nouakchott *Mauritania* 18°9N 15°58W **94** E2
Nouméa *N. Cal.* 22°17S 166°30E **99** E12
Nova Friburgo *Brazil* 22°16S 42°30W **122** D2
Nova Iguaçu *Brazil* 22°45S 43°28W **122** D2
Nova Scotia □ *Canada* 45°10N 63°0W **113** C16
Nova Venécia *Brazil* 18°45S 40°24W **122** C2
Novara *Italy* 45°28N 8°38E **68** B3
Novaya Zemlya *Russia* 75°0N 56°0E **76** B6
Novi Pazar *Serbia* 43°12N 20°28E **69** C9
Novi Sad *Serbia* 45°18N 19°52E **69** B8
Novocherkassk *Russia* 47°27N 40°15E **71** E7
Novokuybyshevsk *Russia* 53°7N 49°58E **70** D8
Novokuznetsk *Russia* 53°45N 87°10E **76** D9
Novomoskovsk *Russia* 54°5N 38°15E **70** D6
Novorossiysk *Russia* 44°43N 37°46E **71** F6
Novoshakhtinsk *Russia* 47°46N 39°58E **71** E6
Novosibirsk *Russia* 55°0N 83°5E **76** D9
Novotroitsk *Russia* 51°10N 58°15E **70** D10
Novyy Urengoy *Russia* 65°48N 76°52E **76** C8
Nowy Sącz *Poland* 49°40N 20°41E **65** D11
Noyabrsk *Russia* 64°34N 76°21E **76** C8
Nu Jiang → *China* 29°58N 97°25E **78** F8
Nu Shan *China* 26°0N 99°20E **78** F8
Nubia *Africa* 21°0N 32°0E **90** D7
Nubian Desert *Sudan* 21°30N 33°30E **95** D12
Nueces → *U.S.A.* 27°51N 97°30W **110** E7
Nueltin L. *Canada* 60°30N 99°30W **108** C10
Nueva Rosita *Mexico* 27°57N 101°13W **114** B4
Nuevitas *Cuba* 21°30N 77°20W **115** C9
Nuevo Laredo *Mexico* 27°30N 99°31W **114** B5
Nuku'alofa *Tonga* 21°10S 175°12W **99** E16
Nukulaelae *Tuvalu* 9°23S 179°52E **99** B14
Nukus *Uzbekistan* 42°27N 59°41E **87** A8
Nullarbor Plain *Australia* 31°10S 129°0E **98** G4
Numan *Nigeria* 9°29N 12°3E **95** G8
Numazu *Japan* 35°7N 138°51E **81** F6
Nunavut □ *Canada* 66°0N 85°0W **109** C11
Nuneaton *U.K.* 52°32N 1°27W **27** G6
Nunivak I. *U.S.A.* 60°10N 166°30W **108** B3
Nunney *U.K.* 51°12N 2°22W **30** D4
Nūoro *Italy* 40°20N 9°20E **68** D3
Nuremberg *Germany* 49°27N 11°3E **64** D6
Nusaybin *Turkey* 37°3N 41°10E **71** G7
Nuuk *Greenland* 64°10N 51°35W **54** C5
Nuweveldberge *S. Africa* 32°10S 21°45E **97** L4
Nyagan *Russia* 62°30N 65°38E **76** C7
Nyahururu *Kenya* 0°2N 36°27E **96** D7
Nyaingêntanglha Shan *China* 30°0N 90°0E **78** F7
Nyâlâ *Sudan* 12°2N 24°58E **95** F10
Nyalam *China* 28°32N 86°4E **78** F6
Nyíregyháza *Hungary* 47°58N 21°47E **65** E11
Nysa *Poland* 50°30N 17°22E **65** C9
Nzérékoré *Guinea* 7°49N 8°48W **94** G4

O

Oa, Mull of *U.K.* 55°35N 6°20W **24** C3
Oadby *U.K.* 52°36N 1°5W **27** G6
Oahe, L. *U.S.A.* 44°27N 100°24W **110** A6
O'ahu *U.S.A.* 21°28N 157°58W **110** H16
Oak Hill *U.S.A.* 37°59N 81°9W **112** G7
Oak Ridge *U.S.A.* 36°1N 84°16W **111** C10
Oakengates *U.K.* 52°41N 2°26W **27** G4
Oakham *U.K.* 52°40N 0°43W **27** G7
Oakland *U.S.A.* 37°48N 122°18W **110** C2
Oates Land *Antarctica* 69°0S 160°0E **55** C11
Oaxaca *Mexico* 17°3N 96°43W **114** D5
Ob → *Russia* 66°45N 69°30E **76** C7
Ob, G. of *Russia* 69°0N 73°0E **76** C8
Oba *Canada* 49°4N 84°7W **109** E11
Oban *U.K.* 56°25N 5°29W **24** B5
Oberhausen *Germany* 51°28N 6°51E **64** C4
Obi, Kepulauan *Indonesia* 1°23S 127°45E **83** E7
Óbidos *Brazil* 1°50S 55°30W **120** C4
Obihiro *Japan* 42°56N 143°12E **81** B8
Obozerskiy *Russia* 63°34N 40°21E **70** B7
Obshchi Syrt *Russia* 52°0N 53°0E **56** E16
Ocala *U.S.A.* 29°11N 82°8W **111** E10
Occidental, Cordillera *Colombia* 5°0N 76°0W **117** C3
Occidental, Grand Erg *Algeria* 30°20N 1°0E **94** B6
Ocean City *U.S.A.* 39°17N 74°35W **113** F10
Oceanside *U.S.A.* 33°12N 117°23W **110** D3
Ochil Hills *U.K.* 56°14N 3°40W **25** B8
Ocho Rios *Jamaica* 18°24N 77°6W **114** a
Oconto *U.S.A.* 44°53N 87°52W **112** C4
Odawara *Japan* 35°20N 139°6E **81** F6
Odense *Denmark* 55°22N 10°23E **63** F6
Oder → *Europe* 53°33N 14°38E **64** B8
Odesa *Ukraine* 46°30N 30°45E **71** E5
Odessa = Odesa *Ukraine* 31°52N 102°23W **110** D6
Odiham *U.K.* 51°15N 0°55W **31** D7
Odintsovo *Russia* 55°40N 37°16E **70** C6
Odisha □ *India* 20°0N 84°0E **85** K14
Odzi *Zimbabwe* 19°0S 32°20E **97** H6
Offa *Nigeria* 8°13N 4°42E **94** G6
Offaly □ *Ireland* 53°15N 7°30W **21** B8
Offenbach *Germany* 50°6N 8°44E **64** C5
Ogaden *Ethiopia* 7°30N 45°30E **89** F3
Ōgaki *Japan* 35°21N 136°37E **81** F5
Ogasawara Gunto *Pac. Oc.* 27°0N 142°0E **102** E6
Ogbomosho *Nigeria* 8°1N 4°11E **94** G6
Ogden *U.S.A.* 41°13N 111°58W **110** B4
Ogdensburg *U.S.A.* 44°42N 75°30W **113** C10
Ogooué → *Gabon* 1°0S 9°0E **96** E1
Ohio □ *U.S.A.* 40°15N 82°45W **112** E6
Ohio → *U.S.A.* 36°59N 89°8W **111** C9
Ohře → *Czechia* 50°30N 14°10E **64** C8
Ohrid, L. *Macedonia* 41°8N 20°52E **69** D9
Oil City *U.S.A.* 41°26N 79°42W **112** E8
Oise → *France* 49°0N 2°4E **66** B5
Oistins *Barbados* 13°4N 59°33W **114** c
Oistins B. *Barbados* 13°4N 59°33W **114** c
Ōita *Japan* 33°14N 131°36E **81** G2
Ojos del Salado, Cerro
 Argentina 27°0S 68°40W **121** E3
Oka → *Russia* 56°20N 43°59E **70** C7

Okara *Pakistan* 30°50N 73°31E **84** D8
Okavango Delta *Botswana* 18°45S 22°45E **97** H4
Okayama *Japan* 34°40N 133°54E **81** F3
Okazaki *Japan* 34°57N 137°10E **81** F5
Okeechobee, L. *U.S.A.* 27°0N 80°50W **111** E10
Okehampton *U.K.* 50°44N 4°0W **29** F5
Okhotsk *Russia* 59°20N 143°10E **77** D15
Okhotsk, Sea of *Asia* 55°0N 145°0E **77** D15
Oki-Shotō *Japan* 36°5N 133°15E **81** E3
Okinawa-Jima *Japan* 26°32N 128°0E **79** F14
Oklahoma □ *U.S.A.* 35°20N 97°30W **110** C7
Oklahoma City *U.S.A.* 35°30N 97°30W **110** C7
Oktyabrskiy *Russia* 54°28N 53°28E **70** D9
Öland *Sweden* 56°45N 16°38E **63** F7
Olavarría *Argentina* 36°55S 60°20W **121** F3
Ólbia *Italy* 40°55N 9°31E **68** D3
Old Basing *U.K.* 51°16N 1°3W **30** D6
Old Crow *Canada* 67°30N 139°55W **108** C6
Old Fletton *U.K.* 52°33N 0°14W **31** A8
Old Leake *U.K.* 53°2N 0°6E **27** F9
Old Town *U.S.A.* 44°56N 68°39W **113** C13
Oldbury *U.K.* 51°38N 2°33W **30** C3
Oldcastle *Ireland* 53°46N 7°10W **19** D7
Oldenburg *Germany* 53°9N 8°13E **64** B5
Oldham *U.K.* 53°33N 2°7W **27** E4
Oldmeldrum *U.K.* 57°20N 2°19W **23** H13
Olean *U.S.A.* 42°5N 78°26W **112** D8
Olekminsk *Russia* 60°25N 120°30E **77** C13
Olenek → *Russia* 73°0N 120°10E **77** B13
Oléron, Î. d' *France* 45°55N 1°15W **66** D3
Ölgiy *Mongolia* 48°56N 89°57E **78** B6
Olímpia *Brazil* 20°44S 48°54W **122** D1
Oliveira *Brazil* 20°39S 44°50W **122** D2
Ollagüe *Chile* 21°15S 68°10W **120** E3
Ollerton *U.K.* 53°12N 1°1W **27** F6
Olmaliq *Uzbekistan* 40°50N 69°35E **76** E7
Olney *U.K.* 52°10N 0°41W **31** B7
Olney *U.S.A.* 38°44N 88°5W **112** F3
Olomouc *Czechia* 49°38N 17°12E **65** D9
Olsztyn *Poland* 53°48N 20°29E **65** B11
Olt → *Romania* 43°43N 24°51E **65** G13
Olympia *Greece* 37°39N 21°39E **69** F9
Olympia *U.S.A.* 47°3N 122°53W **110** A2
Olympus, Mt. *Greece* 40°6N 22°23E **69** D10
Olympus, Mt. *U.S.A.* 47°48N 123°43W **110** A2
Omagh *U.K.* 54°36N 7°19W **18** B7
Omaha *U.S.A.* 41°17N 95°58W **111** B7
Oman ■ *Asia* 23°0N 58°0E **89** C6
Oman, G. of *Asia* 24°30N 58°30E **87** E9
Ombersley *U.K.* 52°16N 2°13W **30** B4
Omdurmân *Sudan* 15°40N 32°28E **95** E12
Ometepec *Mexico* 16°41N 98°25W **114** D5
Omsk *Russia* 55°0N 73°12E **76** D8
Ōmuta *Japan* 33°5N 130°26E **81** G2
Ondangwa *Namibia* 17°57S 16°4E **97** H3
Öndörhaan *Mongolia* 47°19N 110°39E **79** B11
Onega → *Russia* 63°58N 38°2E **70** B6
Onega, L. *Russia* 61°44N 35°22E **70** B6
Onega B. *Russia* 64°24N 36°38E **70** B6
Oneida *U.S.A.* 43°6N 75°39W **113** D10
O'Neill *U.S.A.* 42°27N 98°39W **110** B7
Oneonta *U.S.A.* 42°27N 75°4W **113** D10
Onitsha *Nigeria* 6°6N 6°42E **94** G7
Onny → *U.K.* 52°24N 2°47W **27** H3
Onslow B. *U.S.A.* 34°20N 77°15W **111** D11
Ontario □ *Canada* 48°0N 83°0W **109** E11
Ontario, L. *N. Amer.* 43°20N 78°0W **112** D8
Ontonagon *U.S.A.* 46°52N 89°19W **112** B3
Oostende *Belgium* 51°15N 2°54E **64** C2
Opava *Czechia* 49°57N 17°58E **65** D9
Opole *Poland* 50°42N 17°58E **65** C9
Oradea *Romania* 47°2N 21°58E **65** E11
Öræfajökull *Iceland* 64°2N 16°39W **63** B2
Oral *Kazakhstan* 51°20N 51°20E **71** D9
Oran *Algeria* 35°45N 0°39W **94** A5
Orange *Australia* 33°15S 149°7E **98** G8
Orange *France* 44°8N 4°47E **66** D6
Orange *U.S.A.* 38°15N 78°7W **112** F8
Orange → *S. Africa* 28°41S 16°28E **97** K3
Orange, C. *Brazil* 4°20N 51°30W **120** B4
Orangeburg *U.S.A.* 33°30N 80°52W **111** D10
Orangeville *Canada* 43°55N 80°5W **112** D7
Ordos *China* 39°50N 110°0E **79** D10
Ordos Desert *China* 39°0N 109°0E **79** D10
Ordu *Turkey* 40°55N 37°53E **71** F6
Örebro *Sweden* 59°20N 15°18E **63** F7
Oregon □ *U.S.A.* 44°0N 121°0W **110** B2
Orekhovo-Zuyevo *Russia* 55°50N 38°55E **70** C6
Orel *Russia* 52°57N 36°3E **70** D6
Orem *U.S.A.* 40°19N 111°42W **110** B4
Orenburg *Russia* 51°45N 55°6E **70** D10
Orford *U.K.* 52°5N 1°35E **31** B12
Orford Ness *U.K.* 52°5N 1°35E **31** B12
Oriental, Cordillera *Colombia* 6°0N 73°0W **117** C3
Oriental, Grand Erg *Algeria* 30°0N 6°30E **94** B7
Orihuela *Spain* 38°7N 0°55W **67** C5
Orinoco → *Venezuela* 9°15N 61°30W **120** B3
Oristano *Italy* 39°54N 8°36E **68** E3
Orizaba *Mexico* 18°51N 97°6W **114** D5
Orizaba, Pico de *Mexico* 18°58N 97°15W **114** D5
Orkhon → *Mongolia* 50°21N 106°0E **78** A10
Orkney □ *U.K.* 59°2N 3°13W **23** D11
Orkney Is. *U.K.* 59°0N 3°0W **23** E12
Orlando *U.S.A.* 28°32N 81°22W **111** E10
Orléanais *France* 48°0N 2°0E **66** C5
Orléans *France* 47°54N 1°52E **66** C4
Orléans, Î. d' *Canada* 46°54N 70°58W **113** B12
Ormara *Pakistan* 25°16N 64°33E **84** G4
Ormesby St. Margaret *U.K.* 52°41N 1°41E **31** A12
Ormoc *Phil.* 11°0N 124°37E **83** B6
Ormskirk *U.K.* 53°35N 2°54W **27** E3
Örnsköldsvik *Sweden* 63°17N 18°40E **63** E7
Oronsay *U.K.* 56°1N 6°15W **24** B3
Orsha *Belarus* 54°30N 30°25E **70** D5
Ortegal, C. *Spain* 43°43N 7°52W **67** A2
Oruro *Bolivia* 18°0S 67°9W **120** D3
Orwell → *U.K.* 51°59N 1°18E **31** C11
Ōsaka *Japan* 34°42N 135°30E **81** F4
Osh *Kyrgyzstan* 40°37N 72°49E **76** E8
Oshakati *Namibia* 17°45S 15°40E **97** H3

INDEX 177

Oshawa — Port Elizabeth

Oshawa *Canada* 43°50N 78°50W **109** E12
Oshkosh *U.S.A.* 44°1N 88°33W **112** C3
Oshogbo *Nigeria* 7°48N 4°37E **94** G6
Osijek *Croatia* 45°34N 18°41E **69** B8
Osizweni *S. Africa* 27°49S 30°7E **97** K6
Oskaloosa *U.S.A.* 41°18N 92°39W **111** B8
Oskarshamn *Sweden* 57°15N 16°27E **63** F7
Öskemen *Kazakhstan* 50°0N 82°36E **76** E9
Oslo *Norway* 59°54N 10°43E **63** F6
Oslofjorden *Norway* 59°20N 10°35E **63** F6
Osmaniye *Turkey* 37°5N 36°10E **71** G6
Osmotherley *U.K.* 54°22N 1°18W **26** D6
Osnabrück *Germany* 52°17N 8°3E **64** B5
Osorno *Chile* 40°25S 73°0W **121** G2
Ossa, Mt. *Australia* 41°52S 146°3E **98** J8
Ossett *U.K.* 53°41N 1°34W **27** E5
Ostend = Oostende *Belgium* 51°15N 2°54E **64** C2
Österdalälven → *Sweden* 60°30N 15°7E **63** E6
Östersund *Sweden* 63°10N 14°38E **63** E6
Ostfriesische Inseln *Germany* 53°42N 7°0E **64** B4
Ostrava *Czechia* 49°51N 18°18E **65** D10
Ostrołęka *Poland* 53°4N 21°32E **65** B11
Ostrów Wielkopolski *Poland* 51°36N 17°44E **65** C9
Ostrowiec-Świętokrzyski *Poland* 50°55N 21°22E **65** C11
Oswaldtwistle *U.K.* 53°43N 2°26W **27** E4
Oswego *U.S.A.* 43°27N 76°31W **112** D9
Oswestry *U.K.* 52°52N 3°3W **27** G2
Otaru *Japan* 43°10N 141°0E **81** B7
Otjiwarongo *Namibia* 20°30S 16°33E **97** J3
Otley *U.K.* 53°54N 1°41W **27** E5
Otranto *Italy* 40°9N 18°28E **69** D8
Otranto, Str. of *Italy* 40°15N 18°40E **69** D8
Ōtsu *Japan* 35°0N 135°50E **81** F4
Ottawa *Canada* 45°26N 75°42W **113** C10
Ottawa *U.S.A.* 41°21N 88°51W **112** E3
Ottawa Is. *Canada* 59°35N 80°10W **109** D11
Otter → *U.K.* 50°38N 3°19W **29** F7
Otterburn *U.K.* 55°14N 2°11W **26** B4
Ottery St. Mary *U.K.* 50°44N 3°17W **29** F7
Ottumwa *U.S.A.* 41°1N 92°25W **111** B8
Ouachita → *U.S.A.* 31°38N 91°49W **111** D8
Ouachita Mts. *U.S.A.* 34°30N 94°30W **111** D8
Ouagadougou *Burkina Faso* 12°25N 1°30W **94** F5
Oubangi → *Dem. Rep. of the Congo* 0°30S 17°50E **96** E3
Oudtshoorn *S. Africa* 33°35S 22°14E **97** L4
Ouezzane *Morocco* 34°51N 5°35W **94** B4
Oughterard *Ireland* 53°26N 9°18W **20** B4
Oujda *Morocco* 34°41N 1°55W **94** B5
Oulton *U.K.* 52°30N 1°43E **31** B12
Oulton Broad *U.K.* 52°28N 1°42E **31** B12
Oulu *Finland* 65°1N 25°29E **63** D9
Oulujärvi *Finland* 64°25N 27°15E **63** E9
Oulujoki → *Finland* 65°1N 25°30E **63** D9
Oundle *U.K.* 52°29N 0°28W **31** B8
Ourense *Spain* 42°19N 7°55W **67** A2
Ouro Fino *Brazil* 22°16S 46°25W **122** D1
Ouro Prêto *Brazil* 20°20S 43°30W **122** D2
Ouse → *E. Sussex, U.K.* 50°47N 0°4E **31** E9
Ouse → *N. Yorks., U.K.* 53°44N 0°55W **27** E7
Outaouais → *Canada* 45°27N 74°8W **109** E12
Outer Hebrides *U.K.* 57°30N 7°15W **22** H2
Outjo *Namibia* 20°5S 16°7E **97** J3
Outwell *U.K.* 52°37N 0°14E **31** A9
Ovalle *Chile* 30°33S 71°18W **121** F2
Ovamboland *Namibia* 18°30S 16°0E **97** H3
Over Wallop *U.K.* 51°9N 1°36W **30** D5
Overton *U.K.* 51°15N 1°15W **30** D6
Oviedo *Spain* 43°25N 5°50W **67** A3
Owatonna *U.S.A.* 44°5N 93°14W **111** B8
Owen Sound *Canada* 44°35N 80°55W **109** E11
Owen Stanley Ra. *Papua N. G.* 8°30S 147°0E **98** B8
Owens L. *U.S.A.* 36°26N 117°57W **110** C3
Owensboro *U.S.A.* 37°46N 87°7W **112** G4
Owo *Nigeria* 7°10N 5°39E **94** G7
Owosso *U.S.A.* 43°0N 84°10W **112** D5
Owston Ferry *U.K.* 53°29N 0°47W **27** F7
Owyhee → *U.S.A.* 43°49N 117°2W **110** B3
Oxford *U.K.* 51°46N 1°15W **30** C6
Oxfordshire □ *U.K.* 51°48N 1°16W **30** C6
Oxnard *U.S.A.* 34°12N 119°11W **110** D3
Oyama *Japan* 36°18N 139°48E **81** E6
Oyem *Gabon* 1°34N 11°31E **96** D2
Oykel → *U.K.* 57°56N 4°26W **23** G9
Oyo *Nigeria* 7°46N 3°56E **94** G6
Ozark Plateau *U.S.A.* 37°20N 91°40W **111** C8
Ozarks, L. of the *U.S.A.* 38°12N 92°38W **111** C8

P

Paarl *S. Africa* 33°45S 18°56E **97** L3
Pab Hills *Pakistan* 26°30N 66°45E **84** F5
Pabaidh = Pabbay *U.K.* 57°46N 7°14W **22** G3
Pabbay *U.K.* 57°46N 7°14W **22** G3
Pabna *Bangla.* 24°1N 89°18E **85** G16
Pacaraima, Sa. *S. Amer.* 4°0N 62°30W **120** B3
Pacasmayo *Peru* 7°20S 79°35W **120** C2
Pachuca *Mexico* 20°7N 98°44W **114** C5
Pacific Ocean 10°0N 140°0W **103** G14
Padang *Indonesia* 1°0S 100°20E **82** E2
Padangsidempuan *Indonesia* 1°30N 99°15E **82** D1
Paddock Wood *U.K.* 51°11N 0°24E **31** D9
Paderborn *Germany* 51°42N 8°45E **64** C5
Padiham *U.K.* 53°48N 2°18W **27** E4
Padre I. *U.S.A.* 27°10N 97°25W **111** E7
Padstow *U.K.* 50°33N 4°58W **29** F4
Padstow B. *U.K.* 50°34N 4°57W **29** F4
Padua *Italy* 45°25N 11°53E **68** B4
Paducah *U.S.A.* 37°5N 88°37W **112** G3
Pag *Croatia* 44°25N 15°3E **68** B6
Pagadian *Phil.* 7°55N 123°30E **83** C6
Page *U.S.A.* 36°57N 111°27W **110** C4
Pāhala *U.S.A.* 19°12N 155°29W **110** J17
Paignton *U.K.* 50°26N 3°35W **29** G6
Paine Grande, Cerro *Chile* 50°59S 73°4W **121** H2
Painesville *U.S.A.* 41°43N 81°15W **112** E7
Painswick *U.K.* 51°47N 2°10W **30** C4
Painted Desert *U.S.A.* 36°0N 111°0W **110** C4
Paintsville *U.S.A.* 37°49N 82°48W **112** G6
País Vasco □ *Spain* 42°50N 2°45W **67** A4
Paisley *U.K.* 55°50N 4°25W **24** C7
Paita *Peru* 5°11S 81°9W **120** C1
Pakistan ■ *Asia* 30°0N 70°0E **84** E7
Pakxe *Laos* 15°5N 105°52E **82** A3
Palagruža *Croatia* 42°24N 16°15E **68** C7
Palakkad *India* 10°46N 76°42E **84** P10
Palani Hills *India* 10°14N 77°33E **84** P10
Palanpur *India* 24°10N 72°25E **84** G8
Palapye *Botswana* 22°30S 27°7E **97** J5
Palau ■ *Palau* 7°30N 134°30E **102** G5
Palawan *Phil.* 9°30N 118°30E **82** C5
Palembang *Indonesia* 3°0S 104°50E **82** E2
Palencia *Spain* 42°1N 4°34W **67** A3
Palermo *Italy* 38°7N 13°22E **68** E5
Palestine *U.S.A.* 31°46N 95°38W **111** D7
Palgrave *U.K.* 52°22N 1°6E **31** B11
Pali *India* 25°50N 73°20E **84** G8
Palikir *Micronesia* 6°55N 158°9E **102** G7
Palk Strait *Asia* 10°0N 79°45E **84** Q11
Palm Springs *U.S.A.* 33°50N 116°33W **110** D3
Palma de Mallorca *Spain* 39°35N 2°39E **67** C7
Palmares *Brazil* 8°41S 35°28W **122** A3
Palmas *Brazil* 10°12S 48°21W **122** B1
Palmas, C. *Liberia* 4°27N 7°46W **94** H4
Palmeira dos Índios *Brazil* 9°25S 36°37W **122** A3
Palmer *U.S.A.* 61°36N 149°7W **108** C5
Palmer Land *Antarctica* 73°0S 63°0W **55** D18
Palmerston North *N.Z.* 40°21S 175°39E **99** J14
Palmira *Colombia* 3°32N 76°16W **120** B2
Palmyra *Syria* 34°36N 38°15E **86** C4
Palmyra Is. *Pac. Oc.* 5°52N 162°5W **103** G11
Palopo *Indonesia* 3°0S 120°16E **83** E6
Palu *Indonesia* 1°0S 119°52E **83** E5
Palu *Turkey* 38°45N 40°0E **71** G7
Pamiers *France* 43°7N 1°39E **66** E4
Pamir *Tajikistan* 37°40N 73°0E **87** B13
Pamlico Sd. *U.S.A.* 35°20N 76°0W **111** C11
Pampa *U.S.A.* 35°32N 100°58W **110** C6
Pampas *Argentina* 35°0S 63°0W **121** F3
Pamplona-Iruña *Spain* 42°48N 1°38W **67** A5
Pana *U.S.A.* 39°23N 89°5W **112** F3
Panaji *India* 15°25N 73°50E **84** M8
Panamá *Panama* 9°0N 79°25W **115** F9
Panama ■ *Cent. Amer.* 8°48N 79°55W **115** F9
Panamá, G. de *Panama* 8°4N 79°20W **115** F9
Panama, Isthmus of *Cent. Amer.* 9°0N 79°0W **115** F8
Panama Canal *Panama* 9°10N 79°37W **115** F9
Panama City *U.S.A.* 30°10N 85°40W **111** D9
Panay *Phil.* 11°10N 122°30E **83** B6
Pančevo *Serbia* 44°52N 20°41E **69** B9
Panevėžys *Lithuania* 55°42N 24°25E **63** F8
Pangani *Tanzania* 5°25S 38°58E **96** F7
Pangbourne *U.K.* 51°29N 1°6W **30** D6
Pangkalpinang *Indonesia* 2°10S 106°10E **82** E3
Pangnirtung *Canada* 66°8N 65°43W **109** C13
Pantar *Indonesia* 8°28S 124°10E **83** F6
Pante Macassar *Timor-Leste* 9°30S 123°58E **83** F6
Pantelleria *Italy* 36°50N 11°57E **68** F4
Panzhihua *China* 26°33N 101°44E **78** F9
Papa Stour *U.K.* 60°20N 1°42W **22** B14
Papa Westray *U.K.* 59°20N 2°55W **23** D12
Papantla *Mexico* 20°27N 97°19W **114** C5
Papeete *Tahiti* 17°32S 149°34W **103** J13
Paphos *Cyprus* 34°46N 32°25E **86** C3
Papua □ *Indonesia* 4°0S 137°0E **83** E9
Papua, G. of *Papua N. G.* 9°0S 144°50E **98** B7
Papua New Guinea ■ *Oceania* 8°0S 145°0E **98** B8
Pará □ *Brazil* 3°20S 52°0W **120** C4
Paracatu *Brazil* 17°10S 46°50W **122** C1
Paracel Is. *S. China Sea* 15°50N 112°0E **82** A4
Paragould *U.S.A.* 36°3N 90°29W **111** C8
Paraguaçú → *Brazil* 12°45S 38°54W **122** B3
Paraguaná, Pen. de *Venezuela* 12°0N 70°0W **120** A3
Paraguarí *Paraguay* 25°36S 57°0W **121** E4
Paraguay ■ *S. Amer.* 23°0S 57°0W **121** E4
Paraguay → *Paraguay* 27°18S 58°38W **121** E4
Paraíba □ *Brazil* 7°0S 36°0W **120** C6
Parakou *Benin* 9°25N 2°40E **94** G6
Paramaribo *Suriname* 5°50N 55°10W **120** B4
Paraná *Argentina* 31°45S 60°30W **121** F3
Paraná *Brazil* 12°30S 47°48W **122** B1
Paraná □ *Brazil* 24°30S 51°0W **121** E4
Paraná → *Argentina* 33°43S 59°15W **121** F4
Paranaguá *Brazil* 25°30S 48°30W **122** E1
Paranaíba → *Brazil* 20°6S 51°4W **120** E4
Paranapanema → *Brazil* 22°40S 53°9W **121** E4
Parbhani *India* 19°8N 76°52E **84** K10
Pardo → *Brazil* 15°40S 39°0W **122** C3
Pardubice *Czechia* 50°3N 15°45E **64** C8
Parecis, Serra dos *Brazil* 13°0S 60°0W **120** D4
Parepare *Indonesia* 4°0S 119°40E **83** E5
Parima, Serra *Brazil* 2°30N 64°0W **120** B3
Pariñas, Pta. *Peru* 4°30S 82°0W **117** D2
Parintins *Brazil* 2°40S 56°50W **120** C4
Pariparit Kyun *Myanmar* 14°52N 93°41E **85** M18
Paris *France* 48°53N 2°20E **66** B5
Paris *U.S.A.* 33°40N 95°33W **111** D7
Park Falls *U.S.A.* 45°56N 90°27W **112** C2
Parkersburg *U.S.A.* 39°16N 81°34W **112** F7
Parla *Spain* 40°14N 3°46W **67** B4
Parma *Italy* 44°48N 10°20E **68** B4
Parnaguá *Brazil* 10°10S 44°38W **122** B2
Parnaíba *Brazil* 2°54S 41°47W **120** C5
Parnaíba → *Brazil* 3°0S 41°50W **120** C5
Pärnu *Estonia* 58°28N 24°33E **63** F8
Paros *Greece* 37°5N 25°12E **69** F11
Parracombe *U.K.* 51°11N 3°56W **29** E6
Parrett → *U.K.* 51°12N 3°1W **30** D2
Parry Is. *Canada* 77°0N 110°0W **109** B9
Parry Sound *Canada* 45°20N 80°0W **109** E12
Parsons *U.S.A.* 37°20N 95°16W **111** C7
Partney *U.K.* 53°12N 0°7E **27** F9
Parton *U.K.* 54°35N 3°34W **26** C1
Partry Mts. *Ireland* 53°40N 9°28W **18** D3
Paru → *Brazil* 1°33S 52°38W **120** C4
Pasadena *Calif., U.S.A.* 34°9N 118°8W **110** D3
Pasadena *Tex., U.S.A.* 29°43N 95°13W **111** E7
Paschimbanga □ *India* 23°0N 88°0E **85** H16
Pascua, I. de *Chile* 27°7S 109°23W **103** K17
Paso Robles *U.S.A.* 35°38N 120°41W **110** C2
Passage West *Ireland* 51°52N 8°21W **20** E6
Passau *Germany* 48°34N 13°28E **64** D7
Passo Fundo *Brazil* 28°10S 52°20W **121** E4
Passos *Brazil* 20°45S 46°37W **122** D1
Pastaza → *Peru* 4°50S 76°52W **120** C2
Pasto *Colombia* 1°13N 77°17W **120** B2
Patagonia *Argentina* 45°0S 69°0W **121** G3
Patan *India* 23°54N 72°14E **84** H8
Pateley Bridge *U.K.* 54°5N 1°44W **26** D5
Paterson *U.S.A.* 40°54N 74°9W **113** E10
Pathankot *India* 32°18N 75°45E **84** C9
Pathein *Myanmar* 16°45N 94°30E **85** L19
Pathfinder Res. *U.S.A.* 42°28N 106°51W **110** B5
Patiala *India* 30°23N 76°26E **84** D9
Patkai Bum *India* 27°0N 95°30E **85** F19
Patmos *Greece* 37°21N 26°36E **69** F12
Patna *India* 25°35N 85°12E **85** G14
Patos *Brazil* 6°55S 37°16W **120** C6
Patos, L. dos *Brazil* 31°20S 51°0W **121** F4
Patos de Minas *Brazil* 18°35S 46°32W **122** C1
Patra *Greece* 38°14N 21°47E **69** E9
Patrington *U.K.* 53°41N 0°1W **27** E8
Patrocínio *Brazil* 18°57S 47°0W **122** C1
Patten *U.S.A.* 46°0N 68°38W **113** C13
Patterdale *U.K.* 54°32N 2°56W **26** C3
Pau *France* 43°19N 0°25W **66** E3
Paulatuk *Canada* 69°25N 124°0W **108** C7
Paulistana *Brazil* 8°9S 41°9W **122** A2
Paull *U.K.* 53°44N 0°14W **27** E8
Paulo Afonso *Brazil* 9°21S 38°15W **122** A3
Pavia *Italy* 45°7N 9°8E **68** B3
Pavlodar *Kazakhstan* 52°33N 77°0E **76** D8
Pavlohrad *Ukraine* 48°30N 35°52E **71** E6
Pavlovo *Russia* 55°58N 43°5E **70** C7
Pawtucket *U.S.A.* 41°53N 71°23W **113** E12
Paxton *U.S.A.* 40°27N 88°6W **112** E3
Payakumbuh *Indonesia* 0°20S 100°35E **82** E2
Payette *U.S.A.* 44°5N 116°56W **110** B3
Payne L. *Canada* 59°30N 74°30W **109** D12
Paysandú *Uruguay* 32°19S 58°8W **121** F4
Payson *U.S.A.* 34°14N 111°20W **110** D4
Paz, B. de la *Mexico* 24°9N 110°25W **114** C2
Pazardzhik *Bulgaria* 42°12N 24°20E **69** C11
Peace → *Canada* 59°0N 111°25W **108** D8
Peace River *Canada* 56°15N 117°18W **108** D8
Peacehaven *U.K.* 50°48N 0°0 **31** E8
Peak District △ *U.K.* 53°24N 1°46W **27** F5
Pearl City *U.S.A.* 21°24N 157°59W **110** H16
Pearl Harbor *U.S.A.* 21°21N 157°57W **110** H16
Pearl River Bridge *China* 22°15N 113°48E **79** a
Peasenhall *U.K.* 52°16N 1°27E **31** B11
Peawanuck *Canada* 55°15N 85°12W **109** D11
Pechora *Russia* 65°10N 57°11E **70** A10
Pechora → *Russia* 68°13N 54°15E **70** A9
Pechora B. *Russia* 68°40N 54°0E **70** A9
Pecos *U.S.A.* 31°26N 103°30W **110** D6
Pecos → *U.S.A.* 29°42N 101°22W **110** E6
Pécs *Hungary* 46°5N 18°15E **65** E10
Pedra Azul *Brazil* 16°2S 41°17W **122** C2
Pedro Afonso *Brazil* 9°0S 48°10W **122** A1
Peebles *U.K.* 55°40N 3°11W **25** C9
Peel *I. of Man* 54°13N 4°40W **19** C12
Peel → *Canada* 67°0N 135°0W **108** C6
Peel Fell *U.K.* 55°18N 2°34W **26** B3
Peel Sd. *Canada* 73°0N 96°0W **108** B10
Pegswood *U.K.* 55°11N 1°39W **26** B5
Pegu Yoma *Myanmar* 19°0N 96°0E **85** K20
Pegwell Bay *U.K.* 51°18N 1°24E **31** D11
Peixe *Brazil* 12°0S 48°40W **122** B1
Pejë *Kosovo* 42°40N 20°17E **69** C9
Pekalongan *Indonesia* 6°53S 109°40E **82** F3
Pekanbaru *Indonesia* 0°30N 101°15E **82** D2
Pekin *U.S.A.* 40°35N 89°40W **112** E3
Peking = Beijing *China* 39°53N 116°21E **79** D12
Pelagie, Is. *Italy* 35°39N 12°33E **68** G5
Pelée, Mt. *Martinique* 14°48N 61°10W **115** D12
Peleng *Indonesia* 1°20S 123°30E **83** E6
Pelješac *Croatia* 42°55N 17°25E **68** C7
Pelly → *Canada* 62°47N 137°19W **108** C6
Pelly Bay *Canada* 68°38N 89°50W **109** C11
Peloponnesos □ *Greece* 37°10N 22°0E **69** F10
Pelotas *Brazil* 31°42S 52°23W **121** F4
Pelvoux, Massif du *France* 44°52N 6°20E **66** D7
Pematangsiantar *Indonesia* 2°57N 99°5E **82** D1
Pemba *Mozam.* 12°58S 40°30E **97** G8
Pemba I. *Tanzania* 5°0S 39°45E **96** F7
Pembridge *U.K.* 52°13N 2°52W **30** B3
Pembroke *Canada* 45°50N 77°7W **109** E12
Pembroke *U.K.* 51°41N 4°55W **28** D4
Pembrokeshire □ *U.K.* 51°52N 4°56W **28** D3
Pembrokeshire Coast △ *U.K.* 51°50N 5°2W **28** D3
Pembury *U.K.* 51°8N 0°20E **31** D9
Pen-y-bont ar Ogwr = Bridgend *U.K.* 51°30N 3°34W **29** D6
Pen-y-Ghent *U.K.* 54°10N 2°14W **26** D4
Penarth *U.K.* 51°26N 3°11W **29** E7
Peñas, G. de *Chile* 47°0S 75°0W **121** G2
Pend Oreille, L. *U.S.A.* 48°10N 116°21W **110** A3
Pendeen *U.K.* 50°9N 5°41W **29** G2
Pendle Hill *U.K.* 53°52N 2°19W **27** E4
Pendleton *U.S.A.* 45°40N 118°47W **110** A3
Penedo *Brazil* 10°15S 36°36W **122** B3
Penetanguishene *Canada* 44°50N 79°55W **112** C8
Penfro = Pembroke *U.K.* 51°41N 4°55W **28** D4
Penicuik *U.K.* 55°50N 3°13W **25** C9
Peninsular Malaysia □ *Malaysia* 4°0N 102°0E **82** D2
Penistone *U.K.* 53°31N 1°37W **27** E5
Penkridge *U.K.* 52°44N 2°6W **27** G4
Penmarch, Pte. de *France* 47°48N 4°22W **66** C1
Penn Yan *U.S.A.* 42°40N 77°3W **112** D9
Pennines *U.K.* 54°45N 2°27W **26** C4
Pennsylvania □ *U.S.A.* 40°45N 77°30W **112** E8
Penong *Australia* 31°56S 133°1E **98** G5
Penrith *U.K.* 54°40N 2°45W **26** C3
Penryn *U.K.* 50°9N 5°7W **29** G3
Pensacola *U.S.A.* 30°25N 87°13W **111** D9
Pensacola Mts. *Antarctica* 84°0S 40°0W **55** E1
Penshurst *U.K.* 51°10N 0°12E **31** D9
Penticton *Canada* 49°30N 119°38W **108** E8
Pentire Pt. *U.K.* 50°35N 4°56W **29** F4
Pentland Firth *U.K.* 58°43N 3°10W **23** E11
Pentland Hills *U.K.* 55°48N 3°25W **25** C9
Penwortham *U.K.* 53°45N 2°46W **27** E3
Penygroes *U.K.* 53°3N 4°17W **28** A5
Penza *Russia* 53°15N 45°5E **70** D8
Penzance *U.K.* 50°7N 5°33W **29** G2
Peoria *U.S.A.* 40°42N 89°36W **112** E3
Perabumulih *Indonesia* 3°27S 104°15E **82** E2
Perdido, Mte. *Spain* 42°40N 0°5E **67** A6
Pereira *Colombia* 4°49N 75°43W **120** B2
Pergamino *Argentina* 33°52S 60°30W **121** F3
Péribonka → *Canada* 48°45N 72°5W **109** E12
Périgueux *France* 45°10N 0°42E **66** D4
Perm *Russia* 58°0N 56°10E **70** C10
Pernambuco □ *Brazil* 8°0S 37°0W **120** C6
Pernik *Bulgaria* 42°35N 23°2E **69** C10
Perpignan *France* 42°42N 2°53E **66** E5
Perranporth *U.K.* 50°20N 5°11W **29** G3
Perranzabuloe *U.K.* 50°19N 5°9W **29** G3
Perryton *U.S.A.* 36°24N 100°48W **110** C6
Perryville *U.S.A.* 37°43N 89°52W **112** G3
Persepolis *Iran* 29°55N 52°50E **87** D8
Pershore *U.K.* 52°7N 2°4W **30** B4
Persian Gulf *Asia* 27°0N 50°0E **87** E7
Perth *Australia* 31°57S 115°52E **98** G2
Perth *Canada* 44°55N 76°15W **112** C9
Perth *U.K.* 56°24N 3°26W **25** B9
Perth & Kinross □ *U.K.* 56°45N 3°55W **23** J9
Peru *U.S.A.* 40°45N 86°4W **112** E4
Peru ■ *S. Amer.* 4°0S 75°0W **120** C2
Peru-Chile Trench *Pac. Oc.* 20°0S 72°0W **103** K20
Perugia *Italy* 43°7N 12°23E **68** C5
Pervomaysk *Ukraine* 48°10N 30°46E **71** E5
Pervouralsk *Russia* 56°59N 59°59E **70** C10
Pésaro *Italy* 43°54N 12°55E **68** C5
Pescara *Italy* 42°28N 14°13E **68** C6
Peshawar *Pakistan* 34°2N 71°37E **84** B7
Pesqueira *Brazil* 8°20S 36°42W **122** A3
Petah Tiqwa *Israel* 32°6N 34°53E **86** C3
Peterborough *Canada* 44°20N 78°20W **109** E12
Peterborough *U.K.* 52°35N 0°15W **31** A8
Peterchurch *U.K.* 52°2N 2°56W **30** B3
Peterculter *U.K.* 57°6N 2°16W **23** H13
Peterhead *U.K.* 57°31N 1°48W **23** G14
Peterlee *U.K.* 54°47N 1°20W **26** C6
Petersburg *Alaska, U.S.A.* 56°48N 132°58W **108** D6
Petersburg *Va., U.S.A.* 37°14N 77°24W **112** G9
Petersfield *U.K.* 51°1N 0°56W **31** D7
Petit Piton *St. Lucia* 13°51N 61°5W **114** b
Petitot → *Canada* 60°14N 123°29W **108** C7
Petitsikapau L. *Canada* 54°37N 66°25W **109** D13
Peto *Mexico* 20°8N 88°55W **114** C7
Petoskey *U.S.A.* 45°22N 84°57W **112** C5
Petra *Jordan* 30°20N 35°22E **86** D3
Petrolândia *Brazil* 9°5S 38°20W **122** A3
Petrolina *Brazil* 9°24S 40°30W **122** A2
Petropavl *Kazakhstan* 54°53N 69°13E **76** D7
Petropavlovsk-Kamchatskiy *Russia* 53°3N 158°43E **77** D16
Petrópolis *Brazil* 22°33S 43°9W **122** D2
Petrozavodsk *Russia* 61°41N 34°20E **70** B5
Petworth *U.K.* 51°0N 0°36W **31** E7
Pevensey *U.K.* 50°49N 0°23E **31** E9
Pevensey Levels *U.K.* 50°50N 0°20E **31** E9
Pewsey *U.K.* 51°20N 1°45W **30** D5
Pewsey, Vale of *U.K.* 51°22N 1°40W **30** D5
Pforzheim *Germany* 48°52N 8°41E **64** D5
Phalodi *India* 27°12N 72°24E **84** F8
Phan Rang -Thap Cham *Vietnam* 11°34N 109°0E **82** B3
Phan Thiet *Vietnam* 11°1N 108°9E **82** B3
Phi Phi, Ko *Thailand* 7°45N 98°46E **82** C1
Philadelphia *U.S.A.* 39°57N 75°9W **113** E10
Philippine Sea *Pac. Oc.* 18°0N 125°0E **72** G14
Philippine Trench *Pac. Oc.* 12°0N 126°6E **83** B7
Philippines ■ *Asia* 12°0N 123°0E **83** B6
Phillips *U.S.A.* 45°42N 90°24W **112** C2
Phitsanulok *Thailand* 16°50N 100°12E **82** A2
Phnom Penh *Cambodia* 11°33N 104°55E **82** B2
Phoenix *U.S.A.* 33°26N 112°4W **110** D4
Phoenix Is. *Kiribati* 3°30S 172°0W **99** A16
Phuket *Thailand* 7°53N 98°24E **82** C1
Piacenza *Italy* 45°1N 9°40E **68** B3
Piatra Neamț *Romania* 46°56N 26°21E **65** E14
Piauí □ *Brazil* 7°0S 43°0W **120** C5
Piauí → *Brazil* 6°38S 42°42W **120** C5
Piave → *Italy* 45°32N 12°44E **68** B5
Picardie *France* 49°50N 3°0E **66** B5
Pichilemu *Chile* 34°22S 72°0W **121** F2
Pickering *U.K.* 54°15N 0°46W **26** D7
Pickering, Vale of *U.K.* 54°14N 0°45W **26** D7
Picos *Brazil* 7°5S 41°28W **120** C5
Picton *Canada* 44°1N 77°9W **112** C9
Pidley *U.K.* 52°23N 0°2W **31** B8
Pidurutalagala *Sri Lanka* 7°10N 80°50E **84** R12
Piedmont *U.S.A.* 34°42N 82°28W **111** D10
Piedras Negras *Mexico* 28°42N 100°31W **114** B4
Piemonte □ *Italy* 45°0N 8°0E **68** B2
Pierre *U.S.A.* 44°22N 100°21W **110** B6
Pietermaritzburg *S. Africa* 29°35S 30°25E **97** K6
Pikes Peak *U.S.A.* 38°50N 105°3W **110** C5
Pikeville *U.S.A.* 37°29N 82°31W **112** G6
Pilar *Paraguay* 26°50S 58°20W **121** E4
Pilcomaya → *Paraguay* 25°21S 57°42W **121** E4
Pilibhit *India* 28°40N 79°50E **84** E11
Pilica → *Poland* 51°52N 21°17E **65** C11
Pilling *U.K.* 53°56N 2°54W **27** E3
Pilton *U.K.* 51°10N 2°36W **30** D3
Pimentel *Peru* 6°45S 79°55W **120** C2
Pinar del Río *Cuba* 22°26N 83°40W **115** C8
Pinatubo, Mt. *Phil.* 15°8N 120°21E **83** A6
Pinchbeck *U.K.* 52°50N 0°9W **27** G8
Pinckneyville *U.S.A.* 38°5N 89°23W **112** F3
Pindus Mts. *Greece* 40°0N 21°0E **69** E9
Pine Bluff *U.S.A.* 34°13N 92°1W **111** D8
Pinega → *Russia* 64°30N 44°19E **70** B8
Pingdingshan *China* 33°43N 113°27E **79** E11
P'ingtung *Taiwan* 22°38N 120°30E **79** G13
Pingxiang *Guangxi Zhuangzu, China* 22°6N 106°46E **78** G10
Pingxiang *Jiangxi, China* 27°43N 113°48E **79** F11
Pinheiro *Brazil* 2°31S 45°5W **120** C5
Pinhoe *U.K.* 50°44N 3°28W **29** F7
Pinsk *Belarus* 52°10N 26°1E **70** D4
Piombino *Italy* 42°55N 10°32E **68** C4
Piotrków Trybunalski *Poland* 51°23N 19°43E **65** C10
Pipmuacan, Rés. *Canada* 49°45N 70°30W **113** A12
Piracicaba *Brazil* 22°45S 47°40W **122** D1
Pirapora *Brazil* 17°20S 44°56W **122** C2
Pireas *Greece* 37°57N 23°42E **69** F10
Pirmasens *Germany* 49°12N 7°36E **64** D4
Pisa *Italy* 43°43N 10°23E **68** C4
Pisagua *Chile* 19°40S 70°15W **120** D2
Pishan *China* 37°30N 78°33E **78** D4
Pistóia *Italy* 43°55N 10°54E **68** C4
Pit → *U.S.A.* 40°47N 122°6W **110** B2
Pitcairn I. *Pac. Oc.* 25°5S 130°5W **103** K14
Piteå *Sweden* 65°20N 21°25E **63** D8
Pitești *Romania* 44°52N 24°54E **65** F13
Pitlochry *U.K.* 56°42N 3°44W **23** J10
Pittsburg *U.S.A.* 37°25N 94°42W **111** C8
Pittsburgh *U.S.A.* 40°26N 79°58W **112** E8
Pittsfield *U.S.A.* 42°27N 73°15W **113** D11
Piura *Peru* 5°15S 80°38W **120** C1
Placentia *Canada* 47°20N 54°0W **109** E14
Placentia B. *Canada* 47°0N 54°40W **109** E14
Placetas *Cuba* 22°15N 79°44W **115** C9
Plainview *U.S.A.* 34°11N 101°43W **110** D6
Plata, Río de la → *S. Amer.* 34°45S 57°30W **121** F4
Platte → *U.S.A.* 39°16N 94°50W **111** C8
Plattsburgh *U.S.A.* 44°42N 73°28W **113** C11
Plauen *Germany* 50°30N 12°8E **64** C7
Playa del Carmen *Mexico* 20°37N 87°4W **114** C7
Plenty, B. of *N.Z.* 37°45S 177°0E **99** H14
Plessisville *Canada* 46°14N 71°47W **113** B12
Pleven *Bulgaria* 43°26N 24°37E **69** C11
Plock *Poland* 52°32N 19°40E **65** B10
Ploiești *Romania* 44°57N 26°5E **65** F14
Plovdiv *Bulgaria* 42°8N 24°44E **69** C11
Plymouth *U.K.* 50°22N 4°10W **29** G5
Plymouth *Ind., U.S.A.* 41°21N 86°19W **112** E4
Plymouth *Wis., U.S.A.* 43°45N 87°59W **112** D4
Plympton *U.K.* 50°23N 4°5W **29** G5
Plymstock *U.K.* 50°21N 4°7W **29** G5
Plynlimon = Pumlumon Fawr *U.K.* 52°28N 3°46W **28** C6
Plzeň *Czechia* 49°45N 13°22E **64** D7
Po → *Italy* 44°57N 12°4E **68** B5
Pocatello *U.S.A.* 42°52N 112°27W **110** B4
Pocklington *U.K.* 53°56N 0°46W **27** E7
Poços de Caldas *Brazil* 21°50S 46°33W **122** D1
Podgorica *Montenegro* 42°30N 19°19E **69** C8
Podolsk *Russia* 55°25N 37°30E **70** C6
Pohang *S. Korea* 36°1N 129°23E **79** D14
Pohnpei *Micronesia* 6°55N 158°10E **102** G7
Point Hope *U.S.A.* 68°21N 166°47W **108** C3
Point L. *Canada* 65°15N 113°4W **108** C8
Point Pleasant *U.S.A.* 38°51N 82°8W **112** F6
Pointe-à-Pitre *Guadeloupe* 16°15N 61°32W **115** D12
Pointe-Noire *Congo* 4°48S 11°53E **96** E2
Poitiers *France* 46°35N 0°20E **66** C4
Poitou *France* 46°40N 0°10W **66** C3
Pokhara *Nepal* 28°14N 83°58E **85** E13
Poland ■ *Europe* 52°0N 20°0E **65** C10
Polatsk *Belarus* 55°30N 28°50E **70** C4
Polden Hills *U.K.* 51°7N 2°50W **30** D3
Polegate *U.K.* 50°49N 0°16E **31** E9
Polesworth *U.K.* 52°37N 1°36W **27** G5
Polevskoy *Russia* 56°26N 60°11E **70** C11
Polokwane *S. Africa* 23°54S 29°25E **97** J5
Polperro *U.K.* 50°20N 4°32W **29** G4
Polruan *U.K.* 50°19N 4°38W **29** G4
Poltava *Ukraine* 49°35N 34°35E **71** E5
Polynesia *Pac. Oc.* 10°0S 162°0W **103** F11
Pomeranian Lakes *Poland* 53°40N 16°37E **65** B9
Ponca City *U.S.A.* 36°42N 97°5W **111** C7
Ponce *Puerto Rico* 18°1N 66°37W **115** D11
Pond Inlet *Canada* 72°40N 77°0W **109** B12
Ponferrada *Spain* 42°32N 6°35W **67** A2
Ponta Grossa *Brazil* 25°7S 50°10W **121** E4
Pontardawe *U.K.* 51°43N 3°51W **28** D6
Pontardulais *U.K.* 51°43N 4°3W **28** D5
Pontarlier *France* 46°54N 6°20E **66** C7
Pontchartrain, L. *U.S.A.* 30°5N 90°5W **111** D9
Ponte Nova *Brazil* 20°25S 42°54W **122** D2
Pontefract *U.K.* 53°42N 1°18W **27** E6
Ponteland *U.K.* 55°3N 1°45W **26** B5
Pontevedra *Spain* 42°26N 8°40W **67** A1
Pontiac *Ill., U.S.A.* 40°53N 88°38W **112** E3
Pontiac *Mich., U.S.A.* 42°38N 83°18W **112** D6
Pontianak *Indonesia* 0°3S 109°15E **82** E3
Pontine Mts. *Turkey* 41°0N 36°45E **71** F6
Pontivy *France* 48°5N 2°58W **66** B2
Pontrilas *U.K.* 51°56N 2°52W **30** C3
Pontypool *U.K.* 51°42N 3°2W **28** D7
Pontypridd *U.K.* 51°36N 3°20W **29** D7
Ponziane, Ísole *Italy* 40°55N 12°57E **68** D5
Poole *U.K.* 50°43N 1°59W **30** E5
Poole Harbour *U.K.* 50°41N 2°0W **30** E5
Pooley Bridge *U.K.* 54°37N 2°48W **26** C3
Poopó, L. de *Bolivia* 18°30S 67°35W **120** D3
Popayán *Colombia* 2°27N 76°36W **120** B2
Poplar Bluff *U.S.A.* 36°46N 90°24W **111** C8
Popocatépetl, Volcán *Mexico* 19°2N 98°38W **114** D5
Porbandar *India* 21°44N 69°43E **84** J6
Porcupine → *U.S.A.* 66°34N 145°19W **108** C5
Pori *Finland* 61°29N 21°48E **63** E8
Porlock *U.K.* 51°13N 3°35W **29** E6
Port Alberni *Canada* 49°14N 124°50W **108** E7
Port Antonio *Jamaica* 18°10N 76°26W **114** a
Port Arthur *U.S.A.* 29°54N 93°56W **111** E8
Port-au-Prince *Haiti* 18°40N 72°20W **115** D10
Port Augusta *Australia* 32°30S 137°50E **98** G6
Port Carlisle *U.K.* 54°57N 3°11W **26** C2
Port-Cartier *Canada* 50°2N 66°50W **109** D13
Port-de-Paix *Haiti* 19°50N 72°50W **115** D10
Port Elgin *Canada* 44°25N 81°25W **112** C7
Port Elizabeth *S. Africa* 33°58S 25°40E **97** L5

Port Ellen | Rochester

Port Ellen *U.K.* 55°38N 6°11W **24** C3
Port Erin *I. of Man* 54°5N 4°45W **19** C12
Port-Gentil *Gabon* 0°40S 8°50E **96** E1
Port Glasgow *U.K.* 55°56N 4°41W **24** C6
Port Harcourt *Nigeria* 4°40N 7°10E **94** H7
Port Hawkesbury *Canada* 45°36N 61°22W **109** E13
Port Hedland *Australia* 20°25S 118°35E **98** E2
Port Hope Simpson *Canada* 52°33N 56°18W **109** D14
Port Huron *U.S.A.* 42°58N 82°26W **112** D6
Port Isaac *U.K.* 50°35N 4°50W **29** F4
Port Isaac B. *U.K.* 50°36N 4°50W **29** F4
Port Lincoln *Australia* 34°42S 135°52E **98** G6
Port Louis *Mauritius* 20°10S 57°30E **91** H9
Port McNeill *Canada* 50°35N 127°6W **108** D7
Port Macquarie *Australia* 31°25S 152°25E **98** G9
Port Maria *Jamaica* 18°22N 76°54W **114** a
Port Morant *Jamaica* 17°54N 76°19W **114** a
Port Moresby *Papua N. G.* 9°24S 147°8E **98** B8
Port Nolloth *S. Africa* 29°17S 16°52E **97** K3
Port of Spain *Trin. & Tob.* 10°40N 61°31W **120** A3
Port Pirie *Australia* 33°10S 138°1E **98** G6
Port Said *Egypt* 31°16N 32°18E **95** B12
Port St. Lucie *U.S.A.* 27°18N 80°21W **111** E10
Port St. Mary *U.K.* 54°5N 4°44W **19** C12
Port Shepstone *S. Africa* 30°44S 30°28E **97** L6
Port Sudan *Sudan* 19°32N 37°9E **95** E13
Port Talbot *U.K.* 51°35N 3°47W **29** D6
Port Vila *Vanuatu* 17°45S 168°18E **99** D12
Port Washington *U.S.A.* 43°23N 87°53W **112** D4
Port William *U.K.* 54°46N 4°35W **24** E6
Portadown *U.K.* 54°25N 6°27W **19** C9
Portaferry *U.K.* 54°23N 5°33W **19** C10
Portage *U.S.A.* 43°33N 89°28W **112** D3
Portage la Prairie *Canada* 49°58N 98°18W **108** E10
Portarlington *Ireland* 53°10N 7°10W **21** B8
Porth Tywyn = Burry Port
U.K. 51°41N 4°15W **28** D5
Porthcawl *U.K.* 51°29N 3°42W **29** E6
Porthleven *U.K.* 50°4N 5°19W **29** G3
Porthmadog *U.K.* 52°55N 4°8W **28** B5
Portknockie *U.K.* 57°42N 2°51W **23** D13
Portland *Maine, U.S.A.* 43°39N 70°16W **113** D12
Portland *Oreg., U.S.A.* 45°32N 122°37W **110** A2
Portland, I. of *U.K.* 50°33N 2°26W **30** E4
Portland Bight *Jamaica* 17°52N 77°5W **114** a
Portland Bill *U.K.* 50°31N 2°28W **29** F9
Portland Pt. *Jamaica* 17°42N 77°11W **114** a
Portlaoise *Ireland* 53°2N 7°18W **21** B8
Portmarnock *Ireland* 53°26N 6°8W **21** B10
Portmore *Jamaica* 17°53N 76°53W **114** a
Porto *Portugal* 41°8N 8°40W **67** B1
Pôrto Alegre *Brazil* 30°5S 51°10W **121** F4
Porto Esperança *Brazil* 19°37S 57°29W **120** D2
Porto Nacional *Brazil* 10°40S 48°30W **122** D1
Porto-Novo *Benin* 6°23N 2°42E **94** G6
Porto Seguro *Brazil* 16°26S 39°5W **122** C3
Porto Tôrres *Italy* 40°50N 8°24E **68** D3
Porto-Vecchio *France* 41°35N 9°16E **66** F8
Porto Velho *Brazil* 8°46S 63°54W **120** C3
Porton *U.K.* 51°8N 1°43W **30** D5
Portpatrick *U.K.* 54°51N 5°7W **24** E5
Portree *U.K.* 57°25N 6°12W **22** H5
Portrush *U.K.* 55°12N 6°40W **19** A8
Portslade *U.K.* 50°50N 0°12W **31** E8
Portsmouth *U.K.* 50°48N 1°6W **30** E6
Portsmouth *N.H., U.S.A.* 43°5N 70°45W **113** D12
Portsmouth *Ohio, U.S.A.* 38°44N 82°57W **112** F6
Portsmouth *Va., U.S.A.* 36°58N 76°23W **111** C11
Portsoy *U.K.* 57°41N 2°41W **23** G12
Portstewart *U.K.* 55°11N 6°43W **19** A8
Porttipahdan tekojärvi *Finland* 68°5N 26°40E **63** D9
Portugal ■ *Europe* 40°0N 8°0W **67** C1
Portumna *Ireland* 53°6N 8°14W **20** B6
Posadas *Argentina* 27°30S 55°50W **121** E4
Posse *Brazil* 14°4S 46°18W **122** B1
Postmasburg *S. Africa* 28°18S 23°5E **97** K4
Potchefstroom *S. Africa* 26°41S 27°7E **97** K5
Potenza *Italy* 40°38N 15°48E **68** D6
Poti *Georgia* 42°10N 41°38E **71** F7
Potiskum *Nigeria* 11°39N 11°2E **95** F8
Potomac → *U.S.A.* 38°0N 76°23W **112** F9
Potosí *Bolivia* 19°38S 65°50W **120** D3
Potsdam *Germany* 52°23N 13°3E **64** B7
Potsdam *U.S.A.* 44°40N 74°59W **113** C10
Potter Heigham *U.K.* 52°42N 1°34E **31** A12
Potterne *U.K.* 51°20N 2°0W **30** D4
Potters Bar *U.K.* 51°42N 0°11W **31** C8
Potterspury *U.K.* 52°5N 0°52W **31** B7
Pottstown *U.S.A.* 40°15N 75°39W **113** E10
Pottsville *U.S.A.* 40°41N 76°12W **113** E9
Pottuvil *Sri Lanka* 6°55N 81°50E **84** R12
Poughkeepsie *U.S.A.* 41°42N 73°56W **113** E11
Poulaphouca Res. *Ireland* 53°8N 6°30W **21** B10
Poulton-le-Fylde *U.K.* 53°51N 2°58W **27** E4
Poundstock *U.K.* 50°44N 4°36W **29** F4
Pouso Alegre *Brazil* 22°14S 45°57W **122** D1
Powder → *U.S.A.* 46°45N 105°26W **110** A5
Powell, L. *U.S.A.* 36°57N 111°29W **110** C4
Powell River *Canada* 49°50N 124°35W **108** E7
Powers *U.S.A.* 45°41N 87°32W **112** C4
Powick *U.K.* 52°10N 2°14W **30** B4
Powys □ *U.K.* 52°20N 3°20W **28** C7
Poyang Hu *China* 29°5N 116°20E **79** F12
Poza Rica *Mexico* 20°33N 97°27W **114** C5
Poznań *Poland* 52°25N 16°55E **65** B9
Pozzuoli *Italy* 40°49N 14°7E **68** D6
Prado *Brazil* 17°20S 39°13W **122** C3
Prague *Czechia* 50°4N 14°25E **64** C8
Praia *Cabo Verde* 15°2N 23°34W **93** E1
Praia Grande *Brazil* 24°0S 46°24W **122** D1
Prairie du Chien *U.S.A.* 43°3N 91°9W **112** D2
Prata *Brazil* 19°25S 48°54W **122** C1
Prato *Italy* 43°53N 11°6E **68** C4
Pratt *U.S.A.* 37°39N 98°44W **110** C7
Prawle Pt. *U.K.* 50°12N 3°44W **29** G6
Praya *Indonesia* 8°39S 116°17E **82** F5
Prees *U.K.* 52°54N 2°40W **27** G3
Preesall *U.K.* 53°55N 2°57W **27** E3
Prescott *Canada* 44°45N 75°30W **113** C10
Prescott *U.S.A.* 34°33N 112°28W **110** D4

Presidencia Roque Saenz Peña
Argentina 26°45S 60°30W **121** E3
Presidente Prudente *Brazil* 22°5S 51°25W **120** E4
Presidio *U.S.A.* 29°34N 104°22W **110** E6
Prespa, L. *Macedonia* 40°55N 21°0E **69** D9
Presque Isle *U.S.A.* 46°41N 68°1W **113** B13
Prestatyn *U.K.* 53°20N 3°24W **28** A7
Prestbury *U.K.* 51°54N 2°2W **30** C4
Presteigne *U.K.* 52°17N 3°0W **28** C7
Preston *Borders, U.K.* 55°49N 2°19W **25** C11
Preston *Dorset, U.K.* 50°38N 2°26W **30** E4
Preston *Lancs., U.K.* 53°46N 2°42W **27** E3
Preston *U.S.A.* 42°6N 111°53W **110** B4
Prestonpans *U.K.* 55°58N 2°58W **25** C10
Prestwich *U.K.* 53°32N 2°17W **27** E4
Prestwick *U.K.* 55°29N 4°37W **24** D6
Pretoria *S. Africa* 25°44S 28°12E **97** K5
Pribilof Is. *U.S.A.* 57°0N 170°0W **108** D2
Price *U.S.A.* 39°36N 110°49W **110** B4
Prieska *S. Africa* 29°40S 22°42E **97** K4
Prilep *Macedonia* 41°21N 21°32E **69** D9
Prince Albert *Canada* 53°15N 105°50W **108** D9
Prince Albert Pen. *Canada* 72°30N 116°0W **108** B8
Prince Albert Sd. *Canada* 70°25N 115°0W **108** B8
Prince Alfred, C. *Canada* 74°20N 124°40W **109** B7
Prince Charles I. *Canada* 67°47N 76°12W **109** C12
Prince Charles Mts. *Antarctica* 72°0S 67°0E **55** D6
Prince Edward I. □ *Canada* 46°20N 63°20W **113** C16
Prince Edward Is. *Ind. Oc.* 46°35S 38°0E **53** G11
Prince George *Canada* 53°55N 122°50W **108** D7
Prince Gustaf Adolf Sea
Canada 78°30N 107°0W **109** B9
Prince of Wales I. *Canada* 73°0N 99°0W **108** B10
Prince of Wales I. *U.S.A.* 55°47N 132°50W **108** D6
Prince Patrick I. *Canada* 77°0N 120°0W **109** B8
Prince Rupert *Canada* 54°20N 130°20W **108** D6
Prince William Sd. *U.S.A.* 60°40N 147°0W **108** C5
Princes Risborough *U.K.* 51°43N 0°49W **31** C7
Princeton *Ill., U.S.A.* 41°23N 89°28W **112** E3
Princeton *Ind., U.S.A.* 38°21N 87°34W **112** F4
Princeton *Ky., U.S.A.* 37°7N 87°53W **112** G4
Princeton *W. Va., U.S.A.* 37°22N 81°6W **112** G7
Princetown *U.K.* 50°33N 4°0W **29** F5
Principe *São Tomé & Príncipe* 1°37N 7°25E **90** F4
Pripet → *Europe* 51°20N 30°15E **65** C16
Pripet Marshes *Europe* 52°10N 27°10E **65** C15
Prishtinë *Kosovo* 42°40N 21°13E **69** C9
Priva *France* 44°45N 4°37E **66** D6
Prizren *Kosovo* 42°13N 20°45E **69** C9
Probolinggo *Indonesia* 7°46S 113°13E **82** F4
Probus *U.K.* 50°17N 4°58W **29** G4
Progreso *Mexico* 21°20N 89°40W **114** C7
Propriá *Brazil* 10°13S 36°51W **122** B3
Provence *France* 43°40N 5°46E **66** E6
Providence *U.S.A.* 41°49N 71°24W **113** E12
Providencia, I. de *Caribbean* 13°25N 81°26W **115** E8
Provins *France* 48°33N 3°15E **66** B5
Provo *U.S.A.* 40°14N 111°39W **110** B4
Prudhoe *U.K.* 54°57N 1°52W **26** C5
Prudhoe Bay *U.S.A.* 70°18N 148°22W **108** B5
Pruszków *Poland* 52°9N 20°49E **65** B11
Prut → *Romania* 45°28N 28°10E **65** F15
Pryluky *Ukraine* 50°30N 32°24E **71** D5
Przemyśl *Poland* 49°50N 22°45E **65** D12
Pskov *Russia* 57°50N 28°25E **70** C4
Puddletown *U.K.* 50°44N 2°20W **30** E4
Pudsey *U.K.* 53°47N 1°40W **27** E5
Puducherry *India* 11°59N 79°50E **84** P11
Puebla *Mexico* 19°3N 98°12W **114** D5
Pueblo *U.S.A.* 38°16N 104°37W **110** C6
Puerto Aisén *Chile* 45°27S 73°0W **121** G2
Puerto Barrios *Guatemala* 15°40N 88°32W **114** D7
Puerto Cabello *Venezuela* 10°28N 68°1W **120** A3
Puerto Cabezas *Nic.* 14°0N 83°30W **115** E8
Puerto Carreño *Colombia* 6°12N 67°22W **120** B3
Puerto Cortés *Honduras* 15°51N 88°0W **114** D7
Puerto Deseado *Argentina* 47°55S 66°0W **121** G3
Puerto La Cruz *Venezuela* 10°13N 64°38W **120** A3
Puerto Madryn *Argentina* 42°48S 65°4W **121** G3
Puerto Maldonado *Peru* 12°30S 69°10W **120** D3
Puerto Montt *Chile* 41°28S 73°0W **121** G2
Puerto Plata *Dom. Rep.* 19°48N 70°45W **115** D10
Puerto Princesa *Phil.* 9°46N 118°45E **83** C5
Puerto Rico ☑ *W. Indies* 18°15N 66°45W **115** D11
Puerto Rico Trench *Atl. Oc.* 19°50N 66°0W **115** D11
Puerto San Julián *Argentina* 49°18S 67°43W **121** G3
Puerto Suárez *Bolivia* 18°58S 57°52W **120** D4
Puerto Wilches *Colombia* 7°21N 73°54W **120** B2
Puertollano *Spain* 38°43N 4°7W **67** C3
Puffin I. *Ireland* 51°50N 10°24W **20** D1
Puget Sound *U.S.A.* 47°50N 122°30W **110** A2
Pukapuka *Cook Is.* 10°53S 165°49W **103** J11
Pula *Croatia* 44°54N 13°57E **68** B5
Pulacayo *Bolivia* 20°25S 66°41W **120** E3
Pulaski *U.S.A.* 37°3N 80°47W **111** C10
Pulborough *U.K.* 50°58N 0°30W **31** E8
Pulham Market *U.K.* 52°26N 1°13E **31** B11
Pulham St. Mary *U.K.* 52°26N 1°16E **31** B11
Pullman *U.S.A.* 46°44N 117°10W **110** A3
Pumlumon Fawr *U.K.* 52°28N 3°46W **28** C6
Pune *India* 18°29N 73°57E **84** K8
Punjab □ *India* 31°0N 76°0E **84** D9
Punjab □ *Pakistan* 32°0N 72°30E **84** E9
Puno *Peru* 15°55S 70°3W **120** D2
Punta Arenas *Chile* 53°10S 71°0W **121** H2
Puntarenas *Costa Rica* 9°0N 50°0E **89** F4
Punxsutawney *U.S.A.* 40°57N 78°59W **112** E8
Purbeck, Isle of *U.K.* 50°39N 1°59W **30** E5
Purfleet *U.K.* 51°29N 0°16E **31** D9
Puri *India* 19°50N 85°58E **85** K14
Purley on Thames *U.K.* 51°29N 1°3W **30** D6
Purnia *India* 25°45N 87°31E **85** G15
Puruliya *India* 23°17N 86°24E **85** H15
Purus → *Brazil* 3°42S 61°28W **120** C3
Putian *China* 25°23N 119°0E **79** F12
Putorana, Gory *Russia* 69°0N 95°0E **77** C10
Puttalam *Sri Lanka* 8°1N 79°55E **84** Q11
Putumayo → *S. Amer.* 3°7S 67°58W **120** C3
Puvirnituq *Canada* 60°2N 77°10W **109** C12
Puy-de-Dôme *France* 45°46N 2°57E **66** D5
Puyehue *Chile* 40°40S 72°37W **121** G2

Pwllheli *U.K.* 52°53N 4°25W **28** B5
Pyatigorsk *Russia* 44°2N 43°6E **71** F7
Pye *Myanmar* 18°49N 95°13E **85** K19
Pyinmana *Myanmar* 19°45N 96°12E **85** K20
Pyramid L. *U.S.A.* 40°1N 119°35W **110** C3
Pyramids *Egypt* 29°58N 31°9E **95** C11
Pyrénées *Europe* 42°45N 0°18E **66** E4

Q

Qaanaaq *Greenland* 77°30N 69°10W **54** B4
Qa'emshahr *Iran* 36°30N 52°53E **87** B8
Qaidam Basin *China* 37°0N 95°0E **78** D8
Qamdo *China* 31°15N 97°6E **78** E8
Qandyaghash *Kazakhstan* 49°28N 57°25E **71** E10
Qaqortoq *Greenland* 60°43N 46°0W **54** C5
Qarqan He → *China* 39°30N 88°30E **78** D6
Qarshi *Uzbekistan* 38°53N 65°48E **87** B11
Qatar ■ *Asia* 25°30N 51°15E **87** E7
Qattâra Depression *Egypt* 29°30N 27°30E **95** C11
Qazvin *Iran* 36°15N 50°0E **86** B7
Qena *Egypt* 26°10N 32°43E **95** C12
Qeqertarsuaq *Greenland* 69°15N 53°38W **54** C5
Qeshm *Iran* 26°55N 56°10E **87** E9
Qianshan *China* 22°15N 113°31E **79** a
Qi'ao Dao *China* 22°25N 113°38E **79** a
Qiemo *China* 38°8N 85°32E **78** D6
Qijiaojing *China* 43°28N 91°36E **78** C7
Qikiqtarjuaq *Canada* 67°33N 63°0W **109** C13
Qilian Shan *China* 38°30N 96°0E **78** D8
Qingdao *China* 36°5N 120°20E **79** D13
Qinghai □ *China* 36°0N 98°0E **78** D8
Qinhuangdao *China* 39°56N 119°30E **79** D12
Qinling Shandi *China* 33°50N 108°10E **79** E10
Qinzhou *China* 21°58N 108°38E **78** G10
Qiqihar *China* 47°26N 124°0E **79** B13
Qira *China* 37°0N 80°48E **78** D5
Qitai *China* 44°2N 89°35E **78** C6
Qitaihe *China* 45°48N 130°51E **79** B15
Qom *Iran* 34°40N 51°0E **87** C7
Qo'qon *Uzbekistan* 40°31N 70°56E **87** A12
Qostanay *Kazakhstan* 53°10N 63°35E **76** D7
Quadring *U.K.* 52°54N 0°10W **27** G8
Quang Ngai *Vietnam* 15°13N 108°58E **82** A3
Quantock Hills *U.K.* 51°8N 3°10W **30** D2
Quanzhou *China* 24°55N 118°34E **79** G12
Quaqtaq *Canada* 60°55N 69°40W **109** C13
Quartu Sant'Elena *Italy* 39°15N 9°10E **68** E3
Québec *Canada* 46°52N 71°13W **113** B12
Québec □ *Canada* 48°0N 74°0W **109** E12
Queen Charlotte Sd. *Canada* 51°0N 128°0W **108** D7
Queen Elizabeth Is. *Canada* 76°0N 95°0W **109** B10
Queen Elizabeth Land
Antarctica 85°0S 60°0W **55** E18
Queen Maud G. *Canada* 68°15N 102°30W **108** C9
Queenborough *U.K.* 51°25N 0°46E **31** D10
Queensbury *U.K.* 53°46N 1°50W **27** E5
Queensferry *U.K.* 55°59N 3°23W **25** C8
Queensland □ *Australia* 22°0S 142°0E **98** E7
Queenstown *N.Z.* 45°1S 168°40E **99** K12
Queenstown *S. Africa* 31°52S 26°52E **97** L5
Queimadas *Brazil* 11°0S 39°38W **122** B3
Quelimane *Mozam.* 17°53S 36°58E **97** H7
Quendale, B. of *U.K.* 59°53N 1°20W **22** C15
Querétaro *Mexico* 20°36N 100°23W **114** C4
Quesnel *Canada* 53°0N 122°30W **108** D7
Quesnel L. *Canada* 52°30N 121°20W **108** D7
Quetta *Pakistan* 30°15N 66°55E **84** D5
Quetzaltenango *Guatemala* 14°50N 91°30W **114** E6
Quezon City *Phil.* 14°37N 121°2E **83** B6
Qui Nhon *Vietnam* 13°40N 109°13E **82** B3
Quibdó *Colombia* 5°42N 76°40W **120** B2
Quilán, C. *Chile* 43°15S 74°30W **121** G2
Quilpie *Australia* 26°35S 144°11E **98** F7
Quimper *France* 48°0N 4°9W **66** B1
Quincy *Ill., U.S.A.* 39°56N 91°23W **111** C8
Quincy *Mass., U.S.A.* 42°14N 71°0W **113** D12
Quito *Ecuador* 0°15S 78°35W **120** C2
Qujing *China* 25°32N 103°41E **78** F9
Qulsary *Kazakhstan* 46°59N 54°1E **71** E9
Qŭnghirot *Uzbekistan* 43°2N 58°50E **87** A9
Quorndon *U.K.* 52°46N 1°10W **27** G6
Quseir *Egypt* 26°7N 34°16E **95** C12
Quzhou *China* 28°57N 118°54E **79** F12

R

Raahe *Finland* 64°40N 24°28E **63** E8
Raasay *U.K.* 57°25N 6°4W **22** H5
Raasay, Sd. of *U.K.* 57°30N 6°8W **22** H5
Raba *Indonesia* 8°36S 118°55E **83** F5
Rabat *Morocco* 34°2N 6°48W **94** B4
Rabaul *Papua N. G.* 4°24S 152°18E **98** A9
Rābigh *Si. Arabia* 22°50N 39°5E **86** F4
Race, C. *Canada* 46°40N 53°5W **109** E14
Rach Gia *Vietnam* 10°5N 105°5E **82** B3
Racine *U.S.A.* 42°44N 87°47W **112** D4
Rackheath *U.K.* 52°40N 1°22E **31** A11
Radcliffe *U.K.* 53°34N 2°18W **27** E4
Radcliffe on Trent *U.K.* 52°57N 1°2W **27** G6
Radford *U.S.A.* 37°8N 80°34W **112** G7
Radley *U.K.* 51°41N 1°14W **30** C6
Radnor Forest *U.K.* 52°17N 3°10W **28** C7
Radom *Poland* 51°23N 21°12E **65** C11
Radstock *U.K.* 51°17N 2°26W **30** D4
Rae Bareli *India* 26°18N 81°20E **85** F12
Rae Isthmus *Canada* 66°40N 87°30W **109** C11
Rafaela *Argentina* 31°10S 61°30W **121** F3
Rafsanjän *Iran* 30°30N 56°5E **87** D9
Ragusa *Italy* 36°55N 14°44E **68** F6
Rahimyar Khan *Pakistan* 28°30N 70°25E **84** E7
Raichur *India* 16°10N 77°20E **84** L10
Raigarh *India* 21°56N 83°25E **85** J13
Rainbow Lake *Canada* 58°30N 119°23W **108** D8
Rainham *U.K.* 51°22N 0°37E **31** D10
Rainier, Mt. *U.S.A.* 46°52N 121°46W **110** A2
Rainworth *U.K.* 53°7N 1°7W **27** F6
Rainy L. *Canada* 48°42N 93°10W **108** E10
Raipur *India* 21°17N 81°45E **85** J12
Raj Nandgaon *India* 21°5N 81°5E **85** J12

Rajahmahendravaram *India* 17°1N 81°48E **85** L12
Rajapalaiyam *India* 9°25N 77°35E **84** Q10
Rajasthan □ *India* 26°45N 73°30E **84** F8
Rajkot *India* 22°15N 70°56E **84** H7
Rajshahi *Bangla.* 24°22N 88°39E **85** G16
Rakhine □ *Myanmar* 19°0N 94°15E **85** K18
Raleigh *U.S.A.* 35°47N 78°39W **111** C11
Rame Head *U.K.* 50°19N 4°13W **29** G5
Ramelton *Ireland* 55°2N 7°39W **18** A6
Ramgarh *India* 23°40N 85°35E **85** H14
Râmnicu Vâlcea *Romania* 45°9N 24°21E **65** F13
Rampside *U.K.* 54°6N 3°9W **26** D2
Rampur *India* 28°50N 79°5E **84** E11
Ramree I. *Myanmar* 19°0N 93°40E **85** K19
Ramsbottom *U.K.* 53°38N 2°19W **27** E4
Ramsbury *U.K.* 51°26N 1°36W **30** D5
Ramsey *I. of Man* 54°20N 4°22W **19** C13
Ramsey *Cambs., U.K.* 52°27N 0°7W **31** B8
Ramsey *Essex, U.K.* 51°55N 1°13E **31** C11
Ramsgate *U.K.* 51°20N 1°25E **31** D11
Rancagua *Chile* 34°10S 70°50W **121** F2
Ranchi *India* 23°19N 85°27E **85** H14
Randalstown *U.K.* 54°45N 6°19W **19** B9
Randers *Denmark* 56°29N 10°1E **63** F6
Rangoon = Yangôn
Myanmar 16°45N 96°20E **85** L20
Rangpur *Bangla.* 25°42N 89°22E **85** G16
Rankin Inlet *Canada* 62°30N 93°0W **108** C10
Rannoch *U.K.* 56°40N 4°20W **23** J8
Rannoch, L. *U.K.* 56°41N 4°20W **23** J8
Rannoch Moor *U.K.* 56°38N 4°48W **23** J8
Rantoul *U.S.A.* 40°19N 88°9W **112** E3
Rapa *French Polynesia* 27°35S 144°20W **103** K13
Rapallo *Italy* 44°21N 9°14E **68** B3
Raper, C. *Canada* 69°44N 67°6W **109** C13
Rapid City *U.S.A.* 44°5N 103°14W **110** B6
Rarotonga *Cook Is.* 21°30S 160°0W **103** K12
Ra's al Khaymah *U.A.E.* 25°50N 55°59E **87** E9
Rasht *Iran* 37°20N 49°40E **86** B7
Rat Islands *U.S.A.* 52°0N 178°0E **108** D1
Ratangarh *India* 28°5N 74°35E **84** E9
Rathcoole *Ireland* 53°17N 6°29W **21** B10
Rathdrum *Ireland* 52°56N 6°14W **21** C10
Rathkeale *Ireland* 52°32N 8°56W **20** C5
Rathlin I. *U.K.* 55°18N 6°14W **19** A9
Ratlam *India* 23°20N 75°0E **84** H9
Ratnagiri *India* 16°57N 73°18E **84** L8
Raton *U.S.A.* 36°54N 104°24W **110** C6
Rattray Hd. *U.K.* 57°38N 1°50W **23** G14
Rauma *Finland* 61°10N 21°30E **63** E8
Raunds *U.K.* 52°21N 0°32W **31** B7
Raurkela *India* 22°14N 84°50E **85** H14
Ravenglass *U.K.* 54°22N 3°24W **26** D2
Ravenna *Italy* 44°25N 12°12E **68** B5
Ravenstonedale *U.K.* 54°26N 2°25W **26** D4
Ravi → *Pakistan* 30°35N 71°49E **84** D7
Rawalpindi *Pakistan* 33°38N 73°8E **84** C8
Rawlins *U.S.A.* 41°47N 107°14W **110** B5
Rawmarsh *U.K.* 53°27N 1°21W **27** F6
Rawson *Argentina* 43°15S 65°5W **121** G3
Rawtenstall *U.K.* 53°42N 2°17W **27** E4
Ray, C. *Canada* 47°33N 59°15W **109** E14
Rayleigh *U.K.* 51°36N 0°37E **31** C10
Rayong *Thailand* 12°40N 101°20E **82** B2
Raz, Pte. du *France* 48°2N 4°47W **66** C1
Rê, Î. de *France* 46°12N 1°30W **66** C3
Reading *U.K.* 51°27N 0°58W **31** D7
Reading *U.S.A.* 40°20N 75°56W **113** E10
Reay Forest *U.K.* 58°22N 4°55E **22** F8
Rebiana Desert *Libya* 24°30N 21°0E **95** D10
Recife *Brazil* 8°0S 35°0W **122** A3
Reconquista *Argentina* 29°10S 59°45W **121** E4
Red → *U.S.A.* 31°1N 91°45W **111** D8
Red Bluff *U.S.A.* 40°11N 122°15W **110** B2
Red Deer *Canada* 52°20N 113°50W **108** D8
Red Dial *U.K.* 54°49N 3°10W **26** C2
Red L. *U.S.A.* 48°8N 94°45W **111** A8
Red Lake *Canada* 51°3N 93°49W **108** D10
Red Oak *U.S.A.* 41°1N 95°14W **111** E7
Red River of the North →
N. Amer. 49°0N 97°15W **108** D10
Red Sea *Asia* 25°0N 36°0E **89** C2
Red Wing *U.S.A.* 44°34N 92°31W **111** B8
Redbridge □ *U.K.* 51°35N 0°7E **31** C9
Redcar *U.K.* 54°37N 1°4W **26** D6
Redding *U.S.A.* 40°35N 122°24W **110** B2
Redditch *U.K.* 52°18N 1°55W **30** B5
Rede → *U.K.* 55°9N 2°13W **26** B4
Redesmouth *U.K.* 55°8N 2°13W **26** B4
Redhill *U.K.* 51°14N 0°9W **31** D8
Redlynch *U.K.* 50°59N 1°41W **30** E5
Redmile *U.K.* 52°54N 0°48W **27** G7
Redmire *U.K.* 54°19N 1°55W **26** D5
Redon *France* 47°40N 2°6W **66** C2
Redruth *U.K.* 50°14N 5°14W **29** G3
Ree, L. *Ireland* 53°35N 8°0W **18** D6
Reedham *U.K.* 52°34N 1°34E **31** A12
Reepham *U.K.* 52°46N 1°6E **31** A11
Reese → *U.S.A.* 40°48N 117°4W **110** B3
Reeth *U.K.* 54°23N 1°56W **26** D5
Regensburg *Germany* 49°1N 12°6E **64** D7
Réggio di Calábria *Italy* 38°6N 15°39E **68** E6
Réggio nell'Emília *Italy* 44°43N 10°36E **68** B4
Regina *Canada* 50°27N 104°35W **108** D9
Reichenbach *Germany* 50°37N 12°17E **64** C7
Reigate *U.K.* 51°14N 0°12W **31** D8
Reims *France* 49°15N 4°1E **66** B6
Reina Adelaida, Arch. *Chile* 52°20S 74°0W **121** H2
Reindeer L. *Canada* 57°15N 102°15W **108** D9
Remanso *Brazil* 9°41S 42°4W **122** A2
Remscheid *Germany* 51°11N 7°12E **64** C4
Rennes *France* 48°7N 1°41W **66** B3
Rennell *Solomon Is.* 11°40S 160°10E **99** C11
Rennes *France* 48°7N 1°41W **66** B3
Reno *U.S.A.* 39°31N 119°48W **110** C3
Repton *U.K.* 52°50N 1°33W **27** G6
Republican → *U.S.A.* 39°4N 96°48W **111** C7
Repulse Bay *Canada* 66°30N 86°30W **109** C11
Resistencia *Argentina* 27°30S 59°0W **121** E4
Resolute *Canada* 74°42N 94°54W **109** B10

Resolution I. *Canada* 61°30N 65°0W **109** C13
Reston *U.K.* 55°51N 2°10W **25** C11
Retford *U.K.* 53°19N 0°56W **27** F7
Rethimno *Greece* 35°18N 24°30E **69** G11
Réunion ☑ *Ind. Oc.* 21°0S 56°0E **91** J9
Reus *Spain* 41°10N 1°5E **67** B6
Reutlingen *Germany* 48°29N 9°12E **64** D5
Revda *Russia* 56°48N 59°57E **70** D10
Revelstoke *Canada* 51°0N 118°10W **108** D8
Revillagigedo, Is. de *Pac. Oc.* 18°40N 112°0W **114** D2
Rewa *India* 24°33N 81°25E **85** G12
Rexburg *U.S.A.* 43°49N 111°47W **110** B4
Rey Malabo *Eq. Guin.* 3°45N 8°50E **96** D1
Reykjavík *Iceland* 64°10N 21°57W **63** B1
Reynosa *Mexico* 26°7N 98°18W **114** B5
Rhayader *U.K.* 52°18N 3°29W **28** C7
Rheidol → *U.K.* 52°25N 4°5W **28** C5
Rheine *Germany* 52°17N 7°26E **64** B4
Rheinland-Pfalz □ *Germany* 50°0N 7°0E **64** C4
Rhine → *Europe* 51°52N 6°2E **64** C4
Rhinelander *U.S.A.* 45°38N 89°25W **112** C3
Rhinns Pt. *U.K.* 55°40N 6°29W **24** C3
Rhins, The *U.K.* 54°52N 5°3W **24** E5
Rhode Island □ *U.S.A.* 41°40N 71°30W **113** E12
Rhodes *Greece* 36°15N 28°10E **69** F13
Rhodope Mts. *Bulgaria* 41°40N 24°20E **69** D11
Rhondda □ *U.K.* 51°39N 3°31W **28** D6
Rhône → *France* 43°28N 4°42E **66** E6
Rhosllanerchrugog *U.K.* 53°1N 3°3W **28** A7
Rhossili *U.K.* 51°34N 4°17W **29** D5
Rhossili B. *U.K.* 51°32N 4°14W **29** D5
Rhum = Rùm *U.K.* 57°0N 6°20W **22** J5
Rhydaman = Ammanford
U.K. 51°48N 3°59W **28** D6
Rhyl *U.K.* 53°20N 3°29W **28** A7
Rhymney *U.K.* 51°46N 3°17W **28** D7
Riau, Kepulauan □ *Indonesia* 0°30N 104°20E **82** D2
Ribble → *U.K.* 53°52N 2°25W **27** E4
Ribeirão Prêto *Brazil* 21°10S 47°50W **122** D1
Riberalta *Bolivia* 11°0S 66°0W **120** D3
Riccall *U.K.* 53°50N 1°3W **27** E6
Rice Lake *U.S.A.* 45°30N 91°44W **112** C2
Richards Bay *S. Africa* 28°48S 32°6E **97** K6
Richfield *U.S.A.* 38°46N 112°5W **110** C4
Richland *U.S.A.* 46°17N 119°18W **110** A3
Richland Center *U.S.A.* 43°21N 90°23W **112** D2
Richlands *U.S.A.* 37°6N 81°48W **112** G7
Richmond *U.K.* 54°25N 1°43W **26** D5
Richmond *Ind., U.S.A.* 39°50N 84°53W **112** F5
Richmond *Ky., U.S.A.* 37°45N 84°18W **112** G5
Richmond *Va., U.S.A.* 37°33N 77°27W **112** G9
Richmond-upon-Thames □
U.K. 51°27N 0°17W **31** D8
Rickmansworth *U.K.* 51°38N 0°29W **31** C8
Ridgecrest *U.S.A.* 35°38N 117°40W **110** C3
Ridgway *U.S.A.* 41°25N 78°44W **112** E8
Ridsdale *U.K.* 55°9N 2°9W **26** B4
Rievaulx *U.K.* 54°16N 1°7W **26** D6
Rift Valley *Africa* 7°0N 30°0E **90** G7
Riga *Latvia* 56°53N 24°8E **63** F8
Riga, G. of *Latvia* 57°40N 23°45E **63** F8
Rīgestān *Afghan.* 30°15N 65°0E **87** D11
Rigolet *Canada* 54°10N 58°23W **109** D14
Rijeka *Croatia* 45°20N 14°21E **68** B6
Rillington *U.K.* 54°9N 0°42W **26** D7
Rimini *Italy* 44°3N 12°33E **68** B5
Rimouski *Canada* 48°27N 68°30W **109** E13
Ringmer *U.K.* 50°53N 0°5E **31** E9
Ringwood *U.K.* 50°50N 1°47W **30** E5
Rio Branco *Brazil* 9°58S 67°49W **120** C3
Rio Claro *Brazil* 22°19S 47°35W **122** D1
Rio Cuarto *Argentina* 33°10S 64°25W **121** F3
Rio de Janeiro *Brazil* 22°54S 43°12W **122** D2
Rio de Janeiro □ *Brazil* 22°50S 43°0W **122** D2
Rio Gallegos *Argentina* 51°35S 69°15W **121** H3
Rio Grande *Brazil* 32°0S 52°20W **121** F4
Rio Grande de Santiago →
Mexico 21°36N 105°26W **114** C3
Rio Grande do Norte □ *Brazil* 5°40S 36°0W **120** C6
Rio Grande do Sul □ *Brazil* 30°0S 53°0W **121** E4
Rio Largo *Brazil* 9°28S 35°50W **122** A3
Rio Muni □ *Eq. Guin.* 1°30N 10°0E **96** D2
Riohacha *Colombia* 11°33N 72°55W **120** A2
Ripley *Derby, U.K.* 53°3N 1°24W **27** F6
Ripley *N. Yorks., U.K.* 54°3N 1°34W **26** D6
Ripon *U.K.* 54°9N 1°31W **26** D6
Ripon *U.S.A.* 43°51N 88°50W **112** D3
Risca *U.K.* 51°36N 3°5W **29** D7
Rishton *U.K.* 53°46N 2°26W **27** E4
Rivera *Uruguay* 31°0S 55°50W **121** F4
Riverhead *U.S.A.* 40°55N 72°40W **113** E11
Riverside *U.S.A.* 33°59N 117°22W **110** D3
Riverton *U.S.A.* 43°2N 108°23W **110** B5
Riviera = Côte d'Azur *France* 43°25N 7°10E **66** E7
Rivière-du-Loup *Canada* 47°50N 69°30W **109** E13
Rivne *Ukraine* 50°40N 26°10E **65** C14
Riyadh *Si. Arabia* 24°41N 46°42E **86** E6
Rize *Turkey* 41°0N 40°30E **71** F7
Rizhao *China* 35°25N 119°30E **79** D12
Roade *U.K.* 52°9N 0°53W **31** B7
Roanne *France* 46°3N 4°4E **66** C6
Roanoke *U.S.A.* 37°16N 79°56W **112** G8
Roanoke → *U.S.A.* 35°57N 76°42W **111** C11
Roberton *U.K.* 55°25N 2°54W **25** D10
Roberval *Canada* 48°32N 72°15W **109** E12
Robin Hood's Bay *U.K.* 54°27N 0°32W **26** D7
Robson, Mt. *Canada* 53°10N 119°10W **108** D8
Roca, C. da *Portugal* 38°40N 9°31W **67** C1
Rocester *U.K.* 52°57N 1°50W **27** G5
Rocha *Uruguay* 34°30S 54°25W **121** F4
Rochdale *U.K.* 53°38N 2°9W **27** E4
Roche *U.K.* 50°24N 4°50W **29** G4
Rochefort *France* 45°56N 0°57W **66** D3
Rochester *Medway, U.K.* 51°23N 0°31E **31** D10
Rochester *Northumberland,*
U.K. 55°17N 2°17W **26** B4
Rochester *Ind., U.S.A.* 41°4N 86°13W **112** E4
Rochester *Minn., U.S.A.* 44°1N 92°28W **111** B8
Rochester *N.H., U.S.A.* 43°18N 70°59W **113** D12
Rochester *N.Y., U.S.A.* 43°10N 77°37W **112** D9

Rochford   São João del Rei

Rochford U.K. 51°34N 0°43E **31** C10
Rock Hill U.S.A. 34°56N 81°1W **111** D10
Rock Island U.S.A. 41°30N 90°34W **112** E2
Rock Springs U.S.A. 41°35N 109°14W **110** B5
Rockall Atl. Oc. 57°37N 13°42W **56** D3
Rockcliffe U.K. 54°57N 3°0W **26** C3
Rockford U.S.A. 42°16N 89°6W **112** D3
Rockhampton Australia 23°22S 150°32E **98** E9
Rockingham U.K. 52°31N 0°43W **31** A7
Rockingham Forest U.K. 52°29N 0°42W **31** B7
Rockland U.S.A. 44°6N 69°7W **113** C13
Rocky Mount U.S.A. 35°57N 77°48W **111** C11
Rocky Mts. N. Amer. 49°0N 115°0W **108** D7
Rodez France 44°21N 2°33E **66** D5
Roding → U.K. 51°31N 0°6E **31** C9
Rodrigues Ind. Oc. 19°45S 63°20E **53** E13
Roe → U.K. 55°6N 6°59W **19** A8
Roes Welcome Sd. Canada 65°0N 87°0W **109** C11
Rogans Seat U.K. 54°26N 2°7W **26** D4
Rogate U.K. 51°31N 0°50W **31** D7
Rogers City U.S.A. 45°25N 83°49W **112** C6
Rohri Pakistan 27°45N 68°51E **84** F6
Rojo, C. Mexico 21°33N 97°20W **114** C5
Rolla U.S.A. 37°57N 91°46W **111** C8
Roma Australia 26°32S 148°49E **98** F8
Romaine → Canada 50°18N 63°47W **109** D13
Romania ■ Europe 46°0N 25°0E **65** F12
Romans-sur-Isère France 45°3N 5°3E **66** D6
Rome Italy 41°54N 12°28E **68** D5
Rome Ga., U.S.A. 34°15N 85°10W **111** D9
Rome N.Y., U.S.A. 43°13N 75°27W **113** D10
Romney Marsh U.K. 39°21N 78°45W **112** F8
Romney Marsh U.K. 51°2N 0°54E **31** D10
Romorantin-Lanthenay France 47°21N 1°45E **66** C4
Romsey U.K. 51°0N 1°29W **30** E6
Rona U.K. 57°34N 5°59W **22** G6
Roncador, Serra do Brazil 12°30S 52°30W **120** D4
Rondônia □ Brazil 11°0S 63°0W **120** D3
Rondonópolis Brazil 16°28S 54°38W **120** D4
Ronge, L. la Canada 55°6N 105°17W **108** D9
Ronne Ice Shelf Antarctica 77°30S 60°0W **55** D18
Roosevelt → Brazil 7°35S 60°20W **120** C3
Roosevelt I. Antarctica 79°30S 162°0W **55** D12
Ropsley U.K. 52°54N 0°30W **27** G7
Roquetas de Mar Spain 36°46N 2°36W **67** D4
Roraima □ Brazil 2°0N 61°30W **120** B3
Roraima, Mt. Venezuela 5°10N 60°40W **120** B3
Rosario Argentina 33°0S 60°40W **121** F3
Rosario Mexico 22°58N 105°53W **114** C3
Rosario de la Frontera
  Argentina 25°50S 65°0W **121** E3
Roscommon Ireland 53°38N 8°11W **18** D5
Roscommon □ Ireland 53°49N 8°23W **18** D5
Roscrea Ireland 52°57N 7°49W **20** C7
Roseau Dominica 15°17N 61°24W **115** D12
Roseburg U.S.A. 43°13N 123°20W **110** B2
Rosedale Abbey U.K. 54°21N 0°52W **26** D7
Rosehearty U.K. 57°42N 2°7W **23** G13
Rosenheim Germany 47°51N 12°7E **64** E7
Rosetown Canada 51°35N 107°59W **108** D9
Roseville U.S.A. 38°45N 121°17W **110** C2
Roslavl Russia 53°57N 32°55E **70** D5
Ross Ice Shelf Antarctica 80°0S 180°0E **55** E12
Ross-on-Wye U.K. 51°54N 2°34W **30** C3
Ross River Canada 62°30N 131°30W **108** C6
Ross Sea Antarctica 74°0S 178°0E **55** D11
Rossall Pt. U.K. 53°55N 3°3W **27** E2
Rossan Pt. Ireland 54°42N 8°47W **18** B4
Rosses, The Ireland 55°2N 8°20W **18** A5
Rossignol L. Canada 44°12N 65°10W **113** C15
Rosslare Ireland 52°17N 6°24W **21** D10
Rosslare Harbour Ireland 52°15N 6°20W **21** D10
Rossosh Russia 50°15N 39°28E **71** D6
Rostock Germany 54°5N 12°8E **64** A7
Rostov Russia 47°15N 39°45E **71** E6
Rote Indonesia 10°50S 123°0E **83** F6
Rothbury U.K. 55°19N 1°58W **26** B5
Rothbury Forest U.K. 55°19N 1°50W **26** B5
Rother → U.K. 50°59N 0°45E **31** E10
Rotherham U.K. 53°26N 1°20W **27** F6
Rothes U.K. 57°32N 3°13W **23** G11
Rothesay U.K. 55°50N 5°3W **24** D3
Rothwell Northants., U.K. 52°25N 0°48W **31** B7
Rothwell W. Yorks., U.K. 53°45N 1°28W **27** E6
Rotorua N.Z. 38°9S 176°16E **99** H14
Rotterdam Neths. 51°55N 4°30E **64** C3
Rottingdean U.K. 50°48N 0°4W **31** E8
Rotuma Fiji 12°25S 177°5E **99** C14
Roubaix France 50°40N 3°10E **66** A5
Rouen France 49°27N 1°4E **66** B4
Round Mt. Australia 30°26S 152°16E **98** G9
Rousay U.K. 59°10N 3°2W **23** D11
Roussillon France 42°30N 2°35E **66** E5
Rouyn-Noranda Canada 48°20N 79°0W **109** E12
Rovaniemi Finland 66°29N 25°41E **63** D9
Rovigo Italy 45°4N 11°47E **68** B4
Rowanburn U.K. 55°5N 2°55W **25** D10
Roxas Phil. 11°36N 122°49E **83** B6
Roxburgh U.K. 55°35N 2°28W **25** C11
Roxby U.K. 53°38N 0°38W **27** E7
Royal Canal Ireland 53°30N 7°13W **21** B8
Royal Leamington Spa U.K. 52°18N 1°31W **30** B5
Royal Tunbridge Wells U.K. 51°7N 0°16E **31** D9
Royal Wootton Bassett U.K. 51°32N 1°55W **30** C5
Royale, Isle U.S.A. 48°0N 88°54W **112** B3
Royan France 45°37N 1°2W **66** D3
Royston U.K. 52°3N 0°0 **31** B8
Royton U.K. 53°34N 2°8W **27** E4
Rub' al Khālī Si. Arabia 19°0N 48°0E **89** D4
Rubery U.K. 52°24N 2°1W **30** B5
Rubh a' Mhail U.K. 55°56N 6°8W **24** C3
Rubha Hunish U.K. 57°42N 6°20W **22** G5
Rubtsovsk Russia 51°30N 81°10E **76** D9
Ruby L. U.S.A. 40°10N 115°28W **110** B3
Rudnyy Kazakhstan 52°57N 63°7E **76** D7
Rudston U.K. 54°6N 0°20W **26** D8
Rufford U.K. 53°38N 2°50W **27** E3
Rufiji → Tanzania 7°50S 39°15E **96** F7
Rugby U.K. 52°23N 1°16W **30** B6

Rugeley U.K. 52°46N 1°55W **27** G5
Rügen Germany 54°22N 13°24E **64** A7
Ruhr → Germany 51°27N 6°43E **64** C4
Ruki → Dem. Rep. of the Congo 0°5N 18°17E **96** E3
Rukwa, L. Tanzania 8°0S 32°20E **96** F6
Rùm U.K. 57°0N 6°20W **22** J5
Rùm, Sound of U.K. 56°55N 6°14W **22** J5
Rumania = Romania ■ Europe 46°0N 25°0E **65** F12
Rumford U.S.A. 44°33N 70°33W **113** C12
Runaway Bay Jamaica 18°27N 77°20W **114** a
Runcorn U.K. 53°21N 2°44W **27** F3
Rundu Namibia 17°52S 19°43E **97** H3
Rungwe Tanzania 9°11S 33°32E **96** G7
Ruo Shui → China 41°0N 100°16E **78** C9
Ruoqiang China 38°55N 88°10E **78** D6
Rupert → U.S.A. 42°37N 113°41W **110** B4
Rupert → Canada 51°29N 78°45W **109** D12
Ruse Bulgaria 43°48N 25°59E **69** C12
Rush Ireland 53°31N 6°6W **21** A10
Rushden U.K. 52°18N 0°35W **31** B7
Rushville Ill., U.S.A. 40°7N 90°34W **112** E2
Rushville Ind., U.S.A. 39°37N 85°27W **112** F5
Ruskington U.K. 53°3N 0°22W **27** F8
Russellville U.S.A. 35°17N 93°8W **111** C8
Russia ■ Eurasia 62°0N 105°0E **77** C11
Rustavi Georgia 41°30N 45°0E **71** F8
Rustenburg S. Africa 25°41S 27°14E **97** K5
Ruthin U.K. 53°6N 3°19W **28** A7
Ruthwell U.K. 55°0N 3°25W **25** E9
Rutog China 33°27N 79°42E **78** E4
Ruvuma → Tanzania 10°29S 40°28E **96** G8
Ruwenzori → Africa 0°30N 29°55E **96** D5
Rwanda ■ Africa 2°0S 30°0E **96** E5
Ryan, L. U.K. 55°0N 5°2W **24** E4
Ryazan Russia 54°40N 39°40E **70** D6
Rybachi Pen. Russia 69°43N 32°0E **70** A5
Rybinsk Russia 58°5N 38°50E **70** C6
Rybinsk Res. Russia 58°30N 38°25E **70** C6
Rydal U.K. 54°27N 2°59W **26** D3
Ryde U.K. 50°43N 1°9W **30** E6
Rye U.K. 50°57N 0°45E **31** E10
Rye → U.K. 54°11N 0°44W **26** D7
Rye Bay U.K. 50°52N 0°49E **31** E10
Ryhope U.K. 54°53N 1°21W **26** C6
Ryton U.K. 52°22N 1°25W **30** B6
Ryukyu Is. Japan 26°0N 126°0E **79** F14
Rzeszów Poland 50°5N 21°58E **65** C11
Rzhev Russia 56°20N 34°20E **70** C5

S

Saale → Germany 51°56N 11°54E **64** C6
Saar → Europe 49°41N 6°32E **64** D4
Saarbrücken Germany 49°14N 6°59E **64** D4
Saaremaa Estonia 58°30N 22°30E **63** F8
Sabadell Spain 41°28N 2°7E **67** B7
Sabah □ Malaysia 6°0N 117°0E **82** D5
Sabhā Libya 27°9N 14°29E **95** C8
Sabinas Mexico 27°51N 101°7W **114** B4
Sabinas Hidalgo Mexico 26°30N 100°10W **114** B4
Sabine → U.S.A. 29°59N 93°47W **111** E8
Sable, C. Canada 43°29N 65°38W **113** D15
Sable, C. U.S.A. 25°9N 81°8W **111** E10
Sable I. Canada 44°0N 60°0W **109** E14
Sachsen □ Germany 50°55N 13°10E **64** C7
Sachsen-Anhalt □ Germany 52°0N 12°0E **64** C7
Saco U.S.A. 43°30N 70°27W **113** D12
Sacramento U.S.A. 38°35N 121°29W **110** C2
Sacramento → U.S.A. 38°3N 121°56W **110** C2
Sacramento Mts. U.S.A. 32°30N 105°30W **110** D5
Sado Japan 38°0N 138°25E **81** D6
Safford U.S.A. 32°50N 109°43W **110** D5
Saffron Walden U.K. 52°1N 0°16E **31** B9
Safi Morocco 32°18N 9°20W **94** B4
Saga Japan 33°15N 130°16E **81** G2
Sagaing Myanmar 21°52N 95°59E **85** J19
Sagar India 23°50N 78°44E **84** H11
Saginaw U.S.A. 43°26N 83°56W **112** D6
Saginaw B. U.S.A. 43°50N 83°40W **112** D6
Sagua la Grande Cuba 22°50N 80°10W **115** C8
Saguenay → Canada 48°22N 71°0W **113** A12
Sagunto Spain 39°42N 0°18W **67** C5
Sahara Africa 23°0N 5°0E **94** D6
Saharanpur India 29°58N 77°33E **84** E10
Sahel Africa 16°0N 5°0E **94** E5
Sahiwal Pakistan 30°45N 73°8E **84** D8
Saidpur Bangla. 25°48N 89°0E **85** G16
St. Abb's Head U.K. 55°55N 2°8W **25** C11
St. Agnes Corn., U.K. 50°19N 5°13W **29** G3
St. Agnes Corn., U.K. 49°54N 6°21W **29** H1
St. Agnes Hd. U.K. 50°19N 5°15W **29** G3
St. Albans U.K. 51°45N 0°19W **31** C8
St. Albans Vt., U.S.A. 44°49N 73°5W **113** C11
St. Albans W. Va., U.S.A. 38°23N 81°50W **112** F7
St. Alban's Head U.K. 50°34N 2°4W **30** E4
St. Andrews U.K. 56°20N 2°47W **25** B10
St. Ann's U.K. 55°14N 3°28W **25** D9
St. Ann's Bay Jamaica 18°26N 77°12W **114** a
St. Anthony Canada 51°22N 55°35W **109** D14
St. Asaph U.K. 53°15N 3°27W **28** A7
St-Augustin Canada 51°13N 58°38W **109** D14
St. Augustine U.S.A. 29°54N 81°19W **111** E10
St. Austell U.K. 50°20N 4°47W **29** G4
St. Bees U.K. 54°30N 3°35W **26** C1
St. Bees Hd. U.K. 54°31N 3°38W **26** C1
St. Blazey U.K. 50°22N 4°43W **29** G4
St. Brides B. U.K. 51°49N 5°9W **28** D2
St-Brieuc France 48°30N 2°46W **66** B2
St. Buryan U.K. 50°4N 5°37W **29** G2
St. Catharines Canada 43°10N 79°15W **112** D8
St. Catherine's Pt. U.K. 50°34N 1°18W **30** E6
St. Charles U.S.A. 38°47N 90°29W **112** F2
St. Clair, L. N. Amer. 42°27N 82°39W **112** D6
St. Clears U.K. 51°49N 4°31W **28** D3
St. Cloud U.S.A. 45°34N 94°10W **111** A8
St. Columb Major U.K. 50°26N 4°58W **29** G3
St. Croix U.S. Virgin Is. 17°45N 64°45W **115** D12
St. David's U.K. 51°53N 5°16W **28** D1
St. David's Head U.K. 51°54N 5°19W **28** D1
St-Denis France 48°56N 2°20E **66** B5

St. Dennis U.K. 50°23N 4°53W **29** G4
St-Dizier France 48°38N 4°56E **66** B6
St. Dominick U.K. 50°29N 4°16W **29** G5
St. Elias, Mt. U.S.A. 60°18N 140°56W **108** C5
St. Elias Mts. N. Amer. 60°33N 139°28W **108** D6
St. Enoder U.K. 50°22N 4°59W **29** G4
St. Erth U.K. 50°9N 5°26W **29** G3
St-Étienne France 45°27N 4°22E **66** D6
St-Félicien Canada 48°40N 72°25W **113** A11
St-Flour France 45°2N 3°6E **66** D5
St. Gallen Switz. 47°26N 9°22E **64** E5
St-Gaudens France 43°6N 0°44E **66** E4
St. George U.S.A. 37°6N 113°35W **110** C4
St-Georges Canada 46°8N 70°40W **113** B12
St. George's Grenada 12°5N 61°43W **115** E12
St. George's Channel Europe 52°0N 6°0W **21** E11
St. Germans U.K. 50°23N 4°19W **29** G5
St. Helena Atl. Oc. 15°58S 5°42W **52** E9
St. Helens U.K. 53°27N 2°44W **27** F3
St. Helens, Mt. U.S.A. 46°12N 122°12W **110** A2
St. Helier Canada 49°10N 2°7W **29** J9
St-Hyacinthe Canada 45°40N 72°58W **109** E12
St. Ignace U.S.A. 45°52N 84°44W **112** C5
St. Issey U.K. 50°30N 4°57W **29** G4
St. Ives Cambs., U.K. 52°20N 0°4W **31** B8
St. Ives Corn., U.K. 50°12N 5°30W **29** G3
St. Ives B. U.K. 50°13N 5°27W **29** G3
St-Jean, L. Canada 48°40N 72°0W **113** A12
St-Jérôme Canada 45°47N 74°0W **113** C11
St. John Canada 45°20N 66°8W **109** E13
St. John's Antigua & B. 17°6N 61°51W **115** D12
St. John's Canada 47°35N 52°40W **109** E14
St. Johns U.S.A. 43°0N 84°33W **112** D5
St. Johns → U.S.A. 30°24N 81°24W **111** D10
St. Johns Chapel U.K. 54°44N 2°10W **26** C4
St. Johnsbury U.S.A. 44°25N 72°1W **113** C11
St. Joseph Mich., U.S.A. 42°6N 86°29W **112** D4
St. Joseph Mo., U.S.A. 39°46N 94°50W **111** C8
St. Joseph, L. Canada 51°10N 90°35W **109** D10
St. Just U.K. 50°7N 5°42W **29** G2
St. Keverne U.K. 50°3N 5°6W **29** G3
St. Kilda U.K. 57°49N 8°34W **22** b
St. Kitts & Nevis ■
  W. Indies 17°20N 62°40W **115** D12
St. Lawrence → Canada 49°30N 66°0W **109** E13
St. Lawrence, Gulf of Canada 48°25N 62°0W **109** E13
St. Lawrence I. U.S.A. 63°30N 170°30W **108** C3
St. Levan U.K. 50°2N 5°41W **29** G2
St-Lô France 49°7N 1°5W **66** B3
St-Louis Senegal 16°8N 16°27W **94** E2
St. Louis U.S.A. 38°37N 90°11W **112** F2
St. Lucia ■ W. Indies 14°0N 60°57W **114** b
St. Mabyn U.K. 50°30N 4°47W **29** F4
St. Magnus B. U.K. 60°25N 1°35W **22** B14
St-Malo France 48°39N 2°1W **66** B2
St-Marc Haiti 19°10N 72°41W **115** D10
St. Margaret's-at-Cliffe U.K. 51°9N 1°23E **31** D11
St-Martin ☒ W. Indies 18°5N 63°5W **115** D12
St. Martins Barbados 13°5N 59°28W **114** c
St. Martin's U.K. 49°58N 6°17W **29** H1
St. Mary Bourne U.K. 51°15N 1°24W **30** D6
St. Mary's Corn., U.K. 49°55N 6°18W **29** H1
St. Mary's Orkney, U.K. 58°54N 2°54W **23** E12
St. Marys U.S.A. 41°26N 78°34W **112** E8
St. Mary's Sd. U.K. 49°54N 6°20W **29** H1
St. Matthew I. U.S.A. 60°24N 172°42W **108** C2
St. Mawes U.K. 50°10N 5°2W **29** G3
St. Merryn U.K. 50°32N 5°1W **29** F3
St. Michael's Mount U.K. 50°7N 5°29W **29** G3
St. Minver U.K. 50°33N 4°53W **29** F4
St. Moritz Switz. 46°30N 9°51E **64** E5
St-Nazaire France 47°17N 2°12W **66** C2
St. Neots U.K. 52°14N 0°15W **31** B8
St-Omer France 50°45N 2°15E **66** A5
St. Osyth U.K. 51°47N 1°5E **31** C11
St. Paul U.S.A. 44°56N 93°5W **111** B8
St. Paul, Î. Ind. Oc. 38°55S 77°34E **53** F13
St. Peter Port U.K. 49°26N 2°33W **29** J8
St. Petersburg Russia 59°55N 30°20E **70** C5
St. Petersburg U.S.A. 27°46N 82°40W **111** E10
St-Pierre-et-Miquelon ☒
  N. Amer. 46°55N 56°10W **109** E14
St-Quentin France 49°50N 3°16E **66** B5
St. Stephen Canada 45°16N 67°17W **113** C14
St. Stephen U.K. 50°21N 4°53W **29** G4
St. Teath U.K. 50°35N 4°45W **29** F4
St. Thomas Canada 42°45N 81°10W **112** D7
St-Tropez France 43°17N 6°38E **66** E7
St. Tudy U.K. 50°33N 4°45W **29** F4
St. Vincent, G. Australia 35°0S 138°0E **98** G6
St. Vincent & the Grenadines ■
  W. Indies 13°0N 61°10W **115** D12
Ste. Genevieve U.S.A. 37°59N 90°2W **112** G2
Ste-Marie Canada 46°26N 71°0W **113** B12
Saintes France 45°45N 0°37W **66** D3
Saintfield U.K. 54°28N 5°49W **19** C10
Saintonge France 45°40N 0°50W **66** D3
Saipan N. Marianas 15°12N 145°45E **102** F6
Saitama Japan 35°54N 139°38E **81** F7
Sajama Bolivia 18°7S 69°0W **120** D3
Sakākah Si. Arabia 30°0N 40°8E **86** D5
Sakakawea, L. U.S.A. 47°30N 101°25W **110** A6
Sakarya Turkey 40°48N 30°25E **71** E5
Sakata Japan 38°55N 139°50E **81** D6
Sakha □ Russia 66°0N 130°0E **77** C13
Sakhalin Russia 51°0N 143°0E **77** D15
Sakurajima Japan 31°35N 130°39E **81** H5
Sala Sweden 59°58N 16°35E **63** F7
Sala-y-Gómez Pac. Oc. 26°28S 105°28W **103** K17
Salado → La Pampa, Argentina 37°30S 67°0W **121** F3
Salado → Santa Fe, Argentina 31°40S 60°41W **121** F3
Salālah Oman 16°56N 53°59E **89** D5
Salamanca Spain 40°58N 5°39W **67** B3
Salamanca U.S.A. 42°10N 78°43W **112** D8
Salar de Uyuni Bolivia 20°30S 67°45W **120** E3
Salavat Russia 53°21N 55°55E **70** D10
Salaverry Peru 8°15S 79°0W **120** C2
Salayar Indonesia 6°7S 120°30E **83** F6
Saldanha S. Africa 33°0S 17°58E **97** L3

Sale Australia 38°6S 147°6E **98** H8
Salé Morocco 34°3N 6°48W **94** B4
Sale U.K. 53°26N 2°19W **27** F4
Salekhard Russia 66°30N 66°35E **76** C7
Salem India 11°40N 78°11E **84** P11
Salem Ind., U.S.A. 38°36N 86°6W **112** F4
Salem Mass., U.S.A. 42°31N 70°53W **113** D12
Salem Ohio, U.S.A. 40°54N 80°52W **112** E7
Salem Oreg., U.S.A. 44°56N 123°2W **110** B2
Salem Va., U.S.A. 37°18N 80°3W **112** G7
Salerno Italy 40°41N 14°47E **68** D6
Salford U.K. 53°30N 2°18W **27** F4
Salford Priors U.K. 52°10N 1°53W **30** B5
Salida U.S.A. 38°32N 106°0W **110** C5
Salina U.S.A. 38°50N 97°37W **110** C7
Salina Cruz Mexico 16°10N 95°12W **114** D5
Salinas Ecuador 2°10S 80°58W **120** C1
Salinas U.S.A. 36°40N 121°39W **110** C2
Salinas → U.S.A. 36°45N 121°48W **110** C2
Salinas Grandes Argentina 30°0S 65°0W **121** E3
Salisbury U.K. 51°4N 1°47W **30** D5
Salisbury U.S.A. 38°22N 75°36W **113** F10
Salisbury I. Canada 63°30N 77°0W **109** C12
Salisbury Plain U.K. 51°14N 1°55W **30** D5
Salmon U.S.A. 45°11N 113°54W **110** A4
Salmon → U.S.A. 45°51N 116°47W **110** A3
Salmon Arm Canada 50°40N 119°15W **108** D8
Salmon River Mts. U.S.A. 44°50N 115°30W **110** B6
Salon-de-Provence France 43°39N 5°6E **66** E6
Salsk Russia 46°28N 41°30E **71** E7
Salt → U.S.A. 33°23N 112°19W **110** D4
Salt Lake City U.S.A. 40°45N 111°53W **110** B4
Salta Argentina 24°57S 65°25W **121** E3
Saltash U.K. 50°24N 4°14W **29** G5
Saltburn-by-the-Sea U.K. 54°35N 0°58W **26** C7
Saltcoats U.K. 55°38N 4°47W **24** C6
Saltee Is. Ireland 52°7N 6°37W **21** D9
Saltfleet U.K. 53°25N 0°11E **27** F9
Saltfleetby U.K. 53°23N 0°10E **27** F9
Saltillo Mexico 25°25N 101°0W **114** B4
Salton Sea U.S.A. 33°15N 115°45W **110** D3
Saltwood U.K. 51°4N 1°2E **31** D11
Salvador Brazil 13°0S 38°30W **122** B3
Salween → Myanmar 16°31N 97°37E **78** G8
Salyan Azerbaijan 39°33N 48°59E **71** G8
Salzburg Austria 47°48N 13°2E **64** E7
Salzgitter Germany 52°9N 10°19E **64** B6
Samara Russia 53°8N 50°6E **70** D9
Samarinda Indonesia 0°30S 117°9E **82** E5
Samarqand Uzbekistan 39°40N 66°55E **87** B11
Sambalpur India 21°28N 84°4E **85** J14
Sambhal India 28°35N 78°37E **84** E11
Sambhar India 26°52N 75°6E **84** F9
Samoa ■ Pac. Oc. 14°0S 172°0W **99** C16
Samos Greece 37°45N 26°50E **69** F12
Samothraki Greece 40°28N 25°28E **69** D11
Sampford Courtenay U.K. 50°47N 3°58W **29** F6
Samsun Turkey 41°15N 36°22E **71** F6
Samui, Ko Thailand 9°30N 100°0E **82** C2
San → Poland 50°45N 21°51E **65** C11
San Ambrosio Pac. Oc. 26°28S 79°53W **103** K20
San Andrés, I. de Caribbean 12°42N 81°46W **115** E8
San Andres Mts. U.S.A. 33°0N 106°30W **110** D5
San Andrés Tuxtla Mexico 18°27N 95°13W **114** D5
San Angelo U.S.A. 31°28N 100°26W **110** D6
San Antonio Chile 33°40S 71°40W **121** F2
San Antonio U.S.A. 29°25N 98°29W **110** E7
San Antonio → U.S.A. 28°30N 96°54W **111** E7
San Antonio Oeste Argentina 40°40S 65°0W **121** G3
San Bernardino U.S.A. 34°7N 117°19W **110** D3
San Bernardino Str. Phil. 12°34N 124°10E **83** B6
San Bernardo Chile 33°40S 70°50W **121** F2
San Blas, C. U.S.A. 29°40N 85°21W **111** E9
San Carlos de Bariloche
  Argentina 41°10S 71°25W **121** G2
San Carlos de Bolivar
  Argentina 36°15S 61°6W **121** F3
San Cristóbal Argentina 30°20S 61°10W **121** F3
San Cristóbal Solomon Is. 10°30S 161°0E **99** C11
San Cristóbal Venezuela 7°46N 72°14W **120** B2
San Cristóbal de las Casas
  Mexico 16°45N 92°38W **114** D6
San Diego U.S.A. 32°42N 117°9W **110** D3
San Felipe Venezuela 10°20N 68°44W **120** A3
San Félix Pac. Oc. 26°23S 80°0W **103** K20
San Fernando Chile 34°30S 71°0W **121** F2
San Fernando Spain 36°28N 6°17W **67** D2
San Fernando de Apure
  Venezuela 7°54N 67°15W **120** B3
San Francisco U.S.A. 37°46N 122°23W **110** C2
San Francisco, C. de Colombia 6°18N 77°29W **117** C3
San Francisco de Macoris
  Dom. Rep. 19°19N 70°15W **115** D10
San Gottardo, P. del Switz. 46°33N 8°33E **64** E5
San Ignacio Bolivia 16°20S 60°55W **120** D3
San Joaquin → U.S.A. 38°4N 121°51W **110** C2
San Jorge, G. Argentina 46°0S 66°0W **121** G3
San José Costa Rica 9°55N 84°2W **115** F8
San Jose Phil. 12°27N 121°4E **83** B6
San Jose U.S.A. 37°20N 121°53W **110** C2
San José → U.S.A. 34°25N 106°45W **110** D5
San José de Chiquitos Bolivia 17°53S 60°50W **120** D3
San José de Jáchal Argentina 30°15S 68°46W **121** F3
San José de Mayo Uruguay 34°27S 56°40W **121** F4
San José del Cabo Mexico 23°3N 109°41W **114** C3
San Juan Argentina 31°30S 68°30W **121** F3
San Juan Puerto Rico 18°28N 66°7W **115** D11
San Juan → Nic. 10°56N 83°42W **115** E8
San Juan → U.S.A. 37°16N 110°26W **110** C4
San Juan de la Maguana
  Dom. Rep. 18°49N 71°12W **115** D10
San Juan de los Morros
  Venezuela 9°55N 67°21W **120** B3
San Juan Mts. U.S.A. 37°30N 107°0W **110** C5
San Lorenzo, Mte. Argentina 47°40S 72°20W **121** G2
San Lucas, C. Mexico 22°52N 109°53W **114** C3
San Luis Argentina 33°20S 66°20W **121** F3
San Luis Obispo U.S.A. 35°17N 120°40W **110** C2
San Luis Potosí Mexico 22°9N 100°59W **114** C4

San Marcos U.S.A. 29°53N 97°56W **110** E7
San Marino ■ Europe 43°56N 12°25E **68** C5
San Matías, G. Argentina 41°30S 64°0W **121** G3
San Miguel El Salv. 13°30N 88°12W **114** E7
San Miguel de Tucumán
  Argentina 26°50S 65°20W **121** E3
San Nicolás Argentina 33°25S 60°10W **121** F3
San Pedro Côte d'Ivoire 4°50N 6°33W **94** H4
San Pedro de las Colonias
  Mexico 25°45N 102°59W **114** B4
San Pedro de Macoris
  Dom. Rep. 18°30N 69°18W **115** D11
San Pedro Sula Honduras 15°30N 88°0W **114** D7
San Pietro Italy 39°8N 8°17E **68** E3
San Rafael Argentina 34°40S 68°21W **121** F3
San Remo Italy 43°49N 7°46E **68** C2
San Salvador El Salv. 13°40N 89°10W **114** E7
San Salvador de Jujuy
  Argentina 24°10S 64°48W **121** E3
San Salvador I. Bahamas 24°0N 74°30W **115** C10
San Severo Italy 41°41N 15°23E **68** D6
San Valentín, Mte. Chile 46°30S 73°30W **121** G2
Sana' = Sanaa Yemen 15°27N 44°12E **89** D3
Sanaa Yemen 15°27N 44°12E **89** D3
Sanaga → Cameroon 3°35N 9°38E **96** D1
Sanandaj Iran 35°18N 47°1E **86** C6
Sancti Spíritus Cuba 21°52N 79°33W **115** C9
Sancy, Puy de France 45°32N 2°50E **66** D5
Sandakan Malaysia 5°53N 118°4E **82** C5
Sanday U.K. 59°16N 2°31W **23** D12
Sandbach U.K. 53°9N 2°21W **27** F4
Sandgate U.K. 51°4N 1°10E **31** D11
Sandhurst U.K. 51°21N 0°48W **31** D7
Sandown U.K. 50°40N 1°10W **30** E6
Sandpoint U.S.A. 48°17N 116°33W **110** A3
Sandray U.K. 56°53N 7°31W **22** J2
Sandringham U.K. 52°51N 0°31E **31** A10
Sandusky U.S.A. 41°27N 82°42W **112** E6
Sandwich U.K. 51°16N 1°21E **31** D11
Sandy U.K. 52°8N 0°17W **31** B8
Sandy U.S.A. 40°32N 111°50W **110** B4
Sandy L. Canada 53°2N 93°0W **108** D10
Sanford, Mt. U.S.A. 62°13N 144°8W **108** C5
Sangihe, Pulau Indonesia 3°35N 125°30E **83** D7
Sangli India 16°55N 74°33E **84** L9
Sangre de Cristo Mts.
  U.S.A. 37°30N 105°20W **110** C5
Sanikluaq Canada 56°32N 79°14W **109** D12
Sankt Pölten Austria 48°12N 15°38E **64** D8
Sankuru →
  Dem. Rep. of the Congo 4°17S 20°25E **96** E4
Sanliurfa Turkey 37°12N 38°50E **71** G6
Sanlúcar de Barrameda Spain 36°46N 6°21W **67** D2
Sanmenxia China 34°47N 111°12E **79** E11
Sanming China 26°15N 117°40E **79** F12
Sanndraigh = Sandray U.K. 56°53N 7°31W **22** J2
Sanquhar U.K. 55°22N 3°54W **25** D8
Sant Feliu de Guixols Spain 41°45N 3°1E **67** B7
Santa Ana El Salv. 14°0N 89°31W **114** E7
Santa Ana U.S.A. 33°46N 117°52W **110** D3
Santa Barbara U.S.A. 34°25N 119°42W **110** D3
Santa Catarina □ Brazil 27°25S 48°30W **121** E5
Santa Clara Cuba 22°20N 80°0W **115** C9
Santa Clarita U.S.A. 34°24N 118°33W **110** D3
Santa Coloma de Gramenet
  Spain 41°27N 2°13E **67** B7
Santa Cruz Bolivia 17°43S 63°10W **120** D3
Santa Cruz U.S.A. 36°58N 122°1W **110** C2
Santa Cruz de Tenerife
  Canary Is. 28°28N 16°15W **94** C2
Santa Cruz Is. Solomon Is. 10°30S 166°0E **99** C12
Santa Cruz Mts. Jamaica 17°58N 77°43W **114** a
Santa Fe Argentina 31°35S 60°41W **121** F3
Santa Fe U.S.A. 35°41N 105°57W **110** C5
Santa Inés, I. Chile 54°0S 73°0W **121** H2
Santa Isabel Solomon Is. 8°0S 159°0E **99** B10
Santa Maria Brazil 29°40S 53°48W **121** E4
Santa Maria U.S.A. 34°57N 120°26W **110** D2
Santa María → Mexico 31°0N 107°14W **114** A3
Santa Marta Colombia 11°15N 74°13W **120** A2
Santa Marta, Sierra Nevada de
  Colombia 10°55N 73°50W **120** A2
Santa Rosa Argentina 36°40S 64°17W **121** F3
Santa Rosa U.S.A. 38°26N 122°43W **110** C2
Santai China 31°5N 104°58E **78** E9
Santana do Livramento
  Brazil 30°55S 55°30W **121** F4
Santander Spain 43°27N 3°51W **67** A4
Santanilla, Is. Honduras 17°22N 83°57W **115** D8
Santarém Brazil 2°25S 54°42W **120** C4
Santarém Portugal 39°12N 8°42W **67** C1
Santiago Chile 33°26S 70°40W **121** F2
Santiago de Compostela Spain 42°52N 8°37W **67** A1
Santiago de Cuba Cuba 20°0N 75°49W **115** D9
Santiago de los Caballeros
  Dom. Rep. 19°30N 70°40W **115** D10
Santiago del Estero
  Argentina 27°50S 64°15W **121** E3
Santo Amaro Brazil 12°30S 38°43W **122** B3
Santo André Brazil 23°39S 46°29W **122** D1
Sant' Antioco Italy 39°4N 8°27E **68** E3
Santo Antônio de Jesus
  Brazil 12°58S 39°16W **122** B3
Santo Domingo Dom. Rep. 18°30N 69°59W **115** D11
Santo Domingo de los Colorados
  Ecuador 0°15S 79°9W **120** C2
Santorini Greece 36°23N 25°27E **69** F11
Santos Brazil 24°0S 46°20W **122** D2
Santos Dumont Brazil 22°55S 43°10W **122** D2
Sanxiang China 34°13N 113°25E **79** a
Sanya China 18°14N 109°29E **79** H10

São Bernardo do Campo
  Brazil 23°45S 46°34W **122** D1
São Borja Brazil 28°39S 56°0W **121** E4
São Caitano Brazil 8°21S 36°6W **122** A3
São Carlos Brazil 22°0S 47°50W **122** D1
São Francisco → Brazil 10°30S 36°24W **122** B3
São Gonçalo Brazil 22°48S 43°5W **122** D2
São João da Boa Vista Brazil 22°0S 46°52W **122** D1
São João de Meriti Brazil 22°48S 43°22W **122** D2
São João del Rei Brazil 21°8S 44°15W **122** D2

São João do Piauí   Sonoyta

São João do Piauí *Brazil* 8°21S 42°15W 122 A2
São José do Rio Preto *Brazil* 20°50S 49°20W 122 D1
São José dos Campos *Brazil* 23°7S 45°52W 122 D1
São Lourenço *Brazil* 22°7S 45°3W 122 D1
São Luís *Brazil* 2°39S 44°15W 120 C5
São Marcos ➤ *Brazil* 18°15S 47°37W 122 C1
São Marcos, B. de *Brazil* 2°0S 44°0W 120 C5
São Mateus *Brazil* 18°44S 39°50W 122 C3
São Paulo *Brazil* 23°32S 46°38W 122 D1
São Paulo □ *Brazil* 22°0S 49°0W 120 E5
São Roque, C. de *Brazil* 5°30S 35°16W 120 C6
São Sebastião do Paraíso
Brazil 20°54S 46°59W 122 D1
São Tomé *São Tomé & Principe* 0°10N 6°39E 90 F4
São Tomé & Príncipe ■ *Africa* 0°12N 6°39E 91 F4
São Vicente *Brazil* 23°57S 46°23W 122 D1
São Vicente, C. de *Portugal* 37°0N 9°0W 67 D1
Saône ➤ *France* 45°44N 4°50E 66 D6
Sapele *Nigeria* 5°50N 5°40E 94 G7
Sapporo *Japan* 43°0N 141°21E 81 B7
Saqqez *Iran* 36°15N 46°20E 86 B6
Sar-e Pol *Afghan.* 36°10N 66°0E 87 B11
Saraburi *Thailand* 14°30N 100°55E 82 B2
Sarajevo *Bos.-H.* 43°52N 18°26E 69 C8
Saranac Lakes *U.S.A.* 44°20N 74°28W 113 C10
Saransk *Russia* 54°10N 45°10E 70 D8
Sarapul *Russia* 56°28N 53°48E 70 C9
Sarasota *U.S.A.* 27°20N 82°32W 111 E10
Saratoga Springs *U.S.A.* 43°5N 73°47W 113 D11
Saratov *Russia* 51°30N 46°2E 71 D8
Sarawak □ *Malaysia* 2°0N 113°0E 82 D4
Sarda ➤ *India* 27°21N 81°23E 85 F12
Sardinia □ *Italy* 40°0N 9°0E 68 D3
Sargasso Sea *Atl. Oc.* 27°0N 72°0W 104 G13
Sargodha *Pakistan* 32°10N 72°40E 84 C8
Sarh *Chad* 9°5N 18°23E 95 G9
Sārī *Iran* 36°30N 53°4E 87 B8
Sariwon *N. Korea* 38°31N 125°46E 79 D14
Sark *U.K.* 49°25N 2°22W 29 J9
Sarlat-la-Canéda *France* 44°54N 1°13E 66 D4
Sarmiento *Argentina* 45°35S 69°5W 121 G3
Sarnia *Canada* 42°58N 82°23W 109 E11
Sarqan *Kazakhstan* 45°24N 79°55E 78 B4
Sarreguemines *France* 49°5N 7°4E 66 B7
Sarthe ➤ *France* 47°33N 0°31W 66 C3
Sasebo *Japan* 33°10N 129°43E 81 G1
Saskatchewan □ *Canada* 54°40N 106°0W 108 D9
Saskatchewan ➤ *Canada* 53°37N 100°40W 108 D9
Saskatoon *Canada* 52°10N 106°38W 108 D9
Sássari *Italy* 40°43N 8°34E 68 D3
Sassnitz *Germany* 54°29N 13°39E 64 A7
Satmala Hills *Maharashtra,
India* 20°15N 74°40E 84 J9
Satmala Hills *Telangana, India* 19°45N 78°45E 84 K11
Satna *India* 24°35N 80°50E 85 G12
Satpura Ra. *India* 21°25N 76°10E 84 J10
Satu Mare *Romania* 47°46N 22°55E 65 E12
Saudi Arabia ■ *Asia* 26°0N 44°0E 89 B3
Sault Ste. Marie *Canada* 46°30N 84°20W 112 B5
Saumur *France* 47°15N 0°5W 66 C3
Saurimo *Angola* 9°40S 20°12E 96 F4
Sava ➤ *Serbia* 44°50N 20°26E 69 B9
Savai'i *Samoa* 13°28S 172°24W 99 C16
Savanna-la-Mar *Jamaica* 18°10N 78°10W 114 a
Savannah *U.S.A.* 32°5N 81°6W 111 D10
Savannah ➤ *U.S.A.* 32°2N 80°53W 111 D10
Savannakhet *Laos* 16°30N 104°49E 82 A2
Savoie □ *France* 45°26N 6°25E 66 D7
Savona *Italy* 44°17N 8°30E 68 B3
Sawatch Range *U.S.A.* 39°0N 106°30W 110 C5
Sawbridgeworth *U.K.* 51°48N 0°9E 31 C9
Sawel Mt. *U.K.* 54°50N 7°2W 19 B7
Sawston *U.K.* 52°8N 0°10E 31 B9
Sawtry *U.K.* 52°27N 0°17W 31 B8
Sawu *Indonesia* 10°35S 121°50E 83 F6
Sawu Sea *Indonesia* 9°30S 121°50E 83 F6
Saxilby *U.K.* 53°16N 0°38W 27 F7
Saxlingham Nethergate *U.K.* 52°32N 1°18E 31 A11
Saxmundham *U.K.* 52°13N 1°30E 31 B12
Saxony = Sachsen □
Germany 50°55N 13°10E 64 C7
Sayan Mts. *Russia* 54°0N 96°0E 77 D10
Saydā *Lebanon* 33°35N 35°25E 86 C3
Sayre *U.S.A.* 41°59N 76°32W 112 E9
Sázava ➤ *Czechia* 49°53N 14°24E 64 D8
Scafell Pike *U.K.* 54°27N 3°14W 26 D2
Scalby *U.K.* 54°18N 0°26W 26 D8
Scalloway *U.K.* 60°9N 1°17W 22 B15
Scalpay *Highl., U.K.* 57°18N 6°0W 22 H6
Scalpay *W. Isles, U.K.* 57°52N 6°40W 22 G4
Scamblesby *U.K.* 53°17N 0°5W 27 F8
Scandicci *Italy* 43°45N 11°11E 68 C4
Scandinavia *Europe* 64°0N 12°0E 56 C8
Scapa Flow *U.K.* 58°53N 3°3W 23 E11
Scarba *U.K.* 56°11N 5°43W 24 E3
Scarborough *U.K.* 54°17N 0°24W 26 D8
Scariff I. *Ireland* 51°44N 10°15W 20 E2
Scarning *U.K.* 52°41N 0°54E 31 A10
Scarp *U.K.* 58°1N 7°8W 22 F3
Schaffhausen *Switz.* 47°42N 8°39E 64 E5
Schelde ➤ *Belgium* 51°15N 4°16E 64 C3
Schenectady *U.S.A.* 42°49N 73°57W 113 D11
Schiehallion *U.K.* 56°40N 4°6W 24 A7
Schleswig *Germany* 54°31N 9°34E 64 A5
Schleswig-Holstein □ *Germany* 54°30N 9°30E 64 A5
Schreiber *Canada* 48°45N 87°20W 112 A4
Schwäbische Alb *Germany* 48°20N 9°30E 64 D5
Schwarzwald *Germany* 48°30N 8°20E 64 D5
Schwerin *Germany* 53°36N 11°22E 64 B6
Schwyz *Switz.* 47°2N 8°39E 64 E5
Scilly Is. *U.K.* 49°56N 6°22W 29 H1
Scioto ➤ *U.S.A.* 38°44N 83°1W 112 F6
Scole *U.K.* 52°22N 1°10E 31 B11
Scone *U.K.* 56°25N 3°24W 25 B9
Scopwick *U.K.* 53°8N 0°24W 27 F8
Scotia Sea *Antarctica* 56°5S 56°0W 55 B18
Scotland □ *U.K.* 57°0N 4°0W 62 C5
Scott I. *Antarctica* 67°0S 179°0E 55 C11
Scottish Borders □ *U.K.* 55°35N 2°50W 25 C10
Scottsbluff *U.S.A.* 41°52N 103°40W 110 B6

Scottsburg *U.S.A.* 38°41N 85°47W 112 F5
Scrabster *U.K.* 58°36N 3°33W 23 E10
Scranton *U.S.A.* 41°25N 75°40W 113 E10
Scremerston *U.K.* 55°44N 2°0W 26 A5
Scunthorpe *U.K.* 53°36N 0°39W 27 E7
Scutari *Albania* 42°4N 19°32E 69 C8
Scutari *Turkey* 41°1N 29°0E 86 A2
Seaford *U.K.* 50°47N 0°7E 31 E9
Seaford *U.S.A.* 38°39N 75°37W 113 F10
Seaforth, L. *U.K.* 57°52N 6°36W 22 G4
Seaham *U.K.* 54°50N 1°20W 26 C6
Seahouses *U.K.* 55°34N 1°39W 26 A5
Seal ➤ *Canada* 59°4N 94°48W 108 D10
Seamer *U.K.* 54°15N 0°26W 26 D8
Seascale *U.K.* 54°24N 3°29W 26 D2
Seaton *Cumb., U.K.* 54°40N 3°31W 26 C1
Seaton *Devon, U.K.* 50°42N 3°5W 29 F7
Seaton Delaval *U.K.* 55°5N 1°33W 26 B5
Seattle *U.S.A.* 47°36N 122°19W 110 A2
Sebastián Vizcaíno, B.
Mexico 28°0N 114°30W 114 B2
Şebinkarahisar *Turkey* 40°22N 38°28E 71 F6
Sedalia *U.S.A.* 38°42N 93°14W 111 C8
Sedan *France* 49°43N 4°57E 66 B6
Sedbergh *U.K.* 54°20N 2°31W 26 D3
Sedgefield *U.K.* 54°40N 1°26W 26 C6
Seend *U.K.* 51°21N 2°4W 30 D4
Segesta *Italy* 37°56N 12°50E 68 F5
Ségou *Mali* 13°30N 6°16W 94 F4
Segovia *Spain* 40°57N 4°10W 67 B3
Séguéla *Côte d'Ivoire* 7°55N 6°40W 94 G4
Sehore *India* 23°10N 77°5E 84 H10
Seil *U.K.* 56°18N 5°38W 24 B4
Seine ➤ *France* 49°26N 0°26E 66 B4
Sekondi-Takoradi *Ghana* 4°58N 1°45W 94 H5
Selborne *U.K.* 51°6N 0°56W 31 D7
Selby *U.K.* 53°47N 1°5W 27 E6
Selebi-Phikwe *Botswana* 21°58S 27°48E 97 J5
Selenge Mörön ➤ *Asia* 52°16N 106°16E 78 A10
Selkirk *Canada* 50°10N 96°55W 108 D10
Selkirk *U.K.* 55°33N 2°50W 25 C10
Selkirk Mts. *Canada* 51°15N 117°40W 108 D8
Sellafield *U.K.* 54°25N 3°29W 26 D2
Selma *U.S.A.* 32°25N 87°1W 111 D9
Selsey *U.K.* 50°44N 0°47W 31 E7
Selsey Bill *U.K.* 50°43N 0°47W 31 E7
Selvas *Brazil* 6°30S 67°0W 120 C3
Selwyn L. *Canada* 60°0N 104°30W 108 C9
Selwyn Mts. *Canada* 63°0N 130°0W 108 C6
Semarang *Indonesia* 7°0S 110°26E 82 F4
Semey *Kazakhstan* 50°30N 80°10E 76 D9
Semnān *Iran* 35°40N 53°23E 87 C8
Sena Madureira *Brazil* 9°5S 68°45W 120 C3
Sendai *Japan* 38°15N 140°53E 81 D7
Seneca L. *U.S.A.* 42°40N 76°54W 112 D9
Senegal ■ *W. Afr.* 14°30N 14°30W 94 F3
Sénégal ➤ *W. Afr.* 15°48N 16°32W 94 E2
Senegambia *Africa* 12°45N 12°0W 90 E2
Senhor-do-Bonfim *Brazil* 10°30S 40°10W 122 B2
Senja *Norway* 69°25N 17°30E 63 D7
Senkaku Is. *E. China Sea* 25°45N 123°30E 79 F13
Senlis *France* 49°13N 2°35E 66 B5
Sennen *U.K.* 50°4N 5°42W 29 G2
Sens *France* 48°11N 3°15E 66 B5
Seoul *S. Korea* 37°31N 126°58E 79 D14
Seph ➤ *U.K.* 54°18N 1°9W 26 D6
Sept-Îles *Canada* 50°13N 66°22W 109 D13
Seram *Indonesia* 3°10S 129°0E 83 E7
Seram Sea *Indonesia* 2°30S 128°30E 83 E7
Serang *Indonesia* 6°8S 106°10E 82 F3
Serbia ■ *Europe* 43°20N 20°0E 69 B9
Serdar *Turkmenistan* 39°4N 56°23E 87 B9
Seremban *Malaysia* 2°43N 101°53E 82 D2
Serengeti Plain *Tanzania* 2°40S 35°0E 96 E7
Sergipe □ *Brazil* 10°30S 37°30W 122 B3
Sergiyev Posad *Russia* 56°20N 38°10E 70 C6
Serhetabat *Turkmenistan* 35°20N 62°18E 87 C10
Serifos *Greece* 37°9N 24°30E 69 F11
Serov *Russia* 59°29N 60°35E 70 C11
Serowe *Botswana* 22°25S 26°43E 97 J5
Serra *Brazil* 20°7S 40°18W 122 D2
Serra de Mesa, Barragem de
Brazil 14°30S 48°30W 122 B1
Serrinha *Brazil* 11°39S 39°0W 122 B3
Sète *France* 43°25N 3°42E 66 E5
Sete Lagoas *Brazil* 19°27S 44°16W 122 C2
Sétif *Algeria* 36°9N 5°26E 94 A7
Settat *Morocco* 33°0N 7°40W 94 B4
Settle *U.K.* 54°5N 2°16W 26 D4
Setúbal *Portugal* 38°30N 8°58W 67 C1
Setúbal, B. de *Portugal* 38°40N 8°56W 67 C1
Seul, Lac *Canada* 50°20N 92°30W 108 D10
Sevan, L. *Armenia* 40°30N 45°20E 71 F8
Sevastopol *Ukraine* 44°35N 33°30E 71 F5
Seven ➤ *U.K.* 54°12N 0°52E 26 D7
Sevenoaks *U.K.* 51°16N 0°11E 31 D9
Severn ➤ *Canada* 56°2N 87°36W 109 C11
Severn ➤ *U.K.* 51°35N 2°40W 30 C3
Severn Beach *U.K.* 51°33N 2°39W 30 C3
Severn Stoke *U.K.* 52°6N 2°12W 30 B4
Severnaya Zemlya *Russia* 79°0N 100°0E 77 B10
Severodvinsk *Russia* 64°27N 39°58E 70 B6
Severomorsk *Russia* 69°5N 33°27E 70 A5
Sevier ➤ *U.S.A.* 39°4N 113°6W 110 C4
Sevier L. *U.S.A.* 38°54N 113°9W 110 C4
Seville *Spain* 37°23N 5°58W 67 D2
Seward *U.S.A.* 60°7N 149°27W 108 C5
Seward Peninsula *U.S.A.* 65°30N 166°0W 108 C3
Seychelles ■ *Ind. Oc.* 5°0S 56°0E 91 G9
Seydişfjörður *Iceland* 65°16N 14°0W 63 A3
Seydişehir *Turkey* 37°25N 31°51E 71 G5
Sfântu Gheorghe *Romania* 45°52N 25°48E 65 F13
Sfax *Tunisia* 34°49N 10°48E 95 B8
Sha Tin *China* 22°23N 114°12E 79 a
Shaanxi □ *China* 35°0N 109°0E 79 C10
Shabeelle ➤ *Somalia* 2°0N 44°0E 89 G3
Shache *China* 38°20N 77°10E 78 D4
Shaftesbury *U.K.* 51°0N 2°11W 30 D4
Shahjahanpur *India* 27°54N 79°57E 84 F11

Shajing *China* 22°44N 113°48E 79 a
Shakhty *Russia* 47°40N 40°16E 71 E7
Shaki *Nigeria* 8°41N 3°21E 94 G6
Shaldon *U.K.* 50°32N 3°31W 29 F6
Shaluli Shan *China* 30°40N 99°55E 78 E8
Shamo, L. *Ethiopia* 5°45N 37°30E 89 F2
Shan □ *Myanmar* 21°30N 98°30E 85 J21
Shandong □ *China* 36°0N 118°0E 79 D12
Shandong Pen. *China* 37°0N 121°0E 79 D13
Shanghai *China* 31°15N 121°26E 79 E13
Shangqiu *China* 34°26N 115°36E 79 E12
Shangrao *China* 28°25N 117°59E 79 F12
Shanklin *U.K.* 50°38N 1°11W 30 E6
Shannon ➤ *Ireland* 52°35N 9°30W 20 C4
Shannon ✈ (SNN) *Ireland* 52°42N 8°57W 20 C5
Shannon, Mouth of the
Ireland 52°30N 9°55W 20 D3
Shantou *China* 23°18N 116°40E 79 G12
Shanxi □ *China* 37°0N 112°0E 79 D11
Shaoguan *China* 24°48N 113°35E 79 G11
Shaoxing *China* 30°0N 120°35E 79 F13
Shaoyang *China* 27°14N 111°25E 79 F11
Shap *U.K.* 54°32N 2°40W 26 C3
Shapinsay *U.K.* 59°3N 2°51W 23 D12
Shaqra' *Si. Arabia* 25°15N 45°16E 86 E6
Sharjah *U.A.E.* 25°23N 55°26E 87 E8
Shark B. *Australia* 25°30S 113°32E 98 F1
Sharm el Sheikh *Egypt* 27°53N 34°18E 86 E3
Sharon *U.S.A.* 41°14N 80°31W 112 E7
Sharpness *U.K.* 51°43N 2°28W 30 C4
Sharya *Russia* 58°22N 45°20E 70 C8
Shasta, Mt. *U.S.A.* 41°25N 122°12W 110 B2
Shawano *U.S.A.* 44°47N 88°36W 112 C3
Shawbury *U.K.* 52°48N 2°39W 27 G3
Shawinigan *Canada* 46°35N 72°50W 109 E12
Shawnee *U.S.A.* 35°20N 96°55W 111 C7
Shebbear *U.K.* 50°51N 4°15W 29 F5
Sheboygan *U.S.A.* 43°46N 87°45W 112 D4
Sheelin, L. *Ireland* 53°48N 7°20W 18 D7
Sheep Haven *Ireland* 55°11N 7°52W 18 A6
Sheerness *U.K.* 51°26N 0°47E 31 D10
Sheffield *U.K.* 53°23N 1°28W 27 F6
Shefford *U.K.* 52°2N 0°20W 31 B8
Shehy Mts. *Ireland* 51°47N 9°15W 20 E4
Shekou *China* 22°30N 113°55E 79 a
Shelburne *Canada* 43°47N 65°20W 113 D15
Shelby *U.S.A.* 48°30N 111°51W 110 A4
Shelbyville *Ill., U.S.A.* 39°24N 88°48W 112 F3
Shelbyville *Ind., U.S.A.* 39°31N 85°47W 112 F5
Shelikhov G. *Russia* 59°30N 157°0E 77 D16
Shelikhov G. *Russia* 40°49N 76°12W 113 E9
Sikkim □ *India* 27°50N 88°30E 85 F16
Shendi *Sudan* 16°46N 33°22E 95 E12
Shenfield *U.K.* 51°38N 0°22E 31 C9
Shenyang *China* 41°48N 123°27E 79 C13
Shenzhen *China* 22°32N 114°5E 79 a
Shenzhen Bao'an Int. ✈ (SZX)
China 22°41N 113°49E 79 a
Shenzhen Wan *China* 22°27N 113°55E 79 a
Shepparton *Australia* 36°23S 145°26E 98 H8
Sheppey, I. of *U.K.* 51°25N 0°48E 31 D10
Shepshed *U.K.* 52°47N 1°18W 27 G6
Shepton Mallet *U.K.* 51°11N 2°33W 30 D3
Sherborne *U.K.* 50°57N 2°31W 30 E3
Sherborne St. John *U.K.* 51°17N 1°7W 30 D6
Sherbrooke *Canada* 45°28N 71°57W 113 C12
Sherburn *U.K.* 54°11N 0°32W 26 D7
Sherburn in Elmet *U.K.* 53°48N 1°15W 27 E6
Shere *U.K.* 51°13N 0°27W 31 D8
Sherfield English *U.K.* 51°1N 1°34W 30 D5
Sheridan *U.S.A.* 44°48N 106°58W 110 B5
Sheriff Hutton *U.K.* 54°5N 1°0W 26 D7
Sherkin I. *Ireland* 51°28N 9°26W 20 E4
Sherman *U.S.A.* 33°38N 96°36W 111 D7
Sherston *U.K.* 51°34N 2°14W 30 C4
Sherwood Forest *U.K.* 53°6N 1°7W 27 F6
Shetland □ *U.K.* 60°30N 1°30W 22 B15
Shetland Is. *U.K.* 60°30N 1°30W 22 B15
Sheung Shui *China* 22°31N 114°7E 79 a
Sheyenne ➤ *U.S.A.* 47°2N 96°50W 111 A7
Shiant Is. *U.K.* 57°54N 6°22W 22 G4
Shibām *Yemen* 15°59N 48°36E 89 D4
Shiel, L. *U.K.* 56°48N 5°34W 22 J6
Shifnal *U.K.* 52°39N 2°23W 27 G4
Shihezi *China* 44°15N 86°2E 78 C6
Shijiazhuang *China* 38°2N 114°28E 79 D11
Shikarpur *Pakistan* 27°57N 68°39E 84 F6
Shikoku □ *Japan* 33°30N 133°30E 81 G3
Shilbottle *U.K.* 55°22N 1°40W 26 B5
Shildon *U.K.* 54°38N 1°38W 26 C5
Shiliguri *India* 26°45N 88°25E 85 F16
Shillelagh *Ireland* 52°45N 6°32W 21 C9
Shillingstone *U.K.* 50°53N 2°15W 30 E4
Shillong *India* 25°35N 91°53E 85 G17
Shimla *India* 31°2N 77°9E 84 D10
Shimonoseki *Japan* 33°58N 130°55E 81 G2
Shin, L. *U.K.* 58°5N 4°30W 23 F8
Shinyanga *Tanzania* 3°45S 33°27E 96 E6
Shipdham *U.K.* 52°38N 0°54E 31 A10
Shiphoirt, L. = Seaforth, L.
U.K. 57°52N 6°36W 22 G4
Shipley *U.K.* 53°50N 1°47W 27 E5
Shipston-on-Stour *U.K.* 52°3N 1°37W 30 B5
Shipton under Wychwood
U.K. 51°51N 1°36W 30 C5
Shīrāz *Iran* 29°42N 52°30E 87 D8
Shire ➤ *Africa* 17°42S 35°19E 97 H7
Shirebrook *U.K.* 53°12N 1°13W 27 F6
Shivamogga *India* 13°57N 75°32E 84 N9
Shivpuri *India* 25°26N 77°42E 84 G10
Shizuishan *China* 39°15N 106°50E 78 D10
Shizuoka *Japan* 34°57N 138°24E 81 F6
Shkodër = Shkodra *Albania* 42°4N 19°32E 69 C8
Shoeburyness *U.K.* 51°32N 0°49E 31 C10
Shoreham-by-Sea *U.K.* 50°50N 0°16W 31 E8
Shreveport *U.S.A.* 32°31N 93°45W 111 D8
Shrewsbury *U.K.* 52°43N 2°45W 27 G3
Shrewton *U.K.* 51°12N 1°54W 30 D5
Shrirampur *India* 22°44N 88°21E 85 H16
Shrivenham *U.K.* 51°36N 1°38W 30 C5
Shropshire □ *U.K.* 52°36N 2°45W 27 G3

Shuangliao *China* 43°29N 123°30E 79 C13
Shuangyashan *China* 46°28N 131°5E 79 B15
Shule *China* 39°25N 76°3E 78 D4
Shule He ➤ *China* 40°20N 92°50E 78 C7
Shumagin Is. *U.S.A.* 55°7N 160°30W 108 D4
Shumen *Bulgaria* 43°18N 26°55E 69 C12
Shunan *Japan* 34°3N 131°50E 81 F2
Shuqrā' *Yemen* 13°22N 45°44E 89 E4
Shwebo *Myanmar* 22°30N 95°45E 85 H19
Shymkent *Kazakhstan* 42°18N 69°36E 87 A12
Si Kiang = Xi Jiang ➤ *China* 22°5N 113°20E 79 G11
Siahan Range *Pakistan* 27°30N 64°40E 84 F4
Sialkot *Pakistan* 32°32N 74°30E 84 C9
Šiauliai *Lithuania* 55°56N 23°15E 63 F8
Šibenik *Croatia* 43°48N 15°54E 68 C6
Siberia *Russia* 60°0N 100°0E 72 B11
Siberut *Indonesia* 1°30S 99°0E 82 E1
Sibi *Pakistan* 29°30N 67°54E 84 E5
Sibiu *Romania* 45°45N 24°9E 65 F13
Sible Hedingham *U.K.* 51°59N 0°37E 31 C10
Sibolga *Indonesia* 1°42N 98°45E 82 D1
Sibsey *U.K.* 53°2N 0°1E 27 F9
Sibu *Malaysia* 2°18N 111°49E 82 D4
Sibuyan Sea *Phil.* 12°30N 122°20E 83 B6
Sichuan □ *China* 30°30N 103°0E 78 E9
Sicily *Italy* 37°30N 14°30E 68 F6
Sicily, Str. of *Medit. S.* 37°35N 11°56E 68 F4
Sicuani *Peru* 14°21S 71°10W 120 D2
Sidbury *U.K.* 50°42N 3°14W 29 F7
Sidi-bel-Abbès *Algeria* 35°13N 0°39W 94 A5
Sidlaw Hills *U.K.* 56°32N 3°2W 25 B9
Sidlesham *U.K.* 50°47N 0°47W 31 E7
Sidmouth *U.K.* 50°40N 3°15W 29 F7
Sidney *Nebr., U.S.A.* 41°8N 102°59W 110 B6
Sidney *Ohio, U.S.A.* 40°17N 84°9W 112 E5
Sidra = Surt *Libya* 31°11N 16°39E 95 B9
Siedlce *Poland* 52°10N 22°20E 65 B12
Siegen *Germany* 50°51N 8°0E 64 C5
Siena *Italy* 43°19N 11°21E 68 C4
Sierra Blanca Peak *U.S.A.* 33°23N 105°49W 110 D5
Sierra Leone ■ *W. Afr.* 9°0N 12°0W 94 G3
Sierra Nevada *Spain* 37°3N 3°15W 67 D4
Sierra Nevada *U.S.A.* 39°0N 120°30W 110 C2
Sierra Vista *U.S.A.* 31°33N 110°18W 110 D4
Sifnos *Greece* 37°0N 24°45E 69 F11
Sighty Crag *U.K.* 55°7N 2°38W 26 B3
Sikar *India* 27°33N 75°10E 84 F9
Sikasso *Mali* 11°18N 5°35W 94 F4
Sikeston *U.S.A.* 36°53N 89°35W 112 G3
Sikhote Alin Ra. *Russia* 45°0N 136°0E 77 E14
Sikkim □ *India* 27°50N 88°30E 85 F16
Silesia *Poland* 51°0N 16°30E 64 C9
Silifke *Turkey* 36°22N 33°58E 71 G5
Siling Co *China* 31°50N 89°20E 78 E6
Silloth *U.K.* 54°52N 3°23W 26 C2
Silsden *U.K.* 53°55N 1°55W 27 E5
Silver City *U.S.A.* 32°46N 108°17W 110 D5
Silvermine Mts. *Ireland* 52°47N 8°15W 20 C6
Silverstone *U.K.* 52°5N 1°2W 30 B6
Silverton *U.K.* 50°49N 3°29W 29 F7
Simao *China* 22°47N 101°5E 78 G9
Simcoe, L. *Canada* 44°25N 79°20W 112 C8
Simeulue *Indonesia* 2°45N 95°45E 82 D1
Simferopol *Ukraine* 44°55N 34°3E 71 F5
Simi *Greece* 36°35N 27°50E 69 F12
Simonsbath *U.K.* 51°8N 3°46W 29 E6
Simonside *U.K.* 55°17N 1°59W 26 B5
Simplonpass *Switz.* 46°15N 8°3E 64 E5
Simpson Desert *Australia* 25°0S 137°0E 98 F6
Simpson Pen. *Canada* 68°34N 88°45W 109 C11
Sinai *Egypt* 29°0N 34°0E 95 C12
Sincelejo *Colombia* 9°18N 75°24W 120 B2
Sinclair's B. *U.K.* 58°31N 3°5W 23 E11
Sind Sagar Doab *Pakistan* 32°0N 71°30E 84 D7
Sindh □ *Pakistan* 26°0N 69°0E 84 G6
Sines *Portugal* 37°56N 8°51W 67 D1
Singapore ■ *Asia* 1°17N 103°51E 82 D2
Singaraja *Indonesia* 8°7S 115°6E 82 F5
Singida *Tanzania* 4°49S 34°48E 96 E6
Singkawang *Indonesia* 1°0N 108°57E 82 D3
Singleton *U.K.* 50°55N 0°46W 31 E7
Sinkiang □ *China* 42°0N 86°0E 78 C6
Sinop *Turkey* 42°1N 35°11E 71 F6
Sintra *Portugal* 38°47N 9°25W 67 C1
Sion *Switz.* 46°14N 7°20E 64 E4
Sion Mills *U.K.* 54°48N 7°29W 18 B7
Sioux City *U.S.A.* 42°30N 96°24W 111 B7
Sioux Falls *U.S.A.* 43°33N 96°44W 111 B7
Sioux Lookout *Canada* 50°10N 91°50W 108 D10
Siping *China* 43°8N 124°21E 79 C13
Sir James MacBrien, Mt.
Canada 62°7N 127°41W 108 C7
Siracusa *Italy* 37°4N 15°17E 68 F6
Sirajganj *Bangla.* 24°25N 89°47E 85 G16
Sīrjān *Iran* 29°30N 55°45E 87 D8
Sirsa *India* 29°33N 75°4E 84 E9
Sirte = Surt *Libya* 31°11N 16°39E 95 B9
Sīstān *Asia* 30°50N 61°0E 87 D10
Sitapur *India* 27°38N 80°45E 85 F12
Sitges *Spain* 41°17N 1°47E 67 B6
Sitka *U.S.A.* 57°3N 135°20W 108 D6
Sittingbourne *U.K.* 51°21N 0°45E 31 D10
Sittwe *Myanmar* 20°18N 92°45E 85 J18
Sivas *Turkey* 39°43N 36°58E 71 G6
Sivrihisar *Turkey* 39°30N 31°35E 71 G5
Sīwa *Egypt* 29°11N 25°31E 95 C11
Siwalik Range *Nepal* 28°0N 83°0E 85 F13
Siwan *India* 26°13N 84°21E 85 F14
Six Cross Roads *Barbados* 13°7N 59°28W 114 c
Sixmilebridge *Ireland* 52°44N 8°46W 20 C5
Sjælland *Denmark* 55°30N 11°30E 63 F6
Skagerrak *Denmark* 57°30N 9°0E 63 F5
Skagway *U.S.A.* 59°28N 135°19W 108 D6
Skeena ➤ *Canada* 54°9N 130°5W 108 D6
Skegness *U.K.* 53°9N 0°20E 27 F9
Skeleton Coast *Namibia* 20°0S 13°0E 97 J2
Skellefteå *Sweden* 64°45N 20°50E 63 E8
Skellefteälven ➤ *Sweden* 64°45N 21°10E 63 E8
Skellingthorpe *U.K.* 53°15N 0°37W 27 F7
Skelmersdale *U.K.* 53°33N 2°48W 27 E3

Skelmorlie *U.K.* 55°52N 4°53W 24 C6
Skelton *Cumb., U.K.* 54°43N 2°51W 26 C3
Skelton *N. Yorks., U.K.* 54°34N 0°58W 26 C7
Skerries, The *U.K.* 53°25N 4°36W 28 A4
Skiathos *Greece* 39°12N 23°30E 69 E10
Skibbereen *Ireland* 51°33N 9°16W 20 E4
Skiddaw *U.K.* 54°39N 3°9W 26 C2
Skien *Norway* 59°12N 9°35E 63 F5
Skikda *Algeria* 36°50N 6°58E 94 A7
Skipsea *U.K.* 53°58N 0°13W 27 E8
Skipton *U.K.* 53°58N 2°3W 27 E4
Skíros *Greece* 38°55N 24°34E 69 E11
Skopelos *Greece* 39°9N 23°47E 69 E10
Skopje *Macedonia* 42°1N 21°26E 69 C9
Skovorodino *Russia* 54°0N 124°0E 77 D13
Skowhegan *U.S.A.* 44°46N 69°43W 113 C13
Skull *Ireland* 51°32N 9°34W 20 E3
Skye *U.K.* 57°15N 6°10W 22 H5
Slaidburn *U.K.* 53°58N 2°26W 27 E4
Slaney ➤ *Ireland* 52°26N 6°33W 21 D9
Slatina *Romania* 44°28N 24°22E 65 F13
Slave ➤ *Canada* 61°18N 113°39W 108 C8
Slave Coast *W. Afr.* 6°0N 2°30E 94 G6
Slave Lake *Canada* 55°17N 114°43W 108 D8
Sleaford *U.K.* 53°0N 0°24W 27 F8
Sleat, Sd. of *U.K.* 57°5N 5°47W 22 H6
Sledmere *U.K.* 54°4N 0°35W 26 D7
Sleeper Is. *Canada* 58°30N 81°0W 109 D11
Sleights *U.K.* 54°27N 0°40W 26 D7
Slieve Aughty *Ireland* 53°4N 8°30W 20 B5
Slieve Bloom *Ireland* 53°4N 7°40W 21 B7
Slieve Donard *Ireland* 54°11N 5°55W 19 C10
Slieve Gamph *Ireland* 54°6N 9°0W 18 C4
Slieve Gullion *Ireland* 54°7N 6°26W 19 C9
Slieve League *Ireland* 54°40N 8°42W 18 B4
Slieve Mish *Ireland* 52°12N 9°50W 20 D3
Slievenamon *Ireland* 52°25N 7°34W 21 D7
Sligo *Ireland* 54°16N 8°28W 18 C4
Sligo □ *Ireland* 54°8N 8°42W 18 C4
Sligo B. *Ireland* 54°18N 8°40W 18 C4
Sliven *Bulgaria* 42°42N 26°19E 69 C12
Slough *U.K.* 51°30N 0°36W 31 C7
Slovak Rep. ■ *Europe* 48°30N 20°0E 65 D10
Slovenia ■ *Europe* 45°58N 14°30E 64 F8
Slovyansk *Ukraine* 48°55N 37°36E 71 E6
Słupsk *Poland* 54°30N 17°3E 65 A9
Slutsk *Belarus* 53°2N 27°31E 70 D4
Slyne Hd. *Ireland* 53°25N 10°10W 18 E1
Smallwood Res. *Canada* 54°5N 64°30W 109 D13
Smederevo *Serbia* 44°40N 20°57E 69 B9
Smerwick Harbour *Ireland* 52°12N 10°23W 20 D2
Smethwick *U.K.* 52°30N 1°57W 27 G5
Smithfield *U.K.* 54°59N 2°51W 26 C3
Smiths Falls *Canada* 44°55N 76°0W 113 C9
Smoky ➤ *Canada* 56°10N 117°21W 108 D8
Smoky Hill ➤ *U.S.A.* 39°4N 96°48W 111 C7
Smolensk *Russia* 54°45N 32°5E 70 D5
Snaefell *I. of Man* 54°16N 4°27W 19 C13
Snainton *U.K.* 54°14N 0°35W 26 D7
Snaith *U.K.* 53°42N 1°1W 27 E6
Snake ➤ *U.S.A.* 46°12N 119°2W 110 A3
Snape *U.K.* 52°10N 1°30E 31 B12
Snettisham *U.K.* 52°53N 0°31E 31 A10
Snizort, L. *U.K.* 57°33N 6°28W 22 G5
Snøhetta *Norway* 62°19N 9°16E 63 E5
Snow Hill *U.S.A.* 38°11N 75°24W 113 F10
Snowdon *U.K.* 53°4N 4°5W 28 A5
Snowdonia *U.K.* 53°7N 3°59W 28 A6
Snowy Mts. *Australia* 36°30S 148°20E 98 H8
Sobat ➤ *South Sudan* 9°22N 31°33E 95 G12
Sobradinho, Represa de *Brazil* 9°30S 42°0W 122 A2
Sobral *Brazil* 3°50S 40°20W 120 C5
Soc Trang *Vietnam* 9°37N 105°50E 82 C3
Sochi *Russia* 43°35N 39°40E 71 F6
Société, Îs. de la
French Polynesia 17°0S 151°0W 103 J12
Socorro *U.S.A.* 34°4N 106°54W 110 D5
Socotra *Yemen* 12°30N 54°0E 89 E5
Söderhamn *Sweden* 61°18N 17°10E 63 E7
Sofia *Bulgaria* 42°45N 23°20E 69 C10
Sognefjorden *Norway* 61°10N 5°50E 63 E5
Sohâg *Egypt* 26°33N 31°43E 95 C12
Soham *U.K.* 52°21N 0°21E 31 B9
Soissons *France* 49°25N 3°19E 66 B5
Sokhumi *Georgia* 43°0N 41°0E 71 F7
Sokodé *Togo* 9°0N 1°11E 94 G6
Sokoto *Nigeria* 13°2N 5°16E 94 F7
Sol, Costa del *Spain* 36°30N 4°30W 67 D3
Solapur *India* 17°43N 75°56E 84 L9
Soldotna *U.S.A.* 60°29N 151°3W 108 C4
Soledad *Colombia* 10°55N 74°46W 120 A2
Solent, The *U.K.* 50°45N 1°25W 30 E6
Solihull *U.K.* 52°26N 1°47W 27 G5
Solikamsk *Russia* 59°38N 56°50E 70 C10
Solingen *Germany* 51°10N 7°5E 64 C4
Söller *Spain* 39°46N 2°43E 67 C7
Sologne *France* 47°40N 1°45E 66 C4
Solomon Is. ■ *Pac. Oc.* 6°0S 155°0E 99 B10
Solomon Sea *Papua N. G.* 7°0S 150°0E 98 B9
Solon *China* 46°32N 121°10E 79 B13
Solothurn *Switz.* 47°13N 7°32E 64 E4
Solway Firth *U.K.* 54°49N 3°35W 26 C1
Somali Pen. *Africa* 7°0N 46°0E 90 F8
Somalia ■ *Africa* 7°0N 47°0E 89 F4
Somaliland □ *Somalia* 10°0N 46°0E 89 E4
Sombrerete *Mexico* 23°38N 103°39W 114 C4
Somerby *U.K.* 52°42N 0°50W 27 G7
Somerset *U.S.A.* 37°5N 84°36W 112 G5
Somersham *U.K.* 52°23N 0°0W 31 B9
Somerset □ *U.K.* 51°9N 3°0W 30 D2
Somerset I. *Canada* 73°30N 93°0W 108 B10
Somerton *U.K.* 51°3N 2°44W 30 D3
Somme ➤ *France* 50°11N 1°38E 66 A4
Songhua Hu *China* 43°35N 126°50E 79 C14
Songhua Jiang ➤ *China* 47°45N 132°30E 79 B15
Songkhla *Thailand* 7°13N 100°37E 82 C2
Sonid Youqi *China* 42°45N 112°48E 79 C11
Sonning *U.K.* 51°28N 0°54W 31 D7
Sonora ➤ *Mexico* 29°5N 110°55W 114 B2
Sonoran Desert *U.S.A.* 33°40N 114°15W 110 D4
Sonoyta *Mexico* 31°51N 112°50W 114 A2

Sopot Poland 54°27N 18°31E 65 A10
Sorel-Tracy Canada 46°0N 73°10W 113 C11
Soria Spain 41°43N 2°32W 67 B4
Sorocaba Brazil 23°31S 47°27W 122 D1
Søroya Norway 70°40N 22°30E 63 C8
Sosnowiec Poland 50°20N 19°10E 65 C10
Soufrière St. Lucia 13°51N 61°3W 114 b
Soufrière Bay St. Lucia 13°51N 61°4W 114 b
Sound, The U.K. 50°20N 4°10W 29 G4
Souris → N. Amer. 49°40N 99°34W 108 E9
Sousse Tunisia 35°50N 10°38E 95 A8
South Africa ■ Africa 32°0S 23°0E 97 L4
South America 10°0S 60°0W 117 E5
South Australia □ Australia 32°0S 139°0E 98 G6
South Ayrshire □ U.K. 55°18N 4°41W 24 D6
South Bend U.S.A. 41°41N 86°15W 112 E4
South Benfleet U.K. 51°33N 0°36E 31 C10
South Brent U.K. 50°25N 3°51W 29 G6
South Carolina □ U.S.A. 34°0N 81°0W 111 D10
South Cave U.K. 53°47N 0°37W 26 D7
South Charleston U.S.A. 38°22N 81°44W 112 F7
South China Sea Asia 10°0N 113°0E 82 C4
South Dakota □ U.S.A. 44°15N 100°0W 110 B7
South Dorset Downs U.K. 50°40N 2°26W 30 E4
South Downs △ U.K. 50°50N 0°50W 31 E7
South East C. Australia 43°40S 146°50E 98 J8
South Elkington U.K. 53°23N 0°4W 27 F8
South Esk → U.K. 56°43N 2°31W 23 J12
South Foreland U.K. 51°8N 1°24E 31 D11
South Georgia Antarctica 54°30S 37°0W 55 B1
South Harris U.K. 57°50N 7°0W 22 G4
South Hayling U.K. 50°47N 0°58W 31 E7
South I. N.Z. 44°0S 170°0E 99 J13
South Korea ■ Asia 36°0N 128°0E 79 D14
South Lanarkshire □ U.K. 55°37N 3°53W 25 C8
South Magnetic Pole Antarctica 64°8S 138°8E 55 C9
South Molton U.K. 51°1N 3°51W 29 E6
South Nahanni → Canada 61°3N 123°21W 108 C7
South Negril Pt. Jamaica 18°16N 78°22W 114 a
South Orkney Is. Antarctica 63°0S 45°0W 55 C18
South Ossetia □ Georgia 42°21N 44°2E 71 F7
South Petherton U.K. 50°57N 2°46W 30 E8
South Petherwin U.K. 50°36N 4°24W 29 F5
South Platte → U.S.A. 41°7N 100°42W 110 B6
South Pole Antarctica 90°0S 0°0E 55 E
South Pt. Barbados 13°2N 59°32W 114 c
South Ronaldsay U.K. 58°48N 2°58W 23 E12
South Sandwich Is. Antarctica 57°0S 27°0W 55 B1
South Saskatchewan → Canada 53°15N 105°5W 108 D9
South Shetland Is. Antarctica 62°0S 59°0W 55 C18
South Shields U.K. 55°0N 1°25W 26 C6
South Sudan ■ Africa 8°0N 30°0E 95 G11
South Tawton U.K. 50°44N 3°55W 29 F6
South Tyne → U.K. 54°59N 2°8W 26 C4
South Uist U.K. 57°20N 7°15W 22 H3
South Woodham Ferrers U.K. 51°39N 0°37E 31 C10
South Yorkshire □ U.K. 53°27N 1°36W 27 F5
Southam U.K. 52°18N 1°23W 30 B6
Southampton U.K. 50°54N 1°23W 30 E6
Southampton I. Canada 64°30N 84°0W 109 C11
Southborough U.K. 51°9N 0°16E 31 D9
Southend-on-Sea U.K. 51°32N 0°44E 31 C10
Southern Alps N.Z. 43°41S 170°11E 99 J13
Southern Indian L. Canada 57°10N 98°30W 108 D10
Southern Ocean 62°0S 60°0E 53 H13
Southern Uplands U.K. 55°28N 3°52W 25 D8
Southery U.K. 52°31N 0°24E 31 A9
Southminster U.K. 51°40N 0°51E 31 C10
Southport U.K. 53°39N 3°0W 27 E2
Southwark □ U.K. 51°29N 0°6W 31 D8
Southwell U.K. 53°4N 0°57W 27 F7
Southwick U.K. 50°50N 0°13W 31 E8
Southwold U.K. 52°20N 1°41E 31 B12
Sovetsk Russia 55°6N 21°50E 63 F8
Sowerby U.K. 54°14N 1°21W 26 D6
Soweto S. Africa 26°14S 27°52E 97 K5
Spain ■ Europe 39°0N 4°0W 67 B4
Spalding U.K. 52°48N 0°9W 27 G8
Spanish Canada 46°12N 82°20W 112 B6
Spanish Town Jamaica 18°0N 76°57W 114 a
Sparkford U.K. 51°2N 2°33W 30 D3
Sparks U.S.A. 39°32N 119°45W 110 C3
Sparta Greece 37°5N 22°25E 69 F10
Sparta U.S.A. 43°56N 90°49W 112 D2
Spartanburg U.S.A. 34°56N 81°57W 111 D10
Spartivento, C. Italy 37°55N 16°4E 68 F7
Speightstown Barbados 13°15N 59°39W 114 c
Speke U.K. 53°21N 2°52W 27 F3
Spencer U.S.A. 43°9N 95°9W 111 B7
Spencer G. Australia 34°0S 137°20E 98 G6
Spennymoor U.K. 54°42N 1°36W 26 C5
Sperrin Mts. U.K. 54°50N 7°0W 19 B7
Spey → U.K. 57°40N 3°6W 23 G11
Spilsby U.K. 53°10N 0°6E 27 F9
Spithead U.K. 50°45N 1°10W 30 E6
Split Croatia 43°31N 16°26E 68 C7
Spofforth U.K. 53°57N 1°27W 27 E6
Spokane U.S.A. 47°40N 117°24W 110 A3
Spooner U.S.A. 45°50N 91°53W 112 C2
Spratly Is. S. China Sea 8°20N 112°0E 82 C4
Spree → Germany 52°32N 13°12E 64 B7
Spring Hall Barbados 13°18N 59°36W 114 c
Springbok S. Africa 29°42S 17°54E 97 K3
Springfield Ill., U.S.A. 39°48N 89°39W 112 F3
Springfield Mass., U.S.A. 42°6N 72°35W 113 D11
Springfield Mo., U.S.A. 37°13N 93°17W 111 C8
Springfield Ohio, U.S.A. 39°55N 83°49W 112 F6
Springfield Oreg., U.S.A. 44°3N 123°1W 110 B2
Springhill Canada 45°40N 64°4W 113 C15
Springs S. Africa 26°13S 28°25E 97 K5
Sproatley U.K. 53°40°11W 27 E8
Spurn Hd. U.K. 53°35N 0°8E 27 E9
Srebrenica Bos.-H. 44°6N 19°18E 69 B8
Sredinnyy Ra. Russia 57°0N 160°0E 77 D16
Sri Lanka ■ Asia 7°30N 80°50E 84 R12
Srikakulam India 18°14N 83°58E 85 K13
Srinagar India 34°5N 74°50E 84 B9
Stacks Mts. Ireland 52°20N 9°34W 20 D3
Staffa U.K. 56°27N 6°21W 24 J3
Stafford U.K. 52°49N 2°7W 27 G4

Staffordshire □ U.K. 52°53N 2°10W 27 G4
Staindrop U.K. 54°36N 1°47W 26 C5
Staines-upon-Thames U.K. 51°26N 0°29W 31 D8
Stainforth U.K. 53°37N 1°0W 27 E7
Stainmore Forest U.K. 54°29N 2°5W 26 D4
Stainton U.K. 53°18N 0°24W 27 F8
Staithes U.K. 54°34N 0°46W 26 C7
Stakhanov Ukraine 48°35N 38°40E 71 E6
Stalbridge U.K. 50°57N 2°23W 30 E4
Stalham U.K. 52°47N 1°31E 31 A12
Stallingborough U.K. 53°35N 0°12W 27 E8
Stalybridge U.K. 53°28N 2°3W 27 F4
Stamford U.K. 52°39N 0°29W 27 G8
Stamford U.S.A. 41°3N 73°32W 113 E11
Stamford Bridge U.K. 54°0N 0°54W 27 E7
Stamfordham U.K. 55°3N 1°53W 26 B5
Standish U.K. 53°35N 2°41W 27 E3
Standish U.S.A. 43°59N 83°57W 112 D6
Stanford on Teme U.K. 52°18N 2°25W 30 B4
Stanhope U.K. 54°45N 2°1W 26 C4
Stanley Falk. Is. 51°40S 59°51W 121 H4
Stanley U.K. 54°53N 1°41W 26 C5
Stannington U.K. 55°7N 1°40W 26 B5
Stanovoy Ra. Russia 55°0N 130°0E 77 D13
Stansted Mountfitchet U.K. 51°54N 0°11E 31 C9
Stanwix U.K. 54°55N 2°56W 26 C3
Stapleford U.K. 52°57N 1°16W 27 G6
Staplehurst U.K. 51°9N 0°34E 31 D10
Stara Zagora Bulgaria 42°26N 25°39E 69 C11
Staraya Russa Russia 57°58N 31°23E 70 C5
Starbuck I. Kiribati 5°37S 155°55W 103 H12
Start B. U.K. 50°15N 3°39W 29 G6
Start Pt. U.K. 50°13N 3°39W 29 G6
Staryy Oskol Russia 51°19N 37°55E 71 D6
State College U.S.A. 40°48N 77°52W 112 E9
Staten, I. = Estados, I. de Los Argentina 54°40S 64°30W 121 H3
Staunton U.K. 51°57N 2°17W 30 C4
Staunton U.S.A. 38°9N 79°4W 112 F8
Stavanger Norway 58°57N 5°40E 63 F5
Staveley Cumb., U.K. 54°23N 2°48W 26 D3
Staveley Derby., U.K. 53°16N 1°21W 27 F6
Stavropol Russia 45°5N 42°0E 71 E7
Steiermark □ Austria 47°26N 15°0E 64 E8
Steinkjer Norway 64°1N 11°31E 63 E6
Stellarton Canada 45°32N 62°30W 113 C16
Stellenbosch S. Africa 33°58S 18°50E 97 L3
Stenhousemuir U.K. 56°2N 3°48W 25 B8
Steornabhaigh = Stornoway U.K. 58°13N 6°23W 22 F5
Stephenville Canada 48°31N 58°35W 109 E14
Steppe Asia 50°0N 50°0E 72 C7
Sterling Colo., U.S.A. 40°37N 103°13W 110 B6
Sterling Ill., U.S.A. 41°48N 89°42W 112 E3
Sterlitamak Russia 53°40N 56°0E 70 D10
Stettiner Haff Germany 53°47N 14°15E 64 B8
Stettler Canada 52°19N 112°40W 108 D8
Steubenville U.S.A. 40°22N 80°37W 112 E7
Stevenage U.K. 51°55N 0°13W 31 C8
Stevens Point U.S.A. 44°31N 89°34W 112 C3
Stevenston U.K. 55°39N 4°45W 24 C6
Stewart Canada 55°56N 129°57W 108 D7
Stewart → Canada 63°19N 139°26W 108 C6
Stewart I. N.Z. 46°58S 167°54E 99 K12
Stewarton U.K. 55°40N 4°32W 24 C6
Steyning U.K. 50°53N 0°18W 31 E8
Steyr Austria 48°3N 14°25E 64 D8
Stikine → Canada 56°40N 132°30W 108 D6
Stillington U.K. 54°6N 1°6W 26 D6
Stillwater U.S.A. 36°7N 97°4W 111 A8
Stiperstones U.K. 52°36N 2°55W 27 G3
Stirling U.K. 56°8N 3°57W 25 B8
Stirling □ U.K. 56°12N 4°18W 24 B7
Stobo U.K. 55°38N 3°17W 25 C9
Stockbridge U.K. 51°7N 1°29W 30 D6
Stockholm Sweden 59°19N 18°4E 63 F7
Stockport U.K. 53°25N 2°9W 27 F4
Stocksbridge U.K. 53°29N 1°35W 27 F5
Stockton U.S.A. 37°58N 121°17W 110 C2
Stockton-on-Tees U.K. 54°35N 1°19W 26 C6
Stoer, Pt. of U.K. 58°16N 5°23W 22 F7
Stoke U.K. 51°26N 0°41E 31 D10
Stoke Ferry U.K. 52°34N 0°31E 31 A10
Stoke Fleming U.K. 50°19N 3°37W 29 G6
Stoke Mandeville U.K. 51°47N 0°47W 31 C7
Stoke-on-Trent U.K. 53°1N 2°11W 27 F4
Stoke Prior U.K. 52°19N 2°4W 30 B4
Stokesley U.K. 54°28N 1°12W 26 D6
Stone Bucks., U.K. 51°48N 0°52W 31 C7
Stone Staffs., U.K. 52°55N 2°9W 27 G4
Stonehaven U.K. 56°59N 2°12W 23 J13
Stonehouse U.K. 51°45N 2°16W 30 C4
Stonham Aspal U.K. 52°12N 1°8E 31 B11
Stony Stratford U.K. 52°3N 0°50W 31 B7
Stony Tunguska → Russia 61°50N 90°13E 77 C10
Stora Lulevatten Sweden 67°10N 19°30E 63 D7
Storavan Sweden 65°45N 18°10E 63 D7
Store Bælt Denmark 55°20N 11°0E 63 F6
Stormberge S. Africa 31°16S 26°17E 97 L5
Stornoway U.K. 58°13N 6°23W 22 F5
Storsjön Sweden 63°9N 14°30E 63 E6
Stort → U.K. 51°46N 0°2E 31 C9
Storuman Sweden 65°5N 17°10E 63 D7
Stotfold U.K. 52°1N 0°13W 31 B8
Stour → Dorset, U.K. 50°43N 1°47W 30 E5
Stour → Kent, U.K. 51°18N 1°22E 31 D11
Stour → Suffolk, U.K. 51°57N 1°4E 31 C11
Stour → Worcs., U.K. 52°21N 2°17W 30 B4
Stourbridge U.K. 52°28N 2°8W 27 G4
Stourport-on-Severn U.K. 52°21N 2°17W 30 B4
Stow U.K. 55°42N 2°50W 25 C10
Stow Bardolph U.K. 52°38N 0°24E 31 A9
Stow-on-the-Wold U.K. 51°56N 1°42W 30 C5
Stowmarket U.K. 52°12N 1°0E 31 B10
Strabane U.K. 54°50N 7°27W 18 B7
Stradbroke U.K. 52°19N 1°16E 31 B11
Stralsund Germany 54°18N 13°4E 64 A7
Strangford L. U.K. 54°30N 5°37W 19 C10
Stranraer U.K. 54°54N 5°1W 24 E5
Strasbourg France 48°35N 7°42E 66 B7
Stratford Canada 43°23N 81°0W 112 D7

Stratford St. Mary U.K. 51°58N 1°0E 31 C10
Stratford-upon-Avon U.K. 52°12N 1°42W 30 B5
Strath Avon → U.K. 57°18N 3°23W 23 H11
Strath Dearn U.K. 57°20N 4°0W 23 H9
Strath Glass U.K. 57°22N 4°42W 23 H8
Strath Halladale U.K. 58°30N 3°51W 23 F10
Strath of Kildonan U.K. 58°14N 3°56W 23 F10
Strath Naver U.K. 58°24N 4°12W 23 F9
Strath Spey U.K. 57°9N 3°49W 23 H10
Strath Tay U.K. 56°40N 3°48W 25 A8
Strathaven U.K. 55°40N 4°5W 24 C7
Strathbogie U.K. 57°25N 2°45W 23 H12
Strathmore Angus, U.K. 56°37N 3°7W 23 J11
Strathmore Highl., U.K. 58°22N 4°40W 23 F8
Strathpeffer U.K. 57°35N 4°32W 23 H8
Strathroy Canada 42°58N 81°38W 112 D7
Strathy Pt. U.K. 58°36N 4°1W 23 E9
Stratton U.K. 50°49N 4°32W 29 F4
Stratton St. Margaret U.K. 51°35N 1°44W 30 C5
Streatley U.K. 51°31N 1°8W 30 C6
Street U.K. 51°8N 2°44W 30 D3
Strensall U.K. 54°3N 1°4W 26 D5
Stretford U.K. 53°28N 2°17W 27 F4
Stroma U.K. 58°41N 3°7W 23 E11
Strómboli Italy 38°47N 15°13E 68 E6
Stromeferry U.K. 57°21N 5°33W 22 H6
Stromness U.K. 58°58N 3°17W 23 E11
Stronsay U.K. 59°7N 2°35W 23 D12
Stroud U.K. 51°45N 2°13W 30 C4
Stuart L. Canada 54°30N 124°30W 108 D7
Studland U.K. 50°39N 1°58W 30 E5
Studley U.K. 52°16N 1°54W 30 B5
Sturgeon Bay U.S.A. 44°50N 87°23W 112 C4
Sturgeon Falls Canada 46°25N 79°57W 112 B8
Sturminster Marshall U.K. 50°47N 2°5W 30 E4
Sturminster Newton U.K. 50°55N 2°18W 30 E4
Sturt Stony Desert Australia 28°30S 141°0E 98 F6
Stuttgart Germany 48°48N 9°11E 64 D5
Stuttgart U.S.A. 34°30N 91°33W 111 D8
Suakin Sudan 19°8N 37°20E 95 E13
Şubā Si. Arabia 27°10N 35°40E 86 E5
Subotica Serbia 46°6N 19°39E 69 A8
Suceava Romania 47°38N 26°16E 65 E14
Suck → Ireland 53°17N 8°3W 20 B6
Sucre Bolivia 19°0S 65°15W 120 D3
Sudan ■ Africa 15°0N 30°0E 95 E11
Sudbury Canada 52°54N 1°45W 27 G5
Sudbury Suffolk, U.K. 52°2N 0°45E 31 B10
Sudd South Sudan 8°20N 30°0E 95 G12
Sudeten Europe 50°20N 16°45E 65 C9
Suez Egypt 29°58N 32°31E 95 C12
Suez, G. of Egypt 28°40N 33°0E 95 C12
Suez Canal Egypt 31°0N 32°20E 95 B12
Suffolk □ U.K. 52°16N 1°0E 31 B11
Sugluk Canada 62°14N 75°38W 109 C12
Şuḥār Oman 24°20N 56°40E 87 E9
Suihua China 46°32N 126°55E 79 B14
Suining China 30°26N 105°35E 78 E10
Suir → Ireland 52°16N 7°9W 21 D8
Sukabumi Indonesia 6°56S 106°50E 82 F3
Sukhona → Russia 61°15N 46°39E 70 C8
Sukkur Pakistan 27°42N 68°54E 84 F6
Sulaiman Range Pakistan 30°30N 69°50E 84 D6
Sulawesi Indonesia 2°0S 120°0E 83 E6
Sullana Peru 4°52S 80°39W 120 C1
Sullom Voe U.K. 60°27N 1°20W 22 B15
Sulu Arch. Phil. 6°0N 121°0E 83 C6
Sulu Sea E. Indies 8°0N 120°0E 83 C6
Sumare Brazil 22°49S 47°16W 122 D1
Sumatra Indonesia 0°40N 100°20E 82 D2
Sumba Indonesia 9°45S 119°35E 83 F5
Sumbawa Indonesia 8°26S 117°30E 82 F5
Sumburgh Hd. U.K. 59°52N 1°17W 22 C15
Summer L. U.S.A. 42°50N 120°45W 110 B3
Summerside Canada 46°24N 63°47W 109 E13
Sumqayit Azerbaijan 40°34N 49°38E 71 F8
Sumter U.S.A. 33°55N 80°21W 111 D10
Sumy Ukraine 50°57N 34°50E 71 D5
Sun Valley U.S.A. 43°42N 114°21W 110 B4
Sunart, L. U.K. 56°43N 5°42W 22 J6
Sunart, L. U.K. 56°42N 5°43W 22 J6
Sunbury U.S.A. 40°52N 76°48W 112 E9
Sunda, Selat Indonesia 6°20S 105°30E 82 F3
Sunda Is. Indonesia 5°0S 105°0E 102 H2
Sundarbans Asia 22°0N 89°0E 85 J16
Sunderland U.K. 54°55N 1°23W 26 C6
Sundsvall Sweden 62°23N 17°17E 63 E7
Sungaipenuh Indonesia 2°1S 101°20E 82 E2
Sunk Island U.K. 53°39N 0°6W 27 E8
Sunninghill U.K. 51°24N 0°39W 31 D7
Sunshine Coast Australia 26°30S 153°0E 98 F9
Superior U.S.A. 46°44N 92°6W 112 B1
Superior, L. N. Amer. 47°0N 87°0W 112 B4
Şūr Lebanon 33°19N 35°16E 86 C3
Sura → Russia 56°6N 46°0E 70 C8
Surabaya Indonesia 7°17S 112°45E 82 F4
Surakarta Indonesia 7°35S 110°48E 82 F4
Surat India 21°12N 72°55E 84 J8
Surgut Russia 61°14N 73°20E 76 C8
Surigao Phil. 9°47N 125°29E 83 C7
Suriname ■ S. Amer. 4°0N 56°0W 120 B4
Surrey □ U.K. 51°15N 0°31W 31 D7
Surt Libya 31°11N 16°39E 95 B9
Surt, Khalīj Libya 31°40N 18°30E 95 B9
Surtsey Iceland 63°20N 20°30W 63 B1
Susquehanna → U.S.A. 39°33N 76°5W 113 F9
Sussex Canada 45°45N 65°37W 113 C15
Sutherland U.K. 58°12N 4°50W 23 F8
Sutlej → Pakistan 29°23N 71°3E 84 E7
Sutterton U.K. 52°55N 0°6W 27 G8
Sutton □ U.K. 51°21N 0°11W 31 D8
Sutton Bridge U.K. 52°47N 0°11E 27 G9
Sutton Coldfield U.K. 52°35N 1°49W 27 G5
Sutton Courtenay U.K. 51°39N 1°16W 30 C6
Sutton in Ashfield U.K. 53°8N 1°16W 27 F6
Sutton-on-Sea U.K. 53°18N 0°16E 27 F9
Sutton Scotney U.K. 51°9N 1°20W 30 D6
Suva Fiji 18°6S 178°30E 99 D14
Suwałki Poland 54°8N 22°59E 65 A12
Suwarrow Is. Cook Is. 13°15S 163°5W 103 J11

Suzhou China 31°19N 120°38E 79 E13
Svalbard Arctic 78°0N 17°0E 54 B8
Svealand Sweden 60°20N 15°0E 63 E7
Sverdrup Chan. Canada 79°56N 96°25W 109 B10
Sverdrup Is. Canada 79°0N 97°0W 109 B10
Svir → Russia 60°30N 32°48E 70 B5
Swadlincote U.K. 52°47N 1°33W 27 G5
Swaffham U.K. 52°39N 0°42E 31 A10
Swakopmund Namibia 22°37S 14°30E 97 J2
Swan Hill Australia 35°20S 143°33E 98 H7
Swan River Canada 52°10N 101°16W 108 D9
Swanage U.K. 50°36N 1°58W 30 E5
Swansea U.K. 51°37N 3°57W 29 D6
Swansea B. U.K. 51°32N 3°57W 29 D6
Swartberge S. Africa 33°20S 22°0E 90 K6
Swaziland = Eswatini ■ Africa 26°30S 31°30E 97 K6
Sweden ■ Europe 57°0N 15°0E 63 F7
Sweetwater U.S.A. 32°28N 100°25W 110 D6
Swellendam S. Africa 34°1S 20°26E 97 L4
Swift Current Canada 50°20N 107°45W 108 D9
Swilly, L. Ireland 55°12N 7°33W 18 A6
Swindon U.K. 51°34N 1°46W 30 C5
Swineshead U.K. 52°57N 0°10W 27 G8
Swinford Ireland 53°57N 8°58W 18 D4
Swinton Borders, U.K. 55°43N 2°15W 25 C11
Swinton Gt. Man., U.K. 53°31N 2°20W 27 E4
Swinton S. Yorks., U.K. 53°29N 1°20W 27 F6
Switzerland ■ Europe 46°30N 8°0E 64 E5
Swords Ireland 53°28N 6°13W 21 B10
Sydney Australia 33°52S 151°12E 98 G9
Sydney Canada 46°7N 60°7W 113 C17
Syktyvkar Russia 61°45N 50°40E 70 B9
Sylhet Bangla. 24°54N 91°52E 85 G17
Sylt Germany 54°54N 8°22E 64 A5
Symington U.K. 55°36N 3°36W 25 C8
Symonds Yat U.K. 51°51N 2°38W 30 C3
Syracuse U.S.A. 43°3N 76°9W 113 D9
Syrdarya → Kazakhstan 46°3N 61°0E 76 E7
Syria ■ Asia 35°0N 38°0E 86 C4
Syrian Desert Asia 32°0N 40°0E 86 C4
Syston U.K. 52°42N 1°3W 27 G6
Syzran Russia 53°12N 48°30E 70 D8
Szczecin Poland 53°27N 14°27E 64 B8
Szechwan = Sichuan □ China 30°30N 103°0E 78 E9
Szeged Hungary 46°16N 20°10E 65 E11
Székesfehérvár Hungary 47°15N 18°25E 65 E10
Szekszárd Hungary 46°22N 18°42E 65 E10
Szolnok Hungary 47°10N 20°15E 65 E11
Szombathely Hungary 47°14N 16°38E 65 E9

T

Tabas Iran 33°35N 56°55E 87 C9
Tablas I. Phil. 12°25N 122°2E 83 B6
Table B. S. Africa 33°35S 18°25E 97 L3
Table Mt. S. Africa 33°58S 18°26E 97 L3
Tabora Tanzania 5°2S 32°50E 96 F6
Tabrīz Iran 38°7N 46°20E 86 B6
Tabuaeran Kiribati 3°51N 159°22W 103 G12
Tabūk Si. Arabia 28°23N 36°36E 86 D6
Tacheng China 46°40N 82°58E 78 B5
Tacloban Phil. 11°15N 124°58E 83 B6
Tacna Peru 18°0S 70°20W 120 D2
Tacoma U.S.A. 47°14N 122°26W 110 A2
Tacuarembó Uruguay 31°45S 56°0W 121 F4
Tadcaster U.K. 53°53N 1°16W 27 E6
Tademaït, Plateau du Algeria 28°30N 2°30E 94 C6
Tadley U.K. 51°21N 1°7W 30 D6
Taganrog Russia 47°12N 38°50E 71 E6
Taguatinga Brazil 12°27S 46°22W 122 B1
Tagus → Europe 38°40N 9°24W 67 C1
Tahiti French Polynesia 17°37S 149°27W 103 J13
Tahoe, L. U.S.A. 39°6N 120°2W 110 C2
Tahoua Niger 14°57N 5°16E 94 F7
Tahta Egypt 26°44N 31°32E 95 C12
Tai Hu China 31°5N 120°10E 79 E13
Tai Po China 22°27N 114°10E 79 a
Tai'an China 36°12N 117°8E 79 D12
T'aichung Taiwan 24°9N 120°37E 79 G13
Tain U.K. 57°49N 4°4W 23 G9
T'ainan Taiwan 23°0N 120°10E 79 G13
T'aipei Taiwan 25°4N 121°29E 79 F13
Taiping Malaysia 4°51N 100°44E 82 D2
Taitao, Pen. de Chile 46°30S 75°0W 121 G2
T'aitung Taiwan 22°43N 121°4E 79 G13
Taiwan ■ Asia 23°30N 121°0E 79 G13
Taiwan Str. Asia 24°40N 120°0E 79 G13
Taiyuan China 37°52N 112°33E 79 D11
Taizhou China 32°28N 119°55E 79 E12
Ta'izz Yemen 13°35N 44°2E 89 E3
Tajikistan ■ Asia 38°30N 70°0E 87 B12
Tak Thailand 16°52N 99°8E 82 A1
Takamatsu Japan 34°20N 134°5E 81 F4
Takaoka Japan 36°47N 137°0E 81 E5
Takasaki Japan 36°20N 139°0E 81 E6
Takeshima = Liancourt Rocks Asia 37°15N 131°52E 81 E2
Takla Makan Desert China 38°0N 83°0E 78 D5
Talara Peru 4°38S 81°18W 120 C1
Talaud, Kepulauan Indonesia 4°30N 126°50E 83 D7
Talavera de la Reina Spain 39°55N 4°46W 67 C3
Talca Chile 35°28S 71°40W 121 F2
Talcahuano Chile 36°40S 73°10W 121 F2
Taldyqorghan Kazakhstan 45°10N 78°45E 76 E8
Talgarth U.K. 52°0N 3°14W 28 D7
Taliabu Indonesia 1°50S 125°0E 83 E6
Tallaght Ireland 53°17N 6°22W 21 B10
Tallahassee U.S.A. 30°27N 84°17W 111 D10
Tallinn Estonia 59°22N 24°48E 63 F8
Taloyoak Canada 69°32N 93°32W 108 C10
Taltal Chile 25°23S 70°33W 121 E2
Tamale Ghana 9°22N 0°50W 94 G5
Tamana Kiribati 2°30S 175°59E 99 A13
Tamanrasset Algeria 22°50N 5°30E 94 D7
Tamar → U.K. 50°27N 4°15W 29 G5
Tambov Russia 52°45N 41°28E 70 D7
Tame → U.K. 52°44N 1°43W 27 G5
Tamerton Foliot U.K. 50°25N 4°11W 29 G5
Tamil Nadu □ India 11°0N 77°0E 84 P10
Tampa U.S.A. 27°56N 82°27W 111 E10

Tampa B. U.S.A. 27°50N 82°30W 111 E10
Tampere Finland 61°30N 23°50E 63 E8
Tampico Mexico 22°13N 97°51W 114 C5
Tamworth Australia 31°7S 150°58E 98 G9
Tamworth U.K. 52°39N 1°41W 27 G5
Tana → Kenya 2°32S 40°31E 96 E8
Tana → Norway 70°30N 28°14E 63 C9
Tana, L. Ethiopia 13°5N 37°30E 89 E2
Tanami Desert Australia 18°50S 132°0E 98 D5
Tanana → U.S.A. 65°10N 151°58W 108 C4
Tandil Argentina 37°15S 59°6W 121 F4
Tandragee U.K. 54°21N 6°24W 19 C9
Tanezrouft Algeria 23°9N 0°11E 94 D6
Tanga Tanzania 5°5S 39°2E 96 F7
Tanganyika, L. Africa 6°40S 30°0E 96 F6
Tanggula Shan China 32°40N 92°10E 78 E7
Tanggula Shankou China 32°42N 92°27E 78 E7
Tangier Morocco 35°50N 5°49W 94 A4
Tangjia China 22°22N 113°35E 79 a
Tangra Yumco China 31°0N 86°38E 78 E6
Tangshan China 39°38N 118°10E 79 D12
Tanimbar, Kepulauan Indonesia 7°30S 131°30E 83 F8
Tanjungbalai Indonesia 2°55N 99°44E 82 D1
Tanjungpandan Indonesia 2°43S 107°38E 82 E3
Tanjungredeb Indonesia 2°9N 117°29E 82 D5
Tanna Vanuatu 19°30S 169°20E 99 D12
Tannu Ola Asia 51°0N 94°0E 77 D10
Tanta Egypt 30°45N 30°57E 95 B12
Tanworth U.K. 52°20N 1°50W 30 B5
Tanzania ■ Africa 6°0S 34°0E 96 F6
Tanzhou China 22°16N 113°28E 79 a
Taolanaro Madag. 25°2S 47°0E 97 K9
Taonan China 45°22N 122°40E 79 B13
Taos U.S.A. 36°24N 105°35W 110 C5
Tapachula Mexico 14°54N 92°17W 114 E6
Tapajós → Brazil 2°24S 54°41W 120 C4
Tapti → India 21°8N 72°41E 84 J8
Taquaritinga Brazil 21°24S 48°30W 122 D1
Tarakan Indonesia 3°20N 117°35E 82 D5
Taransay U.K. 57°54N 7°0W 22 G3
Táranto Italy 40°28N 17°14E 68 D7
Táranto, G. di Italy 40°8N 17°20E 68 D7
Tarasaigh = Taransay U.K. 57°54N 7°0W 22 G3
Tarawa Kiribati 1°30N 173°0E 102 G9
Taraz Kazakhstan 42°54N 71°22E 87 A12
Tarbagatay, Khrebet Kazakhstan 48°0N 83°0E 76 E9
Tarbat Ness U.K. 57°52N 3°47W 23 G10
Tarbela Dam Pakistan 34°8N 72°52E 84 B8
Tarbert Argyll & Bute, U.K. 55°52N 5°25W 24 C5
Tarbert W. Isles, U.K. 57°54N 6°49W 22 G4
Tarbes France 43°15N 0°3E 66 E4
Tarcoola Australia 30°44S 134°36E 98 G5
Taree Australia 31°50S 152°30E 98 G9
Tarfaya Morocco 27°55N 12°55W 94 C3
Târgoviște Romania 44°55N 25°27E 65 F13
Târgu Jiu Romania 45°5N 23°19E 65 F12
Târgu Mureş Romania 46°31N 24°38E 65 E13
Tarija Bolivia 21°30S 64°40W 120 E3
Tarim Basin China 40°0N 84°0E 78 C5
Tarim He → China 39°30N 88°30E 78 C6
Tarleton U.K. 53°41N 2°50W 27 E3
Tarn → France 44°5N 1°6E 66 E4
Tarnów Poland 50°3N 21°0E 65 C11
Taroudannt Morocco 30°30N 8°52W 94 B4
Tarporley U.K. 53°10N 2°40W 27 F3
Tarragona Spain 41°5N 1°17E 67 B6
Tarsus Turkey 36°58N 34°55E 71 G5
Tartu Estonia 58°20N 26°44E 63 F9
Tarțūs Syria 34°55N 35°55E 86 C3
Tashkent Uzbekistan 41°20N 69°10E 87 A12
Tasiilaq Greenland 65°40N 37°20W 54 C6
Tasikmalaya Indonesia 7°18S 108°12E 82 F3
Tasman Sea Pac. Oc. 36°0S 160°0E 99 H10
Tasmania □ Australia 42°0S 146°30E 98 J8
Tassili n' Ajjer Algeria 25°47N 8°1E 94 C7
Tatar Str. Russia 50°0N 141°0E 77 E14
Tatarstan □ Russia 55°30N 51°30E 70 C9
Tatnam, C. Canada 57°16N 91°0W 109 D10
Tatra Slovakia 49°20N 20°0E 65 D11
Tattenhall U.K. 53°7N 2°46W 27 F3
Tatuí Brazil 23°25S 47°53W 122 D1
Tatvan Turkey 38°31N 42°15E 71 G7
Taubaté Brazil 23°0S 45°36W 122 D1
Tauern Austria 47°15N 12°40E 64 E7
Taunggyi Myanmar 20°50N 97°0E 85 J20
Taunton U.K. 51°1N 3°5W 30 D2
Taunton U.S.A. 41°54N 71°6W 113 E12
Taunus Germany 50°13N 8°34E 64 C5
Taurus Mts. Turkey 37°0N 32°30E 71 G5
Tavan Bogd Uul Mongolia 49°10N 87°49E 78 B6
Tavistock U.K. 50°33N 4°9W 29 F5
Taw → U.K. 51°4N 4°4W 29 E5
Tawas City U.S.A. 44°16N 83°31W 112 C6
Tawau Malaysia 4°20N 117°55E 82 D5
Taxkorgan Tajik Zizhixian China 37°49N 75°14E 78 D4
Tay → U.K. 56°37N 3°38W 25 A8
Tay, Firth of U.K. 56°25N 3°8W 25 B9
Tay, L. U.K. 56°32N 4°8W 24 A7
Taylor, Mt. U.S.A. 35°14N 107°37W 110 C5
Tayport U.K. 56°27N 2°52W 25 B10
Taz → Russia 67°32N 78°40E 76 C8
Taza Morocco 34°16N 4°6W 94 B5
Tbilisi Georgia 41°43N 44°50E 71 F7
Tebay U.K. 54°26N 2°35W 26 D3
Tébessa Algeria 35°22N 8°8E 94 A7
Tees → U.K. 54°37N 1°10W 26 C6
Teesdale U.K. 54°37N 2°10W 26 C4
Teesside U.K. 54°36N 1°15W 26 C6
Tegal Indonesia 6°52S 109°8E 82 F3
Tegid, L. = Bala, L. U.K. 52°53N 3°37W 28 B6
Tegucigalpa Honduras 14°5N 87°14W 114 E7
Tehrān Iran 35°41N 51°25E 87 C7
Tehuantepec Mexico 16°21N 95°13W 114 D5
Tehuantepec, G. de Mexico 15°50N 95°12W 114 D5
Tehuantepec, Istmo de Mexico 17°15N 94°30W 114 D6
Teifi → U.K. 52°5N 4°41W 28 C4
Teign → U.K. 50°32N 3°32W 29 F6

182 INDEX

Teignmouth Ural Mts.

Teignmouth *U.K.* 50°33N 3°31W **29 F6**
Tejen *Turkmenistan* 37°23N 60°31E **87 B10**
Tekirdağ *Turkey* 40°58N 27°30E **71 F4**
Tel Aviv-Jaffa *Israel* 32°4N 34°48E **86 C3**
Tela *Honduras* 15°40N 87°28W **114 D7**
Telangana □ *India* 17°30N 78°30E **84 K11**
Telegraph Creek *Canada* 58°0N 131°10W **108 D6**
Teles Pires → *Brazil* 7°21S 58°3W **120 C4**
Telford *U.K.* 52°40N 2°27W **27 G4**
Tell City *U.S.A.* 37°57N 86°46W **112 G4**
Telpos Iz *Russia* 63°16N 59°13E **70 B10**
Teluk Intan *Malaysia* 4°3N 101°0E **82 D2**
Tema *Ghana* 5°41N 0°0 **94 G5**
Teme → *U.K.* 52°11N 2°13W **30 B4**
Temirtau *Kazakhstan* 50°5N 72°56E **76 D8**
Témiscaming *Canada* 46°44N 79°5W **112 B8**
Temple *U.S.A.* 31°6N 97°21W **111 D7**
Temple Combe *U.K.* 51°0N 2°24W **30 D4**
Temple Ewell *U.K.* 51°8N 1°17E **31 D11**
Temple Sowerby *U.K.* 54°38N 2°36W **26 C3**
Templemore *Ireland* 52°47N 7°51W **20 C7**
Temuco *Chile* 38°45S 72°40W **121 F2**
Tenali *India* 16°15N 80°35E **85 L12**
Tenbury Wells *U.K.* 52°19N 2°35W **30 B3**
Tenby *U.K.* 51°40N 4°42W **28 D4**
Tenerife *Canary Is.* 28°15N 16°35W **94 C2**
Tengchong *China* 25°0N 98°28E **78 G8**
Tengger Desert *China* 38°0N 104°10E **78 D9**
Tennant Creek *Australia* 19°30S 134°15E **98 D5**
Tennessee □ *U.S.A.* 36°0N 86°30W **111 C9**
Tennessee → *U.S.A.* 37°4N 88°34W **111 C9**
Tenterden *U.K.* 51°4N 0°42E **31 D10**
Teófilo Otoni *Brazil* 17°50S 41°30W **122 C2**
Tepic *Mexico* 21°30N 104°54W **114 C4**
Teraina *Kiribati* 4°43N 160°25W **103 G12**
Téramo *Italy* 42°39N 13°42E **68 C5**
Teresina *Brazil* 5°9S 42°45W **120 C5**
Termiz *Uzbekistan* 37°15N 67°15E **87 B11**
Ternate *Indonesia* 0°45N 127°25E **83 D7**
Terni *Italy* 42°34N 12°37E **68 C5**
Ternopil *Ukraine* 49°30N 25°40E **65 D13**
Terrace *Canada* 54°30N 128°35W **108 D7**
Terrassa *Spain* 41°34N 2°1E **67 B7**
Terre Haute *U.S.A.* 39°28N 87°25W **112 F4**
Terschelling *Neths.* 53°25N 5°20E **64 B3**
Teruel *Spain* 40°22N 1°8W **67 B5**
Tesiyn Gol → *Mongolia* 50°40N 93°20E **78 A7**
Teslin *Canada* 60°10N 132°43W **108 C6**
Test → *U.K.* 50°56N 1°29W **30 E6**
Tetbury *U.K.* 51°38N 2°10W **30 C4**
Tete *Mozam.* 16°13S 33°33E **97 H6**
Tetney *U.K.* 53°29N 0°1W **27 F8**
Tétouan *Morocco* 35°35N 5°21W **94 A4**
Tetovo *Macedonia* 42°1N 20°59E **69 C9**
Teuco → *Argentina* 25°35S 60°11W **121 E3**
Teutoburger Wald *Germany* 52°5N 8°22E **64 B5**
Teviot → *U.K.* 55°29N 2°38W **25 D10**
Teviotdale *U.K.* 55°25N 2°50W **25 D10**
Teviothead *U.K.* 55°20N 2°56W **25 D10**
Tewkesbury *U.K.* 51°59N 2°9W **30 C4**
Texarkana *U.S.A.* 33°26N 94°3W **111 D8**
Texas □ *U.S.A.* 31°40N 98°30W **110 D7**
Texel *Neths.* 53°5N 4°50E **64 B3**
Teynham *U.K.* 51°20N 0°50E **31 D10**
Tezpur *India* 26°40N 92°45E **85 F18**
Thabana Ntlenyana *Lesotho* 29°30S 29°16E **97 K5**
Thabazimbi *S. Africa* 24°40S 27°21E **97 J5**
Thailand ■ *Asia* 16°0N 102°0E **82 A2**
Thailand, G. of *Asia* 11°30N 101°0E **82 B2**
Thal Desert *Pakistan* 31°10N 71°30E **84 D7**
Thalassery *India* 11°45N 75°30E **84 P9**
Thame *U.K.* 51°45N 0°58W **31 C7**
Thame → *U.K.* 51°39N 1°9W **30 C6**
Thames → *Canada* 42°20N 82°25W **112 D6**
Thames → *U.K.* 51°29N 0°34E **31 D10**
Thane *India* 19°12N 72°59E **84 K8**
Thanet, I. of *U.K.* 51°21N 1°20E **31 D11**
Thanjavur *India* 10°48N 79°12E **84 P11**
Thar Desert *India* 28°0N 72°0E **84 F8**
Thargomindah *Australia* 27°58S 143°46E **98 F7**
Thasos *Greece* 40°40N 24°40E **69 D11**
Thatcham *U.K.* 51°24N 1°15W **30 D6**
Thatta *Pakistan* 24°42N 67°55E **84 G5**
Thaxted *U.K.* 51°57N 0°22E **31 C9**
The Pas *Canada* 53°45N 101°15W **108 D9**
Theale *U.K.* 51°26N 1°5W **30 D6**
Thebes *Egypt* 25°40N 32°35E **95 C12**
Thelon → *Canada* 64°16N 96°4W **108 C9**
Thermopolis *U.S.A.* 43°39N 108°13W **110 B5**
Thermopylæ *Greece* 38°48N 22°35E **69 E10**
Thessalon *Canada* 46°20N 83°30W **112 B6**
Thessaloniki *Greece* 40°38N 22°58E **69 D10**
Thetford *U.K.* 52°25N 0°45E **31 B10**
Thetford Mines *Canada* 46°8N 71°18W **109 E12**
Thiers *France* 45°52N 3°33E **66 D5**
Thiès *Senegal* 14°50N 16°51W **94 F2**
Thika *Kenya* 1°1S 37°5E **96 E7**
Thimphu *Bhutan* 27°31N 89°45E **85 F16**
Thionville *France* 49°20N 6°10E **66 B7**
Thira = Santorini *Greece* 36°23N 25°27E **69 F11**
Thirlmere *U.K.* 54°32N 3°4W **26 C2**
Thirsk *U.K.* 54°14N 1°19W **26 D6**
Thiruvananthapuram *India* 8°41N 77°0E **84 Q10**
Thlewiaza → *Canada* 60°29N 94°40W **108 D9**
Thomasville *U.S.A.* 30°50N 83°59W **111 D10**
Thompson *Canada* 55°45N 97°52W **108 D10**
Thornaby on Tees *U.K.* 54°33N 1°18W **26 C6**
Thornbury *U.K.* 51°36N 2°31W **30 C3**
Thorndon *U.K.* 52°17N 1°9E **31 B11**
Thorne *U.K.* 53°37N 0°57W **27 E7**
Thorney *U.K.* 52°37N 0°6W **31 A8**
Thornham *U.K.* 52°58N 0°35E **31 A10**
Thornthwaite *U.K.* 54°37N 3°13W **26 C2**
Thornton *U.K.* 53°52N 2°59W **27 E3**
Thornton Dale *U.K.* 54°15N 0°42W **26 D7**
Thorpe *U.K.* 52°38N 1°22E **31 A11**
Thorpe le Soken *U.K.* 51°51N 1°11E **31 C11**
Thrace *Europe* 41°0N 27°0E **69 D12**
Thrace, Sea of *Greece* 40°30N 25°0E **69 D11**
Thrapston *U.K.* 52°24N 0°32W **31 B7**
Three Gorges Dam *China* 30°45N 111°15E **79 E11**
Threlkeld *U.K.* 54°37N 3°3W **26 C2**
Threshfield *U.K.* 54°4N 2°1W **26 D4**
Thrissur *India* 10°30N 76°18E **84 P10**
Thunder B. *U.S.A.* 45°0N 83°20W **112 C6**
Thunder Bay *Canada* 48°20N 89°15W **112 A3**
Thüringer Wald *Germany* 50°35N 11°0E **64 C6**
Thurlby *U.K.* 52°45N 0°22W **27 G8**
Thurles *Ireland* 52°41N 7°49W **20 C7**
Thurmaston *U.K.* 52°40N 1°5W **27 G6**
Thursby *U.K.* 54°51N 3°2W **26 C2**
Thurso *U.K.* 58°36N 3°32W **23 E10**
Thurso → *U.K.* 58°36N 3°32W **23 E10**
Thurston I. *Antarctica* 72°0S 100°0W **55 D16**
Tian Shan *Asia* 40°30N 76°0E **78 C4**
Tianjin *China* 39°7N 117°12E **79 D12**
Tianjun *China* 38°0N 98°0E **78 D8**
Tianmen *China* 30°39N 113°9E **79 E11**
Tianshui *China* 34°32N 105°40E **78 E10**
Tiaret *Algeria* 35°20N 1°21E **94 A6**
Tibasti, Sarir *Libya* 22°50N 18°30E **95 D9**
Tiber → *Italy* 41°44N 12°14E **68 D5**
Tiberias, L. = Galilee, Sea of *Israel* 32°45N 35°35E **86 C3**
Tibesti *Chad* 21°0N 17°30E **95 D9**
Tibet = Xizang Zizhiqu □ *China* 32°0N 88°0E **78 E6**
Tibet, Plateau of *Asia* 32°0N 86°0E **72 E10**
Tiburón, I. *Mexico* 29°0N 112°25W **114 B2**
Ticehurst *U.K.* 51°3N 0°25E **31 D9**
Ticino → *Italy* 45°9N 9°14E **68 B3**
Tickhill *U.K.* 53°26N 1°6W **27 F6**
Ticonderoga *U.S.A.* 43°51N 73°26W **113 D11**
Tideswell *U.K.* 53°17N 1°47W **27 F5**
Tieling *China* 42°20N 123°55E **79 C13**
Tierra de Campos *Spain* 42°10N 4°50W **67 A3**
Tierra del Fuego, I. Grande de *Argentina* 54°0S 69°0W **121 H3**
Tiffin *U.S.A.* 41°7N 83°11W **112 E6**
Tignish *Canada* 46°58N 64°2W **113 B15**
Tigris → *Asia* 31°0N 47°25E **86 D6**
Tijuana *Mexico* 32°32N 117°1W **114 A1**
Tikhoretsk *Russia* 45°56N 40°5E **71 E7**
Tikhvin *Russia* 59°35N 33°30E **70 C5**
Tikrīt *Iraq* 34°35N 43°37E **86 C5**
Tiksi *Russia* 71°40N 128°45E **77 B13**
Tilburg *Neths.* 51°31N 5°6E **64 C3**
Tilbury *U.K.* 51°27N 0°22E **31 D9**
Till → *U.K.* 55°41N 2°13W **26 A4**
Tillicoultry *U.K.* 56°9N 3°45W **25 B8**
Tilmanstone *U.K.* 51°12N 1°18E **31 D11**
Tilt → *U.K.* 56°46N 3°51W **23 J10**
Timaru *N.Z.* 44°23S 171°14E **99 J13**
Timişoara *Romania* 45°43N 21°15E **65 F11**
Timmins *Canada* 48°28N 81°25W **109 E11**
Timor *Asia* 9°0S 125°0E **83 F7**
Timor-Leste ■ *Asia* 8°50S 126°0E **83 F7**
Timor Sea *Ind. Oc.* 12°0S 127°0E **72 K14**
Tingewick *U.K.* 51°59N 1°2W **30 C6**
Tingri *China* 28°34N 86°38E **78 F6**
Tinogasta *Argentina* 28°5S 67°32W **121 E3**
Tinos *Greece* 37°33N 25°8E **69 F11**
Tintagel *U.K.* 50°39N 4°46W **29 F4**
Tintagel Hd. *U.K.* 50°40N 4°47W **29 F4**
Tipperary *Ireland* 52°28N 8°10W **20 D6**
Tipperary □ *Ireland* 52°37N 7°55W **20 C7**
Tipton *U.K.* 52°32N 2°4W **27 G4**
Tipton *U.S.A.* 41°46N 91°8W **112 E2**
Tiptree *U.K.* 51°48N 0°46E **31 C10**
Tiranë *Albania* 41°18N 19°49E **69 D8**
Tiraspol *Moldova* 46°55N 29°35E **65 E15**
Tirebolu *Turkey* 40°58N 38°45E **71 F6**
Tiree *U.K.* 56°31N 6°55W **24 A2**
Tiree, Passage of *U.K.* 56°30N 6°30W **24 B2**
Tirich Mir *Pakistan* 36°15N 71°55E **84 A7**
Tirol □ *Austria* 47°3N 10°43E **64 E6**
Tiruchchirappalli *India* 10°45N 78°45E **84 P11**
Tirunelveli *India* 8°45N 77°45E **84 Q10**
Tiruppur *India* 11°5N 77°22E **84 P10**
Tisa → *Serbia* 45°15N 20°17E **69 B9**
Tisbury *U.K.* 51°4N 2°5W **30 D4**
Tisdale *Canada* 52°50N 104°0W **108 D9**
Titchfield *U.K.* 50°50N 1°15W **30 E6**
Titicaca, L. *S. Amer.* 15°30S 69°30W **120 D3**
Titusville *U.S.A.* 41°38N 79°41W **112 E8**
Tiverton *U.K.* 50°54N 3°29W **29 F7**
Tivoli *Italy* 41°58N 12°45E **68 D5**
Tizi-Ouzou *Algeria* 36°42N 4°3E **94 A6**
Tlaxiaco *Mexico* 17°25N 97°35W **114 D5**
Tlemcen *Algeria* 34°52N 1°21W **94 B5**
Toamasina *Madag.* 18°10S 49°25E **97 H9**
Toba, Danau *Indonesia* 2°30N 98°30E **82 D1**
Toba Kakar *Pakistan* 31°30N 69°0E **84 D6**
Tobago *Trin. & Tob.* 11°10N 60°30W **120 A3**
Tobermory *Canada* 45°12N 81°40W **112 C7**
Tobermory *U.K.* 56°38N 6°5W **24 A3**
Tobol → *Russia* 58°10N 68°12E **76 D7**
Tobolsk *Russia* 58°15N 68°10E **76 D7**
Tocantins → *Brazil* 1°45S 49°10W **120 C5**
Toddington *U.K.* 51°57N 0°32W **31 C7**
Todmorden *U.K.* 53°43N 2°6W **27 E4**
Todos os Santos, B. de *Brazil* 12°48S 38°38W **122 B3**
Toe Hd. *U.K.* 57°50N 7°8W **22 G3**
Togliatti *Russia* 53°32N 49°24E **70 D8**
Togo ■ *W. Afr.* 8°30N 1°35E **94 G6**
Tok *U.S.A.* 63°20N 142°59W **108 C5**
Tokachi-Dake *Japan* 43°17N 142°5E **81 B8**
Tokat *Turkey* 40°22N 36°35E **71 F6**
Tokelau Is. ☑ *Pac. Oc.* 9°0S 171°45W **99 B16**
Tokushima *Japan* 34°4N 134°34E **81 F4**
Tōkyō *Japan* 35°43N 139°45E **81 F6**
Toledo *Spain* 39°50N 4°2W **67 C3**
Toledo *U.S.A.* 41°39N 83°33W **112 E6**
Toledo, Montes de *Spain* 39°33N 4°20W **67 C3**
Toliara *Madag.* 23°21S 43°40E **97 J8**
Tolima *Colombia* 4°40N 75°19W **120 B2**
Tollesbury *U.K.* 51°45N 0°51E **31 C10**
Toluca *Mexico* 19°17N 99°40W **114 D5**
Tomah *U.S.A.* 43°59N 90°30W **112 D2**
Tomakomai *Japan* 42°38N 141°36E **81 B7**
Tomaszów Mazowiecki *Poland* 51°30N 20°2E **65 C10**
Tombador, Serra do *Brazil* 12°0S 58°0W **120 D4**
Tombigbee → *U.S.A.* 31°8N 87°57W **111 D9**
Tombouctou *Mali* 16°50N 3°0W **94 E5**
Tomini, Teluk *Indonesia* 0°10S 121°0E **83 E6**
Tomintoul *U.K.* 57°15N 3°23W **23 H11**
Tomsk *Russia* 56°30N 85°5E **76 D9**
Tonbridge *U.K.* 51°11N 0°17E **31 D9**
Tone → *U.K.* 50°58N 3°20W **29 F7**
Tong *U.K.* 52°40N 2°17W **27 G4**
Tonga ■ *Pac. Oc.* 19°50S 174°30W **99 D16**
Tonga Trench *Pac. Oc.* 18°0S 173°0W **99 D16**
Tongareva *Cook Is.* 9°0S 158°0W **103 H12**
Tongatapu Group *Tonga* 21°0S 175°0W **99 E16**
Tongchuan *China* 35°6N 109°3E **79 D10**
Tonghua *China* 41°42N 125°58E **79 C14**
Tongliao *China* 43°38N 122°18E **79 C13**
Tongling *China* 30°55N 117°48E **79 E12**
Tongue *U.K.* 58°29N 4°25W **23 F9**
Tongue → *U.S.A.* 46°25N 105°52W **110 A5**
Tonk *India* 26°6N 75°54E **84 F9**
Tonkin, G. of *Asia* 20°0N 108°0E **78 G10**
Tonlé Sap *Cambodia* 13°0N 104°0E **82 B2**
Tonopah *U.S.A.* 38°4N 117°14W **110 C3**
Toowoomba *Australia* 27°32S 151°56E **98 F9**
Topeka *U.S.A.* 39°3N 95°40W **111 C7**
Topolobampo *Mexico* 25°36N 109°3W **114 B3**
Topsham *U.K.* 50°41N 3°28W **29 F7**
Tor B. *U.K.* 50°25N 3°33W **29 G6**
Torbay □ *U.K.* 50°26N 3°31W **29 G6**
Torneälven → *Europe* 65°50N 24°12E **63 D8**
Torneträsk *Sweden* 68°24N 19°15E **63 D7**
Tornio *Finland* 65°50N 24°12E **63 D8**
Toro, Cerro del *Chile* 29°10S 69°50W **121 E3**
Toronto *Canada* 43°39N 79°20W **112 D8**
Torpoint *U.K.* 50°23N 4°13W **29 G5**
Torquay *U.K.* 50°27N 3°32W **29 G6**
Torre del Greco *Italy* 40°47N 14°22E **68 D6**
Torrejón de Ardoz *Spain* 40°27N 3°29W **67 B4**
Torrelavega *Spain* 43°20N 4°5W **67 A3**
Torremolinos *Spain* 36°38N 4°30W **67 D3**
Torrens, L. *Australia* 31°0S 137°50E **98 G6**
Torrent *Spain* 39°27N 0°28W **67 C5**
Torreón *Mexico* 25°33N 103°26W **114 B4**
Torres Strait *Australia* 9°50S 142°20E **98 C7**
Torridge → *U.K.* 51°0N 4°13W **29 E5**
Torridon, L. *U.K.* 57°35N 5°50W **22 G6**
Torthorwald *U.K.* 55°6N 3°32W **25 D8**
Tortosa *Spain* 40°49N 0°31E **67 B6**
Toruń *Poland* 53°2N 18°39E **65 B10**
Torver *U.K.* 54°20N 3°6W **26 D2**
Tory I. *Ireland* 55°16N 8°13W **18 A5**
Toscana □ *Italy* 43°25N 11°0E **68 C4**
Toshka, Buheirat en *Egypt* 22°50N 31°0E **95 D12**
Totland *U.K.* 50°41N 1°32W **30 E5**
Totley *U.K.* 53°20N 1°32W **27 F5**
Totnes *U.K.* 50°26N 3°42W **29 G6**
Totton *U.K.* 50°55N 1°29W **30 E6**
Tottori *Japan* 35°30N 134°15E **81 F4**
Toubkal, Djebel *Morocco* 31°0N 8°0W **94 B4**
Touggourt *Algeria* 33°6N 6°4E **94 B7**
Toul *France* 48°40N 5°53E **66 B6**
Toulon *France* 43°10N 5°55E **66 E6**
Toulouse *France* 43°37N 1°27E **66 E4**
Touraine *France* 47°20N 0°30E **66 C4**
Tournai *Belgium* 50°35N 3°25E **64 C2**
Tournon-sur-Rhône *France* 45°4N 4°50E **66 D6**
Tours *France* 47°22N 0°40E **66 C4**
Towanda *U.S.A.* 41°46N 76°27W **112 E9**
Towcester *U.K.* 52°8N 0°59W **31 B7**
Town Yetholm *U.K.* 55°33N 2°17W **25 C11**
Townsville *Australia* 19°15S 146°45E **98 D8**
Towraghondī *Afghan.* 35°13N 62°16E **84 B3**
Towson *U.S.A.* 39°24N 76°36W **112 F9**
Toyama *Japan* 36°40N 137°15E **81 E5**
Toyohashi *Japan* 34°45N 137°25E **81 F5**
Toyota *Japan* 35°3N 137°7E **81 F5**
Trabzon *Turkey* 41°0N 39°45E **71 F6**
Trafalgar, C. *Spain* 36°10N 6°2W **67 D2**
Trail *Canada* 49°5N 117°40W **108 E8**
Tralee *Ireland* 52°16N 9°42W **20 D3**
Tralee B. *Ireland* 52°17N 9°55W **20 D3**
Tramore *Ireland* 52°10N 7°10W **21 D8**
Tramore B. *Ireland* 52°9N 7°10W **21 D8**
Tranent *U.K.* 55°57N 2°57W **25 C10**
Trang *Thailand* 7°33N 99°38E **82 C1**
Transantarctic Mts. *Antarctica* 85°0S 170°0W **55 E12**
Transnistria □ *Moldova* 47°20N 29°15E **65 E15**
Transylvania *Romania* 46°30N 24°0E **65 E12**
Transylvanian Alps *Romania* 45°30N 25°0E **65 F13**
Trápani *Italy* 38°1N 12°29E **68 E5**
Trasimeno, L. *Italy* 43°8N 12°6E **68 C5**
Traverse City *U.S.A.* 44°46N 85°38W **112 C5**
Trawbreaga B. *Ireland* 55°20N 7°25W **18 A7**
Trawsfynydd *U.K.* 52°54N 3°55W **28 B6**
Tredegar *U.K.* 51°47N 3°14W **28 D7**
Trefaldwyn = Montgomery *U.K.* 52°34N 3°8W **28 B7**
Trefnynw = Monmouth *U.K.* 51°48N 2°42W **28 D8**
Tregaron *U.K.* 52°14N 3°56W **28 C6**
Treinta y Tres *Uruguay* 33°16S 54°17W **121 F4**
Trelew *Argentina* 43°10S 65°20W **121 G3**
Trent → *U.K.* 53°41N 0°42W **27 E7**
Trentham *U.K.* 52°58N 2°11W **27 G4**
Trento *Italy* 46°4N 11°8E **68 A4**
Trenton *Canada* 44°10N 77°34W **112 C9**
Trenton *U.S.A.* 40°14N 74°46W **113 E10**
Tres Arroyos *Argentina* 38°26S 60°20W **121 F3**
Três Corações *Brazil* 21°44S 45°15W **122 D1**
Três Lagoas *Brazil* 20°50S 51°43W **120 E4**
Três Pontas *Brazil* 21°23S 45°29W **122 D1**
Tres Puntas, C. *Argentina* 47°0S 66°0W **121 G3**
Três Rios *Brazil* 22°6S 43°15W **122 D2**
Tresco *U.K.* 49°57N 6°20W **29 H1**
Treviso *Italy* 45°40N 12°15E **68 B5**
Trevose Hd. *U.K.* 50°32N 5°3W **29 F3**
Tribal Areas □ *Pakistan* 33°0N 70°0E **84 C7**
Trier *Germany* 49°45N 6°38E **64 D4**
Trieste *Italy* 45°40N 13°46E **68 B5**
Trim *Ireland* 53°33N 6°48W **19 D8**
Trimdon *U.K.* 54°42N 1°24W **26 C6**
Trimley *U.K.* 51°59N 1°20E **31 C11**
Trincomalee *Sri Lanka* 8°38N 81°15E **84 Q12**
Trindade *Atl. Oc.* 20°20S 29°50W **52 F8**
Trinidad *Bolivia* 14°46S 64°50W **120 D3**
Trinidad *Cuba* 21°48N 80°0W **115 C9**
Trinidad *U.S.A.* 37°10N 104°31W **110 C6**
Trinidad & Tobago ■ *W. Indies* 10°30N 61°20W **115 E12**
Trinity → *U.S.A.* 29°45N 94°43W **111 E8**
Trinity B. *Canada* 48°20N 53°10W **109 E14**
Trinity Is. *U.S.A.* 56°33N 154°25W **108 D4**
Tripoli *Lebanon* 34°31N 35°50E **86 C3**
Tripoli *Libya* 32°49N 13°7E **95 B8**
Tripolitania *Libya* 31°0N 13°0E **95 B8**
Tripura □ *India* 24°0N 92°0E **85 H18**
Tristan da Cunha *Atl. Oc.* 37°6S 12°20W **52 F9**
Trnava *Slovakia* 48°23N 17°35E **65 D9**
Trois-Rivières *Canada* 46°25N 72°34W **109 E12**
Trollhättan *Sweden* 58°17N 12°20E **63 F6**
Trombetas → *Brazil* 1°55S 55°35W **120 C4**
Tromsø *Norway* 69°40N 18°56E **63 D7**
Tronador *Argentina* 41°10S 71°50W **121 G2**
Trondheim *Norway* 63°36N 10°25E **63 E6**
Trondheimsfjorden *Norway* 63°35N 10°30E **63 E6**
Troon *U.K.* 55°33N 4°39W **24 C6**
Trossachs, The *U.K.* 56°14N 4°24W **24 B7**
Trostan *U.K.* 55°3N 6°10W **19 A9**
Trotternish *U.K.* 57°32N 6°15W **22 G5**
Trou Gras Pt. *St. Lucia* 13°51N 60°53W **114 b**
Trout L. *N.W.T., Canada* 60°40N 121°14W **108 C7**
Trout L. *Ont., Canada* 51°20N 93°15W **108 D10**
Trowbridge *U.K.* 51°18N 2°12W **30 D4**
Troy *Turkey* 39°57N 26°12E **71 G4**
Troy *Ala., U.S.A.* 31°48N 85°58W **111 D9**
Troy *N.Y., U.S.A.* 42°44N 73°41W **113 D11**
Troy *Ohio, U.S.A.* 40°2N 84°12W **112 E5**
Troyes *France* 48°19N 4°3E **66 B6**
Trujillo *Honduras* 16°0N 86°0W **114 D7**
Trujillo *Peru* 8°6S 79°0W **120 C2**
Trujillo *Venezuela* 9°22N 70°38W **120 B2**
Truk *Micronesia* 7°25N 151°46E **102 G7**
Trull *U.K.* 51°0N 3°6W **30 E2**
Trumpington *U.K.* 52°10N 0°7E **31 B9**
Truro *Canada* 45°21N 63°14W **109 E13**
Truro *U.K.* 50°16N 5°4W **29 G3**
Tsavo *Kenya* 2°59S 38°28E **96 E7**
Tseung Kwan *China* 22°19N 114°15E **79 a**
Tshikapa *Dem. Rep. of the Congo* 6°28S 20°48E **96 F4**
Tsiigehtchic *Canada* 67°15N 134°0W **108 C6**
Tsimlyansk Res. *Russia* 48°0N 43°0E **71 E7**
Tskhinvali *Georgia* 42°14N 44°1E **71 F7**
Tsuchiura *Japan* 36°5N 140°15E **81 E7**
Tsuen Wan *China* 22°22N 114°6E **79 a**
Tsugaru Str. *Japan* 41°35N 141°0E **81 C7**
Tsumeb *Namibia* 19°9S 17°44E **97 H3**
Tsuruoka *Japan* 38°44N 139°50E **81 D6**
Tsushima *Japan* 34°20N 129°20E **81 F1**
Tuam *Ireland* 53°31N 8°51W **18 D4**
Tuamotu, Îs. *French Polynesia* 17°0S 144°0W **103 J13**
Tuapse *Russia* 44°5N 39°10E **71 F6**
Tubarão *Brazil* 28°30S 49°0W **121 E5**
Tübingen *Germany* 48°31N 9°4E **64 D5**
Tubruq *Libya* 32°7N 23°55E **95 B10**
Tubuaï, Îs. *French Polynesia* 25°0S 150°0W **103 K13**
Tucson *U.S.A.* 32°13N 110°58W **110 D4**
Tucumcari *U.S.A.* 35°10N 103°44W **110 C6**
Tucupita *Venezuela* 9°2N 62°3W **120 B3**
Tucuruí *Brazil* 3°42S 49°44W **120 C5**
Tucuruí, Represa de *Brazil* 4°0S 49°30W **120 C5**
Tuen Mun *China* 22°23N 113°57E **79 a**
Tuguegarao *Phil.* 17°35N 121°42E **83 A6**
Tuktoyaktuk *Canada* 69°27N 133°2W **108 C6**
Tula *Russia* 54°13N 37°38E **70 D6**
Tulancingo *Mexico* 20°5N 98°22W **114 C5**
Tulare *U.S.A.* 36°13N 119°21W **110 C3**
Tulcán *Ecuador* 0°48N 77°43W **120 B2**
Tulcea *Romania* 45°13N 28°46E **65 F15**
Tulita *Canada* 64°57N 125°30W **108 C7**
Tulla *Ireland* 52°53N 8°46W **20 C5**
Tullamore *Ireland* 53°16N 7°31W **21 B7**
Tulle *France* 45°16N 1°46E **66 D4**
Tullow *Ireland* 52°49N 6°45W **21 C9**
Tulsa *U.S.A.* 36°10N 95°55W **111 C7**
Tumaco *Colombia* 1°50N 78°45W **120 B2**
Tumbes *Peru* 3°37S 80°27W **120 C1**
Tummel → *U.K.* 56°42N 4°5W **23 J9**
Tummel, L. *U.K.* 56°43N 3°55W **23 J10**
Tumucumaque, Serra *Brazil* 2°0N 55°0W **120 B4**
Tunis *Tunisia* 36°50N 10°11E **95 A8**
Tunisia ■ *Africa* 33°30N 9°10E **95 A7**
Tunja *Colombia* 5°33N 73°25W **120 B2**
Tunstall *U.K.* 52°9N 1°27E **31 B11**
Tupaciguara *Brazil* 18°35S 48°42W **122 C1**
Tupelo *U.S.A.* 34°16N 88°43W **111 D9**
Tupiza *Bolivia* 21°30S 65°40W **120 E3**
Turfan Basin *China* 42°40N 89°25E **78 C6**
Turgutlu *Turkey* 38°30N 27°43E **71 G4**
Turin *Italy* 45°3N 7°40E **68 B2**
Turkana, L. *Africa* 3°30N 36°5E **96 D7**
Turkey ■ *Eurasia* 39°0N 36°0E **71 G6**
Türkmenabat *Turkmenistan* 39°6N 63°34E **87 B10**
Türkmenbashi *Turkmenistan* 40°5N 53°5E **87 A8**
Turkmenistan ■ *Asia* 39°0N 59°0E **87 B9**
Turks & Caicos Is. ☑ *W. Indies* 21°20N 71°20W **115 C10**
Turku *Finland* 60°30N 22°19E **63 E8**
Turnberry *U.K.* 55°18N 4°49W **24 D6**
Turneffe Is. *Belize* 17°20N 87°50W **114 D7**
Turpan *China* 43°58N 89°10E **78 C6**
Turriff *U.K.* 57°32N 2°27W **23 G13**
Tuscaloosa *U.S.A.* 33°12N 87°34W **111 D9**
Tuscany = Toscana □ *Italy* 43°25N 11°0E **68 C4**
Tutbury *U.K.* 52°51N 1°41W **27 G5**
Tuticorin *India* 8°50N 78°12E **84 Q11**
Tutuila *Amer. Samoa* 14°19S 170°50W **99 C16**
Tutume *Botswana* 20°30S 27°5E **97 J5**
Tuul Gol → *Mongolia* 48°30N 104°25E **78 B9**
Tuva □ *Russia* 51°30N 95°0E **77 D10**
Tuvalu ■ *Pac. Oc.* 8°0S 178°0E **99 B14**
Tuxford *U.K.* 53°14N 0°54W **27 F7**
Tuxpan *Mexico* 20°57N 97°24W **114 C5**
Tuxtla Gutiérrez *Mexico* 16°45N 93°7W **114 D6**
Tuz Gölü *Turkey* 38°42N 33°18E **71 G5**
Tuzla *Bos.-H.* 44°34N 18°41E **69 B8**
Tver *Russia* 56°55N 35°59E **70 C6**
Tweed → *U.K.* 55°45N 2°0W **25 C11**
Tweedmouth *U.K.* 55°45N 2°0W **26 A5**
Tweedshaws *U.K.* 55°27N 3°29W **25 D9**
Twenty *U.K.* 52°47N 0°17W **27 G8**
Twin Falls *U.S.A.* 42°34N 114°28W **110 B4**
Two Harbors *U.S.A.* 47°2N 91°40W **112 B2**
Two Rivers *U.S.A.* 44°9N 87°34W **112 C4**
Twyford *Hants., U.K.* 51°1N 1°19W **30 D6**
Twyford *Wokingham, U.K.* 51°28N 0°51W **31 D7**
Tychy *Poland* 50°9N 18°59E **65 C10**
Tydd St. Mary *U.K.* 52°45N 0°7E **27 G9**
Tyler *U.S.A.* 32°21N 95°18W **111 D7**
Tyndrum *U.K.* 56°26N 4°42W **24 B6**
Tyne → *U.K.* 54°59N 1°32W **26 C5**
Tyne & Wear □ *U.K.* 55°6N 1°17W **26 B6**
Tynemouth *U.K.* 55°1N 1°26W **26 B6**
Tyrol = Tirol □ *Austria* 47°3N 10°43E **64 E6**
Tyrrhenian Sea *Medit. S.* 40°0N 12°30E **68 E5**
Tyumen *Russia* 57°11N 65°29E **76 D7**
Tywardreath *U.K.* 50°21N 4°42W **29 G4**
Tywi → *U.K.* 51°48N 4°21W **28 D5**
Tywyn *U.K.* 52°35N 4°5W **28 B5**
Tzaneen *S. Africa* 23°47S 30°9E **97 J6**

U

U.S.A. = United States of America ■ *N. Amer.* 37°0N 96°0W **110 C7**
U.S. Virgin Is. ☑ *W. Indies* 18°20N 65°0W **115 D12**
Uaupés → *Brazil* 0°2N 67°16W **120 B3**
Ubá *Brazil* 21°8S 43°0W **122 D2**
Ubaitaba *Brazil* 14°18S 39°20W **122 B3**
Ube *Japan* 33°56N 131°15E **81 G2**
Uberaba *Brazil* 19°50S 47°55W **122 C1**
Uberlândia *Brazil* 19°0S 48°20W **122 C1**
Ubon Ratchathani *Thailand* 15°15N 104°50E **82 A2**
Ucayali → *Peru* 4°30S 73°30W **120 C2**
Uckfield *U.K.* 50°58N 0°7E **31 E9**
Udagamandalam *India* 11°30N 76°44E **84 P10**
Udaipur *India* 24°36N 73°44E **84 G8**
Uddingston *U.K.* 55°49N 4°5W **24 C7**
Údine *Italy* 46°3N 13°14E **68 A5**
Udmurtia □ *Russia* 57°30N 52°30E **70 C9**
Udon Thani *Thailand* 17°29N 102°46E **82 A2**
Udupi *India* 13°25N 74°42E **84 N9**
Uele → *Dem. Rep. of the Congo* 3°45N 24°45E **96 D4**
Ufa *Russia* 54°45N 55°55E **70 D10**
Uffculme *U.K.* 50°54N 3°20W **29 F7**
Ufford *U.K.* 52°8N 1°23E **31 B11**
Uganda ■ *Africa* 2°0N 32°0E **96 D6**
Ugborough *U.K.* 50°22N 3°53W **29 G6**
Uibhist a Deas = South Uist *U.K.* 57°20N 7°15W **22 H3**
Uibhist a Tuath = North Uist *U.K.* 57°40N 7°15W **22 G3**
Uig *U.K.* 57°35N 6°21W **22 G5**
Uinta Mts. *U.S.A.* 40°45N 110°30W **110 B4**
Uitenhage *S. Africa* 33°40S 25°28E **97 L5**
Ujjain *India* 23°9N 75°43E **84 H9**
Ukhta *Russia* 63°34N 53°41E **70 B9**
Ukiah *U.S.A.* 39°9N 123°13W **110 C2**
Ukraine ■ *Europe* 49°0N 32°0E **71 E5**
Ulaan-Uul *Mongolia* 46°4N 100°49E **78 B9**
Ulaangom *Mongolia* 50°5N 92°10E **78 A7**
Ulan Bator *Mongolia* 47°55N 106°53E **78 B10**
Ulan Ude *Russia* 51°45N 107°40E **77 D11**
Ulceby Cross *U.K.* 53°15N 0°7E **27 F9**
Ulhasnagar *India* 19°15N 73°10E **84 K8**
Uliastay *Mongolia* 47°56N 97°28E **78 B8**
Ullapool *U.K.* 57°54N 5°9W **22 G7**
Ulleungdo *S. Korea* 37°30N 130°30E **81 E2**
Ullswater *U.K.* 54°34N 2°52W **26 C3**
Ulm *Germany* 48°23N 9°58E **64 D5**
Ulsan *S. Korea* 35°20N 129°15E **79 D14**
Ulster □ *U.K.* 54°35N 6°30W **19 B9**
Ulukhaktok *Canada* 70°44N 117°44W **108 B8**
Ulungur He → *China* 47°1N 87°24E **78 B6**
Uluru *Australia* 25°23S 131°5E **98 F5**
Ulva *U.K.* 56°29N 6°13W **24 B3**
Ulverston *U.K.* 54°13N 3°5W **26 D2**
Ulyanovsk *Russia* 54°20N 48°25E **70 D8**
Uman *Ukraine* 48°40N 30°12E **71 E5**
Umeå *Sweden* 63°45N 20°20E **63 E8**
Umeälven → *Sweden* 63°45N 20°20E **63 E8**
Umlazi *S. Africa* 29°59S 30°54E **97 L6**
Umm al Qaywayn *U.A.E.* 25°30N 55°35E **87 E8**
Umnak I. *U.S.A.* 53°15N 168°20W **108 D3**
Umuahia *Nigeria* 5°31N 7°26E **94 G7**
Unalakleet *U.S.A.* 63°52N 160°47W **108 C3**
Unalaska *U.S.A.* 53°53N 166°32W **108 D3**
Unalaska I. *U.S.A.* 53°35N 166°50W **108 D3**
'Unayzah *Si. Arabia* 26°6N 43°58E **86 E5**
Uncia *Bolivia* 18°25S 66°40W **120 D3**
Ungava, Pén. d' *Canada* 60°0N 74°0W **109 D12**
Ungava B. *Canada* 59°30N 67°30W **109 D13**
União dos Palmares *Brazil* 9°10S 36°2W **122 A3**
Unimak I. *U.S.A.* 54°45N 164°0W **108 D3**
Union City *U.S.A.* 36°26N 89°3W **112 G3**
Uniontown *U.S.A.* 39°54N 79°44W **112 F8**
United Arab Emirates ■ *Asia* 23°50N 54°0E **87 F8**
United Kingdom ■ *Europe* 53°0N 2°0W **62 E6**
United States of America ■ *N. Amer.* 37°0N 96°0W **110 C7**
Unst *U.K.* 60°44N 0°53W **22 A16**
Unzen-Dake *Japan* 32°45N 130°17E **81 G2**
Upavon *U.K.* 51°18N 1°48W **30 D5**
Upington *S. Africa* 28°25S 21°15E **97 K4**
'Upolu *Samoa* 13°58S 172°0W **99 C16**
Upper Heyford *U.K.* 51°56N 1°15W **30 C6**
Upper Klamath L. *U.S.A.* 42°25N 121°55W **110 B2**
Uppingham *U.K.* 52°36N 0°43W **27 G7**
Uppsala *Sweden* 59°53N 17°38E **63 F7**
Upton *U.K.* 53°13N 2°53W **27 F3**
Upton-upon-Severn *U.K.* 52°3N 2°12W **30 B4**
Upwey *U.K.* 50°39N 2°29W **30 E4**
Ur *Iraq* 30°55N 46°25E **86 D6**
Ural → *Kazakhstan* 47°0N 51°48E **71 E9**
Ural Mts. *Eurasia* 60°0N 59°0E **70 C10**

Uranium City   **Whittington**

Place	Coords
Uranium City *Canada*	59°34N 108°37W 108 D9
Uraricoera → *Brazil*	3°2N 60°30W 120 B3
Urbana *Ill., U.S.A.*	40°7N 88°12W 112 E3
Urbana *Ohio, U.S.A.*	40°7N 83°45W 112 E6
Ure → *U.K.*	54°5N 1°20W 26 D5
Urganch *Uzbekistan*	41°40N 60°41E 87 A10
Urmia *Iran*	37°40N 45°0E 86 B6
Urmia, L. *Iran*	37°50N 45°30E 86 B6
Urmston *U.K.*	53°27N 2°21W 27 F4
Uruaçu *Brazil*	14°30S 49°10W 122 B1
Uruapan *Mexico*	19°24N 102°3W 114 D4
Urubamba → *Peru*	10°43S 73°48W 120 D2
Uruguai → *Brazil*	26°0S 53°30W 121 E4
Uruguaiana *Brazil*	29°50S 57°0W 121 E4
Uruguay ■ *S. Amer.*	32°30S 56°30W 121 F4
Uruguay → *S. Amer.*	34°12S 58°18W 117 G5
Ürümqi *China*	43°45N 87°45E 78 C6
Usa → *Russia*	66°16N 59°49E 70 A10
Uşak *Turkey*	38°43N 29°28E 71 F4
Usakos *Namibia*	21°54S 15°31E 97 J3
Usedom *Germany*	53°55N 14°2E 64 B8
Ushant *France*	48°28N 5°6W 66 B1
Ushuaia *Argentina*	54°50S 68°23W 121 H3
Usk → *U.K.*	51°33N 2°58W 29 D8
Usolye Sibirskoye *Russia*	52°48N 103°40E 77 D11
Uspallata, P. de *Argentina*	32°37S 69°22W 121 F3
Usselby *U.K.*	53°26N 0°21W 27 F8
Ussuriysk *Russia*	43°48N 131°59E 81 B2
Ust-Ilimsk *Russia*	58°3N 102°39E 77 D11
Ust-Kut *Russia*	56°50N 105°42E 77 D11
Ústi nad Labem *Czechia*	50°41N 14°3E 64 C8
Ústica *Italy*	38°42N 13°11E 68 E5
Usu *China*	44°27N 84°40E 78 C5
Usumacinta → *Mexico*	18°24N 92°38W 114 D6
Utah □ *U.S.A.*	39°20N 111°30W 110 C4
Utah L. *U.S.A.*	40°12N 111°48W 110 B4
Utica *U.S.A.*	43°6N 75°14W 113 D10
Utrecht *Neths.*	52°5N 5°8E 64 B3
Utsunomiya *Japan*	36°30N 139°50E 81 E6
Uttar Pradesh □ *India*	27°0N 80°0E 84 F12
Uttaradit *Thailand*	17°36N 100°5E 82 A2
Uttarakhand □ *India*	30°0N 79°30E 84 D11
Uttoxeter *U.K.*	52°54N 1°52W 27 G5
Uusikaupunki *Finland*	60°47N 21°25E 63 E8
Uvalde *U.S.A.*	29°13N 99°47W 110 E7
Uvira *Dem. Rep. of the Congo*	3°22S 29°3E 96 E5
Uvs Nuur *Mongolia*	50°20N 92°30E 78 A7
Uyuni *Bolivia*	20°28S 66°47W 120 E3
Uzbekistan ■ *Asia*	41°30N 65°0E 87 A10
Uzhhorod *Ukraine*	48°36N 22°18E 65 D12

V

Place	Coords
Vaal → *S. Africa*	29°4S 23°38E 97 K4
Vaasa *Finland*	63°6N 21°38E 63 E8
Vadakara *India*	11°35N 75°40E 84 P9
Vadodara *India*	22°20N 73°10E 84 H8
Vadsø *Norway*	70°3N 29°50E 63 C9
Vaduz *Liech.*	47°8N 9°31E 64 E5
Váh → *Slovakia*	47°43N 18°7E 65 D9
Vail *U.S.A.*	39°40N 106°20W 110 C5
Vaila *U.K.*	60°12N 1°36W 22 B14
Val-d'Or *Canada*	48°7N 77°47W 109 E12
Valdai Hills *Russia*	57°0N 33°30E 70 C5
Valdés, Pen. *Argentina*	42°30S 63°45W 121 G3
Valdez *U.S.A.*	61°7N 146°16W 108 C5
Valdivia *Chile*	39°50S 73°14W 121 F2
Valdosta *U.S.A.*	30°50N 83°17W 111 D10
Vale of Glamorgan □ *U.K.*	51°28N 3°25W 29 E7
Valença *Brazil*	13°20S 39°5W 122 B3
Valence *France*	44°57N 4°54E 66 D6
Valencia *Spain*	39°27N 0°23W 67 C5
Valencia *Venezuela*	10°11N 68°0W 120 A3
Valencia □ *Spain*	39°20N 0°40W 67 C5
Valencia, G. de *Spain*	39°30N 0°20E 67 C6
Valencia I. *Ireland*	51°54N 10°22W 20 E2
Valenciennes *France*	50°20N 3°34E 66 A5
Valera *Venezuela*	9°19N 70°37W 120 B2
Valladolid *Mexico*	20°41N 88°12W 114 C7
Valladolid *Spain*	41°38N 4°43W 67 B3
Valledupar *Colombia*	10°29N 73°15W 120 A2
Vallejo *U.S.A.*	38°7N 122°14W 110 C2
Vallenar *Chile*	28°30S 70°50W 121 E2
Valletta *Malta*	35°54N 14°31E 68 G6
Valley *U.K.*	53°16N 4°34W 28 A4
Valley City *U.S.A.*	46°55N 98°0W 110 A7
Valparaíso *Chile*	33°2S 71°40W 121 F2
Van *Turkey*	38°30N 43°20E 71 G7
Van, L. *Turkey*	38°30N 43°0E 71 G7
Van Buren *U.S.A.*	47°10N 67°58W 113 B13
Van Wert *U.S.A.*	40°52N 84°35W 112 E5
Vanadzor *Armenia*	40°48N 44°30E 71 F7
Vancouver *Canada*	49°15N 123°7W 108 E7
Vancouver *U.S.A.*	45°38N 122°40W 110 A2
Vancouver I. *Canada*	49°50N 126°0W 108 E7
Vandalia *U.S.A.*	38°58N 89°6W 112 F3
Vanderhoof *Canada*	54°0N 124°0W 108 D7
Vänern *Sweden*	58°47N 13°30E 63 F6
Vännäs *Sweden*	63°58N 19°48E 63 E7
Vannes *France*	47°40N 2°47W 66 C2
Vanrhynsdorp *S. Africa*	31°36S 18°44E 97 L3
Vantaa *Finland*	60°18N 24°56E 63 E8
Vanua Levu *Fiji*	16°33S 179°15E 99 D14
Vanuatu ■ *Pac. Oc.*	15°0S 168°0E 99 D12
Varanasi *India*	25°22N 83°0E 85 G13
Varangerfjorden *Norway*	70°3N 29°25E 63 C9
Varberg *Sweden*	57°6N 12°20E 63 F6
Vardø *Norway*	70°23N 31°5E 63 C10
Varese *Italy*	45°48N 8°50E 68 B3
Varginha *Brazil*	21°33S 45°25W 122 D1
Varna *Bulgaria*	43°13N 27°56E 69 C12
Vasa Barris → *Brazil*	11°10S 37°10W 122 B3
Västerås *Sweden*	59°37N 16°38E 63 F7
Västervik *Sweden*	57°43N 16°33E 63 F7
Vaté *Vanuatu*	17°40S 168°25E 99 D12
Vatersay *U.K.*	56°55N 7°32W 22 J2
Vatican City ■ *Europe*	41°54N 12°27E 68 D5
Vatnajökull *Iceland*	64°30N 16°48W 63 B2
Vättern *Sweden*	58°25N 14°30E 63 F6
Vaughn *U.S.A.*	34°36N 105°13W 110 D5
Vava'u Group *Tonga*	18°40S 174°0W 99 D16

Place	Coords
Vega *Norway*	65°40N 11°55E 63 D6
Vegreville *Canada*	53°30N 112°5W 108 D8
Vélez-Málaga *Spain*	36°48N 4°5W 67 D3
Velhas → *Brazil*	17°13S 44°49W 122 C2
Velikiy Novgorod *Russia*	58°30N 31°25E 70 C5
Velikiye Luki *Russia*	56°25N 30°32E 70 C5
Veliko Tarnovo *Bulgaria*	43°5N 25°41E 69 C11
Velikonda Range *India*	14°45N 79°10E 84 M11
Vellore *India*	12°57N 79°10E 84 N11
Velsk *Russia*	61°10N 42°0E 70 B7
Vendée □ *France*	46°50N 1°35W 66 C3
Vendôme *France*	47°47N 1°3E 66 C4
Venézia, G. di *Italy*	45°15N 13°0E 68 B5
Venezuela ■ *S. Amer.*	8°0N 66°0W 120 B3
Venezuela, G. de *Venezuela*	11°30N 71°0W 120 A2
Vengurla *India*	15°53N 73°45E 84 M8
Venice *Italy*	45°27N 12°21E 68 B5
Ventnor *U.K.*	50°36N 1°12W 30 E6
Ventoux, Mt. *France*	44°10N 5°17E 66 D6
Ventspils *Latvia*	57°25N 21°32E 63 F8
Veracruz *Mexico*	19°11N 96°8W 114 D5
Veraval *India*	20°53N 70°27E 84 J7
Vercelli *Italy*	45°19N 8°25E 68 B3
Verde → *U.S.A.*	33°33N 111°40W 110 D4
Verdun *France*	49°9N 5°24E 66 B6
Vereeniging *S. Africa*	26°38S 27°57E 97 K5
Verkhoyansk *Russia*	67°35N 133°25E 77 C14
Verkhoyansk Ra. *Russia*	66°0N 129°0E 77 C13
Vermont □ *U.S.A.*	44°0N 73°0W 113 D11
Vernal *U.S.A.*	40°27N 109°32W 110 B5
Vernon *Canada*	50°20N 119°15W 108 D8
Vernon *U.S.A.*	34°9N 99°17W 110 D7
Verona *Italy*	45°27N 10°59E 68 B4
Versailles *France*	48°48N 2°7E 66 B5
Vert, C. *Senegal*	14°45N 17°30W 94 F2
Verviers *Belgium*	50°37N 5°52E 64 C3
Verwood *U.K.*	50°52N 1°52W 30 E5
Veryan *U.K.*	50°13N 4°56W 29 G4
Veryan B. *U.K.*	50°13N 4°51W 29 G4
Vesoul *France*	47°40N 6°11E 66 C7
Vesterålen *Norway*	68°45N 15°0E 63 D7
Vestfjorden *Norway*	67°55N 14°0E 63 D6
Vesuvio *Italy*	40°49N 14°26E 68 D6
Veszprém *Hungary*	47°8N 17°57E 65 E9
Vianópolis *Brazil*	16°40S 48°35W 122 C1
Viaréggio *Italy*	43°52N 10°14E 68 C4
Vicenza *Italy*	45°33N 11°33E 68 B4
Vichada → *Colombia*	4°55N 67°50W 120 B3
Vichy *France*	46°9N 3°26E 66 C5
Vickerstown *U.K.*	54°6N 3°15W 26 D2
Vicksburg *U.S.A.*	32°21N 90°53W 111 D8
Victoria *Canada*	48°30N 123°25W 108 E7
Victoria *China*	22°17N 114°11E 79 a
Victoria □ *Australia*	28°48N 97°0W 111 E7
Victoria □ *Australia*	37°0S 144°0E 98 H7
Victoria, L. *Africa*	1°0S 33°0E 96 E6
Victoria Falls *Zimbabwe*	17°58S 25°52E 97 H5
Victoria I. *Canada*	71°0N 111°0W 108 B8
Victoria Ld. *Antarctica*	75°0S 160°0E 55 D11
Victoria Str. *Canada*	69°31N 100°30W 108 C9
Victoriaville *Canada*	46°4N 71°56W 113 B12
Vidin *Bulgaria*	43°59N 22°50E 69 C10
Viedma, L. *Argentina*	49°30S 72°30W 121 G2
Vienna *Austria*	48°12N 16°22E 64 D9
Vienne *France*	45°31N 4°53E 66 D6
Vienne → *France*	47°13N 0°5E 66 C4
Vientiane *Laos*	17°58N 102°36E 82 A2
Vierge Pt. *St. Lucia*	13°49N 60°53W 114 b
Vierzon *France*	47°13N 2°5E 66 C5
Vietnam ■ *Asia*	19°0N 106°0E 82 A3
Vieux Fort *St. Lucia*	13°46N 60°58W 114 b
Vigévano *Italy*	45°19N 8°51E 68 B3
Vigo *Spain*	42°12N 8°41W 67 A1
Vijayapura *India*	16°50N 75°55E 84 L9
Vijayawada *India*	16°31N 80°39E 85 L12
Vikna *Norway*	64°55N 10°58E 63 E6
Vila Nova de Gaia *Portugal*	41°8N 8°37W 67 B1
Vila Velha *Brazil*	20°20S 40°17W 122 D2
Vilaine → *France*	47°30N 2°27W 66 C2
Vilhelmina *Sweden*	64°35N 16°39E 63 E7
Vilhena *Brazil*	12°40S 60°5W 120 D3
Vilkitski Str. *Russia*	78°0N 103°0E 77 B11
Villa Bella *Bolivia*	10°25S 65°22W 120 D3
Villa María *Argentina*	32°20S 63°10W 121 F3
Villach *Austria*	46°37N 13°51E 64 E7
Villahermosa *Mexico*	17°59N 92°55W 114 D6
Villajoyosa *Spain*	38°30N 0°12W 67 C5
Villarrica *Paraguay*	25°40S 56°30W 121 E4
Villavicencio *Colombia*	4°9N 73°37W 120 B2
Ville-Marie *Canada*	47°20N 79°30W 112 B8
Villeneuve-sur-Lot *France*	44°24N 0°42E 66 D4
Vilnius *Lithuania*	54°38N 25°19E 63 G9
Vilyuy → *Russia*	64°24N 126°26E 77 C13
Vilyuysk *Russia*	63°40N 121°35E 77 C13
Viña del Mar *Chile*	33°0S 71°30W 121 F2
Vincennes *U.S.A.*	38°41N 87°32W 112 F4
Vindhya Ra. *India*	22°50N 77°0E 84 H10
Vineland *U.S.A.*	39°29N 75°2W 113 F10
Vinnytsya *Ukraine*	49°15N 28°30E 65 D15
Virden *Canada*	49°50N 100°56W 108 E9
Vire *France*	48°50N 0°53W 66 B3
Virgenes, C. *Argentina*	52°19S 68°21W 121 H3
Virgin → *U.S.A.*	36°28N 114°21W 110 C4
Virgin Is. (British) □ *W. Indies*	18°30N 64°30W 115 D12
Virgin Is. (U.S.) □ *W. Indies*	18°20N 65°0W 115 D12
Virginia *S. Africa*	28°8S 26°55E 97 K5
Virginia □ *U.S.A.*	47°31N 92°32W 111 A8
Virginia □ *U.S.A.*	37°30N 78°45W 112 G8
Virginia Beach *U.S.A.*	36°49N 76°9W 111 C11
Viroqua *U.S.A.*	43°34N 90°53W 112 D2
Vis *Croatia*	43°4N 16°10E 68 C7
Visalia *U.S.A.*	36°20N 119°18W 110 C3
Visby *Sweden*	57°37N 18°18E 63 F7
Viscount Melville Sd. *Canada*	74°10N 108°0W 109 B9
Vishakhapatnam *India*	17°45N 83°20E 85 L13
Vistula → *Poland*	54°22N 18°55E 65 A10
Vitebsk *Belarus*	55°10N 30°15E 70 C5
Viterbo *Italy*	42°25N 12°6E 68 C5
Viti Levu *Fiji*	17°30S 177°30E 99 D14

Place	Coords
Vitim → *Russia*	59°26N 112°34E 77 D12
Vitória *Brazil*	20°20S 40°22W 122 D2
Vitória da Conquista *Brazil*	14°51S 40°51W 122 B2
Vitoria-Gasteiz *Spain*	42°50N 2°41W 67 A4
Vittória *Italy*	36°57N 14°32E 68 F6
Vizianagaram *India*	18°6N 83°30E 85 K13
Vladikavkaz *Russia*	43°0N 44°35E 71 F7
Vladimir *Russia*	56°15N 40°30E 70 C7
Vladivostok *Russia*	43°10N 131°53E 77 E14
Vlissingen *Neths.*	51°26N 3°34E 64 C2
Vlorë *Albania*	40°32N 19°28E 69 D8
Vltava → *Czechia*	50°21N 14°30E 64 D8
Voe *U.K.*	60°21N 1°16W 22 B15
Vogelsberg *Germany*	50°31N 9°12E 64 C5
Vohimena, Tanjon' i *Madag.*	25°36S 45°8E 97 K9
Voi *Kenya*	3°25S 38°32E 96 E7
Vojvodina □ *Serbia*	45°20N 20°0E 69 B9
Volga → *Russia*	46°0N 48°30E 71 E8
Volga Hts. *Russia*	51°0N 46°0E 71 D8
Volgodonsk *Russia*	47°33N 42°5E 71 E7
Volgograd *Russia*	48°40N 44°25E 71 E7
Volgograd Res. *Russia*	50°0N 45°20E 71 D8
Vologda *Russia*	59°10N 39°45E 70 C6
Volos *Greece*	39°24N 22°59E 69 E10
Volsk *Russia*	52°5N 47°22E 70 D8
Volta → *Ghana*	5°46N 0°41E 94 G6
Volta, L. *Ghana*	7°30N 0°0 94 G6
Volta Redonda *Brazil*	22°31S 44°5W 122 D2
Volzhskiy *Russia*	48°56N 44°46E 71 E7
Vorkuta *Russia*	67°48N 64°20E 70 A11
Voronezh *Russia*	51°40N 39°10E 71 D6
Vosges *France*	48°20N 7°10E 66 B7
Vostok I. *Kiribati*	10°5S 152°23W 103 J12
Votkinsk *Russia*	57°0N 53°55E 70 C9
Vratsa *Bulgaria*	43°15N 23°30E 69 C10
Vryburg *S. Africa*	26°55S 24°45E 97 K4
Vryheid *S. Africa*	27°45S 30°47E 97 K6
Vulcano *Italy*	38°24N 14°58E 68 E6
Vung Tau *Vietnam*	10°21N 107°4E 82 B3
Vyazma *Russia*	55°10N 34°15E 70 C5
Vyborg *Russia*	60°43N 28°47E 70 B4
Vychegda → *Russia*	61°18N 46°36E 70 B8
Vyrnwy, L. *U.K.*	52°48N 3°31W 28 B6
Vyshniy Volochek *Russia*	57°30N 34°30E 70 C5

W

Place	Coords
Waal → *Neths.*	51°37N 5°0E 64 C3
Wabasca → *Canada*	58°22N 115°20W 108 D8
Wabash *U.S.A.*	40°48N 85°49W 112 E5
Wabash → *U.S.A.*	37°48N 88°2W 112 G3
Waco *U.S.A.*	31°33N 97°9W 111 D7
Wad Medani *Sudan*	14°28N 33°30E 95 F12
Waddesdon *U.K.*	51°51N 0°55W 31 C7
Waddingham *U.K.*	53°27N 0°32W 27 F7
Waddington *U.K.*	53°10N 0°32W 27 F7
Waddington, Mt. *Canada*	51°23N 125°15W 108 D7
Wadebridge *U.K.*	50°31N 4°51W 29 F4
Wadhurst *U.K.*	51°3N 0°20E 31 D9
Wadi Halfa *Sudan*	21°53N 31°19E 95 D12
Wager B. *Canada*	65°26N 88°40W 109 C11
Wagga Wagga *Australia*	35°7S 147°24E 98 H8
Wah *Pakistan*	33°45N 72°40E 84 C8
Wahiawā *U.S.A.*	21°30N 158°2W 110 H15
Waigeo *Indonesia*	0°20S 130°40E 83 E8
Wailuku *U.S.A.*	20°53N 156°30W 110 H16
Wainfleet All Saints *U.K.*	53°7N 0°15E 27 F9
Wakayama *Japan*	34°15N 135°15E 81 F4
Wake I. *Pac. Oc.*	19°18N 166°36E 102 F8
Wakefield *Jamaica*	18°26N 77°42W 114 a
Wakefield *U.K.*	53°41N 1°29W 27 E6
Wakkanai *Japan*	45°28N 141°35E 81 A7
Walberswick *U.K.*	52°19N 1°40E 31 B12
Wałbrzych *Poland*	50°45N 16°18E 64 C9
Walbury Hill *U.K.*	51°21N 1°28W 30 D6
Waldron *U.S.A.*	50°56N 0°13E 31 E9
Wales □ *U.K.*	52°19N 4°43W 28 C4
Walgett *Australia*	30°0S 148°5E 98 G8
Walker L. *U.S.A.*	38°42N 118°43W 110 C3
Walla Walla *U.S.A.*	46°4N 118°20W 110 A3
Wallaceburg *Canada*	42°34N 82°23W 112 D6
Wallachia *Romania*	44°35N 26°30E 65 F13
Wallasey *U.K.*	53°25N 3°2W 27 F2
Wallingford *U.K.*	51°35N 1°8W 30 C6
Wallis & Futuna, Îs. □ *Pac. Oc.*	13°18S 176°10W 99 C15
Walls *U.K.*	60°14N 1°33W 22 B14
Wallsend *U.K.*	54°59N 1°31W 26 C5
Walmer *U.K.*	51°11N 1°25E 31 D11
Walney, I. of *U.K.*	54°6N 3°15W 26 D2
Walpole *U.K.*	52°45N 0°13E 31 A9
Walsall *U.K.*	52°35N 1°58W 27 G5
Walsenburg *U.S.A.*	37°38N 104°47W 110 C6
Walsoken *U.K.*	52°41N 0°11E 31 A9
Waltham *U.S.A.*	53°31N 0°7W 27 E8
Waltham Abbey *U.K.*	51°41N 0°1E 31 C9
Waltham Forest □ *U.K.*	51°35N 0°0 31 C9
Waltham on the Wolds *U.K.*	52°50N 0°48W 27 G7
Walton-on-the-Naze *U.K.*	51°51N 1°17E 31 C11
Walvis Bay *Namibia*	23°0S 14°28E 97 J2
Wamba *Dem. Rep. of the Congo*	2°10N 27°57E 96 D5
Wanborough *U.K.*	51°33N 1°42W 30 C5
Wandsworth □ *U.K.*	51°27N 0°11W 31 D8
Wanganui *N.Z.*	39°56S 175°3E 99 H14
Wanleweyne *Somalia*	2°37N 44°54E 89 G3
Wansbeck → *U.K.*	55°10N 1°32W 26 B6
Wantage *U.K.*	51°35N 1°25W 30 C6
Wanxian *China*	30°42N 108°20E 78 E10
Wanzai *China*	22°12N 113°31E 79 a
Wapakoneta *U.S.A.*	40°34N 84°12W 112 E5
Warangal *India*	17°58N 79°35E 84 L11
Warboys *U.K.*	52°24N 0°4W 31 B8
Ward *Ireland*	53°26N 6°20W 21 B10
Wardha *India*	20°45N 78°39E 84 J11
Wardington *U.K.*	52°8N 1°17W 30 B6
Wardle *U.K.*	53°7N 2°35W 27 F3
Ward's Stone *U.K.*	54°2N 2°36W 26 D4
Ware *U.K.*	51°49N 0°0 31 C8
Wareham *U.K.*	50°41N 2°7W 30 E5
Wark *U.K.*	55°6N 2°14W 26 B4
Warkworth *U.K.*	55°21N 1°37W 26 B5

Place	Coords
Warley *U.K.*	52°30N 1°59W 27 H5
Warminster *U.K.*	51°12N 2°10W 30 D4
Warrego → *Australia*	30°24S 145°21E 98 G8
Warren *Mich., U.S.A.*	42°28N 83°1W 112 D6
Warren *Ohio, U.S.A.*	41°14N 80°49W 112 E7
Warren *Pa., U.S.A.*	41°51N 79°9W 112 E8
Warri *Nigeria*	5°30N 5°41E 94 G7
Warrington *U.K.*	53°24N 2°35W 27 F3
Warrnambool *Australia*	38°25S 142°40E 98 H7
Warsaw *Poland*	52°14N 21°0E 65 B11
Warta → *Poland*	52°35N 14°39E 64 B8
Warwick *U.K.*	52°18N 1°35W 30 B5
Warwick *U.S.A.*	41°42N 71°28W 113 E12
Warwickshire □ *U.K.*	52°14N 1°38W 30 B5
Wasatch Ra. *U.S.A.*	40°0N 111°30W 110 B4
Wash, The *U.K.*	52°58N 0°20E 31 A9
Washburn *U.S.A.*	46°40N 90°54W 112 B2
Washford *U.K.*	51°9N 3°21W 30 D2
Washington *U.K.*	54°55N 1°30W 26 C6
Washington *U.S.A.*	38°53N 77°2W 112 F9
Washington *Ind., U.S.A.*	38°40N 87°10W 112 F4
Washington *Pa., U.S.A.*	40°10N 80°15W 112 E7
Washington □ *U.S.A.*	47°30N 120°30W 110 A2
Washington, Mt. *U.S.A.*	44°16N 71°18W 113 C12
Washington I. *U.S.A.*	45°23N 86°54W 112 C4
Wasilla *U.S.A.*	61°35N 149°26W 108 C5
Wast Water *U.K.*	54°26N 3°18W 26 D2
Watampone *Indonesia*	4°29S 120°25E 83 E6
Watchet *U.K.*	51°10N 3°19W 30 D2
Waterbeach *U.K.*	52°16N 0°12E 31 B9
Waterford *Ireland*	52°15N 7°8W 21 D8
Waterford □ *Ireland*	52°10N 7°40W 21 D7
Waterford Harbour *Ireland*	52°8N 6°58W 21 D9
Watergate B. *U.K.*	50°26N 5°4W 29 G3
Waterloo *Canada*	43°30N 80°32W 112 D7
Waterloo *Ill., U.S.A.*	38°20N 90°9W 112 F2
Waterloo *Iowa, U.S.A.*	42°30N 92°21W 111 B8
Watersmeet *U.S.A.*	46°16N 89°11W 112 B3
Watertown *N.Y., U.S.A.*	43°59N 75°55W 113 D10
Watertown *S. Dak., U.S.A.*	44°54N 97°7W 111 B7
Watertown *Wis., U.S.A.*	43°12N 88°43W 112 D3
Waterville *U.S.A.*	44°33N 69°38W 113 C13
Watford *U.K.*	51°40N 0°24W 31 C8
Watlington *Norfolk, U.K.*	52°40N 0°24E 31 A9
Watlington *Oxon., U.K.*	51°38N 1°0W 30 C6
Watrous *Canada*	51°40N 105°25W 108 D9
Watsa *Dem. Rep. of the Congo*	3°4N 29°30E 96 D5
Watseka *U.S.A.*	40°47N 87°44W 112 E4
Watson Lake *Canada*	60°6N 128°49W 108 C7
Watton *U.K.*	52°34N 0°51E 31 A10
Wau *South Sudan*	7°45N 28°1E 95 G11
Waukegan *U.S.A.*	42°22N 87°50W 112 D4
Waukesha *U.S.A.*	43°1N 88°14W 112 D3
Waupaca *U.S.A.*	44°21N 89°5W 112 C3
Waupun *U.S.A.*	43°38N 88°44W 112 D3
Wausau *U.S.A.*	44°58N 89°38W 112 C3
Wauwatosa *U.S.A.*	44°4N 89°18W 112 C3
Waveney → *U.K.*	43°3N 88°0W 112 D4
Waver → *U.K.*	52°35N 1°39E 31 A12
Wawa *Canada*	54°50N 3°15W 26 C2
Waycross *U.S.A.*	47°59N 84°47W 112 B5
Wayne *U.S.A.*	31°13N 82°21W 111 D10
Waynesboro *U.S.A.*	38°13N 82°27W 112 F6
Waynesburg *U.S.A.*	38°4N 78°53W 112 F8
Wazirabad *Pakistan*	39°54N 80°11W 112 F7
Weald, The *U.K.*	32°30N 74°8E 84 C9
Wear → *U.K.*	51°4N 0°20E 31 D9
Weardale *U.K.*	54°55N 1°23W 26 C6
Wearhead *U.K.*	54°44N 2°5W 26 C4
Weaver → *U.K.*	54°45N 2°13W 26 C4
Weaverham *U.K.*	53°17N 2°35W 27 F3
Webster Springs *U.S.A.*	53°16N 2°35W 27 F3
Weddell Sea *Antarctica*	38°29N 80°25W 112 F7
Wedmore *U.K.*	72°30S 40°0W 55 D1
Wednesbury *U.K.*	51°13N 2°48W 30 D3
Wednesfield *U.K.*	52°34N 2°1W 27 G4
Weedon Bec *U.K.*	52°37N 2°2W 27 G4
Weifang *China*	52°15N 1°5W 30 B6
Weihai *China*	36°44N 119°7E 79 D12
Weipa *Australia*	37°30N 122°6E 79 D12
Welch *U.S.A.*	12°40S 141°50E 98 C7
Weldon *U.K.*	37°26N 81°35W 112 G7
Welford *Northants., U.K.*	55°17N 1°45W 26 B5
Welford *W. Berkshire, U.K.*	52°25N 1°3W 30 B6
Welkom *S. Africa*	51°27N 1°24W 30 C6
Welland *Canada*	28°0S 26°46E 97 K5
Welland → *U.K.*	43°0N 79°15W 112 D8
Wellesley Is. *Australia*	52°51N 0°5W 27 G8
Wellingborough *U.K.*	16°42S 139°30E 98 D6
Wellington *N.Z.*	52°19N 0°41E 31 B9
Wellington *Telford & Wrekin, U.K.*	41°19S 174°46E 99 J13
Wellington, I. *Chile*	52°42N 2°30W 27 G3
Wellington Chan. *Canada*	49°30S 75°0W 121 G1
Wells *U.K.*	75°0N 93°0W 109 B10
Wells-next-the-Sea *U.K.*	51°13N 2°39W 30 D3
Wellsboro *U.S.A.*	52°57N 0°51E 31 A10
Wellsville *U.S.A.*	41°45N 77°18W 112 E9
Welney *U.K.*	42°7N 77°57W 112 D9
Wels *Austria*	52°31N 0°15E 31 A9
Welshpool *U.K.*	48°9N 14°1E 64 D8
Welton *U.K.*	52°39N 3°8W 28 B7
Welwyn Garden City *U.K.*	53°18N 0°29W 27 F8
Wem *U.K.*	51°48N 0°12W 31 C8
Wemindji *Canada*	52°52N 2°44W 27 G3
Wemyss Bay *U.K.*	53°0N 78°49W 109 D12
Wenatchee *U.S.A.*	55°53N 4°53W 24 D6
Wendover *U.K.*	47°25N 120°19W 110 A2
Wenlock Edge *U.K.*	51°45N 0°44W 31 C7
Wensleydale *U.K.*	52°30N 2°43W 27 H3
Wensu *China*	54°17N 2°0W 26 D4
Wensum → *U.K.*	41°15N 80°10E 78 C5
Wenzhou *China*	52°40N 1°15E 31 A11
Weobley *U.K.*	28°0N 120°38E 79 F13
	52°11N 2°50W 30 B3

Place	Coords
Weser → *Germany*	53°36N 8°28E 64 B5
West Antarctica *Antarctica*	80°0S 90°0W 55 D15
West Auckland *U.K.*	54°38N 1°43W 26 C5
West Bank □ *Asia*	32°6N 35°13E 86 C3
West Bend *U.S.A.*	43°25N 88°11W 112 D3
West Bengal = Paschimbanga □ *India*	23°0N 88°0E 85 H16
West Berkshire □ *U.K.*	51°25N 1°17W 30 D6
West Beskids *Europe*	49°30N 19°0E 65 D10
West Bridgford *U.K.*	52°55N 1°8W 27 G6
West Bromwich *U.K.*	52°32N 1°59W 27 G5
West Burra *U.K.*	60°5N 1°21W 22 B15
West Calder *U.K.*	55°51N 3°33W 25 C8
West Coker *U.K.*	50°55N 2°40W 30 E3
West Falkland *Falk. Is.*	51°40S 60°0W 121 H3
West Fen *U.K.*	53°5N 0°5W 27 F8
West Frankfort *U.S.A.*	37°54N 88°55W 111 C9
West Grinstead *U.K.*	50°58N 0°19W 31 E8
West Haddon *U.K.*	52°20N 1°3W 30 B6
West Kirby *U.K.*	53°23N 3°11W 27 F2
West Linton *U.K.*	55°46N 3°21W 25 C8
West Lulworth *U.K.*	50°37N 2°14W 30 E4
West Malling *U.K.*	51°17N 0°26E 31 D9
West Meon *U.K.*	51°1N 1°5W 30 D6
West Mersea *U.K.*	51°46N 0°56E 31 C10
West Midlands □ *U.K.*	52°26N 2°0W 27 H5
West Moors *U.K.*	50°49N 1°53W 30 E5
West Palm Beach *U.S.A.*	26°43N 80°3W 111 E10
West Point *U.S.A.*	32°32N 76°48W 112 G9
West Rasen *U.K.*	53°23N 0°24W 27 F8
West Seneca *U.S.A.*	42°51N 78°48W 112 D8
West Siberian Plain *Russia*	62°0N 75°0E 72 B9
West Sussex □ *U.K.*	50°55N 0°30W 31 E8
West Yorkshire □ *U.K.*	53°45N 1°40W 27 E5
Westbourne *U.K.*	50°51N 0°55E 31 E7
Westbrook *U.S.A.*	43°41N 70°22W 113 D12
Westbury *Shrops., U.K.*	52°41N 2°55W 27 G3
Westbury *Wilts., U.K.*	51°15N 2°11W 30 D4
Westbury-on-Severn *U.K.*	51°50N 2°25W 30 C4
Wester Ross *U.K.*	57°37N 5°0W 22 H7
Westerham *U.K.*	51°16N 0°5E 31 D9
Western Australia □ *Australia*	25°0S 118°0E 98 F2
Western Ghats *India*	14°0N 75°0E 84 N9
Western Isles = Eilean Siar □ *U.K.*	57°30N 7°10W 22 G3
Western Sahara ■ *Africa*	25°0N 13°0W 94 D3
Westerwald *Germany*	50°38N 7°56E 64 C4
Westfield *U.K.*	50°55N 0°35E 31 E10
Westhill *U.K.*	57°9N 2°19W 23 H13
Westhoughton *U.K.*	53°33N 2°31W 27 E3
Westmeath □ *Ireland*	53°33N 7°34W 18 D6
Westminster *U.S.A.*	39°34N 76°59W 112 F9
Westmoreland *Barbados*	13°13N 59°37W 114 c
Weston *U.K.*	52°51N 2°1W 27 G4
Weston *U.S.A.*	39°2N 80°28W 112 F7
Weston-super-Mare *U.K.*	51°21N 2°58W 30 D3
Westport *Ireland*	53°48N 9°31W 18 D2
Westray *U.K.*	59°18N 3°0W 23 D11
Westruther *U.K.*	55°45N 2°35W 25 C10
Westward Ho! *U.K.*	51°2N 4°15W 29 E5
Wetar *Indonesia*	7°48S 126°30E 83 F7
Wetaskiwin *Canada*	52°55N 113°24W 108 D8
Wetherby *U.K.*	53°56N 1°23W 27 E6
Wetwang *U.K.*	54°1N 0°35W 27 D7
Wewak *Papua N. G.*	3°38S 143°41E 98 A7
Wexford *Ireland*	52°20N 6°28W 21 D10
Wexford □ *Ireland*	52°20N 6°25W 21 D10
Wexford Harbour *Ireland*	52°20N 6°25W 21 D10
Wey → *U.K.*	51°22N 0°27W 31 D8
Weybourne *U.K.*	52°57N 1°9E 31 A11
Weybridge *U.K.*	51°22N 0°27W 31 D8
Weyburn *Canada*	49°40N 103°50W 108 E9
Weymouth *U.K.*	50°37N 2°28W 30 E4
Wha Ti *Canada*	63°8N 117°16W 108 C8
Whale Cove *Canada*	62°10N 92°34W 108 C10
Whales, B. of *Antarctica*	78°0S 160°0W 55 D12
Whalley *U.K.*	53°49N 2°24W 27 E4
Whalsay *U.K.*	60°22N 0°59W 22 B16
Whalton *U.K.*	55°7N 1°46W 26 B6
Whangarei *N.Z.*	35°43S 174°21E 99 H13
Whaplode *U.K.*	52°42N 0°3W 27 G8
Wharfe → *U.K.*	53°51N 1°9W 27 E6
Wharfedale *U.K.*	54°6N 2°1W 26 D4
Wheatley Hill *U.K.*	54°45N 1°23W 26 C6
Wheeler Pk. *U.S.A.*	38°57N 114°15W 110 C4
Wheeling *U.S.A.*	40°4N 80°43W 112 E7
Whernside *U.K.*	54°14N 2°24W 26 D4
Whicham *U.K.*	54°15N 3°22W 26 D2
Whimple *U.K.*	50°46N 3°20W 29 F7
Whipsnade *U.K.*	51°51N 0°32W 31 C7
Whissendine *U.K.*	52°43N 0°46W 27 G7
Whitburn *U.K.*	55°52N 3°40W 25 C8
Whitby *U.K.*	54°29N 0°37W 26 D7
Whitchurch *Devon, U.K.*	50°32N 4°9W 29 F5
Whitchurch *Hants., U.K.*	51°14N 1°20W 30 D6
Whitchurch *Hereford, U.K.*	51°51N 2°39W 30 C3
Whitchurch *Shrops., U.K.*	52°59N 2°40W 27 G3
White → *Ark., U.S.A.*	33°57N 91°5W 111 D8
White → *Ind., U.S.A.*	38°25N 87°45W 112 F4
White → *Utah, U.S.A.*	40°4N 109°41W 110 B5
White Esk → *U.K.*	55°13N 3°11W 25 D9
White Horse, Vale of *U.K.*	51°37N 1°30W 30 C5
White Horse Hill *U.K.*	51°34N 1°33W 30 C5
White Mts. *Calif., U.S.A.*	37°30N 118°15W 110 C3
White Mts. *N.H., U.S.A.*	44°15N 71°15W 111 B12
White Nile → *Sudan*	15°38N 32°31E 95 E12
White Sea *Russia*	66°30N 38°0E 70 A6
Whiteadder Water → *U.K.*	55°51N 2°25W 25 D11
Whitecourt *Canada*	54°10N 115°45W 108 D8
Whitefish Pt. *U.S.A.*	46°45N 84°59W 112 B5
Whitehall *U.K.*	44°22N 91°19W 112 C2
Whitehaven *U.K.*	54°33N 3°35W 26 C1
Whitehorse *Canada*	60°43N 135°3W 108 C6
Whitesand B. *U.K.*	50°21N 4°18W 29 G5
Whitewater *U.S.A.*	42°50N 88°44W 112 D3
Whithorn *U.K.*	54°44N 4°26W 24 E7
Whitley Bay *U.K.*	55°3N 1°27W 26 B6
Whitney, Mt. *U.S.A.*	36°35N 118°18W 110 C3
Whitstable *U.K.*	51°21N 1°3E 31 D11
Whittington *Derby., U.K.*	53°16N 1°26W 27 F6
Whittington *Shrops., U.K.*	52°52N 3°0W 27 G3

Whittlesey   Zwolle

Whittlesey U.K.	52°33N 0°8W	31 A8
Whittlesford U.K.	52°7N 0°9E	31 B9
Whitwell Derby, U.K.	53°17N 1°12W	27 F6
Whitwell I. of W., U.K.	50°36N 1°15W	30 E6
Whitwick U.K.	52°45N 1°22W	27 G6
Whitworth U.K.	53°39N 2°11W	27 E4
Wholdaia L. Canada	60°43N 104°20W	108 C9
Whyalla Australia	33°2S 137°30E	98 G6
Wiarton Canada	44°40N 81°10W	112 C7
Wiay U.K.	57°24N 7°13W	22 H3
Wichita U.S.A.	37°42N 97°20W	111 C7
Wichita Falls U.S.A.	33°54N 98°30W	108 D7
Wick U.K.	58°26N 3°5W	23 F11
Wickford U.K.	51°36N 0°33E	31 C10
Wickham U.K.	50°54N 1°11W	30 E6
Wickham Market U.K.	52°9N 1°23E	31 B11
Wicklow Ireland	52°59N 6°3W	21 C10
Wicklow □ Ireland	52°57N 6°25W	21 C10
Wicklow Hd. Ireland	52°58N 6°0W	21 C11
Wicklow Mts. △ Ireland	53°6N 6°21W	21 B11
Wickwar U.K.	51°36N 2°23W	30 C4
Widdrington U.K.	55°15N 1°35W	26 B5
Widecombe U.K.	50°34N 3°49W	29 F6
Widemouth U.K.	50°47N 4°34W	29 F4
Widnes U.K.	53°23N 2°45W	27 F3
Wiener Neustadt Austria	47°49N 16°16E	64 E9
Wiesbaden Germany	50°4N 8°14E	64 C5
Wigan U.K.	53°33N 2°38W	27 E3
Wight, Isle of □ U.K.	50°41N 1°17W	30 E6
Wigmore U.K.	52°19N 2°51W	30 B3
Wigston U.K.	52°35N 1°6W	27 G6
Wigton U.K.	54°50N 3°10W	26 C2
Wigtown U.K.	54°53N 4°27W	24 E7
Wigtown B. U.K.	54°46N 4°15W	24 E7
Wilhelm, Mt. Papua N. G.	5°50S 145°1E	98 B8
Wilhelmshaven Germany	53°31N 8°7E	64 B5
Wilkes-Barre U.S.A.	41°15N 75°53W	113 E10
Wilkes Land Antarctica	69°0S 120°0E	55 D9
Wilkins Ice Shelf Antarctica	70°30S 72°0W	55 D17
Willemstad Curaçao	12°5N 68°55W	115 C11
Willenhall U.K.	52°36N 2°2W	27 G4
Willesborough U.K.	51°8N 0°56E	31 D10
Williams Lake Canada	52°10N 122°10W	108 C7
Williamsburg U.S.A.	37°16N 76°43W	112 G9
Williamson U.S.A.	37°41N 82°17W	112 G6
Williamsport U.S.A.	41°15N 77°1W	112 E9
Willingdon U.K.	50°47N 0°17E	31 E9
Williston U.S.A.	48°9N 103°37W	110 A6
Williston L. Canada	56°0N 124°0W	108 C7
Williton U.K.	51°9N 3°19W	30 D2
Willmar U.S.A.	45°7N 95°3W	111 A7
Willoughby U.K.	53°13N 0°12E	27 F8
Wilmington Del., U.S.A.	39°45N 75°33W	113 F10
Wilmington N.C., U.S.A.	34°14N 77°55W	111 D11
Wilmslow U.K.	53°19N 2°13W	27 F4
Wilnecote U.K.	52°36N 1°39W	27 G5
Wilton U.K.	51°5N 1°51W	30 D5
Wiltshire □ U.K.	51°18N 1°53W	30 D5
Wimblington U.K.	52°31N 0°4E	31 A9
Wimborne Minster U.K.	50°48N 1°59W	30 E5
Wincanton U.K.	51°3N 2°24W	30 D4
Winchelsea U.K.	50°55N 0°43E	31 E10
Winchester U.K.	51°4N 1°18W	30 D6
Winchester Ky., U.S.A.	37°59N 84°11W	112 G6
Winchester Va., U.S.A.	39°11N 78°10W	112 F8
Wind → U.S.A.	43°12N 108°12W	110 B5
Wind River Range U.S.A.	43°0N 109°30W	110 B5
Windermere U.K.	54°23N 2°55W	26 D3
Windhoek Namibia	22°35S 17°4E	97 J3
Windrush → U.K.	51°43N 1°24W	30 C6
Windsor Canada	42°18N 83°0W	109 E11
Windsor U.K.	51°29N 0°36W	31 D7
Windward Is. W. Indies	13°0N 61°0W	115 E12
Windward Passage Caribbean	20°0N 74°0W	115 D10
Wing U.K.	51°53N 0°43W	31 C7
Wingham U.K.	51°16N 1°13E	31 D11
Winisk → Canada	55°17N 85°5W	109 D11
Winkleigh U.K.	50°50N 3°58W	29 F6
Winkler Canada	49°10N 97°56W	108 E10
Winneba Ghana	5°25N 0°36W	94 G5
Winnebago, L. U.S.A.	44°0N 88°26W	112 D3
Winnemucca U.S.A.	40°58N 117°44W	110 B3
Winnipeg Canada	49°54N 97°9W	108 E10
Winnipeg, L. Canada	52°0N 97°0W	108 D10
Winnipegosis L. Canada	52°30N 100°0W	108 C9
Winona U.S.A.	44°3N 91°39W	111 B8
Winooski U.S.A.	44°29N 73°11W	113 C11
Winsford U.K.	53°12N 2°31W	27 F3
Winslow U.K.	51°57N 0°52W	31 C7
Winslow U.S.A.	35°2N 110°42W	110 C4
Winster U.K.	53°9N 1°39W	27 F6
Winston-Salem U.S.A.	36°6N 80°15W	111 C10
Winterborne Abbas U.K.	50°42N 2°33W	30 E4
Winterthur Switz.	47°30N 8°44E	64 E5
Winterton N. Lincs., U.K.	53°39N 0°37W	27 E7
Winterton Norfolk, U.K.	52°43N 1°41E	31 A12
Winton Australia	22°24S 143°3E	98 E7
Wirksworth U.K.	53°6N 1°35W	27 F5
Wirral U.K.	53°25N 3°0W	27 F2
Wisbech U.K.	52°41N 0°9E	31 A9
Wisborough Green U.K.	51°2N 0°30W	31 D7
Wisconsin □ U.S.A.	44°45N 89°30W	111 B9
Wisconsin Rapids U.S.A.	44°23N 89°49W	112 C3
Wishaw U.K.	55°46N 3°54W	25 C8
Wiske → U.K.	54°19N 1°27W	26 D6
Witham U.K.	51°48N 0°40E	31 C10
Witham → U.K.	52°59N 0°2W	27 G8
Withern U.K.	53°18N 0°8E	27 F9
Withernsea U.K.	53°44N 0°1E	27 E9
Witley U.K.	51°9N 0°39W	31 D7
Witney U.K.	51°48N 1°28W	30 C6
Wittersham U.K.	51°0N 0°43E	31 D10
Wiveliscombe U.K.	51°2N 3°19W	30 D2
Wivenhoe U.K.	51°51N 0°59E	31 C10
Wkra → Poland	52°27N 20°44E	65 B11
Wloclawek Poland	52°40N 19°3E	65 B10
Woburn U.K.	51°59N 0°36W	31 C7
Woburn Sands U.K.	52°1N 0°39W	31 B7
Wodonga Australia	36°5S 146°50E	98 H8
Woking U.K.	51°19N 0°34W	31 D7
Wokingham U.K.	51°24N 0°49W	31 D7
Wolf Rock U.K.	49°57N 5°49W	29 H2
Wolfsburg Germany	52°25N 10°48E	64 B6
Wolin Poland	53°50N 14°37E	64 B8
Wollaston L. Canada	58°7N 103°10W	108 D9
Wollaston Pen. Canada	69°30N 115°0W	108 C8
Wollongong Australia	34°25S 150°54E	98 G9
Wolsingham U.K.	54°44N 1°52W	26 C5
Wolverhampton U.K.	52°35N 2°7W	27 G4
Wolverton U.K.	52°3N 0°47W	31 B7
Wolviston U.K.	54°38N 1°18W	26 C6
Wombwell U.K.	53°32N 1°25W	27 E6
Wönsan N. Korea	39°11N 127°27E	79 D14
Wonston U.K.	51°8N 1°18W	30 D6
Woodbridge U.K.	52°6N 1°20E	31 B11
Woodbury U.K.	50°41N 3°24W	29 F7
Woodhall Spa U.K.	53°10N 0°12W	27 F8
Woodhouse U.K.	53°21N 1°21W	27 F6
Woodley U.K.	51°27N 0°53W	31 D7
Woodroffe, Mt. Australia	26°20S 131°45E	98 F5
Woods, L. of the N. Amer.	49°15N 94°45W	108 E10
Woodstock N.B., Canada	46°11N 67°37W	109 E13
Woodstock Ont., Canada	43°10N 80°45W	112 D7
Woodstock U.K.	51°51N 1°20W	30 C6
Woodstock U.S.A.	42°19N 88°27W	112 D3
Wookey U.K.	51°13N 2°41W	30 D3
Wookey Hole U.K.	51°14N 2°40W	30 D3
Wool U.K.	50°40N 2°12W	30 E4
Woolacombe U.K.	51°10N 4°13W	29 E5
Wooler U.K.	55°33N 2°1W	26 A4
Woonsocket U.S.A.	42°0N 71°31W	113 E11
Wootton Wawen U.K.	52°16N 1°47W	30 B6
Worcester S. Africa	33°39S 19°27E	97 L3
Worcester U.K.	52°11N 2°12W	30 B4
Worcester U.S.A.	42°16N 71°48W	113 D12
Worcestershire □ U.K.	52°13N 2°10W	30 B4
Worfield U.K.	52°34N 2°21W	27 G4
Workington U.K.	54°39N 3°33W	26 C1
Worksop U.K.	53°18N 1°7W	27 F6
Worms Germany	49°37N 8°21E	64 D5
Wortham U.K.	52°21N 1°3E	31 B11
Worthing Barbados	13°5N 59°35W	114 c
Worthing U.K.	50°49N 0°21W	31 E8
Worthington U.S.A.	43°37N 95°36W	111 B7
Wotton under Edge U.K.	51°37N 2°20W	30 C4
Wragby U.K.	53°18N 0°17W	27 F8
Wrangel I. Russia	71°0N 180°0E	77 B19
Wrangell U.S.A.	56°28N 132°23W	108 D6
Wrangell Mts. U.S.A.	61°30N 142°0W	108 C5
Wrangle U.K.	53°3N 0°7E	27 F9
Wrath, C. U.K.	58°38N 5°1W	22 E7
Wrekin, The U.K.	52°41N 2°32W	27 G3
Wrentham U.K.	52°23N 1°40E	31 B12
Wrexham U.K.	53°3N 3°0W	28 A8
Wrexham □ U.K.	53°1N 2°58W	28 D3
Wrigley Canada	63°16N 123°37W	108 C7
Writtle U.K.	51°44N 0°27E	31 C9
Wrocław Poland	51°5N 17°5E	65 C9
Wroughton U.K.	51°31N 1°47W	30 C5
Wroxham U.K.	52°42N 1°24E	31 A11
Wu Jiang → China	29°40N 107°20E	78 D10
Wuhai China	39°39N 106°48E	78 D10
Wuhan China	30°31N 114°18E	79 E11
Wuhu China	31°22N 118°21E	79 E12
Wuppertal Germany	51°16N 7°12E	64 C4
Würzburg Germany	49°46N 9°55E	64 D5
Wushi China	41°9N 79°13E	78 C4
Wutongqiao China	29°22N 103°50E	78 D9
Wuwei China	37°57N 102°34E	78 D9
Wuxi China	31°33N 120°18E	79 E13
Wuyi Shan China	27°0N 117°0E	79 F12
Wuzhong China	38°2N 106°12E	78 D10
Wuzhou China	23°30N 111°18E	79 G11
Wye U.K.	51°10N 0°57E	31 D10
Wye → U.K.	51°38N 2°40W	30 C3
Wylye → U.K.	51°5N 1°51W	30 D5
Wymondham Leics., U.K.	52°45N 0°42W	27 G7
Wymondham Norfolk, U.K.	52°35N 1°7E	31 A11
Wyndham Australia	15°33S 128°3E	98 D4
Wyoming □ U.S.A.	43°0N 107°30W	110 B5
Wyre → U.K.	53°52N 2°57W	27 E3
Wyre Forest U.K.	52°24N 2°24W	27 H4

X

Xaçmaz Azerbaijan	41°31N 48°42E	71 F8
Xai-Xai Mozam.	25°6S 33°31E	97 J6
Xalapa Mexico	19°32N 96°55W	114 D5
Xankändi Azerbaijan	39°52N 46°49E	71 G8
Xenia U.S.A.	39°41N 83°56W	112 F6
Xi Jiang → China	22°5N 113°20E	79 G11
Xiaguan China	25°32N 100°16E	78 F9
Xiamen China	24°25N 118°4E	79 G12
Xi'an China	34°15N 109°0E	79 E10
Xiang Jiang → China	28°55N 112°50E	79 F11
Xiangfan China	32°2N 112°8E	79 E11
Xianggang = Hong Kong □ China	22°11N 114°14E	79 a
Xiangtan China	27°51N 112°54E	79 F11
Xiantao China	30°25N 113°25E	79 E11
Xianyang China	34°20N 108°40E	79 E10
Xichang China	27°51N 102°19E	78 F9
Xigazê China	29°5N 88°45E	78 F6
Xilinhot China	43°52N 116°2E	79 C12
Ximiao China	40°59N 100°12E	78 C9
Xinghua China	32°58N 119°48E	79 E12
Xingu → Brazil	1°30S 51°53W	120 C4
Xingyi China	25°3N 104°59E	78 F9
Xining China	36°34N 101°40E	78 D9
Xinwan China	22°47N 113°40E	79 a
Xinxiang China	35°18N 113°50E	79 D11
Xinyang China	32°6N 114°3E	79 E11
Xinyi China	34°23N 118°21E	79 E12
Xique-Xique Brazil	10°50S 42°40W	122 B2
Xixiang China	22°34N 113°52E	79 a
Xizang Zizhiqu □ China	32°0N 88°0E	78 E6
Xuanhua China	40°40N 115°2E	79 C12
Xuwen China	20°20N 110°10E	79 G11
Xuzhou China	34°18N 117°10E	79 E12

Y

Y Drenewydd = Newtown U.K.	52°31N 3°19W	28 B7
Y Fenni = Abergavenny U.K.	51°49N 3°1W	28 D7
Y Gelli Gandryll = Hay-on-Wye U.K.	52°5N 3°8W	28 C7
Y Trallwng = Welshpool U.K.	52°39N 3°8W	28 B7
Ya'an China	29°58N 103°5E	78 F9
Yablonovyy Ra. Russia	53°0N 114°0E	77 D12
Yacuiba Bolivia	22°0S 63°43W	120 E3
Yakeshi China	49°17N 120°44E	79 B13
Yakima U.S.A.	46°36N 120°31W	110 A2
Yakutat U.S.A.	59°33N 139°44W	108 D6
Yakutsk Russia	62°5N 129°50E	77 C13
Yala Thailand	6°33N 101°18E	82 C2
Yalong Jiang → China	26°40N 101°55E	78 F9
Yalta Ukraine	44°30N 34°10E	71 F5
Yalu Jiang → China	39°55N 124°19E	79 D13
Yamagata Japan	38°15N 140°15E	81 D7
Yamaguchi Japan	34°10N 131°32E	81 F2
Yamal Pen. Russia	71°0N 70°0E	76 B7
Yambol Bulgaria	42°30N 26°30E	69 C12
Yamethin Myanmar	20°29N 96°18E	85 J20
Yamoussoukro Côte d'Ivoire	6°49N 5°17W	94 G4
Yampa → U.S.A.	40°32N 108°59W	110 B5
Yamuna → India	25°30N 81°53E	85 G12
Yamzho Yumco China	28°48N 90°35E	78 F7
Yan'an China	36°35N 109°26E	79 D10
Yanbu 'al Baḩr Si. Arabia	24°5N 38°5E	86 E4
Yancheng China	33°23N 120°8E	79 E13
Yangambi Dem. Rep. of the Congo	0°47N 24°24E	96 D4
Yangjiang China	21°50N 111°59E	79 G11
Yangôn Myanmar	16°45N 96°20E	85 L20
Yangquan China	37°58N 113°31E	79 D11
Yangtse = China	31°48N 121°10E	79 E13
Yangzhou China	32°21N 119°26E	79 E12
Yanji China	42°59N 129°30E	79 C14
Yankton U.S.A.	42°53N 97°23W	111 B7
Yanqi China	42°5N 86°35E	78 C6
Yantai China	37°34N 121°22E	79 D13
Yantian China	22°35N 114°16E	79 a
Yaoundé Cameroon	3°50N 11°35E	96 D2
Yap Pac. Oc.	9°30N 138°10E	102 G5
Yapen Indonesia	1°50S 136°0E	83 E9
Yaqui → Mexico	27°37N 110°39W	114 B2
Yaraka Australia	24°53S 144°3E	98 E7
Yarcombe U.K.	50°51N 3°5W	29 F7
Yare → U.K.	52°35N 1°38E	31 A12
Yaren Nauru	0°33S 166°55E	102 H8
Yarkant He → China	40°26N 80°59E	78 C5
Yarkhun → Pakistan	36°17N 72°30E	84 A8
Yarm U.K.	54°31N 1°21W	26 C6
Yarmouth Canada	43°50N 66°7W	109 E13
Yarmouth U.K.	50°42N 1°29W	30 E6
Yaroslavl Russia	57°35N 39°55E	70 C6
Yarrow U.K.	55°33N 3°1W	25 C9
Yarumal Colombia	6°58N 75°24W	120 B2
Yāsūj Iran	30°31N 51°31E	87 D7
Yate U.K.	51°32N 2°25W	30 C4
Yathkyed L. Canada	62°40N 98°0W	108 C10
Yatsushiro Japan	32°30N 130°40E	81 G2
Yatton U.K.	51°23N 2°49W	30 D3
Yavari → Peru	4°21S 70°2W	120 C2
Yaxley U.K.	52°31N 0°16W	31 A8
Yazd Iran	31°55N 54°27E	87 D8
Yazoo → U.S.A.	32°22N 90°54W	111 D8
Yazoo City U.S.A.	32°51N 90°25W	111 D8
Yealmpton U.K.	50°21N 4°1W	29 G5
Yecheng China	37°54N 77°26E	78 D4
Yelets Russia	52°40N 38°30E	70 D6
Yell U.K.	60°35N 1°5W	22 A15
Yell Sd. U.K.	60°33N 1°15W	22 A15
Yellow = Huang He → China	37°55N 118°50E	79 D12
Yellow Sea China	35°0N 123°0E	79 D13
Yellowhead Pass Canada	52°53N 118°25W	108 D8
Yellowknife Canada	62°27N 114°29W	108 C8
Yellowstone → U.S.A.	47°59N 103°59W	110 A6
Yellowstone Nat. Park △ U.S.A.	44°40N 110°30W	110 B5
Yemen ■ Asia	15°0N 44°0E	89 E3
Yenisey → Russia	71°50N 82°40E	76 B9
Yeo → U.K.	51°24N 2°54W	30 D3
Yeola India	20°2N 74°30E	84 J9
Yeovil U.K.	50°57N 2°38W	30 E3
Yes Tor U.K.	50°41N 4°0W	29 F5
Yerevan Armenia	40°10N 44°31E	71 F7
Yevpatoriya Ukraine	45°15N 33°20E	71 E5
Yeysk Russia	46°40N 38°12E	71 E6
Yibin China	28°45N 104°32E	78 F9
Yichang China	30°40N 111°20E	79 E11
Yichun China	47°44N 128°52E	79 B14
Yilehuli Shan China	51°20N 124°20E	79 A13
Yinchuan China	38°30N 106°15E	78 D10
Yingkou China	40°37N 122°18E	79 C13
Yining China	43°58N 81°10E	78 C5
Yixing China	31°21N 119°48E	79 E12
Yiyang China	28°35N 112°18E	79 F11
Yogyakarta Indonesia	7°49S 110°22E	82 F4
Yokkaichi Japan	34°55N 136°38E	81 F5
Yokohama Japan	35°27N 139°28E	81 F6
Yokosuka Japan	35°20N 139°40E	81 F6
Yonago Japan	35°25N 133°19E	81 F3
Yong'an China	25°59N 117°25E	79 F12
Yongzhou China	26°17N 111°37E	79 F11
Yonkers U.S.A.	40°56N 73°52W	113 E11
Yonne → France	48°23N 2°58E	66 B5
York U.K.	53°58N 1°6W	27 E6
York U.S.A.	39°58N 76°44W	112 F9
York, C. Australia	10°42S 142°31E	98 C7
York, Vale of U.K.	54°15N 1°25W	26 D6
Yorkshire Dales △ U.K.	54°12N 2°10W	26 D4
Yorkshire Wolds U.K.	54°8N 0°31W	26 D7
Yorkton Canada	51°11N 102°28W	108 D9
Yosemite Nat. Park △ U.S.A.	37°45N 119°40W	110 C3
Yoshkar Ola Russia	56°38N 47°55E	70 C8
Youghal Ireland	51°56N 7°52W	20 E7
Youghal B. Ireland	51°55N 7°49W	20 E7
Youlgreave U.K.	53°11N 1°40W	27 F5
Youngstown U.S.A.	41°6N 80°39W	112 E7
Yoxall U.K.	52°46N 1°47W	27 G5
Yoxford U.K.	52°16N 1°31E	31 B12
Yozgat Turkey	39°51N 34°47E	71 G5
Yr Wyddgrug = Mold U.K.	53°9N 3°8W	28 A7
Yreka U.S.A.	41°44N 122°38W	110 B2
Ystalyfera U.K.	51°46N 3°48W	28 D6
Ythan → U.K.	57°19N 1°59W	23 H14
Yu Jiang → China	23°22N 110°3E	79 G11
Yuan Jiang → China	28°55N 111°50E	79 F11
Yuanping China	38°42N 112°46E	79 D11
Yuba City U.S.A.	39°8N 121°37E	110 G3
Yucatán Mexico	19°30N 89°0W	114 D7
Yucatán Channel Caribbean	22°0N 86°30W	114 C7
Yuen Long China	22°26N 114°2E	79 a
Yueyang China	29°21N 113°5E	79 F11
Yukon □ Canada	63°0N 135°0W	108 C6
Yukon → U.S.A.	62°32N 163°54W	108 C3
Yulin China	38°20N 109°30E	79 D10
Yuma U.S.A.	32°43N 114°37W	110 D4
Yumen China	39°50N 97°30E	78 D8
Yungas Bolivia	17°0S 66°0W	120 D3
Yunnan □ China	25°0N 102°0E	78 G9
Yurimaguas Peru	5°55S 76°7W	120 C2
Yushu China	33°5N 96°55E	78 E8
Yutian China	36°52N 81°42E	78 D5
Yuxi China	24°30N 102°35E	78 G9
Yuzhno-Sakhalinsk Russia	46°58N 142°45E	77 E15
Yuzhou China	34°10N 113°28E	79 E11
Yvetot France	49°37N 0°44E	66 B4

Z

Zāb al Kabīr → Iraq	36°1N 43°24E	86 B5
Zābol Iran	32°0N 67°0E	87 D10
Zabrze Poland	50°18N 18°50E	65 C10
Zacatecas Mexico	22°47N 102°35W	114 C4
Zadar Croatia	44°8N 15°14E	68 B6
Zagaoua Chad	15°30N 22°24E	95 E10
Zagazig Egypt	30°40N 31°30E	95 B12
Zagreb Croatia	45°50N 15°58E	68 B7
Zagros Mts. Iran	33°45N 48°5E	86 C6
Zāhedān Iran	29°30N 60°50E	87 D10
Zahlah Lebanon	33°52N 35°50E	86 C3
Zakynthos Greece	37°47N 20°54E	69 F9
Zalantun China	48°0N 122°43E	79 B13
Zambezi → Africa	18°35S 36°20E	97 H7
Zambia ■ Africa	15°0S 28°0E	97 G5
Zamboanga Phil.	6°59N 122°3E	83 C6
Zamora Mexico	19°59N 102°16W	114 D4
Zamora Spain	41°30N 5°45W	67 B3
Zamość Poland	50°43N 23°15E	65 C12
Zanda China	31°32N 79°50E	78 E4
Zanesville U.S.A.	39°56N 82°1W	112 F6
Zanjān Iran	36°40N 48°35E	86 B7
Zanzibar Tanzania	6°12S 39°12E	96 F7
Zaouiet Reggâne Algeria	26°32N 0°3E	94 C6
Zaoyang China	32°10N 112°45E	79 E11
Zaozhuang China	34°50N 117°35E	79 E12
Zapala Argentina	39°0S 70°5W	121 F2
Zaporozhye Ukraine	47°50N 35°10E	71 E6
Zaragoza Spain	41°39N 0°53W	67 B5
Zaranj Afghan.	30°55N 61°55E	87 D10
Zárate Argentina	34°7S 59°0W	121 F4
Zaria Nigeria	11°0N 7°40E	94 F7
Zarzis Tunisia	33°31N 11°2E	95 B8
Zaskar Mts. India	33°15N 77°30E	84 C10
Zaysan, L. Kazakhstan	48°0N 83°0E	76 E9
Zayü China	28°48N 97°27E	78 F8
Zeebrugge Belgium	51°19N 3°12E	64 C2
Zeil, Mt. Australia	23°30S 132°23E	98 E5
Zelenograd Russia	56°1N 37°12E	70 C6
Zenica Bos.-H.	44°10N 17°57E	68 B7
Zhangjiabian China	22°33N 113°28E	79 a
Zhangjiakou China	40°48N 114°55E	79 C11
Zhangye China	38°50N 100°23E	78 D9
Zhangzhou China	24°30N 117°35E	79 G12
Zhanjiang China	21°15N 110°20E	79 G11
Zhaoqing China	23°0N 112°20E	79 G11
Zhaotong China	27°20N 103°44E	78 F9
Zhejiang □ China	29°0N 120°0E	79 F13
Zhengzhou China	34°45N 113°34E	79 E11
Zhezqazghan Kazakhstan	47°44N 67°40E	76 E7
Zhigansk Russia	66°48N 123°27E	77 C13
Zhlobin Belarus	52°55N 30°0E	70 D5
Zhob Pakistan	31°20N 69°31E	84 D6
Zhongdian China	27°48N 99°42E	78 F8
Zhongshan China	22°26N 113°20E	79 a
Zhuhai China	22°17N 113°34E	79 a
Zhumadian China	32°59N 114°2E	79 E11
Zhuzhou China	27°49N 113°12E	79 F11
Zhytomyr Ukraine	50°20N 28°40E	65 C15
Zibo China	36°47N 118°3E	79 D12
Zielona Góra Poland	51°57N 15°31E	64 C8
Zigong China	29°15N 104°48E	78 F9
Ziguinchor Senegal	12°35N 16°20W	94 F2
Žilina Slovakia	49°12N 18°42E	65 D10
Zimbabwe ■ Africa	19°0S 30°0E	97 H5
Zinder Niger	13°48N 9°0E	94 F7
Ziway, L. Ethiopia	8°0N 38°50E	89 F2
Zlatoust Russia	55°10N 59°40E	70 C10
Zlín Czechia	49°14N 17°40E	65 D9
Zonguldak Turkey	41°28N 31°50E	71 F5
Zrenjanin Serbia	45°22N 20°23E	69 B9
Zug Switz.	47°10N 8°31E	64 E5
Zunyi China	27°42N 106°53E	78 F10
Zürich Switz.	47°22N 8°32E	64 E5
Zuwärah Libya	32°58N 12°1E	95 B8
Zvishavane Zimbabwe	20°17S 30°2E	97 J6
Zwelitsha S. Africa	32°55S 27°22E	97 L5
Zwickau Germany	50°44N 12°30E	64 C7
Zwolle Neths.	52°31N 6°6E	64 B4

Published in Great Britain in 2019 by Philip's, a division of Octopus Publishing Group Limited (www.octopusbooks.co.uk)
Carmelite House
50 Victoria Embankment
London EC4Y 0DZ

An Hachette UK Company (www.hachette.co.uk)

Ninety-ninth edition

ISBN 978-1-84907-492-6 (HARDBACK EDITION)
ISBN 978-1-84907-493-3 (PAPERBACK EDITION)

Printed in Malaysia

A CIP catalogue record for this book is available from the British Library.

Details of other Philip's titles and services can be found on our website at www.philips-maps.co.uk

Philip's World Atlases are published in association with The Royal Geographical Society (with The Institute of British Geographers).
The Society was founded in 1830 and given a Royal Charter in 1859 for 'the advancement of geographical science'. Today it is a leading world centre for geographical learning – supporting education, teaching, research and expeditions, and promoting public understanding of the subject.
Further information about the Society and how to join may be found on its website at: www.rgs.org

Royal Geographical Society
with IBG
Advancing geography and geographical learning

PHOTOGRAPHIC ACKNOWLEDGEMENTS
Alamy Stock Photo/Eduardo Blanco p. 37c, /Derek Croucher p. 37t, /Peter Reynolds/LGPL p.36, /Kevin Schafer p. 85 /ian woolcock p. 37b; China RSGS p. 16tl; ClaudioDivizia/iStockphoto p. 43; Digital Globe p. 11; Lavizzara/Dreamstime using data supplied by NASA p.116; NASA pp. 13t, 13tc, 13bc; NPA Satellite Mapping, CGG Services (UK) Ltd (www.cgg.com) pp. 10, 16tr, 14b, 88, 130; Tower Hamlets Local History Library and Archives p. 14t; USGS pp. 12, 13b, 16b, 16br.
Front cover/p.1, 9, 17, 49 7 123 Horvath Zoltan/Dreamstime.com